# SQL Server 2014 with PowerShell v5 Cookbook

Over 150 real-world recipes to simplify database management, automate repetitive tasks, and increase your productivity

**Donabel Santos**

[PACKT] enterprise 🞧
PUBLISHING
professional expertise distilled

BIRMINGHAM - MUMBAI

# SQL Server 2014 with PowerShell v5 Cookbook

First published: November 2015

Production reference: 1251115

Published by Packt Publishing Ltd.
Livery Place
35 Livery Street
Birmingham B3 2PB, UK.

ISBN 978-1-78528-332-1

www.packtpub.com

# Credits

**Author**
Donabel Santos

**Reviewers**
David Cobb
Chrissy LeMaire
Patrik Lindström
Fabrice Romelard
Dave Wentzel

**Commissioning Editor**
Dipika Gaonkar

**Acquisition Editors**
Aaron Lazar
Neha Nagwekar

**Content Development Editor**
Aparna Mitra

**Technical Editors**
Madhunikita Sunil Chindarkar
Manali Gonsalves

**Copy Editor**
Rashmi Sawant

**Project Coordinator**
Izzat Contractor

**Proofreader**
Safis Editing

**Indexer**
Priya Sane

**Production Coordinator**
Shantanu N. Zagade

**Cover Work**
Shantanu N. Zagade

# About the Author

**Donabel Santos** (SQL Server MVP) is a business intelligence architect, trainer/instructor, consultant, author, and principal at QueryWorks Solutions (http://www.queryworks.ca/), based in Vancouver, Canada. She works primarily with SQL Server for database/data warehouse, reporting, and ETL solutions. She scripts and automates tasks with T-SQL and PowerShell and creates corporate dashboards and visualizations with Tableau and Power BI.

She is a Microsoft Certified Trainer (MCT) and an accredited Tableau trainer. She provides consulting and corporate training to clients and also conducts some of Tableau's fundamental and advanced classes in Canada. She is the lead instructor for SQL Server and Tableau (Visual Analytics) courses at British Columbia Institute of Technology (BCIT) Part-time Studies (PTS).

She is a self-professed data geek. Her idea of fun is working with data, SQL Server, PowerShell, and Tableau. She authored two books from Packt Publishing: *SQL Server 2012 with PowerShell v3 Cookbook,* and *PowerShell and SQL Server Essentials.* She has also contributed to *PowerShell Deep Dives, Manning Publications.* She blogs at http://sqlbelle.com/ and tweets at @sqlbelle.

# Acknowledgments

Writing a book is a lot of work and indeed a labor of love. I think the hardest part is the time it takes away from spending with your loved ones. It's the time that can never be replaced, and the least I can do is express my gratitude to them in this corner of the book.

To my dearest Chiyo and the twins, Kristina and Jayden, I hope you will always remember that Tita/Agim loves you all very much. Tita/Agim will always be here for you, whenever you need me.

To Eric, it still feels like it was just yesterday when you first brought me that cup of coffee one midnight while I was cramming for a project at BCIT. I usually drink coffee with milk and sugar, and you brought one that was piping hot, unsweetened, and black (that I was not able to drink at all). Who knew we'd still be together. Thank you for everything. Here's to more coffees, green smoothies, veggie juices, anime and Korean dramas... to a lifetime of crazy adventures together. I love you.

To Papa and Mama, you have always given me strength and inspiration. Thank you for everything that you've done for us. I love you both very much.

To JR and RR—no matter what happens, you will always be my baby brothers, and I will always be your big sis and be there for you.

To Catherine and Lisa, thank you for being the sisters I never had. I am very happy to call you both sisters. To Veronica, you're a cool girl. Just follow your dreams. We're here for you.

To my in-laws—Mom Lisa, Dad Richard, Ama, Aunt Rose, and David—thank you for being my family.

To my BCIT family—Kevin Cudihee, Elsie Au, Joanne Atha, Vaani Nadhan, Cynthia van Ginkel, Steve Eccles, Dean Hildebrand, Charlie Blattler, Bob Langelaan, and Paul Mills—thank you. A special thanks to Kevin Cudihee. Thank you for giving me the chance to teach at BCIT and for believing that I can. 12 years and counting, I still love every minute that I teach. I will always be grateful. And to Elsie Au, thank you for the friendship all these years.

To my UBC family—I am fortunate to work in a great place with great, smart, fun, and passionate people who I deeply admire and learn from. To my teammates, coworkers, acquaintances, and friends, especially Joe Xing, Min Zhu, Jason Metcalfe, Tom Yerex, Jing Zhu, Suzanne Landry, George Firican, Mai Bui, Amy Matsubara, Mary Mootatamby, Shirley Tsui, Lynda Campbell, Cindy Lee, Pat Carew, Stan Tian, and to my truly wonderful director, Pradeep Nair, and our managing director, Ana-Maria Hobrough. It is a privilege to work with all of you.

To the Packt team, to Neha Nagwekar for contacting me to author this book, and Akshay Nair, Aparna Mitra, and Aaron Lazar, who all have helped me throughout the process, thank you so much.

To Chrissy LeMaire, David Wentzel, David Cobb, and Patrik Lindström—my sincerest thank you for your help in reviewing the recipes and content and for all your thoughtful and constructive feedback and corrections. I appreciate your time and learned a lot from your comments, corrections, and suggestions. Thank you for helping me make this book better.

I have learned so much from so many other people—from all the Microsoft Product teams, the SQL Server and PowerShell MVPs, each technology's communities, and bloggers. Thank you all for selflessly sharing your knowledge and for keeping these wonderful communities alive.

There are so many other people who inspired me and helped me along the way, including friends, students (and former students), and acquaintances. Thank you to all of you.

And most importantly, thank you Lord, for all the miracles and blessings in my life.

# About the Reviewers

**David Cobb** is a system architect for CheckAlt Payment Solutions, providers of automated and electronic check transaction processing since 2005. He is a Microsoft Certified Trainer, training people on SQL Server since 2002. He is also the principal consultant for Cobb Information Technologies, Inc, founded in 1996, providing technology consulting with a focus on SQL Server. David blogs occasionally at http://daveslog.com.

He has reviewed *Pro PowerShell for Microsoft Azure*, and *Hyper-V for VMware Administrators*, for Apress.

> I would like to thank Eivina, Noah, and Evan for making my workplace an exciting place to be.

**Chrissy LeMaire** is a PowerShell MVP and currently works as a SQL Server DBA at NATO Special Operations Headquarters in Belgium. She is an avid scripter and has attended the Monad session at the Microsoft's Professional Developers Conference in Los Angeles back in 2005 and has worked and played with PowerShell ever since.

She is currently pursuing an MS degree in systems engineering at Regis University. In her spare time, she tweets (@cl) and maintains two websites, `https://blog.netnerds.net` and `http://www.realcajunrecipes.com`.

She has also worked as a technical reviewer for *Windows PowerShell Cookbook*, by Lee Holmes, *O'Reilly Media*, and *Automating Microsoft Azure with PowerShell* by John Chapman and Aman Dhally, *Packt Publishing*.

**Patrik Lindström** has worked as an IT consultant since 1991. He has worked with SQL Server since 1997. He has worked with BI solutions on the SQL Server stack in media, retail, and finance industries. He started using PowerShell in 2008 at one of the world's largest fashion retailers for measuring the performance of a SQL Server-based system. Currently he works as a DevOps consultant at one of the largest banks in Scandinavia.

He is interested in a wide range of technologies such as C#, JavaScript, functional programming and of course, SQL and PowerShell. If there is a problem, he will find the right tool and get the problem solved.

You can find his resume at `https://careers.stackoverflow.com/patriklindstrom`, or you can take a look at his code at `https://github.com/patriklindstrom/`.

Besides facilitating development, he enjoys practicing Shorinji Kempo—in which he received a second degree black belt. He trains with his youngest son Olle, at the Stockholm Södra Branch. He and his wife Jane, regularly train with their Great Dane, Baaghida. Patrick also practices open water swimming with his older brother, Fredrik Döberl.

**Fabrice Romelard** is a French IT system and network engineer with great experience in development (.NET since the start of this technology). He then moved to Microsoft SQL Server DBA and SharePoint architect. He is now a DevOps engineer. He is currently working for a global company in the industrial certification in Geneva.

Microsoft gives the MVP (Most Valuable Professional) honor since 2003 to different technologies (.NET developer, SQL Server DBA, and SharePoint architect).

After doing an executive MBA in risk management, his day at work is a mix between the administration of his SharePoint farms, DBA on the corporate SQL Server, infrastructure architect for internal projects, and DevOps for all the applications he has to manage. He also manages the due diligence and risk assessments executed by the corporate IT department.

He has published many articles about Microsoft technologies, risk management, and due diligence on his blogs.

---

I would like to thank the publisher team for giving me the opportunity to review this book and the authors who did a great job on the content. This book will give you many tips and tricks for your daily DBA job.

---

**Dave Wentzel** is an independent consultant who specializes in SQL Server performance management and Big Data integration. He uses PowerShell for zero downtime database deployments and automation, freeing up time for life's more important passions.

# www.PacktPub.com

## Support files, eBooks, discount offers, and more

For support files and downloads related to your book, please visit www.PacktPub.com.

Did you know that Packt offers eBook versions of every book published, with PDF and ePub files available? You can upgrade to the eBook version at www.PacktPub.com and as a print book customer, you are entitled to a discount on the eBook copy. Get in touch with us at service@ packtpub.com for more details.

At www.PacktPub.com, you can also read a collection of free technical articles, sign up for a range of free newsletters and receive exclusive discounts and offers on Packt books and eBooks.

https://www2.packtpub.com/books/subscription/packtlib

Do you need instant solutions to your IT questions? PacktLib is Packt's online digital book library. Here, you can search, access, and read Packt's entire library of books.

## Why subscribe?

- ▸ Fully searchable across every book published by Packt
- ▸ Copy and paste, print, and bookmark content
- ▸ On demand and accessible via a web browser

## Free access for Packt account holders

If you have an account with Packt at www.PacktPub.com, you can use this to access PacktLib today and view 9 entirely free books. Simply use your login credentials for immediate access.

## Instant updates on new Packt books

Get notified! Find out when new books are published by following @PacktEnterprise on Twitter or the *Packt Enterprise* Facebook page.

# Table of Contents

# Preface

PowerShell is a powerful and flexible task automation platform and scripting language from Microsoft. Many Microsoft applications, such as Windows Server, Microsoft Exchange, and Microsoft SharePoint now ship with PowerShell cmdlets that can be used for automated and streamlined integration. SQL Server database professionals can also leverage PowerShell to simplify database tasks using built-in cmdlets, the improved SQLPS module, the flexible SQL Server Management Objects (SMO), or by leveraging any of the readily available .NET classes.

*SQL Server 2014 with PowerShell V5 Cookbook*, provides easy-to-follow, practical examples for the busy database professional. There are over 150 recipes in this book, and you're guaranteed to find one that you can use right away!

You start off with basic topics to get you going with SQL Server and PowerShell scripts and progress into more advanced topics to help you manage and administer your SQL Server databases.

The first few chapters demonstrate how to work with SQL Server settings and objects, including exploring objects, creating databases, configuring server settings, and performing inventories. The book then dives deep into more administration topics such as backup and restore, managing security, and configuring AlwaysOn. Additional development and Business Intelligence (BI)-specific topics are also explored, including how to work with SQL Server Integration Services (SSIS), SQL Server Reporting Services (SSRS), and SQL Server Analysis Services (SSAS).

A short PowerShell primer is also provided as a supplement in the *Appendix*, which the database professional can use as a refresher or occasional reference material. Packed with more than 150 practical, ready-to-use scripts, *SQL Server 2014 with PowerShell V5 Cookbook* will be your go-to reference in automating and managing SQL Server.

# What this book covers

*Chapter 1, Getting Started with SQL Server and PowerShell,* provides an introduction on how to work with SQL Server and PowerShell, including an introduction to SQL Server Management Objects (SMO). This chapter provides a recipe to install SQL Server using PowerShell and helps you explore and discover SQL Server-related objects and cmdlets.

*Chapter 2, SQL Server and PowerShell Basic Tasks,* provides scripts and snippets of code that accomplish some basic SQL Server tasks using PowerShell. Tasks include listing SQL Server instances, discovering SQL Server services, configuring SQL Server, importing/exporting records in SQL Server, and creating objects such as tables, indexes, stored procedures, and functions. Some recipes also teach you how to work with Azure SQL Database.

*Chapter 3, Basic Administration,* explores how administrative tasks can be accomplished in PowerShell. Some recipes deal with how to create SQL Server instances and database inventories, how to check disk space, running processes, and SQL Server jobs. Other recipes show you how to attach/detach/copy databases, add files to databases, and execute a query to multiple SQL Server instances

*Chapter 4, Security,* focuses on how to work with SQL Server service accounts, manage logins/users/permissions, and monitor login attempts and also how to work with database roles, credentials, and proxies.

*Chapter 5, Backup and Restore,* teaches you what you already know about SQL Server backup and restore procedures and shows you how these tasks can be done using PowerShell. Many recipes use SQL Server-specific cmdlets, such as `Backup-SqlDatabase` and `Restore-SqlDatabase` wherever possible, but also utilize SQL Server Management Objects (SMO) to get more information on backup metadata. Some recipes also help you tackle backup and restore to Azure BLOB storage.

*Chapter 6, Advanced Administration,* discusses some of the most advanced features of SQL Server and how you can work with them in PowerShell. Recipes in this chapter include how to work with LocalDB, database snapshots, Filestream, FileTable, Full-Text Index, memory-optimized tables, security objects such as certificates, symmetric and asymmetric keys, and setting up Transparent Data Encryption (TDE).

*Chapter 7, Audit and Policies,* focuses on how to work with SQL Server tracking and auditing capabilities and SQL Server Policy Based Management (PBM). This chapter also explores how to work with SQL Server Profiler trace files and events programmatically.

*Chapter 8, High Availability with AlwaysOn,* covers specific recipes that can help you manage and automate SQL Server AlwaysOn, including how to install the failover cluster feature, enabling AlwaysOn, creating AlwaysOn availability groups and listeners, and testing the availability group failover.

*Chapter 9, SQL Server Development*, provides snippets and guidance on how you can work with XML, XSL, JSON, binary data, files in FileTable, and CLR assemblies with SQL Server and PowerShell.

*Chapter 10, Business Intelligence*, covers how PowerShell can help you automate and manage any BI-related tasks, including how to manage and execute SQL Server Integration Services (SSIS) packages, list and download SQL Server Reporting Services (SSRS) reports, and backup and restore SQL Server Analysis Services (SSAS) cubes.

*Chapter 11, Helpful PowerShell Snippets*, covers a variety of recipes that are not SQL Server-specific, but you may find them useful when working with SQL Server and PowerShell. Recipes include snippets for creating files that use timestamps, using Invoke-Expression, compressing files, reading event logs, embedding C# code, extracting data from a web service, and exporting a list of processes to CSV or XML.

*Appendix A, PowerShell Primer*, offers a brief primer on PowerShell fundamentals for the SQL Server professional. This chapter includes sections on how to run PowerShell scripts, understand PowerShell syntax, and convert scripts into functions to make them more reusable.

*Appendix B, Creating a SQL Server VM*, provides a step-by-step tutorial on how to create and configure the virtual machine that was used for this book.

# What you need for this book

For the purpose of this book, the requirements are as follows:

- VMWare Workstation or Player (if you are going to build a virtual machine)
- Windows Server 2012 R2 Trial
- SQL Server 2014 Developer Edition

PowerShell V5 is bundled with Windows Management Framework (WMF) 5. WMF 5 is supported by the following operating systems:

- Windows Server 2012 R2
- Windows 8.1 Pro
- Windows 8.1 Enterprise
- Windows Server 2012
- Windows 7 SP1
- Windows Server 2008 R2 SP1

WMF 5 requires .NET Framework 4.5.

# Who this book is for

This book is written for SQL Server administrators and developers who want to leverage PowerShell to work with SQL Server. A little bit of scripting background will be helpful but not necessary.

# Sections

In this book, you will find several headings that appear frequently (Getting ready, How to do it, How it works, There's more, and See also).

To give clear instructions on how to complete a recipe, we use these sections as follows:

## Getting ready

This section tells you what to expect in the recipe, and describes how to set up any software or any preliminary settings required for the recipe.

## How to do it...

This section contains the steps required to follow the recipe.

## How it works...

This section usually consists of a detailed explanation of what happened in the previous section.

## There's more...

This section consists of additional information about the recipe in order to make the reader more knowledgeable about the recipe.

## See also

This section provides helpful links to other useful information for the recipe.

# Conventions

In this book, you will find a number of text styles that distinguish between different kinds of information. Here are some examples of these styles and an explanation of their meaning.

Code words in text, database table names, folder names, filenames, file extensions, pathnames, dummy URLs, user input, and Twitter handles are shown as follows: "We can include other contexts through the use of the `include` directive."

A block of code is set as follows:

```
#set connection to mixed mode
#note that this authentication will fail if mixed mode
#is not enabled in SQL Server
$server.ConnectionContext.set_LoginSecure($false)
```

When we wish to draw your attention to a particular part of a code block, the relevant lines or items are set in bold:

```
$server.Databases["AdventureWorks2014"].Tables |
Get-Member -MemberType "Property" |
Where-Object Definition -Like "*Smo*"
```

Any command-line input or output is written as follows:

```
(Get-Command -Module "*SQL*" -CommandType Cmdlet).Count
```

**New terms** and **important words** are shown in bold. Words that you see on the screen, for example, in menus or dialog boxes, appear in the text like this: "Open up your PowerShell console, **PowerShell ISE**, or your favorite PowerShell editor."

 Warnings or important notes appear in a box like this.

 Tips and tricks appear like this.

# Reader feedback

Feedback from our readers is always welcome. Let us know what you think about this book—what you liked or disliked. Reader feedback is important for us as it helps us develop titles that you will really get the most out of.

To send us general feedback, simply e-mail `feedback@packtpub.com`, and mention the book's title in the subject of your message.

If there is a topic that you have expertise in and you are interested in either writing or contributing to a book, see our author guide at `www.packtpub.com/authors`.

# Customer support

Now that you are the proud owner of a Packt book, we have a number of things to help you to get the most from your purchase.

## Downloading the example code

You can download the example code files from your account at `http://www.packtpub.com` for all the Packt Publishing books you have purchased. If you purchased this book elsewhere, you can visit `http://www.packtpub.com/support` and register to have the files e-mailed directly to you.

## Downloading the color images of this book

We also provide you with a PDF file that has color images of the screenshots/diagrams used in this book. The color images will help you better understand the changes in the output. You can download this file from `https://www.packtpub.com/sites/default/files/downloads/3321EN_ColorImages.pdf`.

## Errata

Although we have taken every care to ensure the accuracy of our content, mistakes do happen. If you find a mistake in one of our books—maybe a mistake in the text or the code—we would be grateful if you could report this to us. By doing so, you can save other readers from frustration and help us improve subsequent versions of this book. If you find any errata, please report them by visiting `http://www.packtpub.com/submit-errata`, selecting your book, clicking on the **Errata Submission Form** link, and entering the details of your errata. Once your errata are verified, your submission will be accepted and the errata will be uploaded to our website or added to any list of existing errata under the Errata section of that title.

To view the previously submitted errata, go to https://www.packtpub.com/books/content/support and enter the name of the book in the search field. The required information will appear under the **Errata** section.

## Piracy

Piracy of copyrighted material on the Internet is an ongoing problem across all media. At Packt, we take the protection of our copyright and licenses very seriously. If you come across any illegal copies of our works in any form on the Internet, please provide us with the location address or website name immediately so that we can pursue a remedy.

Please contact us at copyright@packtpub.com with a link to the suspected pirated material.

We appreciate your help in protecting our authors and our ability to bring you valuable content.

## Questions

If you have a problem with any aspect of this book, you can contact us at questions@packtpub.com, and we will do our best to address the problem.

# 1
# Getting Started with SQL Server and PowerShell

In this chapter, we will cover:

- ▶ Working with the sample code
- ▶ Installing SQL Server using PowerShell
- ▶ Installing SQL Server Management Objects
- ▶ Loading SMO assemblies
- ▶ Exploring the SQL Server PowerShell hierarchy
- ▶ Discovering SQL-related cmdlets and modules
- ▶ Creating a SQL Server Instance Object
- ▶ Exploring SMO Server Objects

## Introduction

If you have been working with Microsoft products, or have been managing or developing on the Microsoft platform, you might be familiar with PowerShell. If not, I can predict that you are bound to encounter it sooner than later. Since you are holding this book, my prediction just came true.

PowerShell is Microsoft's automation platform, which includes both a shell (often referred to as console) and a scripting language that allows one to streamline, integrate, and automate multiple tasks and applications. But why learn another technology and language? Why bother? If you have experience as a system administrator pre-PowerShell, you probably know the pain of trying to integrate heterogeneous systems using some kind of scripting.

Windows, at its core, is very **Graphical User Interface** (**GUI**)-driven with a lot of point-and-click, but this point-and-click is not so great when you have to do it several times over as you try to tie together systems and automate tasks.

Historically, the scripting solution would have involved a multitude of languages, including VBScript, Jscript, Perl, or Python; a batch file; and even a little bit of C, C++, or C#. System administrators had to be really creative and resourceful—duct taping a solution using a mishmash of languages in the absence of a real solution. It was messy, not flexible, and painful to maintain.

Enter PowerShell! PowerShell allows an administrator, or developer, to do more tasks in a faster, easier, and better way using a scripting language, now understood by many, in the Microsoft family of applications. PowerShell is now the one language you need to know if you want to automate and integrate either, within one application (for example, SQL Server), or between Microsoft and even non-Microsoft applications. Since many Microsoft products such as Windows Server, Exchange, SharePoint, and SQL Server have support for PowerShell, getting one system to talk to another is just a matter of discovering what cmdlets, functions, or modules need to be pulled into the script. The good thing is, even if the product does not have support for PowerShell yet, it most likely has .NET or .com support, which PowerShell can easily use.

PowerShell has become a major player in the automation and integration arena, and it will continue to be, for the foreseeable future.

## Working with SQL Server and PowerShell

Before we dive into the recipes, let's go over a few important concepts and terminologies that will help you understand how SQL Server and PowerShell can work together.

### Running as an administrator

Most of our recipes will perform possible queries and changes in your SQL Server instance or Windows Server. This will require elevated privileges both on your database side and in the PowerShell side. To ensure you can run the recipes in this book without getting access errors, you will need to execute the console or the ISE as administrator. One way to do this is by right-clicking on the PowerShell icon in your task bar and selecting to run either program as administrator.

You can confirm that you've launched either program as administrator by checking the title bar. You should see **Administrator** added to your title bar.

```
Administrator: Windows PowerShell                              _ □ X
PS C:\> Get-Help Compress-Archive

NAME
    Compress-Archive

SYNOPSIS
    The Compress-Archive cmdlet can be used to zip/compress one or more
    files/directories.

SYNTAX
    Compress-Archive [-Path] <String[]> [-DestinationPath] <String>
    [-CompressionLevel <String>] [-Update] [-WhatIf] [-Confirm]
    [<CommonParameters>]
```

## Execution Policy

The **Execution Policy** settings in PowerShell determine what is allowed or not allowed to be run in PowerShell.

 See *Execution Policy* section in, *Appendix A, PowerShell Primer*, for further explanation of different execution policies.

For security reasons, PowerShell will not run automatically unless it is authorized in the settings. This is to prevent scripts from different sources, for example, the ones downloaded from the Internet, from potentially running malicious or destructive code.

To run the recipes in this book, you will need at least a `RemoteSigned` setting. To get this, run the following code:

```
Set-ExecutionPolicy RemoteSigned
```

## Running scripts

If you save your PowerShell code in a file, you need to ensure it has a `.ps1` extension. Otherwise, PowerShell will not run it. Unlike traditional scripts, you cannot run a PowerShell script by double clicking the file. Instead, you can run this script from the PowerShell console simply by calling the name. For example, if you have a script called `myscript.ps1` located in the `C:\Scripts` directory, you can provide the full path to the file to invoke it:

```
PS C:\> C:\Scripts\myscript.ps1
```

You can also change your directory to where the script is saved, and invoke it like this (notice there is a dot and backslash in front of the file):

```
PS C:\Scripts> .\myscript.ps1
```

If the file or path to the file has spaces, then you will need to enclose the full path and file name in single or double quotes. Before PowerShell v3, you would need to use the call (`&`) operator prior to the script name. From PowerShell v3 onwards, you do not need to specify the call operator anymore, but it will still work if you do:

```
PS C:\Scripts> & '.\my script.ps1'
```

If you want to retain the variables and functions included in the script in memory, so that it's available in your session globally, then you will need to dot source the script. Dot source means prepending the filename, or path to the file, with a dot and a space:

```
PS C:\Scripts> . .\myscript.ps1
PS C:\Scripts> . '.\my script.ps1'
```

 To learn more about how to invoke code and executables in PowerShell, see http://social.technet.microsoft.com/wiki/contents/articles/7703.powershell-running-executables.aspx.

## Running different PowerShell versions

If you are running PowerShell v3, v4, or v5, you can choose to run an older version of PowerShell. To do this, simply invoke the shell or start your session with a `-Version` parameter and provide the version you want to use:

```
Powershell.exe -Version 2
```

You can check that the change was made by using the $PSVersionTable variable.
You should now see the PSVersion value reverted to the value you provided to
the -Version parameter:

```
Administrator: Windows PowerShell                                    -  □  x

PS C:\> PowerShell -Version 2
Windows PowerShell
Copyright (C) 2009 Microsoft Corporation. All rights reserved.

PS C:\> $PSVersionTable

Name                             Value
----                             -----
CLRVersion                       2.0.50727.8009
BuildVersion                     6.1.7600.16385
PSVersion                        2.0
WSManStackVersion                2.0
PSCompatibleVersions             {1.0, 2.0}
SerializationVersion             1.1.0.1
PSRemotingProtocolVersion        2.1
```

## Line continuation

Understanding how line continuation works in PowerShell will be crucial when working with
the recipes in this book.

You will encounter a line of PowerShell code that may be wider than the width of the page you
are reading. For example, consider the following code:

```
#create your SQL Server SMO instance
$server = New-Object -TypeName
Microsoft.SqlServer.Management.Smo.Server -ArgumentList
$instanceName
```

The preceding code, which creates a SQL Server instance, is meant to be written in a single
line (no line breaks), otherwise it will not execute. However, to make the line more readable,
some snippets may be broken into multiple lines as long as the line continuation character, a
backtick (`), is provided at the end of the line just before the carriage return. Check out the
following code:

```
$server = New-Object `
        -TypeName `
        Microsoft.SqlServer.Management.Smo.Server `
        -ArgumentList $instanceName
```

Adding the line breaks cleans up the code a little bit and makes it more readable. But do you
see the backtick at the end of each line? You probably have to squint to see it. It's probably
not obvious that the backtick is the last character before the carriage return.

The backtick (`) character in the U.S. keyboard is the key above the left *Tab* key, and to the left of the number *1* key. It shares the key with the tilde (~) sign. Check this post for the visual location of the backtick key in localized keyboards: `http://superuser.com/questions/254076/how-do-i-type-the-tick-and-backtick-characters-on-windows`.

For this book, I will try to avoid backticks for line continuation. Please assume that a long line of code in the recipes, although wrapping in your page, should be written as just a single line. You can also confirm the syntax by downloading the code from the Packt Publishing website.

Where possible, I will break down the code into more readable chunks without using the backtick. For example, consider a long line of code like this:

```
$server.Databases | Get-Member -MemberType "Property" | Where-
Object Definition -Like "*Smo*"
```

The preceding line can be rewritten into multiple lines using the pipe (|) operator at the end of each line:

```
$server.Databases |
Get-Member -MemberType "Property" |
Where-Object Definition -Like "*Smo*"
```

If I have to use the backtick, I will call your attention to it in the code comments.

## PowerShell modules

Modules are a way to extend PowerShell. Modules can add cmdlets and providers, and load functions, variables, aliases and other tools to your session.

For our recipes, we will use the SQLPS module a lot. To load this module, you can use the `Import-Module` cmdlet:

```
Import-Module SQLPS
```

Note that running this command will change your current working directory to:

```
PS SQLSERVER:>
```

# Working with the sample code

This recipe simply walks you through how you can work with the scripts in this book. Samples in this book have been created and tested against SQL Server 2014 on Windows Server 2012 R2.

## How to do it...

If you want to use your current machine without creating a separate VM, as illustrated in *Create a SQL Server VM* section in *Appendix B*, follow these steps to prepare your machine:

1.  Install SQL Server 2014 on your current operating system—either Windows 7 or Windows Server 2012 R2. A list of supported operating systems for SQL Server 2014 is available at `http://msdn.microsoft.com/en-us/library/ms143506.aspx`.

2.  Microsoft provides really good documentation (both MSDN and TechNet) on how to install SQL Server, and the different ways you can install SQL Server. I encourage you to read the installation tutorial, as well as the installation notes that come with your software (`https://msdn.microsoft.com/en-us/library/ms143219.aspx`)

3.  Install PowerShell v5. At the time of writing this book, only the **Windows Management Framework** (**WMF**) 5.0 Production Preview was available. You can download it from `http://www.microsoft.com/en-us/download/details.aspx?id=48729`. The installation instructions are also bundled in the download. At the time of writing this book, WMF 5.0 Production Preview can be installed on Windows 7 SP1, Windows 8.1 Pro/Enterprise, Windows Server 2008 R2, Windows Server 2012, and Windows Server 2012 R2.

4.  By the time this book is in your hands, PowerShell v5 might be available and be bundled in the newer Microsoft operating systems. This download includes, as stated in the download page, updates to Windows PowerShell, **Desired State Configuration** (**DSC**) of Windows PowerShell and Windows PowerShell ISE. It also includes Package Management and Network Switch cmdlets.

5.  If you are planning to use the console, set the execution policy to `RemoteSigned` in the console. This setting will enable us to run the scripts presented in this book.

    1.  Right-click on **Windows PowerShell** on your taskbar and choose **Run as Administrator**.

    2.  Set execution policy to `RemoteSigned` by executing the following on the console:

        ```
        Set-ExecutionPolicy RemoteSigned
        ```

6.  If you are planning to use the PowerShell **Integrated Scripting Environment** (**ISE**), set the execution policy to `RemoteSigned`. We will be using the improved ISE in many samples in this book.

    1.  Right-click on **Windows PowerShell** on your taskbar and choose **Run ISE as Administrator**.

    2.  Set the execution policy to `RemoteSigned` by executing the following on the script editor:

        ```
        Set-ExecutionPolicy RemoteSigned
        ```

## See also

▸ Keep up to date with PowerShell news, articles, tips, and tricks from the PowerShell team blog at `http://blogs.msdn.com/b/powershell/`.

▸ Check out the SQL Server PowerShell documentation on MSDN at `https://msdn.microsoft.com/en-us/library/hh245198.aspx`

# Installing SQL Server using PowerShell

If you're really eager to dive into PowerShell and start installing SQL Server, this recipe will give you a taste of installing SQL Server with PowerShell using the SQL Server `setup.exe` file and a configuration file.

## Getting ready

Get your SQL Server binaries ready. If you have it burned on a DVD, place your copy in the DVD drive. If you have it as an ISO or image file, mount the files now.

You will also need to identify the service accounts you want to use for the SQL Server services you want to install, as well as the locations for all the files that SQL Server will save on your system. In order to perform a completely automated install, the following script will need to be adjusted to use the default service account credentials, or specify the usernames and passwords within the `$command` variable.

In this exercise, we will generate a configuration (`.ini`) first, and then use this for the installation.

## How to do it...

The steps to install a standalone SQL Server instance are as follows:

1. Generate the configuration file using the following steps:

    1. Load your SQL Server install disk or image and launch the `setup.exe` file.

    2. Go through the Wizard and enter all the configuration values.

    3. Once you get to the **Ready to Install** screen, note the **Configuration file path**:

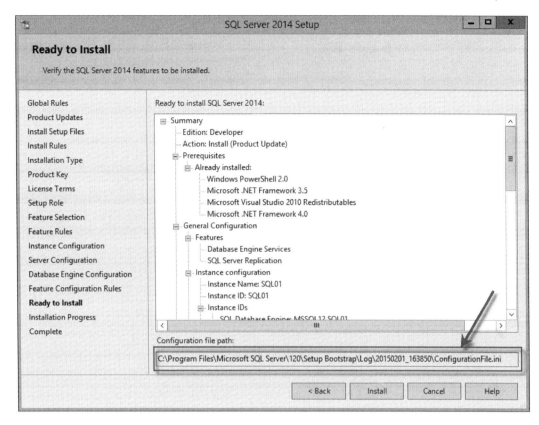

4. Cancel the installation using the Wizard.

2. Change the configuration file to enable a silent install. Open the `.ini` file and make the following changes:

   1. Change the `QUIET` setting to `True`:

      ```
      QUIET="True"
      ```

   2. Comment out the `UIMODE` setting by putting a semicolon before it:

      ```
      ;UIMODE="Normal"
      ```

   3. Add the `IAcceptSQLServerLicenseTerms` value:

      ```
      IAcceptSQLServerLicenseTerms="True"
      ```

3. Save your `.ini` file.
4. Run your PowerShell ISE as administrator.

5. Add the following code to your script editor:

```
#change this to the location of your configuration file
$configfile = "C:\Configurations\SQL_ConfigurationFile.ini"

#we are still using the setup.exe that comes with
#the SQL Server bits
#adjust the path below to where your setup.exe is
$command = "D:\setup.exe /ConfigurationFile=$($configfile)"

#run the command
Invoke-Expression -Command $command
```

6. Change the location of the `$configfile` variable to the location where you saved your `.ini` file. Change the location of the executable as well. In the preceding script, the executable is in the `D:\` directory.

7. Execute the code.

## How it works...

SQL Server can be installed different ways:

▶ **Using Wizard**: You may choose to install SQL Server using the wizard-driven GUI approach, which starts by double-clicking on the `setup.exe` file that comes with your SQL Server binary (`https://technet.microsoft.com/en-us/library/ms143219.aspx`).

▶ **Via command prompt**: You can also install SQL Server using the command prompt by invoking `setup.exe` from the command prompt, and providing all the configuration values in the proper setup parameters (`https://technet.microsoft.com/en-us/library/ms144259.aspx`).

▶ **Via configuration file**: You can install SQL Server still by using the setup executable, but instead of providing all the values in the command prompt, use a configuration file that will host all the configuration values. Visit `https://technet.microsoft.com/en-us/library/dd239405.aspx` for more information.

▶ **Via SysPrep**: Install SQL Server using SysPrep. It is Microsoft's system preparation tool that allows administrators to deploy an image to multiple servers and/or workstations. Visit `https://technet.microsoft.com/en-us/library/ee210664.aspx` for more information.

In the recipe, we went with the third option and installed SQL Server using a configuration file. We are simply going to wrap a few components in PowerShell. You might be asking, "Why not script the whole process in PowerShell instead of using the executable and configuration file?" The answer is, we can do so, and there may be cases where that's the best approach. However, for simple and straightforward installations, it will be easiest to reuse as much of SQL Server's robust, tried-and-true installation process and wrap it inside PowerShell.

The SQL Server configuration file, which has the `.ini` extension, is a text file that contains installation parameter key-value pairs based on your entries and selections within the wizard. The format you will find in the file looks like this:

```
;comment or description
PARAMETERNAME = "value"
```

Some of the common parameters that will be specified in the configuration file include the following:

| Parameter | Description |
| --- | --- |
| ACTION | This is required to start the installation. It accepts only a single value of `Install`. |
| IACCEPTSQLSERVERLICENSETERMS | This is required for unattended installations, and it accepts *End User License Agreement*. |
| UPDATEENABLED | This specifies whether the installation should discover and include product updates, and it accepts `True` or `False`. |
| FEATURES | This specifies components to install, for example, `SQLENGINE`, `AS`, `RS`, `IS`, `SSMS`, or `REPLICATION`. |
| INSTANCENAME | This is a SQL Server instance name. |
| AGTSVCACCOUNT | This is a SQL Agent service account. |
| AGTSVCSTARTUPTYPE | This is a SQL Agent startup type, and it accepts any of the following values: `Automatic`, `Manual`, or `Disabled`. |
| SQLCOLLATION | This is the SQL Server instance collation. |
| SQLSVCACCOUNT | This is the SQL Server database engine service account. |
| SQLSYSADMINACCOUNTS | These are the SQL Server system admin accounts. |
| TCPENABLED | This specifies whether an instance has TCP enabled. |

The list of supported settings is outlined at `https://technet.microsoft.com/en-us/library/ms144259.aspx`.

You can create the `.ini` file from scratch, but it would be best to at least start with the configuration file you get with the wizard. From here, you can adjust and provide additional settings.

Once we've finalized the `.ini` file, the next step is to compose the actual command that needs to be executed. In the following code, we are simply creating a string that contains the path to the `setup.exe` and passing in a single parameter for the `ConfigurationFile`:

```
$command = "D:\setup.exe /ConfigurationFile=$($configfile)"
```

Alternatively, you can also dynamically build the contents `.ini` file using PowerShell and then pass this configuration file to `setup.exe`, just like how we built `$command` previously.

Once the command string is ready, we can use the `Invoke-Expression` PowerShell cmdlet to run the expression contained by the `$command` variable:

```
Invoke-Expression -Command $command
```

Instead of using the `.ini` file, you can also dynamically build all the parameters in a long string based on specific conditions or cases. You can take advantage of PowerShell's logic operators and other constructs when you do this. You should be able to compose the complete command and use `Invoke-Expression` to perform the actual installation:

```
$command = 'D:\setup.exe /ACTION=Install /Q /INSTANCENAME="SQL01"
/IACCEPTSQLSERVERLICENSETERMS /FEATURES=SQLENGINE,REPLICATION
SQLSYSADMINACCOUNTS="QUERYWORKS\Administrator"'
```

## There's more...

You can also take advantage of **Desired State Configuration** (**DSC**), which was introduced in PowerShell v4 and works with Windows Server 2012 R2, to install SQL Server.

DSC is a set of language extensions that will allow you to specify a *desired state*, or a set of ideal configurations, for your servers. This simplifies the configuration of new SQL Server instances, because all you have to do is to identify the *desired state* for your SQL Server installations and reuse the script for every deployment.

These are the simplified steps to take advantage of DSC:

1. Write a configuration script.
2. Run the configuration script to create a **Management Object Framework** (**MOF**).
3. Copy the MOF to the server you're installing SQL Server to. After the installation, at some point, you will want your server to pull the updated MOF automatically.
4. Apply the configuration to the target server and start the installation process.

The PowerShell team made the **xSqlPs** PowerShell module available, which is currently an experimental module, in the Technet Script Center (`https://gallery.technet.microsoft.com/scriptcenter/xSqlps-PowerShell-Module-aed9426c`). Here is a description of the xSqlPs module from the site:

> *The xSqlPs module is a part of the Windows PowerShell Desired State Configuration resource kit, which is a collection of DSC resources produced by the PowerShell team. This module contains the xSqlServerInstall, xSqlHAService, xSqlHAEndpoint, xSqlHAGroup, and xWaitForSqlHAGroup resources.*

To install SQL Server, you will need to work with **xSqlServerInstall**. The PowerShell team has provided an excellent tutorial on how to use this DSC resource. This is a good starting script for a SQL Server Enterprise installation, and you can adjust it as needed. By the time this book is in your hands, the scripts in the module may have already been updated, or moved from an experimental to stable state. Please note that these scripts are also provided *as is*, with no support or warranty from Microsoft.

 If you are looking for a good tutorial on DSC, check out the *Microsoft Virtual Academy* site (`http://www.microsoftvirtualacademy.com/liveevents/getting-started-with-powershell-desired-state-configuration-dsc`).

# Installing SQL Server Management Objects

SQL **Server Management Objects** (**SMO**) was introduced with SQL Server 2005 to allow SQL Server to be accessed and managed programmatically. SMO can be used in any .NET language, including C#, VB.NET, and PowerShell. Since SQL Server does not ship with many cmdlets, SMO is the key to automating most SQL Server tasks. SMO is also backwards compatible with previous versions of SQL Server, extending support all the way to SQL Server 2000.

SMO comprises two distinct classes: the `Instance` classes and the `Utility` classes.

The `Instance` classes are the SQL Server objects. Properties of objects such as the server, databases, and tables can be accessed and managed using the instance classes.

The `Utility` classes are helper or utility classes that accomplish common SQL Server tasks. These classes belong to one of four groups: `Transfer`, `Backup`, and `Restore` classes, or the `Scripter` class.

To gain access to the SMO libraries, SMO needs to be installed and the SQL Server-related assemblies need to be loaded.

## Getting ready

There are a few ways to install SMO:

> ► If you are installing SQL Server 2014 or already have SQL Server 2014, SMO can be installed by installing **Client Tools SDK**. Get your install disk or image ready.

> ► If you want just SMO installed without installing SQL Server, download the SQL Server Feature 2014 Pack.

## How to do it...

If you are installing SQL Server or already have SQL Server, perform the following steps:

1. Load up your SQL Server install disk or image, and launch the `setup.exe` file.

2. Select **New SQL Server standalone installation or add features to an existing installation**.

3. Choose your installation type and click on **Next**.

4. In the **Feature Selection** window, make sure you select **Client Tools SDK**.

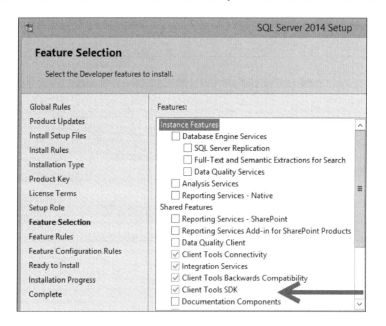

5. Complete your installation

After this, you should already have all the binaries needed to use SMO.

If you are not installing SQL Server, you must install SMO using the SQL Server Feature Pack on the machine you are using SMO with. The steps are as follows:

1. Open your web browser. Go to your favorite search engine and search for **SQL Server 2014 Feature Pack**.

2. Download the package.

3. Double-click on the `SharedManagementObjects.msi` to install.

## There's more...

By default, the SMO assemblies in SQL Server 2014 will be installed in `<SQL Server Install Directory>\120\SDK\Assemblies`. This is shown in the following screenshot:

| Local Disk (C:) ▸ Program Files (x86) ▸ Microsoft SQL Server ▸ 120 ▸ SDK ▸ Assemblies ▸ | |
|---|---|
| Name | Date modified |
| Microsoft.SqlServer.DTSPipelineWrap.dll | 2/21/2014 4:27 AM |
| Microsoft.SQLServer.DTSRuntimeWrap.dll | 2/21/2014 4:27 AM |
| Microsoft.SQLServer.ManagedDTS.dll | 2/21/2014 4:27 AM |
| Microsoft.SqlServer.Management.Collector.dll | 2/21/2014 5:27 AM |
| Microsoft.SqlServer.Management.CollectorEnum.dll | 2/21/2014 5:27 AM |
| Microsoft.SqlServer.Management.Sdk.Sfc.dll | 2/20/2014 8:44 PM |
| Microsoft.SqlServer.Management.Utility.dll | 2/21/2014 5:26 AM |
| Microsoft.SqlServer.Management.UtilityEnum.dll | 2/21/2014 5:26 AM |
| Microsoft.SqlServer.Management.XEvent.dll | 2/21/2014 5:26 AM |
| Microsoft.SqlServer.Management.XEventDbScoped.dll | 2/21/2014 5:26 AM |
| Microsoft.SqlServer.Management.XEventDbScopedEnum.dll | 2/21/2014 5:26 AM |
| Microsoft.SqlServer.Management.XEventEnum.dll | 2/21/2014 5:26 AM |
| Microsoft.SqlServer.OlapEnum.dll | 2/21/2014 4:26 AM |
| Microsoft.SqlServer.PipelineHost.dll | 2/21/2014 4:26 AM |
| Microsoft.SqlServer.PolicyEnum.dll | 2/20/2014 8:44 PM |
| Microsoft.SqlServer.RegSvrEnum.dll | 2/21/2014 5:26 AM |
| Microsoft.SqlServer.Rmo.dll | 2/21/2014 5:26 AM |
| Microsoft.SqlServer.ServiceBrokerEnum.dll | 2/20/2014 8:44 PM |
| Microsoft.SqlServer.Smo.dll | 2/20/2014 8:44 PM |
| Microsoft.SqlServer.SmoExtended.dll | 2/21/2014 5:26 AM |
| Microsoft.SqlServer.SqlEnum.dll | 2/20/2014 8:44 PM |
| Microsoft.SqlServer.SQLTaskConnectionsWrap.dll | 2/21/2014 4:26 AM |
| Microsoft.SqlServer.SqlWmiManagement.dll | 2/21/2014 5:26 AM |
| Microsoft.SqlServer.SString.dll | 2/21/2014 5:27 AM |
| Microsoft.SqlServer.TransactSql.ScriptDom.dll | 2/21/2014 4:26 AM |
| Microsoft.SqlServer.Types.dll | 2/21/2014 4:28 AM |
| Microsoft.SqlServer.WmiEnum.dll | 2/21/2014 5:26 AM |

# Loading SMO assemblies

Before you can use the SMO library, the assemblies need to be loaded. With the introduction of the SQLPS module, this step is easier than ever.

## Getting ready

In this recipe, we assume you have already installed SMO on your machine.

## How to do it...

To load SMO assemblies via the SQLPS module, perform the following steps:

1. Open up your PowerShell console, PowerShell ISE, or your favorite PowerShell Editor.

2. Type the import-module command as follows:

   ```
   Import-Module SQLPS
   ```

3. Confirm that the module is loaded by running the following. This should give the name of the module if it is loaded:

   ```
   Get-Module
   ```

## How it works...

The way to load SMO assemblies has changed between different versions of PowerShell and SQL Server. Before the SQLPS module and in PowerShell v1, loading assemblies could be done explicitly using the `Load()` or `LoadWithPartialName()` methods. The `LoadWithPartialName()` accepts the partial name of the assembly and loads from the application directory or the **Global Assembly Cache** (**GAC**):

```
[void] [Reflection.Assembly] ::LoadWithPartialName("Microsoft.SqlSer
ver.Smo")
```

Although you may still see `LoadWithPartialName()` in some older scripts, this method is now obsolete and should not be used with any new development.

The method `Load()` requires the fully qualified name of the assembly:

```
[void] [Reflection.Assembly] ::Load("Microsoft.SqlServer.Smo,
Version=9.0.242.0, Culture=neutral,
PublicKeyToken=89845dcd8080cc91")
```

In PowerShell v2, assemblies can be added by using `Add-Type`:

```
Add-Type -AssemblyName "Microsoft.SqlServer.Smo"
```

When the SQLPS module was shipped with SQL Server 2012, loading these assemblies one by one became unnecessary, as long as the SQLPS module is loaded using the following code:

```
Import-Module SQLPS
```

There may be cases where you will still want to load specific DLL versions if you are dealing with specific SQL Server versions. Alternatively, you might want to load only specific assemblies without loading the whole SQLPS module. In this case, the `Add-Type` command is still the viable method of bringing the assemblies in.

## There's more...

When you import the SQLPS module, you might see an error about conflicting or unapproved verbs:

> **WARNING**: The names of some imported commands from the module **SQLPS** include unapproved verbs that might make them less discoverable. To find the commands with unapproved verbs, run the `Import-Module` command again with the `Verbose` parameter.
> For a list of approved verbs, type `Get-Verb`.

This means there are some cmdlets that do not conform to the PowerShell naming convention, but the module and its containing cmdlets are still all loaded into your host. To suppress this warning, import the SQLPS module with the `-DisableNameChecking` parameter.

> Learn how to load SMO assemblies using PowerShell from the MSDN at `https://msdn.microsoft.com/en-us/library/hh245202(v=sql.120).aspx`.

## See also

▶ The *Installing SQL Server Management Objects* recipe.

# Exploring the SQL Server PowerShell hierarchy

SQL Server started shipping with the SQLPS module in SQL Server 2012. The SQLPS module allows PowerShell to access SQL Server-specific cmdlets and functions, and also loads commonly used assemblies when working with SQL Server. This continues to be the case in SQL Server 2014.

Launching PowerShell from SQL **Server Management Studio** (**SSMS**) launches a Windows PowerShell session which imports the SQLPS module automatically, and sets the current context to the item the PowerShell session was launched from. Database administrators and developers can then start navigating the object hierarchy from there.

## Getting ready

To follow this recipe, you should log in to SQL Server 2014 Management Studio.

## How to do it...

In this recipe, we will navigate the SQL Server PowerShell hierarchy by launching a PowerShell session from SQL Server Management Studio:

1.  Right-click on your instance node.
2.  Click on **Start PowerShell**.

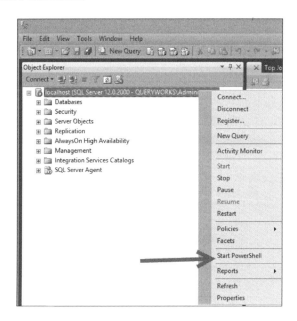

Note that this will launch a PowerShell session and load the SQLPS module. This window looks similar to a command prompt, with a prompt set to the SQL Server object you launched this window from. In the following screenshot, **ROGUE** refers to the name of my local machine:

Note the starting path in this window. The screen now shows how you could get to the default instance if you were to navigate using the PowerShell console or ISE:

```
PS SQLSERVER:\SQL\<SQL instance name>\DEFAULT>
```

3. Type `dir`. This should give you a list of all objects directly accessible from the current server instance; in our case, from the default SQL Server instance **ROGUE**. Note that `dir` is an alias for the cmdlet `Get-ChildItem`.

This is similar to the objects you can find under the instance node in **Object Explorer** in SQL Server Management Studio.

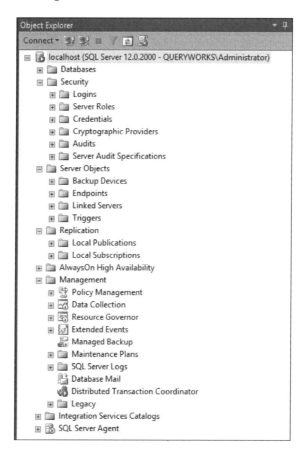

4. While our PowerShell window is open, let's explore the SQL Server `PSDrive` or the SQL Server data store which PowerShell treats as a series of items. Type `cd \`. This will change the path to the root of the current drive, which is our SQL Server `PSDrive`.

5. Type `dir`. This will list all items accessible from the root SQL Server `PSDrive`. You should see something similar to the following screen:

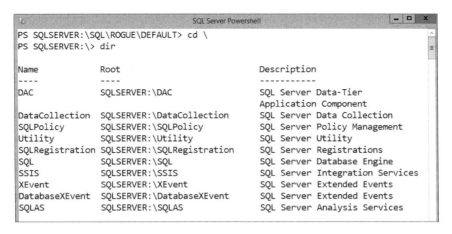

6. Close this window.

7. Go back to **Management Studio** and right-click on one of your user databases.

8. Click on **Start PowerShell**. Note that this will launch another PowerShell session with a path that points to the database you right-clicked from:

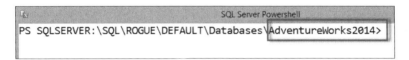

Note the starting path of this window is different from the starting path where you first launched PowerShell in the earlier steps. If you type `dir` from this location, you will see all items that are under the `AdventureWorks2014` database.

```
PS SQLSERVER:\SQL\ROGUE\DEFAULT\Databases\AdventureWorks2014> dir
ApplicationRoles
Assemblies
AsymmetricKeys
Certificates
DatabaseAuditSpecifications
Defaults
ExtendedProperties
ExtendedStoredProcedures
Federations
FileGroups
FullTextCatalogs
FullTextStopLists
LogFiles
PartitionFunctions
PartitionSchemes
PlanGuides
Roles
Rules
Schemas
```

You can see some of the items enumerated in this screenshot in SQL Server Management Studio **Object Explorer**, if you expand the **AdventureWorks2014** database node:

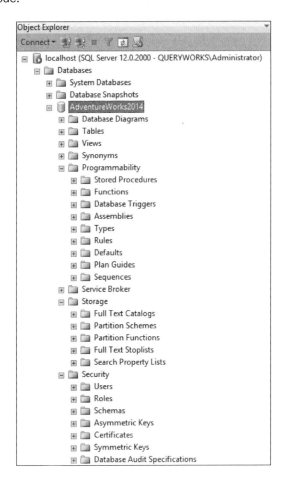

## How it works...

When PowerShell is launched through SSMS, a *context-sensitive* PowerShell session is created and it automatically loads the SQLPS module. This will be evident in the prompt, which by default shows the current path of the object from which the **Start PowerShell** menu item was clicked from.

```
PS SQLSERVER:\SQL\ROGUE\DEFAULT\Databases\AdventureWorks2014>
```

The SQLPS module was not always loaded when PowerShell was launched from SSMS. With SQL Server 2008/2008 R2 it was shipped with a SQLPS utility, which is also referred to as a mini shell. When you started PowerShell from SSMS, it was not a full PowerShell console that was launched. It was a constrained, closed shell preloaded with SQL Server extensions was loaded. This shell was meant to be used for SQL Server *only*, which proved to be quite limiting because DBAs and developers often need to load additional snapins and modules in order to integrate SQL Server with other systems through PowerShell. At that time, the alternative way was to launch a full-fledged PowerShell session and depending on your PowerShell version, either load snapins or load the SQLPS module.

Since SQL Server 2012, the *original* constrained mini shell has been deprecated. When you launch a PowerShell session from SSMS in SQL Server 2012 onwards, what is launched is the full-fledged PowerShell console, with the updated SQLPS module loaded by default.

Once the SQLPS module is loaded, SQL Server becomes exposed as a PowerShell Drive (`PSDrive`), which allows traversing of objects as if they are folders and files. Familiar commands for traversing directories are supported in this provider, such as `dir` or `ls`. Note that these familiar commands are often just aliases to the real cmdlet name, in this case, `Get-ChildItem`.

When you launch PowerShell from SSMS, you can immediately start navigating the SQL Server PowerShell hierarchy.

# Discovering SQL-related cmdlets and modules

In order to be good at working with SQL Server and PowerShell, knowing how to explore and discover cmdlets, snapins, and modules is necessary.

## Getting ready

Launch **PowerShell ISE** as administrator. If you prefer the console, you can also launch that instead, but ensure you are running it as administrator.

## How to do it...

In this recipe, we will explore SQL-related cmdlets and modules:

1. To find out how many SQL-related cmdlets are in your system, type the following in your PowerShell editor and run:

```
#how many commands from modules that
#have SQL in the name
(Get-Command -Module "*SQL*" -CommandType Cmdlet).Count
```

2. To list the SQL-related cmdlets, type the following in your PowerShell editor and run:

```
#list all the SQL-related commands
Get-Command -Module "*SQL*" –CommandType Cmdlet |
Select-Object CommandType, Name, ModuleName |
Sort-Object -Property ModuleName, CommandType, Name |
Format-Table –AutoSize
```

3. To see which of these modules are loaded in your PowerShell session, type the following in your editor and run:

```
Get-Module -Name "*SQL*"
```

If you have already used any of the cmdlets in the previous step, then you should see both SQLPS and SQLASCMDLETS. Otherwise, you will need to load these modules before you can use them.

4. To explicitly load these modules, type the following and run:

```
Import-Module -Name "SQLPS"
```

Note that SQLASCMDLETS will be loaded when you load SQLPS.

## How it works...

At the core of PowerShell, we have cmdlets. A cmdlet (pronounced *commandlet*) is defined in MSDN as *lightweight command that is used in the Windows PowerShell environment*. It can be a compiled, reusable .NET code or an advanced function, or it can be a workflow that typically performs a very specific task. All cmdlets follow the verb-noun naming notation.

PowerShell ships with many cmdlets. In addition, many applications now also ship with their own cmdlets. For example, SharePoint has a fair number of PowerShell cmdlets that help with installation, configuration, and administration of the farm, sites, and everything in between. A list of cmdlets for SharePoint 2013 can be found at https://technet.microsoft.com/en-us/library/ff678226.aspx.

A legacy way of extending PowerShell is by registering additional snapins. A **Snapin** is a binary, or a DLL, that can contain a cmdlet. You can create your own snapin by building your own .NET source, compiling, and registering the snapin. You will always need to register snapins before you can use them. Snapins are a popular way of extending PowerShell.

The following table summarizes common tasks with snapins:

| Task | Syntax |
| --- | --- |
| List loaded Snapins | Get-PSSnapin |
| List Installed Snapins | Get-PSSnapin -Registered |
| Show commands in a Snapin | Get-Command -Module "SnapinName" |
| Load a specific Snapin | Add-PSSnapin "SnapinName" |

Since PowerShell v2, modules are introduced as the improved and preferred method of extending PowerShell. A module is a package that can contain cmdlets, providers, functions, variables, and aliases. In PowerShell v2, modules are not loaded by default, so required modules need to be explicitly imported.

Common tasks with modules are summarized in the following table:

| Task | Syntax |
|------|--------|
| List loaded Modules | `Get-Module` |
| List Installed Modules | `Get-Module -ListAvailable` |
| Show commands in a Module | `Get-Command -Module "ModuleName"` |
| Load a specific Module | `Import-Module -Name "ModuleName"` |

One of the improved features of PowerShell v3 onwards is support for autoloading modules. You do not need to always explicitly load modules before using the contained cmdlets. Using the cmdlets in your script is enough to trigger PowerShell to load the module that contains it.

SQL Server 2014 modules are located at `PowerShell | Modules` in the install directory.

| Local Disk (C:) ▸ Program Files (x86) ▸ Microsoft SQL Server ▸ 120 ▸ Tools ▸ PowerShell ▸ Modules ▸ |
|---|

| Name ▲ | Date modified | Type | Size |
|--------|---------------|------|------|
| SQLASCMDLETS | 8/21/2014 7:13 PM | File folder | |
| SQLPS | 8/21/2014 7:13 PM | File folder | |

## There's more...

You can get a list of SQLPS and SQLASCMDLETS by running the following command:

```
Get-Command -CommandType Cmdlet -Module SQLPS,SQLASCMDLETS|
Select-Object Name, Module |
Sort-Object Module, Name |
Format-Table -AutoSize
```

Here's the list of cmdlets as of this version of SQL Server 2014:

```
CommandType Name                              ModuleName
----------- ----                              ----------
     Cmdlet Add-RoleMember                    SQLASCMDLETS
     Cmdlet Backup-ASDatabase                 SQLASCMDLETS
     Cmdlet Invoke-ASCmd                      SQLASCMDLETS
     Cmdlet Invoke-ProcessCube                SQLASCMDLETS
     Cmdlet Invoke-ProcessDimension           SQLASCMDLETS
```

```
Cmdlet  Invoke-ProcessPartition                       SQLASCMDLETS
Cmdlet  Merge-Partition                               SQLASCMDLETS
Cmdlet  New-RestoreFolder                             SQLASCMDLETS
Cmdlet  New-RestoreLocation                           SQLASCMDLETS
Cmdlet  Remove-RoleMember                             SQLASCMDLETS
Cmdlet  Restore-ASDatabase                            SQLASCMDLETS
Cmdlet  Add-SqlAvailabilityDatabase                   SQLPS
Cmdlet  Add-SqlAvailabilityGroupListenerStaticIp      SQLPS
Cmdlet  Add-SqlFirewallRule                           SQLPS
Cmdlet  Backup-SqlDatabase                            SQLPS
Cmdlet  Convert-UrnToPath                             SQLPS
Cmdlet  Decode-SqlName                                SQLPS
Cmdlet  Disable-SqlAlwaysOn                           SQLPS
Cmdlet  Enable-SqlAlwaysOn                            SQLPS
Cmdlet  Encode-SqlName                                SQLPS
Cmdlet  Get-SqlCredential                             SQLPS
Cmdlet  Get-SqlDatabase                               SQLPS
Cmdlet  Get-SqlInstance                               SQLPS
Cmdlet  Get-SqlSmartAdmin                             SQLPS
Cmdlet  Invoke-PolicyEvaluation                       SQLPS
Cmdlet  Invoke-Sqlcmd                                 SQLPS
Cmdlet  Join-SqlAvailabilityGroup                     SQLPS
Cmdlet  New-SqlAvailabilityGroup                      SQLPS
Cmdlet  New-SqlAvailabilityGroupListener              SQLPS
Cmdlet  New-SqlAvailabilityReplica                    SQLPS
Cmdlet  New-SqlBackupEncryptionOption                 SQLPS
Cmdlet  New-SqlCredential                             SQLPS
Cmdlet  New-SqlHADREndpoint                           SQLPS
Cmdlet  Remove-SqlAvailabilityDatabase                SQLPS
Cmdlet  Remove-SqlAvailabilityGroup                   SQLPS
Cmdlet  Remove-SqlAvailabilityReplica                 SQLPS
Cmdlet  Remove-SqlCredential                          SQLPS
Cmdlet  Remove-SqlFirewallRule                        SQLPS
Cmdlet  Restore-SqlDatabase                           SQLPS
Cmdlet  Resume-SqlAvailabilityDatabase                SQLPS
Cmdlet  Set-SqlAuthenticationMode                     SQLPS
Cmdlet  Set-SqlAvailabilityGroup                      SQLPS
Cmdlet  Set-SqlAvailabilityGroupListener              SQLPS
Cmdlet  Set-SqlAvailabilityReplica                    SQLPS
Cmdlet  Set-SqlCredential                             SQLPS
```

```
Cmdlet  Set-SqlHADREndpoint              SQLPS
Cmdlet  Set-SqlNetworkConfiguration      SQLPS
Cmdlet  Set-SqlSmartAdmin                SQLPS
Cmdlet  Start-SqlInstance                SQLPS
Cmdlet  Stop-SqlInstance                 SQLPS
Cmdlet  Suspend-SqlAvailabilityDatabase  SQLPS
Cmdlet  Switch-SqlAvailabilityGroup      SQLPS
Cmdlet  Test-SqlAvailabilityGroup        SQLPS
Cmdlet  Test-SqlAvailabilityReplica      SQLPS
Cmdlet  Test-SqlDatabaseReplicaState     SQLPS
Cmdlet  Test-SqlSmartAdmin               SQLPS
```

To learn more about these cmdlets, use the `Get-Help` cmdlet. For example, here's the command to learn more about `Invoke-Sqlcmd`:

```
Get-Help  Invoke-Sqlcmd
Get-Help  Invoke-Sqlcmd -Detailed
Get-Help  Invoke-Sqlcmd -Examples
Get-Help  Invoke-Sqlcmd -Full
```

You can also check out the MSDN article on *SQL Server Database Engine Cmdlets* at `http://msdn.microsoft.com/en-us/library/cc281847.aspx`.

When you load the SQLPS module, several assemblies are loaded into your host.

To get a list of SQLServer-related assemblies loaded with the SQLPS module, use the following script, which will work in both PowerShell v2 and v3:

```
Import-Module SQLPS -DisableNameChecking

[AppDomain]::CurrentDomain.GetAssemblies() |
Where-Object {$_.FullName -match "SqlServer" } |
Select-Object FullName
```

If you want to run on v3 or newer versions, you can take advantage of the simplified syntax:

```
Import-Module SQLPS -DisableNameChecking

[AppDomain]::CurrentDomain.GetAssemblies() |
Where-Object FullName -Match "SqlServer" |
Select-Object FullName
```

This will show you all the loaded assemblies, including their public key tokens:

```
FullName
--------
Microsoft.SqlServer.Smo, Version=12.0.0.0, Culture=neutral, PublicKeyToken=89845dcd8080cc91
Microsoft.SqlServer.Dmf, Version=12.0.0.0, Culture=neutral, PublicKeyToken=89845dcd8080cc91
Microsoft.SqlServer.SqlWmiManagement, Version=12.0.0.0, Culture=neutral, PublicKeyToken=89845dcd8080cc91
Microsoft.SqlServer.ConnectionInfo, Version=12.0.0.0, Culture=neutral, PublicKeyToken=89845dcd8080cc91
Microsoft.SqlServer.SmoExtended, Version=12.0.0.0, Culture=neutral, PublicKeyToken=89845dcd8080cc91
Microsoft.SqlServer.Management.RegisteredServers, Version=12.0.0.0, Culture=neutral, PublicKeyToken=8...
Microsoft.SqlServer.Management.Sdk.Sfc, Version=12.0.0.0, Culture=neutral, PublicKeyToken=89845dcd808...
Microsoft.SqlServer.SqlEnum, Version=12.0.0.0, Culture=neutral, PublicKeyToken=89845dcd8080cc91
Microsoft.SqlServer.RegSvrEnum, Version=12.0.0.0, Culture=neutral, PublicKeyToken=89845dcd8080cc91
Microsoft.SqlServer.WmiEnum, Version=12.0.0.0, Culture=neutral, PublicKeyToken=89845dcd8080cc91
Microsoft.SqlServer.ServiceBrokerEnum, Version=12.0.0.0, Culture=neutral, PublicKeyToken=89845dcd8080...
Microsoft.SqlServer.Management.Collector, Version=12.0.0.0, Culture=neutral, PublicKeyToken=89845dcd8...
Microsoft.SqlServer.Management.CollectorEnum, Version=12.0.0.0, Culture=neutral, PublicKeyToken=89845...
Microsoft.SqlServer.Management.Utility, Version=12.0.0.0, Culture=neutral, PublicKeyToken=89845dcd808...
Microsoft.SqlServer.Management.UtilityEnum, Version=12.0.0.0, Culture=neutral, PublicKeyToken=89845dc...
Microsoft.SqlServer.Management.HadrDMF, Version=12.0.0.0, Culture=neutral, PublicKeyToken=89845dcd808...
Microsoft.SqlServer.Management.PSSnapins, Version=12.0.0.0, Culture=neutral, PublicKeyToken=89845dcd8...
Microsoft.SqlServer.Management.PSProvider, Version=12.0.0.0, Culture=neutral, PublicKeyToken=89845dcd...
Microsoft.SqlServer.SqlClrProvider, Version=12.0.0.0, Culture=neutral, PublicKeyToken=89845dcd8080cc91
Microsoft.SqlServer.SString, Version=12.0.0.0, Culture=neutral, PublicKeyToken=89845dcd8080cc91
Microsoft.SqlServer.Management.XEventDbScoped, Version=12.0.0.0, Culture=neutral, PublicKeyToken=8984...
Microsoft.SqlServer.Management.XEvent, Version=12.0.0.0, Culture=neutral, PublicKeyToken=89845dcd8080...
Microsoft.SqlServer.Management.IntegrationServices, Version=12.0.0.0, Culture=neutral, PublicKeyToken...
Microsoft.SqlServer.BatchParser, Version=12.0.0.0, Culture=neutral, PublicKeyToken=89845dcd8080cc91
```

# Creating a SQL Server Instance Object

Most of what you will need to do in SQL Server will require a connection to an instance. One way to do this is by creating an instance object via SMO.

## Getting ready

Open up your PowerShell console, **PowerShell ISE**, or your favorite PowerShell editor.

You will need to note what your instance name is. If you have a default instance, you can use your machine name. If you have a named instance, the format will be `<machine name>\<instance name>`.

## How to do it...

If you are connecting to your instance using Windows authentication and using your current Windows login, the steps are as follows:

1. Import the SQLPS module:

   ```
   #import SQLPS module
   Import-Module SQLPS –DisableNameChecking
   $VerbosePreference = "SilentlyContinue"
   ```

2. Store your instance name in a variable:

```
#create a variable for your instance name
$instanceName = "localhost"
```

3. If you are connecting to your instance using Windows authentication from the account you are logged in as:

```
#create your server instance
$server = New-Object -TypeName
Microsoft.SqlServer.Management.Smo.Server -ArgumentList
$instanceName
```

If you are connecting using **SQL Authentication**, you will need to know the username and password that you will use to authenticate. In this case, you will need to add the following code, which will set the connection to mixed mode and prompt for the username and password:

```
#set connection to mixed mode
$server.ConnectionContext.set_LoginSecure($false)

#set the login name
#of course we don't want to hardcode credentials here
#so we will prompt the user
#note password is passed as a SecureString type
$credentials = Get-Credential

#remove leading backslash in username
$login = $credentials.UserName $server.ConnectionContext.set_
Login($login)
$server.ConnectionContext.set_SecurePassword($credentials.Password)

#check connection string
#note though that this outputs your password in clear text
$server.ConnectionContext.ConnectionString

Write-Verbose "Connected to $($server.Name)"
Write-Verbose "Logged in as $($server.ConnectionContext. Login)"
```

## How it works...

Before you can access or manipulate SQL Server programmatically, you will often need to create references to its objects. At the most basic level is the server.

The server instance is using the type `Microsoft.SqlServer.Management.Smo.Server`. By default, connections to the server are using a trusted connection, meaning it uses the Windows account you're currently using when you log into the server. So all it needs is the instance name in its argument list:

```
#create your server instance
$server = New-Object -TypeName
Microsoft.SqlServer.Management.Smo.Server -ArgumentList
$instanceName
```

However, if you need to connect using a SQL login, you will need to set the `ConnectionContext.LoginSecure` property of the SMO Server class setting to `false`:

```
#set connection to mixed mode
#note that this authentication will fail if mixed mode
#is not enabled in SQL Server
$server.ConnectionContext.set_LoginSecure($false)
```

You will also need to explicitly set the username and the password. The best way to accomplish this is to prompt the user for the credentials:

```
#prompt
$credentials = Get-Credential
```

The `Get-Credential` cmdlet will display a popup window that will capture the login and password entered by the user:

```
$login = $credentials.UserName
```

Once we have the login, we can pass it to the `set_Login` method. The password is already a `SecureString` type, which means it is encrypted. This is the data type required by the `set_SecurePassword` method, so no further conversion is needed. The commands are as follows:

```
$server.ConnectionContext.set_Login($login)
$server.ConnectionContext.set_SecurePassword($credentials.Password
)
```

Should you want to hardcode the username and just prompt for the password, you can also do this:

```
$login = "belle"

#prompt
$credentials = Get-Credential –Credential $login
```

In the script, you will also notice that we are using `Write-Verbose` instead of `Write-Host` to display our results. This is because we want to control the output without always going back to our script and removing the `Write-Host` command.

By default, the script will not display any output, that is, the $VerbosePreference special variable is set to SilentlyContinue. If you want to run the script in verbose mode, you simply need to add this in the beginning of your script:

```
$VerbosePreference = "Continue"
```

When you are done, you just need to change the value to SilentlyContinue:

```
$VerbosePreference = "SilentlyContinue"
```

## See also

  ▸ The recipe *Loading SMO assemblies*.
  ▸ The recipe *Creating a SQL Server Instance Object*.

# Exploring SMO Server Objects

SMO comes with a hierarchy of objects that are accessible programmatically. For example, when we create an SMO server variable, we can then access databases, logins, and database level triggers. Once we get a handle of individual databases, we can then traverse the tables, stored procedures and views that it contains. Since many tasks involve SMO objects, you will be at an advantage if you know how to discover and navigate these objects.

## Getting ready

Open up your PowerShell console, **PowerShell ISE**, or your favorite PowerShell editor.

You will also need to note what your instance name is. If you have a default instance, you can use your machine name. If you have a named instance, the format will be <machine name>\<instance name>.

## How to do it...

In this recipe, we will start exploring the hierarchy of objects with SMO:

1. Import the SQLPS module as follows:

```
Import-Module SQLPS -DisableNameChecking
```

2. Create a server instance as follows:

```
$instanceName = "localhost"

#code below all in one line
$server = New-Object -TypeName
Microsoft.SqlServer.Management.Smo.Server -ArgumentList
$instanceName
```

3. Get the SMO objects directly accessible from the `$server` object:

```
$server |
Get-Member -MemberType "Property" |
Where-Object Definition -Like "*Smo*"
```

> If you are using PowerShell v2, you will have to change the `Where-Object` cmdlet usage to use the curly braces { } and the `$_` variable:
>
> ```
> Where-Object {$_.Definition -like "Smo*" }
> ```

4. Now, let's check SMO objects under databases:

```
$server.Databases |
Get-Member -MemberType "Property" |
Where-Object Definition -Like "*Smo*"
```

5. To check out the tables, you can type and execute the following:

```
$server.Databases["AdventureWorks2014"].Tables |
Get-Member -MemberType "Property" |
Where-Object Definition -Like "*Smo*"
```

## How it works...

SMO contains a hierarchy of objects. At the very top there is a server object, which in turn contains objects such as `Databases`, `Configuration`, `SqlMail`, `LoginCollection`, and so on. These objects in turn contain other objects, for example, `Databases` is a collection that contains `Database` objects, and a `Database` contains `Tables`.

> You can check out the SMO Object Model Diagram from the MSDN at https://msdn.microsoft.com/en-ca/library/ms162209.aspx.

One way to navigate through the hierarchy is by creating a server instance first. From here, you can use `Get-Member` to figure out which properties belong to that object. Once you find out, you can start creating additional variables for the member objects and then use `Get-Member` on them. Lather, rinse, and repeat.

## See also

- The recipe *Loading SMO assemblies*.
- The recipe *Creating a SQL Server Instance Object*.

# 2
# SQL Server and PowerShell Basic Tasks

In this chapter, we will cover:

- ▶ Listing SQL Server instances
- ▶ Discovering SQL Server services
- ▶ Starting/stopping SQL Server services
- ▶ Listing SQL Server configuration settings
- ▶ Changing SQL Server Instance configurations
- ▶ Searching for database objects
- ▶ Scripting SQL Server Stored Procedures
- ▶ Creating a database
- ▶ Altering database properties
- ▶ Dropping a database
- ▶ Changing a database owner
- ▶ Creating a table
- ▶ Creating a view
- ▶ Creating a stored procedure
- ▶ Creating a user defined function
- ▶ Creating a trigger
- ▶ Creating an index
- ▶ Executing a query / SQL script

- ▸ Performing bulk export using Invoke-SqlCmd
- ▸ Performing bulk export using the bcp command-line utility
- ▸ Performing bulk import using BULK INSERT
- ▸ Performing bulk import using the bcp command-line utility
- ▸ Connecting to an Azure SQL database
- ▸ Creating a table in an Azure SQL database

# Introduction

In this chapter, we will discuss scripts and snippets of code that accomplish basic SQL Server tasks using PowerShell. We will start with simple tasks such as listing SQL Server instances and creating objects such as tables, indexes, stored procedures, and functions to get you comfortable with working with SQL Server programmatically.

You will find that many of the recipes can be accomplished using PowerShell and **SQL Management Objects** (**SMO**). SMO is a library that exposes SQL Server classes that allow programmatic manipulation and automation of many database tasks. For some recipes, we will also explore alternative ways of accomplishing the same tasks using different native PowerShell cmdlets.

 SMO is explained in more detail in *Chapter 1, Getting Started with SQL Server and PowerShell.*

However, even if we are exploring how to create some common database objects using PowerShell, keep in mind that PowerShell will not always be the best tool for the task. There will be tasks that are best completed using **T-SQL**. It is still good to know what is possible in PowerShell and how to do it, so you know that you have alternatives depending on your requirements or situation.

For the recipes, we are going to use PowerShell ISE quite a lot.

If you prefer running the script from the PowerShell console rather than running the commands from the ISE, you can save the scripts in a .ps1 file and run it from the PowerShell console.

# Listing SQL Server instances

In this recipe, we will list all SQL Server instances in the local network.

## Getting ready

Log in to the server that has your SQL Server development instance as an administrator.

## How to do it...

Let's look at the steps to list your SQL Server instances:

1.  Open **PowerShell ISE** as administrator.

2.  Let's use the `Start-Service` cmdlet to start the SQL Browser service:

    ```
    Import-Module SQLPS -DisableNameChecking

    #out of the box, the SQLBrowser is disabled. To enable:
    Set-Service SQLBrowser -StartupType Automatic

    #sql browser must be installed and running for us
    #to discover SQL Server instances
    Start-Service "SQLBrowser"
    ```

3.  Next, you need to create a `ManagedComputer` object to get access to instances. Type the following script and run:

    ```
    $instanceName = "localhost"
    $managedComputer = New-Object
    Microsoft.SqlServer.Management.Smo.Wmi.ManagedComputer
    $instanceName

    #list server instances
    $managedComputer.ServerInstances
    ```

Your result should look similar to the one shown in the following screenshot:

```
ServerProtocols : {Np, Sm, Tcp}
Parent          : Microsoft.SqlServer.Management.Smo.Wmi.ManagedComputer
Urn             : ManagedComputer[@Name='localhost']/ServerInstance[@Name='MSSQLSERVER']
Name            : MSSQLSERVER
Properties      : {}
UserData        :
State           : Existing

ServerProtocols : {Np, Sm, Tcp}
Parent          : Microsoft.SqlServer.Management.Smo.Wmi.ManagedComputer
Urn             : ManagedComputer[@Name='localhost']/ServerInstance[@Name='SQL01']
Name            : SQL01
Properties      : {}
UserData        :
State           : Existing
```

Notice that `$managedComputer.ServerInstances` gives you not only instance names, but also additional properties such as `ServerProtocols`, `Urn`, `State`, and so on.

4.  Confirm that these are the same instances you see from **SQL Server Management Studio**.

5.  Open **SQL Server Management Studio**. Go to **Connect | Database Engine**.

6.  In the **Server Name** dropdown, click on **Browse for More**.

7.  Select the **Network Servers** tab and check the instances listed. Your screen should look similar to this:

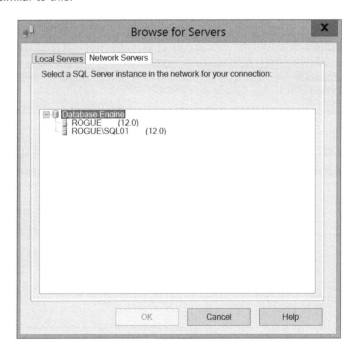

## How it works...

All services in a Windows operating system are exposed and accessible using **Windows Management Instrumentation** (**WMI**). WMI is Microsoft's framework for listing, setting, and configuring any Microsoft-related resource. This framework follows **Web-based Enterprise Management** (**WBEM**). The *Distributed Management Task Force, Inc.* (`http://www.dmtf.org/standards/wbem`) defines WBEM as follows:

> *A set of management and Internet standard technologies developed to unify the management of distributed computing environments. WBEM provides the ability for the industry to deliver a well-integrated set of standard-based management tools, facilitating the exchange of data across otherwise disparate technologies and platforms.*

In order to access SQL Server WMI-related objects, you can create a WMI `ManagedComputer` instance:

```
$managedComputer = New-Object
Microsoft.SqlServer.Management.Smo.Wmi.ManagedComputer
$instanceName
```

The `ManagedComputer` object has access to a `ServerInstance` property, which in turn lists all available instances in the local network. These instances however, are only identifiable if the SQL Server Browser service is running.

> The **SQL Server Browser** is a Windows Service that can provide information on installed instances in a box. You need to start this service if you want to list the SQL Server-related services.

## There's more...

The `Services` instance of the `ManagedComputer` object can also provide similar information, but you will have to filter for the server type `SqlServer`:

```
#list server instances
$managedComputer.Services |
Where-Object Type -eq "SqlServer" |
Select-Object Name, State, Type, StartMode, ProcessId
```

Your result should look like this:

```
Name       : MSSQL$SQL01
State      : Existing
Type       : SqlServer
StartMode  : Auto
ProcessId  : 1620

Name       : MSSQLSERVER
State      : Existing
Type       : SqlServer
StartMode  : Auto
ProcessId  : 1956
```

Instead of creating a WMI instance by using the `New-Object` method, you can also use the `Get-WmiObject` cmdlet when creating your variable. `Get-WmiObject`, however, will not expose exactly the same properties exposed by the `Microsoft.SqlServer.Management.Smo.Wmi.ManagedComputer` object.

To list instances using `Get-WmiObject`, you will need to discover what namespace is available in your environment:

```
$hostName = "localhost"

$namespace = Get-WMIObject -ComputerName $hostName -Namespace
root\Microsoft\SQLServer -Class "__NAMESPACE" |
            Where-Object Name -like "ComputerManagement*"
#see matching namespace objects
$namespace

#see namespace names
$namespace | Select-Object -ExpandProperty "__NAMESPACE"
$namespace | Select-Object -ExpandProperty "Name"
```

 If you are using PowerShell v2, you will have to change the `Where-Object` cmdlet usage to use the curly braces { } and the $_ variable. Recall the $_ variable contains the current pipeline object:

```
Where-Object {$_.Name -like "ComputerManagement*" }
```

For SQL Server 2014, the namespace value is:

```
ROOT\Microsoft\SQLServer\ComputerManagement12
```

This value can be derived from `$namespace.__NAMESPACE` and `$namespace.Name`. Once you have the namespace, you can use this with `Get-WmiObject` to retrieve the instances. We can use the `SqlServiceType` property to filter.

According to MSDN (`http://msdn.microsoft.com/en-us/library/ms179591.aspx`), these are the values of `SqlServiceType`:

| SqlServiceType | Description |
|---|---|
| 1 | SQL Server Service |
| 2 | SQL Server Agent Service |
| 3 | Full-Text Search Engine Service |
| 4 | Integration Services Service |
| 5 | Analysis Services Service |
| 6 | Reporting Services Service |
| 7 | SQL Browser Service |

Thus, to retrieve the SQL Server instances, we need to provide the full namespace `ROOT\Microsoft\SQLServer\ComputerManagement12`. We also need to filter for SQL Server Service type, or `SQLServiceType = 1`. The code is as follows:

```
Get-WmiObject -ComputerName $hostName
-Namespace "$($namespace.__NAMESPACE)\$($namespace.Name)"
-Class SqlService |
Where-Object SQLServiceType -eq 1 |
Select-Object ServiceName, DisplayName, SQLServiceType |
Format-Table –AutoSize
```

Your result should look similar to the following screenshot:

```
ServiceName DisplayName              SQLServiceType
----------- -----------              --------------
MSSQL$SQL01 SQL Server (SQL01)                    1
MSSQLSERVER SQL Server (MSSQLSERVER)              1
```

Yet another way to list all the SQL Server instances in the local network is by using the `System.Data.Sql.SQLSourceEnumerator` class, instead of `ManagedComputer`. This class has a static method called `Instance.GetDataSources` that will list all SQL Server instances:

```
[System.Data.Sql.SqlDataSourceEnumerator]:
:Instance.GetDataSources() |
Format-Table -AutoSize
```

When you execute, your result should look similar to the following:

```
ServerName  InstanceName  IsClustered  Version
----------  ------------  -----------  -------
ROGUE                     No           12.0.2000.8
ROGUE       SQL01         No           12.0.2000.8
```

If you have multiple SQL Server versions, you can use the following code to display your instances:

```
#list services using WMI
foreach ($path in $namespace)
{
Write-Verbose "SQL Services in:$($path._NAMESPACE)\$($path.Name)"
Get-WmiObject -ComputerName $hostName `
-Namespace "$($path._NAMESPACE)\$($path.Name)" `
-Class SqlService |
Where-Object SQLServiceType -eq 1 |
Select-Object ServiceName, DisplayName, SQLServiceType |
Format-Table -AutoSize
}
```

# Discovering SQL Server services

In this recipe, we will enumerate all SQL Server services and list their statuses.

## Getting ready

Check which SQL Server services are installed in your instance. Go to **Start | Run** and type `services.msc`. You should see a screen similar to this:

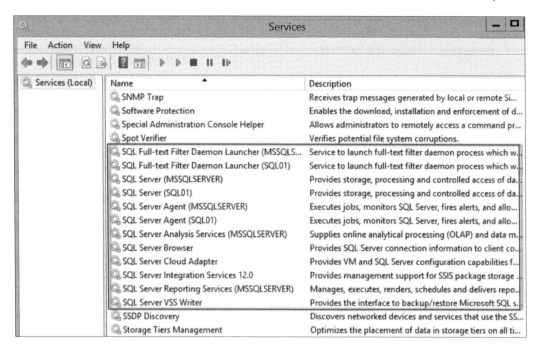

## How to do it...

Let's assume you are running this script on the server box:

1. Open **PowerShell ISE** as administrator.

2. Add the following code and execute:

```
Import-Module SQLPS -DisableNameChecking

#you can replace localhost with your instance name
$instanceName = "localhost"
$managedComputer = New-Object
Microsoft.SqlServer.Management.Smo.Wmi.ManagedComputer
$instanceName

#list services
$managedComputer.Services |
Select-Object Name, Type, ServiceState, DisplayName |
Format-Table -AutoSize
```

Your result will look similar to the one shown in the following screenshot:

```
Name                              Type SeviceState DisplayName
----                              ---- ------------ -----------
MsDtsServer120      SqlServerIntegrationService    Stopped SQL Server Integration Services 12.0
MSSQL$SQL01                       SqlServer         Running SQL Server (SQL01)
MSSQLFDLauncher                           9         Running SQL Full-text Filter Daemon Launcher (MSSQLSERVER)
MSSQLFDLauncher$SQL01                      9         Running SQL Full-text Filter Daemon Launcher (SQL01)
MSSQLSERVER                       SqlServer         Running SQL Server (MSSQLSERVER)
MSSQLServerOLAPService        AnalysisServer        Running SQL Server Analysis Services (MSSQLSERVER)
ReportServer                     ReportServer       Stopped SQL Server Reporting Services (MSSQLSERVER)
SQLAgent$SQL01                     SqlAgent         Stopped SQL Server Agent (SQL01)
SQLBrowser                        SqlBrowser        Running SQL Server Browser
SQLSERVERAGENT                     SqlAgent         Stopped SQL Server Agent (MSSQLSERVER)
```

Items listed in your screen will vary depending on the features installed and running in your instance

3. Confirm that these are the services that exist in your server. Check your services window.

## How it works...

Services that are installed on a system can be queried using WMI. Specific services for SQL Server are exposed through SMO's WMI `ManagedComputer` object. Some of the exposed properties are as follows:

- `ClientProtocols`
- `ConnectionSettings`
- `ServerAliases`
- `ServerInstances`
- `Services`

## There's more...

An alternative way to get SQL Server-related services is by using `Get-WMIObject`. We will need to pass in the host name as well as the SQL Server WMI Provider for the `ComputerManagement` namespace. For SQL Server 2014, this value is `ROOT\Microsoft\SQLServer\ComputerManagement12`.

The script to retrieve the services is provided here. Note that we are dynamically composing the WMI namespace. The code is as follows:

```
$hostName = "localhost"

$namespace = Get-WMIObject -ComputerName $hostName -NameSpace
root\Microsoft\SQLServer -Class "__NAMESPACE" |
            Where-Object Name -like "ComputerManagement*"

Get-WmiObject -ComputerName $hostname -Namespace "$($namespace.__
NAMESPACE)\$($namespace.Name)" -Class SqlService |
Select-Object ServiceName
```

If you have multiple SQL Server versions installed and want to see just the most recent version's services, you can limit to the latest namespace by adding Select-Object -Last 1:

```
$namespace = Get-WMIObject -ComputerName $hostName -NameSpace root\
Microsoft\SQLServer -Class "__NAMESPACE" |
            Where-Object Name -like "ComputerManagement*"   |
            Select-Object -Last 1
```

Yet another alternative but *less accurate* way of listing possible SQL Server related services is the following snippet of code:

```
#alterative - but less accurate
Get-Service *SQL*
```

This uses the `Get-Service` cmdlet and filters base on the service name. This is less accurate because this grabs all processes that have `SQL` in the name, but may not necessarily be related to SQL Server. For example, if you have `MySQL` installed, it will get picked up as a process. Conversely, this will not pick up SQL Server-related services that do not have `SQL` in the name, such as `ReportServer`.

## See also

▸ The *Listing SQL Server instances* recipe.

# Starting/stopping SQL Server services

This recipe describes how to start and/or stop SQL Server services.

## Getting ready

Check which SQL Services are installed in your machine. Go to **Start | Run** and type
`services.msc`. You should see a screen similar to this:

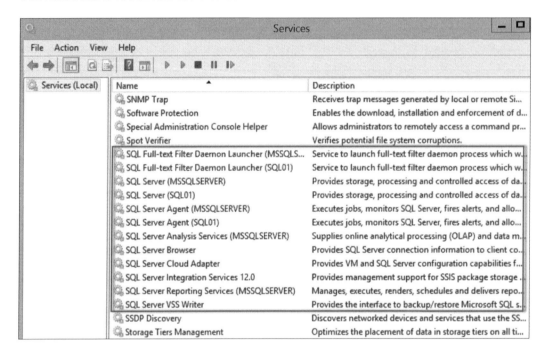

## How to do it...

Let's look at the steps to toggle your SQL Server services states:

1. Open **PowerShell ISE** as administrator.

2. Add the following code:

```
$verbosepreference = "Continue"
$services = @("SQLBrowser", "ReportServer")
$hostName = "localhost"

$services |
ForEach-Object {
```

```
$service = Get-Service -Name $_
if($service.Status -eq "Stopped")
{
    Write-Verbose "Starting $($service.Name) ...."
    Start-Service -Name $service.Name
}
else
{
    Write-Verbose "Stopping $($service.Name) ...."
    Stop-Service -Name $service.Name
}
}
$verbosepreference = "SilentlyContinue"
```

 Be careful; the status may return prematurely as "started" when in fact the service is still in the "starting" state.

3. Execute and confirm that the service status has changed accordingly. Go to **Start | Run** and type Services.msc.

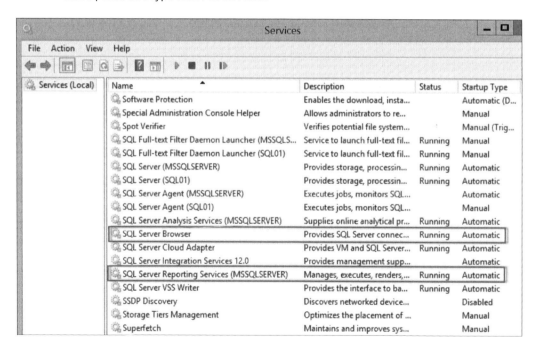

For example, in our sample, both **SQLBrowser** and **ReportServer** were initially running. Once the script was executed, both services were stopped.

## How it works...

In this recipe, we picked two services, **SQLBrowser** and **ReportServer**, which we want to manipulate and save into an array:

```
$services = @("SQLBrowser", "ReportServer")
```

We then pipe the array contents to a `Foreach-Object` cmdlet, so we can determine what action to perform for each service. For our purposes, if the service is stopped, we want to start it. Otherwise we stop it. The code is as follows:

```
$services |
ForEach-Object {
    $service = Get-Service -Name $_
    if($service.Status -eq "Stopped")
    {
        Write-Verbose "Starting $($service.Name) ...."
        Start-Service -Name $service.Name
    }
    else
    {
        Write-Verbose "Stopping $($service.Name) ...."
        Stop-Service -Name $service.Name
    }
}
```

You may also want to determine dependent services, or services that rely on a particular service. It will be good to consider synchronizing the starting/stopping of these dependent services with the main service they depend on.

To identify dependent services, you can use the `DependentServices` property of the `System.ServiceProcess.ServiceController` class:

```
$services |
ForEach-Object {
    $service = Get-Service -Name $_
    Write-Verbose "Services Dependent on $($service.Name)"
    $service.DependentServices |
    Select-Object Name
}
```

To get the list of properties and methods of the `System.ServiceProcess.ServiceController` class, which is the class returned by `Get-Service` cmdlet, you can use the following snippet:

```
Get-Service |
Get-Member
```

An alternative way of working with SQL Server services is by using the `Microsoft.SqlServer.Management.Smo.Wmi.ManagedComputer` class. The code is as follows:

```
Import-Module SQLPS -DisableNameChecking

$verbosepreference = "Continue"

#list services you want to start/stop here
#if you want to use the database engine, use MSSQLSERVER for
#the default instance
$services = @("SQLBrowser", "ReportServer")
$instanceName = "localhost"


#create a ManagedComputer variable
$managedComputer = New-Object
Microsoft.SqlServer.Management.Smo.Wmi.ManagedComputer
$instanceName

#go through each service and toggle the state
$services |
ForEach-Object {
    $service = $managedComputer.Services[$_]
    switch($service.ServiceState)
    {
        "Running"
        {
            Write-Verbose "Stopping $($service.Name)"
            $service.Stop()
        }
        "Stopped"
        {
            Write-Verbose "Starting $($service.Name)"
            $service.Start()
        }
    }
}

$verbosepreference = "SilentlyContinue"
```

When using the `Smo.Wmi.ManagedComputer` object, you can simply use the `Stop` method provided with the class and the `Start` method to start the service.

To get the list of properties and methods available with the `Smo.Wmi.ManagedComputer` class, you can use the following snippet:

```
#make sure you have created a ManagedComputer
#instance before you run this
$managedComputer |
Get-Member
```

## There's more...

To explore available cmdlets that can help manage and maintain services, use the following command:

```
Get-Command -Name *Service* -CommandType Cmdlet
```

This will enumerate all cmdlets that have `Service` in the name:

```
CommandType        Name
-----------        ----
Cmdlet             Get-Service
Cmdlet             New-Service
Cmdlet             New-WebServiceProxy
Cmdlet             Restart-Service
Cmdlet             Resume-Service
Cmdlet             Set-Service
Cmdlet             Start-Service
Cmdlet             Stop-Service
Cmdlet             Suspend-Service
```

All of these cmdlets relate to Windows services, with the exception of `New-WebServiceProxy`, which is described in MSDN as a cmdlet that *creates a Web service proxy object that lets you use and manage the Web service in Windows PowerShell.*

Here is a brief comparison between these service-oriented cmdlets and the methods available for the `Service` object of `Microsoft.SqlServer.Management.Smo.Wmi.ManagedComputer`, as discussed in the recipe:

| Service methods | Service-related cmdlets |
|-----------------|-------------------------|
| `Start()` | `Start-Service` |
| `Stop()` | `Stop-Service` |
| `Continue()` | `Resume-Service` |
| `Pause()` | `Suspend-Service` |
| `Refresh()` | |
| | `Restart-Service` |

There isn't necessarily a one-to-one mapping between the methods of the `Service` class and the `Service` cmdlets. For example, there is a `Restart-Service` cmdlet, but there isn't any `Restart` method. This should not raise alarm bells though.

Although it may seem that some methods or cmdlets may be missing, it is important to note PowerShell is a rich scripting platform and language. In addition to its own cmdlets, it leverages the whole .NET platform. Whatever you can do in the .NET platform, you can probably do using PowerShell. Even if you think something is not doable when you look at a specific class or object, there is most likely a cmdlet somewhere that can perform that same task, or vice versa. If you still cannot find your ideal solution, you can create your own—be it a class, a module, a cmdlet, or a function.

## See also

► The *Discovering SQL Server services* recipe.

# Listing SQL Server configuration settings

This recipe walks through how to list SQL Server configurable and nonconfigurable instance settings using PowerShell.

## How to do it...

Let's look at the steps involved in listing SQL Server configuration settings:

1. Open **PowerShell ISE** as administrator.
2. Import the SQLPS module and create a new SMO Server Object:

```
#import SQL Server module
Import-Module SQLPS -DisableNameChecking

#replace this with your instance name
$instanceName = "localhost"
$server = New-Object -TypeName
Microsoft.SqlServer.Management.Smo.Server -ArgumentList
$instanceName
```

To explore what members and methods are included in the SMO server, use the following:

```
#Explore: get all properties available for a server object
#see http://msdn.microsoft.com/en-us/library/ms212724.aspx
```

```
$server |
Get-Member |
Where-Object MemberType -eq "Property"
```

First, let's explore the `Information` class.

```
#The Information class lists nonconfigurable
#instance settings, like BuildNumber,
#OSVersion, ProductLevel etc
#This also includes settings specified during install

$server.Information.Properties |
Select-Object Name, Value |
Format-Table -AutoSize
```

This is a partial list of values that will be returned:

```
Name                                                                                        Value
----                                                                                        -----
BuildNumber                                                                                  2000
Edition                                                                   Developer Edition (64-bit)
ErrorLogPath          C:\Program Files\Microsoft SQL Server\MSSQL12.MSSQLSERVER\MSSQL\Log
HasNullSaPassword
IsCaseSensitive                                                                             False
IsFullTextInstalled                                                                          True
IsXTPSupported                                                                               True
Language                                                                   English (United States)
MasterDBLogPath       C:\Program Files\Microsoft SQL Server\MSSQL12.MSSQLSERVER\MSSQL\DATA
MasterDBPath          C:\Program Files\Microsoft SQL Server\MSSQL12.MSSQLSERVER\MSSQL\DATA
MaxPrecision                                                                                    38
NetName                                                                                     ROGUE
OSVersion                                                                                6.3 (9600)
PhysicalMemory                                                                               10999
Platform                                                                                   NT x64
Processors                                                                                       4
Product                                                                        Microsoft SQL Server
RootDirectory         C:\Program Files\Microsoft SQL Server\MSSQL12.MSSQLSERVER\MSSQL
VersionMajor                                                                                    12
VersionMinor                                                                                     0
VersionString                                                                           12.0.2000.8
Collation                                                                   SQL_Latin1_General_CP1_CI_AS
EngineEdition                                                                                    3
IsClustered                                                                                 False
IsSingleUser                                                                                False
ProductLevel                                                                                   RTM
BuildClrVersionString                                                                   v4.0.30319
```

3.  Next, let's look at the `Settings` class.

    ```
    #The Settings lists some instance level
    #configurable settings, like LoginMode,
    #BackupDirectory etc

    $server.Settings.Properties |
    Select-Object Name, Value |
    Format-Table -AutoSize
    ```

You should get a result similar to the one shown in the following screenshot:

```
Name                                                                          Value
----                                                                          -----
AuditLevel                                                                      All
BackupDirectory                                                             C:\Temp
DefaultFile       C:\Program Files\Microsoft SQL Server\MSSQL12.MSSQLSERVER\MSSQL\DATA\
DefaultLog        C:\Program Files\Microsoft SQL Server\MSSQL12.MSSQLSERVER\MSSQL\DATA\
LoginMode                                                                  Integrated
MailProfile
NumberOfLogFiles                                                                 -1
PerfMonMode                                                                    None
TapeLoadWaitTime                                                                 -1
```

4. The `UserOptions` class lists user-specific options:

```
#The UserOptions include options that can be set
#for user connections, for example
#AnsiPadding, AnsiNulls, NoCount, QuotedIdentifier

$server.UserOptions.Properties |
Select-Object Name, Value |
Format-Table -AutoSize
```

We get the following output:

```
Name                           Value
----                           -----
AbortOnArithmeticErrors        False
AbortTransactionOnError        False
AnsiNullDefaultOff             False
AnsiNullDefaultOn              False
AnsiNulls                      False
AnsiPadding                    False
AnsiWarnings                   False
ConcatenateNullYieldsNull      False
CursorCloseOnCommit            False
DisableDefaultConstraintCheck  False
IgnoreArithmeticErrors         False
ImplicitTransactions           False
NoCount                        False
NumericRoundAbort              False
QuotedIdentifier               False
```

5. The `Configuration` class contains instance-specific settings, which are similar to what you will see when you run `sp_configure`:

```
#The Configuration class contains instance-specific
#settings, like AgentXPs, clr enabled, xp_cmdshell
#You will normally see this when you run
#the stored procedure sp_configure

$server.Configuration.Properties |
Select-Object DisplayName, RunValue, ConfigValue |
Format-Table –AutoSize
```

We get the following output:

```
DisplayName                          RunValue ConfigValue
-----------                          -------- -----------
recovery interval (min)                     0           0
allow updates                               0           0
user connections                            0           0
locks                                       0           0
open objects                                0           0
fill factor (%)                             0           0
disallow results from triggers              0           0
nested triggers                             1           1
server trigger recursion                    1           1
remote access                               1           1
default language                            0           0
cross db ownership chaining                 0           0
max worker threads                          0           0
network packet size (B)                  4096        4096
show advanced options                       0           0
remote proc trans                           0           0
c2 audit mode                               0           0
default full-text language               1033        1033
two digit year cutoff                    2049        2049
index create memory (KB)                    0           0
priority boost                              0           0
remote login timeout (s)                   10          10
remote query timeout (s)                  600         600
cursor threshold                           -1          -1
set working set size                        0           0
user options                                0           0
affinity mask                               0           0
max text repl size (B)                  65536       65536
```

## How it works...

Most SQL Server settings and configurations are exposed using SMO or WMI, which allows for these values to be programmatically retrieved.

At the core of accessing configuration details is the SMO Server (`Microsoft.SqlServer.Management.Smo.Server`) class. This class exposes a SQL Server instance's properties, some of which are configurable and some are not.

To create an SMO Server class, you will need to know your instance name and pass it as an argument:

```
#replace this with your instance name
$instanceName = "localhost"
$server = New-Object -TypeName
Microsoft.SqlServer.Management.Smo.Server -ArgumentList
$instanceName
```

There are four main properties that store settings/configurations that we looked at in this recipe:

| Server Property | Description |
| --- | --- |
| Information | This includes nonconfigurable instance settings, such as `BuildNumber`, `Edition`, `OSVersion`, and `ProductLevel`. This also includes settings specified during install, for example, `Collation`, `MasterDBPath`, and `MasterDBLogPath`. |
| Settings | This lists some instance level configurable settings, such as `LoginMode` and `BackupDirectory`. |
| UserOptions | This has options that can be set for user connections, such as `AnsiWarnings`, `AnsiNulls`, `AnsiPadding`, and `NoCount`. |
| Configuration | This contains instance-specific settings such as `AgentXPs`, `remote access`, `clr enabled`, and `xp_cmdshell`, which you will normally see and set when you use the `sp_configure` system stored procedure. |

## There's more...

Check out the MSDN for complete documentation on SMO classes:

`http://msdn.microsoft.com/en-us/library/ms212724.aspx`

# Changing SQL Server Instance configurations

This recipe discusses how to change instance configuration settings using PowerShell.

## Getting ready

For this recipe, we will perform the following tasks:

- Change fill factor to 60 percent
- Enable SQL Server Agent
- Set Minimum Server Memory to 500 MB
- Change authentication method to `Mixed`

## How to do it...

Let's change some SQL Server settings using PowerShell:

1. Open **PowerShell ISE** as administrator.

2. Import the SQLPS module and create a new SMO Server Object:

```
#import SQL Server module
Import-Module SQLPS -DisableNameChecking

#replace this with your instance name
$instanceName = "localhost"
$server = New-Object -TypeName
Microsoft.SqlServer.Management.Smo.Server -ArgumentList
$instanceName
```

3. Add the following script and run:

```
<#
run value vs config value
config_value," is what the setting has been set to (but may
or may not be what SQL Server is actually running now. Some
settings don't go into effect until SQL Server has been
restarted, or until the RECONFIGURE WITH OVERRIDE option
has been run, as appropriate.) And the last column,
"run_value," is the value of the setting currently in
effect.
#>

#change FillFactor
$server.Configuration.FillFactor.ConfigValue = 60

#enable SQL Server Agent extended stored procedures
$server.Configuration.AgentXPsEnabled.ConfigValue = 1

#change minimum server memory to 500MB; MB is default
$server.Configuration.MinServerMemory.ConfigValue = 500

$server.Configuration.Alter()

#confirm changes
$server.Configuration.Properties |
Select-Object DisplayName, ConfigValue |
Format-Table -AutoSize
```

```
#change authentication mode
$server.Settings.LoginMode = [Microsoft.SqlServer.Management.Smo.
ServerLoginMode]::Mixed

#you can also simply provide this without the whole
#enumeration value but simply a string:
#$server.Settings.LoginMode = "Mixed"

$server.Alter()

#confirm changes
$server.settings.LoginMode
```

4. Confirm the changes. To confirm fill factor, use the following steps:

    1. Go to **SQL Server Management Studio**.

    2. Connect to your instance.

    3. Right-click on your instance and select **Properties** from the pop-up menu.

    4. Go to **Database Settings** and check whether your fill factor has changed:

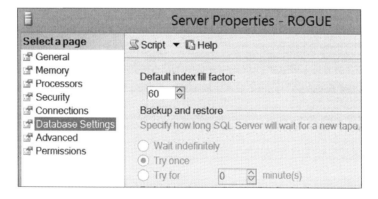

5. A side effect of enabling SQL Server Agent extended stored procedures is enabling SQL Server Agent. To confirm SQL Server Agent has been enabled, use the following steps:

    1. Go to **SQL Server Management Studio**.

    2. Connect to your instance.

3. Check whether **SQL Server Agent** for the instance you modified is now running.

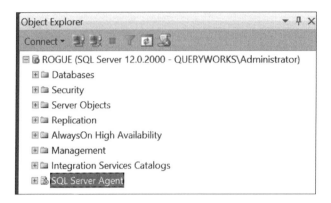

6. To confirm minimum server memory settings, use the following steps:

   1. Go to **SQL Server Management Studio**.

   2. Right-click on your instance and select **Properties**.

   3. Go to **Memory** and check whether the value has changed to what you set it to.

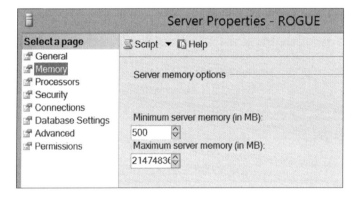

7. To confirm the authentication mode change, use the following steps:

   1. Go to **SQL Server Management Studio**.

   2. Connect to your instance.

   3. Right-click on your instance and select **Properties**.

   4. Go to **Security** and check whether the instance is now in **SQL Server and Windows Authentication** mode.

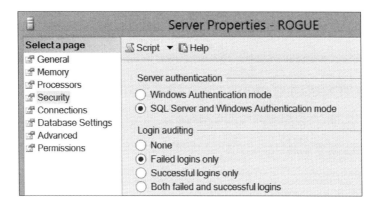

## How it works...

Depending on what server properties you need to change, you may need to determine which of the following classes you may need to access: `Settings`, `UserOptions`, or `Configuration`.

Once you have determined which class and property you want to change, you can change the values and invoke the `Alter()` method:

```
#to make Configuration changes permanent
$server.Configuration.Alter()
```

```
#to make Settings changes permanent
$server.Alter()
```

## There's more...

When you run `sp_configure`, you will see a result that shows both `run value` and `config value`:

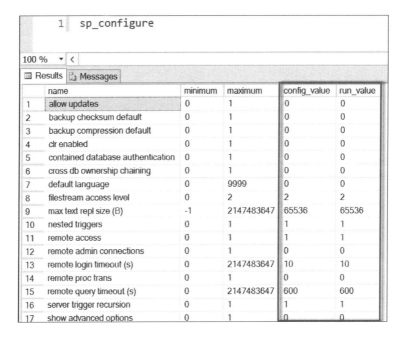

| | name | minimum | maximum | config_value | run_value |
|---|---|---|---|---|---|
| 1 | allow updates | 0 | 1 | 0 | 0 |
| 2 | backup checksum default | 0 | 1 | 0 | 0 |
| 3 | backup compression default | 0 | 1 | 0 | 0 |
| 4 | clr enabled | 0 | 1 | 0 | 0 |
| 5 | contained database authentication | 0 | 1 | 0 | 0 |
| 6 | cross db ownership chaining | 0 | 1 | 0 | 0 |
| 7 | default language | 0 | 9999 | 0 | 0 |
| 8 | filestream access level | 0 | 2 | 2 | 2 |
| 9 | max text repl size (B) | -1 | 2147483647 | 65536 | 65536 |
| 10 | nested triggers | 0 | 1 | 1 | 1 |
| 11 | remote access | 0 | 1 | 1 | 1 |
| 12 | remote admin connections | 0 | 1 | 0 | 0 |
| 13 | remote login timeout (s) | 0 | 2147483647 | 10 | 10 |
| 14 | remote proc trans | 0 | 1 | 0 | 0 |
| 15 | remote query timeout (s) | 0 | 2147483647 | 600 | 600 |
| 16 | server trigger recursion | 0 | 1 | 1 | 1 |
| 17 | show advanced options | 0 | 1 | 0 | 0 |

There is often confusion between `run_value` and `config_value`. The `config_value` variable is what value the setting is set to. The `run_value` variable is what SQL Server is currently using. Sometimes, a new value may be set (`config_value`) but it isn't used by SQL Server until the instance is restarted, or until `RECONFIGURE` is run.

## See also

▸ The *Listing SQL Server configuration settings* recipe.

# Searching for database objects

In this recipe, we will search database objects based on a search string using PowerShell.

## Getting ready

We will use the `AdventureWorks2014` database in this recipe and look for SQL Server objects with the word `Product` in it.

To get an idea of what we are expecting to retrieve, run the following script in **SQL Server Management Studio**:

```
USE AdventureWorks2014
GO
SELECT
  *
FROM
  sys.objects
WHERE
  name LIKE '%Product%'
    -- check only for table, view, function
    -- or stored procedure
  AND [type] IN ('U', 'FN', 'P', 'V')
ORDER BY
  [type]
```

This will get you 23 results. Remember this number.

## How to do it...

Let's see how we can search for objects in your SQL Server database using PowerShell:

1. Open **PowerShell ISE** as administrator.

2. Import the `SQLPS` module and create a new SMO Server Object:

   ```
   #import SQL Server module
   Import-Module SQLPS -DisableNameChecking

   #replace this with your instance name
   $instanceName = "localhost"
   $server = New-Object -TypeName
   Microsoft.SqlServer.Management.Smo.Server -ArgumentList
   $instanceName
   ```

3. Add the following script and run:

   ```
   $databaseName = "AdventureWorks2014"
   $db = $server.Databases[$databaseName]

   #what keyword are we looking for?
   $searchString = "Product"

   #create empty array, we will store results here
   $results = @()

   #now we will loop through all database SMO
   #properties and look of objects that match
   #the search string
   $db |
   ```

```
Get-Member -MemberType Property |
Where-Object Definition -like "*Smo*" |
ForEach-Object {
    $type = $_.Name
    $db.$type |
    Where-Object Name -like "*$searchstring*" |
    ForEach-Object {
        $result = [PSCustomObject] @{
            ObjectType = $type
            ObjectName = $_.Name
        }
        $results += $result
    }
}

#display results
$results |
Format-Table -AutoSize

#export results to csv file
$file = "C:\Temp\SearchResults.csv"
$results | Export-Csv -Path $file -NoTypeInformation

#display file contents in notepad
notepad $file
```

Your result will look like this:

```
ObjectType           ObjectName
----------           ----------
Schemas              Production
StoredProcedures     uspGetWhereUsedProductID
Tables               Product
Tables               ProductCategory
Tables               ProductCostHistory
Tables               ProductDescription
Tables               ProductDocument
Tables               ProductInventory
Tables               ProductListPriceHistory
Tables               ProductModel
Tables               ProductModelIllustration
Tables               ProductModelProductDescriptionCulture
Tables               ProductPhoto
Tables               ProductProductPhoto
Tables               ProductReview
Tables               ProductSubcategory
Tables               ProductVendor
Tables               SpecialOfferProduct
UserDefinedFunctions ufnGetProductDealerPrice
UserDefinedFunctions ufnGetProductListPrice
UserDefinedFunctions ufnGetProductStandardCost
Views                vProductAndDescription
Views                vProductModelCatalogDescription
Views                vProductModelInstructions
XmlSchemaCollections ProductDescriptionSchemaCollection
```

## How it works...

After creating our usual SMO Server Object, we created an SMO database handle to our
`AdventureWorks2014` database:

```
$databasename = "AdventureWorks2014"
$db = $server.Databases[$databasename]
```

We also defined our search string. Our goal is to get all database objects that have the word
`Product` in it:

```
#what keyword are we looking for?
$searchString = "Product"
```

We also create an empty array with the following code, where we can save our search results
as `records`. This will enable us to display our final results in a tabular fashion when we're
done with our iteration.

```
$results = @()
```

The following line allows us to go through all the database-related SMO properties:

```
$db |
Get-Member -MemberType Property |
Where-Object Definition -like "*Smo*"
```

From here, we query the contents of each SMO property for members that contain the
keyword we're looking for:

```
#now we will loop through all database SMO
#properties and look of objects that match
#the search string
$db |
Get-Member -MemberType Property |
Where-Object Definition -like "*Smo*" |
ForEach-Object {
   $type = $_.Name
   $db.$type |
     Where-Object Name -like "*$searchstring*" |
   ForEach-Object {
      $result = [PSCustomObject] @{
         ObjectType = $type
         ObjectName = $_.Name
      }
      $results += $result
   }
}
```

In the inner `Foreach-Object` block, we are building a `PSCustomObject` that will store the two fields we want to return: `ObjectType` and `ObjectName`. A `PSCustomObject` allows you to wrap a set of custom labels and values into a PowerShell object that can easily be used with, and piped to, other cmdlets. This `PSCustomObject` that we created, which stores the matched database objects with our search string, will be then be stored into the `$results` array. We also strip out the substring `Microsoft.SqlServer.Management.Smo` from the resulting object types for brevity. The code is as follows:

```
$db |
Get-Member -MemberType Property |
Where-Object Definition -like "*Smo*" |
ForEach-Object {
    $type = $_.Name
    $db.$type |
    Where-Object Name -like "*$searchstring*" |
    ForEach-Object {
        $result = [PSCustomObject] @{
            ObjectType = $type
            ObjectName = $_.Name
        }
        $results += $result
    }
}
```

Lastly, we export our results to a CSV file using the `Export-Csv` cmdlet, and display the contents in notepad:

```
#export results to csv file
$file = "C:\Temp\SearchResults.csv"
$results | Export-Csv -Path $file -NoTypeInformation

#display file contents
notepad $file
```

When you inspect your results, you will notice two extra objects that were not captured in our T-SQL statement in the *Getting ready* section. If we compare the two approaches, our PowerShell approach is more complete. In addition to the expected 23 results, PowerShell has also captured:

▶ **Production**: Schema object

▶ **ProductDescriptionSchemaCollection**: XmlSchemaCollection object

## There's more...

Another way to iterate through the objects is by using the `EnumObjects` method of the SMO database variable $db:

```
$searchString = "Product"

$db.EnumObjects() |
Where-Object Name -like "*$searchString*" |
Select DatabaseObjectTypes, Name |
Format-Table -AutoSize
```

Yes, there is still yet another alternative. You can look for objects that match the search string by going through the $db object properties one by one:

```
#long version is to enumerate explicitly each object type
$db.Tables |
Where-Object Name -like "*$searchstring*"

$db.StoredProcedures |
Where-Object Name -like "*$searchstring*"

$db.Triggers |
Where-Object Name -like "*$searchstring*"

$db.UserDefinedFunctions |
Where-Object Name -like "*$searchstring*"

#etc
```

This method is longer and less flexible, but it still gets you what you need. This would be a faster alternative if you know exactly what type of object you are looking for.

## See also

- The *Exploring SMO Server Objects* recipe of *Chapter 1, Getting Started with SQL Server and PowerShell*

# Scripting SQL Server Stored Procedures

In this recipe, we will explore how to script SQL Server objects, specifically; how to script all non-system and unencrypted stored procedures in a database and save them individually in their own `.sql` files.

## Getting ready

We will use the `AdventureWorks2014` database in this recipe. Before we start, let's check which stored procedures are available in this database so that we can cross-check against the scripts we are going to create later.

Open **SQL Server Management Studio** and navigate to the **Programmability** node under **AdventureWorks2014**. You should see a list of stored procedures as shown in the following screenshot:

## How to do it...

Let's see how we can script stored procedures in your SQL Server database using PowerShell:

1. Open **PowerShell ISE** as administrator.

2. Import the SQLPS module and create a new SMO Server Object:

```
#import SQL Server module
Import-Module SQLPS -DisableNameChecking
```

```
#replace this with your instance name
$instanceName = "localhost"
$server = New-Object -TypeName
Microsoft.SqlServer.Management.Smo.Server -ArgumentList
$instanceName
```

3. Specify the database that contains the objects you want to script:

```
$dbName = "AdventureWorks2014"
$db = $server.Databases[$dbName]
```

4. Add the following script. Change the `$filename` value to point to a directory and folder that exists in your system. Once the change is done, run the script:

```
#create a Scripter object
$script = New-Object Microsoft.SqlServer.Management.Smo.Scripter
$server

#create a ScriptingOptions object
$scriptOptions = New-Object Microsoft.SqlServer.Management.Smo.
ScriptingOptions

$scriptOptions.AllowSystemObjects = $false
$scriptOptions.ScriptSchema = $true
$scriptOptions.IncludeDatabaseContext = $true
$scriptOptions.SchemaQualify = $true
$scriptOptions.ScriptBatchTerminator = $true
$scriptOptions.NoExecuteAs = $true
$scriptOptions.Permissions = $true
$scriptOptions.ToFileOnly = $true
#assign the options to the Scripter object
$script.Options = $scriptOptions

#iterate over the objects you want to script
#in our case, stored procedures
#exclude any system objects or encrypted stored procedures
$db.StoredProcedures |
Where-Object IsSystemObject -eq $false |
Where-Object IsEncrypted -eq $false |
Foreach-Object {

    #current stored procedure
    $sp = $_

    #specify one file per stored procedure
   #change the directory/folder to one that exists
  #in your system
```

```
$filename = "C:\DATA\$($dbname)_$($sp.Name).sql"
$script.Options.FileName = $filename

#script current object
$script.Script($sp)

}
```

5. Once the script finishes, go to the directory where the script saved the files. You should find all the stored procedure scripts there, as shown in the following screenshot:

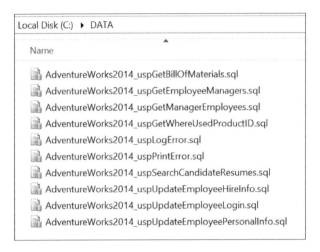

6. You can script SQL objects from **SQL Server Management Studio** by right-clicking on an object.

## How it works...

You can script SQL objects from **SQL Server Management Studio** by right-clicking on an object and choosing the corresponding **Script** option, as shown in the following screenshot:

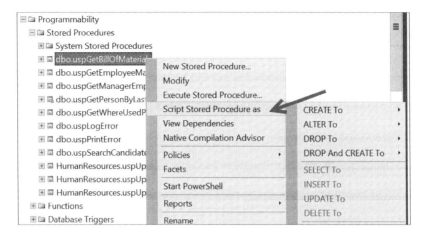

SMO provides a few classes that allow you to script out the definitions of database objects programmatically. The `Microsoft.SqlServer.Management.Smo.Scripter` class is the main class that retrieves the definition for the objects. We first need to create an instance of this class, and then pass the current server instance as an argument:

```
$script = New-Object Microsoft.SqlServer.Management.Smo.Scripter
$server
```

The second class is the `Microsoft.SqlServer.Management.Smo.ScriptingOptions` class, which allows us to provide additional scripting options. An instance of this is also required:

```
$scriptOptions = New-Object
Microsoft.SqlServer.Management.Smo.ScriptingOptions
```

In the `ScriptingOptions` instance, we can set how we want the script to be generated. There are a number of other options that can be programmatically set. In our recipe, the options we've specified are: excluding system objects, schema qualifying objects, including the database context, scripting the schema, and scripting the batch terminators and permissions. The code is as follows:

```
$scriptOptions.AllowSystemObjects = $false
$scriptOptions.ScriptSchema = $true
$scriptOptions.IncludeDatabaseContext = $true
$scriptOptions.SchemaQualify = $true
$scriptOptions.ScriptBatchTerminator = $true
$scriptOptions.NoExecuteAs = $true
$scriptOptions.Permissions = $true
$scriptOptions.ToFileOnly = $true
```

The `Scripter` class also needs an object or a collection of objects to script. Since we want to create a single file per stored procedure, we are using the `Scripter` object in the `Foreach-Object` cmdlet and calling it for each non-system stored procedure that is identified. The code is as follows:

```
$db.StoredProcedures |
Where-Object IsSystemObject -eq $false |
Where-Object IsEncrypted -eq $false |
Foreach-Object {

    #current stored procedure
    $sp = $_

    #specify one file per stored procedure
    $filename = "C:\DATA\$($dbname)_$($sp.Name).sql"
    $script.Options.FileName = $filename

    #script current object
    $script.Script($sp)

}
```

The filename corresponds to the database that owns the stored procedure and the stored procedure name. We make sure the block that generates the filename captures this:

```
    #specify one file per stored procedure
    $filename = "C:\DATA\$($dbname)_$($sp.Name).sql"
    $script.Options.FileName = $filename
```

Scripting other objects in SQL Server should be similar to this recipe. For example if you wanted to script user defined functions, instead of using the `StoredProcedures` member, you should use the `UserDefinedFunctions` member and change the filenames accordingly:

```
$db.StoredProcedures
```

## There's more...

Check out the MSDN for all the possible options you can set when programmatically scripting SQL Server objects:

```
https://msdn.microsoft.com/en-us/library/microsoft.sqlserver.
management.smo.scriptingoptions.aspx
```

# Creating a database

This recipe walks through creating a database with default properties using PowerShell.

## Getting ready

In this example, we are going to create a database called TestDB, and we assume that this database does not yet exist in your instance.

For your reference, the equivalent T-SQL code of this task is as follows:

```
CREATE DATABASE TestDB
```

## How to do it...

Follow these steps to create a simple database in SQL Server:

1. Open **PowerShell ISE** as administrator.

2. Import the SQLPS module and create a new SMO Server Object:

```
#import SQL Server module
Import-Module SQLPS -DisableNameChecking

#replace this with your instance name
$instanceName = "localhost"
$server = New-Object -TypeName Microsoft.SqlServer.Management.Smo.
Server -ArgumentList $instanceName
```

3. Add the following script and run:

```
#database TestDB with default settings
#assumption is that this database does not yet exist
$dbName = "TestDB"
$db = New-Object -TypeName Microsoft.SqlServer.Management.Smo.
Database($server, $dbName)
$db.Create()

#to confirm, list databases in your instance
$server.Databases |
Select Name, Status, Owner, CreateDate
```

## How it works...

There are two key steps in creating a database using SMO and PowerShell: creating an SMO Server Object and creating an SMO database object.

To create the SMO Server Object, we need to use the `Microsoft.SqlServer.Management.Smo.Server` class and pass the SQL Server instance name as argument:

```
$server = New-Object -TypeName
Microsoft.SqlServer.Management.Smo.Server -ArgumentList
$instanceName
```

To create the SMO database object, we need to use the `Microsoft.SqlServer.Management.Smo.Database` class. The SMO database constructor requires both the SMO Server handle and a database object.

```
$dbName = "TestDB"
$db = New-Object -TypeName
Microsoft.SqlServer.Management.Smo.Database($server, $dbName)
```

The final action is to call the database object's `Create` method, which performs the actual database creation:

```
$db.Create()
```

Many SMO objects are consistent with the methods. You will see the `Create` method again in several recipes used in this chapter.

# Altering database properties

This recipe shows you how to change database properties using SMO and PowerShell.

## Getting ready

Create a database called `TestDB` by following the steps in the *Creating a database* recipe.

Using `TestDB`, we will perform the following tasks:

- ▸ Change `ANSI NULLS Enabled` to `False`
- ▸ Change `ANSI PADDING Enabled` to `False`
- ▸ Change compatibility version to `110` (SQL Server 2012)
- ▸ Restrict user access to `RESTRICTED_USER`
- ▸ Set the database to `Read Only`

## How to do it...

Let's look at the steps involved in altering databases using PowerShell:

1. Open **PowerShell ISE** as administrator.

2. Import the SQLPS module and create a new SMO Server Object:

```
#import SQL Server module
Import-Module SQLPS -DisableNameChecking

#replace this with your instance name
$instanceName = "localhost"
$server = New-Object -TypeName Microsoft.SqlServer.Management.Smo.
Server -ArgumentList $instanceName
```

Add the following script and run:

```
#database
$dbName = "TestDB"

#we are going to assume db exists
$db = $server.Databases[$dbName]

#DatabaseOptions
#change ANSI NULLS and ANSI PADDING
$db.DatabaseOptions.AnsiNullsEnabled = $false
$db.DatabaseOptions.AnsiPaddingEnabled = $false


#change compatibility level to SQL Server 2012
#available CompatibilityLevel values
#for SQL Server 2014 are
#Version 2008 ('Version100')
#Version 2012 ('Version110')
#Version 2014 ('Version120')
$db.AutoUpdateStatisticsEnabled = $true
$db.CompatibilityLevel =
[Microsoft.SqlServer.Management.Smo.CompatibilityLevel]::
Version110
$db.Alter()

#Change database access
#DatabaseUserAccess enumeration values:
#multiple, restricted, single
```

```
$db.DatabaseOptions.UserAccess =
[Microsoft.SqlServer.Management.Smo.DatabaseUserAccess]::
Restricted
$db.Alter()


#some options are not available through the
#DatabaseOptions property
#so we will need to access the database object directly
#set to readonly
$db.DatabaseOptions.ReadOnly = $true
$db.Alter()
```

3. Confirm the changes. To start confirming, use the following steps:

   1. Go to **SQL Server Management Studio**.

   2. Connect to your instance.

   You will notice right away in your **Object Explorer** that your database is grayed out and the status has changed to **(Restricted User / Read-Only)**, as shown in the following screenshot:

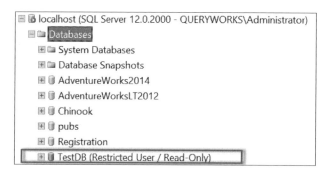

4. To confirm **ANSI NULLS, ANSI PADDING**, and **Compatibility Level**, use the following steps:

   1. Right-click on the **TestDB** database and select **Properties**.

   2. Go to the **Options** tab and check whether the respective options have been changed:

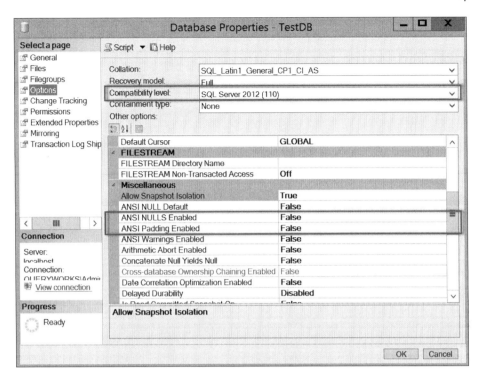

## How it works...

To alter database properties, you will need to create an SMO handle to your database:

```
#we are going to assume db exists
$db = $server.Databases[$dbName]
```

After this, you will need to investigate which of the properties contains the setting you want to change. For example, **ANSI NULLS**, **ANSI WARNINGS**, database access restriction options, and **ReadOnly**, are available through the DatabaseOptions property of your database object:

```
#DatabaseOptions
#change ANSI NULLS and ANSI PADDING
$db.DatabaseOptions.AnsiNullsEnabled = $false
$db.DatabaseOptions.AnsiPaddingEnabled = $false

#Change database access
#DatabaseUserAccess enum values:
#multiple, restricted, single
```

```
$db.DatabaseOptions.UserAccess = [Microsoft.SqlServer.Management.Smo.
DatabaseUserAccess]::Restricted
$db.Alter()

#set to readonly
$db.DatabaseOptions.ReadOnly = $true
$db.Alter()
```

The properties `AutoUpdateStatisticsEnabled` and `CompatibilityLevel` are directly accessible from the $db object, this can be done as follows:

```
$db.AutoUpdateStatisticsEnabled = $true
$db.CompatibilityLevel =
[Microsoft.SqlServer.Management.Smo.
CompatibilityLevel]::Version110
```

 Note that for SQL Server 2014, the earliest version you can set the compatibility level to, is SQL Server 2008 (Version 100).

Once you've set the new values, you can persist the changes by invoking the `Alter` method of your database object:

```
$db.Alter()
```

Finding exactly which property the settings you are looking for reside in, is half the battle, so it's a great idea to familiarize yourself with the properties of the object you are changing. Technet and MSDN are great resources; there are books, numerous articles, and blog posts too. However, remember there is help at your fingertips. The `Get-Member` cmdlet is your friend. It helps you explore all the properties and methods available for a class:

```
$db | Get-Member
```

## See also

▶ The *Changing SQL Server Instance configurations* recipe.

# Dropping a database

This recipe shows how you can drop a database using PowerShell and SMO.

## Getting ready

This task assumes you have created a database called `TestDB`. If you don't have it, create the database `TestDB` by following the steps in the *Creating a database* recipe.

## How to do it...

Here are the steps to drop your `TestDB` database:

1. Open **PowerShell ISE** as administrator.

2. Import the SQLPS module and create a new SMO Server Object:

```
#import SQL Server module
Import-Module SQLPS -DisableNameChecking

#replace this with your instance name
$instanceName = "localhost"
$server = New-Object -TypeName
Microsoft.SqlServer.Management.Smo.Server -ArgumentList
$instanceName
```

3. Add the following script and run:

```
$dbName = "TestDB"

#need to check if database exists, and if it does, drop it
$db = $server.Databases[$dbName]
if ($db)
{
    #we will use KillDatabase instead of Drop
    #Kill database will drop active connections before
    #dropping the database
    $server.KillDatabase($dbName)
}
```

## How it works...

To drop an SMO server or database object, you can simply invoke the `Drop` method. However, if you have ever tried dropping a database before, you might have already experienced being blocked by active connections to that database. For this reason, we chose the `KillDatabase` method, which will kill active connections before dropping the database. This option is also available in **SQL Server Management Studio** when you drop a database from **Object Explorer**. When you right-click on a database, the **Delete Object** window will appear. At the bottom of the window, there is a checkbox called **Close existing connections**.

# Changing database owner

This recipe shows how to programmatically change a SQL Server database owner.

## Getting ready

This task assumes you have created a database called `TestDB`, and a Windows account `QUERYWORKS\srogers`. `QUERYWORKS\srogers` has been created in our test VM.

For more information, see *Appendix B, Create a SQL Server VM.*

If you don't have it, create the database `TestDB` by following the steps in the *Creating a database* recipe.

## How to do it...

Let's look at the steps involved in changing a database owner:

1. Open **PowerShell ISE** as administrator.

2. Import the SQLPS module and create a new SMO Server Object:

```
#import SQL Server module
Import-Module SQLPS -DisableNameChecking

#replace this with your instance name
$instanceName = "localhost"
$server = New-Object -TypeName Microsoft.SqlServer.Management.Smo.
Server -ArgumentList $instanceName
```

3. Add the following script and run:

```
#create database handle
$dbName = "TestDB"
$db = $server.Databases[$dbName]

#display current owner
$db.Owner

#change owner
#SetOwner requires two parameters:
#loginName and overrideIfAlreadyUser
#make sure you provide a login that exists in your environment
#if you don't have any domain users, you can use "sa"
$db.SetOwner("QUERYWORKS\srogers", $true)

#refresh db
$db.Refresh()

#check Owner value
$db.Owner
```

4. Check the following:

    1. Open **SQL Server Management Studio**.

    2. Locate the **AdventureWorks2008R2** database.

    3. Right-click and select **Properties**.

    4. Select **Options**.

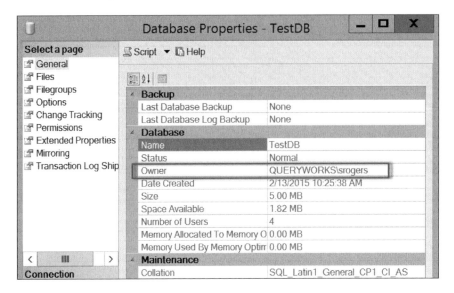

## How it works...

Changing the database owner is a short and straightforward task in PowerShell. First, you need to create a database handle.

The only other action required is invoking the `SetOwner` method of the `Microsoft.SqlServer.Management.Smo.Database` class, which requires two parameters:

▸ `LoginName`

▸ `OverrideIfAlreadyUser`

The `OverrideIfAlreadyUser` option can be set to either `true` or `false`. If set to `true`, which means the login already exists as a user in the target database, the user is dropped and added as owner again. If set to `false` and the login is already mapped to that database, the `SetOwner` method will produce an error.

▶   The *Altering database properties* recipe.

# Creating a table

This recipe shows how to create a table using PowerShell and SMO.

## Getting ready

We will use the `AdventureWorks2014` database to create a table named `Student`, which has five columns and two default constraints. To give you a better idea of what we are trying to achieve, the equivalent T-SQL script needed to create this table is as follows:

```
USE AdventureWorks2014
GO
CREATE TABLE [dbo].[Student] (
   [StudentID] [INT] IDENTITY(1,1) NOT NULL,
   [FName] [VARCHAR](50) NULL,
   [LName] [VARCHAR](50) NOT NULL,
   [DateOfBirth] [DATETIME] NULL,
   [Age]   AS
(DATEPART(YEAR,GETDATE())-DATEPART(YEAR,[DateOfBirth])),
     CONSTRAINT [PK_Student_StudentID] PRIMARY KEY CLUSTERED
   (
     [StudentID] ASC
   )
)

GO
ALTER TABLE [dbo].[Student] ADD  CONSTRAINT [DF_Student_LName]
 DEFAULT ('Doe') FOR [LName]
GO

ALTER TABLE [dbo].[Student] ADD  CONSTRAINT [DF_Student_DateOfBirth]
DEFAULT ('1800-00-00') FOR [DateOfBirth]
GO
```

## How to do it...

Let's create the `Student` table using PowerShell:

1. Open **PowerShell ISE** as administrator.

2. Import the `SQLPS` module and create a new SMO Server Object:

```
#import SQL Server module
Import-Module SQLPS -DisableNameChecking

#replace this with your instance name
$instanceName = "localhost"
$server = New-Object -TypeName
Microsoft.SqlServer.Management.Smo.Server -ArgumentList
$instanceName
```

3. Next, add code to set up the database and table names, and to drop the table if it already exists:

```
$dbName = "AdventureWorks2014"
$tableName = "Student"
$db = $server.Databases[$dbName]
$table = $db.Tables[$tableName]

#if table exists drop
if($table)
{
    $table.Drop()
}
```

4. Add the following script to create the table and run:

```
#table class on MSDN
#http://msdn.microsoft.com/en-us/library/ms220470.aspx
$table = New-Object -TypeName
Microsoft.SqlServer.Management.SMO.Table -ArgumentList $db,
$tableName

#column class on MSDN
#http://msdn.microsoft.com/en-
us/library/microsoft.sqlserver.management.smo.column.aspx
#column 1
$col1Name = "StudentID"
$type = [Microsoft.SqlServer.Management.SMO.DataType]::Int
$col1 = New-Object -TypeName
Microsoft.SqlServer.Management.SMO.Column -ArgumentList
$table, $col1Name, $type
```

```
$col1.Nullable = $false
$col1.Identity = $true
$col1.IdentitySeed = 1
$col1.IdentityIncrement = 1
$table.Columns.Add($col1)

#column 2 - nullable
$col2Name = "FName"
$type = [Microsoft.SqlServer.Management.SMO.DataType]::VarChar(50)
$col2 =  New-Object -TypeName Microsoft.SqlServer.Management.SMO.
Column -ArgumentList
$table, $col2Name, $type
$col2.Nullable = $true
$table.Columns.Add($col2)

#column 3 - not nullable, with default value
$col3Name = "LName"
$type = [Microsoft.SqlServer.Management.SMO.DataType]::VarChar(50)
$col3 =  New-Object -TypeName
Microsoft.SqlServer.Management.SMO.Column -ArgumentList
$table, $col3Name, $type
$col3.Nullable = $false
$col3.AddDefaultConstraint("DF_Student_LName").Text =
"'Doe'"

$table.Columns.Add($col3)

#column 4 - nullable, with default value
$col4Name = "DateOfBirth"
$type = [Microsoft.SqlServer.Management.SMO.DataType]::DateTime
$col4 =  New-Object -TypeName
Microsoft.SqlServer.Management.SMO.Column -ArgumentList
$table, $col4Name, $type
$col4.Nullable = $true
$col4.AddDefaultConstraint("DF_Student_DateOfBirth").Text =
"'1800-00-00'"
$table.Columns.Add($col4)

#column 5
$col5Name = "Age"
$type = [Microsoft.SqlServer.Management.SMO.DataType]::Int
$col5 =  New-Object -TypeName
Microsoft.SqlServer.Management.SMO.Column -ArgumentList
$table, $col5Name, $type
$col5.Nullable = $false
```

```
$col5.Computed = $true
$col5.ComputedText = "YEAR(GETDATE()) - YEAR(DateOfBirth)"
$table.Columns.Add($col5)

$table.Create()
```

5.  Make `StudentID` the primary key as follows:

```
#make StudentID a clustered PK

#note this is just a "placeholder" right now for PK
#no columns are added in this step
$PK = New-Object -TypeName
Microsoft.SqlServer.Management.SMO.Index -ArgumentList
$table, "PK_Student_StudentID"
$PK.IsClustered = $true
$PK.IndexKeyType =
[Microsoft.SqlServer.Management.SMO.IndexKeyType]::
DriPrimaryKey

#identify columns part of the PK
$PKcol = New-Object -TypeName
Microsoft.SqlServer.Management.SMO.IndexedColumn
-ArgumentList $PK, $col1Name
$PK.IndexedColumns.Add($PKcol)
$PK.Create()
```

6.  Check whether the table has been created with the correct columns and constraints. The steps are as follows:

    1.  Open **SQL Server Management Studio**.

    2.  Go to the `AdventureWorks2014` database and expand **Tables**.

    3.  Expand **Columns**, **Keys**, **Constraints**, and **Indexes**, as shown in the following screenshot:

```
⊟ ▦ dbo.Student
   ⊟ ▭ Columns
        ⸙ StudentID (PK, int, not null)
        ▣ FName (varchar(50), null)
        ▣ LName (varchar(50), not null)
        ▣ DateOfBirth (datetime, null)
        ▤ Age (Computed, int, null)
   ⊟ ▭ Keys
        ⸙ PK_Student_StudentID
   ⊟ ▭ Constraints
        ▦ DF_Student_DateOfBirth
        ▦ DF_Student_LName
   ⊞ ▭ Triggers
   ⊟ ▭ Indexes
        ⸙ PK_Student_StudentID (Clustered)
   ⊞ ▭ Statistics
```

## How it works...

To create a table, the first step is to create an SMO table object:

```
$table = New-Object -TypeName
Microsoft.SqlServer.Management.SMO.Table -ArgumentList $db,
$tableName
```

After this, all columns have to be defined one by one and added to the table before the Create method of the Microsoft.SqlServer.Management.SMO.Table class is invoked.

Let's take this step by step. To create a column, we first need to identify the data type we are storing in the column, and the properties of that column.

Column data types in SMO are defined in Microsoft.SqlServer.Management.SMO. DataType. Every T-SQL data type is pretty much represented in this enumeration. To use a data type, the format should be as follows:

```
[Microsoft.SqlServer.Management.SMO.DataType]::DataType
```

To create a column, you will have to specify the table variable, the data type, the column name, and whether it is possible to make it null or not:

```
$col1Name = "StudentID"
$type = [Microsoft.SqlServer.Management.SMO.DataType]::Int
$col1 =  New-Object -TypeName Microsoft.SqlServer.Management.SMO.
Column
-ArgumentList $table, $col1Name, $type
$col1.Nullable = $false
```

Common column properties will now be accessible to your column variable. Some common properties are as follows:

- ▸ `Nullable`
- ▸ `Computed`
- ▸ `ComputedText`
- ▸ Default constraint (by using the `AddDefaultConstraint` method)

For example consider the following code:

```
#column 4 - nullable, with default value
$col4Name = "DateOfBirth"
$type = [Microsoft.SqlServer.Management.SMO.DataType]::DateTime
$col4 =  New-Object -TypeName Microsoft.SqlServer.Management.SMO.
Column -ArgumentList  $table, $col4Name, $type
$col4.Nullable = $true
$col4.AddDefaultConstraint("DF_Student_DateOfBirth").Text = "'1800-00-
00'"
```

There are additional properties that are exposed depending on the data type you've chosen. For example, `[Microsoft.SqlServer.Management.SMO.DataType]::Int` will allow you to specify whether this is an identity and let you set the seed and increment. `[Microsoft.SqlServer.Management.SMO.DataType]::Varchar` will allow you to set the length.

Once you have set the properties, you can add these columns to your table:

```
$table.Columns.Add($col1)
$table.Columns.Add($col4)
```

When everything is set up, you can then invoke the table's `Create` method:

```
$table.Create()
```

To create a primary key, you will need to create two other SMO objects. The first one is the index object. For this object, you can specify what type of index this is and whether it is clustered or nonclustered:

```
$PK = New-Object -TypeName
Microsoft.SqlServer.Management.SMO.Index -ArgumentList $table,
"PK_Student_StudentID"
$PK.IsClustered = $true
$PK.IndexKeyType =
[Microsoft.SqlServer.Management.SMO.IndexKeyType]::DriPrimaryKey
```

The second object, `IndexedColumn`, specifies which columns are part of the index:

```
#identify columns part of the PK
$PKcol = New-Object -TypeName
Microsoft.SqlServer.Management.SMO.IndexedColumn
-ArgumentList $PK, $colName
```

If this column is an included column, simply set the `IsIncluded` property of the `IndexedColumn` object to `true`.

Once you've created all index columns, you can add them to the index and invoke the index's `Create` method:

```
$PK.IndexedColumns.Add($PKcol)
$PK.Create()
```

You might be thinking right now, that what we've just gone over is a long winded way to create a table. You're right. It is a more verbose way to create a table. However, keep in mind this is *just one more way* to get things done. When you need to create a table and T-SQL is just a faster way to do it, go for it. However, knowing how to do it in PowerShell and SMO is just one more tool in your arsenal for those scenarios where you might need to create the tables dynamically or more flexibly. For example, it'll be useful if you need to import the definitions stored in Excel, CSV, of XML files from multiple users.

## There's more...

Check out the complete list of SMO `DataType` classes from the MSDN at `http://msdn.microsoft.com/en-us/library/microsoft.sqlserver.management.smo.datatype.aspx`.

## See also

▶ The *Create an index* recipe.

# Creating a view

This recipe shows how to create a view using PowerShell and SMO.

## Getting ready

We will use the `Person.Person` table in the `AdventureWorks2014` database for this recipe.

To give you an idea what we are attempting to create in this recipe, this is the T-SQL equivalent.

```
CREATE VIEW dbo.vwVCPerson
AS
SELECT
   TOP 100
  BusinessEntityID,
  LastName,
  FirstName
FROM
  Person.Person
WHERE
    PersonType = 'IN'
GO
```

## How to do it...

Let's check out the steps to create a view using PowerShell:

1. Open **PowerShell ISE** as administrator.

2. Import the SQLPS module and create a new SMO Server object:
```
#import SQL Server module
Import-Module SQLPS -DisableNameChecking

#replace this with your instance name
$instanceName = "localhost"
$server = New-Object -TypeName Microsoft.SqlServer.Management.Smo.
Server -ArgumentList $instanceName
```

Add the following script and run:

```
$dbName = "AdventureWorks2014"
$db = $server.Databases[$dbName]
$viewName = "vwVCPerson"
$view = $db.Views[$viewName]

#if view exists, drop it
if ($view)
{
    $view.Drop()
}

$view = New-Object -TypeName Microsoft.SqlServer.Management.SMO.
View -ArgumentList $db, $viewName, "dbo"
```

```
#TextMode = false meaning we are not
#going to explicitly write the CREATE VIEW header
$view.TextMode = $false
$view.TextBody = @"
SELECT
    TOP 100
  BusinessEntityID,
  LastName,
  FirstName
FROM
  Person.Person
WHERE
    PersonType = 'IN'
"@

$view.Create()
```

Test the view from PowerShell by running the following code:

```
#code below all in one line
$result = Invoke-Sqlcmd -Query "SELECT * FROM vwVCPerson"
-ServerInstance $instanceName -Database $dbName

#display results
$result | Format-Table -AutoSize
```

3. Check whether the view has been created. Open **SQL Server Management Studio**. Go to the `AdventureWorks2014` database and expand **Views**, as shown in the following screenshot:

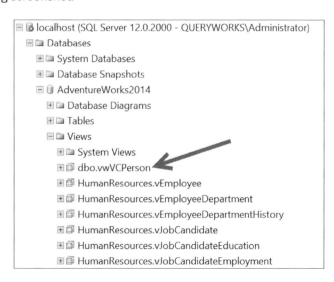

## How it works...

To create a view using SMO and PowerShell, you first need to create an SMO view variable, which requires three parameters: database handle, view name, and schema. The code is as follows:

```
$view = New-Object -TypeName Microsoft.SqlServer.Management.SMO.View
-ArgumentList $db, $viewName, "dbo"
```

You can optionally set the view owner:

```
$view.Owner = "QUERYWORKS\srogers"
```

The crux of the view creation is the view definition. You have the option to set the TextMode property to either True or False.

```
$view.TextMode = $false
$view.TextBody = @"
SELECT
    TOP 100
  BusinessEntityID,
  LastName,
  FirstName
FROM
  Person.Person
WHERE
    PersonType = 'IN'
"@
```

If you set the TextMode property to false, it means you are letting SMO construct the view header for you:

```
$view.TextMode = $false
```

If you set the TextMode property to true, it means you have to define the TextHeader property:

```
$view.TextMode = $true
$view.TextHeader = "CREATE VIEW dbo.vwVCPerson AS "
$view.TextBody = @"
SELECT
    TOP 100
  BusinessEntityID,
  LastName,
  FirstName
FROM
  Person.Person
WHERE
    PersonType = 'IN'
"@
```

When all the pieces are in place, you can then invoke the view's `Create` method:

```
$view.Create()
```

## There's more...

When creating database objects such as views, stored procedures, or functions, you are often required to write blocks of code for the object definition. Although you can technically put all these in one line, it is best to put them in a multiline format for readability.

To embed these blocks of code in PowerShell, you will need to use `here-string`. A `here-string` literal starts with an `@"` and is ended by `"@`, which must be the first character in its own line:

```
$view.TextBody = @"
SELECT
    TOP 100
  BusinessEntityID,
  LastName,
  FirstName
FROM
  Person.Person
WHERE
    PersonType = 'IN'
"@
```

This construction might remind you a little bit of a C-style comment, which starts with `/*` and ends with `*/`, albeit using different characters.

# Creating a stored procedure

This recipe shows how to create an encrypted stored procedure using SMO and PowerShell.

## Getting ready

The T-SQL equivalent of the encrypted stored procedure we are about to recreate in PowerShell is as follows:

```
CREATE PROCEDURE [dbo].[uspGetPersonByLastName]
@LastName [varchar](50)
WITH ENCRYPTION
AS

SELECT
    TOP 10
```

```
        BusinessEntityID,
        LastName
FROM
        Person.Person
WHERE
        LastName = @LastName
```

## How to do it...

Follow these steps to create the uspGetPersonByLastName stored procedure using PowerShell:

1. Open **PowerShell ISE** as administrator.

2. Import the SQLPS module and create a new SMO Server Object:

```
#import SQL Server module
Import-Module SQLPS -DisableNameChecking

#replace this with your instance name
$instanceName = "localhost"
$server = New-Object -TypeName
Microsoft.SqlServer.Management.Smo.Server -ArgumentList
$instanceName
```

Add the following script and run:

```
$dbName = "AdventureWorks2014"
$db = $server.Databases[$dbName]

#storedProcedure class on MSDN:
#http://msdn.microsoft.com/
en-us/library/microsoft.sqlserver.
management.smo.storedprocedure.aspx

$sprocName = "uspGetPersonByLastName"
$sproc = $db.StoredProcedures[$sprocName]
#if stored procedure exists, drop it
if ($sproc)
{
    $sproc.Drop()
}

$sproc = New-Object -TypeName
Microsoft.SqlServer.Management.SMO.StoredProcedure
-ArgumentList $db, $sprocName
```

```
#TextMode = false means stored procedure header
#is not editable as text
#otherwise our text will contain the CREATE PROC block
$sproc.TextMode = $false
$sproc.IsEncrypted = $true

#specify parameter type
$paramtype = [Microsoft.SqlServer.Management.SMO.
Datatype]::VarChar(50)

#create parameter using specified type
$param = New-Object -TypeName Microsoft.SqlServer.Management.SMO.
StoredProcedureParameter
-ArgumentList $sproc,"@LastName",$paramtype

#add parameter to stored procedure
$sproc.Parameters.Add($param)

#Set the TextBody property to define the stored procedure.
$sproc.TextBody =  @"
SELECT
    TOP 10
    BusinessEntityID,
    LastName
FROM
    Person.Person
WHERE
    LastName = @LastName
"@

# Create the stored procedure on the instance of SQL
Server.
$sproc.Create()

#if later on you need to change properties,
can use the Alter method
```

3. Check whether the stored procedure has been created. The steps are as follows:

    1. Open **SQL Server Management Studio**.
    2. Go to AdventureWorks2014 database.
    3. Expand **Programmability | Stored Procedures**.

4. Check whether the stored procedure is there.

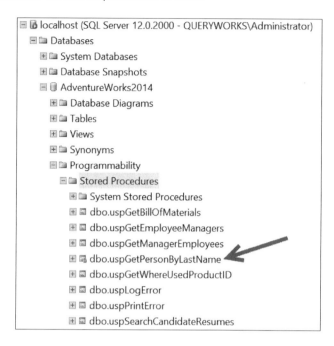

5. Test the stored procedure from PowerShell. In the same session, type the following code and run:

```
$lastName = "Abercrombie"

#code below all in one line
$result = Invoke-Sqlcmd -Query "EXEC uspGetPersonByLastName
@LastName='$LastName'" -ServerInstance "$instanceName"
-Database $dbName

$result | Format-Table -AutoSize
```

## How it works...

To create a stored procedure, you first need to initialize an SMO StoredProcedure object. When creating this object, you need to pass the database handle and the stored procedure name as parameters:

```
$sproc = New-Object -TypeName
Microsoft.SqlServer.Management.SMO.StoredProcedure -ArgumentList
$db, $sprocName
```

You can then set some properties of the stored procedure object, such as whether it's encrypted or not:

```
$sproc.IsEncrypted = $true
```

If you specify TextMode = $true, you will need to create the stored procedure header yourself. If you have parameters, these will have to be defined in your text header.
For example consider the following:

```
$sproc.TextMode = $true
$sproc.TextHeader = @"
CREATE PROCEDURE [dbo].[uspGetPersonByLastName]
   @LastName [varchar](50)
AS
"@
$sproc.TextBody TextBody =   @"
SELECT
    TOP 10
    BusinessEntityID,
    LastName
FROM
    Person.Person
WHERE
    LastName = @LastName
"@
```

Otherwise, if you set TextMode = $false, you are technically allowing PowerShell to autogenerate this header for you based on the other properties and parameters you have set. You will also have to create the parameter objects one by one and add them to the stored procedure. The code is as follows:

```
$sproc.TextMode = $false

#specify parameter type
$paramtype =
[Microsoft.SqlServer.Management.SMO.Datatype]::VarChar(50)

#create parameter using specified type
$param = New-Object -TypeName
Microsoft.SqlServer.Management.SMO.StoredProcedureParameter
-ArgumentList $sproc,"@LastName",$paramtype

#add parameter to stored procedure
$sproc.Parameters.Add($param)
```

When creating the stored procedure, use `here-string` as you set the definition to the `TextBody` property of the stored procedure object:

```
$sproc.TextBody =   @"
SELECT
   TOP 10
   BusinessEntityID,
   LastName
FROM
   Person.Person
WHERE
   LastName = @LastName
"@
```

Once the header, definition, and properties of the stored procedure are in place, you can invoke the `Create` method, which sends the `CREATE PROC` statement to SQL Server and creates the stored procedure. The code is as follows:

```
# Create the stored procedure on the instance of SQL Server.
$sproc.Create()
```

# Creating a trigger

This recipe shows how to programmatically create a trigger in SQL Server using SMO and PowerShell

## Getting ready

For this recipe, we will use the `Person.Person` table in the `AdventureWorks2014` database. We will create a trivial `AFTER` trigger that merely displays values from the inserted and deleted tables upon firing.

The following is the T-SQL equivalent of what we are going to accomplish programmatically in this section:

```
CREATE TRIGGER [Person].[tr_u_Person]
ON [Person].[Person]
AFTER  UPDATE
AS

  SELECT
     GETDATE() AS UpdatedOn,
     SYSTEM_USER AS UpdatedBy,
     i.LastName AS NewLastName,
     i.FirstName AS NewFirstName,
```

```
      d.LastName AS OldLastName,
      d.FirstName AS OldFirstName
   FROM
      inserted i
      INNER JOIN deleted d
      ON i.BusinessEntityID = d.BusinessEntityID
```

## How to do it...

Let's follow these steps to create an AFTER trigger in PowerShell:

1. Open **PowerShell ISE** as administrator.

2. Import the SQLPS module and create a new SMO Server object:

```
#import SQL Server module
Import-Module SQLPS -DisableNameChecking

#replace this with your instance name
$instanceName = "localhost"
$server = New-Object -TypeName
Microsoft.SqlServer.Management.Smo.Server -ArgumentList
$instanceName
```

3. Add the following script and run:

```
$dbName = "AdventureWorks2014"
$db = $server.Databases[$dbName]
$tableName = "Person"
$schemaName = "Person"

#get a handle to the Person.Person table
$table = $db.Tables |
        Where-Object Schema -like "$schemaName" |
        Where-Object Name -like "$tableName"

$triggerName = "tr_u_Person"
#note here we need to check triggers attached to table
$trigger = $table.Triggers[$triggerName]

#if trigger exists, drop it
if ($trigger)
{
    $trigger.Drop()
}
```

```
$trigger = New-Object -TypeName
Microsoft.SqlServer.Management.SMO.Trigger -ArgumentList
$table, $triggerName
$trigger.TextMode = $false

#this is just an update trigger
$trigger.Update = $true
$trigger.Insert = $false
$trigger.Delete = $false

#3 options for ActivationOrder: First, Last, None
$trigger.InsertOrder = [Microsoft.SqlServer.Management.SMO.Agent.
ActivationOrder]:
:None
$trigger.ImplementationType = [Microsoft.SqlServer.Management.SMO.
ImplementationType]::
TransactSql

#simple example
$trigger.TextBody = @"
  SELECT
      GETDATE() AS UpdatedOn,
      SYSTEM_USER AS UpdatedBy,
      i.LastName AS NewLastName,
      i.FirstName AS NewFirstName,
      d.LastName AS OldLastName,
      d.FirstName AS OldFirstName
  FROM
      inserted i
      INNER JOIN deleted d
      ON i.BusinessEntityID = d.BusinessEntityID

"@

$trigger.Create()
```

4. Check whether the stored procedure has been created. Open **SQL Server SQL Server Management Studio** and check under the `Person.Person` table, as shown in the following screenshot:

5. Test the stored procedure from PowerShell:

```
$firstName = "Frankk"

$result = Invoke-Sqlcmd -Query @"
UPDATE Person.Person
SET FirstName = '$firstName'
WHERE BusinessEntityID = 2081
"@ -ServerInstance "$instanceName" -Database $dbName

$result | Format-Table –AutoSize
```

Your result should look similar to the following:

| UpdatedOn | UpdatedBy | NewLastName | NewFirstName | OldLastName | OldFirstName |
| --- | --- | --- | --- | --- | --- |
| 2/14/2015 10:07:20 PM | QUERYWORKS\Administrator | Zhang | Frankk | zhang | Frank |

## How it works...

The code for this section is quite long, so we will break it down here.

To create a trigger, you need to create a refcrence to both the instance and the database first. This is something we have done for most of the recipes in this chapter, if you have skipped the previous recipes.

A trigger is bound to a table or view. You will need to create a variable that points to the table you want the trigger to attach to:

```
$tableName = "Person"
$schemaName = "Person"

$table = $db.Tables |
        Where-Object Schema -like "$schemaName" |
        Where-Object Name -like "$tableName"
```

For the purpose of this recipe, if the trigger exists, we will drop it:

```
$trigger = $table.Triggers[$triggerName]

#if trigger exists, drop it
if ($trigger)
{
   $trigger.Drop()
}
```

Next, you need to create an SMO trigger object:

```
$trigger = New-Object -TypeName
Microsoft.SqlServer.Management.SMO.Trigger -ArgumentList $table,
$triggerName
```

Next, set the `TextMode` property. If set to `true`, this means you have to define the trigger header text yourself. Otherwise, SMO will automatically generate this for you.

```
$trigger.TextMode = $false
```

You will also need to define what type of DML trigger this is. Your options are INSERT, UPDATE, and/or DELETE triggers. Our example is just an update trigger, so the `Insert` and `Update` properties need to be set to `$false`:

```
#this is just an update trigger
$trigger.Update = $true
$trigger.Insert = $false
$trigger.Delete = $false
```

You can also optionally define the trigger order. There are three possible values for the trigger activation order: `First`, `Last`, and `None`. This can be specified as an enumeration value in the format:

```
[Microsoft.SqlServer.Management.SMO.Agent.ActivationOrder]::
<Value>
```

By default, there is no guarantee in what order the triggers will be run by SQL Server (that is, `None`), but you have the option to set it to `First` or `Last`. In our example, we leave it as default (that is, `None`), but we still explicitly define it for readability:

```
$trigger.InsertOrder =
[Microsoft.SqlServer.Management.SMO.Agent.ActivationOrder]::None
```

Our trigger is also a T-SQL trigger. SQL Server SMO also supports SQLCLR triggers, which will require the enumeration value `SqlClr`.

```
$trigger.ImplementationType =
[Microsoft.SqlServer.Management.SMO.ImplementationType]::
TransactSql
```

To specify the trigger definition, you can set the value of the trigger's `TextBody` property. You can use `here-string` to assign the trigger code block to the `TextBody`:

```
#simple example
$trigger.TextBody = @"
  SELECT
     GETDATE() AS UpdatedOn,
     SYSTEM_USER AS UpdatedBy,
     i.LastName AS NewLastName,
     i.FirstName AS NewFirstName,
     d.LastName AS OldLastName,
     d.FirstName AS OldFirstName
  FROM
     inserted i
     INNER JOIN deleted d
     ON i.BusinessEntityID = d.BusinessEntityID

"@
```

When ready, invoke the `Create()` method of the trigger:

```
$trigger.Create()
```

# Creating an index

This recipe shows how to create a nonclustered index with an included column using PowerShell and SMO.

## Getting ready

We will use the `Person.Person` table in the `AdventureWorks2014` database. We will create a nonclustered index on `FirstName`, `LastName`, and include `MiddleName`. The T-SQL equivalent of this task is as follows:

```
CREATE NONCLUSTERED INDEX [idxLastNameFirstName]
ON [Person].[Person]
(
  [LastName] ASC,
  [FirstName] ASC
)
INCLUDE ([MiddleName])
GO
```

## How to do it...

Let's check out how we can create an index using PowerShell:

1. Open **PowerShell ISE** as administrator.

2. Import the SQLPS module and create a new SMO Server object:

```
#import SQL Server module
Import-Module SQLPS -DisableNameChecking

#replace this with your instance name
$instanceName = "localhost"
$server = New-Object -TypeName
Microsoft.SqlServer.Management.Smo.Server -ArgumentList
$instanceName
```

3. Add the following script and run:

```
$dbName = "AdventureWorks2014"
$db = $server.Databases[$dbName]

$tableName = "Person"
$schemaName = "Person"

$table = $db.Tables |
        Where-Object Schema -like "$schemaName" |
        Where-Object Name -like "$tableName"


$indexName = "idxLastNameFirstName"
$index = $table.Indexes[$indexName]
#if index exists, drop it
if ($index)
{
    $index.Drop()
}

$index = New-Object -TypeName
Microsoft.SqlServer.Management.SMO.Index -ArgumentList
$table, $indexName

#first index column, by default sorted ascending
#last parameter $false specifies descending = false
$idxCol1 = New-Object -TypeName Microsoft.SqlServer.Management.
SMO.IndexedColumn
-ArgumentList $index, "LastName", $false
$index.IndexedColumns.Add($idxCol1)
```

```
#second index column, by default sorted ascending
#last parameter $false specifies descending = false
$idxCol2 = New-Object -TypeName
Microsoft.SqlServer.Management.SMO.IndexedColumn
-ArgumentList $index, "FirstName", $false
$index.IndexedColumns.Add($idxCol2)

#included column
$inclCol1 = New-Object -TypeName
Microsoft.SqlServer.Management.SMO.IndexedColumn
-ArgumentList $index, "MiddleName"
$inclCol1.IsIncluded = $true
$index.IndexedColumns.Add($inclCol1)

#Set the index properties.
<#
None            - no constraint
DriPrimaryKey   - primary key
DriUniqueKey    - unique constraint
#>
$index.IndexKeyType =
[Microsoft.SqlServer.Management.SMO.IndexKeyType]::None
$index.IsClustered = $false
$index.FillFactor = 70

#Create the index on the instance of SQL Server.
$index.Create()
```

4.  Check whether the stored procedure has been created.

## How it works...

The first step to create an index is to create an SMO index object, which requires both the table/view handle and the index name:

```
$index = New-Object -TypeName
Microsoft.SqlServer.Management.SMO.Index -ArgumentList $table,
$indexName
```

The next step is to identify all index columns using the `IndexedColumn` property of the `Microsoft.SqlServer.Management.SMO.Index` class:

```
#first index column, by default sorted ascending
#last parameter $false specifies descending = false
$idxCol1 = New-Object -TypeName
Microsoft.SqlServer.Management.SMO.IndexedColumn -ArgumentList
$index, "LastName", $false
$index.IndexedColumns.Add($idxCol1)

#second index column, by default sorted ascending
#last parameter $false specifies descending = false
$idxCol2 = New-Object -TypeName
Microsoft.SqlServer.Management.SMO.IndexedColumn -ArgumentList
$index, "FirstName", $false
$index.IndexedColumns.Add($idxCol2)
```

Optionally, you can add included columns, that is, columns that "tag along" with the index but are not part of the indexed columns. The code is as follows:

```
#included column
$inclCol1 = New-Object -TypeName Microsoft.SqlServer.Management.SMO.
IndexedColumn -ArgumentList $index, "MiddleName"
$inclCol1.IsIncluded = $true
$index.IndexedColumns.Add($inclCol1)
```

The type of the index can be specified using the `IndexKeyType` property of the `Microsoft.SqlServer.Management.SMO.IndexedColumn` class, which accepts three possible values:

- ▸ `None`: This is a not a unique value
- ▸ `DriPrimaryKey`: This is a primary key
- ▸ `DriUniqueKey`: This is a unique key

Additional properties can also be set, including fill factor and whether this key is clustered or not. The code is as follows:

```
$index.IndexKeyType = [Microsoft.SqlServer.Management.SMO.
IndexKeyType]::None
$index.IsClustered = $false
$index.FillFactor = 70
```

When all properties are set, invoke the `Create()` method of the SMO index object:

```
#Create the index on the instance of SQL Server.
$index.Create()
```

## There's more...

The SMO index object also supports different kinds of indexes:

| Index type | What to set |
| --- | --- |
| Filtered | `HasFilter` <br> `FilterDefinition` |
| FullText | `IsFullTextKey = $true` |
| XML | `IsXMLIndex= $true` |
| Spatial | `IsSpatialIndex = $true` |

To get more information about index options that can be programmatically set, check out the MSDN documentation on SMO indexes:

```
http://msdn.microsoft.com/en-us/library/microsoft.sqlserver.
management.smo.index.aspx
```

## See also

▶ The *Creating a table* recipe.

# Executing a query/SQL script

This recipe shows how you can execute either a hardcoded query or a SQL Script from PowerShell.

## Getting ready

Create a file in your `C:\Temp` folder called `SampleScript.sql`. This should contain the following:

```
SELECT TOP 10 *
FROM Person.Person
```

## How to do it...

The following are the steps in executing a query / SQL script:

1. Open **PowerShell ISE** as administrator.

2. Import the SQLPS module and create a new SMO Server Object:

   ```
   #import SQL Server module
   Import-Module SQLPS -DisableNameChecking

   #replace this with your instance name
   $instanceName = "localhost"
   $server = New-Object -TypeName
   Microsoft.SqlServer.Management.Smo.Server -ArgumentList
   $instanceName
   ```

3. Add the following script and run:

   ```
   $dbName = "AdventureWorks2014"
   $db = $server.Databases[$dbName]

   #execute a passthrough query, and export to a CSV file

   #line continuation in code below only happens at
   #the pipe (|) delimiter
   Invoke-Sqlcmd -Query "SELECT * FROM Person.Person"
   -ServerInstance "$instanceName" -Database $dbName |
   Export-Csv -LiteralPath
   "C:\Temp\ResultsFromPassThrough.csv"
   -NoTypeInformation
   ```

```
#execute the SampleScript.sql, and display
#results to screen

#line continuation in code below only happens at
#the pipe (|) delimiter
Invoke-SqlCmd -InputFile "C:\Temp\SampleScript.sql"
-ServerInstance "$instanceName" -Database $dbName |
Select-Object FirstName, LastName, ModifiedDate |
Format-Table
```

## How it works...

Start warming up to the `Invoke-Sqlcmd` cmdlet. We will be using it a lot in this book.

As the name suggests, this cmdlet allows you to run T-SQL code, scripts, and commands supported by the SQLCMD utility. This also allows you to run XQuery code. `Invoke-Sqlcmd` is your all-purpose SQL utility cmdlet.

To get more information about `Invoke-Sqlcmd`, use the `Get-Help` cmdlet:

```
Get-Help Invoke-Sqlcmd -Full
```

In this recipe, we looked at two ways to use `Invoke-Sqlcmd`. First, we specify a query to run and we use the `-Query` option:

```
#execute a passthrough query, and export to a CSV file

#line continuation in code below only happens at
#the pipe (|) delimiter
Invoke-Sqlcmd -Query "SELECT * FROM Person.Person"
-ServerInstance "$instanceName" -Database $dbName |
Export-Csv -LiteralPath C:\Temp\ResultsFromPassThrough.csv"
-NoTypeInformation
```

For the second way, which requires running a SQL Script, we need to specify the `InputFile` switch:

```
#execute the SampleScript.sql, and display
#results to screen

#line continuation in code below only happens at
#the pipe (|) delimiter
Invoke-SqlCmd -InputFile "C:\Temp\SampleScript.sql"
-ServerInstance "$instanceName" -Database $dbName |
Select-Object FirstName, LastName, ModifiedDate |
Format-Table
```

# Performing bulk export using Invoke-SqlCmd

This recipe shows how to export contents of a table to a CSV file using PowerShell and the `Invoke-SqlCmd` cmdlet.

## Getting ready

Make sure you have access to the `AdventureWorks2014` database. We will use the `Person.Person` table. Create a `C:\Temp` folder, if you don't already have it in your system.

## How to do it...

Follow these steps to perform a bulk export using PowerShell and `Invoke-sqlcmd`:

1. Open **PowerShell ISE** as administrator.

2. Import the SQLPS module and create a new SMO Server Object:

```
#import SQL Server module
Import-Module SQLPS -DisableNameChecking

#replace this with your instance name
$instanceName = "localhost"
$server = New-Object -TypeName
Microsoft.SqlServer.Management.Smo.Server -ArgumentList
$instanceName
```

3. Add the following script and run:

```
#database handle
$dbName = "AdventureWorks2014"
$db = $server.Databases[$dbName]

#export file name
$exportfile = "C:\Temp\Person_Person.csv"

$query = @"
SELECT
    *
FROM
    Person.Person
"@
Invoke-Sqlcmd -Query $query -ServerInstance "$instanceName"
-Database $dbName |
Export-Csv -LiteralPath $exportfile -NoTypeInformation
```

## How it works...

In this recipe, we export the results of a query to a CSV file. There are two core pieces to the export approach in this recipe.

The first piece is executing the query, and we use the `Invoke-Sqlcmd` cmdlet for this. We specify the instance and database, and then send a query to SQL Server through this cmdlet:

```
Invoke-Sqlcmd -Query $query -ServerInstance "$instanceName"
-Database $dbName |
Export-Csv -LiteralPath $exportfile -NoTypeInformation
```

The second piece is piping the results to the `Export-Csv` cmdlet and specifying the file the results are supposed to be stored to. We also specify the `-NoTypeInformation` variable so the cmdlet will omit the `#TYPE` .NET information type as the first line in the file:

```
Invoke-Sqlcmd -Query $query -ServerInstance "$instanceName"
-Database $dbName |
Export-Csv -LiteralPath $exportfile -NoTypeInformation
```

## See also

The *Execute a query / SQL script* recipe.

# Performing bulk export using the bcp command-line utility

This recipe shows how to export contents of a table to a CSV file using PowerShell and bcp.

## Getting ready

Make sure you have access to the `AdventureWorks2014` database. We will export the `Person.Person` table to a pipe (|) delimited, timestamped text file.

Create a `C:\Temp\Exports` folder, if you don't already have it in your system.

## How to do it...

These are the steps to perform bulk export using `bcp`:

1. Open **PowerShell ISE** as administrator.

2. Add the following script and run:

```
$server = "localhost"
$table = "AdventureWorks2014.Person.Person"
$curdate = Get-Date -Format "yyyy-MM-dd_hmmtt"

$foldername = "C:\Temp\Exports\"

#format file name
$formatfilename = "$($table)_$($curdate).fmt"

#export file name
$exportfilename = "$($table)_$($curdate).csv"

$destination_exportfilename =
"$($foldername)$($exportfilename)"
$destination_formatfilename =
"$($foldername)$($formatfilename)"

#command to generate format file
$cmdformatfile = "bcp $table format nul -T -c -t `"|`" -r
`"\n`" -f `"$($destination_formatfilename)`" -S$($server)"

#command to generate the export file
$cmdexport = "bcp $($table) out
`"$($destination_exportfilename)`" -S$($server) -T -f
`"$destination_formatfilename`""

#run the format file command
Invoke-Expression $cmdformatfile

#delay 1 sec, give server some time to generate the format
file
#sleep helps us avoid race conditions
Start-Sleep -s 1

#run the export command
Invoke-Expression $cmdexport

#check the folder for generated file
explorer.exe $foldername
 How it works...
```

Using SQL Server's bcp is often the faster way to export records out of SQL Server. It is also often preferred because bcp offers flexibility in the export format.

The default export format of `bcp` uses a tab (`\t`) as a field delimiter and a carriage return newline character (`\r\n`) as a row delimiter. If you want to change this, you will need to create and use a format file that specifies how you want the export to be formatted.

In our recipe, we first timestamped both the format file and the export filenames:

```
$curdate = Get-Date -Format "yyyy-MM-dd_hmmtt"

$foldername = "C:\Temp\Exports\"

#format file name
$formatfilename = "$($table)_$($curdate).fmt"

#export file name
$exportfilename = "$($table)_$($curdate).csv"

$destination_exportfilename = "$($foldername)$($exportfilename)"
$destination_formatfilename = "$($foldername)$($formatfilename)"
```

What we are going for is a filename that has the database name, schema name, table name, and current system time attached to it:

```
AdventureWorks2014.Person.Person_2015-02-20_913PM
```

We then create the string that will generate the format file as follows:

```
#command to generate format file
$cmdformatfile = "bcp $table format nul -T -c -t `"|`" -r `"\n`"
-f `"$($destination_formatfilename)`" -S$($server)"
```

The format file specifies that the export should:

- Use the character data type (`-c`)
- Use a pipe as a column delimiter (`-t "|"`)
- Use a newline as a row terminator (`-r "\n"`)

 Note that because the actual command requires double quotes, when we construct the command, we need to escape the double quote within the command with a backtick (`` ` ``).

The command that is generated should be similar to the following:

```
bcp AdventureWorks2014.Person.Person format nul -T -c -t "|" -r
"\n" -f "C:\Temp\Exports\AdventureWorks2014.Person.Person_2015-02-
20_913PM.fmt" -Slocalhost
```

We also construct the command that will export the records using the format file we just created:

```
#command to generate the export file
$cmdexport = "bcp $($table) out `"$($destination_exportfilename)`"
-S$($server) -T -f `"$destination_formatfilename`""
```

This will give us something similar to the following:

```
bcp AdventureWorks2014.Person.Person out "C:\Temp\Exports\
AdventureWorks2014.Person.Person_2015-02-20_913PM.csv" -Slocalhost
-T -f "C:\Temp\Exports\ AdventureWorks2014.Person.Person_2015-02-
20_913PM.fmt"
```

When the strings containing the commands are complete, we can execute the command using the `Invoke-Expression` cmdlet. We run the format file creation command first and then sleep. We use the `Start-Sleep` cmdlet to pause for 1 second to ensure the format file has been created first before we invoke the command to do the actual export. The code is as follows:

```
#run the format file command
Invoke-Expression $cmdformatfile

#delay 1 sec, give server some time to generate
#the format file
#sleep helps us avoid race conditions
Start-Sleep -s 1

#run the export command
Invoke-Expression $cmdexport
```

If we don't wait, there is a chance that all the commands will have been executed really fast, and the command to export will run before the format file has been generated. This will lead to an error, because the `bcp` command will not be able to find the format file.

Lastly, we open **Windows Explorer** so we can inspect the files we generated:

```
#check the folder for generated file
explorer.exe $foldername
```

## There's more...

Read more about the bcp format file options from `http://msdn.microsoft.com/en-us/library/ms191516.aspx`.

## See also

▶ The *Performing bulk export using Invoke-SqlCmd* recipe.

# Performing bulk import using BULK INSERT

This recipe will walk through how to import contents of a CSV file to SQL Server using PowerShell and `BULK INSERT`.

## Getting ready

To do a test import, we need to create a `Person` table similar to the `Person.Person` table from the `AdventureWorks2014` database, with some slight modifications.

We will create this in the `Test` schema; we will remove some of the constraints and keep this table as simple and independent as we can.

To create the table we need for this exercise, open up **SQL Server Management Studio** and run the following code:

```
CREATE SCHEMA [Test]
GO
CREATE TABLE [Test].[Person](
   [BusinessEntityID] [int] NOT NULL PRIMARY KEY,
   [PersonType] [nchar](2) NOT NULL,
   [NameStyle] [dbo].[NameStyle] NOT NULL,
   [Title] [nvarchar](8) NULL,
   [FirstName] [dbo].[Name] NOT NULL,
   [MiddleName] [dbo].[Name] NULL,
   [LastName] [dbo].[Name] NOT NULL,
   [Suffix] [nvarchar](10) NULL,
   [EmailPromotion] [int] NOT NULL,
   [AdditionalContactInfo] [xml] NULL,
   [Demographics] [xml] NULL,
   [rowguid] [uniqueidentifier] ROWGUIDCOL  NOT NULL,
   [ModifiedDate] [datetime] NOT NULL
)

GO
```

For this recipe, we will import the file you generated from the previous recipe, *Performing Bulk Export using the bcp command-line utility*. Rename this file as `Person.Person.csv` and save this in the folder `C:\Temp\Exports`.

## How to do it...

Let's follow these steps to perform a bulk import using BULK INSERT:

1. Open **PowerShell ISE** as administrator.

2. Let's add some helper functions first. Type the following and execute:

```
Import-Module SQLPS -DisableNameChecking

function Import-Person {
<#
.SYNOPSIS
    Very simple function to get number
    of records in Test.Person
.NOTES
    Author      : Donabel Santos
.LINK
    http://www.sqlbelle.com
#>
param(
    [string]$instanceName,
    [string]$dbName,
    [string]$fileName
)
$query = @"
TRUNCATE TABLE Test.Person
GO
BULK INSERT AdventureWorks2014.Test.Person
    FROM `'$fileName`'
    WITH
        (
            FIELDTERMINATOR ='|',
            ROWTERMINATOR ='\n'
        )
SELECT COUNT(*) AS NumRecords
FROM AdventureWorks2014.Test.Person
"@

#check number of records
#code below should be in one line
Invoke-Sqlcmd -Query $query -ServerInstance $instanceName
-Database $dbName
}
```

3.  Now, let's invoke the function in the same session as follows:

```
$instanceName = "localhost"
$dbName = "AdventureWorks2014"
$fileName = "C:\Temp\Exports\Person.Person.csv"
Import-Person $instanceName $dbName $fileName
```

## How it works...

To import records in a CSV or text file into a SQL Server table using the `BULK INSERT` command, we need to construct the `BULK INSERT` T-SQL statement and execute this statement using the `Invoke-Sqlcmd` cmdlet:

```
Invoke-Sqlcmd -Query $query -ServerInstance $instanceName
-Database $dbName
```

However, we have done things a little bit differently than our previous recipes. In this recipe, we first created a function that encapsulates all the core import tasks.

To create a function, you first need to create a function header:

```
function Import-Person {
```

The function header starts with the keyword `function`, followed by the function name in the verb-noun format. The body of the function is encapsulated by opening and closing curly braces (`{ }`).

Right after the function header, we also create a **comment-based help** header comment:

```
<#
.SYNOPSIS
    Very simple function to get number
    of records in Test.Person
.NOTES
    Author    : Donabel Santos
.LINK
    http://www.sqlbelle.com
#>
```

Block comments in PowerShell start with `<#` and end with `#>`. In addition, this is a special type of block comment that allows this function's comments to be displayed in a `Get-Help` cmdlet. If we use the following command now:

```
Get-Help Import-Person
```

We will get an output similar to the help you get for any other cmdlet:

```
PS SQLSERVER:\> Get-Help Import-Person

NAME
    Import-Person

SYNOPSIS
    Very simple function to get number
    of records in Test.Person


SYNTAX
    Import-Person [[-instanceName] <String>] [[-dbName] <String>] [[-fileName] <String>]
    [<CommonParameters>]


DESCRIPTION


RELATED LINKS
    http://www.sqlbelle.com

REMARKS
    To see the examples, type: "get-help Import-Person -examples".
    For more information, type: "get-help Import-Person -detailed".
    For technical information, type: "get-help Import-Person -full".
    For online help, type: "get-help Import-Person -online"
```

After the function header and comment, comes the parameters. Our `Import-Person` function accepts three parameters: instance name, database name, and filename. The code is as follows:

```
param(
    [string]$instanceName,
    [string]$dbName,
    [string]$fileName
)
```

Next, we have the function definition. We start by creating `here-string` that contains our T-SQL statement:

```
$query = @"
TRUNCATE TABLE Test.Person
GO
BULK INSERT AdventureWorks2014.Test.Person
    FROM `'$fileName`'
    WITH
        (
            FIELDTERMINATOR ='|',
            ROWTERMINATOR ='\n'
        )
```

```
SELECT COUNT(*) AS NumRecords
FROM AdventureWorks2014.Test.Person
"@
```

After our query is constructed, we pass this to the `Invoke-Sqlcmd` cmdlet, which in turn sends and executes this in our SQL Server instance. The command is as follows:

```
Invoke-Sqlcmd -Query $query -ServerInstance "$instanceName"
-Database $dbName
```

Functions in PowerShell are local-scoped by default, but maintain a global scope when run through ISE. In our recipe, once you run the first part of the script that has the function definition, this function can be invoked any time in the current session. We can see that the `Import-Person` function simplifies our task and needs only the instance name, database name, and filename:

```
$instanceName = "localhost"
$dbName = "AdventureWorks2014"
$fileName = "C:\Temp\Exports\Person.Person.csv"
Import-Person $instanceName $dbName $filename
```

If you are using the shell and you want this function to persist globally across different scopes, save the script as a `.ps1` file and dot source it. Another way is to prepend the function name with `global`:

```
function global:Import-Person {
```

## See also

▶ The *Executing a query / SQL script* recipe.

▶ The *Performing bulk import using the bcp command-line utility* recipe.

# Performing bulk import using the bcp command-line utility

This recipe will walk through the process of importing the contents of a CSV file to SQL Server using PowerShell and `bcp`.

## Getting ready

To do a test import, let's first create a Person table similar to the `Person.Person` table from the `AdventureWorks2014` database, with some slight modifications. We will create this in the `Test` schema, and we will remove some of the constraints and keep this table as simple and independent as we can.

If `Test.Person` does not yet exist in your environment, let's create it. Open up **SQL Server Management Studio** and run the following code:

```
CREATE SCHEMA [Test]
GO
CREATE TABLE [Test].[Person](
   [BusinessEntityID] [int] NOT NULL PRIMARY KEY,
   [PersonType] [nchar](2) NOT NULL,
   [NameStyle] [dbo].[NameStyle] NOT NULL,
   [Title] [nvarchar](8) NULL,
   [FirstName] [dbo].[Name] NOT NULL,
   [MiddleName] [dbo].[Name] NULL,
   [LastName] [dbo].[Name] NOT NULL,
   [Suffix] [nvarchar](10) NULL,
   [EmailPromotion] [int] NOT NULL,
   [AdditionalContactInfo] [xml] NULL,
   [Demographics] [xml] NULL,
   [rowguid] [uniqueidentifier] ROWGUIDCOL  NOT NULL,
   [ModifiedDate] [datetime] NOT NULL
)

GO
```

For this recipe, we will import the file you generated from the preceding recipe, *Performing bulk export using the bcp command-line utility*. Rename this file as `Person.Person.csv` and save this in the folder `C:\Temp\Exports`.

## How to do it...

Let's follow these steps to perform a bulk import using `bcp`:

1.  Open **PowerShell ISE** as administrator.

2.  Let's add some helper functions first. Type the following and then run:
    ```
    Import-Module SQLPS -DisableNameChecking
    $instanceName = "localhost"
    $dbName = "AdventureWorks2014"
    ```

```
function Truncate-Table {
<#
.SYNOPSIS
    Very simple function to truncate
    records from Test.Person
.NOTES
    Author     : Donabel Santos
.LINK
    http://www.sqlbelle.com
#>
param([string]$instanceName,[string]$dbName)

$query = @"
TRUNCATE TABLE Test.Person
"@

#check number of records
#code below should be in a single line
Invoke-Sqlcmd -Query $query -ServerInstance $instanceName
-Database $dbName
}


function Get-PersonCount {
<#
.SYNOPSIS
    Very simple function to get number
    of records in Test.Person
.NOTES
    Author     : Donabel Santos
.LINK
    http://www.sqlbelle.com
#>
param([string]$instanceName,[string]$dbName)
$query = @"
SELECT COUNT(*) AS NumRecords
FROM Test.Person
"@

#check number of records
#code below should be in a single line
Invoke-Sqlcmd -Query $query -ServerInstance $instanceName
-Database $dbName
}
```

3.  Add the following script and run:

```
#let's clean up the Test.Person table first
Truncate-Table $instanceName $dbName

$server = "localhost"
$table = "AdventureWorks2014.Test.Person"
$importfile = "C:\Temp\Exports\Person.Person.csv"


#command to import from csv
$cmdimport = "bcp $($table) in `"$($importfile)`" -S$server
-T -c -t `"|`" -r `"\n`" "

#run the import command
Invoke-Expression $cmdimport

#delay 1 sec, give server some time to import records
#sleep helps us avoid race conditions
Start-Sleep -s 2

Get-PersonCount $instanceName $dbName
```

## How it works...

Performing a bulk import using bcp is a straightforward task: we need to use the
Invoke-Expression cmdlet and pass in the bcp command. In this recipe, however,
we have cleaned up our script a little bit and started off with a couple of helper functions.

The first helper function, Truncate-Table, is a simple helper function that truncates
the Test.Person table that we want to import the records to. This function passes the
TRUNCATE TABLE command to SQL Server using the Invoke-Sqlcmd cmdlet. To use this
function, simply use the following command:

```
Truncate-Table $instanceName $dbName
```

The second helper function, Get-PersonCount, simply returns a count of the records that
have been imported into the Test.Person table. It uses the Invoke-Sqlcmd cmdlet.
To invoke the Get-PersonCount function, use the following command:

```
Get-PersonCount $instanceName $dbName
```

The core of this recipe is in the construction of the `bcp` import command:

```
$server = "localhost"
$table = "AdventureWorks2014.Test.Person"
$importfile = "C:\Temp\Exports\ Person.Person.csv"

#command to import from csv
$cmdimport = "bcp " + $table + " in " + '"' + $importfile + '"'
+ " -S $server -T -c -t `"|`" -r `"\n`" "
```

This will give us the `bcp` command that points to the import file, and it specifies the pipe as the field delimiter, and newline as the row delimiter:

```
bcp AdventureWorks2014.Test.Person in "C:\Temp\Exports\ Person.Person.
csv" -T -c -t "|" -r "\n"
```

Once this command is constructed, we just need to pass this to the `Invoke-Sqlcmd` expression:

```
Invoke-Expression $cmdimport
```

We also added a little bit of delay here (2 seconds) using the `Start-Sleep` cmdlet to allow `INSERT` before we count the records. This is a very simple way to avoid race conditions, but it is sufficient for our requirements.

## See also

▶ The *Performing bulk import using BULK INSERT* recipe.

▶ The *Performing bulk export using the bcp command-line utility* recipe.

# Connecting to an Azure SQL database

In this recipe, we will connect to an Azure-hosted SQL Server database.

## Getting ready

There are a number of prerequisites before you can follow through with this recipe. First, you must already have a Windows Azure account. If you do not, you will need to set one up.

You also need to have the Azure PowerShell cmdlets. If you do not have these installed yet, you can get them by installing the Microsoft Web Platform Installer from `http://go.microsoft.com/fwlink/p/?linkid=320376&clcid=0x409`. Note that this requires .NET 4.5

In addition, you also need to already have an Azure SQL database to connect to. You need to note your server name, database name, your username, and your password. You will need these when connecting to your instance in the recipe.

## How to do it...

The steps to connect to your Azure SQL database using PowerShell are as follows:

1. Open **PowerShell ISE** as administrator.

2. If you haven't already done so yet, you will need to set up connectivity between your workstation and Windows Azure. Execute the following commands one by one:

    1. Get your Azure subscription:

    ```
    Get-AzurePublishSettingsFile
    ```

    This will download a settings file to your local machine. Note where this is stored or move this to a folder that you prefer.

    2. Import your settings file using the following command:

    ```
    Import-AzurePublishSettingsFile -PublishSettingsFile
    "C:\DATA\your-credentials.publishsettings"
    ```

    3. Set up a firewall rule to allow your workstation. You will need to replace the IP address in the sample below with your workstation's IP address:

    ```
    #get Azure SQL Database ServerName
    $servername = Get-AzureSqlDatabaseServer | Select-Object
    -First 1 -ExpandProperty ServerName
     "YourAzureSqlDatabaseServerName"


    New-AzureSqlDatabaseServerFirewallRule -ServerName
    $servername -RuleName 'ServerIP' -StartIpAddress '<replace
    with your external IP>' -EndIpAddress '<replace with your
    external IP>'


    #you can use the following to get your external IP
    $externalip = (Invoke-WebRequest <url>).Content.Trim()
    ```

3. Connect to your SQL Azure database:

    ```
    $server = Get-AzureSqlDatabase -ServerName $servername
    ```

4. Check the database properties:

    ```
    $server
    ```

Your screen should look similar to the following:

```
Name                                          : master
CollationName                                 : SQL_Latin1_General_CP1_CI_AS
Edition                                       : System
MaxSizeGB                                     : 5
MaxSizeBytes                                  : 5368709120
ServiceObjectiveName                          : System2
ServiceObjectiveAssignmentStateDescription    :
CreationDate                                  : 2/21/2015 8:50:41 AM
RecoveryPeriodStartDate                       :

Name                                          : School
CollationName                                 : SQL_Latin1_General_CP1_CI_AS
Edition                                       : Standard
MaxSizeGB                                     : 250
MaxSizeBytes                                  : 268435456000
ServiceObjectiveName                          : S0
ServiceObjectiveAssignmentStateDescription    :
CreationDate                                  : 2/21/2015 8:52:30 AM
RecoveryPeriodStartDate                       : 2/21/2015 8:58:07 AM
```

## How it works...

To connect to your Azure SQL database, you first need to make sure your environment is set up. This includes installing Azure cmdlets and setting up your workstation to access your Azure server by adding subscription and firewall rules. Alternatively, you can use a certificate to set up that trust between your instance and your workstation.

Connecting to the instance is pretty straightforward. You can do this using an Azure cmdlet called `Get-AzureSqlDatabase`, which simply accepts a server name and connects to your instance as long as the subscription and firewall rules are in place:

```
$server = Get-AzureSqlDatabase -ServerName $servername
```

## There's more...

Microsoft provides additional cmdlets if you are working with Azure using PowerShell. This requires downloading the Azure cmdlets. Before you install the Microsoft Web Platform Installer, which contains the Azure cmdlets, you will not find any Azure-related cmdlets. The following should yield no result:

```
Get-Command "*Azure*"
```

After you install, you should find more than 500 Azure-related cmdlets when you run the following:

```
(Get-Command "*Azure*").Count
```

Within this set, you should find more than a handful related to SQL Server when you run the following:

```
Get-Command "*Azure*Sql*"
```

## There's more...

- Check out the article *How to install and configure Azure PowerShell* for more details on setting up PowerShell for Azure and how to use `Get-AzurePublishSettingsFile` at `http://azure.microsoft.com/en-us/documentation/articles/install-configure-powershell`.

- To learn more about the Azure SQL Database cmdlets, check out the MSDN page at `https://msdn.microsoft.com/en-us/library/dn546726.aspx`.

# Creating a table in an Azure SQL database

In this recipe, we will create a table in your Azure SQL database.

## Getting ready

The prerequisites for this recipe are similar to the previous recipe, *Connecting to an Azure SQL database*. You must have the following:

- A Windows Azure account
- Azure PowerShell modules installed
- An existing Azure SQL database
- Azure subscription set up in your workstation
- Firewall rules to allow your workstation to connect to your Azure database

To follow along, you need to note your Azure server name, database name, your username, and your password. You will need these when connecting to your instance in the recipe.

If you are not sure you have the prerequisites, I recommend that you go back to the previous recipe, *Connecting to an Azure SQL database*, to ensure you can successfully connect to Azure using PowerShell.

## How to do it...

Let's create a table in your Azure SQL database using PowerShell:

1. Open **PowerShell ISE** as administrator.

2. Use the following script to connect to your Azure database and run a query that creates your table. Make sure you replace the relevant variables with your own connection settings:

```
Import-Module SQLPS -DisableNameChecking

$query = @"
CREATE TABLE Student
(
    ID INT PRIMARY KEY,
    FName VARCHAR(100),
    LName VARCHAR(100)
)
"@

$azureserver = "yourAzureServer.database.windows.net"
$database = "School"
$username = "yourusername"
$password = "yourpassword"
Invoke-SqlCmd -ServerInstance $azureserver -Database
$database -Username $username -Password $password -Query
$query
```

3. Check whether the table has been created. You can do this using PowerShell:

```
$query = @"
SELECT *
FROM INFORMATION_SCHEMA.TABLES
"@

Invoke-SqlCmd -ServerInstance $azureserver -Database
$database -Username $username -Password $password -Query
$query
```

Now, you should see the table you just created.

| TABLE_CATALOG | TABLE_SCHEMA | TABLE_NAME | TABLE_TYPE |
| --- | --- | --- | --- |
| School | sys | database_firewall_rules | VIEW |
| School | dbo | Student | BASE TABLE |

4. Alternatively, you can connect to your Azure SQL database using **SQL Server Management Studio** (**SSMS**). Provide the server name, username, and password in SSMS when you connect. Once connected, navigate to the **Tables** node and find the table you just created. This is shown in the following screenshot:

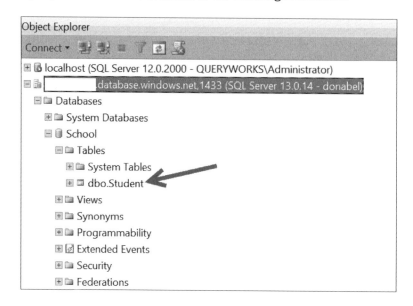

## How it works...

You can use the `Invoke-SqlCmd` cmdlet to send queries to your Azure SQL database in the same way you would for an on-premise instance of SQL Server. You just need to make sure you've already set up your workstation to have access to the Azure server.

To create the table, simply specify the query that creates the table. Pass this query to the `Invoke-SqlCmd` cmdlet along with the server and database information:

```
Invoke-SqlCmd -ServerInstance $azureserver -Database $database
-Username $username -Password $password -Query $query
```

# 3
# Basic Administration

In this chapter, we will cover:

- Creating a SQL Server instance inventory
- Creating a SQL Server database inventory
- Listing installed hotfixes and Service Packs
- Listing running/blocking processes
- Killing a blocking process
- Checking disk space usage
- Setting up WMI server event alerts
- Detaching a database
- Attaching a database
- Copying a database
- Executing a SQL query to multiple servers
- Creating a filegroup
- Adding a secondary data file to a filegroup
- Increasing data file size
- Moving an index to a different filegroup
- Checking index fragmentation
- Reorganizing/rebuilding an index
- Running DBCC commands
- Setting up Database Mail
- Listing SQL Server Jobs
- Adding a SQL Server operator

- ▸ Creating a SQL Server Job
- ▸ Adding a SQL Server event alert
- ▸ Running a SQL Server Job
- ▸ Scheduling a SQL Server Job

# Introduction

In this chapter, we will tackle more administrative tasks that can be accomplished using PowerShell. PowerShell can help automate a lot of the repetitive, tedious, mundane tasks that used to take so many clicks to accomplish. Some of the tasks we will look at include checking disk space, checking instance and database properties, creating WMI alerts, and managing SQL Server jobs.

# Creating a SQL Server instance inventory

In this recipe, we will export SQL Server instance properties to a text file.

## How to do it...

Let's see how to create a SQL Server instance inventory file:

1. Open **PowerShell ISE** as administrator.

2. Import the SQLPS module and create a new SMO Server Object:

```
#import SQL Server module
Import-Module SQLPS -DisableNameChecking

#replace this with your instance name
$instanceName = "localhost"
$server = New-Object -TypeName
Microsoft.SqlServer.Management.Smo.Server -ArgumentList
$instanceName
```

3. Add the following script and run:

```
#specify folder and filename to be produced
$folder = "C:\Temp"
$currdate = Get-Date -Format "yyyy-MM-dd_hmmtt"
$filename = "$($instanceName)_$($currdate).csv"
$fullpath = Join-Path $folder $filename

#export all "server" object properties
$server |
```

```
Get-Member |
Where-Object Name -ne "SystemMessages" |
Where-Object MemberType -eq "Property" |
Select-Object Name,
@{Name="Value";Expression={$server.($_.Name)}} |
Export-Csv -Path $fullpath -NoTypeInformation

#jobs are also extremely important to monitor
#export all job names + last run date and result
$server.JobServer.Jobs |
Select-Object
@{Name="Name";Expression={"Job: $($_.Name)"}},
    @{Name="Value";Expression={"Last run:
$($_.LastRunDate) ($($_.LastRunOutcome))" }} |
Export-Csv -Path $fullpath -NoTypeInformation -Append

#show file in explorer
explorer $folder
```

## How it works...

Using PowerShell, you can regularly take an inventory of your SQL Server instances, that is, get a list of the SQL Server instances and their properties, for auditing and archiving purposes. It will be easier to detect changes if you know what your baseline properties are. In this recipe, we save the properties into a text file in the `C:\Temp` directory. Alternatively, if you want to use the server temp directory, you can use the following command:

```
$folder = [environment]::GetEnvironmentVariable("temp","machine")
```

If you want to use the user temp directory, you can use the following command:

```
$folder = $env:temp
```

There are different ways of extracting different SQL Server settings using PowerShell. What we used in this recipe is a fairly simple script, but exhaustive.

Let's dissect the first part first. The full block of code is as follows:

```
$server |
Get-Member |
Where-Object Name -ne "SystemMessages" |
Where-Object MemberType -eq "Property" |
Select-Object Name,
@{Name="Value";Expression={$server.($_.Name)}} |
Export-Csv -Path $fullpath -NoTypeInformation
```

The first few lines retrieve all properties and methods of the server object:

```
$server |
Get-Member |
```

The next part is as follows:

```
Where-Object Name -ne "SystemMessages" |
Where-Object MemberType -eq "Property" |
```

It retrieves all nonsystem message properties. We filter out all system messages because this will list all system messages stored in the system, which will clutter our inventory. The code up to this line would normally lead to a result that looks similar to the one shown in the following screenshot:

```
   TypeName: Microsoft.SqlServer.Management.Smo.Server

Name                          MemberType Definition
----                          ---------- ----------
ActiveDirectory               Property   Microsoft.SqlServer.Management.Smo.ServerActiveDirectory ActiveDirectory {get;}
AffinityInfo                  Property   Microsoft.SqlServer.Management.Smo.AffinityInfo AffinityInfo {get;}
AuditLevel                    Property   Microsoft.SqlServer.Management.Smo.AuditLevel AuditLevel {get;set;}
Audits                        Property   Microsoft.SqlServer.Management.Smo.AuditCollection Audits {get;}
AvailabilityGroups            Property   Microsoft.SqlServer.Management.Smo.AvailabilityGroupCollection AvailabilityGroups
BackupDevices                 Property   Microsoft.SqlServer.Management.Smo.BackupDeviceCollection BackupDevices {get;}
BackupDirectory               Property   string BackupDirectory {get;set;}
BrowserServiceAccount         Property   string BrowserServiceAccount {get;}
BrowserStartMode              Property   Microsoft.SqlServer.Management.Smo.ServiceStartMode BrowserStartMode {get;}
BuildClrVersion               Property   version BuildClrVersion {get;}
BuildClrVersionString         Property   string BuildClrVersionString {get;}
BuildNumber                   Property   int BuildNumber {get;}
ClusterName                   Property   string ClusterName {get;}
ClusterQuorumState            Property   Microsoft.SqlServer.Management.Smo.ClusterQuorumState ClusterQuorumState {get;}
ClusterQuorumType             Property   Microsoft.SqlServer.Management.Smo.ClusterQuorumType ClusterQuorumType {get;}
Collation                     Property   string Collation {get;}
CollationID                   Property   int CollationID {get;}
ComparisonStyle               Property   int ComparisonStyle {get;}
ComputerNamePhysicalNetBIOS   Property   string ComputerNamePhysicalNetBIOS {get;}
Configuration                 Property   Microsoft.SqlServer.Management.Smo.Configuration Configuration {get;}
ConnectionContext             Property   Microsoft.SqlServer.Management.Common.ServerConnection ConnectionContext {get;}
```

Notice that this only lists the properties of the server, but not the actual values on these properties.

The next line allows us to display the property name and the actual property value:

```
Select-Object Name,
@{Name="Value";Expression={$server.($_.Name)}} |
```

This is at the core of retrieving the inventory. Here, we select the name of the property and also select the property value:

```
@{Name="Value";Expression={$server.($_.Name)}}
```

The `$server.($_.Name)` retrieves the current property in the pipe. For example, if the current property in the pipeline is `Collation`, then this would be translated to `$server.Collation`.

The last part of this line exports the results to a text, **comma-separated value** (**CSV**) file:

```
Export-Csv -Path $fullpath -NoTypeInformation
```

If you want to have a different delimiter, just add the `-Delimiter` parameter, for example:

```
Export-Csv -Path $fullpath -Delimiter "|" -NoTypeInformation
```

The `-NoTypeInformation` removes the headers from the file. The resulting Excel file should look similar to the following screenshot, which shows the first few lines of the resulting inventory file:

| | Name | Value |
|---|---|---|
| 1 | Name | Value |
| 2 | ActiveDirectory | |
| 3 | AffinityInfo | Microsoft.SqlServer.Management.Smo.AffinityInfo |
| 4 | AuditLevel | All |
| 5 | Audits | |
| 6 | AvailabilityGroups | |
| 7 | BackupDevices | |
| 8 | BackupDirectory | C:\Temp |
| 9 | BrowserServiceAccount | NT AUTHORITY\LOCALSERVICE |
| 10 | BrowserStartMode | Auto |
| 11 | BuildClrVersion | 4.0.30319 |
| 12 | BuildClrVersionString | 4.0.30319 |
| 13 | BuildNumber | |
| 14 | ClusterName | |
| 15 | ClusterQuorumState | NotApplicable |
| 16 | ClusterQuorumType | NotApplicable |
| 17 | Collation | SQL_Latin1_General_CP1_CI_AS |
| 18 | CollationID | |
| 19 | ComparisonStyle | |
| 20 | ComputerNamePhysicalNetBIOS | ROGUE |
| 21 | Configuration | Microsoft.SqlServer.Management.Smo.Configuration |

This is not where we stop our script though. We also append job information from the server, including the last run date and last run result:

```
$server.JobServer.Jobs |
Select-Object @{Name="Name";Expression={"Job: $($_.Name)"}},
      @{Name="Value";Expression={"Last run: $($_.LastRunDate)
($($_.LastRunOutcome))" }} |
Export-Csv -Path $fullpath -NoTypeInformation -Append
```

To get the job details, we have to use `$server.JobServer.Jobs` instead of `$server` only. We list the properties of the `Jobs` object: `Name`, `LastRunDate`, and `LastRunOutcome`.

The job details are appended at the end of the file, as shown in the following screenshot:

| | A | |
|---|---|---|
| 103 | Triggers | |
| 104 | Urn | Server[@Name='ROGUE'] |
| 105 | UserData | |
| 106 | UserDefinedMessages | |
| 107 | UserOptions | Microsoft.SqlServer.Management.Smo.UserOptions |
| 108 | Version | 12.0.2000 |
| 109 | VersionMajor | |
| 110 | VersionMinor | |
| 111 | VersionString | 12.0.2000.8 |
| 112 | Job: Agent history clean up: distribution | Last run: 02/26/2015 08:40:00 (Succeeded) |
| 113 | Job: Backup Database | Last run: 10/23/2014 12:35:28 (Succeeded) |
| 114 | Job: Distribution clean up: distribution | Last run: 02/26/2015 08:35:00 (Succeeded) |
| 115 | Job: Expired subscription clean up | Last run: 02/26/2015 01:00:00 (Succeeded) |
| 116 | Job: Export Client Data | Last run: 10/23/2014 12:34:39 (Failed) |
| 117 | Job: Reinitialize subscriptions having data validation failures | Last run: 01/01/0001 00:00:00 (Unknown) |
| 118 | Job: Replication agents checkup | Last run: 02/26/2015 08:40:00 (Succeeded) |
| 119 | Job: Replication monitoring refresher for distribution. | Last run: 01/01/0001 00:00:00 (Unknown) |
| 120 | Job: ROGUE-Registration-1 | Last run: 11/28/2014 09:02:39 (Failed) |
| 121 | Job: ROGUE-Registration-Registration-1 | Last run: 10/25/2014 12:24:01 (Succeeded) |
| 122 | Job: ROGUE-Registration-Registration-ROGUE\SQL2014-3 | Last run: 11/28/2014 09:02:39 (Failed) |
| 123 | Job: syspolicy_purge_history | Last run: 02/26/2015 02:00:00 (Succeeded) |
| 124 | Job: Test Job | Last run: 11/28/2014 10:24:25 (Failed) |
| 125 | | |

## There's more...

There are different ways to extract inventory information. The recipe just loops through all properties exposed with SMO and exports them to our CSV file. However, you may prefer to extract *specific properties* and eliminate ones that are not applicable to your inventory. This will entail exploring the SMO object model, and working with `Get-Member` to nail down exactly which properties you want exported. With this approach, the resulting CSV is going to be more concise and relevant to your needs.

These are examples of more explicitly defined properties:

```
$server.Information.EngineEdition
$server.Information.Collation
$server.Settings.LoginMode
$server.Settings.MailProfile

$server.Configuration.AgentXPsEnabled
$server.Configuration. DatabaseMailEnabled
```

To export to CSV, you can store these properties in `PSCustomObject` which can be piped to the `Export-Csv` cmdlet:

```
#export some "server" object properties
#capture info you want to capture into a PSCustomObject
#the PSCustomObject will make it easier to export to CSV

$result = [PSCustomObject] @{
 EngineEdition        = $server.Information.EngineEdition
 Collation            = $server.Information.Collation
 LoginMode            = $server.Settings.LoginMode
 MailProfile          = $server.Settings.MailProfile
 AgentXPsEnabled      = $server.Configuration.AgentXPsEnabled
}

$result |
Export-Csv -Path $fullpath -NoTypeInformation
```

## See also

 ▸  The *Creating a SQL Server database inventory* recipe.

# Creating a SQL Server database inventory

This recipe will explain the process of retrieving database properties and saving it to a file.

## Getting ready

Log in to your SQL Server instance. Check which user databases are available for you to investigate. The same databases should appear in your resulting file after you run the PowerShell script.

## How to do it...

To create a SQL Server Database Inventory, follow these steps:

1.  Open **PowerShell ISE** as administrator.

2.  Import the SQLPS module and create a new SMO Server object:

```
#import SQL Server module
```

```
Import-Module SQLPS -DisableNameChecking

#replace this with your instance name
$instanceName = "localhost"
$server = New-Object -TypeName
Microsoft.SqlServer.Management.Smo.Server -ArgumentList
$instanceName
```

Add the following script and run:

```
#specify folder and filename to be produced
$folder = "C:\Temp"
$currdate = Get-Date -Format "yyyy-MM-dd_hmmtt"
$filename = "$($instanceName)_db_$($currdate).csv"
$fullpath = Join-Path $folder $filename

$result = @()

#get properties of all databases in instance
$server.Databases |
ForEach-Object {

    #current database in pipeline
    $db = $_

    #capture info you want to capture
    #into a PSCustomObject
    #this make it easier to export to CSV
    $item = [PSCustomObject] @{
        DatabaseName       = $db.Name
        CreateDate         = $db.CreateDate
        Owner              = $db.Owner
        RecoveryModel      = $db.RecoveryModel
        SizeMB             = $db.Size
        DataSpaceUsage     = ($db.DataSpaceUsage/1MB).
ToString("0.00")
        IndexSpaceUsage    =
($db.IndexSpaceUsage/1MB).ToString("0.00")
        Collation          = $db.Collation
        Users              = (($db.Users | ForEach-Object
{$_.Name}) -Join ",")
        UserCount          = $db.Users.Count
        TableCount         = $db.Tables.Count
        SPCount            = $db.StoredProcedures.Count
        UDFCount           = $db.UserDefinedFunctions.Count
        ViewCount          = $db.Views.Count
        TriggerCount       = $db.Triggers.Count
```

```
        LastBackupDate      = $db.LastBackupDate
        LastDiffBackupDate  = $db.LastDifferentialBackupDate
        LastLogBackupDate   = $db.LastBackupDate
    }
    #create a new "row" and add to the results array
    $result += $item
}

#export result to CSV
#note CSV can be opened in Excel, which is handy
$result |
Export-Csv -Path $fullpath -NoTypeInformation

#view folder in Windows Explorer
explorer $folder
```

## How it works...

We have taken a slightly different approach with the database inventory compared to the previous server inventory.

In this recipe, we first constructed our filename with a timestamp:

```
#specify folder and filename to be produced
$folder = "C:\Temp"
$currdate = Get-Date -Format "yyyy-MM-dd_hmmtt"
$filename = "$($instanceName)_db_$($currdate).csv"
$fullpath = Join-Path $folder $filename
```

We then created an empty array where we can store our data:

```
$result = @()
```

In the next step, we created PSCustomObject to capture the information we want from our databases and store each record in our $result array. The PSCustomObject instance helps us create our nice tabular result that we can easily export into our CSV file. The code is as follows:

```
$server.Databases |
ForEach-Object {

    #current database in pipeline
    $db = $_

    #capture info you want to capture
    #into a PSCustomObject
    #this make it easier to export to CSV
```

```
$item = [PSCustomObject] @{
    DatabaseName        = $db.Name
    CreateDate          = $db.CreateDate
    Owner               = $db.Owner
    RecoveryModel       = $db.RecoveryModel
    SizeMB              = $db.Size
    DataSpaceUsage      = ($db.DataSpaceUsage/1MB).ToString("0.00")
    IndexSpaceUsage     = ($db.IndexSpaceUsage/1MB).ToString("0.00")
    Collation           = $db.Collation
    Users               =
(($db.Users | ForEach-Object {$_.Name}) -Join ",")
    UserCount           = $db.Users.Count
    TableCount          = $db.Tables.Count
    SPCount             = $db.StoredProcedures.Count
    UDFCount            = $db.UserDefinedFunctions.Count
    ViewCount           = $db.Views.Count
    TriggerCount        = $db.Triggers.Count
    LastBackupDate      = $db.LastBackupDate
    LastDiffBackupDate  = $db.LastDifferentialBackupDate
    LastLogBackupDate   = $db.LastBackupDate
}
#create a new "row" and add to the results array
$result += $item
}
```

When you export, you can simply take what is stored in $result and pass this to Export-Csv. The code is as follows:

```
$result |
Export-Csv -Path $fullpath -NoTypeInformation
```

The first few columns in your result should look like the following screenshot:

| | A | B | C | D | E |
|---|---|---|---|---|---|
| 1 | DatabaseName | CreateDate | Owner | RecoveryModel | SizeMB |
| 2 | AdventureWorks2014 | 9/6/2014 2:01:44 PM | QUERYWORKS\Administrator | Simple | 303.25 |
| 3 | AdventureWorksLT2012 | 9/6/2014 2:03:14 PM | QUERYWORKS\Administrator | Simple | 9.0625 |
| 4 | Chinook | 10/20/2014 9:42:09 PM | QUERYWORKS\Administrator | Full | 6 |
| 5 | distribution | 10/25/2014 12:21:58 PM | sa | Simple | 8.25 |
| 6 | master | 4/8/2003 9:13:36 AM | sa | Simple | 6.25 |
| 7 | model | 4/8/2003 9:13:36 AM | sa | Full | 3.9375 |
| 8 | msdb | 2/20/2014 8:49:38 PM | sa | Simple | 16.3125 |
| 9 | pubs | 9/6/2014 1:58:12 PM | QUERYWORKS\Administrator | Full | 4 |
| 10 | Registration | 10/20/2014 3:59:33 PM | QUERYWORKS\Administrator | Full | 19 |
| 11 | tempdb | 2/27/2015 6:28:51 AM | sa | Simple | 8.75 |
| 12 | TestDB | 2/13/2015 10:25:38 AM | QUERYWORKS\srogers | Full | 16.25 |

A database has many properties that you may or may not want to capture in an inventory file. You can optionally select which properties you want to export. Remember you can adjust this script as necessary to capture more properties than those we've listed out.

## See also

▶  The *Creating a SQL Server instance inventory* recipe.

# Listing installed hotfixes and Service Packs

In this recipe, we will check which Service Pack and hotfixes/patches are installed on our server.

## How to do it...

Let's explore the ways to list hotfixes and Service Packs:

1. Open **PowerShell ISE** as administrator.

2. Import the SQLPS module and create a new SMO Server object:

```
#import SQL Server module
Import-Module SQLPS -DisableNameChecking

#replace this with your instance name
$instanceName = "localhost"
$server = New-Object -TypeName
Microsoft.SqlServer.Management.Smo.Server -ArgumentList
$instanceName
```

To list the version of SQL Server and Service Pack level, add the following script and run:

```
#the version format is:
#major.minor.build.buildminor
#this should tell you collectively at what
#level your install is
$server.Information.VersionString

#version of SQL Server:
#'RTM' = Original release version
#'SPn' = Service pack version
#'CTP', = Community Technology Preview version
$server.Information.ProductLevel

#to get hotfixes/updates/patches, we can use
```

```
#the Get-Hotfix cmdlet
#Get-Hotfix wraps the WMI class Win32_QuickFixEngineering
#but this may miss some updates or properties,
#depending on your OS
#this also does not include updates that are supplied by
#Microsoft Windows Installer (MSI)

#get all hotfixes
#note the Get-Hotfix cmdlet does not list updates
#applied by MSI (Microsoft Installer)
Get-Hotfix

#check if a specific hotfix is installed
Get-Hotfix -Id "KB2620704"
```

## How it works...

The script for this task can be divided into two separate parts. The first part is specifically an SQL Server script that allows us to check which version and Service Pack has been installed in our instance.

The code that gives us the Service Pack level is straightforward:

```
#version of SQL Server
#'RTM' = Original release version
#'SPn' = Service pack version
#'CTP', = Community Technology Preview version
$server.Information.ProductLevel
```

The block that gives us the version string provides a little bit more information than you might guess:

```
#the version format is:
#major.minor.build.buildminor
#this should tell you collectively at what
#level your install is
$server.Information.VersionString
```

You may get a version such as 12.0.2480.0, which is a SQL Server with cumulative update 6 (build number 2480.0). When you install a hotfix or service pack, it should tell you what build your instance is going to be.

The second part of the script that uses `Get-Hotfix` is not SQL Server-specific. The `Get-Hotfix` cmdlet can query either the local or a remote machine for installed hotfixes. Simply calling `Get-Hotfix` will list all installed hotfixes, or you can also pass a specific hotfix number (or **KB** number) and it will query that specific item for you:

```
#check if a specific hotfix is installed
Get-Hotfix -Id "KB2620704"
```

Note that there is a documented limitation of `Get-Hotfix`. It is documented in MSDN (`http://msdn.microsoft.com/en-us/library/dd315358.aspx`):

> *This cmdlet uses the Win32_QuickFixEngineering WMI class, which represents small system-wide updates of the operating system. Starting with Windows Vista, this class returns only the updates supplied by Component Based Servicing (CBS). It does not include updates that are supplied by Microsoft Windows Installer (MSI) or the Windows update site.*

To get a complete picture of all updates, see Laerte Junior's Simple-Talk article *List updates, hotfixes, and Service Packs with Simple Commands* at `http://www.simple-talk.com/blogs/2011/09/08/list-updates-hotfixes-and-service-packs-with-simple-commands/`.

## There's more...

Some of the terms used in this recipe may be vaguely familiar to you. If so, let's define some of these terms. After all, you may hear it again and again in your dealings with your network administrator, system administrator, or your DBA:

| Terminology | Description | Cycle |
|---|---|---|
| **RTM** | This is short for **Release to Manufacturing**. It is the version of the product that is released to the market. | N/A |
| **Hotfix** | This is also referred to as **Quick Fix Engineering** (**QFE**). It is designed to address single or isolated issues, usually on a per client basis. It has to be specifically requested from Microsoft, either through a support call or from the site (`https://support.microsoft.com/contactus/emailcontact.aspx?scid=sw;%5BLN%5D;1422&WS=hotfix`).<br><br>It is distributed by Microsoft's **Customer Service and Support** (**CSS**) and cannot be redistributed by clients. | N/A |

| Terminology | Description | Cycle |
|---|---|---|
| **Cumulative Update (CU)** | This is a package that contains a bundle of hotfixes that have passed an *acceptance criteria*<br><br>Since it's not fully regression tested, it should not be applied by all customers. | Every 2 months |
| **Service Pack** | According to Microsoft official terminology guide: *is a tested, cumulative set of all hotfixes, security updates, critical updates, and update.* | Every 12-18 months |

For more information on additional terminologies, visit `http://support.microsoft.com/kb/824684`.

There is a comprehensive, unofficial guide to the SQL Server builds. You can check it out at `http://sqlserverbuilds.blogspot.com/`.

In addition, Microsoft has a best practice guide on applying hotfixes and Service Packs that can be found at `http://technet.microsoft.com/en-us/library/cc750077.aspx#XSLTsection127121120120`.

# Listing running/blocking processes

This recipe lists processes in your SQL Server instance and their status.

## Getting ready

In order to see blocking processes in your list, we will have to force some blocking queries.

Open **SQL Server Management Studio** and connect to the instance you want to test. We will assume you have `AdventureWorks2014`. If not, you can use a different database and table altogether.

Open two new query windows for that connection. Type and run the following in the two query windows:

```
USE AdventureWorks2014
GO

BEGIN TRAN
SELECT *
FROM dbo.ErrorLog
WITH (TABLOCKX)
```

# How to do it...

Let's see how to list running and blocking processes in SQL Server using PowerShell:

1. Open **PowerShell ISE** as administrator.

2. Import the SQLPS module and create a new SMO Server object:

```
#import SQL Server module
Import-Module SQLPS -DisableNameChecking

#replace this with your instance name
$instanceName = "localhost"
$server = New-Object -TypeName
Microsoft.SqlServer.Management.Smo.Server -ArgumentList
$instanceName
```

Run the following script to see all processes:

```
#List all processes
$server.EnumProcesses() |
Select-Object Name, Spid, Command, Status,
Login, Database, BlockingSpid |
Format-Table -AutoSize
```

You should see something similar to the following screenshot:

| Name | Spid | Command | Status | Login | Database | BlockingSpid |
| --- | --- | --- | --- | --- | --- | --- |
| 1 | 1 | UNKNOWN TOKEN | background | sa | master | 0 |
| 2 | 2 | UNKNOWN TOKEN | background | sa | master | 0 |
| 3 | 3 | UNKNOWN TOKEN | background | sa | master | 0 |
| 4 | 4 | LOG WRITER | background | sa | master | 0 |
| 5 | 5 | LAZY WRITER | background | sa | master | 0 |
| 6 | 6 | RECOVERY WRITER | background | sa | master | 0 |
| 7 | 7 | SIGNAL HANDLER | background | sa | master | 0 |
| 8 | 8 | XTP_THREAD_POOL | background | sa | master | 0 |
| 9 | 9 | TASK MANAGER | sleeping | sa | master | 0 |
| 10 | 10 | XTP_CKPT_AGENT | background | sa | master | 0 |
| 11 | 11 | LOCK MONITOR | background | sa | master | 0 |
| 12 | 12 | TASK MANAGER | sleeping | sa | master | 0 |
| 13 | 13 | TRACE QUEUE TASK | background | sa | master | 0 |
| 14 | 14 | SYSTEM_HEALTH_MONITOR | background | sa | master | 0 |
| 15 | 15 | RECEIVE | background | sa | master | 0 |
| 16 | 16 | UNKNOWN TOKEN | background | sa | master | 0 |
| 17 | 17 | TASK MANAGER | sleeping | sa | master | 0 |
| 18 | 18 | TASK MANAGER | background | sa | master | 0 |
| 19 | 19 | CHECKPOINT | background | sa | master | 0 |
| 20 | 20 | BRKR TASK | background | sa | master | 0 |
| 21 | 21 | TASK MANAGER | sleeping | sa | master | 0 |
| 22 | 22 | TASK MANAGER | sleeping | sa | master | 0 |
| 23 | 23 | TASK MANAGER | sleeping | sa | master | 0 |
| 24 | 24 | TASK MANAGER | sleeping | sa | master | 0 |
| 25 | 25 | TASK MANAGER | sleeping | sa | master | 0 |
| 26 | 26 | TASK MANAGER | sleeping | sa | master | 0 |
| 28 | 28 | TASK MANAGER | sleeping | sa | master | 0 |

3. To list blocking processes, run the following code:

```
#List blocking Processes
#This assumes you already ran the SQL Script in the
#prep section to create the blocking processes
#Otherwise you may not see any results
$server.EnumProcesses() |
Where-Object BlockingSpid -ne 0 |
Select-Object Name, Spid, Command, Status,
Login, Database, BlockingSpid |
Format-Table -AutoSize
```

4. Your result should show the blocking process you produced in the prep section:

| Name | Spid | Command | Status | Login | Database | BlockingSpid |
|------|------|---------|--------|-------|----------|--------------|
| 55 | 55 | SELECT | suspended | QUERYWORKS\Administrator | AdventureWorks2014 | 54 |

5. Go back to your SSMS windows and rollback your transactions.

## How it works...

The SMO Server object has a method named `EnumProcesses` that simplifies the listing of running processes in an instance. Once the SMO server object is instantiated, all you need to invoke is the `EnumProcesses` method:

```
$server.EnumProcesses() |
Select-Object Name, Spid, Command, Status,
Login, Database, BlockingSpid |
Format-Table –AutoSize
```

If you wish to display processes that are blocked, this command can be filtered to show processes where the `BlockingSpid` is not zero (0), that is, blocked:

```
Where-Object BlockingSpid -ne 0 |
```

There are a number of overloads for the `EnumProcesses` method. An overload means you can call the same method with different parameters. Without any parameter, it returns all processes. Other overloads allow you to perform the following operations:

▶ List processes excluding system processes

▶ List information for a specific process ID

▶ List processes for a specific login

The result returned by `EnumProcesses` is similar to the information you get from the system stored procedure `sp_who2`. The information includes the following:

- ► Name
- ► Login
- ► Host
- ► Status
- ► Command
- ► Database
- ► Blocking SPID

## There's more...

To learn more about the `EnumProcesses` method, including ways to use the method with the different overloads, visit `http://msdn.microsoft.com/en-us/library/microsoft.sqlserver.management.smo.server.enumprocesses(v=sql.110).aspx`.

## See also

- ► The *Killing a blocking process* recipe.

# Killing a blocking process

This recipe illustrates how you can kill a blocking process in SQL Server.

## Getting ready

In order to see blocking processes in your list, we will have to force some blocking queries. If you have already done the prep work in the *Listing running/blocking processes* section, you do not need to do this prep section. If you haven't, go ahead and perform the following steps:

1. Open **SQL Server Management Studio** and connect to the instance you want to test. We will assume you have `AdventureWorks2014`. If not, you can use a different database and table altogether.

2. Open two new query windows for that connection. Type and run the following in the two query windows:

```
USE AdventureWorks2014
GO

BEGIN TRAN
```

```
SELECT *
FROM dbo.ErrorLog
WITH (TABLOCKX)
```

## How to do it...

These are the steps to kill a blocking SQL Server process in PowerShell:

1. Open **PowerShell ISE** as administrator.

2. Import the SQLPS module and create a new SMO Server object:

```
#import SQL Server module
Import-Module SQLPS -DisableNameChecking

#replace this with your instance name
$instanceName = "localhost"
$server = New-Object -TypeName
Microsoft.SqlServer.Management.Smo.Server -ArgumentList
$instanceName
```

Add the following script and run:

```
$VerbosePreference = "Continue"

#This assumes you already ran the SQL script in the
#prep section to create the blocking processes
#Otherwise you may not see any results
$server.EnumProcesses() |
Where-Object BlockingSpid -ne 0 |
ForEach-Object {
    Write-Verbose "Killing SPID $($_.BlockingSpid)"
    $server.KillProcess($_.BlockingSpid)
}

$VerbosePreference = "SilentlyContinue"
```

## How it works...

To kill a blocking process in PowerShell using SMO simply requires the invocation of the
KillProcess method of the SMO Server class:

```
$server.KillProcess($_.BlockingSpid)
```

However, this entails knowing which process ID needs to be killed. In this recipe, we've also identified via scripting which processes are blocking and then killing them. Thus, we need to identify all blocking processes. The code is as follows:

```
$server.EnumProcesses() |
Where-Object BlockingSpid -ne 0 |
ForEach-Object {
    Write-Verbose "Killing SPID $($_.BlockingSpid)"
    $server.KillProcess($_.BlockingSpid)
}
```

Once we've identified all blocking processes, we can kill the processes. In our recipe, we also display which process ID we are killing:

```
$server.EnumProcesses() |
Where-Object BlockingSpid -ne 0 |
ForEach-Object {
    Write-Verbose "Killing SPID $($_.BlockingSpid)"
    $server.KillProcess($_.BlockingSpid)
}
```

## There's more...

We have all run into a situation where SQL Server is running a process that is out of control and is blocking other transactions from finishing. Perhaps the offending process contains a query that is missing a join (or has an accidental cross join) or is simply using too many resources (like memory). Using PowerShell scripting can help reduce manual errors of accidentally killing a process that wasn't blocking.

 Killing a process can be considered a *drastic* measure. Use this script with extreme caution.

## See also

▸ The *Listing running/blocking processes* recipe.

# Checking disk space usage

This recipe shows how to list disks available for your SQL Server instance, how much is used, and how much is available.

## How to do it...

Follow these steps to check the disk space usage:

1. Open **PowerShell ISE** as administrator.

2. Add the following script and run:

```
#get server list
$servers = @("localhost")

#this can come from a file instead of hardcoding
#the servers
#servers = Get-Content <filename>

Get-WmiObject -ComputerName $servers -Class Win32_Volume |
ForEach-Object {
    $drive = $_
    $item  = [PSCustomObject] @{
        Name = $drive.Name
        DeviceType = switch ($drive.DriveType)
                     {
                       0 {"Unknown"}
                       1 {"No Root Directory"}
                       2 {"Removable Disk"}
                       3 {"Local Disk"}
                       4 {"Network Drive"}
                       5 {"Compact Disk"}
                       6 {"RAM"}
                     }
        SizeGB = "{0:N2}" -f ($drive.Capacity/1GB)
        FreeSpaceGB = "{0:N2}" -f ($drive.FreeSpace/1GB)
        FreeSpacePercent = "{0:P0}" -f
($drive.FreeSpace/$drive.Capacity)
    }
    $item
} |
Format-Table -AutoSize
```

The result would look similar to the following screenshot:

```
Name DeviceType   SizeGB FreeSpaceGB FreeSpacePercent
---- ----------   ------ ----------- ----------------
C:\  Local Disk   120.00 95.15       79 %
D:\  Compact Disk 2.43   0.00        0 %
```

# How it works...

An essential task for a database administrator is to know how much disk the database server is consuming. An automated script can help the administrator create an accurate profile of the database server storage and allows for scaling the system.

For this recipe, we enlist the help of the **Windows Management Instrumentation** (**WMI**) `Win32_Volume` class:

```
Get-WmiObject -ComputerName $servers -Class Win32_Volume
```

 WMI is further discussed in *Chapter 2, SQL Server and PowerShell Basic Tasks*.

Using WMI, we can list all drives recognized on the target machine, including removable drives, local hard drives, network disks, compact disks, RAM disks, and clustered and mounted drives.

According to MSDN (`http://msdn.microsoft.com/en-us/library/windows/desktop/aa394515(v=vs.85).aspx`):

> *The Win32_Volume class represents an area of storage on a hard disk. The class returns local volumes that are formatted, unformatted, mounted, or offline.*

We use `Win32_Volume` instead of `Win32_LogicalDisk` for the following reasons:

▸ `Win32_Volume` does not manage floppy disk drives, but `Win32_LogicalDisk` does. Since we're dealing with databases, we do not need the floppy disk drives. Databases will not be stored in floppy disks.

▸ `Win32_Volume` enumerates all volumes, even those that do not have driven letters. This is useful for databases that are stored in volume mountpoints.

For the purpose of this recipe, we list all disks. In reality, you will most likely always filter to show just the local and networked hard drives. In the script, once we capture the disks using the `Win32_Volume` class, we pipe this to the `Select-Object` cmdlet, where we format our output. We use `PSCustomObject` to format the pertinent values we want displayed. Note that in some of the values, we used for format specifiers. For example, we have used `{0:N1}` for single decimal numeric values, and `{0:P0}` for 0 decimal percent.

An alternative to using `PSCustomObject` is to use the `Name` and `Expression` pair in the `Select-Object` cmdlet:

```
Select @{Name="Name";Expression={$_.Name}},
```

We can also shorten this by using `N` for `Name` and `E` for `Expression`:

```
Select @{N="Name";E={$_.Name}},
```

If you were to use this format, your code would look something like this:

```
Get-WmiObject -ComputerName $servers -Class Win32_Volume |
Select-Object @{N="Name";E={$_.Name}},
      @{N="DriveLetter";E={$_.DriveLetter}},
    @{N="DeviceType";
        E={switch ($_.DriveType)
            {
                0 {"Unknown"}
                1 {"No Root Directory"}
                2 {"Removable Disk"}
                3 {"Local Disk"}
                4 {"Network Drive"}
                5 {"Compact Disk"}
                6 {"RAM"}
            }};
        },
    @{N="Size(GB)";E={"{0:N1}" -f($_.Capacity/1GB)}},
    @{N="FreeSpace(GB)";E={"{0:N1}" -f($_.FreeSpace/1GB)}},
    @{N="FreeSpacePercent";E={
            if ($_.Capacity -gt 0)
            {
                "{0:P0}" -f($_.FreeSpace/$_.Capacity)
            }
            else
            {
                0
            }
        }
    } |
Format-Table -AutoSize
```

## There's more...

Learn more about the `Win32_Volume` by visiting http://msdn.microsoft.com/en-us/library/windows/desktop/aa394515(v=vs.85).aspx.

For more information on `Win32_LogicalDisk`, visit http://msdn.microsoft.com/en-us/library/windows/desktop/aa394173(v=vs.85).aspx.

You can also check out the standard .NET format specifiers at `http://msdn.microsoft.com/en-us/library/dwhawy9k(v=vs.110).aspx`.

# Setting up WMI server event alerts

In this recipe, we will set up a simple WMI server event alert for a DDL event.

## Getting ready

We will set up an alert that creates a text file with timestamp every time there is a DDL login event (any of `CREATE`, `ALTER`, or `DROP`). We will utilize the WMI provider for server events in this exercise.

These are the values you will need to know:

| Item | Value |
|------|-------|
| Namespace (if using default instance) | `root\Microsoft\SqlServer\ServerEvents\MSSQLServer` |
| Namespace (if using named instance) | `root\Microsoft\SqlServer\ServerEvents\InstanceName` |
| WMI query | `SELECT * FROM DDL_LOGIN_EVENTS` |
| `DDL_LOGIN_EVENTS` Properties (partial list) | `SQLInstance`<br>`LoginName`<br>`PostTime`<br>`SPID`<br>`ComputerName`<br>`LoginType` |

For WMI events hitting SQL Server, you will also need to ensure that the SQL Server Broker is running on your target database. In our case, we need to ensure the broker is running on the `msdb` database. We can use the following snippet in T-SQL and run it in SQL Server Management Studio to find that out:

```
SELECT
  is_broker_enabled, *
FROM
  sys.databases
ORDER BY
  name
```

Check the `is_broker_enabled` field of `msdb` in the result:

| | is_broker_enabled | name | database_id |
|---|---|---|---|
| 1 | 0 | AdventureWorks2014 | 7 |
| 2 | 0 | AdventureWorksLT2012 | 8 |
| 3 | 0 | Chinook | 6 |
| 4 | 1 | distribution | 10 |
| 5 | 0 | master | 1 |
| 6 | 0 | model | 3 |
| 7 | 1 | msdb | 4 |
| 8 | 1 | pubs | 5 |
| 9 | 0 | Registration | 9 |
| 10 | 1 | tempdb | 2 |
| 11 | 0 | TestDB | 11 |

Alternatively, you can use PowerShell to ensure the broker is running on the `msdb` database:

```
$server.databases["msdb"].BrokerEnabled
```

If service broker is not running on `msdb`, run the following T-SQL statement from SQL Server Management Studio:

```
ALTER DATABASE msdb
SET ENABLE_BROKER
```

Alternatively, you can do this using PowerShell:

```
$database.BrokerEnabled = $true
$database.Alter()
```

## How to do it...

Let's look at the steps needed to set up WMI Server Event Alerts:

1. Open **PowerShell ISE** as administrator.
2. Add the following script and run:

```
$namespace = "root\Microsoft\SqlServer\ServerEvents\MSSQLSERVER"

#WQL for Login Events
#note we will capture CREATE, DROP, ALTER
#if you want to more specific, use these events
#DROP_LOGIN, CREATE_LOGIN, ALTER_LOGIN
```

```
$query = "SELECT * FROM DDL_LOGIN_EVENTS"

#register the event
#if the event is triggered, it will respond by
#creating a timestamped file containing event
#details
Register-WMIEvent -Namespace $namespace -Query $query
-SourceIdentifier "SQLLoginEvent" -Action {
  $date = Get-Date -Format "yyyy-MM-dd_hmmtt"
  $filename = "C:\Temp\LoginEvent-$($date).txt"
  New-Item -ItemType file $filename

$msg = @"

DDL Login Event Occurred`n
PostTime: $($event.SourceEventArgs.NewEvent.PostTime)
Instance: $($event.SourceEventArgs.NewEvent.SQLInstance)
LoginType: $($event.SourceEventArgs.NewEvent.LoginType)
LoginName: $($event.SourceEventArgs.NewEvent.LoginName)
SID:        $($event.SourceEventArgs.NewEvent.SID)
SPID:       $($event.SourceEventArgs.NewEvent.SPID)
TSQLCommand:
$($event.SourceEventArgs.NewEvent.TSQLCommand)


"@

$msg |
Out-File -FilePath $filename -Append
}
```

3. This sets up the alert. You will see a screen like this:

```
Id   Name           PSJobTypeName   State       HasMoreData   Location   Command
--   ----           -------------   -----       -----------   --------   -------
2    SQLLoginEvent                  NotStarted  False                    ...
```

4. Test firing a DDL event and check if the file gets created as response to the event:

    1. Open SQL Server Management Studio.

    2. In a new query window, execute the following code that should trigger the DDL LOGIN WMI event:

```
USE [master]
GO
```

```
CREATE LOGIN [eric]
WITH PASSWORD=N'P@ssword',
DEFAULT_DATABASE=[master],
CHECK_EXPIRATION=OFF,
CHECK_POLICY=OFF
GO
```

5. Go to your `Temp` folder, and check if there is a file created for the `LoginEvent`:

6. Open the `LoginEvent` file to see the entries. The file contains details of the event information, including post time, instance name, login, SID and T-SQL statement used to create the new login has been captured in this file as shown in the following figure:

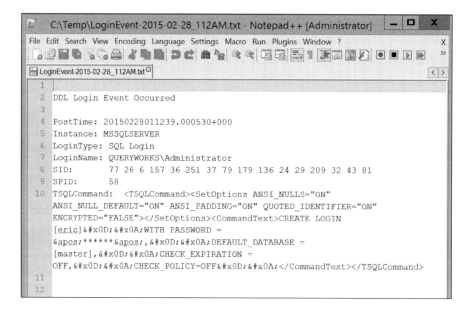

Note that this is a fairly generic log. If you want to narrow down exactly what login event has happened, you can attach this to more specific events such as DROP_LOGIN, CREATE_LOGIN, or ALTER_LOGIN.

## How it works...

We are utilizing WMI and **WMI Query Language** (**WQL**) in this recipe. However, before we can put this into place, Service Broker has to be enabled in your instance, as specified in the *Getting Ready* section. The Service Broker is what the WMI provider uses to send the SQL Server instance events.

WMI is further discussed in *Chapter 2, SQL Server and PowerShell Basic Tasks*.

1. The first thing to identify is which namespace to use. For our purposes, because we want to capture the SQL Server events from the default instance. Our namespace will be:

```
$namespace =
"root\Microsoft\SqlServer\ServerEvents\MSSQLSERVER"
```

2. If you have a named instance, simply replace MSSQLSERVER with the instance name.

3. The next step is to identify which WQL query we need to capture the events we want to be alerted on. In our case, it is just DDL_LOGIN_EVENTS. The other available events that you can query are listed in MSDN's *WMI Provider for Server Events Classes and Properties* article. The code is as follows:

```
#WQL for Login Events
#note this will capture CREATE, DROP, ALTER
#if you want to more specific, use these events
#ROP_LOGIN, CREATE_LOGIN, ALTER_LOGIN
$query = "SELECT * FROM DDL_LOGIN_EVENTS"
```

Another way to explore the SQL Server WMI Events is to use a tool such as WMI Explorer, which is available in CodePlex (`https://wmie.codeplex.com/`). It is inspired by PowerShell **WMI Explorer** created by Marc van Orsouw (the PowerShell guy).

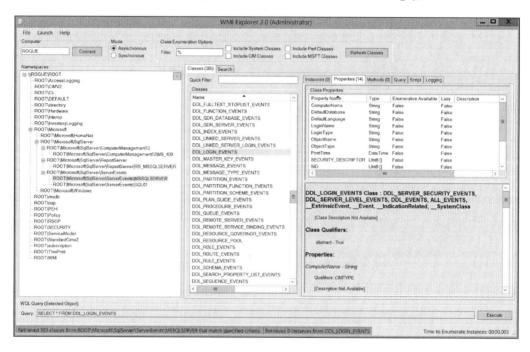

Marc has provided instructions on his blog on how to use this tool, which is pretty straightforward. Once you navigate to the `root\Microsoft\SqlServer\ServerEvents\MSSQLSERVER` namespace and the `DDL_LOGIN_EVENTS` class, the supported properties and methods will be displayed on the right-hand side pane.

After you finalize namespace and WQL query, you need to register this as a WMI event. When registering this event, we will specify an `Action` section to create a log file with a timestamp each time the event is triggered. This log file will contain event properties such as `PostTime`, `LoginType`, `LoginName`, `SID`, `SPID`, and the T-SQL command that caused the event trigger to fire. The code is as follows:

```
Register-WMIEvent -Namespace $namespace -Query
$query -SourceIdentifier "SQLLoginEvent" -Action {
  $date = Get-Date -Format "yyyy-MM-dd_hmmtt"
  $filename = "C:\Temp\LoginEvent-$($date).txt"
  New-Item –ItemType file $filename

$msg = @"

DDL Login Event Occurred`n
```

```
PostTime:   $($event.SourceEventArgs.NewEvent.PostTime)
Instance:   $($event.SourceEventArgs.NewEvent.SQLInstance)
LoginType:  $($event.SourceEventArgs.NewEvent.LoginType)
LoginName:  $($event.SourceEventArgs.NewEvent.LoginName)
SID:        $($event.SourceEventArgs.NewEvent.SID)
SPID:       $($event.SourceEventArgs.NewEvent.SPID)
TSQLCommand:  $($event.SourceEventArgs.NewEvent.TSQLCommand)


"@


$msg |
Out-File -FilePath $filename -Append
}
```

The `Register-WmiEvent` translates the query into SQL Server event notifications, which is handled by the Service Broker.

To unregister the event, use the `Unregister-Event` cmdlet:

```
Unregister-Event "SQLLoginEvent"
```

One caveat about the `Register-WmiEvent` is that it's a temporary registered event. This means it will go away if the program hosting it stops or the server gets restarted.

# There's more...

The article *WMI Provider for Server Events Classes and Properties* can be found at `https://msdn.microsoft.com/en-us/library/ms186449.aspx`.

To learn more about *DDL Event Groups*, check out MSDN at `https://msdn.microsoft.com/en-us/library/bb510452.aspx`.

Also, check out the MSDN article on *Understanding the WMI Provider for Server Events* at `http://msdn.microsoft.com/en-us/library/ms181893.aspx`.

WQL will become more and more important as you work with more WMI events. There is an excellent free e-book provided by one of the prominent bloggers in the PowerShell community, Ravikanth Chaganti. You can download his WQL e-book from `http://www.ravichaganti.com/blog/?p=1979`.

One tool that can help you explore the WMI properties and events is Marc van Orsouw's PowerShell WMI Explorer, explored in the following article by PowerShell MVP Jeffery Hicks `https://4sysops.com/archives/free-mow-powershell-wmi-browser/`

# Detaching a database

In this recipe, we will detach a database programmatically.

## Getting ready

For the purpose of this recipe, let's create a database called TestDB and put its data files in the C:\DATA folder. Open up **SQL Server Management Studio** and run the following code:

```
IF DB_ID('TestDB') IS NOT NULL
DROP DATABASE TestDB
GO

CREATE DATABASE [TestDB]
 CONTAINMENT = NONE
 ON  PRIMARY
( NAME = N'TestDB', FILENAME = N'C:\DATA\TestDB.mdf' , SIZE =
4096KB , FILEGROWTH = 1024KB ),
 FILEGROUP [FG1]
( NAME = N'data1', FILENAME = N'C:\DATA\data1.ndf' ,
SIZE = 4096KB , FILEGROWTH = 1024KB ),
 FILEGROUP [FG2]
( NAME = N'data2', FILENAME = N'C:\DATA\data2.ndf' ,
SIZE = 4096KB , FILEGROWTH = 1024KB )
 LOG ON
( NAME = N'TestDB_log', FILENAME =
N'C:\DATA\TestDB_log.ldf' , SIZE = 1024KB , FILEGROWTH = 10%)
GO
```

## How to do it...

To detach a database programmatically, follow these steps:

1. Open **PowerShell ISE** as administrator.

2. Import the SQLPS module and create a new SMO Server object:

```
#import SQL Server module
Import-Module SQLPS -DisableNameChecking

#replace this with your instance name
$instanceName = "localhost"
$server = New-Object -TypeName
Microsoft.SqlServer.Management.Smo.Server -ArgumentList
$instanceName
```

Add the following script and run:

```
$databaseName = "TestDB"

#parameters   accepted are databasename, boolean
#flag for updatestatistics, and boolean flag
#for removeFulltextIndexFile
$server.DetachDatabase($databaseName, $false, $false)
```

## How it works...

Detaching a database programmatically is fairly straightforward. The `DetachDatabase` method of the `$server` object accepts three parameters: database name, an `updateStatistics` Boolean flag, and a `removeFulltextIndexFile` Boolean flag. The command is as follows:

```
$server.DetachDatabase($databasename, $false, $false)
```

There is another overload of the `DetachDatabase` method that accepts only two parameters: database name and the `updateStatistics` flag.

In addition, note that there are settings that may prevent you from detaching your databases, such as:

▶ Insufficient privileges on the instance

▶ Database is being replicated

▶ Database has a snapshot

You can read the full documentation from MSDN at `http://msdn.microsoft.com/en-us/library/ms190794.aspx`.

## There's more...

Capturing the `mdf`, `ndf`, and `ldf` information can be useful especially if you plan to detach the database and reattach it right away to a different instance.

One way to get this information is by using the `mdf` file to extract all the other data and log files that the detached database uses. You can supply the `mdf` full file path to two methods to get all information about the data and log files:

```
$server.EnumDetachedDatabaseFiles($mdfname)
$server.EnumDetachedLogFiles($mdfname)
```

From the script, you can easily pass this information to your *Attach database* script or code block.

▶   The *Attaching a database* recipe.

# Attaching a database

In this recipe, we will programmatically attach a database with a primary data file (`mdf`), log file (`ldf`), and multiple secondary data files (`ndf`).

## Getting ready

Before we can attach a database, we must have the data files and optional log files to attach. If you have not completed the section *Detach a database*, complete the following steps.

When we attach the database, we will set `QUERYWORKS\srogers` as the owner. This principal has been created with our development VM. Feel free to replace the appropriate code with a login available with your system.

We will first create a database called `TestDB`. Open up **SQL Server Management Studio** and run the following code:

```
IF DB_ID('TestDB') IS NOT NULL
DROP DATABASE TestDB
GO

CREATE DATABASE [TestDB]
 CONTAINMENT = NONE
 ON  PRIMARY
( NAME = N'TestDB', FILENAME = N'C:\DATA\TestDB.mdf' , SIZE =
4096KB , FILEGROWTH = 1024KB ),
 FILEGROUP [FG1]
( NAME = N'data1', FILENAME = N'C:\DATA\data1.ndf' ,
SIZE = 4096KB
, FILEGROWTH = 1024KB ),
 FILEGROUP [FG2]
( NAME = N'data2', FILENAME =
N'C:\DATA\data2.ndf' , SIZE = 4096KB
, FILEGROWTH = 1024KB )
 LOG ON
( NAME = N'TestDB_log', FILENAME =
N'C:\DATA\TestDB_log.ldf' ,
SIZE = 1024KB , FILEGROWTH = 10%)
GO
```

Once you have this, perform the steps in the previous recipe, *Detaching a database*. Alternatively, you can detach from SSMS by going to **Object Explorer** | **TestDB** | **Tasks** | **Detach**:

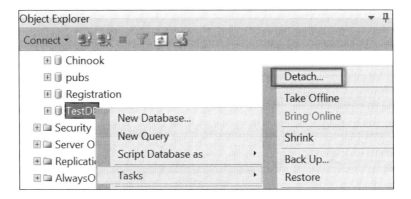

## How to do it...

Let's look at the steps in attaching a database:

1. Open **PowerShell ISE** as administrator.

2. Import the SQLPS module and create a new SMO Server object:

```
#import SQL Server module
Import-Module SQLPS -DisableNameChecking

#replace this with your instance name
$instanceName = "localhost"
$server = New-Object -TypeName
Microsoft.SqlServer.Management.Smo.Server -ArgumentList
$instanceName
```

3. Add the following script and run:

```
$databasename = "TestDB"
$owner = "sa"

#identify the primary data file
#this typically has the .mdf extension
#copy this to an easily referenced location
$mdfname = "C:\DATA\TestDB.mdf"

#FYI only
#view detached database info
$server.DetachedDatabaseInfo($mdfname) |
```

```
Format-Table

#attachdatabase accepts a StringCollection, so we need
#to add our files in this collection
$filecoll = New-Object
System.Collections.Specialized.StringCollection

#add all data files
#this includes the primary data file
$server.EnumDetachedDatabaseFiles($mdfname) |
Foreach-Object {
    $filecoll.Add($_)
}

#add all log files

$server.EnumDetachedLogFiles($mdfname) |
ForEach-Object {
    $filecoll.Add($_)
}


<#
http://msdn.microsoft.com/en-us/library/microsoft.sqlserver.
management.smo.attachoptions.aspx
None        Value = 0. There are no attach options.
EnableBroker  Value = 1. Enables Service Broker.
NewBroker     Value = 2. Creates a new Service Broker .
ErrorBrokerConversations  Value = 3. Stops all current
active Service Broker conversations at the save point and
issues an error message.
RebuildLog    Value = 4. Rebuilds the log.
#>

$server.AttachDatabase($databasename, $filecoll, $owner,
[Microsoft.SqlServer.Management.Smo.AttachOptions]::None)
```

## How it works...

Attaching a database requires a little bit more work compared to detaching a database. For detaching a database, all you really need to know and supply is the instance details and the database name.

For attaching a database, you also will need to supply at minimum all the files (primary data, secondary data, and log) that the database used to use. You can attach a database without supplying log files. SQL Server will recreate new log files for you. While log files are technically *optional*, it is best if you have preserved the log files if this will be needed later on for any point-in-time restore (applicable only to **Bulk Logged and Full Recovery Model**).

 Backup and restore is covered in *Chapter 5, Backup and Restore*, Bulk Logged, and Full are discussed in this chapter.

Before we can attach the database, we first need to identify the primary data file:

```
#identify the primary data file
#this typically has the .mdf extension
$mdfname = "C:\DATA\TestDB.mdf"
```

Note that the primary data files *do not have to have* the .mdf extension, although it is conventional to use this extension.

We also need to create a StringCollection object that will store all other related data and log files to the database we are attaching. We will pass this as parameter to the AttachDatabase method of the SMO server object:

```
#attachdatabase accepts a StringCollection, so we need
#to add our files in this collection
$filecoll = New-Object System.Collections.Specialized.StringCollection
```

Once we have our primary data file path and our StringCollection object, we can start adding all the data files listed in the mdf header into our collection:

```
#add all data files
$server.EnumDetachedDatabaseFiles($mdfname) |
Foreach-Object {
    $filecoll.Add($_)
}
```

You can also add all the log file information if this is available. If not, you can choose to rebuild the log when you attach:

```
$server.EnumDetachedLogFiles($mdfname) |
ForEach-Object {
    $filecoll.Add($_)
}
```

If you need to change the location of the files, you will need to replace the path before you add the filename to the collection, for example:

```
$newpath = "C:\Temp"
$server.EnumDetachedDatabaseFiles($mdfname) |
Foreach-Object {
    $newfile = Join-Path $newpath (Split-Path $_ -Leaf)
    $filecoll.Add($newfile)
}
```

You can also reset a few additional properties, including the database owner:

```
$owner = "sa"
```

Once ready, you can invoke the `AttachDatabase` method, which accepts four parameters: database name, file collection, owner, and attachment options. The command is as follows:

```
$server.AttachDatabase($databasename, $filecoll, $owner,
[Microsoft.SqlServer.Management.Smo.AttachOptions]::None)
```

There are five attach options: `None`, `EnableBroker`, `NewBroker`, `ErrorBrokerConversations`, and `RebuildLog`. If you want to change the attach option, simply replace the enumeration value to `[Microsoft.SqlServer.Management.Smo.AttachOptions]::<NewValue>`. If you do not have the log files handy, be sure to choose `RebuildLog`.

## There's more...

Read more about the `AttachDatabase` options at `http://msdn.microsoft.com/en-us/library/microsoft.sqlserver.management.smo.attachoptions(v=sql.110).aspx`.

## See also

- The *Detaching a database* recipe.

# Copying a database

In this recipe, we will look at how to copy a database using PowerShell and SMO.

## Getting ready

In this recipe, we will create a copy of the database `TestDB` and call it `TestDB_Copy`. We will assume you have the `TestDB` database already created from previous recipes. If you do not have it, you can also substitute this with any database you already have in your instance.

## How to do it...

Let's list the steps required to copy a database using PowerShell.

1. Open **PowerShell ISE** as administrator.

2. Import the SQLPS module and create a new SMO Server object:

```
#import SQL Server module
Import-Module SQLPS -DisableNameChecking

#replace this with your instance name
$instanceName = "localhost"
$server = New-Object -TypeName
Microsoft.SqlServer.Management.Smo.Server -ArgumentList
$instanceName
```

Add the following script and run:

```
$databasename = "TestDB"
$sourcedatabase = $server.Databases[$databasename]

#Create a database to hold the copy of your database
$dbnamecopy = "$($databasename)_copy"

$dbcopy = New-Object -TypeName
Microsoft.SqlServer.Management.SMO.Database -Argumentlist
$server, $dbnamecopy
$dbcopy.Create()

#need to specify source database
#Use SMO Transfer Class
$transfer = New-Object -TypeName
Microsoft.SqlServer.Management.SMO.Transfer -Argumentlist
$sourcedatabase
$transfer.CopyAllTables = $true
$transfer.Options.WithDependencies = $true
$transfer.Options.ContinueScriptingOnError = $true
$transfer.DestinationDatabase = $dbnamecopy
$transfer.DestinationServer = $server.Name
$transfer.DestinationLoginSecure = $true
$transfer.CopySchema = $true

#perform the actual transfer
$transfer.TransferData()
```

3. Check that the database has been created. Go to **SQL Server Management Studio** and inspect the user databases in **Object Explorer**. You may need to refresh **Object Explorer**:

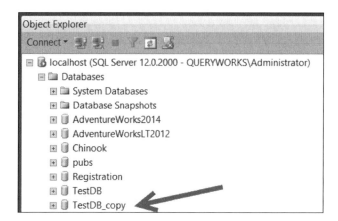

## How it works...

Copying a database using SMO is made a lot simpler by the `Microsoft.SqlServer.Management.SMO.Transfer` class. To create a database copy, we first need to create an empty database that will eventually hold the *copied* database:

```
#Create a database to hold the copy of your database
$dbnamecopy = "$($databasename)_copy"

$dbcopy = New-Object -TypeName
Microsoft.SqlServer.Management.SMO.Database -Argumentlist $server,
$dbnamecopy
$dbcopy.Create()
```

We will then need to create an SMO `Transfer` class, which accepts the source database as a parameter:

```
$transfer = New-Object -TypeName
Microsoft.SqlServer.Management.SMO.Transfer -Argumentlist
$sourcedatabase
```

In the transfer object, you can specify properties you want either brought over, or excluded, when the copy happens:

```
$transfer.CopyAllTables = $true
$transfer.Options.WithDependencies = $true
$transfer.Options.ContinueScriptingOnError = $true
```

```
$transfer.DestinationDatabase = $dbnamecopy
$transfer.DestinationServer = $server.Name
$transfer.DestinationLoginSecure = $true
$transfer.CopySchema = $true
```

When you are ready to bring the data and schema over, you can use the `TransferData` method, which copies the structure and transfers over the records to the destination database:

```
#if you want to perform the actual transfer
#you should use the TransferData method
$transfer.TransferData()
```

There is also an option to just script out the transfer if you wish to just generate the copy script. You can achieve this using the `ScriptTransfer` method:

```
#if you want to only produce a script that will
#"copy" your database, use the ScriptTransfer method
$transfer.ScriptTransfer()
```

## There's more...

To learn more about the SMO `Transfer` class, check out the MSDN documentation at `http://msdn.microsoft.com/en-us/library/microsoft.sqlserver.management.smo.transfer.aspx`.

# Executing SQL query to multiple servers

This recipe executes a predefined SQL query to multiple SQL Server instances specified in a text file.

## Getting ready

In this recipe, we will connect to multiple SQL Server instances and execute a SQL command against all of them.

Identify the available instances for you to run your query on. Once you have identified all the instances you want to execute the command to, create a text file in `C:\Temp` called `sqlinstances.txt` and put each instance name per line in that file. For example:

```
localhost
localhost\SQL01
```

## How to do it...

Let's list the steps required to complete the task:

1. Open **PowerShell ISE** as administrator.

2. Import the SQLPS module:

   ```
   #import SQL Server module
   Import-Module SQLPS -DisableNameChecking
   ```

3. Add the following script and run:

   ```
   #replace this with your own file that contains
   #a list of instances you want to send the query to

   $instances = Get-Content "C:\Temp\sqlinstances.txt"
   $query = "SELECT @@SERVERNAME 'SERVERNAME', @@VERSION
   'VERSION'"
   $databasename = "master"
   $instances |
   ForEach-Object {

       $server = New-Object -TypeName Microsoft.SqlServer.Management.
   Smo.Server -ArgumentList $_

       Invoke-Sqlcmd -ServerInstance $_ -Database $databasename -Query
   $query
   }
   ```

## How it works...

In this script, we are leveraging the `Invoke-Sqlcmd` cmdlet to accomplish our task.

We first get all the instances and temporarily store them in a variable. Note that you can alternatively just pipe the results of the `Get-Content` cmdlet to the succeeding cmdlets in the pipeline:

```
$instances = Get-content "C:\Temp\sqlinstances.txt"
```

Next, we just define the global query we want to execute, and the database we want to execute it against, regardless of the instance. The code is as follows:

```
$query = "SELECT @@SERVERNAME 'SERVERNAME', @@VERSION 'VERSION'"
$databasename = "master"
```

The core of the recipe is iterating through all instances. For each instance, we create a new SMO server object and use the `Invoke-Sqlcmd` cmdlet to execute the query. Note that what we are passing in the pipeline is the instance name; thus, we need to refer to it as $_ when we create the SMO server object. The code is as follows:

```
$instances |
ForEach-Object {
    $server = New-Object -TypeName Microsoft.SqlServer.Management.Smo.
Server -ArgumentList $_
    Invoke-Sqlcmd -ServerInstance $_  -Database $databasename -Query
$query
}
```

## See also

► The *Executing a query/SQL script* recipe of *Chapter 2, SQL Server and PowerShell Basic Tasks*

# Creating a filegroup

This recipe describes how to create a filegroup programmatically using PowerShell and SMO.

## Getting ready

We will add a filegroup called `FGActive` to your `TestDB` database. In this recipe, this is the T-SQL equivalent of what we are trying to accomplish:

```
ALTER DATABASE [TestDB]
ADD FILEGROUP [FGActive]
GO
```

## How to do it...

These are the steps to add a filegroup to your database:

1. Open **PowerShell ISE** as administrator.

2. Import the SQLPS module and create a new SMO Server object:

```
#import SQL Server module
Import-Module SQLPS -DisableNameChecking

#replace this with your instance name
$instanceName = "localhost"
```

```
$server = New-Object -TypeName
Microsoft.SqlServer.Management.Smo.Server -ArgumentList
$instanceName
```

Add the following script and run:

```
$databasename = "TestDB"
$database = $server.Databases[$databasename]
$fgname = "FGActive"

#For purposes of this recipe, we are going to drop this
#filegroup if it exists, so we can recreate it without
#any issues
if ($database.FileGroups[$fgname])
{
    $database.FileGroups[$fgname].Drop()
}

#create the filegroup
$fg = New-Object -TypeName Microsoft.SqlServer.Management.SMO.
Filegroup -Argumentlist
$database, $fgname
$fg.Create()
```

3.  Log in to **Management Studio** and confirm that the filegroup has been added:

    1.  Right-click on the **TestDB** database and go to **Properties**.

    2.  On the left-hand side pane, click on **Filegroups** and check whether the **FGActive** filegroup is there:

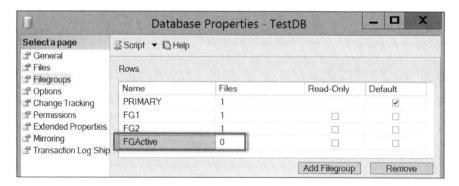

## How it works...

Adding a filegroup can be accomplished with very little code in PowerShell. This task entails creating the file `Microsoft.SqlServer.Management.SMO.Filegroup` object and invoking its `Create` method.

```
$fg = New-Object -TypeName Microsoft.SqlServer.Management.SMO.
Filegroup -Argumentlist $database, $fgname
$fg.Create()
```

If you want to make this filegroup the default filegroup, it will require adding data files to this filegroup first.

Once data files are added, you can use the following block to make a filegroup the default one:

```
#make sure there's a data file before you set a
#filegroup default
#otherwise you will get an error
$fg = $database.FileGroups[$fgname]
$fg.IsDefault = $true
$fg.Alter()
```

## See also

▶   The *Adding a secondary data file to a filegroup* recipe.

# Adding a secondary data file to a filegroup

This recipe walks you through how to add a secondary data file to a filegroup using PowerShell and SMO.

## Getting ready

In this recipe, we will add a secondary data file to the FGActive filegroup we created for the TestDB database in the previous recipe. If you don't have this filegroup yet, you can follow the recipe, *Creating a filegroup*. Alternatively, you can execute the following T-SQL statement in SQL Server Management Studio to create the filegroup:

```
ALTER DATABASE [TestDB]
ADD FILEGROUP [FGActive]
GO
```

In this recipe, we will accomplish this T-SQL equivalent:

```
ALTER DATABASE [TestDB]
ADD FILE (
NAME = N'datafile1',
FILENAME = N'C:\Temp\datafile1.ndf')
TO FILEGROUP [FGActive]
GO
```

## How to do it...

To add secondary data files to an existing filegroup, follow these steps:

1. Open **PowerShell ISE** as administrator.

2. Import the SQLPS module and create a new SMO Server object:

```
#import SQL Server module
Import-Module SQLPS -DisableNameChecking

#replace this with your instance name
$instanceName = "localhost"
$server = New-Object -TypeName
Microsoft.SqlServer.Management.Smo.Server -ArgumentList
$instanceName
```

Add the following script and run:

```
$databasename = "TestDB"
$fgname = "FGActive"

$database = $server.Databases[$databasename]
$fg = $database.FileGroups[$fgname]

#Define a DataFile object on the file group and set the
logical file name.
$df = New-Object -TypeName
Microsoft.SqlServer.Management.SMO.DataFile -ArgumentList
$fg, "datafile1"

#Make sure to have a directory created to hold the
designated data file
```

```
$df.FileName = "c:\\Temp\\datafile1.ndf"

#Call the Create method to create the data file on the
instance of SQL Server.
$df.Create()
```

## How it works...

After setting up your $server and $database SMO objects, you will need to get a handle to the filegroup you want the secondary file added to. You can get a handle to the FileGroups property through the $database SMO object:

```
$fg = $database.FileGroups[$fgname]
```

Once the filegroup handle is in place, you can create a Microsoft.SqlServer. Management.SMO.DataFile object and specify the logical filename:

```
#Define a DataFile object on the file group and set the logical
file name
$df = New-Object -TypeName
Microsoft.SqlServer.Management.SMO.DataFile -ArgumentList $fg,
"datafile1"

#Make sure to have a directory created to hold the designated data
file
$df.FileName = "c:\\Temp\\datafile1.ndf"
The last step is to invoke the Create method of the DataFile
object:
#Call the Create method to create the data file on the instance of
SQL Server.
$df.Create()
```

## See also

- ▶ The *Creating a filegroup* recipe.

# Increase data file size

In this recipe, we will increase the size of an existing secondary data file.

## Getting ready

We will use the `datafile1` data file in the `TestDB` database, which was created in the recipe *Adding secondary data files to a filegroup*. We will increase the size to 1 GB. Feel free to substitute this with a secondary data file from a database that exists in your environment.

This recipe will accomplish this T-SQL equivalent:

```
ALTER DATABASE [TestDB]
MODIFY FILE (
NAME = N'datafile1',
SIZE = 2048KB)
GO
```

## How to do it...

To adjust the size of a secondary data files to an existing filegroup, follow these steps:

1.  Open **PowerShell ISE** as administrator.

2.  Import the SQLPS module and create a new SMO Server object:

```
#import SQL Server module
Import-Module SQLPS -DisableNameChecking

#replace this with your instance name
$instanceName = "localhost"
$server = New-Object -TypeName
Microsoft.SqlServer.Management.Smo.Server -ArgumentList
$instanceName
```

Add the following script and run:

```
$databasename = "TestDB"
$fgname = "FGActive"
$dfname = "datafile1"

$database = $server.Databases[$databasename]
$fg = $database.FileGroups[$fgname]
$df = $fg.Files[$dfname]

#Size is measured in KB
$df.Size = 2048
$df.Alter()
```

## How it works...

In SQL Server, you can define multiple filegroups and each of these filegroups can contain a set of data files. To adjust the size of a data file, we first need to get a handle to the filegroup that contains the data file:

```
$fg = $database.FileGroups[$fgname]
```

Once the filegroup handle is in place, you specify the data file you want to modify:

```
$database = $server.Databases[$databasename]
$fg = $database.FileGroups[$fgname]
$df = $fg.Files[$dfname]
```

Size is a property of the `Microsoft.SqlServer.Management.SMO.DataFile` object measured in KB, which can be set as follows:

```
$df.Size = 2048
```

When you're ready to apply the changes, invoke the `Alter` method of the `DataFile` object:

```
$df.Alter()
```

Other properties that you can set for a data file include:

▸ Name

▸ FileName

▸ Growth

▸ GrowthType

▸ MaxSize

Learn more about the `DataFile` class, including its properties and methods, from the MSDN documentation page at `https://msdn.microsoft.com/en-us/library/microsoft.sqlserver.management.smo.datafile.aspx`.

## See also

▸ The *Creating a filegroup* recipe.

▸ The *Adding a secondary data file to a filegroup* recipe.

# Moving an index to a different filegroup

This recipe illustrates how to move indexes to a different filegroup.

## Getting ready

Using the `TestDB` database, or any database of your choice, let's create a table called `Student` with a clustered primary key.

Open **SQL Server Management Studio** and execute the following code:

```
USE TestDB
GO


-- this table is going to be stored to
-- the default filegroup
IF OBJECT_ID('Student') IS NOT NULL
DROP TABLE Student
GO
CREATE TABLE Student
(
ID INT IDENTITY(1,1) NOT NULL,
FName VARCHAR(50),
CONSTRAINT [PK_Student] PRIMARY KEY CLUSTERED
([ID] ASC)
)
GO
-- insert some sample data
-- nothing fancy, every student will be called Joe for now :)
INSERT INTO Student(FName)
VALUES('Joe')
GO 20
INSERT INTO Student(FName)
SELECT FName FROM Student
GO 10


-- check how many records are inserted
-- this should give 20480
SELECT COUNT(*) FROM Student
```

We want to move the table to a different filegroup called `FGStudent`. Feel free to replace this with your choice of filegroup. Note that the filegroup must already exist.

The T-SQL equivalent of what we are trying to accomplish in this recipe is as follows:

```
CREATE UNIQUE CLUSTERED INDEX PK_Student
ON dbo.Student
(
    ID ASC
)
WITH (DROP_EXISTING=ON, ONLINE=ON)
ON FGStudent
GO
```

## How to do it...

Let's see the steps required to complete the task:

1. Open **PowerShell ISE** as administrator.

2. Import the SQLPS module and create a new SMO Server object:

```
#import SQL Server module
Import-Module SQLPS -DisableNameChecking

$VerbosePreference = "continue"

#replace this with your instance name
$instanceName = "localhost"
$server = New-Object -TypeName
Microsoft.SqlServer.Management.Smo.Server -ArgumentList
$instanceName
```

Add the following script and run:

```
$databasename = "TestDB"
$database = $server.Databases[$databasename]
$tablename = "Student"
$table = $database.Tables[$tablename]

#display which filegroup the table is on now
Write-Verbose "Current: $($table.FileGroup)"

#now move to a different filegroup
#make sure this filegroup already exists
#if not, create it
```

```
$fgname = "FGStudent"

if (!($database.FileGroups[$fgname]))
{
    $fg = New-Object -TypeName
Microsoft.SqlServer.Management.SMO.Filegroup -ArgumentList
$database, $fgname
    $fg.Create()
}


$fg = $database.FileGroups[$fgname]

#create a datafile and specify the filename
$df = New-Object -TypeName
Microsoft.SqlServer.Management.SMO.DataFile -ArgumentList
$fg, "studentdata"

#create a datafile and specify the filename
$df.FileName = "c:\Temp\studentdata.ndf"

#create the datafile
$df.Create()

#now let's recreate the clustered index
#onto the new filegroup
$clusteredindex = $table.Indexes |
Where-Object IsClustered -eq $true

$clusteredindex.FileGroup = $fgname
$clusteredindex.Recreate()

#display which filegroup the table is on now
$table.Refresh()

#display which filegroup the table is on now
Write-Verbose "New: $($table.FileGroup)"
```

## How it works...

Your indexes might outgrow your initial space allocation for them, or you may want to place them into a different disk purely for performance reasons. There will be a number of reasons to move your indexes to a different filegroup. The good news is PowerShell and SMO can accomplish this task.

For purposes of our exercise, the first few steps are creating a filegroup called `FGStudent` and adding a secondary data file into the new filegroup.

 See the recipes *Create a filegroup* and *Adding a secondary data file to a filegroup* for additional information.

For this recipe, we will be moving our clustered index into a different filegroup. Since the `Student` table has a clustered index, the clustered index becomes synonymous to the table. In SQL Server, the clustered index stores the data rows. Therefore, to move the table to a different filegroup in this case means moving the clustered index to the new filegroup.

To start off, we need to capture the clustered index. The following code implicitly creates a `Microsoft.SqlServer.Management.Smo.Index` object when you access the `$table.Indexes` object and assign it to the `$clusteredindex` variable:

```
$clusteredindex = $table.Indexes |
Where-Object IsClustered -eq $true
```

After getting the clustered index and storing it to a variable, we will need to specify the new filegroup this clustered index should belong to:

```
$clusteredindex.FileGroup = $fgname
```

Once you've specified the filegroup, you can invoke the `Recreate` method of the `Microsoft.SqlServer.Management.Smo.Index` object. Note that we are recreating the index—not simply creating it—because the index already exists. The `Recreate` method is equivalent to `CREATE...WITH DROP EXISTING`:

```
$clusteredindex.Recreate()
```

To check, you can refresh the table and see which filegroup the index is attached to:

```
#display which filegroup the table is on now
$table.Refresh()

#display which filegroup the table is on now
Write-Verbose "New: $($table.FileGroup)"
```

## There's more...

To move nonclustered indexes to a different filegroup, you have to follow the same method described in the previous recipe. Here's an example:

```
$idxname = $table.Indexes["idxname"]
$idxname.FileGroup = $fgname
```

```
$idxname.Recreate()
$idxname.Refresh()
$idxname.FileGroup
```

If you are dealing with a clustered index that is not a primary key, you can also consider the `DropAndMove` method of the `Microsoft.SqlServer.Management.Smo.Index` object. This method drops the clustered index and recreates it in the specified filegroup:

```
$idxname.DropAndMove($fgname)
```

## See also

▸ The *Creating a filegroup* recipe.

▸ The *Adding a secondary data file to a filegroup* recipe.

▸ The *Creating an index* recipe of *Chapter 2, SQL Server and PowerShell Basic Tasks*

# Checking index fragmentation

In this recipe, we will look at the steps to display index fragmentation using SMO and PowerShell.

## Getting ready

We will investigate the index fragmentation of the `Person.Person` table in the `AdventureWorks2014` database.

## How to do it...

Let's see the steps required to complete the task:

1. Open **PowerShell ISE** as administrator.

2. Import the SQLPS module and create a new SMO Server object:

```
#import SQL Server module
Import-Module SQLPS -DisableNameChecking

#replace this with your instance name
$instanceName = "localhost"
$server = New-Object -TypeName Microsoft.SqlServer.Management.Smo.
Server -ArgumentList $instanceName
```

3. Add the following script and run:

```
$databasename = "AdventureWorks2014"
$database = $server.Databases[$databasename]

$tableName = "Person"
$schemaName = "Person"

$table = $database.Tables |
        Where-Object Schema -like $schemaName |
        Where-Object Name -like $tableName

#From MSDN:
#EnumFragmentation enumerates a list of
#fragmentation information for the index
#using the default fast fragmentation option.
$table.Indexes |
Foreach-Object {
  $item = $_
  $item.EnumFragmentation() |
  Select-Object Index_Name,
                Index_Type,
                Pages,
               @{Name="AvgFragmentation";
Expression={($_.AverageFragmentation).ToString("0.0000")}}
} |
Format-Table -AutoSize
```

The result will look similar to the one shown in the following screenshot:

| Index_Name | Index_Type | Pages | AvgFragmentation |
|---|---|---|---|
| AK_Person_rowguid | | 65 | 0.0000 |
| idxLastNameFirstName | | 146 | 0.0000 |
| IX_Person_LastName_FirstName_MiddleName | | 108 | 8.3333 |
| PK_Person_BusinessEntityID | | 3809 | 0.1838 |
| PK_Person_BusinessEntityID | | 1 | 0.0000 |
| PK_Person_BusinessEntityID | | 1 | 0.0000 |
| PXML_Person_AddContact | | 3 | 0.0000 |
| PXML_Person_Demographics | | 2152 | 0.0000 |
| XMLPATH_Person_Demographics | | 1389 | 0.9359 |
| XMLPATH_Person_Demographics | | 1 | 0.0000 |
| XMLPROPERTY_Person_Demographics | | 1391 | 1.0784 |
| XMLPROPERTY_Person_Demographics | | 1 | 0.0000 |
| XMLVALUE_Person_Demographics | | 1389 | 1.0799 |
| XMLVALUE_Person_Demographics | | 1 | 0.0000 |

## How it works...

The SMO Index class provides a method called `EnumFragmentation` of the `Microsoft.SqlServer.Management.Smo.Index` object that can enumerate fragmentation of indexes in a table.

You can invoke the `EnumFragmentation` method against all indexes in a table. This method provides the following information:

```
Index_Name
Index_ID
Depth
Pages
Rows
MinimumRecordSize
MaximumRecordSize
AverageRecordSize
ForwardedRecords
AveragePageDensity
IndexType
PartitionNumber
GhostRows
VersionGhostRows
AverageFragmentation
```

In the script, we looped through all the indexes in the table and invoked the `EnumFragmentation` method for each. For each index we display the index name, type, number of pages, and the `AverageFragmentation` property (formatted to display four decimal places). The code is as follows:

```
$table.Indexes |
Foreach-Object {
   $item = $_
   $item.EnumFragmentation() |
   Select-Object Index_Name,
                 Index_Type,
                 Pages,
@{Name="AvgFragmentation";Expression={($_.AverageFragmentation).
ToString("0.0000")}}
} |
Format-Table -AutoSize
```

You can read more on the EnumFragmentation method of the Microsoft.SqlServer. Management.Smo.Index object from MSDN, including options you can specify (http://msdn.microsoft.com/en-us/library/microsoft.sqlserver.management.smo.index.enumfragmentation.aspx).

## See also

▶ The *Reorganizing/rebuilding an index* recipe.

# Reorganizing/rebuilding an index

This recipe demonstrates how to reorganize or rebuild an index.

## Getting ready

We will iterate through all the indexes in the Person.Person table in the AdventureWorks2014 database for this exercise.

## How to do it...

Let's see how to reorganize or rebuild indexes programmatically:

1.  Open **PowerShell ISE** as administrator.

2.  Import the SQLPS module and create a new SMO Server object:

```
#import SQL Server module
Import-Module SQLPS -DisableNameChecking

#replace this with your instance name
$instanceName = "localhost"
$server = New-Object -TypeName
Microsoft.SqlServer.Management.Smo.Server -ArgumentList
$instanceName
```

Add the following script and run:

```
$VerbosePreference = "Continue"

$databasename = "AdventureWorks2014"
$database = $server.Databases[$databasename]

$tableName = "Person"
$schemaName = "Person"

$table = $database.Tables |
        Where-Object Schema -like $schemaName |
        Where-Object Name -like $tableName

#From MSDN:
#EnumFragmentation enumerates a list of
#fragmentation information
#for the index using the default fast fragmentation option.
$table.Indexes |
ForEach-Object {
   $index = $_
   $index.EnumFragmentation() |
   ForEach-Object {
        $item = $_
        #reorganize if 10 and 30% fragmentation
        if($item.AverageFragmentation -ge  10 -and
           $item.AverageFragmentation -le 30  -and
           $item.Pages -ge 1000)
        {
           Write-Verbose "Reorganizing $index.Name ... "
           $index.Reorganize()
        }
        #rebuild if more than 30%
        elseif ($item.AverageFragmentation -gt 30 -and
               $item.Pages -ge 1000)
        {
           Write-Verbose "Rebuilding $index.Name ... "
           $index.Rebuild()
        }
   }
}

$VerbosePreference = "SilentlyContinue"
```

## How it works...

The `EnumFragmentation` method allows additional information about indexes to be extracted, such as average fragmentation and number of pages. Instead of just blindly rebuilding or reorganizing all indexes, we can check these properties and put more smarts as to when the indexes need to be reorganized, or rebuilt (if at all).

These are the rules of thumb:

- If fragmentation is more than 30 percent and if pages are more than or equal to 1,000, rebuild
- If fragmentation is between 10 percent and 30 percent and pages are more than or equal to 1,000, reorganize

It's more of a guideline to have 1,000 pages for the index page count (documented in articles and discussed in conferences). Paul Randal has a post explaining where this number comes from: `http://www.sqlskills.com/blogs/paul/where-do-the-books-online-index-fragmentation-thresholds-come-from/`. I have used this number in a benchmarking exercise and 1,000 worked well in that environment. Test this on your system; you may find that the number of pages that works for you are a little bit higher or a little bit lower.

To use this conditional rebuild/reorganize strategy in PowerShell, you can use an `if-else` statement to divert the action to the correct code block, depending on the fragmentation and pages values:

```
#reorganize if 10 and 30% fragmentation
if($item.AverageFragmentation -ge  10 -and
   $item.AverageFragmentation -le 30  -and
   $item.Pages -ge 1000)
{
   Write-Verbose "Reorganizing $index.Name ... "
   $index.Reorganize()
}
#rebuild if more than 30%
elseif ($item.AverageFragmentation -gt 30 -and
        $item.Pages -ge 1000)
{
   Write-Verbose "Rebuilding $index.Name ... "
   $index.Rebuild()
}
```

## See also

- The *Checking index fragmentation* recipe.

# Running DBCC commands

This recipe shows you some of the DBCC commands that can be run using PowerShell.

## How to do it...

Follow these steps to run DBCC commands:

1. Open **PowerShell ISE** as administrator.

2. Import the SQLPS module and create a new SMO Server object:

```
#import SQL Server module
Import-Module SQLPS -DisableNameChecking

#replace this with your instance name
$instanceName = "localhost"
$server = New-Object -TypeName
Microsoft.SqlServer.Management.Smo.Server -ArgumentList
$instanceName
```

3. Some DBCC commands are built into SMO, so you can just call the methods:

```
$databasename = "AdventureWorks2014"
$database = $server.Databases[$databasename]
#RepairType Values: AllowDataLost, Fast, None, Rebuild
$database.CheckTables
([Microsoft.SqlServer.Management.Smo.RepairType]::None)
```

## How it works...

Not all DBCC commands are wrapped in SMO methods. Some of the available methods are on a database level are as follows:

- ▶ CheckAllocations
- ▶ CheckAllocationsDataOnly
- ▶ CheckCatalog
- ▶ CheckTables
- ▶ CheckTablesDataOnly

To invoke the SMO DBCC methods, you need to get a handle to the database first:

```
$databasename = "AdventureWorks2014"
$database = $server.Databases[$databasename]
```

The `CheckTables` method requires a parameter for `RepairType`, which can be one of the following: `AllowDataLost`, `Fast`, `None`, or `Rebuild`.

```
$database.CheckTables([Microsoft.SqlServer.Management.Smo.
RepairType]::None)
```

For other DBCC commands that are not nicely wrapped in methods, you can still use the `Invoke-Sqlcmd` cmdlet:

```
$query = "DBCC SHRINKFILE(TestDB_Log)"
Invoke-Sqlcmd -ServerInstance $instanceName -Query $query
```

# Setting up Database Mail

This recipe demonstrates how to set up Database Mail programmatically using PowerShell.

## Getting ready

The assumption in this recipe is that Database Mail is not yet configured on your instance.

These are the settings we will use for this recipe:

| Setting | Value |
| --- | --- |
| Mail Server | `mail.queryworks.local` |
| Mail Server Port | `25` |
| E-mail address for Database Mail profile | `dbmail@queryworks.local` |
| SMTP authentication | Basic authentication |
| Credentials for e-mail address | Username is `dbmail@queryworks.local` |
| | Password is `<some password>` |

## How to do it...

To set up Database Mail, follow these steps:

1. Open **PowerShell ISE** as administrator.
2. Import the SQLPS module and create a new SMO Server object:
   ```
   #import SQL Server module
   Import-Module SQLPS -DisableNameChecking

   #replace this with your actual server name
   ```

```
$instanceName = "localhost"

$server = New-Object -TypeName
Microsoft.SqlServer.Management.Smo.Server -ArgumentList
$instanceName
```

Add the following script block to create a Database Mail account and run:

```
#enable DatabaseMail
#this is similar to an sp_configure TSQL command
$server.Configuration.DatabaseMailEnabled.ConfigValue = 1
$server.Configuration.Alter()
$server.Refresh()

#set up account
$accountName = "DBMail"
$accountDescription = "QUERYWORKS Database Mail"
$displayName = "QUERYWORKS mail"
$emailAddress = "dbmail@queryworks.local"
$replyToAddress = "dbmail@queryworks.local"
$mailServerAddress = "mail.queryworks.local"

$account = New-Object -TypeName Microsoft.SqlServer.Management.
SMO.Mail.MailAccount
-Argumentlist $server.Mail, $accountName,
$accountDescription, $displayName, $emailAddress
$account.ReplyToAddress = $replyToAddress
$account.Create()
```

3. Check **SQL Server Management Studio** and confirm that a new account has been created in Database Mail. The steps are as follows:

   1. Open **SQL Server Management Studio**.
   2. Expand the **Management** node.
   3. Right-click on **Database Mail** and choose **Configure Database Mail**.
   4. In the **Select Configuration Task** window, select the **Manage Database Mail accounts and profiles** radio button.
   5. In the **Manage Profiles and Accounts** window, select the option **View, change, or delete an existing account**.

4. Visually check the **Modify Existing Account** page. See what settings have been saved from executing your PowerShell script. You will see that **Anonymous Authentication** has been selected in the **SMTP authentication** by default.

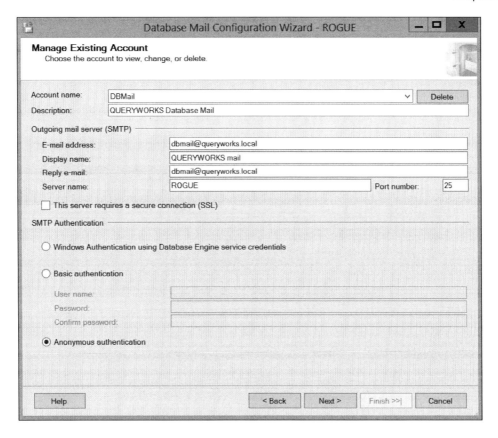

5. After you've confirmed the account, cancel out of the wizard and go back to your **PowerShell ISE**

6. Now we are going to configure the account to use. Add the following to the script and run:

```
#default mail server that was saved in previous script
#was the server name, we need to change this to the
#appropriate mail server
$mailserver = $account.MailServers[$instanceName]
$mailserver.Rename($mailServerAddress)
$mailserver.Alter()

#default SMTP authentication is Anonymous Authentication
#we need to set this to use proper authentication
$mailserver.SetAccount("dbmail@queryworks.local",
"some password")
$mailserver.Port = 25
$mailserver.Alter()
```

7. Check the **Modify Existing Account** window from **Management Studio** again. Check whether these new settings have been saved.

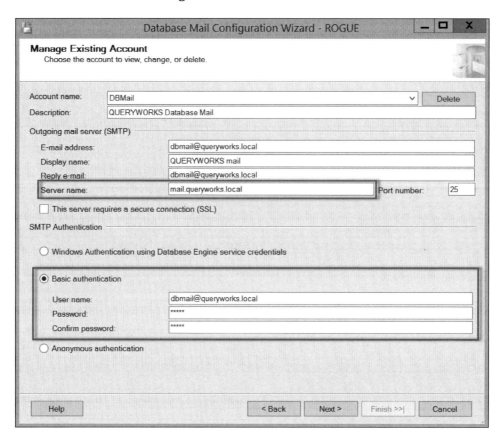

8. After confirming the new settings, cancel out of the wizard and go back to your **PowerShell ISE**.

9. To add a Database Mail profile, add the following code to the script and run:

```
#create a profile
$profileName = "DB Mail Profile"
$profileDescription= "Default DB Mail Profile"

if($mailProfile)
{
  $mailProfile.Drop()
}
```

```
$mailProfile = New-Object -TypeName
Microsoft.SqlServer.Management.SMO.Mail.MailProfile
-ArgumentList $server.Mail, $profileName,
$profileDescription
$mailProfile.Create()
$mailProfile.Refresh()
```

10. Check the settings from **SQL Server Management Studio**. The steps are as follows:

    1. Go back to the **Manage Profiles and Accounts** window, but this time select **View, change, or delete an existing profile**.

    2. Visually check the **Manage Existing Profile** page. You will see that apart from the name and description, the window is still fairly empty.

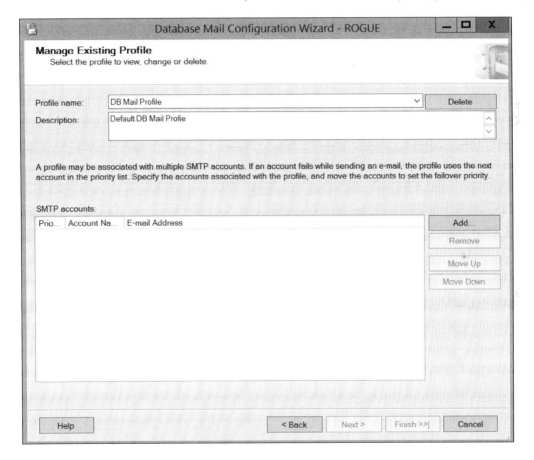

11. After confirming that the new profile has been created, cancel out of the wizard and go back to your **PowerShell ISE**.

12. Next we will attach the Database Mail account to the profile and make it the default profile. Add the following code to the script and run:

```
#add account to the profile
$mailProfile.AddAccount($accountName, 0)
$mailProfile.AddPrincipal('public', 1)
$mailProfile.Alter()
```

13. Check the settings from **SQL Server Management Studio**. The steps are as follows:

    1.  Go back to the **Manage Profiles and Accounts** window, but this time select **View, change, or delete an existing profile**.

    2.  Visually check the **Manage Profile Security** page. You will see that the default profile that has been saved.

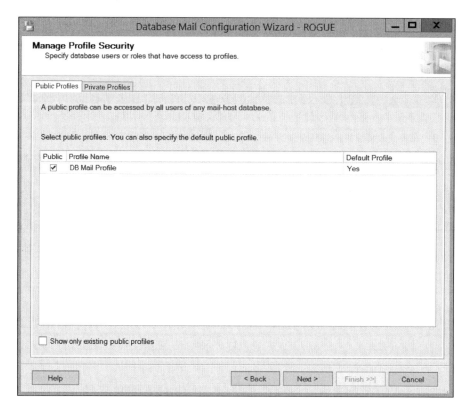

14. After confirming, cancel out of the wizard and go back to **PowerShell ISE**.

15. To link the mail profile to SQL Server Agent, add the following code to the script and run:

```
#link this mail profile to SQL Server Agent
$server.JobServer.AgentMailType = 'DatabaseMail'
```

```
$server.JobServer.DatabaseMailProfile = $profileName
$server.JobServer.Alter()

#restart SQL Server Agent
$managedComputer = New-Object
Microsoft.SqlServer.Management.Smo.Wmi.ManagedComputer
$instanceName
$servicename = "SQLSERVERAGENT"
$service = $managedComputer.Services[$servicename]
$service.Stop()
$service.Start()
```

 Since we are restarting **SQL Server Agent**, you may need to wait a few minutes for to be connected again.

16. Once **SQL Server Agent** is back, check the new settings from **Management Studio**. The steps are as follows:

    1.  Right-click on **SQL Server Agent** and go to **Properties**.

    2.  Click on **Alert System** from the left-hand side pane.

17. Check the settings. The **Enable Mail Profile** option should be checked.

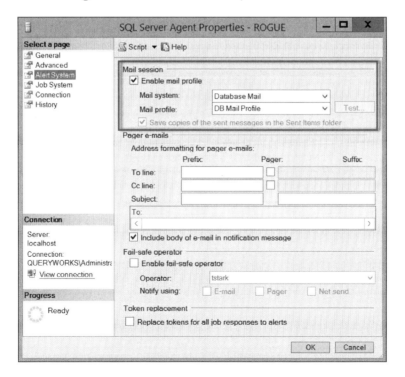

18. Manually test sending an e-mail. Right-click on **Database Mail** and choose **Send Test E-mail**, as shown in the following screenshot:

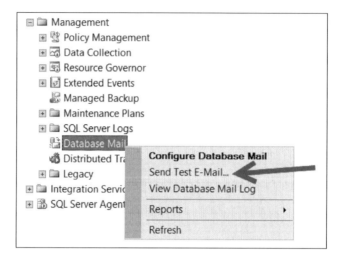

19. Check your mail client to see whether you have received the e-mail.

## How it works...

Database Mail is a feature introduced in SQL Server 2005 that simplifies the sending of e-mails from your SQL Server instance. With Database Mail, you can set up the following:

▶ **Accounts**: This can store the e-mail accounts and associated credentials that Database Mail can use to send e-mails.

▶ **Profiles**: This can store multiple accounts. If an account in a profile fails, the next one in the queue will be used.

Database Mail is a disabled service by default. To start using it, you first need to enable it:

```
#enable DatabaseMail
#this is similar to an sp_configure TSQL command
$server.Configuration.DatabaseMailEnabled.ConfigValue = 1
$server.Configuration.Alter()
```

This statement is equivalent to the following T-SQL statement:

```
EXEC sp_configure 'Database Mail XPs', 1
GO
RECONFIGURE
GO
```

To continue setting up Database Mail, you need to set up an account first:

```
#set up account
$accountName = "DBMail"
$accountDescription = "QUERYWORKS Database Mail"
$displayName = "QUERYWORKS mail"
$emailAddress = "dbmail@queryworks.local"
$replyToAddress = "dbmail@queryworks.local"
$mailServerAddress = "mail.queryworks.local"

$account = New-Object -TypeName
Microsoft.SqlServer.Management.SMO.Mail.MailAccount -Argumentlist
$server.Mail, $accountName, $accountDescription, $displayName,
$emailAddress
$account.ReplyToAddress = $replyToAddress
$account.Create()
```

The next step is to create a profile:

```
$mailProfile = New-Object -TypeName Microsoft.SqlServer.Management.
SMO.Mail.MailProfile -ArgumentList $server.Mail, $profileName,
$profileDescription
$mailProfile.Create()
$mailProfile.Refresh()
```

Once both the account(s) and profile are set up, you need to add the accounts to the mail profile:

```
#add account to the profile
$mailProfile.AddAccount($accountName, 0)
$mailProfile.AddPrincipal('public', 1)
$mailProfile.Alter()
```

The main reason behind setting up Database Mail is to use this with SQL Server Agent. If this is not set up, SQL Server Agent will not be able to alert operators for a job via e-mails. Setting up the Alert for SQL Server Agent is a key step and is often missed. The code is as follows:

```
#link this mail profile to SQL Server Agent
$server.JobServer.AgentMailType = 'DatabaseMail'
$server.JobServer.DatabaseMailProfile = $profileName
$server.JobServer.Alter()
```

Once the Database Mail profile is hooked to SQL Server Agent, you also need to restart the server before you can start using it.

# Listing SQL Server Jobs

This recipe illustrates how to list SQL Server Jobs using PowerShell.

## Getting ready

Do a visual check of your SQL Server Jobs in your instance. You should see the following jobs after you run the script in this recipe:

```
☐ 📇 SQL Server Agent
  ☐ 📁 Jobs
      📄 Agent history clean up: distribution
      📄 Backup Database
      📄 Distribution clean up: distribution
      📄 Expired subscription clean up
      📄 Export Client Data
      📄 Reinitialize subscriptions having data validation failures
      📄 Replication agents checkup
      📄 Replication monitoring refresher for distribution.
      📄 ROGUE-Registration-1
      📄 ROGUE-Registration-Registration-1
      📄 ROGUE-Registration-Registration-ROGUE\SQL2014-3
      📄 syspolicy_purge_history
      📄 Test Job
  📇 Job Activity Monitor
```

## How to do it...

These are the steps to list SQL Server Jobs:

1. Open **PowerShell ISE** as administrator.
2. Import the SQLPS module and create a new SMO Server object:

```
#import SQL Server module
Import-Module SQLPS -DisableNameChecking

#replace this with your instance name
$instanceName = "localhost"
$server = New-Object -TypeName
Microsoft.SqlServer.Management.Smo.Server -ArgumentList
$instanceName
```

Add the following script and run:

```
$jobs=$server.JobServer.Jobs
$jobs |
Select-Object Name, OwnerLoginName,
LastRunDate, LastRunOutcome |
Sort-Object -Property Name |
Format-Table -AutoSize
```

## How it works...

Listing SQL Server Jobs is a short, simple task in PowerShell. To list the jobs, you first need to get a handle to the JobServer.Jobs object:

```
$jobs=$server.JobServer.Jobs
```

Once you have the jobs, you can query the properties you are interested in:

```
$jobs |
Select-Object Name, OwnerLoginName,
LastRunDate, LastRunOutcome |
Sort-Object -Property Name |
Format-Table -AutoSize
```

Each `Job` object exposes a variety of information about the job. Here is a partial list of properties available with a `Job` object, which includes `Category`, `DateCreated`, `LastRunDate`, `LastRunOutcome`, `VersionNumber`, and `JobSchedules`:

```
Parent                   : [ROGUE]
Category                 : [Uncategorized (Local)]
CategoryType             : 1
CurrentRunRetryAttempt   : 0
CurrentRunStatus         : Idle
CurrentRunStep           : 0 (unknown)
DateCreated              : 10/23/2014 12:32:02 PM
DateLastModified         : 10/23/2014 12:35:23 PM
DeleteLevel              : Never
Description              : No description available.
EmailLevel               : Never
EventLogLevel            : Never
HasSchedule              : True
HasServer                : True
HasStep                  : True
IsEnabled                : True
JobID                    : 5f8cdd39-4072-4da0-8ff4-c8187bf220c2
JobType                  : Local
LastRunDate              : 10/23/2014 12:35:28 PM
LastRunOutcome           : Succeeded
NetSendLevel             : Never
NextRunDate              : 3/1/2015 4:00:00 AM
NextRunScheduleID        : 18
OperatorToEmail          :
OperatorToNetSend        :
OperatorToPage           :
OriginatingServer        : ROGUE
OwnerLoginName           : QUERYWORKS\Administrator
PageLevel                : Never
StartStepID              : 1
VersionNumber            : 4
Name                     : Backup Database
CategoryID               : 0
JobSteps                 : {Step 1}
JobSchedules             : {Every night}
```

If you want to list only the failed jobs, pipe the results and filter for `LastRunOutcome` of `"Failed"`:

```
$jobs=$server.JobServer.Jobs
$jobs |
Where-Object LastRunOutcome -like "Failed" |
Select-Object Name, OwnerLoginName,
LastRunDate, LastRunOutcome |
Format-Table -AutoSize
```

## There's more...

You can learn more about the SQL Server `Job` class and explore its properties and methods at `http://msdn.microsoft.com/en-us/library/microsoft.sqlserver.management.smo.agent.job.aspx`.

## See also

▸ The *Creating a SQL Server Job* recipe.

# Adding a SQL Server operator

In this recipe, we'll see how you can create a SQL Server operator using SMO and PowerShell.

## Getting ready

For this recipe, we will create an operator with the following settings:

| Setting operator | Value |
|---|---|
| Name | tstark |
| E-mail | tstark@queryworks.local |

If you do not have this account set up in your system, you can substitute this with another available account in your environment that has an e-mail address. To set up an operator, you must be a `sysadmin` for your instance.

## How to do it...

To create an operator, follow these steps:

1. Open **PowerShell ISE** as administrator.

2. Import the SQLPS module and create a new SMO Server object:

```
#import SQL Server module
Import-Module SQLPS -DisableNameChecking

#replace this with your instance name
$instanceName = "localhost"
$server = New-Object -TypeName Microsoft.SqlServer.Management.Smo.
Server -ArgumentList $instanceName
```

Add the following script and run:

```
$jobserver      = $server.JobServer
$operatorName   = "tstark"
$operatorEmail = "tstark@queryworks.local"

$operator = New-Object  Microsoft.SqlServer.Management.Smo.Agent.
Operator
-ArgumentList $jobserver, $operatorName
$operator.EmailAddress = $operatorEmail
$operator.Create()

#verify by listing operators
$jobserver.Operators
```

3. Open **SQL Server Management Studio** and check if the operator has been created. Go to **SQL Server Agent | Operators**.

## How it works...

To create an operator, you must first get a handle to the JobServer object of your instance:

```
$jobserver      = $server.JobServer
```

An operator will require a name and a method to be contacted. We are going to use e-mail in this case, but you can also specify the NetSendAddress and PagerAddress properties of the Microsoft.SqlServer.Management.Smo.Agent.Operator object:

```
$operatorName   = "tstark"
$operatorEmail = "tstark@queryworks.local"

$operator = New-Object  Microsoft.SqlServer.Management.Smo.Agent.
Operator
-ArgumentList $jobserver, $operatorName
$operator.EmailAddress = $operatorEmail
```

Once these settings are in place, you can just invoke the `Create` method of the `Microsoft.SqlServer.Management.Smo.Agent.Operator` object to persist the operator in the instance:

```
$operator.Create()
```

## There's more...

To learn more about the SQL Server `Operator` class, check out the MSDN entry at `http://msdn.microsoft.com/en-us/library/microsoft.sqlserver.management.smo.agent.operator.aspx`.

## See also

- ▸ The *Creating a SQL Server Job* recipe.
- ▸ The *Adding a SQL Server event alert* recipe.

# Creating a SQL Server Job

In this recipe, we will create a simple SQL Server job programmatically.

## Getting ready

We are going to create a simple job called `Test Job` and set up `tstark` as our operator. We added `tstark` as an operator in the recipe *Adding a SQL Server operator*. If you don't have `tstark`, choose another SQL Server operator that's available in your instance.

## How to do it...

Let's look at the steps required to create a SQL Server `Job` programmatically:

1. Open **PowerShell ISE** as administrator.
2. Import the SQLPS module and create a new SMO Server object:

```
#import SQL Server module
Import-Module SQLPS -DisableNameChecking

#replace this with your instance name
$instanceName = "localhost"
$server = New-Object -TypeName Microsoft.SqlServer.Management.Smo.
Server -ArgumentList $instanceName
```

Add the following script and run:

```
$jobName = "Test Job"

#we will drop our test job if it exists already
if($server.JobServer.Jobs[$jobName])
{
    $server.JobServer.Jobs[$jobName].Drop()
}


$job = New-Object -TypeName
Microsoft.SqlServer.Management.SMO.Agent.Job -Argumentlist
$server.JobServer, $jobName

#Specify which operator to inform
$operatorName = "tstark"
$operator = $server.JobServer.Operators[$operatorName]
$job.OperatorToEmail = $operator.Name

#Specify completion action
#Values can be: Never, OnSuccess, OnFailure, Always
$job.EmailLevel =
[Microsoft.SqlServer.Management.SMO.Agent.
CompletionAction]::OnFailure

#create
$job.Create()

#apply to local instance of SQL Server
#for local we need to specify "(local)"
$job.ApplyToTargetServer("(local)")

#now let's add a simple T-SQL Job Step
$jobStep = New-Object
Microsoft.SqlServer.Management.Smo.Agent.
JobStep($job, "Test Job Step")
$jobStep.Subsystem =
[Microsoft.SqlServer.Management.Smo.Agent.AgentSubSystem]::
TransactSql
$jobStep.Command = "SELECT GETDATE()"
```

```
$jobStep.OnSuccessAction =
[Microsoft.SqlServer.Management.Smo.Agent.
StepCompletionAction]::QuitWithSuccess
$jobStep.OnFailAction =
[Microsoft.SqlServer.Management.Smo.Agent.
StepCompletionAction]::QuitWithFailure

#create the job
$jobStep.Create()
```

3. Check from **SQL Server Management Studio** if this job has been created.

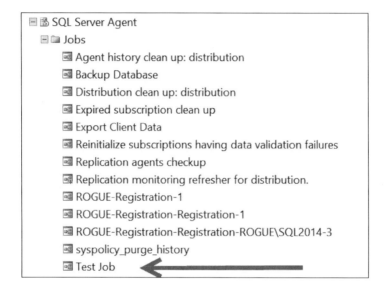

4. Go to **Steps**, and you should see the T-SQL step we added:

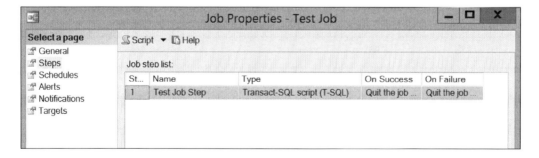

5.  Go to **Notifications**, and you should see `tstark` was added as the operator to receive the e-mail notifications:

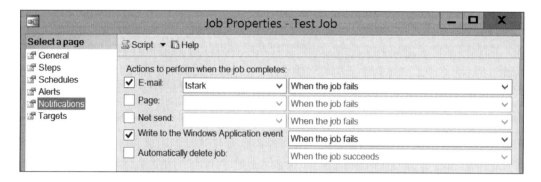

## How it works...

To create a `Job` programmatically, first create a `Microsoft.SqlServer.Management.SMO.Agent.Job` object:

```
$job = New-Object -TypeName
Microsoft.SqlServer.Management.SMO.Agent.Job -Argumentlist
$server.JobServer, "Test Job"
```

Next, specify the `operator` (this is an optional step):

```
#Specify which operator to inform and the completion action.
$operatorName = "tstark"
$operator = $server.JobServer.Operators[$operatorName]
$job.OperatorToEmail = $operator.Name
```

For the notification you can select either by e-mail, net send, or pager. You will also need to specify when the alert should happen. This can be either `Never`, `OnSuccess`, `OnFailure`, or `Always`. The code is as follows:

```
$job.EmailLevel =
[Microsoft.SqlServer.Management.SMO.Agent.CompletionAction]::
OnFailure
```

When ready, invoke the `Create` method of the `Microsoft.SqlServer.Management.SMO.Agent.Job` object. We also need to specify the target server (in our case, just the local instance of SQL Server):

```
$job.ApplyToTargetServer("(local)")
```

To add a job step, you can use the `JobStep` method of the SMO Agent class:

```
#now let's add a simple T-SQL Job Step
$jobStep = New-Object Microsoft.SqlServer.Management.Smo.Agent.
JobStep($job,
"Test Job Step")
```

We can create different types of job steps in SQL Server, and this is defined in PowerShell as `AgentSubSystem`. The possible values for this `Microsoft.SqlServer.Management.Smo.Agent.AgentSubSystem` enumeration are as follows:

- `TransactSql`
- `ActiveScripting`
- `CmdExec`
- `Snapshot`
- `LogReader`
- `Distribution`
- `Merge`
- `QueueReader`
- `AnalysisQuery`
- `AnalysisCommand`
- `Ssis`
- `PowerShell`

For our simple step, we will use a T-SQL subsystem. We will also attach a simple T-SQL statement to this step to retrieve the current system date as a `command`:

```
$jobStep.Subsystem =
[Microsoft.SqlServer.Management.Smo.Agent.AgentSubSystem]::
TransactSql
$jobStep.Command = "SELECT GETDATE()"
```

We can also define the failure and completion actions:

```
$jobStep.OnSuccessAction =
[Microsoft.SqlServer.Management.Smo.Agent.StepCompletionAction]::
QuitWithSuccess
$jobStep.OnFailAction =
[Microsoft.SqlServer.Management.Smo.Agent.StepCompletionAction]::
QuitWithFailure
```

When ready, we can create the job step by invoking the `Create` method of the `Microsoft.SqlServer.Management.Smo.Agent.JobStep` object:

```
$jobStep.Create()
```

## There's more...

Check out MSDN for *Microsoft.SqlServer.Management.Smo.Agent.AgentSubSystem* enumeration (`http://msdn.microsoft.com/en-us/library/microsoft.sqlserver.management.smo.agent.agentsubsystem.aspx`).

## See also

- ▸ The *Listing SQL Server Jobs* recipe
- ▸ The *Adding a SQL Server operator* recipe

# Adding a SQL Server event alert

In this recipe, we'll see the steps for adding a SQL Server event alert.

## How to do it...

Let's list the steps required to complete the task:

1. Open **PowerShell ISE** as administrator.

2. Import the SQLPS module and create a new SMO Server object:

```
#import SQL Server module
Import-Module SQLPS -DisableNameChecking

#replace this with your instance name
$instanceName = "localhost"
$server = New-Object -TypeName Microsoft.SqlServer.Management.Smo.
Server -ArgumentList $instanceName
```

Add the following script and run:

```
$jobserver = $server.JobServer
#for purposes of our exercise, we will drop this
#alert if it  already exists
$alertname = "Test Alert"
$alert = $jobserver.Alerts[$alertname]

#if our test alert exists, we will drop it first
```

```
if($alert)
{
  $alert.Drop()
}

#Alert accepts a JobServer and an alert name
$alert  = New-Object
Microsoft.SqlServer.Management.Smo.Agent.Alert $jobserver,
$alertname
$alert.Severity = 10

#Raise Alert when Message contains
$alert.EventDescriptionKeyword = "failed"

#Set notification message
$alert.NotificationMessage = "This is a test alert,
dont worry"

$alert.Create()
```

## How it works...

To create an alert, you will first need to create a `Microsoft.SqlServer.Management.Smo.Agent.Alert` object:

```
$alert  = New-Object
Microsoft.SqlServer.Management.Smo.Agent.Alert $jobserver, "Test
Alert"
```

This alert is a `SQLServerEvent` alert type by default. The available values for the `AlertType` property that you can specify programmatically, as documented in MSDN, are as follows:

- ▶ `SQLServerEvent`: This specifies an error or event generated by the SQL Server
- ▶ `SqlServerPerformanceCondition`: This specifies a condition applied to a specified SQL Server performance counter
- ▶ `NonSqlServerEvent`: This specifies a system event
- ▶ `WmiEvent`: This specifies an event raised by **WMI**

The `AlertType` property is a read-only property. To choose an event alert type, you will need to set the properties required for that alert type. For example, if you want to create a `WmiEvent` alert, you will need to set the values for `WmiEventNamespace` and `WmiEventQuery`.

For the `SQLServerEvent` alert event type, we will need to specify either error number or severity. You can also optionally specify a keyword that can trigger this notification. The code is as follows:

```
$alert.Severity = 10

#Raise Alert when Message contains
$alert.EventDescriptionKeyword = "failed"
```

Once the alert settings have been provided, you can also add a notification message:

```
$alert.NotificationMessage = "This is a test alert, dont worry"
```

To create the alert, just invoke the `Create` method of the `Microsoft.SqlServer.Management.Smo.Agent.Alert` object:

```
$alert.Create()
```

## There's more...

SQL Server provides a mechanism to alert DBAs and other database staff of possible issues or thresholds reached by the instances. If you navigate to SQL Server Agent and expand **Alerts**, you should see all the alerts set up in your instance.

You can find **Alerts** under the **SQL Server Agent** node in **SQL Server Management Studio**. When you first set up a SQL Server Agent Alert, you will see the following window:

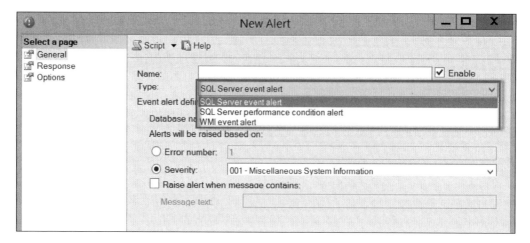

The following table summarizes the types of alerts you can set up in SQL Server:

| Alert type | Description |
|---|---|
| SQL Server Event Alert | This is typically used for specific error numbers, severity, or keywords that exist in the error message. |
| SQL Server Performance Condition Alert | This is typically set up if a performance threshold is reached, for example, if data file size exceeds 100 GB. |
| WMI Event Alert | This is used for WMI events that you want to flag within SQL Server, for example, if you want to monitor if a file gets created or a deadlock is detected in one of the instances. |

To learn more about the `Alert` class, check out the MSDN documentation at `http://msdn.microsoft.com/en-us/library/microsoft.sqlserver.management.smo.agent.alert.aspx`.

## See also

▸ The *Setting up WMI server event alerts* recipe.

# Running an SQL Server Job

In this recipe, we will see how you can run a SQL Server Job programmatically.

## Getting ready

In this recipe, we assume you have a job called `Test Job` in your development environment that you can run. This was created in the *Creating a SQL Server Job* recipe. If you do not have this job, pick another job in your system that you can run.

## How to do it...

These are the steps to run a SQL Server Job:

1. Open **PowerShell ISE** as administrator.

2. Import the SQLPS module and create a new SMO Server Object:

```
#import SQL Server module
Import-Module SQLPS -DisableNameChecking

#replace this with your instance name
$instanceName = "localhost"
$server = New-Object -TypeName
Microsoft.SqlServer.Management.Smo.Server -ArgumentList
$instanceName
```

Add the following script and run:

```
$jobserver = $server.JobServer
$jobname = "Test Job"

$job = $jobserver.Jobs[$jobname]
$job.Start()

#sleep to wait for job to finish
#check last run date
Start-Sleep -s 1
$job.Refresh()
$job.LastRunDate
```

## How it works...

The first step is to get a handle to your instance's JobServer object:

```
$jobserver = $server.JobServer
$jobname = "Test Job"
```

You also need to specify the name of the job you want to run. Once you get a handle to the name, you can just invoke the method Start of the JobServer.Job object:

```
$job = $jobserver.Jobs[$jobname]
$job.Start()
```

If you want to start your job at a specified step, you can pass in the job step name to the Start method.

To check if it ran recently, you can check the last run date by using the `LastRunDate` property:

```
$job.Refresh()
$job.LastRunDate
```

An alternative way to check when the job last ran is to go to **SQL Server Management Studio**, go to that job, right-click, and select **View Job History**. The window that will appear should show a history of the times this job has been run, including the job run status.

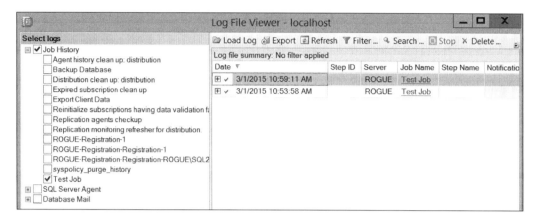

### See also

▸ The *Scheduling a SQL Server Job* recipe.

# Scheduling a SQL Server Job

In this recipe, we will demonstrate how to schedule a SQL Server Job using PowerShell and SMO.

## Getting ready

In this recipe, we assume you have a job called `Test Job` in your development environment that you can run. This was created in the *Creating a SQL Server Job* recipe. If you do not have this job, pick another job in your system that you can use.

We will schedule this job to run every weekend night at 10 P.M.

## How to do it...

Let's look at the steps to schedule a SQL Server Job using PowerShell:

1. Open **PowerShell ISE** as administrator.

2. Import the SQLPS module and create a new SMO Server object:

```
#import SQL Server module
Import-Module SQLPS -DisableNameChecking

#replace this with your instance name
$instanceName = "localhost"
$server = New-Object -TypeName Microsoft.SqlServer.Management.Smo.
Server -ArgumentList $instanceName
```

Add the following script and run:

```
$jobserver = $server.JobServer
$jobname = "Test Job"

$job = $jobserver.Jobs[$jobname]
$jobschedule = New-Object -TypeName
Microsoft.SqlServer.Management.SMO.Agent.JobSchedule
-ArgumentList $job, "Every Weekend Night 10PM"

#Values for FrequencyTypes are:
#AutoStart, Daily, Monthly, MonthlyRelative, OneTime,
#OnIdle, Weekly, unknown
$jobschedule.FrequencyTypes =
[Microsoft.SqlServer.Management.SMO.Agent.FrequencyTypes]::
Weekly

#schedule for every Saturday and Sunday
#can also use 65
$jobschedule.FrequencyInterval =
[Microsoft.SqlServer.Management.SMO.Agent.WeekDays]::
WeekEnds

#set time
#3 parameters - hours, mins, days
#if we don't specify time, it will start at midnight
$starttime = New-Object -TypeName TimeSpan
-ArgumentList 22, 0, 0
$jobschedule.ActiveStartTimeOfDay = $starttime

#frequency of recurrence
```

```
$jobschedule.FrequencyRecurrenceFactor = 1
$jobschedule.ActiveStartDate = "01/01/2015"

#Create the job schedule on the instance of SQL Agent.
$jobschedule.Create()
```

3.  Check the schedule from **SQL Server Management Studio**. The steps are as follows:

    1.  Go to **Management Studio**.
    2.  Under **SQL Server Agent**, double-click on **Test Job**.

4.  Click on **Schedules** on the left-hand side pane. Confirm that the schedule that was created.

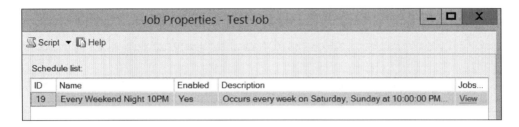

## How it works...

To schedule a job, you first need to get a handle to the job you are scheduling:

```
$job = $jobserver.Jobs[$jobname]
```

The next step is to create a `Microsoft.SqlServer.Management.SMO.Agent.JobSchedule` object. You need to pass the job object and the name of the schedule:

```
$jobschedule =  New-Object -TypeName
Microsoft.SqlServer.Management.SMO.Agent.JobSchedule
-ArgumentList $job, "Every Weekend Night 10PM"
```

For this recipe, we wanted to schedule it every Saturday and Sunday at 10 P.M. The settings that need to be set are as follows:

►   FrequencyTypes

►   FrequencyInterval

►   ActiveStartTimeOfDay

►   FrequencyRecurrenceFactor

►   ActiveStartDate

You will notice that depending on the schedule you want to set, you may need to skip some of the settings or set different properties altogether.

 More scheduling examples are provided in the *There's more...* section.

Because the schedule happens every week, we need to set the `FrequencyType` to `Weekly`:

```
$jobschedule.FrequencyTypes =
[Microsoft.SqlServer.Management.SMO.Agent.FrequencyTypes]::Weekly
```

The different values available for `FrequencyTypes` are as follows:

- `AutoStart`
- `Daily`
- `Monthly`
- `MonthlyRelative`
- `OneTime`
- `OnIdle`
- `Weekly`
- `Unknown`

For `FrequencyInterval`, we are setting our job to be run every weekend:

```
#every Saturday and Sunday
#can also use 65
$jobschedule.FrequencyInterval =
[Microsoft.SqlServer.Management.SMO.Agent.WeekDays]::WeekEnds
```

The valid `FrequencyInterval` values are as follows:

| FrequencyInterval | Numeric value | Notes |
|---|---|---|
| WeekDays.Sunday | 1 | $2^0$ |
| WeekDays.Monday | 2 | $2^1$ |
| WeekDays.Tuesday | 4 | $2^2$ |
| WeekDays.Wednesday | 8 | $2^3$ |
| WeekDays.Thursday | 16 | $2^4$ |
| WeekDays.Friday | 32 | $2^5$ |

| FrequencyInterval | Numeric value | Notes |
|---|---|---|
| `WeekDays.Saturday` | 64 | $2^6$ |
| `WeekDays.WeekDays` | 62 | Monday to Friday |
| `WeekDays.WeekEnds` | 65 | Saturday and Sunday |
| `WeekDays.EveryDay` | 127 | Sunday to Saturday |

As documented in MSDN, if you decide to mix and match the days, you will have to use logical OR to get the value. For example, if you want to schedule a job for Wednesday (8) and Thursday (16), the value you assign to `FrequencyInterval` should be *8+16 = 24.*

To specify that the job needs to run at 10 P.M., we need to use a `TimeSpan` object, which accepts three parameters for hour, minute, and second:

```
$starttime =  New-Object -TypeName TimeSpan -ArgumentList 22, 0, 0
$jobschedule.ActiveStartTimeOfDay = $starttime
```

To set the start date, we need to set the `ActiveStartDate` property of the `JobSchedule` object:

```
$jobschedule.ActiveStartDate = "01/01/2015"
```

The `FrequencyRecurrenceFactor` variable specifies how often in this time period the job should run (in this case, only once):

```
#frequency of recurrence
$jobschedule.FrequencyRecurrenceFactor = 1
```

The last piece is to invoke the `Create()` method:

```
#Create the job schedule on the instance of SQL Agent.
$jobschedule.Create()
```

## There's more...

There are a variety of possible schedules that you may need to set up for jobs in your instance. Here are a few more samples with different variations to get you started:

▶ **Every Weekend at 10 P.M.**

```
$jobschedule.FrequencyTypes =
[Microsoft.SqlServer.Management.SMO.Agent.FrequencyTypes]::
Weekly

#every Saturday and Sunday
```

```
$jobschedule.FrequencyInterval =
[Microsoft.SqlServer.Management.SMO.Agent.WeekDays]::
WeekEnds

#10PM
$starttime =  New-Object -TypeName TimeSpan -ArgumentList
22, 0, 0
$jobschedule.ActiveStartTimeOfDay = $starttime
$jobschedule.FrequencyRecurrenceFactor = 1
```

▶ **Every Weekday from 8 A.M. to 4 P.M., every half hour**

```
$jobschedule.FrequencyTypes =
[Microsoft.SqlServer.Management.SMO.Agent.FrequencyTypes]::
Weekly

#every weekday
$jobschedule.FrequencyInterval = 62

#every half hour
$jobschedule.FrequencySubDayTypes =
[Microsoft.SqlServer.Management.SMO.Agent.
FrequencySubDayTypes]::Minute
$jobschedule.FrequencySubDayInterval = 30

#from 8-4
$starttime =  New-Object -TypeName TimeSpan -ArgumentList
8, 0, 0
$jobschedule.ActiveStartTimeOfDay = $starttime
$endtime = New-Object -TypeName TimeSpan -ArgumentList
16, 0, 0
$jobschedule.ActiveEndTimeOfDay = $endtime
```

▶ **Every month end at 11:30 P.M.**

```
$jobschedule.FrequencyTypes =
[Microsoft.SqlServer.Management.SMO.Agent.FrequencyTypes]::
MonthlyRelative
$jobschedule.FrequencyRelativeIntervals =
[Microsoft.SqlServer.Management.SMO.Agent.
FrequencyRelativeIntervals]::Last

#month end can fall any day, so we'll have to set
#interval to everyday
```

```
$jobschedule.FrequencyInterval =
[Microsoft.SqlServer.Management.SMO.Agent.
MonthlyRelativeWeekDays]::EveryDay

$jobschedule.FrequencyRecurrenceFactor = 1

#start at 11:30 PM
#3 params - hours, mins, days
$starttime =  New-Object -TypeName TimeSpan
-ArgumentList 23, 30, 0
$jobschedule.ActiveStartTimeOfDay = $starttime
```

▶ **Every Tuesday and Thursday at 12 P.M.**

```
$jobschedule.FrequencyTypes =
[Microsoft.SqlServer.Management.SMO.Agent.FrequencyTypes]::
Weekly

#every Tuesday and Thursday
#Tuesday = 4, Thursday = 16
#Final value = 4 + 16 = 20
$jobschedule.FrequencyInterval = 20
$jobschedule.FrequencyRecurrenceFactor = 1

#noon
#3 params - hours, mins, days
$starttime =  New-Object -TypeName TimeSpan -ArgumentList
12, 00, 0
$jobschedule.ActiveStartTimeOfDay = $ starttime
```

▶ **Every third Friday of the month at 6 A.M.**

```
$jobschedule.FrequencyTypes =
[Microsoft.SqlServer.Management.SMO.Agent.FrequencyTypes]::
MonthlyRelative

$jobschedule.FrequencyRelativeIntervals =
[Microsoft.SqlServer.Management.SMO.Agent.
FrequencyRelativeIntervals]::Third

$jobschedule.FrequencyInterval =
[Microsoft.SqlServer.Management.SMO.Agent.
MonthlyRelativeWeekDays]::Friday

$jobschedule.FrequencyRecurrenceFactor = 1

#start at 10:30 PM
```

```
$starttime =  New-Object -TypeName TimeSpan -ArgumentList
6, 00, 0
$jobschedule.ActiveStartTimeOfDay = $starttime
```

▶ **Every last Thursday of the month 11 P.M.**

```
$jobschedule.FrequencyTypes =
[Microsoft.SqlServer.Management.SMO.Agent.FrequencyTypes]::
MonthlyRelative

$jobschedule.FrequencyRelativeIntervals =
[Microsoft.SqlServer.Management.SMO.Agent.
FrequencyRelativeIntervals]::Last

$jobschedule.FrequencyInterval =
[Microsoft.SqlServer.Management.SMO.Agent.
MonthlyRelativeWeekDays]::Thursday

$jobschedule.FrequencyRecurrenceFactor = 1

#11PM
$starttime =  New-Object -TypeName TimeSpan -ArgumentList
23, 00, 0
$jobschedule.ActiveStartTimeOfDay = $starttime
```

It is important to be familiar with the different combinations of the FrequencyType and FrequencyInterval values when setting the SQL Server Job schedule programmatically.

You can learn more about FrequencyType from the MSDN page at http://msdn. microsoft.com/en-us/library/microsoft.sqlserver.management.smo.agent. frequencytypes.aspx.

The FrequencyInterval documentation can be found at http://msdn.microsoft. com/en-us/library/microsoft.sqlserver.management.smo.agent. jobschedule.frequencyinterval.aspx.

## See also

▶ The *Listing SQL Server Jobs* recipe
▶ The *Creating a SQL Server Job* recipe
▶ The *Running an SQL Server Job* recipe

# 4
# Security

In this chapter, we will cover:

- ▶ Listing SQL Server service accounts
- ▶ Changing SQL Server service accounts
- ▶ Listing authentication mode
- ▶ Changing authentication mode
- ▶ Listing SQL Server log errors
- ▶ Listing failed login attempts
- ▶ Enabling Common Criteria compliance
- ▶ Listing logins, users, and database mappings
- ▶ Listing login/user roles and permissions
- ▶ Creating a user-defined server role
- ▶ Creating a login
- ▶ Assigning permissions and roles to a login
- ▶ Creating a database user
- ▶ Assigning permissions to a database user
- ▶ Creating a database role
- ▶ Fixing orphaned users
- ▶ Creating a credential
- ▶ Creating a proxy

# Introduction

PowerShell can help database administrators and developers to automate security tasks. Whether you need to monitor repeated failed login attempts by parsing out event logs, or manage roles and permissions when the number of users in the system is very high, PowerShell can help you deliver. This chapter will show you the classes and snippets of scripts that will help you manage your SQL Server logins and database users programmatically.

# Listing SQL Server service accounts

We will list service accounts in this recipe.

## How to do it...

These are the steps for listing SQL Server service accounts:

1.  Open **PowerShell ISE** as an administrator.

2.  Import the SQLPS module as follows:

    ```
    #import SQL Server module
    Import-Module SQLPS -DisableNameChecking
    ```

3.  Add the following script and run:

    ```
    #replace localhost with your machine name
    #make sure you open the appropriate firewall ports
    $instanceName = "localhost"
    $managedComputer = New-Object
    Microsoft.SqlServer.Management.Smo.Wmi.ManagedComputer
    $instanceName

    #list services
    $managedComputer.Services |
    Select-Object Name, ServiceAccount, ServiceState |
    Format-Table -AutoSize
    ```

You should see a list of services and their service accounts in a format like this:

```
Name                       ServiceAccount                      ServiceState
----                       --------------                      ------------
MsDtsServer120             QUERYWORKS\sqlservice                Stopped
MSSQL$SQL01                NT Service\MSSQL$SQL01               Running
MSSQLFDLauncher            NT Service\MSSQLFDLauncher           Running
MSSQLFDLauncher$SQL01      NT Service\MSSQLFDLauncher$SQL01     Running
MSSQLSERVER                QUERYWORKS\sqlservice                Running
MSSQLServerOLAPService     QUERYWORKS\sqlservice                Running
ReportServer               QUERYWORKS\sqlservice                Running
SQLAgent$SQL01             NT Service\SQLAgent$SQL01            Stopped
SQLBrowser                 NT AUTHORITY\LOCALSERVICE            Running
SQLSERVERAGENT             QUERYWORKS\sqlservice                Running
```

## How it works...

A service account is an account created for the exclusive purpose of running a service. To list service accounts, we can use a `Wmi.ManagedComputer` object:

```
$managedComputer = New-Object
Microsoft.SqlServer.Management.Smo.Wmi.ManagedComputer
$instanceName
```

The `ManagedComputer` instance has a property called `ServiceAccount`, which is what we want to list. It has additional properties, such as `Name` and `ServiceState`, which will be useful to know when you are checking service accounts:

```
#list services
$managedComputer.Services |
Select-Object Name, ServiceAccount, ServiceState |
Format-Table -AutoSize
```

Alternatively, instead of the `Wmi.ManagedComputer` object, we can use the `Get-WmiObject` cmdlet to list the service accounts.

To use `Get-WmiObject`, we must first identify the hostname and the SQL Server namespace:

```
$hostname = "localhost"

$namespace = Get-WMIObject -ComputerName $hostName -NameSpace
root\Microsoft\SQLServer -Class "__NAMESPACE" |
            Where-Object Name -like "ComputerManagement*"
```

For SQL Server 2014, this value is as follows:

```
ROOT\Microsoft\SQLServer\ComputerManagement12
```

This value is different for different SQL Server versions. It is ROOT\Microsoft\SQLServer\ComputerManagement10 for SQL Server 2008 and ROOT\Microsoft\SQLServer\ComputerManagement11 for SQL Server 2012.

We can then use the following snippet with the Get-WmiObject cmdlet to list all the SQL Server services and service accounts. The service account is stored in the StartName property:

```
#code should be all in one line
Get-WmiObject -ComputerName $hostname
-Namespace "$($namespace.__NAMESPACE)\$($namespace.Name)"
-Class SqlService |
Select-Object ServiceName,
        DisplayName,
        @{Name="ServiceAccount";Expression={$_.StartName}} |
Format-Table -AutoSize
```

## See also

- The *Changing SQL Server service account* recipe.
- The *Listing SQL Server Instances* recipe of *Chapter 2, SQL Server and PowerShell Basic Tasks*

# Changing SQL Server service account

We will see how to change SQL Server accounts in this recipe.

## Getting ready

For this recipe, you will need to create another Windows/Domain account that you can use to change the service account to.

In this recipe, we will change the service account for SQLSERVERAGENT from QUERYWORKS\sqlservice to QUERYWORKS\sqlagent, which are available in the **Virtual Machine** (**VM**) created in *Appendix B, Creating a SQL Server VM* if you've created the same VM. If you are using a different environment, you must substitute these with accounts that already exist in your system.

## How to do it...

Let's explore the code required to change a SQL Server service account:

1. Open **PowerShell ISE** as an administrator.

2. Import the `SQLPS` module and create a new `Wmi.ManagedComputer` object as follows:

```
#import SQL Server module
Import-Module SQLPS -DisableNameChecking

#default SQL Server instance
$instanceName = "localhost"

$managedComputer = New-Object -TypeName
Microsoft.SqlServer.Management.Smo.Wmi.ManagedComputer
-ArgumentList $instanceName
```

Add the following script and run:

```
#get handle to service
#below is the SQL Server Agent service for the default
$servicename = "SqlAgent"
$sqlservice = $managedComputer.Services |
Where-Object Type -eq $servicename

#prompt for the new service account credential
$username = "QUERYWORKS\sqlagent"
$credential = Get-Credential -credential $username

#change service account
$sqlservice.SetServiceAccount($credential.UserName,
$credential.GetNetworkCredential().Password)
```

3. Confirm that the service account has changed:

```
#list services
$managedComputer.Services |
Where-Object Name -eq $servicename |
Select-Object Name, ServiceAccount,
DisplayName, ServiceState |
Format-Table -AutoSize
```

## How it works...

To change the service account, the first step is to get a handle to the service that you want to change. In this recipe, we get a handle to SQLSERVERAGENT, that is, we create a PowerShell variable that points to our SQL Server Agent service:

```
#get handle to service
$servicename = "SQLSERVERAGENT"
$sqlservice = $managedComputer.Services |
Where-Object Type -eq $servicename
```

In this recipe, we opted to prompt for the credential:

```
#prompt for the new service account credential
$username = "QUERYWORKS\sqlagent"
$credential = Get-Credential -credential $username
```

The Get-Credential cmdlet prompts for both the username and the password. Since we pass in the username, the username is already populated in the dialog box that appears:

The Get-Credential cmdlet stored the password as SecureString. A SecureString type is text that is encrypted using the Windows Data Protection API (http://msdn.microsoft.com/en-us/library/ms995355.aspx).

It's good news because now our password is stored securely (not in plain text). There's a caveat though. The SetServiceAccount method of the Smo.Wmi.ManagedComputer service class accepts a string password, not a SecureString password. This means that to set the new service account's password, we need to convert the password back into a readable string that the SetServiceAccount method can accept. This can be done by using $credential.GetNetworkCredential().password, which provides the text equivalent of the password:

```
$sqlservice.SetServiceAccount($credential.UserName,
$credential.GetNetworkCredential().Password)
```

Another alternative, albeit a much less secure one, is to pass the password in clear text (I think I hear you saying "Nooooo" in the background):

```
#make sure no one is looking
#over your shoulder
$username = "QUERYWORKS\sqlagent01"
$password = "P@ssword"
$sqlservice.SetServiceAccount($username, $password)
```

This snippet is provided to you for reference only. I highly discourage you from embedding your passwords in your script in clear text.

Another popular alternative to Get-Credential and embedding the credentials in your script is to make the username and password parameters in your script. For more information, visit https://technet.microsoft.com/en-us/library/hh847743.aspx.

## There's more...

It is definitely important to understand what service accounts are and how to manage them. Here are a few helpful resources related to service accounts:

- ▶ *Service Accounts Step-by-Step Guide* (http://msdn.microsoft.com/en-us/library/dd548356(WS.10).aspx)
- ▶ *Create Windows PowerShell Scripts that Accept Credentials* (http://msdn.microsoft.com/en-us/magazine/ff714574.aspx)

## See also

The *Listing SQL Server service accounts* recipe.

# Listing authentication mode

In this recipe, we will list the currently enabled authentication mode in your SQL Server instance, using PowerShell and SMO.

## Getting ready

Confirm which authentication mode your instance is running. Go to **SQL Server Management Studio** and log in to your instance. Once logged in, right-click on the instance and go to **Properties | Security**:

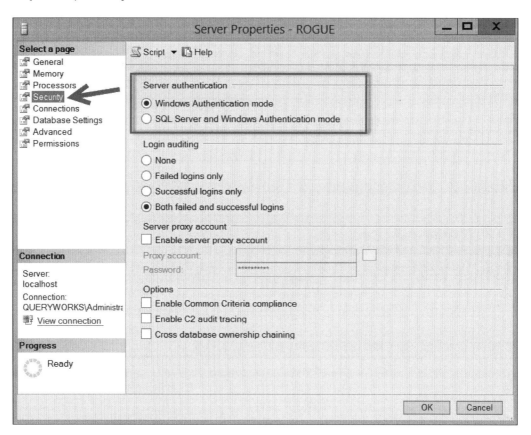

## How to do it...

Let's list the steps required to list your instance's current authentication mode:

1. Open **PowerShell ISE** as an administrator.

2. Import the `SQLPS` module and create a new SMO Server Object as follows:

```
#import SQL Server module
Import-Module SQLPS -DisableNameChecking

#replace this with your instance name
$instanceName = "localhost"
$server = New-Object -TypeName
Microsoft.SqlServer.Management.Smo.Server -ArgumentList
$instanceName
```

3. Add the following script and run:

```
#display login mode
$server.settings.LoginMode
```

## How it works...

This is a very short and straightforward recipe. To display the login mode, you need to have a handle to the instance first:

```
$instanceName = "localhost"
$server = New-Object -TypeName
Microsoft.SqlServer.Management.Smo.Server
-ArgumentList $instanceName
```

Once the server handle is established, you need to access the server object's `Settings.LoginMode` property:

```
#display login mode
$server.settings.LoginMode
```

This should display the current authentication mode of your instance.

## See also

▶ The *Changing authentication mode* recipe.

# Changing authentication mode

In this recipe, we will change SQL Server authentication mode.

## Getting ready

Confirm which authentication mode your instance is running. Go to **SQL Server Management Studio** and log in to your instance. Once logged in, right-click on the instance and go to **Properties | Security** (this is similar to what we did in the previous recipe):

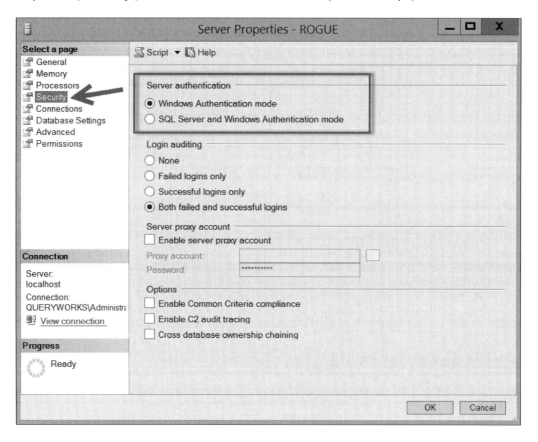

In this recipe, we will change the authentication mode from Integrated to Mixed. Feel free to do the reverse if your settings are different from what is presented in the preceding image.

## How to do it...

Let's explore the steps required to complete the task:

1. Open **PowerShell ISE** as an administrator.

2. Import the `SQLPS` module and create a new SMO Server Object as follows:

```
#import SQL Server module
Import-Module SQLPS -DisableNameChecking

#replace this with your instance name
$instanceName = "localhost"
$server = New-Object -TypeName
Microsoft.SqlServer.Management.Smo.Server
-ArgumentList $instanceName
```

Add the following script and run:

```
#according to MSDN, there are four (4) possible
#values for LoginMode:
#Normal, Integrated, Mixed and Unknown
$server.settings.LoginMode =
[Microsoft.SqlServer.Management.Smo.ServerLoginMode]::Mixed
$server.Alter()
$server.Refresh()

#display login mode
$server.settings.LoginMode
```

## How it works...

To change the authentication mode, you first need to get a handle to the server instance. Once you have the handle, you can assign a valid `LoginMode` enumeration value to the `LoginMode` property:

```
$server.settings.LoginMode =
[Microsoft.SqlServer.Management.Smo.ServerLoginMode]::Mixed
```

There are four possible values: `Normal`, `Integrated`, `Mixed`, and `Unknown`. Once the new authentication mode is assigned, you can invoke the `Alter` method of the SMO server object. Optionally, you can also call the `Refresh` method if you want to display the new value right away:

```
$server.Alter()
$server.Refresh()
```

>  Note that while the GUI may reflect the change in authentication mode, the actual change will not take effect until the SQL Server service is restarted.

## There's more...

Authentication mode in SQL Server identifies how login accounts can connect to an instance. There are two *well-known* modes: `Mixed` and `Integrated`.

However, if you check out the valid enumeration values for `LoginMode` on MSDN, there are four:

| LoginMode | Description |
|---|---|
| Normal | SQL authentication only |
| Integrated | Windows authentication only |
| Mixed | SQL and Windows authentication |
| Unknown | Unknown |

It is interesting to note that the two *lesser-known* modes, `Normal` and `Unknown`, are not accessible using **SQL Server Management Studio**. If you do try to set these values using PowerShell and SMO, it will disable **Authentication Mode** in **SQL Server Management Studio**:

```
$server.settings.LoginMode =
[Microsoft.SqlServer.Management.Smo.ServerLoginMode]::Normal
$server.Alter()
$server.Refresh()
```

In **SQL Server Management Studio**, after you set the `ServerLoginMode` to `Normal`, you will see that your **Server authentication** section is grayed out and disabled.

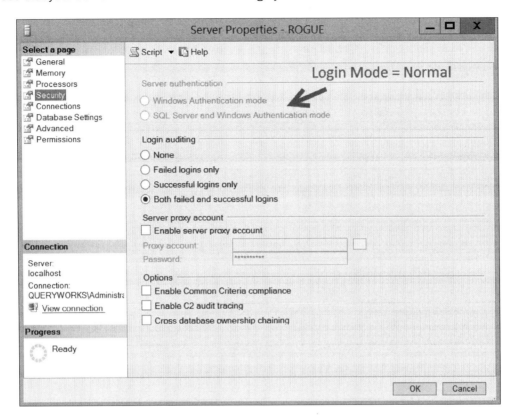

For our purposes, we only need to be concerned with `Mixed` and `Integrated`. `Normal` and `Unknown` are legacy values, and they should not be used in today's production environments.

Check out the MSDN article explaining the different `ServerLoginMode` enumeration values at `http://msdn.microsoft.com/en-us/library/microsoft.sqlserver.management.smo.serverloginmode.aspx`.

## More on legacy LoginMode values

Tibor Karaszi wrote a blog post called *Watch out for old stuff*, which explains the four `ServerLoginMode` values and where we might encounter them (`http://sqlblog.com/blogs/tibor_karaszi/archive/2010/09/15/watch-out-for-old-stuff.aspx`)

## See also

► The *Listing authentication mode* recipe.

# Listing SQL Server log errors

In this recipe, we will list SQL Server log errors past a specific date.

## Getting ready

Go to **SQL Server Management Studio** and log in to your instance. Once logged in, expand **SQL Server Agent | Error Logs | Current**.

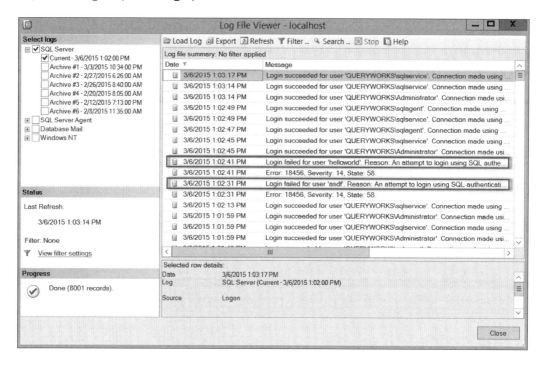

For our recipe, we will check the logs that have *failed* entries past March 1, 2015. Feel free to change these parameters when you do this recipe.

## How to do it...

Let's check how we can list SQL Server errors using PowerShell:

1. Open **PowerShell ISE** as an administrator.

2. Import the `SQLPS` module and create a new SMO Server Object as follows:

```
#import SQL Server module
Import-Module SQLPS -DisableNameChecking


#replace this with your instance name
$instanceName = "localhost"
$server = New-Object -TypeName
Microsoft.SqlServer.Management.Smo.Server -ArgumentList
$instanceName
```

Add the following script and run:

```
#According to MSDN:
#ReadErrorLog: returns A StringCollection system object
#value that contains an enumerated list of errors from
#the SQL Server error log.
[datetime]$date = "2015-03-01"


$server.ReadErrorLog() |
Where-Object Text -like "*failed*" |
Where-Object LogDate -ge $date |
Format-Table -AutoSize
```

Your result should look similar to the following screenshot:

```
LogDate              ProcessInfo Text
-------              ----------- ----
3/6/2015 1:02:31 PM Logon       Login failed for user 'asdf'. Reason: An attempt to login
3/6/2015 1:02:41 PM Logon       Login failed for user 'helloworld'. Reason: An attempt to
```

3. Confirm that these entries exist in **Error Logs** via **SQL Server Management Studio**.

4. Open **SQL Server Management Studio** and connect to your instance. Expand **SQL Server Agent | Error Logs**.

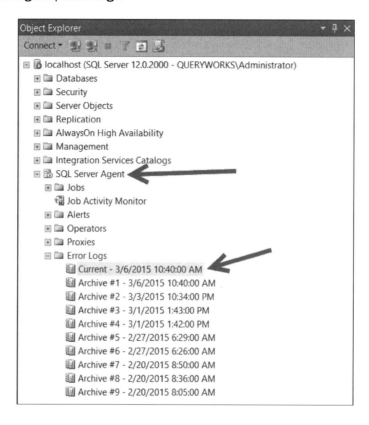

5. Double-click on **Current Error Log**. By default, this opens **SQL Server Agent** logs. Change the selected log to **SQL Server**.

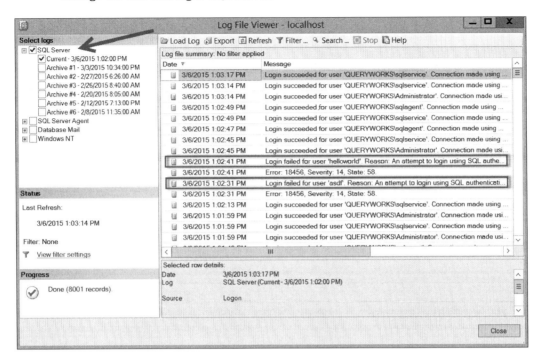

6. To filter, click on the **Filter** icon. Add the `failed` string in the **Message Contains text** field and check the **Apply filter** checkbox.

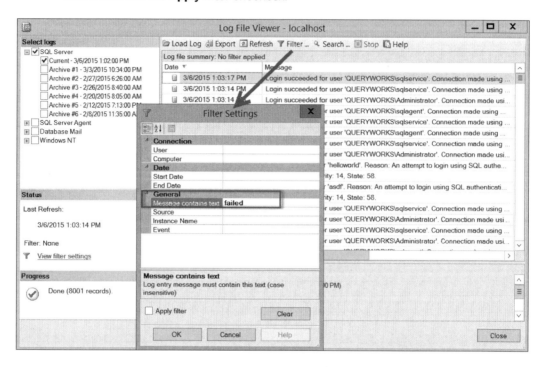

7. Click **OK** to see the filtered log events.

8. If you want to get generic errors from the event log, add the following script and run:

```
#if you want to get all the generic errors from the Event
Log, you can use this
Get-EventLog Application -Source "MSSQLSERVER"
-EntryType Error
```

You will get the following output:

```
Index Time          EntryType  Source        InstanceID  Message
----- ----          ---------  ------        ----------  -------
209410 Mar 01 11:56  Error      MSSQLSERVER   3221242525  c:\\Temp\\datafile1.ndf:
206745 Feb 28 08:23  Error      MSSQLSERVER   3221226385  Could not find database
206702 Feb 28 07:58  Error      MSSQLSERVER   3221226385  Could not find database
```

9. To check this, you can go to **Administrative Tools | Event Viewer | Application | Filter Current Log**. Check **Error**, **Critical**, and **Warning** under **Event level**, and choose **MSSQLSERVER** under **Event sources**. This is shown in the following screenshot:

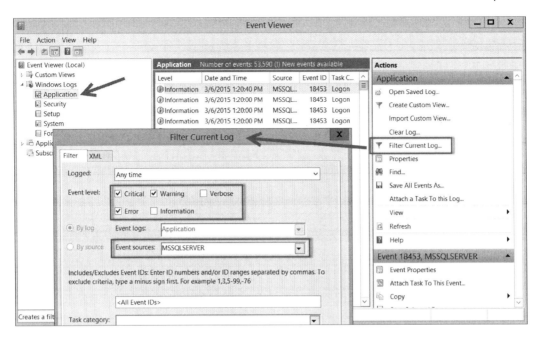

10. This should give you a list of errors pertaining only to the default instance
**MSSQLSERVER**.

## How it works...

SMO provides a way to easily retrieve and display SQL Server-related errors. This is through
the `ReadErrorLog` method of the SMO server object. The `ReadErrorLog` method retrieves
a list of errors in the SQL Server error log. In our recipe, we filtered only the log entries that
contained the word `failed`, and only those that occurred after March 1, 2015.

```
[datetime]$date = "2015-03-01"

$server.ReadErrorLog() |
Where-Object Text -like "*failed*" |
Where-Object LogDate -ge $date |
Format-Table -AutoSize
```

You can change this snippet to look for other keywords that you want to filter on, or to retrieve
entries before or after specific dates.

> You can read more about the `ReadErrorLog` method from MSDN at
> http://msdn.microsoft.com/en-us/library/ms210384.aspx.

Instead of using the `ReadErrorLog` method, an alternative is to use the `Get-EventLog` cmdlet and filter by source and keyword:

```
Get-EventLog Application -Source "MSSQLSERVER" -Message "*failed*"
```

The `Get-EventLog` cmdlet also supports a number of switches that allow you to further filter and sort results. If you want to display strictly `Error` entry types, you can use the following:

```
Get-EventLog Application -Source "MSSQLSERVER" -EntryType Error
```

## See also

▸ The *Listing failed login attempts* recipe.

# Listing failed login attempts

This recipe lists failed login attempts in your SQL Server instance.

## Getting ready

In order to get some entries in this recipe, you will need to simulate some failed login attempts in your SQL Server instance, if you don't already have any previous failed logins. One way to do this is to try logging in to SQL Server using **SQL Server Management Studio** and providing an incorrect username or password.

## How to do it...

To check the failed login attempts, follow these steps:

1. Open **PowerShell ISE** as an administrator.

2. Import the `SQLPS` module and create a new SMO Server Object as follows:

```
#import SQL Server module
Import-Module SQLPS -DisableNameChecking

#replace this with your instance name
$instanceName = "localhost"
$server = New-Object -TypeName
Microsoft.SqlServer.Management.Smo.Server -ArgumentList
$instanceName
```

3. Add the following script and run:

```
#According to MSDN:
#ReadErrorLog returns A StringCollection system object
#value that contains an enumerated list of errors
#from the SQL Server error log.

$server.ReadErrorLog() |
Where-Object ProcessInfo -Like "*Logon*" |
Where-Object Text -Like "*Login failed*" |
Format-Table -AutoSize
```

```
LogDate                  ProcessInfo Text
-------                  ----------- ----
3/6/2015 1:02:31 PM Logon     Login failed for user 'asdf'. Reason: An attempt to login
3/6/2015 1:02:41 PM Logon     Login failed for user 'helloworld'. Reason: An attempt to
```

## How it works...

One way to get failed login attempts is by using the `ReadErrorLog` method of the SMO Server Object and filtering by the `ProcessInfo` and `Text` properties. The `ProcessInfo` property we are targeting is `Logon`, and we want to display any login activities that have `failed`:

```
$server.ReadErrorLog() |
Where-Object ProcessInfo -like "*Logon*" |
Where-Object Text -like "*Login failed*" |
Format-List
```

## See also

▸ The *Listing SQL Server log errors* recipe.

# Enabling Common Criteria compliance

In this recipe, we are going to enable SQL Server's Common Criteria compliance feature.

## How to do it...

These are the steps to enable Common Criteria compliance using PowerShell:

1. Open **PowerShell ISE** as an administrator.

2. Import the `SQLPS` module as follows:

```
#import SQL Server module
Import-Module SQLPS -DisableNameChecking
```

3. Add the following script and run:

```
#replace this with your instance name
$instanceName = "localhost"
$server = New-Object -TypeName Microsoft.SqlServer.Management.Smo.
Server
-ArgumentList $instanceName

$server.Configuration.CommonCriteriaComplianceEnabled.ConfigValue
= $true
$server.Configuration.Alter()
```

You can confirm this from **SQL Server Management Studio**. Right-click on your instance, click on **Properties**, and select the **Security** page from the **Select a page** pane. In the **Options** section at the bottom, you should see the **Enable Common Criteria compliance** checkbox checked.

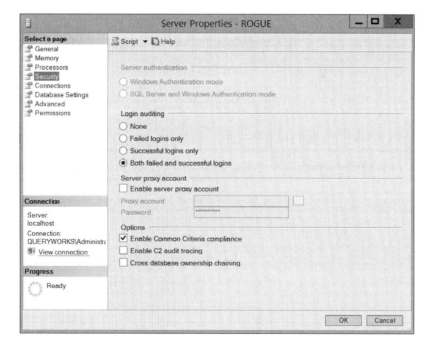

## How it works...

The Common Criteria is a set of security standards maintained by the **International Standards Organization** (**ISO**) that some organizations and companies, such as governments and financial institutions, may need to adhere to. This Common Criteria compliance feature was introduced in SQL Server 2005 SP1, but is only available in the Enterprise, Developer, and Evaluation editions. This feature replaces the deprecated C2 audit feature tracing.

To enable this feature in SQL Server using PowerShell, we simply have to toggle the value of the SMO server object's `Configuration.CommonCriteriaComplianceEnabled.ConfigValue` property to `true`. The `Alter` method needs to be invoked to ensure this new setting is saved to the server:

```
$server.Configuration.CommonCriteriaComplianceEnabled.
ConfigValue = $true
$server.Configuration.Alter()
```

## There's more...

When enabled, the Common Criteria enables the following, as documented in MSDN (`https://msdn.microsoft.com/en-us/library/bb326650.aspx`):

- ▶ Memory allocation is overwritten with a known pattern of bits before memory is reallocated to a new resource. This meets the **Residual Information Protection** criteria.

- ▶ Login auditing is enabled, which includes successful and unsuccessful login attempts and all attempts in between. This information can also be viewed from `sys.dm_exec_sessions`. This meets the **ability to view login statistics** criteria.

- ▶ Table-level `DENY` overrides column-level `GRANT`. This meets the **column GRANT should not override table DENY** criteria.

Common Criteria is further explained, including the framework, goals, and evaluation criteria, at `http://en.wikipedia.org/wiki/Common_Criteria`.

You can learn more about the versions of SQL Server that have been certified by Common Critera (CC, ISO15408) at this Microsoft page `http://www.microsoft.com/en-us/server-cloud/products/sql-server/resources.aspx`.

The Common Criteria feature in SQL Server is documented on this MSDN page at `https://msdn.microsoft.com/en-us/library/bb326650.aspx`.

▶ The *Listing SQL Server configuration settings* recipe of *Chapter 2, SQL Server and PowerShell Basic Tasks*

▶ The *Changing SQL Server Instance configurations* recipe of *Chapter 2, SQL Server and PowerShell Basic Tasks*

# Listing logins, users, and database mappings

This recipe lists logins and their corresponding usernames through database mappings.

## Getting ready

To check logins and their database mappings in **SQL Server Management Studio**, log in to SSMS. Go to the **Security** folder, expand **Logins**, and double-click on a particular login. This will show you the **Login Properties** window. Click on the **User Mapping** option on the left-hand pane, as shown in the following screenshot:

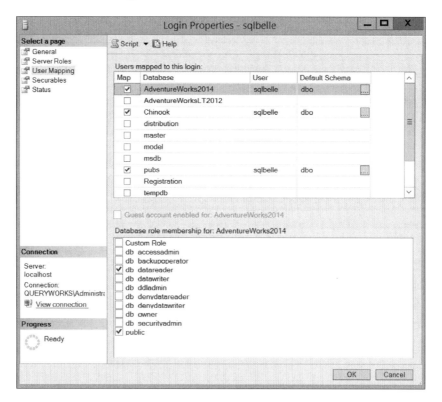

# How to do it...

To list logins, users, and database mappings, let's use the following steps:

1. Open **PowerShell ISE** as an administrator.

2. Import the `SQLPS` module and create a new SMO Server Object as follows:

```
#import SQL Server module
Import-Module SQLPS -DisableNameChecking

#replace this with your instance name
$instanceName = "localhost"
$server = New-Object -TypeName
Microsoft.SqlServer.Management.Smo.Server
-ArgumentList $instanceName
```

Add the following script and run:

```
#display login info
#these are two different ways of displaying login info
$server.Logins
$server.EnumWindowsUserInfo()

#List users, and database mappings
$server.Databases |
ForEach-Object {
    #capture database object
    $database = $_

    #capture users in this database
    $users = $database.Users

    #get only non-system objects
    $users |
    Where-Object IsSystemObject -eq $false |
    ForEach-Object {
        $result = [PSCustomObject] @{
            Login = $_.Login
            User = $_.Name
            DBName = $database.Name
            LoginType = $_.LoginType
            UserType = $_.UserType
        }
        #display current object
        $result
    }
} |
Format-Table -AutoSize
```

We should get a result similar to this:

```
Login                             User                              DBName                LoginType   UserType
-----                             ----                              ------                ---------   --------
QUERYWORKS\killua                 QUERYWORKS\killua                 AdventureWorks2014    WindowsUser SqlLogin
NT AUTHORITY\NETWORK SERVICE      NT AUTHORITY\NETWORK SERVICE      AdventureWorksLT2012  WindowsUser SqlLogin
QUERYWORKS\gon                    QUERYWORKS\gon                    AdventureWorksLT2012  WindowsUser SqlLogin
kurapika                          kurapika                          Chinook                           SqlLogin    SqlLogin
QUERYWORKS\gon                    QUERYWORKS\gon                    Chinook               WindowsUser SqlLogin
QUERYWORKS\killua                 QUERYWORKS\killua                 Chinook               WindowsUser SqlLogin
sqlbelle                          sqlbelle                          Chinook                           SqlLogin    SqlLogin
##MS_AgentSigningCertificate##    ##MS_AgentSigningCertificate##    master                Certificate Certificate
##MS_PolicyEventProcessingLogin## ##MS_PolicyEventProcessingLogin## master                            SqlLogin    SqlLogin
##MS_PolicyEventProcessingLogin## ##MS_PolicyEventProcessingLogin## msdb                              SqlLogin    SqlLogin
##MS_PolicyTsqlExecutionLogin##   ##MS_PolicyTsqlExecutionLogin##   msdb                              SqlLogin    SqlLogin
                                  MS_DataCollectorInternalUser      msdb                                          NoLogin
QUERYWORKS\killua                 QUERYWORKS\killua                 pubs                  WindowsUser SqlLogin
sqlbelle                          sqlbelle                          pubs                              SqlLogin    SqlLogin
                                  wolverine                         pubs                              SqlLogin    NoLogin
sqlservice                        sqlservice                        Registration                      SqlLogin    SqlLogin
```

## How it works...

To display just logins, you can use the server object and the `Logins` property:

```
$server.Logins
```

This gives you, by default, a list of logins, login types, and creation dates:

```
Name                             Login Type     Created
----                             ----------     -------
##MS_PolicyEventProcessingLogin## SqlLogin       2/20/2014 8:49 PM
##MS_PolicyTsqlExecutionLogin##   SqlLogin       2/20/2014 8:49 PM
distributor_admin                SqlLogin       10/25/2014 12:21 PM
eric                             SqlLogin       2/28/2015 1:12 AM
kurapika                         SqlLogin       10/23/2014 6:48 AM
NT AUTHORITY\SYSTEM              WindowsUser    8/21/2014 7:15 PM
NT SERVICE\MSSQLSERVER           WindowsUser    8/21/2014 7:15 PM
NT SERVICE\SQLSERVERAGENT        WindowsUser    8/21/2014 7:15 PM
NT SERVICE\SQLWriter             WindowsUser    8/21/2014 7:15 PM
NT SERVICE\Winmgmt               WindowsUser    8/21/2014 7:15 PM
QUERYWORKS\Administrator         WindowsUser    8/21/2014 7:15 PM
QUERYWORKS\gon                   WindowsUser    10/20/2014 12:04 PM
QUERYWORKS\killua                WindowsUser    10/20/2014 12:04 PM
QUERYWORKS\sqlagent              WindowsUser    3/6/2015 10:36 AM
QUERYWORKS\srogers               WindowsUser    2/13/2015 10:26 AM
QUERYWORKS\todinson              WindowsUser    2/13/2015 10:27 AM
QUERYWORKS\tstark                WindowsUser    2/13/2015 10:27 AM
```

An alternative way, if you are only interested in Windows accounts, is using the `EnumWindowsUserInfo` method of the SMO server class, which returns Windows users who have been explicitly given SQL Server access:

```
$server.EnumWindowsUserInfo()
```

This gives you a result similar to the following screenshot, which lists the account name, type, privilege, mapped login name, and permission path:

```
account name       : QUERYWORKS\Administrator
type               : user
privilege          : admin
mapped login name  : QUERYWORKS\Administrator
permission path    :

account name       : QUERYWORKS\sqlagent
type               : user
privilege          : admin
mapped login name  : QUERYWORKS\sqlagent
permission path    :

account name       : QUERYWORKS\srogers
type               : user
privilege          : admin
mapped login name  : QUERYWORKS\srogers
permission path    :
```

To display only database users, we can get a handle to a specific database and use the `Users` property of the database handle.

The most straightforward way of getting all the mappings is by looping through all the databases, and getting a handle to all users in that database. Once there is a handle to the database object's `Users`, you can display properties such as `Login`, `User`, `LoginType`, and `UserType`. Note that we can use `PSCustomObject` to temporarily save only the fields we want to capture. This also helps us structure the results, display them as we wish, or even export them later on if needed. The code is as follows:

```
#List users, and database mappings
$server.Databases |
ForEach-Object {
    #capture database object
    $database = $_

    #capture users in this database
    $users = $database.Users

    #get only non-system objects
    $users |
    Where-Object IsSystemObject -eq $false |
    ForEach-Object {
        $result = [PSCustomObject] @{
            Login = $_.Login
            User = $_.Name
```

```
        DBName = $database.Name
        LoginType = $_.LoginType
        UserType = $_.UserType
    }
    #display current object
    $result
  }
} |
Format-Table –AutoSize
```

## There's more...

Logins and users are two terms that are often used interchangeably, but shouldn't be. A login is a server principal that is used for authenticating who can connect and who will have access on the instance level.

SQL Server supports two types of logins: a Windows login and a SQL login. A Windows login is a Windows-level principal, meaning this is seen and shared with the Windows OS or domain. A SQL login is a SQL Server principal or a login known only to SQL Server.

A user, on the other hand, is a database principal. This means it is a database-level object, not a server-level object. A user is often mapped to a valid login using the login's security ID. There are cases when a user isn't mapped; this is when the user is orphaned. This can happen when the database has been moved or restored to a different SQL Server Instance that does not contain the original login. This can also happen when a login has been removed from the instance, and the related database users have not been cleaned up or reassigned.

## See also

The *Listing login/user roles and permissions* recipe.

# Listing login/user roles and permissions

This recipe shows how you can list login and user related database mappings, roles, and permissions for a specific database.

## How to do it...

Let's check the code needed to list logins, their database mappings, assigned roles, and permissions:

1.  Open **PowerShell ISE** as an administrator.

2. Import the `SQLPS` module and create a new SMO Server Object as follows:

```
#import SQL Server module
Import-Module SQLPS -DisableNameChecking

#replace this with your instance name
$instanceName = "localhost"
$server = New-Object -TypeName
Microsoft.SqlServer.Management.Smo.Server -ArgumentList
$instanceName
```

Add the following script and run:

```
#list all databases you want to query in an array
#alternatively you can read this from a file
$databases = @("AdventureWorks2014")

#we will temporarily store results in an array
#so it will easier to read and export
$results = @()

$databases |
ForEach-Object {
   #capture current database object
   $database = $server.Databases[$_]

   #capture users in this database
   $users = $database.Users

   #get all database users and list
   #their properties and permissions
   $users |
   Sort-Object -Property Name |
   Where-Object IsSystemObject -eq $false |
   ForEach-Object {
      $user = $_

      #list all object permissions of current user
      $database.EnumObjectPermissions($user.Name) |
      ForEach-Object {
         $perm = $_
         $item = [PSCustomObject] @{
            Login = $user.Login
            DBUser = $user.Name
            DBName = $database.Name
            DBRoles = ($user.EnumRoles())
```

```
                    Object = $perm.ObjectName
                    Permission = $perm.PermissionType
                }
                #display current object
                $results += $item
            }
        }
    }


    #display results
    $results |
    Format-Table -AutoSize
```

3.  You should see a result similar to what is shown in the following screenshot:

```
Login                DBUser              DBName          DBRoles       Object                    Permission
-----                ------              ------          -------       ------                    ----------
QUERYWORKS\tstark QUERYWORKS\tstark AdventureWorks2014 {db_datawriter} vEmployee                 SELECT
QUERYWORKS\tstark QUERYWORKS\tstark AdventureWorks2014 {db_datawriter} vEmployeeDepartment       SELECT
QUERYWORKS\tstark QUERYWORKS\tstark AdventureWorks2014 {db_datawriter} vEmployeeDepartmentHistory VIEW DEFINITION
QUERYWORKS\tstark QUERYWORKS\tstark AdventureWorks2014 {db_datawriter} vJobCandidate             VIEW DEFINITION
sqlbelle             sqlbelle            AdventureWorks2014 {db_datareader} uspGetBillOfMaterials  EXECUTE
sqlbelle             sqlbelle            AdventureWorks2014 {db_datareader} uspGetEmployeeManagers VIEW DEFINITION
```

## How it works...

A database mapping determines which logins are related to which database users. A database user is a database-level principal that is mapped to a server login via a security ID.

To display the database mappings, we will need to loop through a database (or databases) and display the mappings using each individual `User` object. In this recipe, we've listed our database in an array, which you can add databases to:

```
$databases = @("AdventureWorks2014")
```

Instead of storing in an array, you can also read the list of databases from a file:

```
$databases = Get-Content "path\to\database\file.txt"
```

For each database, we can list all the database users and we ignore all system objects (such as `sys`, `guest`, or `information_schema`):

```
$users |
Sort-Object -Property Name |
Where-Object IsSystemObject -eq $false |
```

For each user, we also display properties such as the database they belong to, the database user name, the corresponding server login, and the role memberships in the current database using the `EnumRoles` method of the `User` class. We also iterate through all the database-specific object-level permissions for the current user by using the `EnumObjectPermissions` method of the database class. The code is as follows:

```
ForEach-Object {
    $user = $_

    #list all object permissions of current user
    $database.EnumObjectPermissions($user.Name) |
    ForEach-Object {
        $perm = $_
        $item = [PSCustomObject] @{
            Login = $user.Login
            DBUser = $user.Name
            DBName = $database.Name
            DBRoles = ($user.EnumRoles())
            Object = $perm.ObjectName
            Permission = $perm.PermissionType
        }
        #display current object
        $results += $item
    }
}
```

Iterating through `EnumObjectPermissions` allows us to capture all permissions granted to an object, for example, a `SELECT` that's granted to a table and more.

Depending on how many database roles and permissions the users have, displaying the results in a tabular format might get truncated. Another option is to just display the result using `Format-List` instead of `Format-Table`.

```
Login       : QUERYWORKS\tstark
DBUser      : QUERYWORKS\tstark
DBName      : AdventureWorks2014
DBRoles     : {db_datawriter}
Object      : vJobCandidate
Permission  : VIEW DEFINITION

Login       : sqlbelle
DBUser      : sqlbelle
DBName      : AdventureWorks2014
DBRoles     : {db_datareader}
Object      : uspGetBillOfMaterials
Permission  : EXECUTE

Login       : sqlbelle
DBUser      : sqlbelle
DBName      : AdventureWorks2014
DBRoles     : {db_datareader}
Object      : uspGetEmployeeManagers
Permission  : VIEW DEFINITION
```

Yet another option is just to export the $results array to a file, using cmdlets such as Export-Csv, among others.

## See also

▶ The *Listing logins, users, and database mappings* recipe.

# Creating a user-defined server role

This recipe walks you through how to create a user-defined server role in SQL Server.

## Getting ready

In this recipe, we will create a user-defined server role called impersonator and add QUERYWORKS\tstark as a member. We are also going to assign this new role permissions to impersonate any login and grant permissions to any unsafe assembly.

The T-SQL equivalent of what we are going to accomplish in this recipe is as follows:

```
-- create custom server role
CREATE SERVER ROLE [impersonator]
AUTHORIZATION [QUERYWORKS\Administrator]
GO

-- add member
ALTER SERVER ROLE [impersonator]
ADD MEMBER [QUERYWORKS\tstark]
GO

-- add permissions for custom role
GRANT IMPERSONATE ANY LOGIN TO [impersonator]
GO
GRANT UNSAFE ASSEMBLY TO [impersonator]
GO
```

If you are not using the QueryWorks VM that was created in *Appendix B, Creating a SQL Server VM*, you must change the names, members, and permissions in this recipe based on what's available in your development environment.

## How to do it...

These are the steps to create a new user-defined server role in SQL Server using PowerShell:

1. Open **PowerShell ISE** as an administrator.

2. Import the `SQLPS` module as follows:

```
#import SQL Server module
Import-Module SQLPS -DisableNameChecking
```

3. Add the following script and run:

```
#replace this with your instance name
$instanceName = "localhost"
$server = New-Object -TypeName
Microsoft.SqlServer.Management.Smo.Server -ArgumentList
$instanceName
$serverRoleName = "impersonator"

#for our exercise, we will drop the role
#if it already exists
if ($server.Roles[$serverRoleName])
{
    "Dropping"
    $server.Roles[$serverRoleName].Drop()
}

#create new server role
$serverRole = New-Object -TypeName
Microsoft.SqlServer.Management.Smo.ServerRole -ArgumentList
$server, $serverRoleName
$serverRole.Owner = "QUERYWORKS\Administrator"
$serverRole.Create()

#add member to this server role
$serverRole.AddMember("QUERYWORKS\tstark")

#assign permissions to this server role
$permissionset = New-Object
Microsoft.SqlServer.Management.Smo.ServerPermissionSet(
[Microsoft.SqlServer.Management.Smo.ServerPermission]::
ImpersonateAnyLogin)
$permissionset.Add(
[Microsoft.SqlServer.Management.Smo.ServerPermission]::
UnsafeAssembly)
```

```
$server.Grant($permissionset, $serverRoleName)
$server.Alter()
$server.Refresh()

#list all custom server roles
$server.Roles |
Where-Object IsFixedRole -eq $false
```

In the following screenshot, you can see the user-defined server roles in the environment:

```
Name               Fixed Role  Created              Owner                    Modified
----               ----------  -------              -----                    --------
impersonator       False       3/7/2015 11:17 PM    QUERYWORKS\Administrator 3/7/2015 11:17 PM
public             False       4/13/2009 12:59 PM   sa                       4/13/2009 12:59 PM
```

## How it works...

The ability to create user-defined server roles was introduced in SQL Server 2012. This was a welcome change because, for some instances, the built-in server roles were just not sufficient. You may want to grant specific groups more or less permissions than what the built-in roles had. Before user-defined roles, a database administrator would have had to assign these specific permissions to each login, which can be tedious. This also makes permission management at that level harder to manage and maintain.

To create user-defined server roles in **SQL Server Management Studio**, you can simply go to the **Security** node and right-click on **Server Roles** to see the **New Server Role** option:

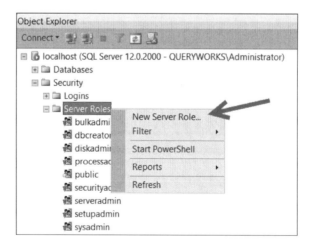

In PowerShell via SMO, this is equivalent to creating an SMO `ServerRole` object by providing an SMO Server Object and the server role name, and invoking the `Create` method:

```
#create new role
$serverRole = New-Object -TypeName
Microsoft.SqlServer.Management.Smo.ServerRole
-ArgumentList $server, $serverRoleName
$serverRole.Owner = "QUERYWORKS\Administrator"
$serverRole.Create()
```

In addition to just creating the server, we can also add members to this role programmatically. The server role object has access to an `AddMember` method that can be passed with the login you wish to include in this:

```
#add member to this server role
$serverRole.AddMember("QUERYWORKS\tstark")
```

To add permissions, an SMO `ServerPermissionSet` object first needs to be created. This accepts a server-level permission to start:

```
#assign permissions to this server role
$permissionset = New-Object
Microsoft.SqlServer.Management.Smo.ServerPermissionSet(
[Microsoft.SqlServer.Management.Smo.ServerPermission]::
ImpersonateAnyLogin)
```

The server-level permission is an enumeration. In PowerShell ISE, you can explore the available values. You can simply type `[Microsoft.SqlServer.Management.Smo.ServerPermission]::` and see a dropdown of the possible values:

To add additional permissions, use the `Add` method from the `PermissionSet` object:

```
$permissionset.Add([Microsoft.SqlServer.Management.Smo.
ServerPermission]::UnsafeAssembly)
```

To grant the permissions, use the `Grant` method of the SMO server object. To persist this on the server, invoke the `Alter` method:

```
$server.Grant($permissionset, $serverRoleName)
$server.Alter()
```

## There's more...

Read more about the `ServerPermissionSet` class from the MSDN at `http://msdn.microsoft.com/en-us/library/microsoft.sqlserver.management.smo.serverpermissionset.aspx`.

Check out all the `ServerPermission` properties at `http://msdn.microsoft.com/en-us/library/microsoft.sqlserver.management.smo.serverpermission.aspx`.

## See also

▸  The *Assigning permissions to a database user* recipe.

# Creating a login

This recipe shows how you can create a SQL login using PowerShell and SMO.

## Getting ready

For this recipe, we will create a SQL login called `eric`. Here's the T-SQL equivalent of what we are trying to accomplish:

```
CREATE LOGIN [eric]
WITH PASSWORD=N'YourSuperStrongPassword',
CHECK_EXPIRATION=OFF
GO
```

## How to do it...

These are the steps to create a login:

1. Open **PowerShell ISE** as an administrator.

2. Import the `SQLPS` module and create a new SMO Server Object as follows:

```
#import SQL Server module
Import-Module SQLPS -DisableNameChecking
```

```
#replace this with your instance name
$instanceName = "localhost"
$server = New-Object -TypeName
Microsoft.SqlServer.Management.Smo.Server -ArgumentList
$instanceName
```

3. Add the following script and run:

```
$loginName = "eric"

#for our recipe
#drop login if it exists
if ($server.Logins.Contains($loginName))
{
    $server.Logins[$loginName].Drop()
}

$login = New-Object -TypeName
Microsoft.SqlServer.Management.Smo.Login -ArgumentList
$server, $loginName

#specify SQL Login
$login.LoginType =
[Microsoft.SqlServer.Management.Smo.LoginType]::SqlLogin
$login.PasswordExpirationEnabled = $false

# prompt for password
$pw = Read-Host "Enter login password" -AsSecureString
$login.Create($pw)
```

## How it works...

The first thing we need to do, after getting an SMO Server Object handle, is create an SMO
Login object:

```
$login = New-Object -TypeName
Microsoft.SqlServer.Management.Smo.Login -ArgumentList $server,
$loginName
```

The next step is to identify what type of login this is. The possible LoginType values are
AsymmetricKey, Certificate, SQLLogin, WindowsGroup, and WindowsUser. In our
recipe, we are using SQLLogin:

```
$login.LoginType =
[Microsoft.SqlServer.Management.Smo.LoginType]::SqlLogin
```

The login object also has a few settable properties such as `PasswordPolicyEnforced` and `PasswordExpirationEnabled`:

```
$login.PasswordExpirationEnabled = $false
```

When ready, you can invoke the `Create` method of the `Login` class. Note that the `Create` method has a few overloads, some of which allow you to pass `LoginCreateOptions`. In our recipe, we are only passing in a password which we collect using a `Read-Host` cmdlet. We prompt the user for the password, instead of us hardcoding it with our script:

```
$pw = Read-Host "Enter login password" -AsSecureString
$login.Create($pw)
```

## See also

▸ The *Assigning permissions and roles to a login* recipe.

▸ The *Creating a database user* recipe.

# Assigning permissions and roles to a login

This recipe shows you how to assign permissions and roles to a login by using PowerShell and SMO.

## Getting ready

If you haven't already done so in the *Creating a login* recipe, create a SQL login name `eric`. Alternatively, choose another login in your system that you want to use for this recipe. We will be assigning the `dbcreator` and `setupadmin` server roles to this login, as well as granting `ALTER` permissions to any setting or database. Here's the T-SQL equivalent of what we are trying to accomplish:

```
ALTER SERVER ROLE [dbcreator]
ADD MEMBER [eric]
GO
ALTER SERVER ROLE [setupadmin]
ADD MEMBER [eric]
GO
GRANT
    ALTER ANY DATABASE,
    ALTER SETTINGS
TO [eric]
```

## How to do it...

Let's list the steps required to complete the task:

1. Open **PowerShell ISE** as an administrator.

2. Import the `SQLPS` module and create a new SMO Server Object as follows:

```
#import SQL Server module
Import-Module SQLPS -DisableNameChecking

#replace this with your instance name
$instanceName = "localhost"
$server = New-Object -TypeName
Microsoft.SqlServer.Management.Smo.Server -ArgumentList
$instanceName
```

3. Add the following script and run:

```
#assumption is this login already exists
$loginName = "eric"

#assign server level roles
$login = $server.Logins[$loginName]
$login.AddToRole("dbcreator")
$login.AddToRole("setupadmin")
$login.Alter()

#grant server level permissions
$permissionset = New-Object
Microsoft.SqlServer.Management.Smo.ServerPermissionSet(
[Microsoft.SqlServer.Management.Smo.ServerPermission]::
AlterAnyDatabase)
$permissionset.Add(
[Microsoft.SqlServer.Management.Smo.ServerPermission]::
AlterSettings)
$server.Grant($permissionset, $loginName)

#confirm server roles
Write-Output "Memberships:"
$login.ListMembers()

#confirm permissions
$server.EnumServerPermissions($loginName) |
Select-Object Grantee, PermissionType, PermissionState |
Format-Table -AutoSize
```

4. You should get a result similar to this screenshot:

```
Memberships:
setupadmin
dbcreator

Grantee PermissionType         PermissionState
------- --------------         ---------------
eric    ALTER ANY DATABASE               Grant
eric    ALTER SETTINGS                   Grant
eric    CONNECT SQL                      Grant
```

## How it works...

After we create an SMO `server` object, we create a handle to the SMO `login` we want to query:

```
$loginName = "eric"

#assign server level roles
$login = $server.Logins[$loginName]
```

The `login` object has an `AddToRole` method that we can use to add the login as a member to fixed server roles:

```
$login.AddToRole("dbcreator")
$login.AddToRole("setupadmin")
```

When we're ready to send this command to SQL Server, we issue the `Alter` method of the login object:

```
$login.Alter()
```

Now, we also have the option to assign specific permissions outside the role for the login. This requires creating a `ServerPermissionSet` object. The following command creates the permission set and adds the `AlterAnyDatabase` permission to the list of permissions that we will be assigning:

```
$permissionset = New-Object
Microsoft.SqlServer.Management.Smo.ServerPermissionSet(
[Microsoft.SqlServer.Management.Smo.ServerPermission]::
AlterAnyDatabase)
```

This permission set can accommodate multiple server-level permissions. In our recipe, we add another permission, `AlterSettings`, by issuing this command:

```
$permissionset.Add([Microsoft.SqlServer.Management.Smo.ServerPermissio
n]::AlterSettings)
```

To finalize the process, we issue the `Grant` statement on the object, with the parameters being the permission set that we have created and the login:

```
$server.Grant($permissionset, $loginName)
```

## There's more...

Read more about the `ServerPermissionSet` class at the MSDN at `http://msdn.microsoft.com/en-us/library/microsoft.sqlserver.management.smo.serverpermissionset.aspx`.

Check out all the `ServerPermission` properties from `http://msdn.microsoft.com/en-us/library/microsoft.sqlserver.management.smo.serverpermission.aspx`.

## See also

▶ The *Creating a login* recipe.
▶ The *Creating a database user* recipe.

# Creating a database user

This recipe shows how to create a database user by using PowerShell and SMO.

## Getting ready

If you haven't already done so in the *Creating a login* recipe, create a SQL login called `eric`. Alternatively, feel free to substitute this with a login that already exists in your system.

In our recipe, we will use a login called `eric`, which we will map to a user called `eric` in the `AdventureWorks2014` database. Here's the T-SQL equivalent of what we are trying to accomplish:

```
USE [AdventureWorks2014]
GO

CREATE USER [eric]
FOR LOGIN [eric]
```

## How to do it...

Here are the steps to create a database user:

1. Open **PowerShell ISE** as an administrator.

2. Import the SQLPS module and create a new SMO Server Object as follows:

```
#import SQL Server module
Import-Module SQLPS -DisableNameChecking

#replace this with your instance name
$instanceName = "localhost"
$server = New-Object -TypeName
Microsoft.SqlServer.Management.Smo.Server -ArgumentList
$instanceName
```

3. Add the following script and run:

```
$loginName = "eric"

#get login
$login = $server.Logins[$loginName]

#add a database mapping
$databasename = "AdventureWorks2014"
$database = $server.Databases[$databasename]

$dbUserName = "eric"

if($database.Users[$dbUserName])
{
    $database.Users[$dbUserName].Drop()
}


#code to create database user is all in one line
$dbuser = New-Object -TypeName
Microsoft.SqlServer.Management.Smo.User -ArgumentList
$database, $dbUserName

$dbuser.Login = $loginName
$dbuser.Create()
```

## How it works...

After creating the SMO server object, create a handle to the login you wish to use:

```
$loginName = "eric"

#get login
$login = $server.Logins[$loginName]
```

Next, you need to get a handle to the database that you want this login to have a corresponding user to. In our case, we will be using `AdventureWorks2014`:

```
$databasename = "AdventureWorks2014"
$database = $server.Databases[$databasename]
```

To create a database user, we need to instantiate a `Microsoft.SqlServer.Management.Smo.User` object, and pass the database and database user name as arguments:

```
$dbUserName = "eric"

#code to create database user is all in one line
$dbuser = New-Object -TypeName
Microsoft.SqlServer.Management.Smo.User -ArgumentList $database,
$dbUserName

$dbuser.Login = $loginName
```

The final step is to issue the `Create` method on the `$dbuser` object:

```
$dbuser.Create()
```

## See also

- ▶ The *Creating a login* recipe.
- ▶ The *Assigning permissions to a database user* recipe.

# Assigning permissions to a database user

This recipe shows how to assign permissions to a database user via SMO and PowerShell.

## Getting ready

In this recipe, we will use the `AdventureWorks2014` database user `eric` we created in previous recipes. We will grant this user the `ALTER` and `CREATE TABLE` permissions. Here's the T-SQL equivalent of what we are trying to accomplish:

```
USE [AdventureWorks2014]
GO
GRANT
  ALTER,
  CREATE TABLE
TO [eric]
```

You can substitute this database user with any database user that you already have in your database.

## How to do it...

To assign permissions and roles to a database user, let's follow these steps:

1. Open **PowerShell ISE** as an administrator.

2. Import the `SQLPS` module and create a new SMO Server Object as follows:
   ```
   #import SQL Server module
   Import-Module SQLPS -DisableNameChecking

   #replace this with your instance name
   $instanceName = "localhost"
   $server = New-Object -TypeName
   Microsoft.SqlServer.Management.Smo.Server -ArgumentList
   $instanceName
   ```

3. Add the following script and run:
   ```
   $databasename = "AdventureWorks2014"
   $database = $server.Databases[$databasename]

   #get a handle to the database user we want
   #to assign permissions to
   $dbusername = "eric"
   $dbuser = $database.Users[$dbusername]
   ```

```
#assign ALTER DATABASE permission
$permissionset = New-Object
Microsoft.SqlServer.Management.Smo.DatabasePermissionSet(
[Microsoft.SqlServer.Management.Smo.DatabasePermission]::
Alter)

#assign CREATE TABLE permission
$permissionset.Add(
[Microsoft.SqlServer.Management.Smo.DatabasePermission]::
CreateTable) | Out-Null

#grant the permissions
$database.Grant($permissionset, $dbuser.Name)

#confirm permissions
$database.EnumDatabasePermissions($dbuser.Name) |
Select-Object PermissionState, PermissionType, Grantee
```

4. When the script successfully finishes executing, you should see a screen similar to this:

```
PermissionState PermissionType                                Grantee
--------------- --------------                                -------
          Grant ALTER                                         eric
          Grant CONNECT                                       eric
          Grant CREATE TABLE                                  eric
```

## How it works...

To add specific permissions to a database user, you must first get a handle to the database user:

```
$dbusername = "eric"
$dbuser = $database.Users[$dbusername]
```

The next step is to define DatabasePermissionSet. This object will contain all the permissions you want to assign to your database user:

```
#assign ALTER DATABASE permission
$permissionset = New-Object
Microsoft.SqlServer.Management.Smo.DatabasePermissionSet(
[Microsoft.SqlServer.Management.Smo.DatabasePermission]::Alter)

#assign CREATE TABLE permission
$permissionset.Add([Microsoft.SqlServer.Management.Smo.
DatabasePermission]::CreateTable) | Out-Null
```

Once you've added all the permissions, invoke the `Grant` method of the database object:

```
#grant the permissions
$database.Grant($permissionset, $dbuser.Name)
```

To list all the permissions for the current database user, we can use the database's `EnumDatabasePermissions` method. This should list whether a GRANT, DENY, or REVOKE permission has been assigned to a particular permission and principal:

```
#confirm permissions
$database.EnumDatabasePermissions($dbuser.Name) |
Select-Object PermissionState, PermissionType, Grantee
```

## There's more...

Read more about the `DatabasePermissionSet` class from the MSDN at `http://msdn.microsoft.com/en-us/library/microsoft.sqlserver.management.smo.databasepermissionset.aspx`.

## See also

  ▸   The *Creating a database user* recipe.

# Creating a database role

In this recipe, we will walk through creating a custom database role.

## Getting ready

In this recipe, we will create a database role called `Custom Role`. Then, we will grant it SELECT permissions to the `HumanResources` schema, and ALTER and CREATE TABLE permissions to the database.

Here's the T-SQL equivalent of what we are trying to accomplish:

```
USE AdventureWorks2014
GO

CREATE ROLE [Custom Role]
GO
```

```
GRANT SELECT
ON SCHEMA::[HumanResources]
TO [Custom Role]

GRANT ALTER, CREATE TABLE
TO [Custom Role]
```

## How to do it...

Let's explore the steps for creating a custom database role:

1. Open **PowerShell ISE** as an administrator.

2. Import the SQLPS module and create a new SMO Server Object:

   ```
   #import SQL Server module
   Import-Module SQLPS -DisableNameChecking

   #replace this with your instance name
   $instanceName = "localhost"
   $server = New-Object -TypeName
   Microsoft.SqlServer.Management.Smo.Server -ArgumentList
   $instanceName
   ```

   Add the following script and run:

   ```
   $databasename = "AdventureWorks2014"
   $database = $server.Databases[$databasename]

   #role
   $rolename = "Custom Role"
   if($database.Roles[$rolename])
   {
       $database.Roles[$rolename].Drop()
   }

   #let's assume this custom role, we want to grant
   #everyone in this role select, insert access
   #to the HumanResources Schema, in addition to the
   #CreateTable permission

   $dbrole = New-Object
   Microsoft.SqlServer.Management.Smo.DatabaseRole
   -ArgumentList $database, $rolename
   $dbrole.Create()
   ```

```
#verify; list database roles
$database.Roles

#create a permission set to contain SELECT permissions
#for the HumanResources schema
$permissionset1 = New-Object Microsoft.SqlServer.Management.Smo.
ObjectPermissionSet(
[Microsoft.SqlServer.Management.Smo.ObjectPermission]::
Select)
$permissionset1.Add([Microsoft.SqlServer.Management.
Smo.ObjectPermission]::Select)
$hrschema = $database.Schemas["HumanResources"]
$hrschema.Grant($permissionset1, $dbrole.Name)

#create another permission set that contains
#CREATE TABLE and ALTER on this database
$permissionset2 = New-Object
Microsoft.SqlServer.Management.Smo.DatabasePermissionSet(
[Microsoft.SqlServer.Management.Smo.DatabasePermission]::
CreateTable)
$permissionset2.Add([Microsoft.SqlServer.Management.
Smo.DatabasePermission]::Alter)
$database.Grant($permissionset2, $dbrole.Name)

#to add member
#assume eric is already a user in the database
$username = "eric"
$dbrole.AddMember($username)

#confirm members of new role
$database.Roles[$rolename].EnumMembers()

#confirm permissions of new role
$database.EnumDatabasePermissions($dbrole.Name) |
Select-Object PermissionState, PermissionType, Grantee |
Format-Table -AutoSize
```

3. The enumerated permissions of the new role should look similar to the following screenshot:

```
PermissionState PermissionType ObjectName          Grantee
--------------- -------------- ----------          -------
          Grant ALTER          AdventureWorks2014 Custom Role
          Grant CREATE TABLE   AdventureWorks2014 Custom Role
```

# How it works...

A database role allows for easier management of users and permissions on the database level. To create a database role, you need to create an instance of an SMO `DatabaseRole` first:

```
$dbrole = New-Object
Microsoft.SqlServer.Management.Smo.DatabaseRole
-ArgumentList $database, "Custom Role"
$dbrole.Create()
```

The next step is to identify what permissions this group needs to have. You will need to create a different permission set for each type of securable you want to assign permissions to.

In our recipe, we created two permission sets. The first one is at the schema level, allowing the database user to use the `SELECT` statement against all objects belonging to the `HumanResources` schema:

```
#create a permission set to contain SELECT permissions
#for the HumanResources schema
$permissionset1 = New-Object
Microsoft.SqlServer.Management.Smo.ObjectPermissionSet(
[Microsoft.SqlServer.Management.Smo.ObjectPermission]::Select)
$permissionset1.Add(
[Microsoft.SqlServer.Management.Smo.ObjectPermission]::Select)
$hrschema = $database.Schemas["HumanResources"]
$hrschema.Grant($permissionset1, $dbrole.Name)
```

Our second permission set pertains to the database securable, allowing `CREATE` and `ALTER` permissions to the `AdventureWorks2014` database:

```
#create another permission set that contains
#CREATE TABLE and ALTER on this database
$permissionset2 = New-Object
Microsoft.SqlServer.Management.Smo.DatabasePermissionSet(
[Microsoft.SqlServer.Management.Smo.DatabasePermission]::
CreateTable)
$permissionset2.Add(
[Microsoft.SqlServer.Management.Smo.DatabasePermission]::Alter)
$database.Grant($permissionset2, $dbrole.Name)
```

The last step in our recipe is to add users to this role. This step does not need to follow granting permissions. This can happen as soon as the role is set up:

```
#to add member
#assume eric is already a user in the database
$username = "eric"
$dbrole.AddMember($username)
```

To confirm that we have successfully added this new member, we can use the `EnumMembers` method of the SMO role object:

```
#confirm members of new role
$database.Roles[$rolename].EnumMembers()
```

To confirm the permissions of the role, we can use the `EnumDatabasePermissions` of the SMO `database` class to display the `PermissionState`, `PermissionType`, `ObjectName`, and `Grantee` properties:

```
#confirm permissions of new role
$database.EnumDatabasePermissions($dbrole.Name) |
Select-Object PermissionState, PermissionType, Grantee |
Format-Table -AutoSize
```

## See also

▸ The *Creating a database user* recipe.

# Fixing orphaned users

This recipe shows how you can remap orphaned database users to valid logins.

## Getting ready

Let's create an *orphaned* user for us to use in this recipe. Open **SQL Server Management Studio** and execute the following T-SQL statements:

```
USE [master]
GO
CREATE LOGIN [baymax]
WITH PASSWORD=N'P@ssword',
DEFAULT_DATABASE=[master],
CHECK_EXPIRATION=OFF,
CHECK_POLICY=OFF
GO
USE [AdventureWorks2014]
GO
CREATE USER [baymax]
FOR LOGIN [baymax]
GO
USE [master]
GO
```

```
DROP LOGIN [baymax]
GO


-- create another SQL login
-- note this will generate a
-- different security ID (SID)
CREATE LOGIN [baymax]
WITH PASSWORD=N'P@ssword',
DEFAULT_DATABASE=[master],
CHECK_EXPIRATION=OFF,
CHECK_POLICY=OFF
```

This code has created an orphaned user called `baymax` in the `AdventureWorks2014`
database. Although we have recreated a login with the same name, this would generate a
different security ID and leave the database user orphaned.

## How to do it...

Let's list the steps to fix orphaned users:

1.  Open **PowerShell ISE** as an administrator.

2.  Import the `SQLPS` module and create a new SMO Server Object:
    ```
    #import SQL Server module
    Import-Module SQLPS -DisableNameChecking


    #replace this with your instance name
    $instanceName = "localhost"
    $server = New-Object -TypeName
    Microsoft.SqlServer.Management.Smo.Server -ArgumentList
    $instanceName
    ```

3.  Add the following script and run:
    ```
    $databasename = "AdventureWorks2014"
    $database = $server.Databases[$databasename]
    $loginname = "baymax"
    $username = "baymax"
    $user = $database.Users[$username]


    #display current status
    $user |
    Select-Object Parent, Name, Login, LoginType, UserType
    ```

4. When the script successfully finishes executing, you should see a screen similar to the following one. We can confirm that baymax is an orphaned user because the Login value in the result is blank, and the UserType is NoLogin.

```
Parent    : [AdventureWorks2014]
Name      : baymax
Login     :
LoginType : SqlLogin
UserType  : NoLogin
```

5. Let's fix the orphaned user by remapping it to the new valid login. Note that we are going to use a combination of T-SQL and the Invoke-Sqlcmd cmdlet to accomplish the remapping because of some issues with SMO, which is discussed in the *There's More...* section. The code is as follows:

```
$query = "ALTER USER $($username) WITH LOGIN=$($loginname)"
Invoke-Sqlcmd -ServerInstance $instanceName
-Query $query -Database $databasename

#display current status
$user.Refresh()
$user |
Select-Object Parent, Name, Login, LoginType, UserType
```

```
Parent    : [AdventureWorks2014]
Name      : baymax
Login     : baymax
LoginType : SqlLogin
UserType  : SqlLogin
```

## How it works...

An orphaned user is a database user that is not mapped anymore to a valid login in the SQL Server instance. This may stem from a number of scenarios, but more often, Windows logins get orphaned when you move a database from one server to another server that belongs to a different domain, for example, from a production to development environment. This also typically happens to SQL logins when you move databases around, even if the source and destination instances belong in the same domain.

To fix an orphaned user, you need to remap this orphaned user to a valid recognized login in your instance. The core of the solution lies in these statements:

```
$query = "ALTER USER $($username) WITH LOGIN=$($loginname)"
Invoke-Sqlcmd -ServerInstance $instanceName -Query $query
-Database $databasename
```

For the most part, we acquired handles to the database `User` objects merely to display the status of the user. While it's still orphaned, the `UserType` will indicate `NoLogin`.

## There's more...

Following the patterns of the previous recipes, you may have thought that we should be able to use SMO to fix our orphaned user. This snippet of code **should** allow us to remap the user:

```
#unfortunately this doesn't work
$user.Login = "baymax"
$user.Alter()
$user.Refresh()
```

The code makes sense syntax-wise; however, when you execute this, it will give an exception:

```
System.Management.Automation.MethodInvocationException: Exception
calling "Alter" with "0" argument(s): "Alter failed for User
'baymax'. " --->
Microsoft.SqlServer.Management.Smo.FailedOperationException: Alter
failed for User 'baymax'.  --->
Microsoft.SqlServer.Management.Smo.SmoException: Modifying the
Login property of the User object is not allowed. You must drop
and recreate the object with the desired property.
```

Therefore, to make it work using SMO, we will need to drop and recreate the database user. Dropping and recreating can work to an extent, but you will have to remember to reassign all permissions and roles to this user. For some situations, this may not be the ideal solution.

## See also

- The *Listing logins, users, and database mappings* recipe.

# Creating a credential

This recipe goes through the code needed for creating a SQL Server credential.

## Getting ready

In this recipe, we will create a credential for a domain account that has access to certain files and folders in our system, `QUERYWORKS\filemanager`. Here's the equivalent T-SQL of what we are trying to accomplish:

```
CREATE CREDENTIAL [filemanagercred]
WITH IDENTITY = N'QUERYWORKS\filemanager',
SECRET = N'YourSuperStrongPassword'
```

You can substitute this with another known Windows account you have in your environment.

## How to do it...

These are the steps to create a credential:

1. Open **PowerShell ISE** as an administrator.

2. Import the `SQLPS` module and create a new SMO Server Object:

   ```
   #import SQL Server module
   Import-Module SQLPS -DisableNameChecking

   #replace this with your instance name
   $instanceName = "localhost"
   $server = New-Object -TypeName
   Microsoft.SqlServer.Management.Smo.Server -ArgumentList
   $instanceName
   ```

3. Add the following script and run:

   ```
   $identity = "QUERYWORKS\filemanager"
   $credentialName = "filemanagercredential"

   #for purposes of our recipe
   #we will drop the credential if it already exists
   if($server.Credentials[$credentialName])
   {
     $server.Credentials[$credentialName].Drop()
   }
   ```

```
$credential=New-Object Microsoft.SqlServer.Management.Smo.
Credential -ArgumentList
$server, $credentialName

#create credential
$credential.Create($identity, "YourSuperStrongPassword")

#list credentials
#confirm new credential is listed
$server.Credentials
```

## How it works...

A credential in SQL Server allows a server principal to connect to resources outside SQL Server using different a identity or username/password combination. This is often used to map SQL Server logins to a Windows account needed to access resources such as files, folders, and/or programs outside SQL Server.

Creating a credential in PowerShell is short and straightforward. To create a credential, you will need to know the username and password of the external account you want to use as the credential:

```
$credential=New-Object
Microsoft.SqlServer.Management.Smo.Credential
-ArgumentList $server, $credentialName
$credential.Create($identity, "YourSuperStrongPassword")
```

Although this recipe shows you how to create the credential by passing the identity and password, I strongly discourage you from hardcoding a clear text password in your script. You can instead use the Get-Credential cmdlet to capture the password.

 The Get-Credential cmdlet is used and discussed further in the *Changing SQL Server service account* recipe.

## See also

- ▸ The *Creating a proxy* recipe.
- ▸ The *Changing SQL Server service account* recipe.

# Creating a proxy

In this recipe, we will create a SQL Server proxy.

## Getting ready

In this recipe, we will map our SQL Server Agent service account (QUERYWORKS\sqlagent) to the credential we created in the previous recipe, filemanagercred. We are also going to grant this proxy rights to run the PowerShell agent steps and the Operating System (CmdExec) steps. Here's the T-SQL equivalent of what we are trying to achieve:

```
EXEC msdb.dbo.sp_add_proxy
@proxy_name = N'filemanagerproxy',
@credential_name = N'filemanagercredential',
@enabled = 1,
@description = N'Proxy Account for PowerShell Agent Job steps'

EXEC msdb.dbo.sp_grant_login_to_proxy
@proxy_name = N'filemanagerproxy',
@login_name = N'QUERYWORKS\sqlagent'

-- PowerShell subsystem
EXEC msdb.dbo.sp_grant_proxy_to_subsystem
@proxy_name = N'filemanagerproxy',
@subsystem_id = 12

-- CmdExec subsystem
EXEC msdb.dbo.sp_grant_proxy_to_subsystem
@proxy_name = N'filemanagerproxy',
@subsystem_id = 12
```

You can substitute this with known SQL Server principals and credentials in your environment.

## How to do it...

These are the steps to create a proxy in SQL Server:

1. Open **PowerShell ISE** as an administrator.

2. Import the SQLPS module and create a new SMO Server Object as follows:

   ```
   #import SQL Server module
   Import-Module SQLPS -DisableNameChecking
   ```

```
#replace this with your instance name
$instanceName = "localhost"
$server = New-Object -TypeName Microsoft.SqlServer.Management.Smo.
Server -ArgumentList $instanceName
```

3.  Add the following script and run:

```
$proxyName = "filemanagerproxy"
$credentialName = "filemanagercredential"
$jobServer = $server.JobServer

#for purposes of our recipe
#we will drop the proxy account if it already exists
if($jobServer.ProxyAccounts[$proxyName])
{
    $jobServer.ProxyAccounts[$proxyName].Drop()
}

#line below to create proxy object
#should be in one line
$proxy = New-Object Microsoft.SqlServer.Management.Smo.Agent.
ProxyAccount
-ArgumentList $jobServer, $proxyName, $credentialName,
$true, "Proxy Account for PowerShell Agent Job steps"

#create the proxy on the server
$proxy.Create()

#add sql server agent account - QUERYWORKS\sqlagent
$agentLogin = "QUERYWORKS\sqlagent"
$proxy.AddLogin($agentLogin)

#add PowerShell and CmdExec Subsystems
$proxy.AddSubSystem(
[Microsoft.SqlServer.Management.Smo.Agent.AgentSubsystem]::
PowerShell)
$proxy.AddSubSystem(
[Microsoft.SqlServer.Management.Smo.Agent.AgentSubsystem]::
CmdExec)

#confirm, list proxy accounts
$jobserver.ProxyAccounts |
ForEach-Object {
    $currProxy = $_
```

```
#put all subsystems in a single string
$subsytems = ($currProxy.EnumSubSystems() |
             Select -ExpandProperty Name) -Join ","

$item = [PSCustomObject] @{
    Proxy = $currProxy.Name
    Credential = $currProxy.CredentialName
    Identity = $currProxy.CredentialIdentity
    Subsystems = $subsytems
}

#display
$item
}
```

4. When the script successfully finishes executing, you should see a screen that lists all the proxies in your system. Confirm that the proxy has been created and subsystems have been assigned.

| Proxy | Credential | Identity | Subsystems |
|-------|-----------|----------|------------|
| [REPL][QUERYWORKS\Administ... | [REPL][QUERYWORKS\Administ... | QUERYWORKS\Administrator | LogReader |
| [REPL][QUERYWORKS\Administ... | [REPL][QUERYWORKS\Administ... | QUERYWORKS\Administrator | Snapshot |
| [REPL][QUERYWORKS\Administ... | [REPL][QUERYWORKS\Administ... | QUERYWORKS\Administrator | Distribution |
| filemanagerproxy | filemanagercredential | QUERYWORKS\filemanager | CmdExec,PowerShell |
| sharedfileuser | sharedfileuser | ROGUE\sharedfileuser | CmdExec,SSIS |

## How it works...

The first step is to create an SMO proxy instance. This is a pretty long line that wraps in the page, but ensure that you don't have any new lines that break it otherwise PowerShell will complain about some syntax errors:

```
#line below to create proxy object
#should be in one line
$proxy=New-Object Microsoft.SqlServer.Management.Smo.Agent.
ProxyAccount -ArgumentList $jobServer, $proxyName, $credentialName,
$true, "Proxy Account for PowerShell Agent Job steps"

#create the proxy on the server
$proxy.Create()
```

To create a proxy, you will need two pieces of information: the server principal (login) you want to use and the SQL Server credential to map it to. In our recipe, we mapped our SQL Server Agent service account QUERYWORKS\sqlagent to a domain account called QUERYWORKS\filemanager via the filemanagercredential credential:

```
$agentLogin = "QUERYWORKS\sqlagent"
$proxy.AddLogin($agentlogin)
```

In SQL Server, when creating proxies, we also need to narrow down which specific subsystems the proxy can be used. In our recipe, we specified the PowerShell and CmdExec subsystems:

```
$proxy.AddSubSystem(
[Microsoft.SqlServer.Management.Smo.Agent.AgentSubsystem]::
PowerShell)
$proxy.AddSubSystem(
[Microsoft.SqlServer.Management.Smo.Agent.AgentSubsystem]::
CmdExec)
```

Other common options include TransactSQL, ActiveScripting, AnalysisCommand, AnalysisQuery, and SSIS.

To confirm, we iterate through all ProxyAccounts and use the EnumSubsystems method of the Microsoft.SqlServer.Management.Smo.Agent.ProxyAccount class to display which subsytems are tied to a proxy:

```
#confirm, list proxy accounts
$jobserver.ProxyAccounts |
ForEach-Object {
   $currProxy = $_

   #put all subsystems in a single string
   $subsytems = ($currProxy.EnumSubSystems() |
                 Select -ExpandProperty Name) -Join ","

   $item = [PSCustomObject] @{
      Proxy = $currProxy.Name
      Credential = $currProxy.CredentialName
      Identity = $currProxy.CredentialIdentity
      Subsystems = $subsytems
   }

   #display
   $item
}
```

You can find the complete enumeration values from the MSDN at `http://msdn.microsoft.com/en-us/library/microsoft.sqlserver.management.smo.agent.agentsubsystem.aspx`.

## There's more...

You will often encounter the need to use proxies when you have some principals that need to access external resources, but you don't want to grant them those extra permissions outside SQL Server. One common scenario is with your SSIS packages. A SQL Server agent would usually not have the extra rights to access files and folders. To avoid granting these extra rights, you will need to map the agent account to another account that already has these rights.

## See also

▸ The *Creating a credential* recipe.

# 5
# Backup and Restore

In this chapter, we will cover:

- ▶ Changing database recovery model
- ▶ Checking last backup date
- ▶ Creating a backup device
- ▶ Listing backup header and file list information
- ▶ Creating a full back up
- ▶ Creating a backup on mirrored media sets
- ▶ Creating a differential backup
- ▶ Creating a transaction log backup
- ▶ Creating a filegroup backup
- ▶ Restoring a database to a point in time
- ▶ Performing an online piecemeal restore
- ▶ Backing up database to Azure Blob storage
- ▶ Restoring database from Azure Blob storage

## Introduction

Knowing how to backup and restore a database is one of the most fundamental skills, that you need to have when managing your database environment.

There are different ways to do backup and restore. It can be done through **SQL Server Management Studio** (**SSMS**) by using stored procedures, or through **SQL Server Integration Services** (**SSIS**). These backup tasks can also be done with PowerShell. With all these different options, the key is to determine which tool is best suited for the particular task.

Doing the backups and restores using PowerShell has its own advantages, including the ability to automate backups across multiple servers and applications, and being able to retrieve, consolidate, and filter all backup histories if needed. SQL Server also comes with backup and restore cmdlets, introduced in SQL Server 2012. In addition, you can still tap into SQL Server Management Objects if you need more flexibility.

# Changing database recovery model

In this recipe, we will explore how to change SQL Server recovery model using PowerShell.

## Getting ready

We will use `AdventureWorks2014` in this exercise and change the recovery model from `Full` to `Simple`. Feel free to substitute this with a database of your choice.

Check what SQL Server recovery model your instance is set to. Using SSMS, open your **Object Explorer**. Right-click on the database you chose, click on **Properties**, and select **Options**:

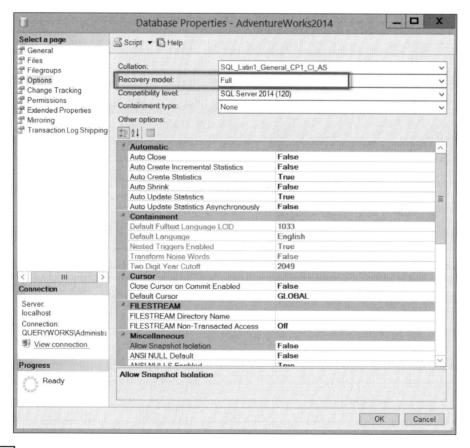

If your database is set to either **Simple** or **Bulk-logged**, change this to **Full** and click on **OK**. Since we will use AdventureWorks2014 in later exercises, we need to change this recovery model back to **Full** after this exercise.

## How to do it...

The steps to change the recovery model are as follows:

1. Open **PowerShell ISE** as administrator.

2. Import the SQLPS module as follows:

   ```
   #import SQL Server module
   Import-Module SQLPS -DisableNameChecking
   ```

3. Add the following script and run:

   ```
   $instanceName = "localhost"
   $server = New-Object -TypeName
   Microsoft.SqlServer.Management.Smo.Server -ArgumentList
   $instanceName

   $databasename = "AdventureWorks2014"
   $database = $server.Databases[$databasename]

   #possible values for RecoveryModel are
   #Full, Simple and BulkLogged
   $database.DatabaseOptions.RecoveryModel =
   [Microsoft.SqlServer.Management.Smo.RecoveryModel]::Simple
   $database.Alter()
   $database.Refresh()

   #list Recovery Model again
   $database.DatabaseOptions.RecoveryModel

   #remember to change the recovery model back
   #to full for the next recipes
   ```

## How it works...

To change a database's RecoveryModel property, get a handle to that database first:

```
$databasename = "AdventureWorks2014"
$database = $server.Databases[$databasename]
```

Once you have the handle, use the `DatabaseOptions` property of the database object to set `RecoveryModel` to `BulkLogged`:

```
#possible values for RecoveryModel are
#Full, Simple and BulkLogged
$database.DatabaseOptions.RecoveryModel =
[Microsoft.SqlServer.Management.Smo.RecoveryModel]::Simple
$database.Alter()
$database.Refresh()
```

## There's more...

`RecoveryModel` is a database property that specifies what backup and restore operations are allowed and permitted. There are three possible values for `RecoveryModel`: `Full`, `BulkLogged`, and `Simple`.

The `Full` and `BulkLogged` recovery models allow the use of log files for backup and restore purposes. The `Full` recovery model uses the transaction log files heavily and allows for point-in-time recovery.

> The `BulkLogged` recovery model logs bulk events minimally. If there are no bulk events in the system, then point-in-time recovery is possible. If there are bulk events, however, point-in-time recoverability will be affected, and it is possible that we'll be unable to recover anything from your log files at all. Check out Paul Randal's blog post *A SQL Server DBA myth a day: (28/30) BULK_LOGGED recovery model* (`http://www.sqlskills.com/BLOGS/PAUL/post/A-SQL-Server-DBA-myth-a-day-(2830)-BULK_LOGGED-recovery-model.aspx`).

The `Simple` recovery model does not support transaction log backups and restores at all. The transaction log tasks are unavailable (disabled) when you are in the `Simple` recovery model. You can visually confirm this when you go to your database properties in SQL Server Management Studio as well. This means point-in-time recovery is not possible, and the window for data loss could be large. Therefore, the `Simple` recovery model is not a recommended setting for production servers; it can be used for development and sandbox servers, or any instance where data loss would not be critical.

The `RecoveryModel` type you choose in your environment will typically be determined by a company's **Recovery Point Objective** (**RPO**) and **Recovery Time Objective** (**RTO**); although, in most cases the recommended setting would be the `Full` recovery model.

Read more about recovery models from the MSDN at `http://msdn.microsoft.com/en-us/library/ms189275.aspx`.

## See also

▸ The *Altering database properties* recipe in *Chapter 2, SQL Server and PowerShell Basic Tasks*.

# Checking last backup date

In this recipe, we will check when databases have been last backed up.

## Getting ready

One way to check when a database was last backed up is through SQL Server Management Studio. Open SSMS and connect to your instance. For example, if you want to see when AdventureWorks2014 was last backed up, you can right-click on this database and select **Properties**. In the **General** page, you should see a section for **Backup**, which should show you when a database and log were last backed up.

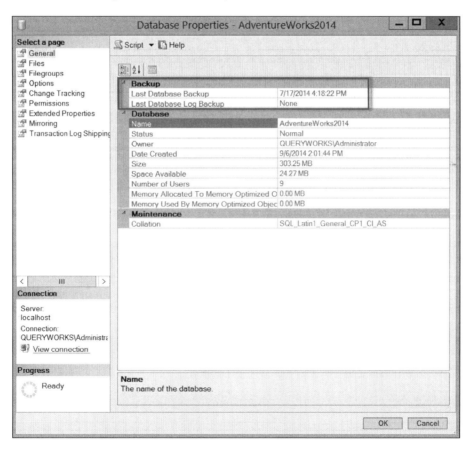

## How to do it...

The steps to check the last backup dates are as follows:

1. Open **PowerShell ISE** as administrator.

2. Import the SQLPS module as follows:

```
#import SQL Server module
Import-Module SQLPS -DisableNameChecking
```

3. Add the following script and run:

```
$instanceName = "localhost"
$server = New-Object -TypeName
Microsoft.SqlServer.Management.Smo.Server -ArgumentList
$instanceName


$server.Databases |
Select-Object Name, RecoveryModel,
LastBackupDate,
LastDifferentialBackupDate,
LastLogBackupDate |
Format-Table -Autosize
```

## How it works...

By default, each database will already contain properties that capture the last backup dates, specifically LastBackupDate, LastDifferentialBackupDate, and LastLogBackupDate. Once you get a handle on the database object, you can simply query these properties. Your result will look similar to the following screenshot:

| Name | RecoveryModel | LastBackupDate | LastDifferentialBackupDate | LastLogBackupDate |
|------|---------------|----------------|----------------------------|-------------------|
| AdventureWorks2014 | Full | 7/17/2014 4:18:22 PM | 1/1/0001 12:00:00 AM | 1/1/0001 12:00:00 AM |
| AdventureWorksLT2012 | Simple | 1/1/0001 12:00:00 AM | 1/1/0001 12:00:00 AM | 1/1/0001 12:00:00 AM |
| Chinook | Full | 10/24/2014 10:11:11 AM | 10/24/2014 10:11:11 AM | 10/23/2014 11:58:41 PM |
| distribution | Simple | 1/1/0001 12:00:00 AM | 1/1/0001 12:00:00 AM | 1/1/0001 12:00:00 AM |
| master | Simple | 1/1/0001 12:00:00 AM | 1/1/0001 12:00:00 AM | 1/1/0001 12:00:00 AM |
| model | Full | 1/1/0001 12:00:00 AM | 1/1/0001 12:00:00 AM | 1/1/0001 12:00:00 AM |
| msdb | Simple | 1/1/0001 12:00:00 AM | 1/1/0001 12:00:00 AM | 1/1/0001 12:00:00 AM |
| pubs | Full | 1/1/0001 12:00:00 AM | 1/1/0001 12:00:00 AM | 1/1/0001 12:00:00 AM |
| Registration | Full | 1/1/0001 12:00:00 AM | 1/1/0001 12:00:00 AM | 1/1/0001 12:00:00 AM |
| tempdb | Simple | 1/1/0001 12:00:00 AM | 1/1/0001 12:00:00 AM | 1/1/0001 12:00:00 AM |
| TestDB | Full | 1/1/0001 12:00:00 AM | 1/1/0001 12:00:00 AM | 1/1/0001 12:00:00 AM |
| TestDB_copy | Full | 1/1/0001 12:00:00 AM | 1/1/0001 12:00:00 AM | 1/1/0001 12:00:00 AM |

Note that when you see a date: **01/01/0001 12:00:00 AM** when querying a backup date, this means that specific type of backup has not been performed yet in that database, if the value is under `LastBackupDate`, then a full backup has not been performed yet. If it falls under `LastDifferentialBackupDate`, then a differential backup hasn't been performed yet. The same holds true if it is under `LastLogBackupDate`.

In the recipe, we simply displayed the results on the screen using the `Format-Table` cmdlet. Alternatively, you can capture the results in a file or a table as per your requirements.

## See also

▶ The *Listing SQL Server configuration settings* recipe in *Chapter 2, SQL Server and PowerShell Basic Tasks*.

▶ The *Listing SQL Server Jobs* recipe in *Chapter 3, Basic Administration*.

# Creating a backup device

This recipe will show how you can create a backup device using PowerShell.

## Getting ready

We are going to create a backup device in this recipe. Here's the T-SQL equivalent of what we are trying to accomplish:

```
EXEC master.dbo.sp_addumpdevice @devtype = N'disk',
    @logicalname = N'Full Backups',
    @physicalname = N'C:\Backup\backupfile.bak'
```

## How to do it...

Let's list the steps required to create a backup device:

1.  Open **PowerShell ISE** as administrator.

2.  Import the `SQLPS` module as follows:

    ```
    #import SQL Server module
    Import-Module SQLPS -DisableNameChecking
    ```

3. Add the following script and run:

```
$instanceName = "localhost"
$server = New-Object -TypeName
Microsoft.SqlServer.Management.Smo.Server -ArgumentList
$instanceName

#this file will be created by PowerShell/SMO
$backupfilename = "Full Backups"
$backupfile = "C:\Backup\backupfile.bak"

#this line should be in a single line
$backupdevice = New-Object Microsoft.SqlServer.Management.Smo.
BackupDevice
-ArgumentList $server, $backupfilename

#BackupDeviceType values are:
#CDRom, Disk, FloppyA, FloppyB, Tape, Pipe, Unknown
$backupdevice.BackupDeviceType = [Microsoft.SqlServer.Management.
Smo.BackupDeviceType]::Disk

$backupdevice.PhysicalLocation = $backupfile

#create the specified backup device
$backupdevice.Create()

#list backup devices to confirm
$server.BackupDevices
```

4. To confirm from SQL Server Management Studio, log in to your instance and expand **Backup Devices**. You should see the new backup device you created in PowerShell.

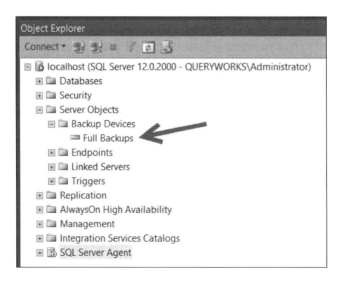

## How it works...

A backup device is a layer of abstraction that allows you to reference a backup media—be it a file, network share, or tape—using a logical name instead of specifying the full physical path.

To create a backup device using PowerShell and SMO, you need to create a handle to an SMO `BackupDevice` object:

```
$backupdevice = New-Object
Microsoft.SqlServer.Management.Smo.BackupDevice -ArgumentList
$server, $backupfilename
```

You will also need to specify `BackupDeviceType` and the physical location of the media. `BackupDeviceType` can be `CDRom`, `Disk`, `FloppyA`, `FloppyB`, `Tape`, `Pipe`, or `Unknown`. The code is as follows:

```
$instanceName = "localhost"
$server = New-Object -TypeName
Microsoft.SqlServer.Management.Smo.Server -ArgumentList
$instanceName

$backupdevice.BackupDeviceType =
[Microsoft.SqlServer.Management.Smo.BackupDeviceType]::Disk

$backupdevice.PhysicalLocation = $backupfile

#create the specified backup device
$backupdevice.Create()
```

## There's more...

Learn more about backup devices, including terminologies, how to use backup devices, mirrored media sets, and archiving SQL Server backups from the following MSDN page:

```
http://msdn.microsoft.com/en-us/library/ms179313.aspx
```

## See also

▶ The *Listing backup header and FileList information* recipe.

# Listing backup header and FileList information

In this recipe, we will see how to list backup header information from a backup file.

## Getting ready

We need to list the existing backup's header information.

 If you do not have any backups in your system yet, you can go back to any of this chapter's Backup recipes prior to performing this recipe.

## How to do it...

To list the header information, follow these steps:

1. Open **PowerShell ISE** as administrator.

2. Import the `SQLPS` module as follows:

```
#import SQL Server module
Import-Module SQLPS -DisableNameChecking
```

3. Add the following script and run:

```
$instanceName = "localhost"
$server = New-Object -TypeName
Microsoft.SqlServer.Management.Smo.Server -ArgumentList
$instanceName

#replace this with your backup file
$backupfile = "AdventureWorks2014.bak"

#replace this with your backup directory
$backupdir = $server.Settings.BackupDirectory

#get full path
$backupfilepath = Join-Path $backupdir $backupfile

#SMO restore object will allow us to
#investigate contents of backup
$smoRestore = New-Object Microsoft.SqlServer.Management.Smo.
Restore
```

```
#add the backup file
$smoRestore.Devices.AddDevice($backupfilepath,
[Microsoft.SqlServer.Management.Smo.DeviceType]::File)

#list backup header
$smoRestore.ReadBackupHeader($server)
```

The following screenshot shows a part of what you will see after you execute the `ReadBackupHeader` method. Notice that you can see the `BackupName`, `BackupType`, `ServerName`, `BackupSize`, `BackupStartDate`, `BackupFinishDate`, and different `LSN` values.

```
BackupName               : AdventureWorks2014-Full Database Backup
BackupDescription        :
BackupType               : 1
ExpirationDate           :
Compressed               : 0
Position                 : 1
DeviceType               : 2
UserName                 : QUERYWORKS\Administrator
ServerName               : ROGUE
DatabaseName             : AdventureWorks2014
DatabaseVersion          : 782
DatabaseCreationDate     : 9/6/2014 2:01:44 PM
BackupSize               : 222394368
FirstLSN                 : 75000000044700111
LastLSN                  : 75000000049400001
CheckpointLSN            : 75000000044700111
DatabaseBackupLSN        : 44000000084000074
BackupStartDate          : 3/14/2015 8:59:24 AM
BackupFinishDate         : 3/14/2015 8:59:35 AM
SortOrder                : 52
CodePage                 : 0
UnicodeLocaleId          : 1033
UnicodeComparisonStyle   : 196609
CompatibilityLevel       : 120
SoftwareVendorId         : 4608
SoftwareVersionMajor     : 12
SoftwareVersionMinor     : 0
SoftwareVersionBuild     : 2000
MachineName              : ROGUE
```

4. To display the file list information, add the following script and run:

```
#get filelist
$smoRestore.ReadFileList($server)
```

The following screenshot shows you a partial screen of the information you will get with `ReadFileList`. Notice that you can see properties such as `LogicalName`, `PhysicalName`, `FileGroupName`, and `Size` of both the data and log files associated with this backup file.

```
LogicalName         : AdventureWorks2014_Data
PhysicalName        : C:\Program Files\Microsoft SQL Server\MSSQL12.MSSQLSERVER\MSSQL\DATA\AdventureWorks2014_Data.mdf
Type                : D
FileGroupName       : PRIMARY
Size                : 248774656
MaxSize             : 35184372080640
FileId              : 1
CreateLSN           : 0
DropLSN             : 0
UniqueId            : fbf02ee2-5f78-44b2-972f-df53a8fe35ee
ReadOnlyLSN         : 0
ReadWriteLSN        : 0
BackupSizeInBytes   : 222167040
SourceBlockSize     : 512
FileGroupId         : 1
LogGroupGUID        :
DifferentialBaseLSN : 44000000084000074
DifferentialBaseGUID : 0ac27e09-66d5-4054-b7e5-db56b879912b
IsReadOnly          : False
IsPresent           : True
TDEThumbprint       :

LogicalName         : AdventureWorks2014_Log
PhysicalName        : C:\Program Files\Microsoft SQL Server\MSSQL12.MSSQLSERVER\MSSQL\DATA\AdventureWorks2014_Log.ldf
Type                : L
FileGroupName       :
Size                : 69206016
MaxSize             : 2199023255552
FileId              : 2
CreateLSN           : 0
DropLSN             : 0
UniqueId            : 1ef63d26-36ae-4d8f-92ae-662d78b25805
ReadOnlyLSN         : 0
```

## How it works...

You will often want to find out more information about the content of your backup files. The backup header and the file list of the backup files allow you to retrieve additional information about the content of a backup file or backup device. Starting with SQL Server 2008, you must have the `CREATE DATABASE` permission before the header information can be listed.

To start, we should identify which backup file and path we want to investigate:

```
#replace this with your backup file
$backupfile = "AdventureWorks2014.bak"

#replace this with your backup directory
$backupdir = $server.Settings.BackupDirectory

#get full path
$backupfilepath = Join-Path $backupdir $backupfile
```

Next, we create a reference to an SMO `Restore` object:

```
$smoRestore = New-Object
Microsoft.SqlServer.Management.Smo.Restore
```

We then add the backup file to this SMO Restore object using the `AddDevice` method. We can specify the full path to the backup file and the type of device. The valid values for `DeviceType` are `File`, `LogicalDevice`, `Pipe`, `Tape`, `Url`, and `VirtualDevice`:

```
$smoRestore.Devices.AddDevice($backupfilepath,
[Microsoft.SqlServer.Management.Smo.DeviceType]::File)
```

The SMO `Restore` object contains a method called `ReadBackupHeader`, which lists all the backup headers for all backup sets contained in a backup device or file. The information it returns includes the following:

- `BackupName` and description
- `BackupType`
- `Compressed`
- `ServerName`
- `DatabaseName`
- `DatabaseVersion` and `DatabaseCreationDate`
- `BackupSize`
- `CheckpointLSN`
- `DatabaseBackupLSN`
- Backup start and finish date

To retrieve the backup header, just invoke the `ReadBackupHeader` method of the `Restore` object and pass in the server object as an argument:

```
$smoRestore.ReadBackupHeader($server)
```

The file list contains the actual database and log files associated in a particular backup set. Listing the file list requires a very similar syntax to when reading the backup header. We need to invoke the method `ReadFileList`, passing the server object as an argument again:

```
$smoRestore.ReadFileList($server)
```

## There's more...

To learn more about the `Restore` class, including its properties and methods, check out `https://msdn.microsoft.com/en-us/library/Microsoft.SqlServer.Management.Smo.Restore.aspx`.

# Creating a full backup

In this recipe, we will see how to create a full database backup using PowerShell.

## Getting ready

Using the `AdventureWorks2014` database, we will create a full, compressed backup of the database to a timestamped backup (`.bak`) file in the `C:\Backup` folder. Feel free to use a database of your choice for this task.

The T-SQL syntax that will be generated by this PowerShell recipe will look similar to the following:

```
BACKUP DATABASE [AdventureWorks2014]
TO   DISK = N'C:\Backup\AdventureWorks2014_Full_20150314092409.bak'
WITH NOFORMAT, INIT,
NAME = N'AdventureWorks2014 Full Backup',
NOSKIP, REWIND, NOUNLOAD, COMPRESSION,
STATS = 10, CHECKSUM
```

## How to do it...

The steps to create a full database backup are as follows:

1.  Open **PowerShell ISE** as administrator.

2.  Import the `SQLPS` module as follows:

    ```
    #import SQL Server module
    Import-Module SQLPS -DisableNameChecking
    ```

3.  Add the following script and run:

    ```
    $instanceName = "localhost"
    $server = New-Object -TypeName
    Microsoft.SqlServer.Management.Smo.Server -ArgumentList
    $instanceName

    $databasename = "AdventureWorks2014"
    $timestamp = Get-Date -format yyyyMMddHHmmss
    $backupfolder = "C:\Backup\"
    $backupfile = "$($databasename)_Full_$($timestamp).bak"
    $fullBackupFile = Join-Path $backupfolder $backupfile

    #note that we are using backticks in this command
    #to allow for a newline for each parameter
    ```

```
#to clearly show parameters used
Backup-SqlDatabase `
-ServerInstance $instanceName `
-Database $databasename `
-BackupFile $fullBackupFile `
-Checksum `
-Initialize `
-BackupSetName "$databasename Full Backup" `
-CompressionOption On
```

Because the **STATS** option is on by default, reporting progress in 10 percent increments, you should notice a progress bar in PowerShell ISE while the database is being backed up:

Note that if you are using the PowerShell console, you will also see a progress bar, although it is slightly different in appearance. Once backup is done, check your `C:\Backup` directory and confirm that the timestamped backup file has been created.

4. Confirm by reading the backup header. Add the following script and run:

```
#confirm by reading the header
$smoRestore = New-Object
Microsoft.SqlServer.Management.Smo.Restore
$smoRestore.Devices.AddDevice($fullBackupFile,
[Microsoft.SqlServer.Management.Smo.DeviceType]::File)
$smoRestore.ReadBackupHeader($server)
$smoRestore.ReadFileList($server)
```

## How it works...

In this recipe, we first create a timestamped filename:

```
$databasename = "AdventureWorks2014"
$timestamp = Get-Date -format yyyyMMddHHmmss
$backupfolder = "C:\Backup\"
$backupfile = "$($databasename)_Full_$($timestamp).bak"
$fullBackupFile = Join-Path $backupfolder $backupfile
```

This will give you a filename similar to this `C:\Backup\AdventureWorks2014_Full_20150314092409.bak`.

Next, we use the `Backup-SqlDatabase` cmdlet. The `Backup-SqlDatabase` cmdlet was introduced in SQL Server 2012 as part of the `SQLPS` module. This cmdlet encapsulates a lot of the options that used to be available only via SMO.

It is imperative for this recipe that we use `Get-Help` for the `Backup-SqlDatabase` cmdlet first to know which parameters are available. The `Backup-SqlDatabase` cmdlet supports several parameter sets, which means it's fairly flexible in the options you can provide.

Here's the first part of the results of `Get-Help` for this cmdlet, just to give you an idea:

```
PS SQLSERVER:\> Get-Help Backup-SqlDatabase

NAME
    Backup-SqlDatabase

SYNOPSIS
    The Backup-SqlDatabase cmdlet performs backup operations on a SQL Server database.

SYNTAX
    Backup-SqlDatabase [-Database] <String> [[-BackupFile] <String[]>] [-BackupAction <BackupActionType>] [-BackupContainer <String>]
    [-BackupDevice <BackupDeviceItem[]>] [-BackupSetDescription <String>] [-BackupSetName <String>] [-BlockSize <Int32>] [-BufferCount
    <Int32>] [-Checksum] [-CompressionOption <BackupCompressionOptions>] [-ContinueAfterError] [-CopyOnly] [-DatabaseFile <String[]>]
    [-DatabaseFileGroup <String[]>] [-EncryptionOption <BackupEncryptionOptions>] [-ExpirationDate <DateTime>] [-FormatMedia]
    [-Incremental] [-Initialize] [-LogTruncationType <BackupTruncateLogType>] [-MaxTransferSize <Int32>] [-MediaDescription <String>]
    [-MediaName <String>] [-MirrorDevices <BackupDeviceList[]>] [-NoRecovery] [-NoRewind] [-PassThru] [-Path <String[]>] [-Restart]
    [-RetainDays <Int32>] [-Script] [-SkipTapeHeader] [-SqlCredential <PSObject>] [-UndoFileName <String>] [-UnloadTapeAfter] [-Confirm]
    [-WhatIf] [<CommonParameters>]

    Backup-SqlDatabase [-DatabaseObject] <Database> [[-BackupFile] <String[]>] [-BackupAction <BackupActionType>] [-BackupContainer
    <String>] [-BackupDevice <BackupDeviceItem[]>] [-BackupSetDescription <String>] [-BackupSetName <String>] [-BlockSize <Int32>]
    [-BufferCount <Int32>] [-Checksum] [-CompressionOption <BackupCompressionOptions>] [-ContinueAfterError] [-CopyOnly] [-DatabaseFile
    <String[]>] [-DatabaseFileGroup <String[]>] [-EncryptionOption <BackupEncryptionOptions>] [-ExpirationDate <DateTime>] [-FormatMedia]
    [-Incremental] [-Initialize] [-LogTruncationType <BackupTruncateLogType>] [-MaxTransferSize <Int32>] [-MediaDescription <String>]
    [-MediaName <String>] [-MirrorDevices <BackupDeviceList[]>] [-NoRecovery] [-NoRewind] [-PassThru] [-Restart] [-RetainDays <Int32>]
    [-Script] [-SkipTapeHeader] [-SqlCredential <PSObject>] [-UndoFileName <String>] [-UnloadTapeAfter] [-Confirm] [-WhatIf]
    [<CommonParameters>]
```

In our recipe, this is the command we executed:

```
Backup-SqlDatabase `
-ServerInstance $instanceName `
-Database $databasename `
-BackupFile $fullBackupFile `
-Checksum `
-Initialize `
-BackupSetName "$databasename Full Backup" `
-CompressionOption On
```

> Note that we used the line continuation character backtick (`` ` ``) for readability purposes so that we can align each parameter on the same position in each line.

Let's explain the options we have chosen in more detail:

| Parameter | Explanation |
|---|---|
| `-ServerInstance $instanceName` | Instance to backup. |
| `-Database $databasename` | Database to backup. |
| `-BackupFile $fullBackupFile` | Backup filename. |

| Parameter | Explanation |
|---|---|
| `-Checksum` | Enable backup checksum, which can be used in restore operation to determine if backup file is corrupt. |
| `-Initialize` | Specifies backup set contained in the file or backup device will be overwritten. |
| `-BackupSetName "$databasename Full Backup"` | Backup set name. |
| `-CompressionOption On` | Specifies whether compression should be applied to the backup file.<br><br>You can also provide the complete enum reference for the `CompressionOption` value:<br><br>`-CompressionOption ([Microsoft.SqlServer.Management.Smo.BackupCompressionOptions]::On)` |

Instead of compressing backups, you can also take advantage of the new `Compress-Archive` cmdlet introduced in PowerShell v5:

```
$backupfile = "C:\Backup\AdventureWorks2014.bak"
$backupzip = "C:\Backup\AdventureWorks2014.zip"

#create the zipped file
Compress-Archive -Path $backupfile -DestinationPath $backupzip
-CompressionLevel Optimal
```

There are currently three supported compression levels for the `Compress-Archive` cmdlet: `Fastest`, `NoCompression`, and `Optimal`. These values should automatically show up as dropdown in PowerShell ISE once you've typed the `-CompressionLevel` parameter:

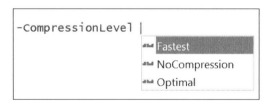

There are two blog posts that discuss the reasons to use compression whenever possible:

▸ Henk van der Valk's *How to increase SQL Database Full Backup speed using compression and Solid State Disks* at `http:// henkvandervalk.com/how-to-increase-sql-database- full-backup-speed-using-compression-and-solid- state-disks`.

▸ Denis Gobo discusses the benefits of compression, including faster backups, restores and file transfers at `http://blogs. lessthandot.com/index.php/datamgmt/dbadmin/ testing-backup-compression-in-sql-server-2008/`.

Once you get familiar with the `Backup-SqlDatabase` cmdlet, you will realize that the command and options for all other backup types will be fairly similar. You will just need to add or change some of the parameters.

## There's more...

Although there is already a cmdlet available for backing up databases, it will be useful to discuss how you can do the backups via SMO. Using SMO may be the more code-heavy way of tackling a database backup in PowerShell, but it is still very powerful and flexible.

The cmdlet can be viewed simply, as a wrapper to the SMO backup methods. Taking a peek at how this is done could be a good exercise.

The first steps in this approach are similar to the steps we have for this recipe: import `SQLPS` and create the SMO server object. After that, create an SMO `Backup` object. The code is as follows:

```
$databasename = "AdventureWorks2014"
$timestamp = Get-Date -format yyyyMMddHHmmss
$backupfolder = "C:\Backup\"
$backupfile = "$($databasename)_Full_$($timestamp).bak"
$fullBackupFile = Join-Path $backupfolder $backupfile

#This belongs in Microsoft.SqlServer.SmoExtended assembly
$smoBackup = New-Object Microsoft.SqlServer.Management.Smo.Backup
```

With a handle to the SMO backup object, you will have more granular control over what values are set to which properties. `Action` can be `Database`, `File`, or `Log`. The code is as follows:

```
$smoBackup.Action =
[Microsoft.SqlServer.Management.Smo.BackupActionType]::Database
$smoBackup.BackupSetName = "$databasename Full Backup"
$smoBackup.Database = $databasename
$smoBackup.MediaDescription = "Disk"
$smoBackup.Devices.AddDevice($fullBackupFile, "File")
$smoBackup.Checksum = $true
$smoBackup.Initialize = $true
$smoBackup.CompressionOption =
[Microsoft.SqlServer.Management.Smo.BackupCompressionOptions]::On
```

You can also optionally set up your own event notification on the backup progress using the `Microsoft.SqlServer.Management.Smo.PercentCompleteEventHandler` and `Microsoft.SqlServer.Management.Common.ServerMessageEventHandler` classes. The code is as follows:

```
#the notification part below is optional
#it just creates an event handler
#that indicates progress every 20%
$smoBackup.PercentCompleteNotification = 20
$percentEventHandler =
[Microsoft.SqlServer.Management.Smo.PercentCompleteEventHandler] {
    Write-Host "Backing up $($databasename)...$($_.Percent)%"
}
$completedEventHandler =
[Microsoft.SqlServer.Management.Common.ServerMessageEventHandler]
{
    Write-Host $_.Error.Message
}
$smoBackup.add_PercentComplete($percentEventHandler)
$smoBackup.add_Complete($completedEventHandler)
```

After setting the properties, you can invoke the `SqlBackup` method of the SMO `Backup` class and pass the server object:

```
#backup
$smoBackup.SqlBackup($server)
```

Alternatively, when you do a restore with SMO, the steps are going to be pretty similar. You will need to create the SMO `Restore` object, set the properties, and call the `SqlRestore` method of the `Restore` class in the end.

### More about backup and PercentCompleteEventHandler

To learn more about the `BackupRestoreBase` and `PercentCompleteHandler` SMO classes, you can refer to the following:

- `BackupRestoreBase` at `http://msdn.microsoft.com/en-us/library/microsoft.sqlserver.management.smo.backuprestorebase.percentcomplete.aspx`

- `PercentCompleteEventHandler` at `http://msdn.microsoft.com/en-us/library/microsoft.sqlserver.management.smo.percentcompleteeventhandler.aspx`

### See also

- The *Creating a backup on Mirrored Media Sets* recipe.
- The *Creating a differential backup* recipe.
- The *Creating a transaction log backup* recipe.
- The *Creating a filegroup backup* recipe.

# Creating a backup on Mirrored Media Sets

In this recipe, we will create a full database backup on mirrored backup files.

### Getting ready

We will use the `AdventureWorks2014` database for this recipe. We will create a mirrored backup of the database, and both timestamped backup files will be stored in `C:\Backup`. Feel free to substitute this with the database you want to use with mirrored backups.

 Note that mirrored backups are only supported in Developer or Enterprise editions of SQL Server. Please ensure you have either of these editions before proceeding with the recipe.

Here's the T-SQL syntax that will be generated by this PowerShell recipe:

```
BACKUP DATABASE [AdventureWorks2014]
TO  DISK = N'AdventureWorks2014.bak'
MIRROR
TO  DISK =
N'C:\Backup\AdventureWorks2014_Full_20150314092409_Copy1.bak'
MIRROR TO  DISK =
N'C:\Backup\AdventureWorks2014_Full_20150314092409_Copy2.bak'
WITH FORMAT, INIT,
NAME = N'AdventureWorks2014 Full Backup', SKIP, REWIND,
NOUNLOAD, COMPRESSION, STATS = 10, CHECKSUM
```

## How to do it...

To create a backup on mirrored media sets, use the following steps:

1.  Open **PowerShell ISE** as administrator.

2.  Import the SQLPS module as follows:

    ```
    #import SQL Server module
    Import-Module SQLPS -DisableNameChecking
    ```

3.  Add the following script and run:

    ```
    $instanceName = "localhost"
    $server = New-Object -TypeName
    Microsoft.SqlServer.Management.Smo.Server -ArgumentList
    $instanceName

    $databasename = "AdventureWorks2014"

    #create filenames, which we will use as Device
    $databasename = "AdventureWorks2014"
    $timestamp = Get-Date -format yyyyMMddHHmmss
    $backupfolder = "C:\Backup\"

    #backup mirror 1
    $backupfile1 = Join-Path $backupfolder
    "$($databasename)_Full_$($timestamp)_Copy1.bak"

    #backup mirror 2
    $backupfile2 = Join-Path $backupfolder
    "$($databasename)_Full_$($timestamp)_Copy2.bak"
    ```

```
#create a backup device list
#in this example, we will only use
#two (2) mirrored media sets
#note a maximum of four (4) is allowed
$backupDevices = New-Object
Microsoft.SqlServer.Management.Smo.BackupDeviceList(2)
#backup mirror 1
$backupDevices.AddDevice($backupfile1,
[Microsoft.SqlServer.Management.Smo.DeviceType]::File)

#backup mirror 2
$backupDevices.AddDevice($backupfile2,
[Microsoft.SqlServer.Management.Smo.DeviceType]::File)

#backup database
#note that we are using backticks in this command
#to allow for a newline for each parameter
#to clearly show parameters used
Backup-SqlDatabase        `
-ServerInstance $instanceName `
-Database $databasename `
-BackupSetName "$databasename Full Backup" `
-Checksum `
-Initialize `
-FormatMedia `
-SkipTapeHeader `
-MirrorDevices $backupDevices `
-CompressionOption On
```

4. Open your `C:\Backup` folder and confirm that the two timestamped backup files have been created.

## How it works...

With SQL Server, it is possible to create a backup with up to four mirrors per media set. Mirrored media sets allow you to have multiple copies of that backup which are stored in different backup devices.

For our recipe, we must create a set of files first, that we will use to save our backup to:

```
#create backup devices
#in this example, we will only use two (2) mirrored media sets
#note a maximum of four (4) is allowed
$databasename = "AdventureWorks2014"
$timestamp = Get-Date -format yyyyMMddHHmmss
```

```
$backupfolder = "C:\Backup\"

#backup mirror 1
$backupfile1 = Join-Path $backupfolder
"$($databasename)_Full_$($timestamp)_Copy1.bak"

#backup mirror 2
$backupfile2 = Join-Path $backupfolder
"$($databasename)_Full_$($timestamp)_Copy2.bak"
```

We then need to add these files' backup devices to our `BackupDeviceList` object. The two parameters that we pass to our `BackupDeviceList` constructor represent the number of backup devices we are adding. A maximum of four devices are allowed for mirrored media. The code is as follows:

```
$backupDevices = New-Object
Microsoft.SqlServer.Management.Smo.BackupDeviceList(2)

#backup mirror 1
$backupDevices.AddDevice($backupfile1,
[Microsoft.SqlServer.Management.Smo.DeviceType]::File)

#backup mirror 2
$backupDevices.AddDevice($backupfile2,
[Microsoft.SqlServer.Management.Smo.DeviceType]::File)
```

In the `Backup-SqlDatabase` cmdlet, the highlighted code below shows the options that enable mirrored backups:

```
#backup database
Backup-SqlDatabase            `
-ServerInstance $instanceName `
-Database $databasename       `
-BackupSetName "$databasename Full Backup" `
-Checksum `
-Initialize `
-FormatMedia `
-SkipTapeHeader `
-MirrorDevices $backupDevices `
-CompressionOption On
```

Note that we used the line continuation character backtick (`` ` ``) for readability purposes, so we can align each parameter on the same position each line.

Let's discuss some of these highlighted options in detail:

| Parameter | Explanation |
|---|---|
| -Initialize | Specifies the backup set contained in the file or backup device will be overwritten |
| -FormatMedia | Overwrites existing media header information, and creates a new media set |
| -SkipTapeHeader | Skip checking backup tape expiration |
| -MirrorDevices | Allows backup on Mirrored Media Sets; accepts a `BackupDeviceList` array |

## There's more...

To learn more about Mirrored Backup Media Sets, hardware requirements, and related tasks, visit http://msdn.microsoft.com/en-us/library/ms175053.aspx.

## See also

- ▸ The *Creating a full backup* recipe.
- ▸ The *Creating a differential backup* recipe.
- ▸ The *Creating a transaction log backup* recipe.
- ▸ The *Creating a filegroup backup* recipe.

# Creating a differential backup

This recipe will discuss how you can create a differential backup on your database.

## Getting ready

We will use the AdventureWorks2014 database for this recipe. We will create a differential compressed backup of the database to a timestamped .bak file in the C:\Backup folder. Feel free to use a database of your choice for this task.

The T-SQL syntax that will be generated by this PowerShell recipe will look like this:

```
BACKUP DATABASE [AdventureWorks2014]
TO  DISK = N'C:\Backup\AdventureWorks2014_Diff_20150314092409.bak'
WITH  DIFFERENTIAL , NOFORMAT, INIT,
NAME = N'AdventureWorks2014 Diff Backup',
NOSKIP, REWIND, NOUNLOAD, COMPRESSION,
STATS = 10, CHECKSUM
```

## How to do it...

Let's list the steps required to create a differential database backup:

1. Open **PowerShell ISE** as administrator.

2. Import the SQLPS module as follows:

```
#import SQL Server module
Import-Module SQLPS -DisableNameChecking
```

3. Add the following script and run:

```
$instanceName = "localhost"
$server = New-Object -TypeName
Microsoft.SqlServer.Management.Smo.Server -ArgumentList
$instanceName

$databasename = "AdventureWorks2014"
$timestamp = Get-Date -format yyyyMMddHHmmss
$backupfolder = "C:\Backup\"
$backupfile = "$($databasename)_Diff_$($timestamp).bak"
$diffBackupFile = Join-Path $backupfolder $backupfile

#note that we are using backticks in this command
#to allow for a newline for each parameter
#to clearly show parameters used
Backup-SqlDatabase    `
-ServerInstance $instanceName `
-Database $databasename `
-BackupFile $diffBackupFile `
-Checksum `
-Initialize `
-Incremental `
-BackupSetName "$databasename Diff Backup" `
-CompressionOption On
```

4. Confirm by reading the backup header. Add the following script and run:

```
#confirm by reading the header
#backup type for differential is 5
#this is a block of code you would want to put
#in a function so you can use anytime
$smoRestore = New-Object
Microsoft.SqlServer.Management.Smo.Restore
$smoRestore.Devices.AddDevice($diffBackupFile,
[Microsoft.SqlServer.Management.Smo.DeviceType]::File)
$smoRestore.ReadBackupHeader($server)
$smoRestore.ReadFileList($server)
```

## How it works...

A differential backup captures all changes to a database since the last full backup. Creating a differential in PowerShell is very similar to creating a full backup using the `Backup-SqlDatabase` cmdlet, with a slight change in the set of options that need to be specified. The code is as follows:

```
Backup-SqlDatabase  `
-ServerInstance $instanceName  `
-Database $databasename  `
-BackupFile $diffBackupFile  `
-Checksum  `
-Initialize  `
-Incremental  `
-BackupSetName "$databasename Diff Backup"  `
-CompressionOption On
```

The one thing that differentiates a full and differential backup is the `-Incremental` option.

More information about options used with the `Backup-SqlDatabase` cmdlet are explained in more detail in the *Create a full backup* recipe.

## There's more...

To do a differential backup using SMO, the code will be similar to the SMO code you would use with a full backup; just add one more line:

```
$smoBackup.Incremental = $true
```

Check out a detailed example and explanation of how to use SMO for backups instead of the `Backup-SqlDatabase` cmdlet in the recipe *Create a full backup*.

## See also

▶ The *Creating a full backup* recipe.

▶ The *Creating a backup on Mirrored Media Sets* recipe.

▶ The *Creating a transaction log backup* recipe.

▶ The *Creating a filegroup backup* recipe.

# Creating a transaction log backup

In this recipe, we will create a transaction log backup.

## Getting ready

We will use the `AdventureWorks2014` database for this recipe. We will create a timestamped transaction log backup file in the `C:\Backup` folder. Feel free to use a database of your choice for this task.

Ensure that the recovery model of the database you are backing up is either `Full` or `BulkLogged`. You can use the recipe *Changing database recovery model* as a reference. Execute the following command to query the current recovery model setting of your database:

```
$database.DatabaseOptions.RecoveryModel
```

You can also check this using SQL Server Management Studio. The steps are as follows:

1. Log in to SSMS.
2. Expand **Databases** and right-click on **AdventureWorks2014**.
3. Go to **Properties | Options** and check the **Recovery Model** value.

The T-SQL syntax that will be generated by this PowerShell recipe will look similar to this:

```
BACKUP LOG [AdventureWorks2014]
TO   DISK = N'C:\Backup\AdventureWorks2014_Txn_20150314235319.bak'
 WITH NOFORMAT, NOINIT, NOSKIP, REWIND, NOUNLOAD, STATS = 10
```

## How to do it...

Let's list the steps required to create a transaction log backup:

1. Open **PowerShell ISE** as administrator.
2. Import the `SQLPS` module as follows:

   ```
   #import SQL Server module
   Import-Module SQLPS -DisableNameChecking
   ```

3. Add the following script and run:

   ```
   $instanceName = "localhost"
   $server = New-Object -TypeName
   Microsoft.SqlServer.Management.Smo.Server -ArgumentList
   $instanceName
   ```

```
#create a transaction log backup
$databasename = "AdventureWorks2014"
$timestamp = Get-Date -format yyyyMMddHHmmss
$backupfolder = "C:\Backup\"
$backupfile = "$($databasename)_Txn_$($timestamp).bak"
$txnBackupFile = Join-Path $backupfolder $backupfile

#note that we are using backticks in this command
#to allow for a newline for each parameter
#to clearly show parameters used
Backup-SqlDatabase `
-BackupAction Log `
-ServerInstance $instanceName `
-Database $databasename `
-BackupFile $txnBackupFile
```

## How it works...

Transaction log backups are only permitted if the database you are backing up is in either the `Full` or `BulkLogged` recovery model. To create a transaction log backup using the `Backup-SqlDatabase` cmdlet, there is one option that must be specified:

```
Backup-SqlDatabase `
-BackupAction Log `
-ServerInstance $instanceName `
-Database $databasename `
-BackupFile $txnBackupFile
```

When backing up databases, one of the important parameters is `BackupAction`. It accepts three valid values: `Database`, `Files`, and `Log`.

You can also optionally use the fully qualified name of the `BackupActionType` enumeration:

```
-BackupAction
([Microsoft.SqlServer.Management.Smo.BackupActionType]::Log
```

The following table lists some additional options that you can specify when doing transaction log backups:

| Parameter | Explanation |
|---|---|
| -NoRecovery | This is required when you are taking tail log backups; it puts the database in the `Restoring` state, and the log is not truncated. |
| -LogTruncationType | This accepts an SMO `BackupTruncateLogType` enumeration value: `NoTruncate`, `Truncate`, or `TruncateOnly`. |

## There's more...

Tail log backups will contain any log records that have not been backed up yet. These backups are usually taken in the event of a disaster, or just before a restore operation. Taking a tail log backup leaves the database in a `Restoring` state, that is, in an inaccessible state to prevent further changes.

To learn more about tail log backups, visit `http://msdn.microsoft.com/en-us/library/ms179314.aspx`.

## See also

▸ The *Creating a backup on Mirrored Media Sets* recipe.

▸ The *Creating a full backup* recipe.

▸ The *Creating a differential backup* recipe.

▸ The *Creating a filegroup backup* recipe.

# Creating a filegroup backup

In this recipe, we will create a filegroup backup using the `Backup-SqlDatabase` PowerShell cmdlet.

## Getting ready

For testing purposes, let's create a small sample database called `StudentDB` that contains a couple of filegroups called `FG1` and `FG2`. Each filegroup will have two data files, which will be saved in the `C:\Temp` folder.

Open up SQL Server Management Studio and run the following script:

```
CREATE DATABASE [StudentDB]
 ON  PRIMARY
( NAME = N'StudentDB', FILENAME = N'C:\Temp\StudentDB.mdf'),
 FILEGROUP [FG1]
( NAME = N'StudentData1', FILENAME = N'C:\Temp\StudentData1.ndf'),
( NAME = N'StudentData2', FILENAME = N'C:\Temp\StudentData2.ndf'),
 FILEGROUP [FG2]
( NAME = N'StudentData3', FILENAME = N'C:\Temp\StudentData3.ndf')
 LOG ON
( NAME = N'StudentDB_log', FILENAME = N'C:\Temp\StudentDB.ldf')
GO
```

We will use this database to do our filegroup backup. Feel free to substitute this with a database that already exists in your instance which already has filegroups.

## How to do it...

These are the steps required to create a filegroup backup:

1. Open **PowerShell ISE** as administrator.

2. Import the SQLPS module as follows:

   ```
   #import SQL Server module
   Import-Module SQLPS -DisableNameChecking
   ```

3. Add the following script and run:

   ```
   $instanceName = "localhost"
   $server = New-Object -TypeName
   Microsoft.SqlServer.Management.Smo.Server -ArgumentList
   $instanceName

   $databasename = "StudentDB"
   $timestamp = Get-Date -format yyyyMMddHHmmss

   #create a file to backup FG1 filegroup
   $backupfolder = "C:\Backup\"
   $backupfile = "$($databasename)_FG1_$($timestamp).bak"
   $fgBackupFile = Join-Path $backupfolder $backupfile

   #note that we are using backticks in this command
   #to allow for a newline for each parameter
   #to clearly show parameters used
   Backup-SqlDatabase `
   -BackupAction Files `
   -DatabaseFileGroup "FG1" `
   -ServerInstance $instanceName `
   -Database $databasename `
   -BackupFile $fgBackupFile `
   -Checksum `
   -Initialize `
   -BackupSetName "$databasename FG1 Backup" `
   -CompressionOption On

   #confirm by reading the header
   #backup type for files is 4
   #this is a block of code you would want to put
   ```

```
#in a function so you can use anytime
$smoRestore = New-Object
Microsoft.SqlServer.Management.Smo.Restore
$smoRestore.Devices.AddDevice($fgBackupFile,
[Microsoft.SqlServer.Management.Smo.DeviceType]::File)

$smoRestore.ReadBackupHeader($server)
```

## How it works...

Backing up filegroups can be considered a practical alternative for **Very Large Databases** (**VLDBs**), where a full backup can take up impractical amounts of space and time. With filegroup backups, you can strategize which filegroups to back up more frequently and which ones less frequently. Filegroup backups also enable you to take advantage of online piecemeal restores for Enterprise Edition of SQL Server, starting with SQL Server 2005.

 See the *Performing an online piecemeal restore* recipe for more details

In our recipe, we chose to backup `FG1`. Our main backup command looks like this:

```
Backup-SqlDatabase `
-BackupAction Files `
-DatabaseFileGroup "FG1" `
-ServerInstance $instanceName `
-Database $databasename `
-BackupFile $fgBackupFile `
-Checksum `
-Initialize `
-BackupSetName "$databasename FG1 Backup" `
-CompressionOption On;
```

Notice the highlighted lines of code. These lines enable the filegroup backups. In `BackupAction`, we have to specify `Files`. The other options for `BackupAction` are `Database` and `Log`.

Once we have specified we want `Files`, we should also pass the filegroup name we want to back up using the `DatabaseFileGroup` parameter.

## There's more...

To learn more about backing up files and filegroups, visit `http://msdn.microsoft.com/en-us/library/ms179401.aspx`.

## See also

- ▶ The *Creating a backup on Mirrored Media Sets* recipe.
- ▶ The *Creating a full backup* recipe.
- ▶ The *Creating a differential backup* recipe.
- ▶ The *Creating a transaction log backup* recipe.
- ▶ The *Performing an online piecemeal restore* recipe.

# Restoring a database to a point-in-time

In this recipe, we will use the different backup files which we have to restore to a point-in-time.

## Getting ready

In this recipe, we will use the `SampleDB` database. The `SampleDB` database has a single filegroup that contains a single data file. We will restore this database to another SQL Server instance, and to a point-in-time using three different backup files from three different backup types:

- ▶ Full backup
- ▶ Differential backup
- ▶ Transaction log backup

You can use the following script to create your files in `B04525 - Ch05 - 10 - Restoring a Database to a Point in Time - Prep.ps1` (this is available in the code bundle available with the book), which is included in the downloadable files for this book. The prep file will perform the following tasks:

1. Create a sample database called `SampleDB`.

2. Create a table called `Record` inside `SampleDB`, which will contain a date/time column that will capture when records are inserted. This column will help verify that our point-in-time restore works.

3. Insert records into the `Record` table at one-minute intervals. This is what your table should look like after the prep file finishes executing:

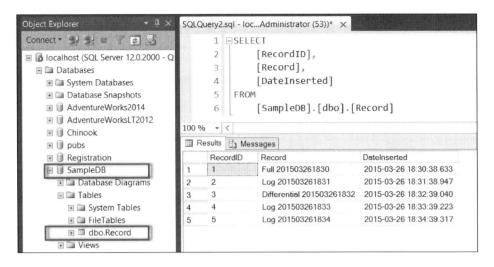

4. Create a full, differential log file and three transaction log backups, which will be stored in a local folder `C:\Backup\`. Each backup file will be timestamped. The following screenshot shows the result of running the prep file. Your files should be similar, just with different timestamp values.

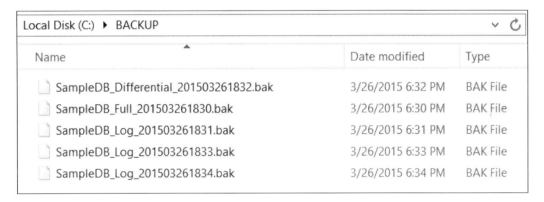

For our recipe, we will restore the database to a new database called `SampleDB_Restored`, up to `2015-03-26 18:33:40`. This means after the point-in-time restore, we should have only four records in the `Record` table:

▶ `Full 201503261830`

▶ `Log 2015032618301`

▶ `Differential 201503261832`

▶ `Log 201503261833`

Again, feel free to substitute this database with your preferred database in your development environment.

## How to do it...

To restore to a point in time using a full, differential log file and several transaction log files, follow these steps:

1. Open **PowerShell ISE** as administrator.

2. Import the SQLPS module as follows:

```
#import SQL Server module
Import-Module SQLPS -DisableNameChecking
```

3. Add the following script and run:

```
$instanceName = "localhost"
$server = New-Object -TypeName Microsoft.SqlServer.Management.Smo.
Server
-ArgumentList $instanceName

$originalDBName = "SampleDB"
$restoredDBName = "SampleDB_Restored"

#location of backups
$backupfilefolder = "C:\Backup\"

#change this to your restore point
$restorepoint = "2015-03-26 18:33:40"

#remove restored database if already exists
if($server.Databases[$restoredDBName])
{
    $server.KillDatabase($restoredDBName)
}


#look for the last full backupfile
#alternatively, you can specify filename
$fullBackupFile =
Get-ChildItem $backupfilefolder -Filter "*Full*" |
Sort-Object -Property LastWriteTime -Descending |
Select-Object -Last 1

#read the filelist info within the backup file
```

```
#so that we know which other files we need to restore
$smoRestore = New-Object
Microsoft.SqlServer.Management.Smo.Restore

$smoRestore.Devices.AddDevice($fullBackupFile.FullName,
[Microsoft.SqlServer.Management.Smo.DeviceType]::File)

$filelist = $smoRestore.ReadFileList($server)

#we are putting the files we read from the filelist
#in an array in case we have multiple data
#and log files associated with the database
$relocateFileList = @()
$relocatePath = "C:\Program Files\Microsoft SQL
Server\MSSQL12.MSSQLSERVER\MSSQL\DATA"

<#
#an alternative to using a static path
#is to dynamically assign the path
#using the following code:
$relocatePath = $server.DefaultFile
if ($relocatePath.Length -eq 0) {
 $ relocatePath = $server.Information.MasterDBPath
}
#>

foreach($file in $fileList)
{
    #restore to different file name since
    #the original and new database will
    #be stored in the same data folder
    $relocateFile = Join-Path $relocatePath
(Split-Path $file.PhysicalName
-Leaf).Replace($originalDBName, $restoredDBName)

    #add to array
    $relocateFileList += New-Object Microsoft.SqlServer.
Management.Smo.RelocateFile
($file.LogicalName, $relocateFile)
}

#note that we have backticks in the
#Restore-SqlDatabase statements to make
#the statement easier to read
```

```
#===========================================================
#restore the full backup to the new instance name
#===========================================================
#note also we have a NoRecovery option because
#we have additional files to restore
Restore-SqlDatabase `
-ReplaceDatabase `
-ServerInstance $instanceName `
-Database $restoredDBName `
-BackupFile $fullBackupFile.FullName `
-RelocateFile $relocateFileList `
-NoRecovery


#===========================================================
#restore last differential
#note the database is still in Restoring State
#===========================================================
$diffBackupFile =
Get-ChildItem $backupfilefolder -Filter "*Diff*" |
Where-Object LastWriteTime -ge
$fullBackupFile.LastWriteTime |
Sort-Object -Property LastWriteTime -Descending |
Select-Object -Last 1

Restore-SqlDatabase `
-ReplaceDatabase `
-ServerInstance $instanceName `
-Database $restoreddbname `
-BackupFile $diffBackupFile.FullName `
-NoRecovery


#===========================================================
#restore all transaction log backups from last
#differential, stop at 2015-03-24 18:33:40,
#just after the 4th record was inserted
#===========================================================

#get all transaction log files after differential
Get-ChildItem $backupfilefolder -Filter "*Log*" |
Where-Object LastWriteTime -gt
$diffBackupFile.LastWriteTime |
Sort-Object -Property LastWriteTime |
```

```
ForEach-Object {
   $logfile = $_

   #restore with NoRecovery if before restorepoint
   if ($logfile.LastWriteTime -lt $restorepoint) {
        Restore-SqlDatabase `
        -ReplaceDatabase `
        -ServerInstance $instanceName `
        -Database $restoreddbname `
        -BackupFile $logfile.FullName `
        -NoRecovery
   }
   else
   {
        #restore last transaction log file
        #with Recovery
        Restore-SqlDatabase `
        -ReplaceDatabase `
        -ServerInstance $instanceName `
        -Database $restoreddbname `
        -BackupFile $logfile.FullName `
        -ToPointInTime $restorepoint

        #exit out of loop
        break
   }
}
```

## How it works...

In this recipe, we are using the `Restore-SqlDatabase` cmdlet, the counterpart of the `Backup-SqlDatabase` cmdlet that was introduced in SQL Server 2012.

Let's get a high-level overview of how to perform a point-in-time restore, and then we can break it down and explain the pieces involved in this recipe:

1. Gather your backup files. Identify upto the last transaction log backup file that contains the point you want to restore to.

2. Restore the last good full backup with NORECOVERY.

3. Restore the last good differential backup taken after the full backup you just restored with NORECOVERY.

4. Restore the transaction logs taken after your differential backup.

- ❑ You can restore **up to and including** the log backup that contains the data to the point in time you want to restore WITH NORECOVERY. You need to restore the last log backup to a point in time, that is, you need to specify up to when to restore. Lastly, restore the database WITH RECOVERY to make the database accessible and ready to use.

- ❑ Alternatively, you can restore all transaction log backup files **before** the log backup that contains the data to the point in time you want to restore WITH NORECOVERY. Next, restore the last log backup WITH RECOVERY to a point in time, that is, you need to specify up to when to restore.

## Gathering your backup files

You need to collect your backup files. They don't necessarily have to live in the same folder or drive, but it would be ideal as it can simplify your restore script; you will have a uniform folder/ drive to refer to. You will also need read permissions for these files.

In our recipe, we simplified these steps. We have collected our full, differential log file and transaction log backup files and stored them in the C:\Backup\ folder for ease of access. If your backup files reside in different locations, you will just need to adjust the directory references in your script appropriately.

Once you have the backup files, assuming you follow a file naming convention, you can filter out all the full backups in your directory. In our sample, we are using the convention databasename_type_timestamp.bak. For this scenario, we can extract that one full backup file by specifying the keyword or pattern in our filename. We use the Get-ChildItem cmdlet to filter for the latest full backup file:

```
#look for the last full backupfile
#alternatively, you can specify filename
$fullBackupFile =
Get-ChildItem $backupfilefolder -Filter "*Full*" |
Sort-Object -Property LastWriteTime -Descending |
Select-Object -Last 1
```

Once you have the full backup handle, you can read filelist, which is stored in that backup file. You can use the ReadFileList method that is available with an SMO Restore object. Reading the filelist can help you automate, by extracting the filenames of the data and log files you will need to restore.

```
#read the filelist info within the backup file
#so that we know which other files we need to restore
$smoRestore = New-Object
Microsoft.SqlServer.Management.Smo.Restore
```

```
$smoRestore.Devices.AddDevice($fullBackupFile.FullName,
[Microsoft.SqlServer.Management.Smo.DeviceType]::File)

$filelist = $smoRestore.ReadFileList($server)
```

When reading the filelist, you can extract the type of file that is stored, as shown in the following screenshot (highlighted with a box outline):

```
LogicalName            : SampleDB
PhysicalName           : C:\Program Files\Microsoft SQL Server\MSSQL12.MSSQLSERVER\MSSQL\DATA\SampleDB.mdf
Type                   : D
FileGroupName          : PRIMARY
Size                   : 3342336
MaxSize                : 35184372080640
FileId                 : 1
CreateLSN              : 0
DropLSN                : 0
UniqueId               : 767dbf31-c17e-4dce-88ba-2745b8d1c83e
ReadOnlyLSN            : 0
ReadWriteLSN           : 0
BackupSizeInBytes      : 2424832
SourceBlockSize        : 512
FileGroupId            : 1
LogGroupGUID           :
DifferentialBaseLSN    : 0
DifferentialBaseGUID   : 00000000-0000-0000-0000-000000000000
IsReadOnly             : False
IsPresent              : True
TDEThumbprint          :
```

The different types of backup files are:

- L is log file
- D is database file
- F is FullText catalog

## Restoring the latest good full backup with NORECOVERY

The first step in restore operations is to restore the latest, good, full backup. This provides you with a baseline that you can restore additional files to. The NORECOVERY option is very important, as it preserves (or does not roll back) uncommitted transactions and allows additional files to be restored. We will be using the NORECOVERY option throughout our restore process.

Because the full backup is always the first file that needs to be restored, all the preparatory work required when moving files also happens at this stage.

For our recipe, we want to restore the database in the same instance as the original. For this reason, we will need to specify different filenames for the restored database's data and log files:

```
(Split-Path $file.PhysicalName -Leaf).
Replace($originalDBName, $restoredDBName)
```

The `Split-Path` parameter with the `-Leaf` switch takes the original file's full path and extracts only the file name. The `Replace` method is then used on the extracted string to replace the original database reference with the new, restored database name.

Our array contains the `Microsoft.SqlServer.Management.Smo.RelocateFile` objects, which will contain the logical and (relocated) physical names of our database files. The full script block that builds the new file list is as follows:

```
#we are putting the files we read from the filelist
#in an array in case we have multiple data
#and log files associated with the database
$relocateFileList = @()
$relocatePath = "C:\Program Files\Microsoft SQL
Server\MSSQL12.MSSQLSERVER\MSSQL\DATA"

foreach($file in $fileList)
{
    #restore to different file name since
    #the original and new database will
    #be stored in the same data folder
    $relocateFile = Join-Path $relocatePath (Split-Path $file.
PhysicalName -Leaf).Replace($originalDBName, $restoredDBName)

    #add to array
    $relocateFileList += New-Object Microsoft.SqlServer.Management.
Smo.RelocateFile($file.LogicalName, $relocateFile)
}
```

To restore the database, we are going to use the `Restore-SqlDatabase` cmdlet. There are two important options that need to be specified here: `RelocateFile` and `NoRecovery`. `RelocateFile` specifies the new file names, and `NoRecovery` specifies that there are additional files to be restored after this:

```
#restore the full backup to the new instance name
#note we have a NoRecovery option, because we have
#additional files to restore
Restore-SqlDatabase `
-ReplaceDatabase `
-ServerInstance $instanceName `
-Database $restoredDBName `
-BackupFile $fullBackupFile.FullName `
-RelocateFile $relocateFileList `
-NoRecovery
```

## Restoring the last good differential backup taken after the full backup you just restored with NORECOVERY

Once the full backup is restored, we can add the last good differential backup following our full backup. This is going to be a less involved process, because at this point we've already restored our base database and relocated our files. We need to restore the differential backup NORECOVERY to prevent uncommitted transactions from being rolled back. The code is as follows:

```
$diffBackupFile =
Get-ChildItem $backupfilefolder -Filter "*Diff*" |
Where-Object LastWriteTime -ge $fullBackupFile.LastWriteTime |
Sort-Object -Property LastWriteTime -Descending |
Select-Object -Last 1

Restore-SqlDatabase `
-ReplaceDatabase `
-ServerInstance $instanceName `
-Database $restoreddbname `
-BackupFile $diffBackupFile.FullName `
-NoRecovery
```

You may, or may not, have a differential backup file in your environment. If you don't have one, don't worry. It does not affect the recoverability of the database as long as you have all the transaction log backup files intact and available for restore.

## Restoring the transaction logs taken after your differential backup

After we restore our differential backup file, we can start restoring our transaction log backup files. These transaction log backup files should be the ones following your differential backup. You may or may not need the complete set of log files following your differential backup. If you need to restore up to the point of a database crash, you will need to restore all transaction log backups including the tail log backup. If not, you will only need the backup files up to the time you want to restore.

For our recipe, we identify all the transaction log files with timestamp after our differential backup file, listing the oldest one first, to the newest one.

 Note that we used a specific naming convention for our log files (that is, adding the word Log on each one) to allow us to easily filter these files:

```
Get-ChildItem $backupfilefolder -Filter "*Log*" |
Where-Object LastWriteTime -gt $diffBackupFile.LastWriteTime |
Sort-Object -Property LastWriteTime
```

We then go through all of the files before the restore point and restore them with `NoRecovery`. The code is as follows:

```
ForEach-Object {
    $logfile = $_

    #restore with NoRecovery if before restorepoint
    if ($logfile.LastWriteTime -lt $restorepoint) {
        Restore-SqlDatabase `
        -ReplaceDatabase `
        -ServerInstance $instanceName `
        -Database $restoreddbname `
        -BackupFile $logfile.FullName `
        -NoRecovery
    }
    else
    {
        #restore last transaction log file
        #with Recovery
        Restore-SqlDatabase `
        -ReplaceDatabase `
        -ServerInstance $instanceName `
        -Database $restoreddbname `
        -BackupFile $logfile.FullName `
        -ToPointInTime $restorepoint

        #exit out of loop
        break
    }
}
```

Once we get to the first file past the restore point, we restore this file with `Recovery` to our specified point-in-time, and exit out of the loop. The code is as follows:

```
ForEach-Object {
    $logfile = $_

    #restore with NoRecovery if before restorepoint
    if ($logfile.LastWriteTime -lt $restorepoint) {
        Restore-SqlDatabase `
        -ReplaceDatabase `
        -ServerInstance $instanceName `
        -Database $restoreddbname `
        -BackupFile $logfile.FullName `
        -NoRecovery
```

```
    }
    else
    {
        #restore last transaction log file
        #with Recovery
        Restore-SqlDatabase `
        -ReplaceDatabase `
        -ServerInstance $instanceName `
        -Database $restoreddbname `
        -BackupFile $logfile.FullName `
        -ToPointInTime $restorepoint

        #exit out of loop
        break
    }
}
```

At this point, once the script breaks out of the loop, all the files up to the restore point have been restored. The database should also be accessible at this point, and all uncommitted transactions should have already been rolled back.

An alternative to the preceding method is to restore all transaction log files with the NoRecovery switch. This could be a safer approach because if we accidentally restore a backup file WITH RECOVERY, the only way to correct it is to redo the entire restore process. This may not be such a big deal for smaller databases, but this could be very time consuming for bigger databases.

If you are going with this method of restoring all log files with NoRecovery, once you have confirmed all the files you need, have been restored, you can restore the database with RECOVERY. One way to achieve this in our recipe is by using a T-SQL statement, and passing the following statement to the Invoke-SqlCmd cmdlet:

```
#get the database out of Restoring state
#make the database accessible
$sql = "RESTORE DATABASE $restoreddbname WITH RECOVERY"
Invoke-Sqlcmd -ServerInstance $instanceName -Query $sql
```

The RESTORE DATABASE command takes the database from the Restoring state to an accessible and ready-to-use state. The RESTORE command rolls back all unfinished transactions and readies the database for use.

## There's more...

As a reference, you can check out how to do point-in-time restore using T-SQL. Visit http://msdn.microsoft.com/en-us/library/ms179451.aspx.

## See also

> ▸ The *Creating a backup on Mirrored Media Sets* recipe.
>
> ▸ The *Creating a full backup* recipe.
>
> ▸ The *Creating a differential backup* recipe.
>
> ▸ The *Creating a transaction log backup* recipe.
>
> ▸ The *Performing an online piecemeal restore* recipe.

# Performing an online piecemeal restore

In this recipe, we will perform an online piecemeal restore.

## Getting ready

We will back up a test database called StudentDB database, which has three filegroups: one primary filegroup and two custom filegroups, FG1 and FG2, in this recipe. FG1 and FG2 will have one secondary data file stored in the C:\DATA folder.

You can use the following script to create your files B04525 - Ch05 - 11 - Performing an Online PieceMeal Restore - Prep.ps1 (this is available in the code bundle available with the book), which is included in the downloadable files for this book. After the script is executed, you should see the following database:

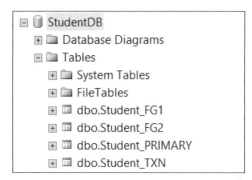

This is how the tables will be structured:

| Table | Filegroup | Data file name | Data file location |
|---|---|---|---|
| Student_PRIMARY | PRIMARY | StudentDB.mdf | Default data directory |
| Student_FG1 | FG1 | Student_FG1_ data | C:\DATA |
| Student_FG2 | FG2 | Student_FG1_ data | C:\DATA |
| Student_TXN | PRIMARY | StudentDB.mdf | Default data directory |

For our recipe, we will restore only the PRIMARY filegroup, and restore filegroup FG2 to a database called StudentDB_RESTORED in our default SQL Server instance. At the end of our task, only the Student_PRIMARY and Student_FG2 tables will be accessible.

Feel free to substitute this with a database available in your development environment that already has separate filegroups and filegroup backups.

## How to do it...

Let's list the steps required to complete the task:

1. Open **PowerShell ISE** as administrator.

2. Import the SQLPS module as follows:

```
#import SQL Server module
Import-Module SQLPS -DisableNameChecking
```

3. Add the following script and run:

```
$instanceName = "localhost"
$server = New-Object -TypeName
Microsoft.SqlServer.Management.Smo.Server
-ArgumentList $instanceName

$backupfolder = "C:\BACKUP\"
$originalDBName = "StudentDB"
$restoredDBName = "StudentDB_Restored"

#folder where data files will be stored
$relocatePath = "C:\Program Files\Microsoft SQL
Server\MSSQL12.MSSQLSERVER\MSSQL\DATA"
```

```
#for this piecemeal restore, we need to specify
#files to restore
#primary filegroup
$primaryfgbackup = "C:\BACKUP\StudentDB_PRIMARY.bak"

#additional filegroup(s) to restore, and filegroup name
$fg2backup = "C:\BACKUP\StudentDB_FG2.bak"
$fg2name = "Student_FG2_data"

#transaction log backup
$txnbackup = "C:\BACKUP\StudentDB_TXN.bak"


#=========================================
#primary fg
#=========================================
#we need to restore to different file name
#since the original and new database will
#be stored in the same data folder
$relocateFileList = @()

$smoRestore = New-Object
Microsoft.SqlServer.Management.Smo.Restore
$smoRestore.Devices.AddDevice($primaryfgbackup ,
[Microsoft.SqlServer.Management.Smo.DeviceType]::File)

#get all the files specified in this backup, and
#change the filename
$smoRestore.ReadFileList($server) |
ForEach-Object {
        $file = $_
        $relocateFile = Join-Path $relocatePath
(Split-Path $file.PhysicalName
-Leaf).Replace($originalDBName, $restoredDBName)
        $relocateFileList += New-Object
Microsoft.SqlServer.Management.Smo.RelocateFile
($file.LogicalName, $relocateFile)
}


#=========================================
#restore primary fg
#Partial switch must be used if restoring primary fg
#needs to be only mdf and ldf
#=========================================
Restore-SqlDatabase `
-Partial `
```

```
-ReplaceDatabase `
-ServerInstance $instanceName `
-Database $restoredDBName `
-BackupFile $primaryfgbackup `
-RelocateFile $relocateFileList `
-NoRecovery


#=======================================
#fg2
#=======================================
$relocateFileList = @()

#for the custom filegroup we want to restore, we want to
#relocate only that filegroup's data files
$smoRestore = New-Object Microsoft.SqlServer.Management.Smo.
Restore
$smoRestore.Devices.AddDevice($fg2backup ,
[Microsoft.SqlServer.Management.Smo.DeviceType]::File)


$smoRestore.ReadFileList($server) |
ForEach-Object {
    $file = $_

    #restore only FG2
    if($file.Type -eq "D" -and $file.FileGroupName
-ne "PRIMARY" -and $file.LogicalName -eq $fg2name)
    {
        $relocateFile = Join-Path $relocatePath
(Split-Path $file.PhysicalName -Leaf).Replace($originalDBName,
$restoredDBName)
        $relocateFileList += New-Object
Microsoft.SqlServer.Management.Smo.RelocateFile
($file.LogicalName, $relocateFile)
    }
}


#=======================================
#restore  fg2
#we don't need the Partial switch anymore
#=======================================
Restore-SqlDatabase   `
-ReplaceDatabase `
-ServerInstance $instanceName `
-Database $restoredDBName `
-BackupFile $fg2backup `
```

```
-RelocateFile $relocateFileList `
-NoRecovery

#=========================================
#restore transaction log backup
#this will restore with recovery
#=========================================
Restore-SqlDatabase `
-ReplaceDatabase `
-ServerInstance $instanceName `
-Database $restoredDBName `
-BackupFile $txnbackup
```

## How it works...

Online piecemeal restore is an Enterprise feature available since SQL Server 2005. This type of restore, also referred to as a partial restore, allows you to stage your restores. Each restore sequence can turn one or more filegroups online, leaving the rest offline. The power of this feature is that as soon as your first filegroups are restored, the objects you have in this filegroup become accessible to your end users or applications.

The first thing you will need to do is line up your files. You will need to specify where the PRIMARY filegroup back up is, any user filegroups you want to restore, and the transaction log backup files. In our recipe, we are also restoring the database to a different instance, so we will need to relocate our database files. For this reason, we must specify what the filegroup names are for the filegroup we are restoring. The code is as follows:

```
#primary filegroup
$primaryfgbackup = "C:\BACKUP\StudentDB_PRIMARY.bak"

#additional filegroup(s) to restore, and filegroup name
$fg2backup = "C:\ BACKUP\StudentDB_FG2.bak"
$fg2name = "Student_FG2_data"

#transaction log backup
$txnbackup = "C:\ BACKUP\StudentDB_TXN.bak"
```

Once we have the files lined up, we need to create an array that contains the files we are relocating. Since we are saving these files in the same folder as the original database's files, we will need to rename our files. In our recipe, we simply replace the reference to the original database name to the new restored name using the string function Replace:

```
$relocateFileList = @()

$smoRestore = New-Object
Microsoft.SqlServer.Management.Smo.Restore
```

```
$smoRestore.Devices.AddDevice($primaryfgbackup ,
[Microsoft.SqlServer.Management.Smo.DeviceType]::File)

#get all the files specified in this backup, and
#change the filename
$smoRestore.ReadFileList($server) |
ForEach-Object {
        $file = $_
        $relocateFile = Join-Path $relocatePath (Split-Path
$file.PhysicalName -Leaf).Replace($originalDBName,
$restoredDBName)
        $relocateFileList += New-Object
Microsoft.SqlServer.Management.Smo.RelocateFile($file.LogicalName,
$relocateFile)
}
```

We can then use our `Restore-SqlDatabase` cmdlet to restore the primary filegroup first with `NORECOVERY`. When restoring the `PRIMARY` filegroup, you will need to specify the option `Partial`. This `Partial` option indicates that we want to start a new piecemeal restore. We only need this in the first restore sequence. The code is as follows:

```
#========================================
#restore primary fg
#partial must be used if restoring primary fg
#needs to be only mdf and ldf
#========================================
Restore-SqlDatabase `
-Partial `
-ReplaceDatabase `
-ServerInstance $instanceName `
-Database $restoredDBName `
-BackupFile $primaryfgbackup `
-RelocateFile $relocateFileList `
-NoRecovery
```

You have the option to bring the database online already, after the primary filegroup is restored. If you are working in simple recovery model, you can simply omit the –NoRecovery option. If your database is in full recovery model, you will need to restore the transaction log backup files first, and omit the –NoRecovery option in the last transaction log backup you are going to restore.

Check out how online piecemeal restores with full recovery model can be accomplished using T-SQL:

https://msdn.microsoft.com/en-us/library/ms175541.aspx

To restore the user filegroups, we are still going to use an array that contains the specific files for specific filegroup(s) we are restoring. We also still need to rename the files, because these files will live in the same path as that of the original database. The code is as follows:

```
$relocateFileList = @()

#for the custom filegroup we want to restore, we want to
#relocate only that filegroup's data files
$smoRestore = New-Object
Microsoft.SqlServer.Management.Smo.Restore
$smoRestore.Devices.AddDevice($fg2backup ,
[Microsoft.SqlServer.Management.Smo.DeviceType]::File)

$smoRestore.ReadFileList($server) |
ForEach-Object {
    $file = $_

    #restore only FG2
    if($file.Type -eq "D" -and $file.FileGroupName -ne "PRIMARY"
-and $file.LogicalName -eq $fg2name)
    {
        #rename
        $relocateFile = Join-Path $relocatePath
(Split-Path $file.PhysicalName -Leaf).Replace($originalDBName,
$restoredDBName)

        $relocateFileList += New-Object
Microsoft.SqlServer.Management.Smo.RelocateFile($file.LogicalName,
$relocateFile)
    }
}
```

Once we have the array of relocated files, we can restore our user filegroup.

Note that for this statement, we no longer need to specify the option `Partial`:

```
#=========================================
#restore  fg2
#don't need partial anymore
#=========================================
Restore-SqlDatabase `
-ReplaceDatabase `
-ServerInstance $instanceName `
-Database $restoredDBName `
-BackupFile $fg2backup `
-RelocateFile $relocateFileList `
-NoRecovery
```

Lastly, we need to restore the transaction log file(s). If there are multiple transaction log files, each transaction log file before the final transaction log file needs to be restored with `NORECOVERY`. The last transaction log file can be restored with `RECOVERY`. In PowerShell, this can be done by simply omitting the `-NoRecovery` switch. The code is as follows:

```
#========================================
#restore transaction log backup
#========================================
Restore-SqlDatabase `
-ReplaceDatabase `
-ServerInstance $instanceName `
-Database $restoreddbname `
-BackupFile $txnbackup
```

You should see something like this after you restore this sequence:

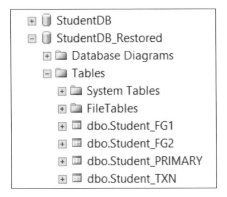

It is a little bit deceiving because it looks like the whole database is already available and accessible. However, since we only restored `FG2`, only objects in `FG2` are truly accessible. If you try to access any of the objects that reside in the unrestored filegroup, you will get an error similar to this:

**Msg 8653, Level 16, State 1, Line 2**

**The query processor is unable to produce a plan for the table or view 'Student_FG1' because the table resides in a filegroup which is not online.**

To restore the rest of your filegroups, you can use the same steps until the final filegroup is restored. Remember to always restore the filegroup and then restore the transaction log backup. Lather, rinse, and repeat.

## There's more...

To learn more about performing piecemeal restores, visit `http://msdn.microsoft.com/en-us/library/ms177425.aspx`.

## See also

▸ The *Creating a filegroup backup* recipe.

# Backing up database to Azure Blob storage

In this recipe we will back up a local database to Azure.

## Getting ready

Before we can back up our databases to Microsoft Azure Blob storage, there are a few things that need to be in place.

1. First, your Azure storage needs to be set up.

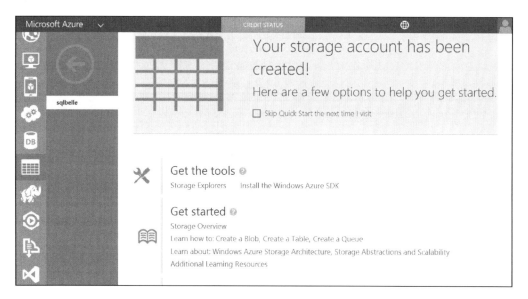

2. Second, you need to have a container.

3. Third, you need to know what your Azure storage access keys are. You can get them from your Azure storage page. The link should be at the bottom of the **storage** page screen, as shown in the following screenshot:

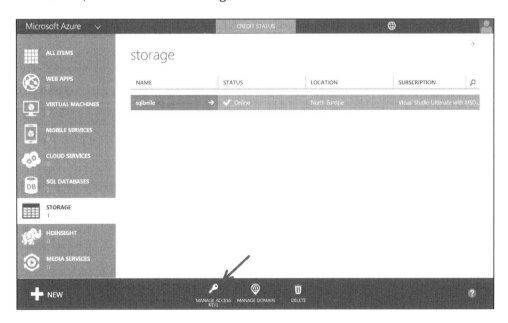

## How to do it...

The steps to back up your database to Azure Blob storage are as follows:

1. Open **PowerShell ISE** as administrator.

2. Import the `SQLPS` module as follows:

```
#import SQL Server module
Import-Module SQLPS -DisableNameChecking
```

3. If one does not already exist, create a credential to use for the remote backup:

```
$instanceName = "localhost"
$AzureStorageAccount = "replaceThisWithAzureStorageAccount"
$storageKey = "replaceThisWithYourStorageKey"
$secureString = ConvertTo-SecureString $storageKey
-AsPlainText -Force
$credentialName = "AzureCredential"

$instanceName |
New-SqlCredential -Name $credentialName  -Identity
$AzureStorageAccount -Secret $secureString
```

4. Add the following script and run:

```
#replace values specific to your Azure account
$blobContainer = "replaceWithYourContainerName"
$backupUrlContainer =
"https://$AzureStorageAccount.blob.core.windows.net/
$blobContainer/"

$server = New-Object -TypeName
Microsoft.SqlServer.Management.Smo.Server -ArgumentList
$instanceName
$databaseName = "SampleDB"

Backup-SqlDatabase `
-ServerInstance $instanceName `
-Database $databaseName `
-BackupContainer $backupUrlContainer `
-SqlCredential $credentialName `
-Compression On
```

## How it works...

Microsoft has become a major player in cloud services. In the context of SQL Server, you can now opt to back up your databases to Azure, or more specifically, Azure Blob storage.

To backup to Azure Blob storage, you must first create a credential that allows you to connect to your Azure storage account. You must create this on every instance that you're going to use remote backup in. The code is as follows:

```
$instanceName = "localhost"
$AzureStorageAccount = "replaceThisWithAzureStorageAccount"
$storageKey = "replaceThisWithYourStorageKey"
$secureString = ConvertTo-SecureString $storageKey
-AsPlainText -Force
$credentialName = "AzureCredential"

$instanceName |
New-SqlCredential -Name $credentialName  -Identity
$AzureStorageAccount -Secret $secureString
```

To perform the actual backup, you can use the existing `Backup-SqlDatabase` cmdlet. Instead of specifying a filename, you have to specify your backup URL container, which will be a combination of your storage account and your Blob container. The code is as follows:

```
#replace values specific to your Azure account
$blobContainer = "replaceWithYourContainerName"
$backupUrlContainer =
"https://$AzureStorageAccount.blob.core.windows.net/
$blobContainer/"

$server = New-Object -TypeName
Microsoft.SqlServer.Management.Smo.Server -ArgumentList
$instanceName
$databaseName = "SampleDB"

Backup-SqlDatabase `
-ServerInstance $instanceName `
-Database $databaseName `
-BackupContainer $backupUrlContainer `
-SqlCredential $credentialName `
-Compression On
```

If you want to simply script the command out and see what this looks like in T-SQL, you can add the `-Script` switch in your `Backup-SqlDatabase` command. This is what the command will look like in T-SQL:

```
BACKUP DATABASE [SampleDB]
TO  URL = N'https://azureURL/container/autogeneratedfilename.bak'
WITH  CREDENTIAL = N'AzureCredential' ,
NOFORMAT, NOINIT, NOSKIP, REWIND, NOUNLOAD,
COMPRESSION,  STATS = 10
GO
```

## There's more...

Read more about SQL Server backup to URL from the MSDN page at `https://msdn.microsoft.com/en-us/library/dn435916.aspx`.

You can see a number of examples on backing up multiple databases on Azure using PowerShell at `https://msdn.microsoft.com/en-us/library/dn223322.aspx`.

In addition, Microsoft provides guidance best practices and troubleshooting when backing up to Azure BLOB storage. Visit `https://msdn.microsoft.com/en-us/library/jj919149.aspx`.

## See also

▶ The *Restoring database from Azure Blob storage* recipe.

# Restoring database from Azure Blob storage

This recipe walks you through how to restore a database to a local instance from a backup stored in Azure.

## Getting ready

For this recipe, you need to have already performed a backup to Azure Blob storage. If you haven't already done so, you can refer to the recipe *Backing up database to Azure Blob storage* to prepare your environment.

## How to do it...

These are the steps to change the recovery model:

1. Open **PowerShell ISE** as administrator.

2. Import the `SQLPS` module as follows:

```
#import SQL Server module
Import-Module SQLPS -DisableNameChecking
```

3. Add the following script and run:

```
$AzureStorageAccount = "replaceThisWithAzureStorageAccount"
$credentialName = "AzureCredential"

#replace values specific to your Azure account
$blobContainer = "replaceWithYourContainerName"
$backupUrlContainer =
"https://$AzureStorageAccount.blob.core.windows.net/
$blobContainer/"

$backupfile = "replacethiswithyourazurefilename.bak"
$backupfileURL = $backupUrlContainer + $backupfile

$instanceName = "localhost"
$server = New-Object -TypeName Microsoft.SqlServer.Management.Smo.
Server -ArgumentList
$instanceName
$databaseName = "SampleDB"



#restore database
#note there are backticks in this command
#so we can place each parameter in its line to
#make the command more readable
Restore-SqlDatabase `
-ServerInstance $instanceName `
-Database $databaseName `
-SqlCredential $credentialName `
-BackupFile $backupfileURL `
-Verbose
```

## How it works...

Restoring a database with a backup file that is stored in Azure Blob storage will be similar to restoring a database where the backup file is restored locally, or on a shared drive. The only difference is; when the database is being restored, instead of a filename, the backup file URL needs to be provided. A credential also needs to be provided in order to access and read the backup file from Azure. The code is as follows:

```
Restore-SqlDatabase `
-ServerInstance $instanceName `
-Database $databaseName `
-SqlCredential $credentialName `
-BackupFile $backupfileURL `
-Verbose
```

If you are restoring the database to the same instance as the original database, you will need to provide the set of new file names that the restored database will use. You can achieve this using a snippet of code we've used in previous recipes that replaces references to the original database with the new database name:

```
$relocateFileList = @()
$relocatePath = "C:\Program Files\Microsoft SQL
Server\MSSQL12.MSSQLSERVER\MSSQL\DATA"

foreach($file in $fileList)
{
    #restore to different file name since
    #the original and new database will
    #be stored in the same data folder
    $relocateFile = Join-Path $relocatePath
(Split-Path $file.PhysicalName -Leaf).Replace($originalDBName,
$restoredDBName)

    #add to array
    $relocateFileList += New-Object
Microsoft.SqlServer.Management.Smo.RelocateFile
($file.LogicalName, $relocateFile)
}
```

Once the array has been populated, you can use the `-RelocateFile` parameter in the `Restore-SqlDatabase` cmdlet:

```
Restore-SqlDatabase `
-ServerInstance $instanceName `
-Database $databaseName `
-RelocateFile $relocateFileList `
-SqlCredential $credentialName `
-BackupFile $backupfileURL `
-Verbose
```

If you wanted to script the command out and see what this looks like in T-SQL, you can add the `-Script` switch in your `Restore-SqlDatabase` command. This is what the command will look like in T-SQL:

```
RESTORE DATABASE [SampleDB]
FROM  URL =
N'https://azureURL/container/autogeneratedfilename.bak'
WITH  CREDENTIAL = N'AzureCredential' ,
NOUNLOAD, STATS = 10
```

## There's more...

Read more about *Restoring From Backups Stored in Windows Azure* from the MSDN page at `https://msdn.microsoft.com/en-us/library/dn449492.aspx`.

## See also

▶ The *Backing up database to Azure Blob storage* recipe.

# 6
# Advanced Administration

In this chapter, we will cover the following topics:

- ▶ Connecting to LocalDB
- ▶ Creating a new LocalDB instance
- ▶ Listing database snapshots
- ▶ Creating a database snapshot
- ▶ Dropping a database snapshot
- ▶ Enabling FileStream
- ▶ Setting up a FileStream Filegroup
- ▶ Adding a FileTable
- ▶ Adding a full-text catalog
- ▶ Adding a full-text index
- ▶ Creating a memory-optimized table
- ▶ Creating a database master key
- ▶ Creating a certificate
- ▶ Creating symmetric and asymmetric keys
- ▶ Setting up Transparent Data Encryption

# Introduction

SQL Server matures and increases its already rich feature sets in each new version. You can now easily store unstructured data and **binary large objects** (**BLOBs**) in SQL Server using FileStream and FileTables. SQL Server also supports different levels of encryption, including column-level encryption and database-level encryption. In this chapter, we will explore how to connect and use LocalDB, set up FileStream and FileTables, configure full-text catalogs and indexes, and enable **Transparent Database Encryption** (**TDE**) in order to encrypt your whole database.

# Connecting to LocalDB

In this recipe, we will connect to the LocalDB database.

## Getting ready

LocalDB is a separate installation from your usual instance. LocalDB needs to be installed before you can follow this recipe.

You can download LocalDB with SQL Server Express from MSDN downloads at `https://www.microsoft.com/en-ca/download/details.aspx?id=42299`.

## How to do it...

Let's take a look at the steps to connect to LocalDB:

1.  Open **PowerShell ISE** as an administrator.

2.  Import the `SQLPS` module and create a new SMO Server object as follows:

    ```
    #import SQL Server module
    Import-Module SQLPS -DisableNameChecking
    ```

3.  Add the following script and run it:

    ```
    $instanceName = "(localdb)\MSSQLLocalDB"
    $server = New-Object -TypeName
    Microsoft.SqlServer.Management.Smo.Server -ArgumentList
    $instanceName

    #list all databases in localdb
    $server.Databases
    ```

# How it works...

LocalDB is a flavor of SQL Server Express that is geared toward developers. You can think of it as a stripped-down version of SQL Server Express—it is a simple installation with no instance configuration or complicated management required.

LocalDB is described by MSDN (`https://msdn.microsoft.com/en-us/library/hh510202.aspx`) as follows:

> *LocalDB is a lightweight version of Express that has all its programmability features, yet runs in user mode and has a fast, zero-configuration installation and short list of pre-requisites. Use this if you need a simple way to create and work with databases from code. It can be bundled with Application and Database Development tools like Visual Studio and or embedded with an application that needs local databases.*

When LocalDB was introduced in SQL Server 2012, you had to connect to it using the `(LocalDB)\v11.0` instance name.

In SQL Server 2014, the LocalDB instance name was changed to `MSSQLLocalDB`. To connect to it, you will have to use `(LocalDB)\MSSQLLocalDB`.

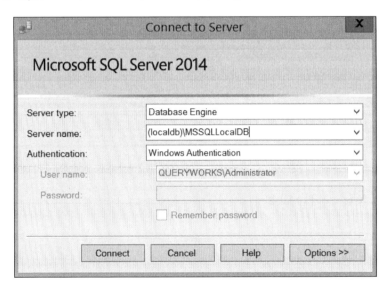

Connecting to LocalDB in PowerShell is not so different from connecting to other databases, as shown in many recipes in this book:

```
$server = New-Object -TypeName
Microsoft.SqlServer.Management.Smo.Server -ArgumentList
$instanceName
```

## There's more...

LocalDB has been introduced as an "improved" SQL Server Express

(http://blogs.msdn.com/b/sqlexpress/archive/2011/07/12/introducing-localdb-a-better-sql-express.aspx).

Alberto Morillo (@sqlcoffee) has put together a concise list of requirements, benefits, and limitations of LocalDB at http://www.sqlcoffee.com/SQLServer2012_0004.htm.

LocalDB is very similar to SQL Server **Compact Edition** (**CE**); however, there are some key differences. For example, SQL Server CE can be embedded in the application, while LocalDB cannot be embedded. There is also better support for programmatic T-SQL, such as stored procedures and CASE statements in LocalDB compared to SQL Server CE.

Erik Jensen has compiled a matrix that shows the difference between SQL Server Compact, SQL Server Express, SQL Server LocalDB, and SQLite (updated for SQL Server 2014) at http://erikej.blogspot.ca/2011/01/comparison-of-sql-server-compact-4-and.html.

## See also

▸ The *Creating a new LocalDB instance* recipe.

# Creating a new LocalDB instance

In this recipe, we will create a new LocalDB instance.

## Getting ready

You need to make sure that LocalDB is installed. You can download LocalDB with SQL Server Express from MSDN downloads at https://www.microsoft.com/en-ca/download/details.aspx?id=42299.

## How to do it...

These are the steps to create a new LocalDB instance:

1. Open **PowerShell ISE** as an administrator.

2. Add the following script and run it:

```
#create new LocalDB instance
$localDBInstance = "NewLocalDB"
$command = "SQLLocalDB create `"$($localDBInstance)`""

#execute the command
Invoke-Expression $command

#confirm by listing all instances
$command = "SQLLocalDB i"
Invoke-Expression $command
```

## How it works...

You can also connect to and manage LocalDB using an executable utility called SQLLocalDB that comes with the installation. Since this method uses the executable and not SMO, you can use Invoke-Expression cmdlet and pass SQLLocalDB as a parameter. To learn more about the operations and parameters available in the SQLLocalDB utility, you can open Command Prompt and run the following command:

```
SQLLocalDB /?
```

One of the operations supported is create (or c) that allows you to create a new LocalDB instance. In our recipe, we will construct a command that we will typically use in a string variable when we are at Command Prompt and pass this variable to the Invoke-Expression cmdlet:

```
#create new LocalDB instance
$localDBInstance = "NewLocalDB"
$command = "SQLLocalDB create `"$($localDBInstance)`""

#execute the command
Invoke-Expression $command
```

## There's more...

Check out the syntax and examples of the `SQLLocalDB` utility on the MSDN page at `https://msdn.microsoft.com/en-us/library/hh212961.aspx`.

## See also

> ▸ The *Connecting to LocalDB* recipe

# Listing database snapshots

In this recipe, we will list the database snapshots that are available in your instance.

## Getting ready

You may choose to create a test snapshot if the instance that you are using does not have any database snapshots. You can use the following T-SQL script, or you can choose to perform the *Creating a database snapshot* recipe first before we proceed with this recipe.

## How to do it...

The following steps walk you through listing database snapshots:

1.  Open **PowerShell ISE** as an administrator.

2.  Import the `SQLPS` module as follows:

    ```
    #import SQL Server module
    Import-Module SQLPS -DisableNameChecking
    ```

3.  Add the following script and run it:

    ```
    $instanceName = "localhost"
    $server = New-Object -TypeName
    Microsoft.SqlServer.Management.Smo.Server -ArgumentList
    $instanceName

    $server.Databases |
    Where-Object IsDatabaseSnapshot -eq $true
    ```

## How it works...

A database snapshot is a static, read-only view of a source database at the time its snapshot was created. Database snapshots are initially created as sparse files, that is, empty files. When the original database changes or gets updated, the original data pages of the source database are copied to the database snapshot, thus preserving what the source database "looked like" at the time the snapshot was created.

Checking snapshots that exist in your instance using PowerShell and SMO is fairly simple because there is a property called `IsDatabaseSnapshot` that flags whether a database is a snapshot or not:

```
$server.Databases |
Where-Object IsDatabaseSnapshot -EQ $true
```

To check which databases are the bases (or sources) of snapshots, you can use the property called `IsDatabaseSnapshotBase`:

```
$server.Databases |
Where-Object IsDatabaseSnapshotBase -EQ $true
```

## There's more...

Read more about database snapshots in SQL Server from the MSDN page at

`https://msdn.microsoft.com/en-us/library/ms175158.aspx`.

## See also

► The *Creating a database snapshot* recipe.

# Creating a database snapshot

In this recipe, we will create a database snapshot.

## Getting ready

SQL Server database snapshots require either the SQL Server Developer or Enterprise edition. You can also use the Evaluation edition, which is similar to the Enterprise edition.

We will use the script called *B04525 - Ch06 - 04 - Creating a Database Snapshot - Prep.ps1* to create a sample database that we will base our snapshot on. The database created in this script will have multiple Filegroups and data files.

Alternatively, you can choose a source database that you would like to serve as the base of your snapshot.

## How to do it...

Let's take a look at the steps to create a database snapshot:

1. Open **PowerShell ISE** as an administrator.

2. Import the `SQLPS` module and create a new SMO Server object as follows:

```
#import SQL Server module
Import-Module SQLPS -DisableNameChecking

$instanceName = "localhost"
$server = New-Object -TypeName
Microsoft.SqlServer.Management.Smo.Server -ArgumentList
$instanceName
```

3. Add the following script and run it:

```
$databaseName = "SnapshotDB"
$databaseSnapshotName = "SnapshotDB_SS"

#source database
$db = $server.Databases[$databaseName]

#for our recipe, drop snapshot if exists
if($server.Databases[$databaseSnapshotName])
{
    $server.Databases[$databaseSnapshotName].Drop()
}

#database snapshot
$dbSnapshot = New-Object -TypeName
Microsoft.SqlServer.Management.Smo.Database -ArgumentList
$instanceName, $databaseSnapshotName

#original database name, which serves as base
$dbSnapshot.DatabaseSnapshotBaseName = $databaseName

#need to recreate all filegroups and files
```

```
#in the snapshot
$db.FileGroups |
ForEach-Object {
    $fg = $_

    #add filegroup to snapshot
    $snapshotFG = New-Object -TypeName
Microsoft.SqlServer.Management.Smo.FileGroup $dbSnapshot,
$fg.Name
    $dbSnapshot.FileGroups.Add($snapshotFG)

    #add files to snapshot
    $fg.Files |
    ForEach-Object {
        $file = $_
        $snapshotFile = New-Object -TypeName
Microsoft.SqlServer.Management.Smo.DataFile $snapshotFG,
$file.Name

        #use different file extension for snapshot
        $snapshotFile.FileName =
"$($db.PrimaryFilePath)\$($file.Name).ss"

        #add file to snapshot filegroup
$dbSnapshot.FileGroups[$snapshotFG.Name].Files.Add
($snapshotFile)

    }

}

#create the snapshot
$dbSnapshot.Create()
```

## How it works...

Creating a database snapshot is similar to creating an actual database. The first step is to create a `Microsoft.SqlServer.Management.Smo.Database` object:

```
$dbSnapshot = New-Object -TypeName
Microsoft.SqlServer.Management.Smo.Database -ArgumentList
$instanceName, $databaseSnapshotName
```

Identifying the base database is a key piece of creating a snapshot. This can be done by assigning the source database's name to the snapshot's `DatabaseSnapshotBaseName` property. Whenever there are changes in the source that affect the original data pages, the original page will be copied to the snapshot:

```
#original database name, which serves as base
$dbSnapshot.DatabaseSnapshotBaseName = $databaseName
```

In addition to specifying the source database, we also need to recreate all the Filegroups and files from the base database.

For the Filegroups, you will do it as follows:

```
#need to recreate all filegroups and files
#in the snapshot
$db.FileGroups |
ForEach-Object {
    $fg = $_

    #add filegroup to snapshot
    $snapshotFG = New-Object -TypeName
Microsoft.SqlServer.Management.Smo.FileGroup $dbSnapshot,
$fg.Name
    $dbsnapshot.FileGroups.Add($snapshotFG)

    #code to add files here

}
```

To add the individual files to their respective Filegroups, we can iterate over all the files in that particular Filegroup and create this in the snapshot. In our case, we create these files with a different extension. Instead of the default `.mdf` or `.ndf` extension, we will use the extension `.ss` which signifies snapshot file:

```
$fg.Files |
ForEach-Object {
    $file = $_
    $snapshotFile = New-Object -TypeName Microsoft.SqlServer.
Management.Smo.DataFile $snapshotFG, $file.Name

    #use different file extension for snapshot
    $snapshotFile.FileName =
"$($db.PrimaryFilePath)\$($file.Name).ss"

    #add file to snapshot filegroup
```

```
$dbSnapshot.FileGroups[$snapshotFG.Name].Files.Add($snapshotFile)

   }
```

If you want to script the T-SQL command instead of executing it from PowerShell, then you can use the `Script` method of the database object:

```
$dbsnapshot.Script()
```

This is what a typical snapshot of the T-SQL script will look like:

```
CREATE DATABASE [SnapshotDB_SS] ON
( NAME = N'SnapshotDB',
  FILENAME = N'C:\Data\SnapshotDB.ss' ),

( NAME = N'SnapshotDB_FG1_data',
  FILENAME = N'C:\Data\SnapshotDB_FG1_data.ss' ),

( NAME = N'SnapshotDB_FG2_data',
  FILENAME = N'C:\Data\SnapshotDB_FG2_data.ss'
)
AS SNAPSHOT OF [SnapshotDB]
```

## See also

▶ The *Listing database snapshots* recipe.

# Dropping a database snapshot

In this recipe, we will drop an existing database snapshot.

## How to do it...

Here are the steps to drop a database snapshot:

1. Open **PowerShell ISE** as an administrator.

2. Import the `SQLPS` module and create a new SMO Server object as follows:

```
#import SQL Server module
Import-Module SQLPS –DisableNameChecking

$instanceName = "localhost"
$server = New-Object -TypeName
Microsoft.SqlServer.Management.Smo.Server -ArgumentList
$instanceName
```

3. Add the following script and run it:

```
$databaseSnapshotName = "SnapshotDB_SS"

#source database
$db = $server.Databases[$databaseName]

#for our recipe, drop snapshot if exists
if($server.Databases[$databaseSnapshotName])
{
    $server.Databases[$databaseSnapshotName].Drop()
}
```

## How it works...

Dropping a database snapshot using PowerShell and SMO is very similar to dropping an actual physical database. You need to create a handle in your database snapshot and use the `Drop` method:

```
$server.Databases[$databaseSnapshotName].Drop()
```

## See also

▶ The *Listing database snapshots* recipe.

▶ The *Creating a database snapshot* recipe.

▶ The *Dropping a database* recipe of *Chapter 2*, *SQL Server and PowerShell Basic Tasks*

# Enabling FileStream

This recipe explains how to enable FileStream in SQL Server.

## How to do it...

Let's take a look at the steps to enable FileStream in SQL Server:

1. Open **PowerShell ISE** as an administrator.

2. Import the `SQLPS` module as follows:

```
#import SQL Server module
Import-Module SQLPS -DisableNameChecking
```

3.  Add the following script and run it:

```
$instanceName = "localhost"
$server = New-Object -TypeName Microsoft.SqlServer.Management.Smo.
Server -ArgumentList $instanceName

<#
These are the FileStreamLevel Enumeration values:
Disabled
TSqlAccess
TSqlFullFileSystemAccess
TSqlLocalFileSystemAccess
#>

#enable
$server.Configuration.FilestreamAccessLevel.ConfigValue =
[Microsoft.SqlServer.Management.Smo.FileStreamLevel]::
TSqlLocalFileSystemAccess
$server.Alter()
```

## How it works...

If you've ever had to maintain folders with images or videos in them, and you had to reference the file paths (or URLs) and other metadata from SQL Server, you might have encountered challenges in keeping these two synchronized.

The FileStream feature in SQL Server allows you to store unstructured data at the filesystem-level, but still maintains the records and transactional consistency at the database-level. FileStream needs to be set up at the engine-level and server-level.

To enable filestream, we can get a handle to the current instance and use the SMO Server Configuration class to set the FilestreamAccessLevel property. Once this is set, the Alter method can be invoked to persist the change:

```
#enable filestream
$server.Configuration.FilestreamAccessLevel.ConfigValue =
[Microsoft.SqlServer.Management.Smo.FileStreamLevel]::
TSqlLocalFileSystemAccess
$server.Alter()
```

The FileStream access can be set using T-SQL using the `sp_configure` system stored procedure or using PowerShell and SMO. The values for the FileStream access are as follows:

| FileStreamLevel enumeration values | sp_configure value | Description |
| --- | --- | --- |
| Disabled | 0 | The FileStream support for an instance is disabled |
| TSqlAccess | 1 | FileStream for T-SQL access is enabled |
| TSqlLocalFileSystemAccess | 2 | FileStream for file I/O access is enabled |
| TSqlFullFileSystemAccess | 3 | FileStream for file I/O access and remote clients access to FileStream is enabled. It cannot be set either by PowerShell/ SMO or `sp_configure` |

You can set the FileStream access from SQL Server Configuration Manager as well.

Note that the `TSqlFullFileSystemAccess` option cannot be set using T-SQL or SMO, but it can only be set from **SQL Server Configuration Manager (SSCM)**. In SSCM, you need to select the **Allow remote clients access to FILESTREAM data** option. This restriction for *filestream access level* from T-SQL is documented in `https://msdn.microsoft.com/en-us/library/cc645956.aspx`.

## There's more...

▸ Read more about SQL Server Filestream from MSDN at `https://msdn.microsoft.com/en-ca/library/gg471497.aspx`.

▸ Check out Microsoft's recommended steps and practices when enabling and configuring Filestream at `https://msdn.microsoft.com/en-us/library/cc645923.aspx`.

## See also

▸ The *Setting up a FileStream filegroup* recipe.

▸ The *Adding a FileTable* recipe.

# Setting up a FileStream filegroup

In this recipe, we will add a Filestream Filegroup to our database.

## Getting ready

Before you can use a FileStream Filegroup, the FileStream feature needs to be first enabled on your instance. If you haven't already enabled it, you can follow the *Enabling Filestream* recipe to enable it.

## How to do it...

Let's take a look at the steps to create a FileStream Filegroup:

1. Open the **PowerShell ISE** as an administrator.

2. Import the `SQLPS` module and create a new SMO Server object as follows:

```
#import SQL Server module
Import-Module SQLPS -DisableNameChecking
```

```
$instanceName = "localhost"
$server = New-Object -TypeName
Microsoft.SqlServer.Management.Smo.Server -ArgumentList
$instanceName
```

3. Create a sample database for this recipe:

```
$databaseName = "FileStreamDB"

#for this recipe only
#drop if it exists
if($server.Databases[$databaseName])
{
    $server.KillDatabase($databaseName)
}

#create the database
$db = New-Object -TypeName
Microsoft.SqlServer.Management.Smo.Database -ArgumentList
$server, $databaseName
$db.Create()
```

4. Add and run the following script to create the FileStream filegroup:

```
#Add filestream filegroup
$fileGroupName = "FilestreamData"
$fg = New-Object -TypeName
Microsoft.SqlServer.Management.SMO.Filegroup -Argumentlist
$db, $fileGroupName

#change the filegroup type
$fg.FileGroupType =
[Microsoft.SqlServer.Management.Smo.FileGroupType]::
FileStreamDataFileGroup
$fg.IsFileStream = $true

#create the filegroup
$fg.Create()

#add data file
$dataFileName = "C:\DATA\FilestreamData"
$dataFile = New-Object -TypeName
Microsoft.SqlServer.Management.SMO.DataFile -ArgumentList
$fg, $dataFileName
```

```
$datafile.FileName = $dataFileName

#create data file
$dataFile.Create()
```

## How it works...

Before you can start with storing your unstructured data in a filesystem using SQL Server, using the FileStream feature, you first need to ensure that a Filegroup is added, which is marked, to accept FileStream.

Using PowerShell and SMO, this can be achieved by adding a Filegroup and setting the type to the `FileStreamDataFileGroup` and `IsFileStream` properties to `true`:

```
#change the filegroup type
$fg.FileGroupType =
[Microsoft.SqlServer.Management.Smo.FileGroupType]::
FileStreamDataFileGroup
$fg.IsFileStream = $true
```

Once these properties are set, the `Create` method can be invoked to persist the changes:

```
#create the filegroup
$fg.Create()
```

The equivalent T-SQL command for this script block is as follows. Notice that the code block that adds the Filegroup has the extra `CONTAINS Filestream` clause, which you will not specify when you add regular Filegroups:

```
ALTER DATABASE FilestreamDB
ADD FILEGROUP FilestreamData
CONTAINS Filestream
```

In the last section, we will add a data file to the Filegroup. The "data file" in this case does not specify an individual file, but a directory that will store the unstructured data:

```
#add data file
$dataFileName = "C:\DATA\FilestreamData"
$dataFile = New-Object -TypeName
Microsoft.SqlServer.Management.SMO.DataFile -ArgumentList $fg,
$dataFileName

$dataFile.FileName = $dataFileName

#create data file
$dataFile.Create()
```

## There's more...

When you are working with the PowerShell ISE, you can take advantage of the Intellisense to see the different valid Filegroup types that you can specify:

```
[Microsoft.SqlServer.Management.Smo.FileGroupType]::
```
> FileStreamDataFileGroup
> MemoryOptimizedDataFileGroup
> RowsFileGroup

On the console, you can use the following code to see the valid values:

```
[Microsoft.SqlServer.Management.Smo.FilegroupType] |
Get-Member |
Out-Host -paging
```

## See also

▶   The *Enabling FileStream* recipe.

# Adding a FileTable

In this recipe, we will create a FileTable.

## Getting ready

Before you can use a FileTable, the FileStream feature needs to be first enabled on your instance. If you haven't already enabled it, you can follow the *Enabling FileStream* recipe to enable it.

In addition, you should also have a Filestream filegroup. You can follow the *Setting up a FileStream filegroup* recipe to prepare this recipe.

## How to do it...

Let's take a look at the steps to create a FileTable using SMO and PowerShell:

1.   Open **PowerShell ISE** as an administrator.
2.   Import the SQLPS module and create a new SMO Server object as follows:
     ```
     #import SQL Server module
     ```

```
Import-Module SQLPS -DisableNameChecking

$instanceName = "localhost"
$server = New-Object -TypeName
Microsoft.SqlServer.Management.Smo.Server -ArgumentList
$instanceName
```

3.  Add the following script and run it:

```
#filestream enabled database
$databaseName = "FileStreamDB"
$db = $server.Databases[$databaseName]

#get handle to filestream filegroup
$filegroupName = "FilestreamData"
$fg = $db.FileGroups[$filegroupName]

#enable filestream on server
$db.FilestreamDirectoryName = "FileTable"
$db.FilestreamNonTransactedAccess =
[Microsoft.SqlServer.Management.Smo.FilestreamNonTransactedAccessT
ype]::Full
$db.Alter()

#for this recipe only
#drop filetable if already exists
$tableName = "MyFiles"
if($db.Tables[$tableName])
{
    $db.Tables[$tableName].Drop()
}

$table = New-Object -TypeName
Microsoft.SqlServer.Management.SMO.Table -ArgumentList $db,
$tableName
$table.IsFileTable = $true
$table.FileTableDirectoryName =  "MyFiles"
$table.Create()
```

## How it works...

FileTables, or a *table of files*, are special tables in SQL Server that allow you to access and manage files if the files are stored in the filesystem. For example, adding a file will be as simple as dragging and dropping the file into the FileTable in Windows Explorer.

First, we need to ensure the database that we are accessing has `FilestreamNonTransactedAccess` set to `Full`. This means that Windows applications can access the stored files without needing transactions. For example, this will allow files to be dragged and dropped via Windows Explorer:

```
#enable filestream on server
$db.FilestreamDirectoryName = "FileTable"
$db.FilestreamNonTransactedAccess =
[Microsoft.SqlServer.Management.Smo.FilestreamNonTransactedAccess
Type]::Full
$db.Alter()
```

The equivalent T-SQL statement of the preceding snippet is as follows:

```
ALTER DATABASE [FileTableDB]
SET FILESTREAM (
   NON_TRANSACTED_ACCESS = FULL,
   DIRECTORY_NAME = N'FileTable'
)
```

After the non-transacted access is set, we can create a FileTable. Creating a FileTable is similar to creating a regular table, but we have to set at least two more properties: `IsFileTable` and `FileTableDirectoryName`:

```
$tableName = "MyFiles"

#for this recipe only
#drop filetable if already exists
if($db.Tables[$tableName])
{
    $db.Tables[$tableName].Drop()
}

$table = New-Object -TypeName
Microsoft.SqlServer.Management.SMO.Table -ArgumentList $db,
$tableName
$table.IsFileTable = $true
$table.FileTableDirectoryName =  "MyFiles"
$table.Create()
```

Once this is created, you can confirm the FileTable from SQL Server Management Studio. Under the database name, you will see the **Tables** folder, and when you expand this, you will see another folder called **FileTables**. When you expand the columns of this table, you will see that there are a number of columns that are already created that will capture the file metadata, as shown in the following screenshot:

When you right-click on the **FileTable** folder, you will see an **Explore FileTable Directory** option.

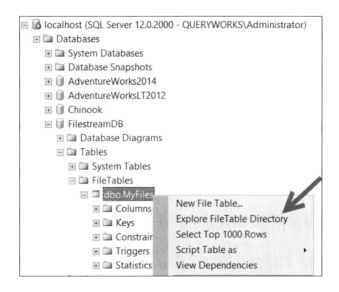

When you click on the FileTable directory, a shared folder will be opened. This is where you can manage your files if they are part of the filesystem.

Note that this feature will only work when SQL Server Management Studio and SQL Server are running on the same machine.

## There's more...

Read more about the `FileTable` feature in SQL Server from the MSDN page at `https://msdn.microsoft.com/en-us/library/ff929144.aspx`. It covers descriptions, considerations, and common tasks.

## See also

> ▸ The *Enabling FileStream* recipe.
> ▸ The *Setting up a FileStream filegroup* recipe.
> ▸ The *Adding files to a FileTable* recipe in *Chapter 9, SQL Server Development*.

# Adding full-text catalog

In this recipe, we will create a full-text catalog.

## Getting ready

In this recipe, a full-text search component needs to be installed on your SQL Server instance.

Run the script *B04525 - Ch06 - 10 - Adding Full-Text Catalog - Prep.ps1* to ready the database we will use in this recipe. This script creates a database called `FullTextCatalogDB` that contains a table called `Documents`.

## How to do it...

Let's take a look at the steps to create a full-text catalog:

1. Open **PowerShell ISE** as an administrator.

2. Import the `SQLPS` module and create a new SMO Server object as follows:

```
#import SQL Server module
Import-Module SQLPS –DisableNameChecking

$instanceName = "localhost"
$server = New-Object -TypeName
Microsoft.SqlServer.Management.Smo.Server -ArgumentList
$instanceName
```

3. Add the following script and run it:

```
$databaseName = "FullTextCatalogDB"
$db = $server.Databases[$databaseName]

$catalogName = "FTC"

$ftc = New-Object -TypeName
Microsoft.SqlServer.Management.Smo.FullTextCatalog
-ArgumentList $db, $catalogName
$ftc.IsAccentSensitive = $true
$ftc.IsDefault = $true
$ftc.Create()
```

## How it works...

A full-text search allows you to search for columns that contain a lot of text for keywords, phrases, or even different forms of a word. In SQL Server, you can do a full-text search on columns that have data types, such as `char`, `varchar`, `nchar`, `nvarchar`, `text`, `ntext`, `image`, `xml`, `varbinary(max)`, or `filestream`.

To enable a full-text search, a full-text catalog must first be created. A full-text catalog is a special storage space used to house full-text indexes that make full-text searches possible.

To create a full-text catalog using PowerShell and SMO, we need to create a `Microsoft.SqlServer.Management.Smo.FullTextCatalog` object. It needs the database object and the full-text catalog names as parameters:

```
$catalogName = "FTC"
```

```
$ftc = New-Object -TypeName
Microsoft.SqlServer.Management.Smo.FullTextCatalog -ArgumentList
$db, $catalogName
```

You can also set properties, such as `IsDefault`, `IsAccentSensitive`, `FileGroup`, and `Owner`:

```
$ftc.IsAccentSensitive = $true
$ftc.IsDefault = $true
```

When you're done setting up the properties, you can invoke the `Create` method to create the catalog:

```
$ftc.Create()
```

The equivalent T-SQL statement to create the catalog is as follows:

```
CREATE FULLTEXT CATALOG [FTC]
WITH ACCENT_SENSITIVITY = ON
AS DEFAULT
```

## There's more...

► Read more about SQL Server's full-text search capabilities at `https://msdn.microsoft.com/en-us/library/ms142571.aspx`.

► To learn more about how to create and manage full-text catalogs, check out the Microsoft documentation at `https://msdn.microsoft.com/en-us/library/bb326035.aspx`.

## See also

► The *Adding a full-text index* recipe.

# Adding full-text index

In this recipe, we will create a full-text index.

## Getting ready

Before we proceed with this recipe, ensure that you have already created a full-text catalog in your instance. If you haven't created one, you can run the *B04525 - Ch06 - 10 - Adding Full-Text Catalog - Prep.ps1* file that creates the sample database and full-text catalog and follow the *Adding a full-text catalog* recipe before proceeding with this recipe.

## How to do it...

Let's take a look at the steps to create a full-text index:

1. Open **PowerShell ISE** as an administrator.

2. Import the `SQLPS` module and create a new SMO Server object as follows:

```
#import SQL Server module
Import-Module SQLPS -DisableNameChecking

$instanceName = "localhost"
$server = New-Object -TypeName
Microsoft.SqlServer.Management.Smo.Server -ArgumentList
$instanceName
```

3. Add the following script and run it:

```
#database
$databaseName = "FullTextCatalogDB"
$db = $server.Databases[$databaseName]

#catalog
$catalogName = "FTC"
$catalog = $db.FullTextCatalogs[$catalogName]

#table
$tableName = "Documents"
$table = $db.Tables[$tableName]

#create full-text index
$fullTextIndex = New-Object -TypeName
Microsoft.SqlServer.Management.SMO.FullTextIndex

#set full-text index properties
$fullTextIndex.Parent = $table
$fullTextIndex.CatalogName = $catalogName
$fulltextIndex.StopListName = "SYSTEM"

#need to establish unique ID for base table
$fullTextIndex.UniqueIndexName = "PK_Documents_DocumentID"
$fullTextIndex.Create()

#specify index column
$documentNameCol = New-Object -TypeName
Microsoft.SqlServer.Management.Smo.FullTextIndexColumn
-ArgumentList $fullTextIndex, "Name"
```

```
$documentNameCol.Language = "English"
$documentNameCol.Create()

#specify a type column
$documentContentCol = New-Object -TypeName
Microsoft.SqlServer.Management.Smo.FullTextIndexColumn
-ArgumentList $fullTextIndex, "Content"
$documentContentCol.Language = "English"
$documentContentCol.TypeColumnName = "Extension"

#create
$documentContentCol.Create()
```

## How it works...

Before you create a full-text index, you must ensure that you already have a full-text catalog set up.

To create a full-text index, we have to create a
`Microsoft.SqlServer.Management.SMO.FullTextIndex` object:

```
#create full-text index
$fullTextIndex = New-Object -TypeName
Microsoft.SqlServer.Management.SMO.FullTextIndex
```

You can set several properties, including the parent table, catalog name, and stop list name. In addition, you also need to specify the unique index in the base table:

```
#set full-text index properties
$fullTextIndex.Parent = $table
$fullTextIndex.CatalogName = $catalogName
$fulltextIndex.StopListName = "SYSTEM"

#need to establish unique ID for base table
$fullTextIndex.UniqueIndexName = "PK_Documents_DocumentID"
$fullTextIndex.Create()
```

The equivalent T-SQL statement to create this index is as follows:

```
CREATE FULLTEXT INDEX ON [dbo].[Documents]
KEY INDEX [PK_Documents_DocumentID]ON ([FTC])
WITH (STOPLIST = [SYSTEM])
```

With a full-text index, you can add additional text columns that can be searched. In our recipe, we add the `Name` columns to our index. This will allow the content of `Name` to be full-text searched:

```
#specify column for index
$documentNameCol = New-Object -TypeName
Microsoft.SqlServer.Management.Smo.FullTextIndexColumn
-ArgumentList $fullTextIndex, "Name"
$documentNameCol.Language = "English"
$documentNameCol.Create()
```

If you were to do this in T-SQL, this would be your script:

```
ALTER FULLTEXT INDEX
ON [dbo].[Documents]
ADD
(
    [Name] LANGUAGE [English]
)
```

Because our table also has another field that specifies the document type, we can add this to our full-text index. We can specify this using the `TypeColumnName` property:

```
$documentContentCol = New-Object -TypeName Microsoft.SqlServer.
Management.Smo.FullTextIndexColumn
-ArgumentList $fullTextIndex, "Content"
$documentContentCol.Language = "English"
$documentContentCol.TypeColumnName = "Extension"
$documentContentCol.Create()
```

The addition of the type column to T-SQL is as follows:

```
ALTER FULLTEXT INDEX
ON [dbo].[Documents]
ADD
(
    [Content] TYPE COLUMN [Extension] LANGUAGE [English]
)
```

## There's more...

You can learn more about how to create and manage full-text indexes at `https://msdn.microsoft.com/en-us/library/cc879306.aspx`.

▸ The *Adding a full-text catalog* recipe.

# Creating a memory-optimized table

In this recipe, we will create a memory-optimized table in SQL Server.

## Getting ready

Memory-optimized tables require SQL Server Developer and the Enterprise or Evaluation edition.

## How to do it...

Let's take a look at the steps to create a memory-optimized table:

1. Open **PowerShell ISE** as an administrator.

2. Import the `SQLPS` module and create a new SMO Server object as follows:

   ```
   #import SQL Server module
   Import-Module SQLPS -DisableNameChecking

   $instanceName = "localhost"
   $server = New-Object -TypeName
   Microsoft.SqlServer.Management.Smo.Server -ArgumentList
   $instanceName
   ```

3. Add the following script and run it:

   ```
   $databaseName = "MemoryOptimizedDB"

   #for this recipe only
   #drop if it exists
   if($server.Databases[$databaseName])
   {
       $server.KillDatabase($databaseName)
   }

   $db = New-Object -TypeName
   Microsoft.SqlServer.Management.Smo.Database -ArgumentList
   $server, $databaseName
   $db.Create()

   #Add memory optimized filegroup
   ```

```
$filegroupName = "MemoryOptimizedData"
$fg = New-Object -TypeName
Microsoft.SqlServer.Management.SMO.Filegroup -Argumentlist
$db, $filegroupName

#set the filegroup type
$fg.FileGroupType =
[Microsoft.SqlServer.Management.Smo.FileGroupType]::
MemoryOptimizedDataFileGroup
$fg.Create()

#add data file
$df = New-Object -TypeName
Microsoft.SqlServer.Management.SMO.DataFile -ArgumentList
$fg, "datafile"

#specify data file path and filename
$df.FileName = "c:\Temp\memoryoptimizeddata1.ndf"

#create data file
$df.Create()

#create table
$tableName = "Student"
$table = New-Object -TypeName
Microsoft.SqlServer.Management.SMO.Table -ArgumentList $db,
$tableName

$col1Name = "StudentID"
$type = [Microsoft.SqlServer.Management.SMO.DataType]::
Int
$col1 =  New-Object -TypeName
Microsoft.SqlServer.Management.SMO.Column -ArgumentList
$table, $col1Name, $type
$col1.Nullable = $false
#$col1.Identity = $true
#$col1.IdentitySeed = 1
#$col1.IdentityIncrement = 1
$table.Columns.Add($col1)

#must have a primary key
#only hash or nonclustered indexes can
#be created in memory optimized

$index = New-Object -TypeName
Microsoft.SqlServer.Management.SMO.Index -Argumentlist
$table, "PK_Student_StudentID"
```

```
$index.IndexType =
[Microsoft.SqlServer.Management.SMO.IndexType]::
NonClusteredIndex
$index.IsClustered = $false
$index.IndexKeyType =
[Microsoft.SqlServer.Management.SMO.IndexKeyType]::
DriPrimaryKey

$indexCol = New-Object -TypeName
Microsoft.SqlServer.Management.SMO.IndexedColumn
-Argumentlist $index, $col1Name
$index.IndexedColumns.Add($indexCol)
$table.Indexes.Add($index)

$table.IsMemoryOptimized = $true
$table.Durability = [Microsoft.SqlServer.Management.Smo.
DurabilityType]::
SchemaAndData

#create table
$table.Create()
```

## How it works...

SQL Server 2014 introduces features, such as In-Memory OLTP in 64-bit Enterprise, Developer, or Evaluation editions, which are designed to make OLTP applications much faster. Using In-Memory OLTP can dramatically make OLTP applications faster. If you have a table that you use heavily, you may consider taking advantage of this new feature. Memory-optimized tables reside in memory. A drawback, however, is that the whole table must fit in the memory.

To start with, we need to create a database with a Filegroup that is memory optimized:

```
#set the filegroup type
$fg.FileGroupType =
[Microsoft.SqlServer.Management.Smo.FileGroupType]::
MemoryOptimizedDataFileGroup
$fg.Create()
```

Once the database is set up, we can create a table that is memory optimized. There are a few requirements that we need to observe. Here are two requirements regarding indexes that are documented in MSDN (`https://msdn.microsoft.com/en-us/library/dn133166.aspx`):

> *Memory-optimized indexes must be created with CREATE TABLE (SQL Server).*
> *Disk-based indexes can be created with CREATE TABLE and CREATE INDEX.*

*Each memory-optimized table must have at least one index. Note that each PRIMARY KEY constraint implicitly creates an index. Therefore, if a table has a primary key, it has an index. A primary key is a requirement for a durable memory-optimized table.*

In our recipe, we need to create an index during our table creation script. We also need to specify that this index is a primary key nonclustered index:

```
#must have a primary key
#only hash or nonclustered indexes can
#be created in memory optimized

$index = New-Object -TypeName
Microsoft.SqlServer.Management.SMO.Index -Argumentlist $table,
"PK_Student_StudentID"
$index.IndexType =
[Microsoft.SqlServer.Management.SMO.IndexType]::NonClusteredIndex
$index.IsClustered = $false
$index.IndexKeyType =
[Microsoft.SqlServer.Management.SMO.IndexKeyType]::DriPrimaryKey

$indexCol = New-Object -TypeName
Microsoft.SqlServer.Management.SMO.IndexedColumn -Argumentlist
$index, $colName
$index.IndexedColumns.Add($indexCol)
$table.Indexes.Add($index)
```

The other requirement that we need to fulfill is to set a couple of table properties to indicate that this table is memory optimized (IsMemoryOptimized) and durable (Durability):

```
$table.IsMemoryOptimized = $true
$table.Durability =
[Microsoft.SqlServer.Management.Smo.DurabilityType]::SchemaAndData
```

Once we set the properties, we can invoke the Create method:

```
$table.Create()
```

The T-SQL equivalent of creating a memory-optimized table looks like this:

```
CREATE TABLE [dbo].[Student]
(
   [StudentID] [int] NOT NULL,
    CONSTRAINT [PK_Student_StudentID] PRIMARY KEY NONCLUSTERED
    (
      [StudentID]
    )
)WITH ( MEMORY_OPTIMIZED = ON , DURABILITY = SCHEMA_AND_DATA )
```

## There's more...

▶ You can learn more about SQL Server's memory-optimized tables at `https://msdn.microsoft.com/en-us/library/dn133165.aspx`.

▶ Guidelines for using indexes in memory-optimized tables can be found on the MSDN page at `https://msdn.microsoft.com/en-us/library/dn133166.aspx`.

▶ You can find the requirements for memory-optimized tables at `https://msdn.microsoft.com/en-us/library/dn170449.aspx`.

▶ Read more about SQL Server Management Objects Support for In-Memory OLTP at `https://msdn.microsoft.com/en-us/library/dn133168.aspx`.

## See also

▶ The *Creating a table* recipe in *Chapter 2, SQL Server and PowerShell Basic Tasks*.

# Creating a database master key

In this recipe, we will create a database master key.

## Getting ready

In this recipe, we will create a database master key for the master database. You can substitute a different database for this exercise if you wish.

The T-SQL equivalent of what we are trying to accomplish is as follows:

```
USE master
GO
CREATE MASTER KEY
ENCRYPTION BY PASSWORD = 'P@ssword'
```

## How to do it...

Let's take a look at the steps required to complete the task:

1. Open **PowerShell ISE** as an administrator.

2. Import the `SQLPS` module and create a new SMO Server object as follows:
   ```
   #import SQL Server module
   Import-Module SQLPS -DisableNameChecking
   ```

```
#replace this with your instance name
$instanceName = "localhost"

$server = New-Object -TypeName Microsoft.SqlServer.Management.Smo.
Server -ArgumentList $instanceName
```

3. Add the following script and run it:

```
$VerbosePreference = "Continue"
$masterdb =  $server.Databases["master"]

if($masterdb.MasterKey -eq $null)
{
    $masterkey = New-Object Microsoft.SqlServer.Management.Smo.
MasterKey -ArgumentList $masterdb

    $masterkey.Create("P@ssword")

    Write-Verbose "Master Key Created :
$($masterkey.CreateDate)"
}
$VerbosePreference = "SilentlyContinue"
```

4. If successful, you will see a one-line message that contains the successful message and the date on which the master key was created as the output.

## How it works...

A database master key is required if you want to do any database-level encryption. It is used to encrypt keys and certificates in a specific database.

Creating a database master key is straightforward. You need to create an SMO `MasterKey` object:

```
$masterkey = New-Object
Microsoft.SqlServer.Management.Smo.MasterKey -ArgumentList
$masterdb

$masterkey.Create("P@ssword")
```

There are a couple of overloads to the `Create` method of the `MasterKey` class. In our recipe, we chose to provide a password. The alternative is to pass both a decryption and encryption password.

If the database master key already exists, you may not necessarily be able to drop it right away. If there are encryption objects already created, that are being protected by the database master key, you must first drop those encryption objects before you drop the database master key. Once there are no more dependent objects, you can use the following PowerShell code to drop the master key:

```
#drop master key
$masterkey.Drop()
```

## There's more...

You can learn more about the `MasterKey` class from the MSDN page at `http://msdn.microsoft.com/en-us/library/microsoft.sqlserver.management.smo.masterkey.aspx`.

## See also

▶ The *Creating a certificate* recipe.

# Creating a certificate

This recipe shows how you can create a certificate using PowerShell and SMO.

## Getting ready

In this recipe, we will create a certificate called `Test Certificate` that is protected by the database master key. You will need to make sure that the database master key has been created first for the database.

The T-SQL equivalent of what we are trying to accomplish in this recipe is as follows:

```
CREATE CERTIFICATE [Test Certificate]
WITH SUBJECT = N'This is a test certificate.',
START_DATE = N'04/10/2015',
EXPIRY_DATE = N'04/10/2017'
```

## How to do it...

Let's take a look at the steps required to complete the task:

1. Open **PowerShell ISE** as an administrator.

2. Import the `SQLPS` module and create a new SMO Server object as follows:

```
#import SQL Server module
Import-Module SQLPS -DisableNameChecking

#replace this with your instance name
$instanceName = "localhost"
$server = New-Object -TypeName
Microsoft.SqlServer.Management.Smo.Server -ArgumentList
$instanceName
```

3. Add the following script and run it:

```
$certificateName = "Test Certificate"
$masterdb = $server.Databases["master"]

if ($masterdb.Certificates[$certificateName])
{
   $masterdb.Certificates[$certificateName].Drop()
}
$certificate = New-Object -TypeName
Microsoft.SqlServer.Management.Smo.Certificate
-argumentlist $masterdb, $certificateName

#set properties
$certificate.StartDate = Get-Date
$certificate.Subject = "This is a test certificate."
$certificate.ExpirationDate = (Get-Date).AddYears(2)
$certificate.ActiveForServiceBrokerDialog = $false

#create certificate
#you can optionally provide a password, but this
#certificate we created is protected by the master key
$certificate.Create("SUppLYStr0NGPassw0RDH3r3")

#display all properties
$certificate |
Select-Object *
```

4. When the certificate is created and the script is executed, the resulting screen will look like this:

```
Parent                        : [master]
ActiveForServiceBrokerDialog  : False
ExpirationDate                : 4/10/2017 12:00:00 AM
ID                            : 261
Issuer                        : This is a test certificate.
LastBackupDate                : 1/1/0001 12:00:00 AM
Owner                         : dbo
PrivateKeyEncryptionType      : Password
Serial                        : 1a 55 d9 87 97 fe 8a 96 4f cd 6d 09 f6 b7 1e bb
Sid                           : {1, 6, 0, 0...}
StartDate                     : 4/10/2015 12:00:00 AM
Subject                       : This is a test certificate.
Thumbprint                    : {119, 109, 104, 211...}
Events                        : Microsoft.SqlServer.Management.Smo.CertificateEvents
Name                          : Test Certificate
Urn                           : Server[@Name='ROGUE']/Database[@Name='master']/Certificate[@Name='Test Certificate']
Properties                    : {Name=ActiveForServiceBrokerDialog/Type=System.Boolean/Writable=True/Value=False,
                                Name=ExpirationDate/Type=System.DateTime/Writable=True/Value=04/10/2017 00:00:00,
                                Name=ID/Type=System.Int32/Writable=False/Value=261,
                                Name=Issuer/Type=System.String/Writable=False/Value=This is a test certificate....}
UserData                      :
State                         : Existing
IsDesignMode                  : False
```

5. To confirm this via T-SQL, we can use the `sys.certificates` DMV to list all the certificates. Open **SQL Server Management Studio** and execute the following T-SQL statement:

```
SELECT *
FROM sys.certificates
WHERE [name] = 'Test Certificate'
```

## How it works...

To create a certificate, you need to first create an SMO Certificate object:

```
$certificate = New-Object -TypeName
Microsoft.SqlServer.Management.Smo.Certificate -argumentlist
$masterdb, $certificateName
```

There are a few properties that we can set for an SMO `Certificate` object. In this recipe, we set the `StartDate`, `Subject`, and `ExpirationDate` properties:

```
$certificate.StartDate = Get-Date
$certificate.Subject = "This is a test certificate."
$certificate.ExpirationDate = (Get-Date).AddYears(2)
$certificate.ActiveForServiceBrokerDialog = $false
```

If you want to create a certificate that is protected by the database master key, you just need to invoke the `Create` method of the `Certificate` class and provide a strong password:

```
$certificate.Create("SUppLYStr0NGPassw0RDH3r3")
```

## There's more...

A certificate is essentially a digitally signed document that binds a public key with an identity and is used to prove authenticity of ownership. This helps prevent malicious impersonations, that is, somebody or something "pretending" to be someone or something they are not.

You can learn more about certificates from the MSDN page at

`http://msdn.microsoft.com/en-us/library/ms189586.aspx`.

## See also

- ▶ The *Creating a database master key* recipe.

# Creating symmetric and asymmetric keys

In this recipe, we will create symmetric and asymmetric keys.

## Getting ready

In this recipe, we will use the `TestDB` database. If you don't already have this database, log in to **SQL Server Management Studio** and execute the following T-SQL code:

```
IF DB_ID('TestDB') IS NULL
CREATE DATABASE TestDB
GO
```

We will also work with a database user called `eric` in our `TestDB` database. This user will map to the SQL login `eric`. Feel free to create this user using the *Creating a database user* recipe of *Chapter 4*, *Security*, as a reference. Alternatively, execute the following T-SQL code from **SQL Server Management Studio** or replace it with an existing login/database user in your system:

```
Use TestDB
GO
CREATE USER [eric]
FOR LOGIN [eric]
```

## How to do it...

Let's take a look at the steps required to complete the task:

1. Open **PowerShell ISE** as an administrator.

2. Import the `SQLPS` module and create a new SMO Server object as follows:

```
#import SQL Server module
Import-Module SQLPS -DisableNameChecking

#replace this with your instance name
$instanceName = "localhost"
$server = New-Object -TypeName
Microsoft.SqlServer.Management.Smo.Server -ArgumentList
$instanceName
```

3. Add the following script and run it:

```
#database handle
$databasename = "TestDB"
$database = $server.Databases[$databasename]

#create a database master key
#if this doesn't exist yet
$dbmk = New-Object
Microsoft.SqlServer.Management.Smo.MasterKey -ArgumentList
$database
$dbmk.Create("P@ssword")


#==========================================================
# Create Asymmetric Key
#==========================================================
#this is equivalent to:
<#
USE TestDB
GO
CREATE ASYMMETRIC KEY [EncryptionAsymmetricKey]
AUTHORIZATION [eric]
WITH ALGORITHM = RSA_2048
#>
$asymk = New-Object
Microsoft.SqlServer.Management.Smo.AsymmetricKey
-ArgumentList $database, "EncryptionAsymmetricKey"

#replace this with a known database user in the
#database you are using for this recipe
$asymk.Owner = "eric"
```

```
$asymk.Create(
[Microsoft.SqlServer.Management.Smo.AsymmetricKeyEncryption
Algorithm]::Rsa2048)

#create certificate first to be used for Symmetric Key
$cert = New-Object -TypeName
Microsoft.SqlServer.Management.Smo.Certificate
-argumentlist $database, "Encryption"
$cert.StartDate = Get-Date
$cert.Subject = "This is a test certificate."
$cert.ExpirationDate = (Get-Date).AddYears(2)
$cert.Create()

#create a symmetric key based on certificate
$symk = New-Object Microsoft.SqlServer.Management.Smo.SymmetricKey
-ArgumentList $database, "EncryptionSymmetricKey"
$symkenc = New-Object
Microsoft.SqlServer.Management.Smo.SymmetricKeyEncryption
([Microsoft.SqlServer.Management.Smo.KeyEncryptionType]::
Certificate, "Encryption")
$symk.Create($symkenc, [Microsoft.SqlServer.Management.Smo.
SymmetricKeyEncryption
Algorithm]::TripleDes)

#list each object we created
$dbmk
$cert.Name
$asymk
$symk
```

4. The resulting screen will look similar to the following screenshot:

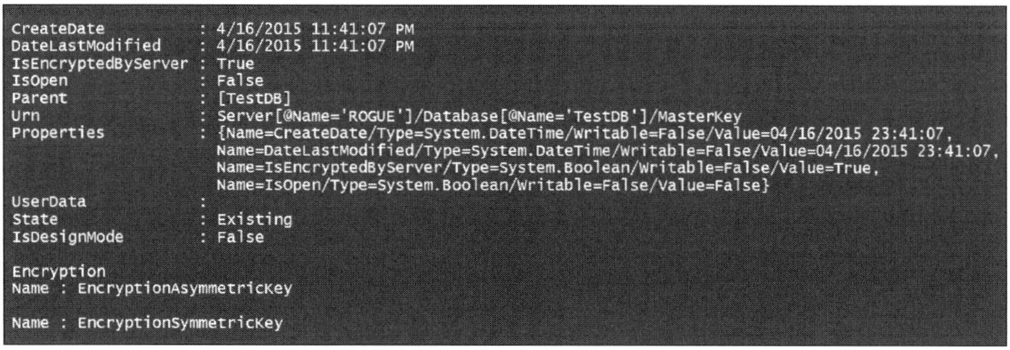

5. Alternatively, you can use the following T-SQL statement to confirm the existence of the database master key, certificate, symmetric, and asymmetric keys that we created in this recipe:

```
SELECT    'DB Master Key' ,
          is_master_key_encrypted_by_server
FROM      sys.databases
WHERE     [name] = 'TestDB'

SELECT    'Certificate' , *
FROM      sys.certificates
WHERE     [name] = 'Encryption'

SELECT    'Asymmetric Key' , *
FROM      sys.asymmetric_keys
WHERE     [name] = 'EncryptionAsymmetricKey'

SELECT    'Symmetric Key' , *
FROM      sys.symmetric_keys
WHERE     [name] = 'EncryptionSymmetricKey'
```

## How it works...

Before we create a symmetric or asymmetric key, we have to first create a database master key. MSDN defines a database master key as follows:

> *a symmetric key that is used to protect the private keys of certificates and asymmetric keys that are present in the database.*

Here is how you would create a database master key using PowerShell and SMO:

```
$dbmk = New-Object Microsoft.SqlServer.Management.Smo.MasterKey
-ArgumentList $database
$dbmk.Create("P@ssword")
```

Once the database master key is in place, we can create our Symmetric and Asymmetric keys. This is equivalent to the following T-SQL statement:

```
USE TestDB
GO
CREATE MASTER KEY ENCRYPTION
BY PASSWORD = 'P@ssword'
```

To create the asymmetric key, you need to create an SMO asymmetric key instance and assign an owner and encryption algorithm. The available `AsymmetricKeyEncryptionAlgorithm` values are `CryptographicProviderDefined`, `Rsa512`, `Rsa1024`, and `Rsa2048`:

```
$asymk = New-Object
Microsoft.SqlServer.Management.Smo.AsymmetricKey -ArgumentList
$database, "EncryptionAsymmetricKey"
#replace this with a known user in your instance
$asymk.Owner = "EncryptionUser"
$asymk.Create([Microsoft.SqlServer.Management.Smo.AsymmetricKey
EncryptionAlgorithm]::Rsa2048)
```

To create a symmetric key, we must first create a certificate:

```
#create certificate first to be used for Symmetric Key
$cert = New-Object -TypeName
Microsoft.SqlServer.Management.Smo.Certificate -argumentlist
$database, "Encryption"
$cert.StartDate = "(Get-Date).AddYears(2)
$cert.Subject = "This is a test certificate."
$cert.ExpirationDate = (Get-Date).AddYears(2)
$cert.Create()
```

If you were to do this in T-SQL, this would be the equivalent script:

```
CREATE CERTIFICATE [Encryption]
WITH SUBJECT = N'This is a test certificate.',
START_DATE = N'04/10/2015',
EXPIRY_DATE = N'04/10/2017'
```

If you want to use dynamic dates, the preceding T-SQL snippet can be adjusted to use Dynamic SQL and retrieve the current date using the T-SQL `GETDATE()` functions, and we can add two years using `DATEADD()`.

To create a symmetric key based on the certificate, we should first instantiate a SMO `SymmetricKey` object:

```
$symk = New-Object Microsoft.SqlServer.Management.Smo.SymmetricKey
 -ArgumentList $database, "EncryptionSymmetricKey"
```

We then need to specify the `SymmetricKey` encryption type. The available values are `SymmetricKey`, `Certificate`, `Password`, `AsymmetricKey`, and `Provider`.

```
$symkenc = New-Object
Microsoft.SqlServer.Management.Smo.SymmetricKeyEncryption
([Microsoft.SqlServer.Management.Smo.KeyEncryptionType]::
Certificate, "Encryption")
```

When we create `SymmetricKey`, we need to also specify which algorithm to use. The available `SymmetricKeyAlgorithm` values are `CryptographicProviderDefined`, `RC2`, `RC4`, `Des`, `TripleDes`, `DesX`, `Aes128`, `Aes192`, `Aes256`, and `TripleDes3Key`:

```
$symk.Create($symkenc,
[Microsoft.SqlServer.Management.Smo.SymmetricKeyEncryption
Algorithm]::TripleDes)
```

The equivalent T-SQL will look like this:

```
CREATE SYMMETRIC KEY [EncryptionSymmetricKey]
WITH ALGORITHM = TRIPLE_DES
ENCRYPTION BY CERTIFICATE [Encryption]
```

## There's more...

Symmetric and asymmetric keys can be used to set up cell-level encryption in SQL Server. The typical steps to set up cell-level encryption are as follows:

1. Create a master key
2. Create a certificate or asymmetric key
3. Create a symmetric key that is protected by a certificate or asymmetric key
4. Open a symmetric key, then encrypt or decrypt and later close a symmetric key

You can learn more about `Symmetric` and `Asymmetric` keys from the MSDN article at

`http://support.microsoft.com/kb/246071`.

Another MSDN article that walks you through the process of encrypting a column of data using T-SQL is available at `http://msdn.microsoft.com/en-us/library/ms179331.aspx`.

## See also

- ▶ The *Creating a database master key* recipe.
- ▶ The *Creating a certificate* recipe.

# Setting up Transparent Data Encryption

This recipe shows how you can set up Transparent Data Encryption using PowerShell and SMO.

## Getting ready

**Transparent Data Encryption** (**TDE**) is supported only in Enterprise, Developer, or Evaluation editions.

In this recipe, we will enable TDE on the `TestDB` database. If you don't already have this test database, log in to SQL Server Management Studio and execute the following T-SQL code:

```
IF DB_ID('TestDB') IS NULL
CREATE DATABASE TestDB
GO
```

You should already have a database master key for this `TestDB` database. If you don't have one, create it using the *Creating a database master key* recipe.

## How to do it...

These are the steps to set up TDE programmatically:

1. Open **PowerShell ISE** as an administrator.

2. Import the `SQLPS` module and create a new SMO Server object as follows:
```
#import SQL Server module
Import-Module SQLPS -DisableNameChecking

#replace this with your instance name
$instanceName = "localhost"

$server = New-Object -TypeName
Microsoft.SqlServer.Management.Smo.Server -ArgumentList
$instanceName
```

3. Add the following script and run it:
```
#if not yet created, create a master key
$masterdb = $server.Databases["master"]

if($masterdb.MasterKey -eq $null)
{
    $masterkey = New-Object Microsoft.SqlServer.Management.Smo.
MasterKey -ArgumentList $masterdb
    $masterkey.Create("P@ssword")
}

#if not yet created, create or obtain a certificate
```

```
#protected by the master key
$certificateName = "Test Certificate"

if ($masterdb.Certificates[$certificateName])
{
  $masterdb.Certificates[$certificateName].Drop()
}
$certificate = New-Object -TypeName Microsoft.SqlServer.
Management.Smo.Certificate -argumentlist $masterdb,
$certificateName

#create certificate protected by the master key
$certificate.StartDate = "April 10, 2015"
$certificate.Subject = "This is a test certificate."
$certificate.ExpirationDate = "April 10, 2017"

#you can optionally provide a password, but this
#certificate we created is protected by the master key
$certificate.Create()

#create a database encryption key
$databaseName = "TestDB"
$database = $server.Databases[$databaseName]

$dbencryption = New-Object
Microsoft.SqlServer.Management.Smo.DatabaseEncryptionKey
$dbencryption.Parent = $database
$dbencryption.EncryptionAlgorithm =
[Microsoft.SqlServer.Management.Smo.DatabaseEncryption
Algorithm]::Aes256
$dbencryption.EncryptionType =
[Microsoft.SqlServer.Management.Smo.DatabaseEncryptionType]::Serve
rCertificate

#associate certificate name
$dbencryption.EncryptorName = $certificateName
$dbencryption.Create()

#enable TDE
$database.EncryptionEnabled = $true
$database.Alter()
$database.Refresh()

#display TDE setting
```

```
$database.EncryptionEnabled

$databasename = "TestDB"
$database = $server.Databases[$databasename]
```

4. The last line should say `True` if Transparent Data Encryption was successfully turned on for `TestDB`.

5. Alternatively, you can use the following T-SQL statement to confirm this:

```
SELECT
    db.name,
    db.is_encrypted,
    dm.encryption_state,
    dm.percent_complete,
    dm.key_algorithm,
    dm.key_length
FROM
    sys.databases db
    LEFT OUTER JOIN sys.dm_database_encryption_keys dm
    ON db.database_id = dm.database_id
```

6. This will give you a list of all your databases in your instance and identify which ones are encrypted.

| | name | is_encrypted | encryption_state | percent_complete | key_algorithm | key_length |
|---|---|---|---|---|---|---|
| 1 | AdventureWorks2014 | 0 | NULL | NULL | NULL | NULL |
| 2 | AdventureWorksLT2012 | 0 | NULL | NULL | NULL | NULL |
| 3 | Chinook | 0 | NULL | NULL | NULL | NULL |
| 4 | distribution | 0 | NULL | NULL | NULL | NULL |
| 5 | FileTableDB | 0 | NULL | NULL | NULL | NULL |
| 6 | FullTextCatalogDB | 0 | NULL | NULL | NULL | NULL |
| 7 | master | 0 | NULL | NULL | NULL | NULL |
| 8 | model | 0 | NULL | NULL | NULL | NULL |
| 9 | msdb | 0 | NULL | NULL | NULL | NULL |
| 10 | pubs | 0 | NULL | NULL | NULL | NULL |
| 11 | Registration | 0 | NULL | NULL | NULL | NULL |
| 12 | SnapshotDB | 0 | NULL | NULL | NULL | NULL |
| 13 | SnapshotDB_SS | 0 | NULL | NULL | NULL | NULL |
| 14 | tempdb | 0 | 3 | 0 | AES | 256 |
| 15 | TestDB | 1 | 3 | 0 | AES | 256 |

The `encryption_state = 3` means that the encryption of that database has already been completed. Also, notice that `tempdb` is also encrypted. By default, if any user databases are encrypted, then `tempdb` also automatically gets encrypted.

## How it works...

Transparent Data Encryption is supported only in Enterprise, Developer, or Evaluation editions.

There are a few preparatory steps required to enable Transparent Data Encryption.

You first need to create a master key. The following script is a simple script to do so, or you can also refer to the *Creating a database master key* recipe:

```
#if not yet created, create a master key
$masterdb =  $server.Databases["master"]

if($masterdb.MasterKey -eq $null)
{
    $masterkey = New-Object
Microsoft.SqlServer.Management.Smo.MasterKey -ArgumentList
$masterdb
    $masterkey.Create("P@ssword")
}
```

You will then need to create a certificate stored in the master database and protected by the database master key for the master database:

```
$certificateName = "Test Certificate"

if ($masterdb.Certificates[$certificateName])
{
  $masterdb.Certificates[$certificateName].Drop()
}
$certificate = New-Object -TypeName Microsoft.SqlServer.Management.
Smo.Certificate -argumentlist $masterdb, $certificateName

#create certificate protected by the master key
$certificate.StartDate = "April 10, 2015"
$certificate.Subject = "This is a test certificate."
$certificate.ExpirationDate = "April 10, 2017"

#you can optionally provide a password, but this
#certificate we created is protected by the master key
$certificate.Create()
```

The preceding script block is equivalent to the following T-SQL command:

```
USE master
GO
```

```
CREATE CERTIFICATE [Encryption]
WITH SUBJECT = N'This is a test certificate.',
START_DATE = N'04/10/2015',
EXPIRY_DATE = N'04/10/2017'
```

After the certificate has been created, the next step is to create a database encryption key that is protected by the certificate. This key is needed to enable Transparent Data Encryption on a user database:

```
#create a database encryption key
$dbencryption = New-Object
Microsoft.SqlServer.Management.Smo.DatabaseEncryptionKey
```

We need to associate this with the database for which we want to turn on the TDE:

```
$databaseName = "TestDB"
$database = $server.Databases[$databaseName]
$dbencryption.Parent = $database
```

When creating a database encryption key, we also need to specify the encryption algorithm. The available encryptions are `Aes128`, `Aes192`, `Aes256`, and `TripleDes`:

```
$dbencryption.EncryptionAlgorithm =
[Microsoft.SqlServer.Management.Smo.DatabaseEncryptionAlgorithm]::
Aes256
```

We also need to associate this key with the certificate that we previously created. The possible `DatabaseEncryptionType` values are `ServerCertificate` and `ServerAsymmetricKey`:

```
$dbencryption.EncryptionType =
[Microsoft.SqlServer.Management.Smo.DatabaseEncryptionType]::
ServerCertificate

#associate certificate name
$dbencryption.EncryptorName = $certificateName
```

You are now ready to create the database encryption key:

```
$dbencryption.Create()
```

The equivalent T-SQL statement to create a database encryption key is as follows:

```
CREATE DATABASE ENCRYPTION KEY
WITH ALGORITHM = AES_256
ENCRYPTION BY SERVER CERTIFICATE [Test Certificate]
```

At this point, the preparatory steps to enable TDE are complete. We can now turn on TDE and alter our target database:

```
#enable TDE
$database.EncryptionEnabled = $true
$database.Alter()
$database.Refresh()
```

In the background, this change generates the following T-SQL statement:

```
ALTER DATABASE [TestDB]
SET ENCRYPTION ON
```

## There's more...

Transparent Data Encryption is introduced in SQL Server 2008 as a solution for database-level encryption. If TDE is turned on, data in the data and log files are encrypted. This will also automatically encrypt `tempdb`.

▸ Read more about Transparent Data Encryption from MSDN at `http://msdn.microsoft.com/en-us/library/bb934049.aspx`.

▸ Check out `encryption_state` values of `sys.dm_database_encryption_keys` from MSDN at `http://msdn.microsoft.com/en-us/library/bb677274.aspx`.

## See also

▸ The *Creating a certificate* recipe.

▸ The *Altering database properties* recipe in *Chapter 2, SQL Server and PowerShell Basic Tasks*.

# 7
# Audit and Policies

In this chapter, we will cover the following topics:

- ▶ Enabling/disabling change tracking
- ▶ Configuring SQL Server Audit
- ▶ Listing facets and their properties
- ▶ Listing policies
- ▶ Exporting a policy
- ▶ Importing a policy
- ▶ Creating a condition
- ▶ Creating a policy
- ▶ Evaluating a policy
- ▶ Running and saving a profile trace event
- ▶ Extracting the contents of a trace file

# Introduction

Part of a SQL Server DBA or developer's regular tasks include tracking changes, auditing databases and tables, and ensuring that instances comply with the organizational policies. SQL Server has features that allow all of these tasks to be accomplished more easily. In this chapter, we will take a look at how to enable tracking and auditing in SQL Server. We will also take a look at how to use PowerShell in order to enable and use **Policy Based Management** (**PBM**) in SQL Server to ensure compliance of settings and configurations with company rules.

# Enabling/disabling change tracking

This recipe shows you how you can enable and disable change tracking in your target database.

## Getting ready

In this recipe, we will use a test database called `TestDB`. If you do not already have this database, log in to **SQL Server Management Studio** and execute the following T-SQL code:

```
IF DB_ID('TestDB') IS NULL
CREATE DATABASE TestDB
GO
```

You need to check which of your databases have *change tracking* enabled. To do this, connect to your instance using **SQL Server Management Studio**, and type in the following T-SQL statement:

```
SELECT
   DB_NAME(database_id) AS 'DB',
   *
FROM
   sys.change_tracking_databases
```

## How to do it...

To enable/disable change tracking, perform the following steps:

1. Open **PowerShell ISE** as an administrator.

2. Import the `SQLPS` module and create a new SMO Server object as follows:

```
#import SQL Server module
Import-Module SQLPS -DisableNameChecking

#replace this with your instance name
$instanceName = "localhost"
$server = New-Object -TypeName
Microsoft.SqlServer.Management.Smo.Server -ArgumentList
$instanceName
```

3. Add the following script and run it:

```
$databaseName = "TestDB"
$database = $server.Databases[$databaseName]

#enable the Change Tracking feature
$database.ChangeTrackingEnabled
$database.ChangeTrackingEnabled = $true
$database.Alter()
$database.Refresh()

#confirm
$database.ChangeTrackingEnabled
```

4. To disable change tracking, you just need to set the `ChangeTrackingEnabled` database property to `false` and invoke the `Alter` method again:

```
$database.ChangeTrackingEnabled = $false
$database.Alter()
```

## How it works...

Change Tracking is a database-level feature that can be turned on or off using the database object's `ChangeTrackingEnabled` property. Once you get a handle to the database, you can set this property to a `true` or `false` Boolean value, followed by an invocation of the `Alter` method:

```
$database.ChangeTrackingEnabled
$database.ChangeTrackingEnabled = $true
$database.Alter()
```

## There's more...

**Change Tracking** (**CT**) is a feature introduced in SQL Server 2008. It is a lightweight solution that enables developers and administrators alike to detect whether changes have been done to a user table they are monitoring. This is a pretty lightweight solution because it only tracks those changes that have occurred and does not keep track of all intermediate changes, which is what the Enterprise feature, **Change Data Capture** (**CDC**), is capable of doing.

► Learn more about Change Tracking from MSDN at `https://msdn.microsoft.com/en-us/library/bb933875.aspx`.

▶ Mike Byrd from Solarwinds has a great article on how to use Change Tracking for near bullet-proof ETL at `http://logicalread.solarwinds.com/sql-server-change-tracking-bulletproof-etl-p1-mb01/#.VXQ0L8-vGUk`.

▶ Leonard Mwangi from Alexander Open Systems also has a great article on Change Tracking in SQL Server Pro, including the downside of this feature at `http://sqlmag.com/sql-server-2012/tracking-changes-sql-server-2012`.

## See also

▶ The *Altering database properties* recipe in *Chapter 2, SQL Server and PowerShell Basic Tasks*.

# Configuring SQL Server Audit

In this recipe, we will set up SQL Server Audit to track failed logins.

## How to do it...

These are the steps required to configure and test SQL Server Audit:

1. Open **PowerShell ISE** as an administrator.

2. Import the `SQLPS` module and create a new SMO Server object as follows:

```
#import SQL Server module
Import-Module SQLPS -DisableNameChecking

$instanceName = "localhost"
$server = New-Object -TypeName
Microsoft.SqlServer.Management.Smo.Server -ArgumentList
$instanceName
```

3. Use the following script to first create SQL Server Audit that uses a file destination:

```
$auditName = "FileAudit"

#if it exists, disable then drop
if($server.Audits[$auditName])
{
    $server.Audits[$auditName].Disable()
    $server.Audits[$auditName].Drop()
}
```

```
$serverAudit = New-Object -TypeName
Microsoft.SqlServer.Management.Smo.Audit $server,
$auditName

#set the destination as file
$serverAudit.DestinationType =
[Microsoft.SqlServer.Management.Smo.AuditDestinationType]::
File

#specify the folder where audit will be saved
$serverAudit.FilePath = "C:\Audit\"

#create
$serverAudit.Create()

#enable
$serverAudit.Enable()
```

4.  Create a Server Audit Specification using the following script:

```
$serverAuditSpecName = "FileSpecAudit"

#if exists, disable then drop
if($server.ServerAuditSpecifications[$serverAuditSpecName])
{
    $server.ServerAuditSpecifications[$serverAuditSpecName].
Disable()
    $server.ServerAuditSpecifications[$serverAuditSpecName].
Drop()
}

$serverAuditSpec = New-Object
Microsoft.SqlServer.Management.Smo.ServerAuditSpecification
$server, $serverAuditSpecName

#which Audit does this belong to?
$serverAuditSpec.AuditName = $auditName

#set up which server event will be monitored/audited
$auditActionType =
[Microsoft.SqlServer.Management.Smo.AuditActionType]::
FailedLoginGroup
```

```
#create the specification detail
$serverAuditSpecDetail = New-Object
Microsoft.SqlServer.Management.Smo.
AuditSpecificationDetail($auditActionType)

#add specification detail to audit specification
$serverAuditSpec.
AddAuditSpecificationDetail($serverAuditSpecDetail)

#create
$serverAuditSpec.Create()

#enable
$serverAuditSpec.Enable()
```

## How it works...

SQL Server Audit allows events to be tracked, monitored, and logged either at the instance-level or database-level. SQL Server Audit leverages extended events, which is a lightweight monitoring system that is built into SQL Server.

There are two main components of SQL Server Audit: SQL Server Audit and SQL Server Audit specification.

A SQL Server Audit is securable at an instance-level. This is where the events will be stored. There are three options for an audit destination: **File, Security Log**, or **Application Log**. You can see these options when you create an **Audit** from SQL Server Management Studio:

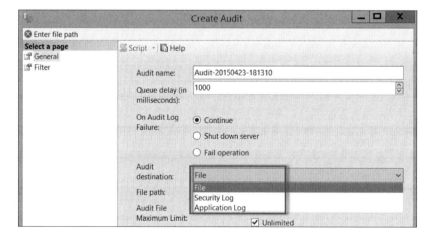

To do this in PowerShell and SMO, you need to create a `Microsoft.SqlServer.Management.Smo.Audit` object after you've initialized your SMO server object:

```
$auditName = "FileAudit"

$serverAudit = New-Object -TypeName
Microsoft.SqlServer.Management.Smo.Audit $server, $auditName
```

You can then set the `DestinationType` property. The three values are `File`, `ApplicationLog`, and `SecurityLog`:

```
#set the destination as file
$serverAudit.DestinationType =
[Microsoft.SqlServer.Management.Smo.AuditDestinationType]::File
```

Since we are setting the audit to a file destination, we need to specify which folder the audit files will be saved in:

```
#specify the folder where audit will be saved
$serverAudit.FilePath = "C:\Audit\"
```

Once the destination type and file path are set, we can create the `Audit`:

```
$serverAudit.Create()
```

By default, SQL Server Audit is created in a disabled state. To enable this, invoke the `Enable` method:

```
$serverAudit.Enable()
```

Once it has been created and enabled, you can see **Audits** from SQL Server Management Studio:

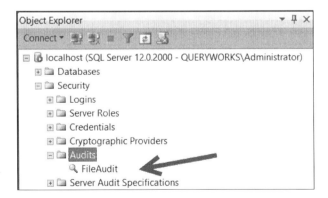

If you want to see what the equivalent T-SQL script would be like, you can invoke the Script method. It will give you the following output:

```
CREATE SERVER AUDIT [FileAudit]
TO FILE
(  FILEPATH = N'C:\Audit\'
  ,MAXSIZE = 0 MB
  ,MAX_ROLLOVER_FILES = 2147483647
  ,RESERVE_DISK_SPACE = OFF
)
WITH
(  QUEUE_DELAY = 1000
  ,ON_FAILURE = CONTINUE
  ,AUDIT_GUID = 'ece733bf-e087-4bbc-971c-474465b1fe8b'
)
ALTER SERVER AUDIT [FileAudit] WITH (STATE = ON)
```

The second component of setting up SQL Server Audit is the Audit Specification. The Audit Specification is where you identify the events or actions that you want to monitor and track. The Audit Specification belongs to an Audit that identifies how the actions are going to be recorded.

 The *SQL Server Audit Action Groups and Actions* are listed at
https://msdn.microsoft.com/en-us/library/cc280663.aspx.

The Audit Specification can also be at the server-level or database-level.

In our recipe, we created a Server Audit specification and specified which Audit it belongs to:

```
$serverAuditSpecName = "FileSpecAudit"

$serverAuditSpec = New-Object
Microsoft.SqlServer.Management.Smo.ServerAuditSpecification
$server, $serverAuditSpecName

#which Audit does this belong to?
$serverAuditSpec.AuditName = $auditName
```

In addition to specifying which audit it's tied to, we also need to specify the actions or events that it needs to monitor. In our case, we want it to monitor failed logins:

```
#set up which server event will be monitored/audited
$auditActionType = [Microsoft.SqlServer.Management.Smo.AuditActionType
]::FailedLoginGroup
```

This action type needs to be an `AuditSpecificationDetail`, which needs to be added to our Server Audit Specification object:

```
#create the specification detail
$serverAuditSpecDetail = New-Object
Microsoft.SqlServer.Management.Smo.AuditSpecificationDetail
($auditActionType)

#add specification detail to audit specification
$serverAuditSpec.AddAuditSpecificationDetail($serverAuditSpecDetail)
```

As with the server audit, this Audit Specification can be created and enabled:

```
#create
$serverAuditSpec.Create()

#enable
$serverAuditSpec.Enable()
```

Once it's created, you can view it from SQL Server Management Studio:

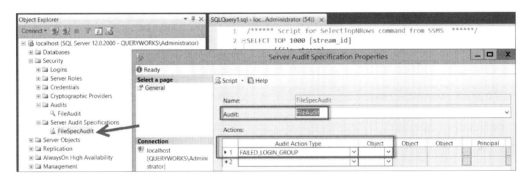

The equivalent T-SQL script to create the Server Audit Specification is as follows:

```
CREATE SERVER AUDIT SPECIFICATION [FileSpecAudit]
FOR SERVER AUDIT [FileAudit]
ADD (FAILED_LOGIN_GROUP)
WITH (STATE = ON)
```

You can now test SQL Server Audit. Go ahead and try to log in with an invalid account. These invalid login attempts will be captured by SQL Server Audit. You can check the entries from SQL Server Management Studio by right-clicking on the **Audit** object and choosing **View Audit Logs**:

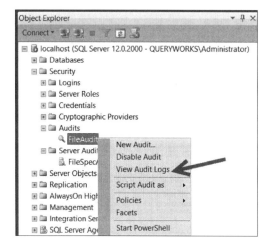

This will open up the **Log File Viewer** prompt, and you can see the entry for the invalid login attempt:

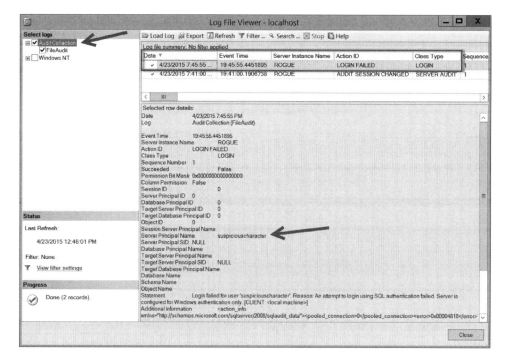

## There's more...

- ► Learn more about SQL Server Audit from the MSDN page at `https://msdn.microsoft.com/en-us/library/cc280386.aspx`.

- ► The SMO Audit class and its properties and methods are documented in MSDN at `https://msdn.microsoft.com/en-us/library/microsoft.sqlserver.management.smo.audit.aspx`.

- ► Learn more about SQL Server Extended Events at `https://msdn.microsoft.com/en-us/library/bb630282.aspx`.

## See also

- ► The *Listing SQL Server log errors* recipe of *Chapter 4, Security*

- ► The *Listing failed login attempts* recipe.

# Listing facets and their properties

In this recipe, we will list all available facets and their properties.

## How to do it...

Let's take a look at the steps for listing facets and their properties:

1. Open **PowerShell ISE** as an administrator. Import the `SQLPS` module as follows:

```
#import SQL Server module
Import-Module SQLPS -DisableNameChecking
```

2. Add the following script and run it:

```
$result = @()

[Microsoft.SqlServer.Management.Dmf.PolicyStore]::Facets |
ForEach-Object {
    $facet = $_
    $facet.FacetProperties |
    ForEach-Object {
        $property = $_
        $item = [PSCustomObject] @{
            Name = $facet.Name
```

```
                    PropertyName = $property.Name
                    PropertyType = $property.PropertyType
                }
                $result += $item
            }
        }

        $result |
        Format-Table
```

3. When the script successfully finishes executing, the resulting screen should display all the facets and their properties.

```
Name                     PropertyName                PropertyType
----                     ------------                ------------
ApplicationRole          CreateDate                  System.DateTime
ApplicationRole          DateLastModified            System.DateTime
ApplicationRole          ID                          System.Int32
ApplicationRole          DefaultSchema               System.String
ApplicationRole          Name                        System.String
AsymmetricKey            ID                          System.Int32
AsymmetricKey            KeyEncryptionAlgorithm      Microsoft.SqlServer.Management
AsymmetricKey            KeyLength                   System.Int32
AsymmetricKey            Owner                       System.String
AsymmetricKey            PrivateKeyEncryptionType    Microsoft.SqlServer.Management
AsymmetricKey            PublicKey                   System.Byte[]
AsymmetricKey            Sid                         System.Byte[]
AsymmetricKey            Thumbprint                  System.Byte[]
AsymmetricKey            ProviderName                System.String
AsymmetricKey            Name                        System.String
Audit                    CreateDate                  System.DateTime
Audit                    DateLastModified            System.DateTime
Audit                    DestinationType             Microsoft.SqlServer.Management
Audit                    Enabled                     System.Boolean
Audit                    FileName                    System.String
Audit                    FilePath                    System.String
Audit                    Guid                        System.Guid
Audit                    ID                          System.Int32
Audit                    MaximumFileSize             System.Int32
Audit                    MaximumFileSizeUnit         Microsoft.SqlServer.Management
Audit                    MaximumRolloverFiles        System.Int64
```

## How it works...

Facets are introduced with SQL Server 2008's **Policy Based Management** (**PBM**) feature. PBM is a feature that allows database administrators and professionals to manage their SQL Server instances by defining policies and identifying which properties in SQL Server are in compliance or violation with these policies.

Facets are defined in MSDN as follows:

> *A set of logical properties that model the behavior or characteristics for certain types of managed targets. Simply, these are the SQL Server components manageable through PBM.*

To explore facets available in SQL Server, you need to connect to the `PolicyStore` class, using the `Microsoft.SqlServer.Management.Dmf.PolicyStore` namespace:

```
[Microsoft.SqlServer.Management.Dmf.PolicyStore]::Facets
```

Note that **Declarative Management Framework** (**DMF**) is the *legacy* PBM name (that is, the name it was given before PBM was released on the market). Although the feature was renamed, not all the libraries were. This is why you will see DMF sprinkled with some of the SMO names.

In this recipe, we iterate through all the facets and display the facet name, facet property name, and type:

```
[Microsoft.SqlServer.Management.Dmf.PolicyStore]::Facets |
ForEach-Object {
```

For each facet, we extract the respective facet properties and store them in an array so that we can view all the facets and their properties in a single tabular view:

```
[Microsoft.SqlServer.Management.Dmf.PolicyStore]::Facets |
ForEach-Object {
    $facet = $_
    $facet.FacetProperties |
    ForEach-Object {
        $property = $_
        $item = [PSCustomObject] @{
            Name = $facet.Name
            PropertyName = $property.Name
            PropertyType = $property.PropertyType
        }
        $result += $item
    }
}

$result |
Format-Table
```

To explore more about facets, use the `$facet` object and pipe it to `Get-Member`:

```
$facet | Get-Member
```

## There's more...

- You can learn more about how to administer SQL Server using Policy Based Management at `https://msdn.microsoft.com/en-us/library/bb510667.aspx`.

- Dan Jones, project manager of the SQL Server Manageability team at Microsoft, explains the origin of the term *facet* on his blog at `http://blogs.msdn.com/b/sqlpbm/archive/2008/05/24/facets.aspx`.

## See also

▶  The *Listing policies* recipe.

▶  The *Creating a policy* recipe.

# Listing policies

In this recipe, we will list policies deployed in our SQL Server instance.

## Getting ready

Check which policies are being used in your environment using **SQL Server Management Studio**. Connect to SSMS and navigate to **Management | Policy Based Management | Policies**:

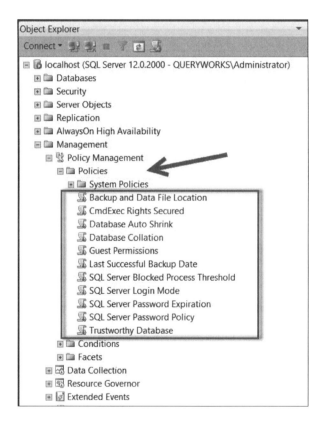

These are the same policies you should get after you run the PowerShell script in this recipe.

## How to do it...

To list policies using PowerShell, perform the following steps:

1. Open **PowerShell ISE** as an administrator.

2. Import the `SQLPS` module as follows:

   ```
   #import SQL Server module
   Import-Module SQLPS -DisableNameChecking
   ```

3. Add the following script and run it:

   ```
   #replace with your server information
   $connectionString =
   "server='localhost';Trusted_Connection=true"

   $conn = New-Object
   Microsoft.SqlServer.Management.Sdk.Sfc.SqlStoreConnection
   ($connectionString)

   #NOTE notice how the namespace is still called DMF
   #DMF - declarative management framework
   #DMF was the old reference to Policy Based Management
   $policyStore = New-Object
   Microsoft.SqlServer.Management.DMF.PolicyStore($conn)

   #display policies for this instance
   $policyStore.Policies |
   Select Name, CreateDate,
   Condition, ObjectSet, Enabled |
   Format-List
   ```

4. When the script successfully finishes executing, the resulting screen will display all the policies registered in your instance:

```
Name        : CmdExec Rights Secured
CreateDate  : 10/25/2014 9:14:45 PM
Condition   : CmdExec Rights for sysadmins Only
ObjectSet   : CmdExec Rights Secured_ObjectSet
Enabled     : False

Name        : Database Auto Shrink
CreateDate  : 10/25/2014 9:14:45 PM
Condition   : Auto Shrink Disabled
ObjectSet   : Database Auto Shrink_ObjectSet
Enabled     : False

Name        : Database Collation
CreateDate  : 10/25/2014 9:14:45 PM
Condition   : Collation Matches master or model
ObjectSet   : Database Collation_ObjectSet
Enabled     : False

Name        : Guest Permissions
CreateDate  : 10/25/2014 9:14:45 PM
Condition   : Has No Database Access
ObjectSet   : Guest Permissions_ObjectSet
Enabled     : False

Name        : Last Successful Backup Date
CreateDate  : 10/25/2014 9:14:45 PM
Condition   : Safe Last Backup Date
ObjectSet   : Last Successful Backup Date_ObjectSet
Enabled     : False
```

## How it works...

To list the policies in your instance, you need to connect to the `PolicyStore` class, which is connected to your SQL Server instance. Note that the `PolicyStore` class requires a different type of `Connection` compared to the SMO server connections that we have been making in the previous recipes.

To connect to the `PolicyStore` class, you first need to create `Sfc.SqlStoreConnection`. This accepts a connection string that identifies your server name, the authentication method, and/or details:

```
$connectionString = "server='localhost';Trusted_Connection=true"

$conn = New-Object
Microsoft.SQlServer.Management.Sdk.Sfc.SqlStoreConnection
($connectionString)
```

Once `Sfc.SqlStoreConnection` has been established, you can connect to the `PolicyStore` class:

```
#NOTE notice how the namespace is still called DMF
#DMF - declarative management framework
```

```
#DMF was the old reference to Policy Based Management
$policyStore = New-Object
Microsoft.SqlServer.Management.DMF.PolicyStore($conn)
```

Once you have a handle to the `PolicyStore` class, you can use the `Policies` object and list the `name`, `create date`, and `condition`, among other properties:

```
$policyStore.Policies |
Select Name, CreateDate, Condition, ObjectSet, Enabled |
Format-List
```

The `PolicyStore` class has several other properties and members that you may find useful as you start scripting to get more information on policies in your instance. You can pipe the `$policyStore` object to the `Get-Member` cmdlet to learn more about this. The methods that you may find useful are `CreatePolicyFromFacet`, `EnumPoliciesOnFacet`, `EnumPolicyCategories`, `ImportPolicy`, `PurgeHealthState`, `Refresh`, and `RepairPolicyAutomation`.

## There's more...

To learn more about the `SqlStoreConnection` class, check out the MSDN documentation page at `http://msdn.microsoft.com/en-us/library/microsoft.sqlserver.management.sdk.sfc.sqlstoreconnection.aspx`.

## See also

▸ The *Listing facets and their properties* recipe.

# Exporting a policy

In this recipe, we will export a policy to an XML file using PowerShell.

## Getting ready

In this recipe, we will export a policy called **Password Expiry** to an XML file. To do this, we must first create this policy. Alternatively, instead of creating this policy, you can substitute this **Password Expiry** policy with another policy that exists in your system. The steps to create this policy are as follows:

1. Log in to **SQL Server Management Studio** and navigate to **Management | Policy Management**.

2. Right-click on **Conditions** and select **New Condition**.

3. Create a new condition as follows:

   1. Set **Name** to **Password Expiry Condition**.

   2. Select **Login Options** for **Facet**.

   3. Use **@PasswordExpirationEnabled = True** for **Expression**.

4. Click on **OK** when done.

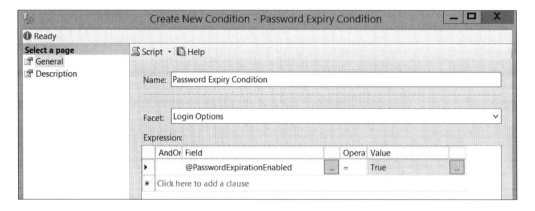

5. Right-click on **Policies** and select **New Policy**.

6. Create a new policy as follows:

   4. Type **Password Expiry** for the **Name** property.

   5. Use "**Password Expiry Condition**" for the **Condition**.

   6. Leave the checkbox for **Against Targets** checked, since we want to target every login.

   7. Change **Evaluation Mode** to **On demand**.

   8. Change **Server Restriction** to **None**.

7. Click on **OK** when done.

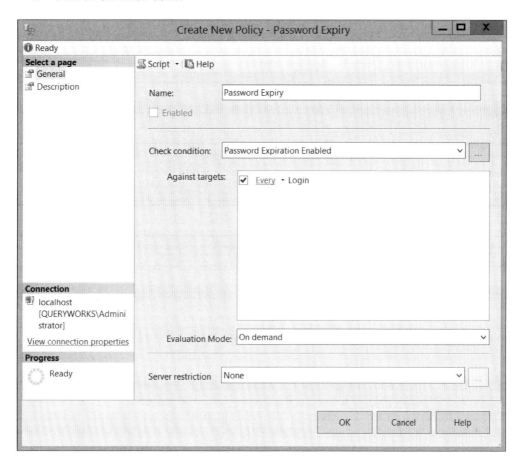

## How to do it...

To export a policy to an XML file, perform the following steps:

1. Open **PowerShell ISE** as an administrator.

2. Import the SQLPS module as follows:

```
#import SQL Server module
Import-Module SQLPS -DisableNameChecking
```

3. Add the following script and run it:

```
$connectionString =
"server='localhost';Trusted_Connection=true"

#policy to export
$policyName = "Password Expiry"

#where to export
$exportFolder = "C:\Temp\"

#set up connection
$conn = New-Object Microsoft.SqlServer.Management.Sdk.Sfc.SqlStore
Connection($connectionString)

#NOTE this is still called DMF, which stands for
#PBM's old name, Declarative Management Framework
$policyStore = New-Object Microsoft.SqlServer.Management.DMF.
PolicyStore($conn)

#get handle to policy you want to export
$policy = $policyStore.Policies[$policyName]

#where to export
$policyFileName = "$($policy.Name).xml"
$exportPath = Join-Path $exportFolder $policyFileName

#create an XML writer, to enable us to
#write an XML file
$XMLWriter = [System.Xml.XmlWriter]::Create($exportPath)
$policy.Serialize($XMLWriter)
$XMLWriter.Close()
```

## How it works...

Policies are stored as XML documents, so these policies can be easily exported as XML files.

To export a policy, you first need to get a handle to the `PolicyStore` class:

```
$policyStore = New-Object
Microsoft.SqlServer.Management.DMF.PolicyStore($conn)
```

Once the connection to the `PolicyStore` class is established, you can get a handle to the policy you want to export:

```
#policy to export
$policyName = "Password Expiry"

#get handle to policy you want to export
$policy = $policyStore.Policies[$policyName]
```

Exporting the policy requires writing the contents of the policy to an XML file in your filesystem. You need to first specify what the exported filename should be and where it should be stored:

```
#where to export
$exportFolder = "C:\Temp\"

#where to export
$policyFileName = "$($policy.Name).xml"
$exportPath = Join-Path $exportFolder $policyFileName
```

To do the actual export, we will need to use the `XMLWriter` class. This will read the policy saved in our SQL Server instance and write it to disk:

```
#create an XML writer, to enable us to
#write an XML file
$XMLWriter = [System.Xml.XmlWriter]::Create($exportPath)
$policy.Serialize($XMLWriter)
$XMLWriter.Close()
```

Once this is done, double-check the file that was created. When you open it, you will see the XML structure used to store your policies. To confirm that the export format is not corrupted, you can choose to delete the current policy you have and import the file that was created by this recipe.

## There's more...

To export a policy from **SQL Server Management Studio**, you can right-click on the policy and select **Export Policy**, as shown in the following screenshot:

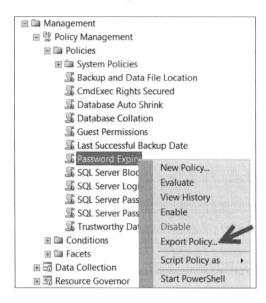

## See also

▸ The *Listing policies* recipe.

▸ The *Importing a policy* recipe.

# Importing a policy

This recipe will show you how you can import a policy stored as an XML file into SQL Server.

## Getting ready

In this recipe, we will use an XML policy that comes with the default SQL Server installation. This policy is called **Database Page Verification.xml** and is stored in `C:\Program Files (x86)\Microsoft SQL Server\120\Tools\Policies\DatabaseEngine\1033`.

Feel free to substitute this with a policy that is available in your system.

## How to do it...

These are the steps required to import a policy using PowerShell:

1. Open **PowerShell ISE** as an administrator.

2. Import the SQLPS module:

```
#import SQL Server module
Import-Module SQLPS -DisableNameChecking
```

3. Add the following script and run it:

```
$connectionString =
"server='localhost';Trusted_Connection=true"

#set up connection
$conn = New-Object
Microsoft.SQlServer.Management.Sdk.Sfc.SqlStoreConnection
($connectionString)

#NOTE this is still called DMF, which stands for
#PBM's old name, Declarative Management Framework
$policyStore = New-Object Microsoft.SqlServer.Management.DMF.
PolicyStore($conn)

#you can replace this with your own file
$policyXmlPath = "C:\Program Files (x86)\Microsoft SQL
Server\120\Tools\Policies\DatabaseEngine\1033\Database
Page Verification.xml"

$xmlReader = [System.Xml.XmlReader]::Create($policyXmlPath)

#ready to import
$policyStore.ImportPolicy($xmlReader,
[Microsoft.SqlServer.Management.Dmf.ImportPolicyEnabledState]::Unc
hanged, $true, $true)

#list policies to confirm
$policyStore.Policies
```

4. All the loaded policies should be listed when the script has finished executing. Check whether the Database Page Verification policy is included in the list or not.

## How it works...

To import a policy defined in an XML file, you will first need to connect to the
PolicyStore class:

```
$connectionString = "server='localhost';Trusted_Connection=true"

#set up connection
$conn = New-Object
Microsoft.SQlServer.Management.Sdk.Sfc.SqlStoreConnection
($connectionString)

#NOTE this is still called DMF, which stands for
#PBM's old name, Declarative Management Framework
$policyStore = New-Object
Microsoft.SqlServer.Management.DMF.PolicyStore($conn)
```

You will also need to specify the file that you want to import. For our recipe, we are using the
one that comes with your SQL Server installation, which is located in the Tools\Policies\
DatabaseEngine folder:

```
#you can replace this with your own file
$policyXmlPath = "C:\Program Files (x86)\Microsoft SQL
Server\120\Tools\Policies\DatabaseEngine\1033\Database Page
Verification.xml"
```

This XML file needs to be created in our script using an XMLReader class:

```
$xmlReader = [System.Xml.XmlReader]::Create($policyXmlPath)
```

Once the XMLReader object is created with the content of the policy, we can use the
ImportPolicy method of the PolicyStore object to import the definition into SQL Server:

```
$policyStore.ImportPolicy($xmlReader,
[Microsoft.SqlServer.Management.Dmf.ImportPolicyEnabledState]::
Unchanged, $true, $true)
```

If you want to import all policies, you can get all the XML files from the default path for the
policies using the Get-ChildItem cmdlet. Iterate through each file and load each of them
using the ImportPolicy method:

```
$xmlPath = "C:\Program Files (x86)\Microsoft SQL
Server\120\Tools\Policies\DatabaseEngine\1033\"

Get-ChildItem -Path "$($xmlPath)*.xml" |
ForEach-Object {
```

```
$xmlReader = [System.Xml.XmlReader]::Create($_.FullName)
$policyStore.ImportPolicy($xmlReader,
[Microsoft.SqlServer.Management.Dmf.ImportPolicyEnabledState]::
Unchanged, $true, $true) |
   Out-Null
}
```

## There's more...

The ImportPolicy class accepts the following four parameters:

▸ An XMLReader that contains the policy

▸ ImportEnabledState

▸ overwriteExistingPolicy: this has a Boolean value

▸ overwriteExistingCondition this has a Boolean value

## See also

▸ The *Listing policies* recipe.

▸ The *Exporting a policy* recipe.

# Creating a condition

In this recipe, we will create a condition that will later be used for a policy, programmatically.

## Getting ready

In this recipe, we will create a condition called xp_cmdshell is disabled that checks the Server Security facet, XPCmdShellEnabled.

## How to do it...

These are the steps required to create a condition:

1. Open **PowerShell ISE** as an administrator.

2. Import the SQLPS module and create a new SQL Server object as follows:

   ```
   #import SQL Server module
   Import-Module SQLPS -DisableNameChecking
   ```

```
$connectionString =
"server='localhost';Trusted_Connection=true"

$conn = New-Object
Microsoft.SQlServer.Management.Sdk.Sfc.SqlStoreConnection
($connectionString)

$policyStore = New-Object
Microsoft.SqlServer.Management.DMF.PolicyStore($conn)
```

3. Add the following script and run it:

```
$conditionName = "xp_cmdshell is disabled"

if ($policyStore.Conditions[$conditionName])
{
    #we cannot delete a condition referenced by a policy
    #before we remove the condition
    #we must remove the dependent policies
        $policyStore.Conditions[$conditionName].
EnumDependentPolicies() |
      ForEach-Object {
          $policy = $_
          $policy.Drop()
      }

    #now remove the condition
    $policyStore.Conditions[$conditionName].Drop()
}

#facet name
#we are retrieving facet name in this manner because
#some facet names are different from the display names

#note this is PowerShell V3 syntax Where-Object syntax
#beginning in Windows PowerShell 3.0, Where-Object adds
#comparison operators as parameters in a Where-Object command
$selectedFacetDisplayName = "Server Security"
$selectedFacet =
[Microsoft.SqlServer.Management.Dmf.PolicyStore]::Facets |
Where-Object DisplayName -eq $selectedFacetDisplayName

#display, for visual reference
$selectedfacet.Name
```

```
#create condition
$condition = New-Object
Microsoft.SqlServer.Management.Dmf.Condition($conn,
$conditionName)
$condition.Facet = $selectedFacet.Name

#a condition consists of a facet, an operator,
#and a value to compare to
$op = [Microsoft.SqlServer.Management.Dmf.OperatorType]::
EQ
$attr = New-Object
Microsoft.SqlServer.Management.Dmf.ExpressionNodeAttribute
("XPCmdShellEnabled")
$value =
[Microsoft.SqlServer.Management.Dmf.ExpressionNode]::
ConstructNode($false)

#create the expression node
#this is equivalent to "@XPCmdShellEnabled = false"
$expressionNode = New-Object
Microsoft.SqlServer.Management.Dmf.ExpressionNodeOperator
($op, $attr, $value)

#display expression node that was constructed
$expressionNode

#assign the expression node to the condition, and create
$condition.ExpressionNode = $expressionNode
$condition.Create()

#confirm by displaying  conditions in PolicyStore
$policyStore.Conditions |
Where-Object Name -eq $conditionName |
Select-Object Name, Facet, ExpressionNode |
Format-Table -AutoSize
```

4. When the script finishes execution of this code, you will see the new condition displayed in the resulting output:

```
Name            : xp_cmdshell is disabled
Facet           : IServerSecurityFacet
ExpressionNode  : @XPCmdShellEnabled = False()
```

To confirm visually from **SQL Server Management Studio**, connect to SSMS.

5. Go to **Management** and then go to **Policy Management | Conditions**.

6. Double-click on the **xp_cmdshell is disabled** condition.

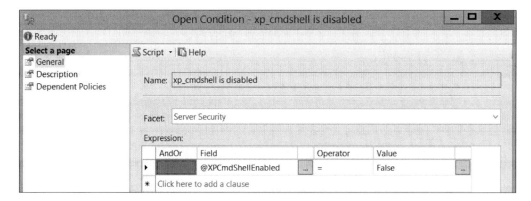

# How it works...

Creating a condition for Policy Based Management requires creating what is called an **expression node**. This is the expression that will be utilized by policies, and evaluated to be true or false:

```
#a condition consists of a facet, an operator,
#and a value to compare to
$op = [Microsoft.SqlServer.Management.Dmf.OperatorType]::EQ
$attr = New-Object
Microsoft.SqlServer.Management.Dmf.ExpressionNodeAttribute
("XPCmdShellEnabled")
$value = [Microsoft.SqlServer.Management.Dmf.ExpressionNode]::
ConstructNode($false)
```

To put these together, we use the `ExpressionNodeOperator` class of the `Microsoft.SqlServer.Management.Dmf` namespace to construct the final expression node. The constructor, or special method to create a new object of this class accepts an operator type, a left expression, and a right expression:

```
#create the expression node
#this is equivalent to "@XPCmdShellEnabled = false"
$expressionNode = New-Object
Microsoft.SqlServer.Management.Dmf.ExpressionNodeOperator
($op, $attr, $value)
```

Some conditions are straightforward and will not require `ExpressionNodeOperator` to construct them. For example, let's take a look at the following conditions:

▶  `@Size <= 100`

▶  `@ID >= 4`

▶  `Name = 'sqlagent'`

The constructed expression node needs to be assigned to the condition object:

```
#assign the expression node to the condition, and create
$condition.ExpressionNode = $expressionNode
```

Once the expression has been assigned, we can invoke the `Create` method of the `Microsoft.SqlServer.Management.Dmf.Condition` class to create the condition in SQL Server:

```
$condition.Create()
```

## There's more...

Here are a few useful links to `ExpressionNodes` and `ExpressionNodeOperator`:

▶ ExpressionNodeOperator: https://msdn.microsoft.com/en-us/library/cc286169.aspx

▶ ExpressionNode: https://msdn.microsoft.com/en-us/library/microsoft.sqlserver.management.dmf.expressionnode.aspx

## See also

▶ The *Creating a policy* recipe.

# Creating a policy

In this recipe, we will create a policy programmatically using PowerShell.

## Getting ready

In this recipe, we will use the condition called `xp_cmdshell is disabled`, which we created in a previous recipe, to create a policy called `xp_cmdshell must be disabled`. Feel free to substitute this with a condition that is available in your instance.

## How to do it...

These are the steps required to create a policy:

1. Open **PowerShell ISE** as an administrator.

2. Import the `SQLPS` module and create a new SQL Server object as follows:

```
#import SQL Server module
Import-Module SQLPS -DisableNameChecking

$connectionString =
"server='localhost';Trusted_Connection=true"
$conn = New-Object
Microsoft.SQlServer.Management.Sdk.Sfc.SqlStoreConnection
($connectionString)
$policyStore = New-Object
Microsoft.SqlServer.Management.DMF.PolicyStore($conn)
```

3. Add the following script and run it:

```
$policyName = "xp_cmdshell must be disabled"
$conditionName = "xp_cmdshell is disabled"

if ($policyStore.Policies[$policyName])
{
    $policyStore.Policies[$policyName].Drop()
}


#facet name this policy refers to
$selectedFacetDisplayName = "Server Security"
$selectedFacet =
[Microsoft.SqlServer.Management.Dmf.PolicyStore]::Facets |
Where-Object DisplayName -eq $selectedFacetDisplayName

#create objectset
#objectset represents a policy-based management
#set of objects
$objectsetName = "$($policyName)_ObjectSet"

#remove first if this object set already exists
if($policyStore.ObjectSets[$objectsetName])
{
    $policyStore.ObjectSets[$objectsetName].Drop()
}

$objectset = New-Object
Microsoft.SqlServer.Management.Dmf.ObjectSet($policyStore,
$objectsetName)
$objectset.Facet = $selectedFacet.Name
$objectset.Create()

#to confirm, display objectset name
$objectset.Name
$policyStore.ObjectSets |
Where-Object Name -eq $objectsetName |
Format-List

#create policy
$policy = New-Object
Microsoft.SQLServer.Management.Dmf.Policy ($conn,
$policyName)
```

```
#assumption here is condition has been pre-created
#if not, see recipe for creating a condition
$policy.Condition=$conditionName
$policy.ObjectSet = $objectsetName
$policy.AutomatedPolicyEvaluationMode=[Microsoft.SqlServer.
Management.Dmf.AutomatedPolicyEvaluationMode]::None
$policy.Create()

#confirm, display policies
$policyStore.Policies |
Where-Object Name -eq $policyName
```

## How it works...

To start, you need to create a Policy instance:

```
#create policy
$policy = New-Object Microsoft.SQLServer.Management.Dmf.Policy
($conn, $policyName)
```

Before you create a policy, you need to make sure that you have condition(s) available that you can use to attach to your policy. In our recipe, we will use the xp_cmdshell is disabled condition.

 The xp_cmdshell is disabled condition is created in the *Create a condition* recipe.

To attach a condition to a policy, you can assign this to the policy's condition property:

```
#assumption here is conditions have been pre-created
$policy.Condition=$conditionName
```

Policy Based Management also requires an object set. An object set is defined in MSDN as an object that *represents a policy-based management set of objects*. The object set provides the target objects for the policy, in our case, our facet:

```
#create objectset
#objectset represents a policy-based management set of objects
$objectsetName = "$($policyName)_ObjectSet"
$objectset = New-Object
Microsoft.SqlServer.Management.Dmf.ObjectSet($policyStore,
$objectsetName)
$objectset.Facet = $selectedfacet.Name
$objectset.Create()
```

You will also need to specify what the evaluation mode is. The valid values for the evaluation mode are as follows:

| Evaluation mode | Description |
|---|---|
| None | No policy checking |
| Enforce | Use DDL triggers to evaluate or prevent policy violations |
| CheckOnChanges | Use event notification to evaluate a policy when changes happen |
| CheckOnSchedule | Use SQL Server Agent to evaluate a policy based on a schedule |

Not all facets support all possible evaluation modes. Most facets support OnDemand (for example, None) and OnSchedule. Aaron Bertrand posted a blog called *Policy-Based Management: Which facets support which evaluation methods?* that provides a way to determine which evaluation methods are supported by each facet (http://sqlblog. com/blogs/aaron_bertrand/archive/2011/10/03/policy-based-management- which-facets-support-which-evaluation-methods.aspx).

For our purposes, we will just choose None or OnDemand:

```
$policy.AutomatedPolicyEvaluationMode=
[Microsoft.SqlServer.Management.Dmf.AutomatedPolicyEvaluationMode]::N
one
```

When ready, invoke the Create method of the policy object:

```
$policy.Create()
```

## There's more...

The complete EvaluationMode enumeration values can be found at http://msdn. microsoft.com/en-us/library/microsoft.sqlserver.management.dmf.automa tedpolicyevaluationmode(v=sql.110).aspx.

## See also

► The *Creating a condition* recipe.

# Evaluating a policy

In this recipe, we will evaluate a policy against our SQL Server instance.

## Getting ready

In this recipe, we will evaluate the xp_cmdshell must be disabled policy, which we created in a previous recipe. We also want to export this to an XML file and there are two different ways of evaluating the policy. Use the *Exporting a policy* recipe to export the xp_cmdshell must be disabled policy and save it in C:\Temp. Alternatively, you can perform the following steps:

1. Log in to **SQL Server Management Studio**.

2. Go to **Management | Policy Management** and select **Policies**.

3. Right-click on the **xp_cmdshell must be disabled** policy and select **Export Policy**.

4. Save this policy in C:\Temp.

Feel free to substitute this with a policy that is available in your instance.

## How to do it...

These are the steps required to evaluate a policy using PowerShell:

1. Open **PowerShell ISE** as an administrator.

2. Import the SQLPS module and create a new SQL Server object as follows:

```
#import SQL Server module
Import-Module SQLPS -DisableNameChecking

$instanceName = "localhost"

$connectionString =
"server='localhost';Trusted_Connection=true"

$conn = New-Object
Microsoft.SQlServer.Management.Sdk.Sfc.SqlStoreConnection
($connectionString)

$policyStore = New-Object
Microsoft.SqlServer.Management.DMF.PolicyStore($conn)
```

3. Add the following script and run it:

```
$policyName = "xp_cmdshell must be disabled"

$policy = $policyStore.Policies[$policyName]

#evaluate using the Evaluate() method
$policy.Evaluate(
[Microsoft.SqlServer.Management.DMF.
AdHocPolicyEvaluationMode]::Check,$conn)

#check evaluation history
Write-Host "$("=" * 100)'n Evaluation Histories'n$("=" *
100)"
$policy.EvaluationHistories

#an alternative way to invoke a policy is
#to use the Invoke-PolicyEvaluation cmdlet instead
#of using the Evaluate() method
#however you need to have a handle to the actual XML file
#this alternative way allows you to capture the results
#which you can save to another XML file
#assuming we have this policy definition in
$file = "C:\Temp\$($policyName).xml"
$result = Invoke-PolicyEvaluation -Policy $file
-TargetServer $instanceName


#display results
Write-Host "$("=" * 100)'n Invocation Result'n$("=" * 100)"
$result
```

4. Your result should look like the following screenshot:

```
====================================================================================================
Evaluation Histories
====================================================================================================

 ID Policy Name                   Result Start Date          End Date            Messages
 -- -----------                   ------ ----------          --------            --------
  9 xp_cmdshell must be disabled  False  4/12/2015 7:34 PM   4/12/2015 7:34 PM
 10 xp_cmdshell must be disabled  False  4/12/2015 7:34 PM   4/12/2015 7:34 PM
 11 xp_cmdshell must be disabled  False  4/12/2015 7:35 PM   4/12/2015 7:35 PM
 12 xp_cmdshell must be disabled  False  4/12/2015 7:36 PM   4/12/2015 7:36 PM
 13 xp_cmdshell must be disabled  False  4/12/2015 7:36 PM   4/12/2015 7:36 PM
 14 xp_cmdshell must be disabled  False  4/12/2015 7:36 PM   4/12/2015 7:36 PM
====================================================================================================
Invocation Result
====================================================================================================
  1 xp_cmdshell must be disabled  False  4/12/2015 7:36 PM   4/12/2015 7:36 PM
```

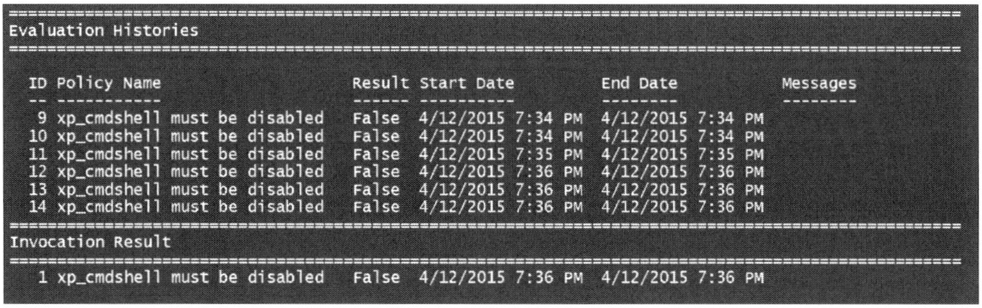

## How it works...

In this recipe, we will cover a couple of ways to evaluate a policy.

The first way is using the `Policy` object. We first need to get a handle to the `Policy` object:

```
$policyName = "xp_cmdshell must be disabled"
$policy = $policyStore.Policies[$policyName]
```

The `policy` object has a method called `Evaluate`, which we can invoke as follows:

```
$policy.Evaluate([Microsoft.SqlServer.Management.DMF.AdHocPolicyEvalua
tionMode]::Check,$conn)
```

The `Evaluate` method returns a Boolean value—`true` if every object you evaluated the policy against is in compliance with the policy, and `false` otherwise.

An alternative way to invoke a policy is using the `Invoke-PolicyEvaluation` cmdlet. You will need to provide the full path of the XML file that contains the policy. This cmdlet also returns the result of the evaluation, also in the XML format, which you can either display or save in a file:

```
$result = Invoke-PolicyEvaluation -Policy $file -TargetServer
$instanceName
```

## There's more...

To get more information on `Invoke-PolicyEvaluation`, type the following command:

```
Get-Help Invoke-PolicyEvaluation
```

You will quickly find out that this cmdlet allows you to:

- Evaluate policies against your target objects
- Retrieve results in an XML format, which you can redirect to an XML file for storage
- Reconfigure objects in the target set

## See also

- The *Creating a policy* recipe.

# Running and saving a profiler trace event

In this recipe, we will run and save a profiler trace event using PowerShell.

## Getting ready

To run and save a profiler trace event, we will need to use the **x86 Version** of PowerShell and/or PowerShell ISE. This is unfortunate, but some of the classes that we need to use are only supported in 32-bit mode.

In this recipe, we will need to use the standard trace **template definition file** (**TDF**) as our starting template for the trace we're going to run. This can be found in `C:\Program Files (x86)\Microsoft SQL Server\120\Tools\Profiler\Templates\Microsoft SQL Server\110\Standard.tdf`.

For our purposes, we are also going to limit the number of events to 10.

## How to do it...

Let's take a look at the steps to run and save a profiler trace event:

1. Open **PowerShell ISE (x86)** as an administrator. Note that it is **important to use the x86 PowerShell console or ISE** for this recipe, otherwise you will get errors when you run the following script.

   If you are using the command line or using this in a script, you can also execute the following command to enter an x86 shell:

   ```
   &"$env:windir\syswow64\windowspowershell\v1.0\
   powershell.exe"
   ```

2. Import the `SQLPS` module and create a new SMO Server object as follows:

   ```
   #import SQL Server module
   Import-Module SQLPS -DisableNameChecking

   #replace this with your instance name
   $instanceName = "localhost"
   $server = New-Object -TypeName
   Microsoft.SqlServer.Management.Smo.Server -ArgumentList
   $instanceName
   ```

3. Import the additional `Microsoft.SqlServer.ConnectionInfo` and `Microsoft.SqlServer.ConnectionInfoExtended` libraries. These are needed to use our `TraceFile` and `TraceServer` classes. You can use the `Add-Type` cmdlet to add these libraries:

```
Add-Type -AssemblyName "Microsoft.SqlServer.ConnectionInfo,
Version=12.0.0.0, Culture=neutral,
PublicKeyToken=89845dcd8080cc91"

Add-Type -AssemblyName
"Microsoft.SqlServer.ConnectionInfoExtended,
Version=12.0.0.0, Culture=neutral,
PublicKeyToken=89845dcd8080cc91"
```

4. Add the following script and run it:

```
#create SqlConnectionInfo object,
#specifically required to run the traces
#need to specifically use the ConnectionInfoBase type
[Microsoft.SqlServer.Management.Common.ConnectionInfoBase]
$conn = New-Object
Microsoft.SqlServer.Management.Common.SqlConnectionInfo
-ArgumentList "localhost"

$conn.UseIntegratedSecurity = $true

#create new TraceServer object
#The TraceServer class can start and read traces
$trcserver = New-Object -TypeName
Microsoft.SqlServer.Management.Trace.TraceServer

#need to get a handle to a Trace Template
#in this case we are using the Standard template
#that comes with Microsoft
$standardTemplate = "C:\Program Files (x86)\Microsoft SQL
Server\120\Tools\Profiler\Templates\Microsoft SQL
Server\120\Standard.tdf"

$trcserver.InitializeAsReader($conn,$standardTemplate) |
Out-Null

$received = 0

#where do you want to write the trace?
#here we compose a timestamped file
$folder = "C:\Temp\"
$currdate = Get-Date -Format "yyyy-MM-dd_hmmtt"
$filename = "$($instanceName)_trace_$($currdate).trc"
$outputtrace = Join-Path $folder $filename
```

```
#number of events to capture
$numevents = 10

#create new TraceFile object
#and initialize as writer
#The TraceFile class can read and write a Trace File
$trcwriter = New-Object
Microsoft.SqlServer.Management.Trace.TraceFile

$trcwriter.InitializeAsWriter($trcserver,$outputtrace) |
Out-Null

while ($trcserver.Read())
{
    #write incoming trace to file
    $trcwriter.Write() | Out-Null
    $received++

    #we don't know how many columns are included
    #in the template so we will have to loop if we
    #want to capture and display all of them

    #get number of columns
    #we need to subtract 1 because column array
    #is zero-based, ie index starts at 0
    $cols = ($trcserver.FieldCount) -1

    #we'll need to dynamically create a hash table to
    #contain the trace events

    #because we need to dynamically build this hash table
    #based on number of columns included in a template,
    #we'll have to store the code to build the hash table
    #as string first and then invoke expression
    #to actually build the hash table in PowerShell
    $hashtablestr = "'$hashtable = '$null; 'n"
    $hashtablestr += "'$hashtablestr = @{   'n"
    for($i = 0;$i -le $cols; $i++)
    {
        $colname = $trcserver.GetName($i)

        #add each column to our hash table
        #we will not capture the binary data
        if($colname -ne "BinaryData")
        {
         $colvalue =
$trcserver.GetValue($trcserver.GetOrdinal($colname))
```

```
            $hashtablestr += "'"$($colname)'"='"$($colvalue)'"
'n"
        }
    }
    $hashtablestr += "}"

    #create the real hash table
    Invoke-Expression $hashtablestr

    #display
    $item = New-Object PSObject -Property $hashtable
    $item | Format-List

    if($received -ge $numevents)
    {
        break
    }
}

$trcwriter.Close()
$trcserver.Close()
```

5.  What you should see in your **PowerShell ISE** results pane is a stream of events that
    are happening in SQL Server, which is similar to what you would see if you were
    running **SQL Server Profiler**.

```
StartTime       : 04/16/2015 22:17:20
CPU             :
Reads           :
EventClass      : ExistingConnection
Duration        :
NTUserName      : Administrator
SPID            : 51
Writes          :
TextData        : -- network protocol: LPC
                  set quoted_identifier on
                  set arithabort off
                  set numeric_roundabort off
                  set ansi_warnings on
                  set ansi_padding on
                  set ansi_nulls on
                  set concat_null_yields_null on
                  set cursor_close_on_commit off
                  set implicit_transactions off
                  set language us_english
                  set dateformat mdy
                  set datefirst 7
                  set transaction isolation level read committed

EndTime         :
ApplicationName : SQL Server Profiler - 27a6f38a-d0bc-49fd-b806-3f4570642be5
LoginName       : QUERYWORKS\Administrator
ClientProcessID : 3632
```

# How it works...

This is a long recipe. There are quite a few things going on here. What we are doing is simulating what you can do, and see, with **SQL Server Profiler** using PowerShell. There will be cases where this will be useful and cases where **SQL Server Profiler** is still the right tool for the job. Regardless, it is good to know how to do it using PowerShell.

To start, it is important to use **PowerShell ISE (x86)**, instead of the usual (x64) version that we have been using in other recipes. The classes that we need to use are only supported in 32-bit mode.

We first need to load a few extra libraries, `ConnectionInfo` and `ConnectionInfoExtended`, because we will need to pass these as arguments to the `TraceServer` class constructor when we are creating our `TraceServer` object:

```
Add-Type -AssemblyName "Microsoft.SqlServer.ConnectionInfo,
Version=12.0.0.0, Culture=neutral,
PublicKeyToken=89845dcd8080cc91"

Add-Type -AssemblyName "Microsoft.SqlServer.ConnectionInfoExtended,
Version=12.0.0.0,
Culture=neutral, PublicKeyToken=89845dcd8080cc91"
```

If you are not sure of the details of the assembly that you want to load, you can use the following script as a reference to display the assembly details, including the name, version, culture, and public key token:

```
[AppDomain]::CurrentDomain.GetAssemblies() |
ForEach-Object {
    $item = $_
    if ($item.FullName.Contains("YourSearchString"))
    {
        $item | Select FullName
    }
}
```

Next, we need to create a `SqlConnectionInfo` connection object that needs to be stored in a `ConnectionInfoBase` class:

```
#create SqlConnectionInfo object,
#specifically required to run the traces
[Microsoft.SqlServer.Management.Common.ConnectionInfoBase]
$conn = New-Object Microsoft.SqlServer.Management.Common.
SqlConnectionInfo
-ArgumentList "localhost"

$conn.UseIntegratedSecurity = $true
```

There are a couple of classes specific to `Trace` that we need to initialize. The first one is the `TraceServer,` which will enable us to start and read the traces:

```
#create new TraceServer object
#The TraceServer class can start and read traces
$trcserver = New-Object -TypeName
Microsoft.SqlServer.Management.Trace.TraceServer
```

We will need to initialize this as `Reader`, and we need to pass our connection object and the path to our **Standard Trace Template**:

```
#need to get a handle to a Trace Template
#in this case we are using the Standard template
#that comes with Microsoft
$standardTemplate = "C:\Program Files (x86)\Microsoft SQL
Server\120\Tools\Profiler\Templates\Microsoft SQL
Server\120\Standard.tdf"

$trcserver.InitializeAsReader($conn,$standardTemplate) |
Out-Null
```

The goal of our recipe is to start and read the trace, as well as write new trace events to a trace file. To achieve this, we need to create a `TraceFile` object, which allows you to write the `Trace` file:

```
#create new TraceFile object
#and initialize as writer
#The TraceFile class can read and write a Trace File
$trcwriter = New-Object Microsoft.SqlServer.Management.Trace.TraceFile

$trcwriter.InitializeAsWriter($trcserver,$outputtrace) |
Out-Null
```

Once the `TraceServer` and `TraceFile` objects are set up, we can start reading the trace. This will need to happen in a loop:

```
while ($trcserver.Read())
```

This start of the while loop will go on as long as there are events being captured by our
`TraceServer` object.

Inside the loop, we do two things. The first thing that we do is we write these events to a trace
file, using our `TraceFile` object called `$trcwriter`:

```
$trcwriter.Write()
```

The second thing that we do is display the trace. For this particular exercise, we want to
capture the events and be able to display them in a tabular fashion if we need to. To do this,
we can store this event data in a hash table and display it before the end of the loop. This is a
little bit challenging to do if you do not know which columns and how many columns are being
captured. This will depend on the trace template you are using. To accommodate different
templates, we'll first determine how many columns are being captured by the `TraceServer`
object. Note that when we retrieve the columns from the `TraceServer` object, the column
index will start at zero (0), so we need to subtract 1 from the total number of columns to avoid
any *index out of bounds* errors:

```
$cols = ($trcserver.FieldCount) -1
```

Based on the columns, we can dynamically build our hash. We can use the `GetName` method
of the `TraceServer` object to get the name of the incoming column and the `GetValue` and
`GetOrdinal` methods of the `TraceServer` class to extract the value of the column coming
in:

```
$hashtablestr = "'$hashtable = '$null; 'n"
$hashtablestr += "'$hashtable = @{  'n"
    for($i = 0;$i -le $cols; $i++)
    {
        $colname = $trcserver.GetName($i)

        #add each column to our hash
        #we will not capture the binary data
        if($colname -ne "BinaryData")
        {
            $colvalue = $trcserver.GetValue($trcserver.
GetOrdinal($colname))

            $hashtablestr += "'"$($colname)'"="'"$($colvalue)'" 'n"
        }
    }
    $hashtablestr += "}"
```

This is an example of the dynamically constructed hash code:

```
$hashtable = $null;
 $hashtable = @{
"EventClass"="SQL:BatchStarting"
"TextData"=" set quoted_identifier off "
"ApplicationName"="SQLAgent - Job Manager"
"NTUserName"="sqlagent"
"LoginName"="QUERYWORKS\sqlagent"
"CPU"=""
"Reads"=""
"Writes"=""
"Duration"=""
"ClientProcessID"="3032"
"SPID"="63"
"StartTime"="09/20/2015 10:32:55"
"EndTime"=""
}
```

We then take this dynamically created code to create the actual hash table using the `Invoke-Expression` cmdlet:

```
Invoke-Expression $hashtablestr
```

Once the hash is created, we can display it on the screen:

```
#display
$item = New-Object PSObject -Property $hashtable
$item | Format-List
```

When we are done with our loop, we need to close both the `TraceServer` and `TraceFile` handles:

```
$trcwriter.Close()
$trcserver.Close()
```

## There's more...

Check out the article in MSDN called *Trace and Replay Objects: A New API for SQL Server Tracking and Replay* at `https://msdn.microsoft.com/en-us/library/ms345134.aspx`

It is a little bit outdated but is still very relevant if you want to work programmatically with traces using .NET languages.

## See also

▶ The *Extracting the contents of a trace file* recipe.

# Extracting the contents of a trace file

In this recipe, we will extract the contents of a trace (.trc) file using PowerShell.

## Getting ready

We will need to use the **x86 Version** of PowerShell and/or PowerShell ISE for this recipe. This is unfortunate, but some of the classes that we need to use are only supported in 32-bit mode.

In this recipe, we will use a previously saved trace (.trc) file. Feel free to substitute this with a trace file that is available.

## How to do it...

Let's take a look at how we can extract the contents of a trace file:

1.  Open **PowerShell ISE** as an administrator.

2.  Import the SQLPS module:

    ```
    #import SQL Server module
    Import-Module SQLPS -DisableNameChecking
    ```

3.  Import additional libraries. These are needed to use our TraceFile and TraceServer classes. We do this as follows:

    ```
    Add-Type -AssemblyName "Microsoft.SqlServer.ConnectionInfo,
    Version=12.0.0.0, Culture=neutral,
    PublicKeyToken=89845dcd8080cc91"

    Add-Type -AssemblyName
    "Microsoft.SqlServer.ConnectionInfoExtended,
    Version=12.0.0.0, Culture=neutral,
    PublicKeyToken=89845dcd8080cc91"
    ```

4.  Add the following script and run it:

    ```
    #get the last trace file we saved in C:\Temp
       $path = Get-ChildItem C:\temp\*.trc |
             Select-Object -First 1
    ```

```
$trcreader = New-Object
Microsoft.SqlServer.Management.Trace.TraceFile
$trcreader.InitializeAsReader($path)

#extract all
$result = @()
while($trcreader.Read())
{
    #let's extract only the ones that
    #took more than 1000ms
    $duration =
$trcreader.GetValue($trcreader.GetOrdinal("Duration"))

    if($duration -ge 1000)
    {
        $cols = ($trcreader.FieldCount) -1

        #we need to dynamically build the hash table string
        #because we don't know how many columns
        #are in the incoming trace file
        $hashtablestr = "'$hashtable = @{   'n"

        for($i = 0;$i -le $cols; $i++)
        {
            $colname = $trcreader.GetName($i)

            #don't include binary data
            if($colName -ne "BinaryData")
            {
                $colvalue = $trcreader.GetValue($trcreader.
GetOrdinal($colname))
                $hashtablestr += "'"$($colname)'"="'"$($colvalue)'"
'n"
            }
        }
        $hashtablestr += "}"

        #create the real hash table
        Invoke-Expression $hashtablestr

        $item = New-Object PSObject -Property $hashtable
        $result += $item
    }
}
```

```
$trcreader.Close()
#display
$result | Format-List
```

Once the script finishes executing, the results on your screen should look similar to the following screenshot:

```
StartTime        : 04/16/2015 22:35:16
CPU              : 16
Reads            : 64
EventClass       : SQL:BatchCompleted
Duration         : 11084
NTUserName       : Administrator
SPID             : 55
Writes           : 0
TextData         : SELECT
                   SCHEMA_NAME(tt.schema_id) AS [Schema],
                   tt.name AS [Name]
                   FROM
                   sys.table_types AS tt
                   INNER JOIN sys.schemas AS stt ON stt.schema_id = tt.schema_id
                   ORDER BY
                   [Schema] ASC,[Name] ASC
EndTime          : 04/16/2015 22:35:16
ApplicationName  : Microsoft SQL Server Management Studio - Transact-SQL IntelliSense
LoginName        : QUERYWORKS\Administrator
ClientProcessID  : 4624
```

## How it works...

To extract the contents of a trace (.trc) file, we first need to load a few extra libraries, ConnectionInfo and ConnectionInfoExtended. These contain the TraceFile class we need to use in this recipe:

```
Add-Type -AssemblyName "Microsoft.SqlServer.ConnectionInfo,
Version=12.0.0.0, Culture=neutral,
PublicKeyToken=89845dcd8080cc91"


Add-Type -AssemblyName
"Microsoft.SqlServer.ConnectionInfoExtended,  Version=12.0.0.0,
Culture=neutral, PublicKeyToken=89845dcd8080cc91"
```

We then need to create a TraceFile object, which is initialized as a reader:

```
#get the last trace file we saved in C:\Temp
$path = Get-ChildItem C:\temp\*.trc |
    Select-Object -First 1
```

```
$trcreader = New-Object
Microsoft.SqlServer.Management.Trace.TraceFile
$trcreader.InitializeAsReader($path)
```

To read all the contents, we need to put the reader in a while loop and keep on iterating while there are events in the trace file to be read:

```
while($trcreader.Read())
```

In our recipe, we only considered events that had a duration longer than `1000ms`:

```
#let's extract only the ones that took more than 1000ms
$duration =
$trcreader.GetValue($trcreader.GetOrdinal("Duration"))
```

The `GetOrdinal` method of the `TraceFile` class allows you to get the *nth* column in which we find `Duration`. Using this, we can pass it to the `GetValue` method of the `TraceFile` class to extract the value in that column position.

Also, note that in our recipe, we extract all the columns except the `BinaryData` column in the trace file. We do this by looping through all the columns and putting them into a hash table that we build dynamically:

```
#we need to dynamically build the hash table string
#because we don't know how many columns are in the
#incoming trace file
$hashtablestr = "'$hashtable = @{  'n"
for($i = 0;$i -le $cols; $i++)
{
    $colname = $trcreader.GetName($i)
    #don't include binary data
    if($colName -ne "BinaryData")
    {
    $colvalue = $trcreader.GetValue($trcreader.GetOrdinal($colname))
    $hashstr += "'"$($colname)'"='"$($colvalue)'" 'n"
    }
}
$hashtablestr += "}"
```

This is an example of the dynamically constructed hash table:

```
$hashtable = $null;
 $hashtable = @{
"EventClass"="SQL:BatchStarting"
"TextData"=" set quoted_identifier off "
"ApplicationName"="SQLAgent - Job Manager"
"NTUserName"="sqlagent"
"LoginName"="QUERYWORKS\sqlagent"
"CPU"=""
"Reads"=""
"Writes"=""
"Duration"=""
"ClientProcessID"="3032"
"SPID"="63"
"StartTime"="09/20/2015 10:32:55"
"EndTime"=""
}
```

Once the hash table string is built, we can use the `Invoke-Expression` cmdlet to create the real hash table:

```
#create the real hash table
Invoke-Expression $hashtablestr
```

We then store this in an array, which we display after the loop is finished:

```
        $item = New-Object PSObject -Property $hashtable
        $result += $item


    }
  }

  $trcreader.Close()
#display
$result | Format-List
```

An alternative to dynamically building the hash table is to explicitly identify the columns you want to include in the hash. This is doable only if you are familiar with the template used when capturing the trace file. The syntax you will use will be similar to this:

```
$hashtable = @{
"EventClass"=$trcreader.GetValue($trcreader.GetOrdinal
("EventClass"))
"TextData"=$trcreader.GetValue($trcreader.GetOrdinal("TextData"))
"Duration"=$trcreader.GetValue($trcreader.GetOrdinal("Duration"))
}
$item = New-Object PSObject -Property $hashtable
$result += $item
```

## See also

> ▸  The *Running and saving a profiler trace event* recipe.

# 8
# High Availability with AlwaysOn

In this chapter, we will cover the following topics:

- ▸ Installing the Failover Cluster feature on Windows
- ▸ Enabling TCP and named pipes in SQL Server
- ▸ Enabling AlwaysOn in SQL Server
- ▸ Creating and enabling a HADR endpoint
- ▸ Granting the CONNECT permission to a HADR endpoint
- ▸ Creating an AlwaysOn Availability Group
- ▸ Joining secondary replicas to an Availability Group
- ▸ Adding an availability database to an Availability Group
- ▸ Creating an Availability Group listener
- ▸ Testing the Availability Group failover
- ▸ Monitoring the health of an Availability Group

# Introduction

There are several **high availability disaster recovery** (**HADR**) solutions supported in SQL Server with the different versions that you may be familiar with or have implemented in your environments, such as transaction log shipping, database mirroring, and transactional replication. On the Windows server-side, you can also use **Windows Server Failover Clustering** (**WSFC**). This chapter focuses on AlwaysOn.

SQL Server AlwaysOn is meant to replace database mirroring, which was deprecated in SQL Server 2012, and addresses the limitations that database mirroring faced. Some of the commonly cited limitations of database mirroring include the following:

▶ Having only one unreadable mirror

▶ Inability to failover multiple dependent databases as groups

SQL Server AlwaysOn addresses these shortcomings. AlwaysOn is an Enterprise-only feature that leverages Windows Server Failover Clustering and provides some of the following benefits:

▶ An AlwaysOn configuration can have up to four readable secondary replicas with different synchronization modes

▶ AlwaysOn secondary replicas allow reporting, backups, and DBCC statements on the secondary replicas

▶ An AlwaysOn configuration does not require shared storage, in contrast to the typical shared storage requirement for clustered SQL Server instances

There are a few prerequisites before AlwaysOn can be configured in your environment. We will cover the high level requirements in this chapter. To read the complete documentation on pre-requisites, visit the following MSDN page:

```
https://msdn.microsoft.com/en-CA/library/ff878487.aspx.
```

For this chapter, we will need to access an environment that will allow us to demonstrate how to configure AlwaysOn. You can build this environment using the SQL Server Developer edition or trial edition, as both of these have all the Enterprise features. The setup is illustrated in the following diagram:

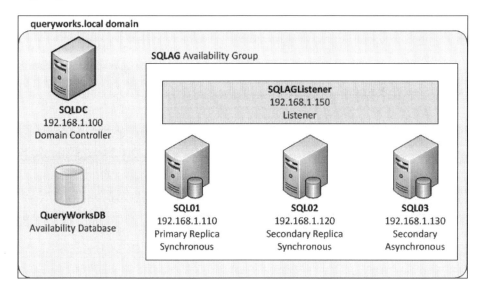

There is a total of four virtual machines in this setup, which are all in the
`queryworks.local` domain:

- ▸ SQLDC: This is a domain controller
- ▸ SQL01: This is a primary replica
- ▸ SQL02: This is a secondary replica
- ▸ SQL03: This is a secondary replica

All these VMs are set up in Windows Server 2012 R2 with Hyper-V feature installed:

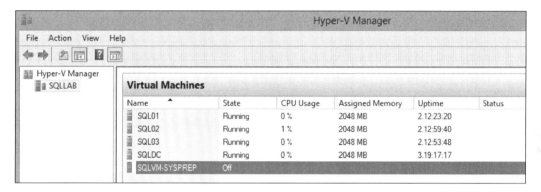

To perform the exercises in this chapter, you will need to have access to a test environment
that has a similar setup.

# Installing the Failover Cluster feature on Windows

In this recipe, we will install the Failover Cluster feature on Windows Server 2012 R2.

## Getting ready

Log in to each of the Windows Server 2012 R2 servers that will participate in the AlwaysOn
configuration and perform the following steps for each of the nodes.

## How to do it...

These are the steps required to install the Failover Cluster feature on each node:

1. Open **PowerShell ISE** as an administrator.

2. Type the following command to check whether the **Failover Clustering** feature is turned on:

```
Get-WindowsFeature Failover* |
Format-Table -Autosize
```

   If it is already installed, you will see a result similar to the following screenshot:

```
PS SQLSERVER:\> C:\Users\Administrator.QUERYWORKS\Documents\Check Failover Cluster.ps1

Display Name                    Name                    Install State
------------                    ----                    -------------
[X] Failover Clustering Failover-Clustering      Installed
```

3. If the feature is not yet installed, install it using the following PowerShell script:

```
Install-WindowsFeature -Name Failover-Clustering `
-IncludeManagementTools
```

## How it works...

Although this task is not directly related to SQL Server, enabling the Failover Clustering feature in Windows Server is essential to AlwaysOn.

PowerShell provides a cmdlet called `Install-WindowsFeature` that enables administrators to install features via a script instead of using the GUI Server Manager. This is how you can install the Failover Clustering feature in the script:

```
Install-WindowsFeature -Name Failover-Clustering `
-IncludeManagementTools
```

This can also be done by navigating to **Server Manager | Add Roles and Features** and adding the component from the **Features** window:

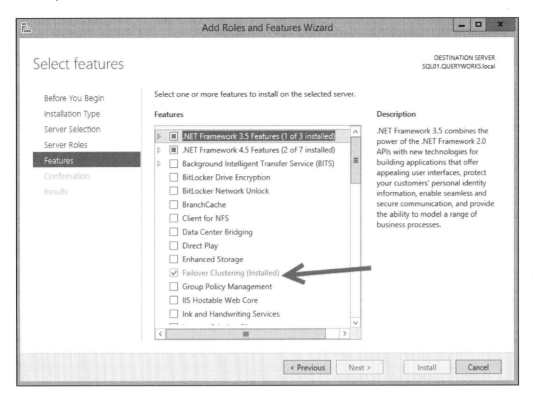

There are additional cmdlets that you can use to test and get more information about your cluster. For example, to get the cluster name, you can use a cmdlet called `Get-Cluster`. When your cluster is set up, you can use a cmdlet called `Get-ClusterNode`, and you will get a list of the nodes that are part of the cluster:

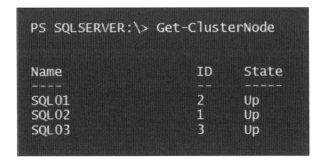

To get the cluster resources, you can use the following cmdlet:

```
Get-ClusterResource
```

To discover additional cluster-related cmdlets, you can use the `Get-Command` cmdlet with the `*Cluster*` name pattern:

```
Get-Command *Cluster*
```

## There's more...

> ▶ Read more about Windows Server Failover Clustering at `https://msdn.microsoft.com/en-us/library/hh831579.aspx`.

> ▶ Another great resource to help you understand how this feature works with SQL Server is the MSDN *Windows Server Failover Clustering (WSFC) with SQL Server* article at `https://msdn.microsoft.com/en-CA/library/hh270278.aspx`.

# Enabling TCP and named pipes in SQL Server

In this recipe, we will enable two network protocols in SQL Server.

## Getting ready

For this recipe, we will execute the code on each of the nodes, both local and remote, that will participate in the AlwaysOn configuration.

To do this, we must first ensure that `PSRemoting` is turned on in every node. Log in to each of the nodes, launch PowerShell or PowerShell ISE as an administrator, and enable remoting using the following script:

```
Enable-PSRemoting -Force
```

In addition, check the currently enabled protocols in SQL Server. You can go to SQL Server Configuration Manager and check these protocols from the **SQL Server Network Configuration** node. By default, **Named Pipes** and **TCP/IP** are disabled:

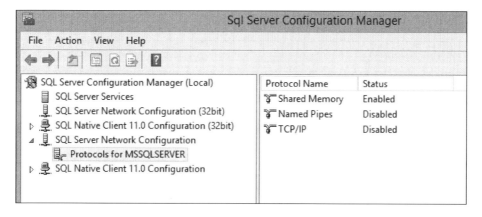

You can also do this check from PowerShell:

```
[System.Reflection.Assembly]::
LoadWithPartialName('Microsoft.SqlServer.SMO')
$instanceName = "SQL01"
$server = New-Object Microsoft.SqlServer.Management.Smo.Server
-ArgumentList $instanceName

#check TCP
$server.TcpEnabled

#check Named Pipe
$server.NamedPipesEnabled
```

## How to do it...

Perform the following steps to enable additional networking protocols in SQL Server:

1. Open **PowerShell ISE** as an administrator.

2. Add the following script and run it:

```
$cred = Get-Credential
foreach ($node in Get-ClusterNode)
{
    Write-Host "Processing $($node.Name)"

    #execute command on the remote hosts
    Invoke-Command -ComputerName $node.Name
-Credential $cred -ScriptBlock {
        Import-Module SQLPS -DisableNameChecking
```

```
#create ManagedComputer object
$wmi = New-Object
Microsoft.SqlServer.Management.Smo.WMI.ManagedComputer

#get current machine name
$computerName = $env:COMPUTERNAME

#compose URI to the server protocol
$uri =
"ManagedComputer[@Name='$($computerName)']/ServerInstance[@
Name='MSSQLSERVER']/ServerProtocol"

#enable TCP
$tcp = $wmi.GetSmoObject($uri + "[@Name='Tcp']")
$tcp.IsEnabled = $true
$tcp.Alter()
$tcp.Refresh()

#enabled named pipe
$np = $wmi.GetSmoObject($uri + "[@Name='Np']")
$np.IsEnabled = $true
$np.Alter()
$np.Refresh()

    }
}
```

3. Once the script finishes the execution, you should be able to confirm that the protocols have been enabled.

## How it works...

SQL Server's network protocols identify what kind of connections are allowed.

A default SQL Server installation will give you three protocols:

- **Shared memory**: This is the simplest protocol and requires that the clients reside in the same machine as the SQL Server instance before they are allowed to connect.

- **Named pipes**: They are useful in local area networks (LANs) and allow memory to be "shared" among processes. According to MSDN, *a part of memory is used by one process to pass information to another process, so that the output of one is the input of the other.*

- **TCP/IP**: This is probably the most common and popular protocol and allows interconnectivity not just within the LAN but also outside it from a WAN.

In AlwaysOn, we will have multiple nodes that may or may not reside in the same network. It is important that these protocols are enabled to ensure smooth interconnectivity between the different instances, roles, and components.

## There's more...

You can explore the concepts introduced in this recipe in more detail:

- ▶ The `Enable-PSRemoting` permission allows remote commands to be executed on a machine. Check out the syntax and usage at `https://msdn.microsoft.com/en-us/library/hh849694.aspx`

- ▶ Learn more about the supported network protocols in SQL Server from the documentation page at `https://msdn.microsoft.com/en-us/library/ms187892.aspx`

- ▶ The official documentation for enabling and disabling network protocols in SQL Server via the GUI or PowerShell can be found at `https://msdn.microsoft.com/en-us/library/ms191294.aspx`

# Enabling AlwaysOn in SQL Server

In this recipe, we will enable the AlwaysOn feature in SQL Server.

## Getting ready

Check whether the AlwaysOn feature is enabled. You can do this from the GUI by launching **SQL Server Configuration Manager**, right-clicking on the SQL Server database engine service, and selecting **Properties**. Click on the **AlwaysOn High Availability** tab:

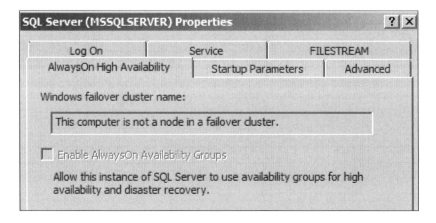

You can also do this using PowerShell by running the following code:

```
$instanceName = "SQL01"
$server = New-Object Microsoft.SqlServer.Management.Smo.Server
-ArgumentList $instanceName

#check AlwaysOn
$server.IsHadrEnabled
```

To check this feature against multiple nodes, you can use the following code snippet:

```
$nodeNames = Get-ClusterNode |
            Select-Object -ExpandProperty Name
Foreach-Object ($instanceName in $nodeNames) {
    $server = New-Object Microsoft.SqlServer.Management.Smo.Server
-ArgumentList $instanceName

    #check AlwaysOn
    $server.IsHadrEnabled
}
```

## How to do it...

Perform the following steps to enable AlwaysOn in SQL Server:

1. Open **PowerShell ISE** as an administrator.

2. Import the SQLPS module as follows:

   ```
   #import SQL Server module
   Import-Module SQLPS -DisableNameChecking
   ```

3. Add the following script and run it:

   ```
   #enable AlwaysOn for all active nodes in the cluster
   foreach ($node in Get-ClusterNode)
   {
       Write-Host "Processing $($node.Name)"

       #enable AlwaysOn
       Enable-SqlAlwaysOn -ServerInstance $node.Name -Force

       #targeting default instance
       $serviceName = "MSSQLSERVER"
       $service = Get-Service -ComputerName $node.Name `
                  -Name $serviceName
   ```

```
#restart service
Stop-Service $service -Force
Start-Service $service
}
```

4. Once the services have been restarted, AlwaysOn should already be enabled. You will be able to see this feature checked in **SQL Server Configuration Manager**:

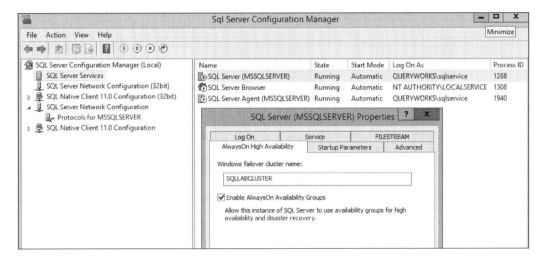

# How it works...

After the Windows Server Failover Clustering feature has been installed, the next component to be enabled is the AlwaysOn feature from the SQL Server instance. There is a PowerShell `Enable-SqlAlwaysOn` cmdlet that enables this task to be scripted and automated:

```
#enable AlwaysOn
Enable-SqlAlwaysOn -ServerInstance $node.Name -Force
```

This feature needs to be enabled for all the nodes in the cluster.

To disable this feature, you can use the `Disable-SqlAlwaysOn` cmdlet.

# There's more...

Check out *Enable and Disable AlwaysOn Availability Groups (SQL Server)* at https://msdn.microsoft.com/en-us/library/ff878259.aspx.

# Creating and enabling the HADR endpoint

In this recipe, we will create and enable the AlwaysOn endpoint for all the nodes.

## Getting ready

For this recipe, we will use port 5022 for the AlwaysOn communication for all the nodes. To ensure that this works, an exception in the firewall needs to be created for this port for all the instances. If you are using an isolated development environment, you need to first turn off the firewall to get this recipe to work, without having to tinker with the firewall.

We are also going to execute the code on all the nodes. For the following recipe to work, PSRemoting needs to be turned on in every node. Log in to each of the nodes, launch PowerShell or PowerShell ISE as an administrator, and enable remoting using the following script:

```
Enable-PSRemoting -Force
```

## How to do it...

The following steps will create and enable the AlwaysOn endpoint:

1. Open **PowerShell ISE** as an administrator.

2. Add the following script and run it:

```
#prompt for credential
$cred = Get-Credential

#process each node
foreach ($node in Get-ClusterNode)
{
    Write-Host "Processing $($node.Name)"

    #execute command on remote hosts
    Invoke-Command -ComputerName $node.Name -Credential
$cred -ScriptBlock {

        Import-Module SQLPS -DisableNameChecking
        $instance = $env:COMPUTERNAME

        #create server object
        $server = New-Object Microsoft.SqlServer.Management.Smo.
Server $instance

        #get a handle to the "AlwaysOnEndpoint"
```

```
$endpoint = $null
$endpoint = $server.Endpoints |
Where-Object EndpointType -eq "DatabaseMirroring" |
Where-Object Name -eq "AlwaysOnEndpoint" |
Select-Object -First 1

#drop if endpoint exists
if($endpoint -ne $null)
{
    #drop endpoint
    Write-Host "Dropping endpoint ..."
    $endpoint.Drop()
}

$port = 5022
$owner = "QUERYWORKS\Administrator"
$endpointName = "AlwaysOnEndpoint"
$path = "SQLSERVER:\SQL\$($instance)\DEFAULT"

$endpoint = New-SqlHADREndpoint -Port $port `
            -Owner $owner -Encryption Supported `
            -EncryptionAlgorithm Aes `
            -Name $endpointName `
            -Path $path
#if successfully created, start the endpoint
if($endpoint -ne $null)
{
    Set-SqlHADREndpoint -InputObject $endpoint `
    -State "Started"

    #this is the SQL Server domain service account
    #make sure this account is added as principal
    #to the SQL Server instance
    $endpointAccount = "QUERYWORKS\sqlservice"

    #assign CONNECT permission to the endpoint
    $permissionSet = New-Object
Microsoft.SqlServer.Management.Smo.ObjectPermissionSet(
[Microsoft.SqlServer.Management.Smo.ObjectPermission]::
Connect)

    $endpoint.Grant($permissionSet,$endpointAccount)
}

  }
}
```

3.  Once the script executes successfully, you should be able to visually check the
    endpoint from SQL Server Management Studio:

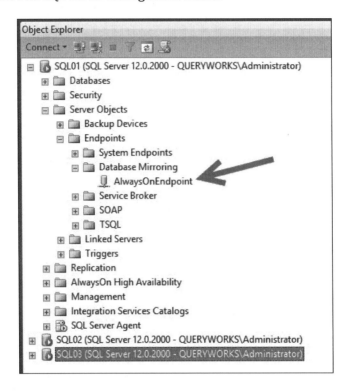

## How it works...

An endpoint is a way to connect to SQL Server. This manifests as a server object that contains
a connection string in the following format:

```
<protocol>://<domain>:<port number>
```

In our case, we will dedicate port 5022 to each of the machine names such as TCP and the
AlwaysOn configuration. Here is an example of the **fully qualified domain name** (**FQDN**):

```
TCP://SQL01.queryworks.local:5022
```

There is an AlwaysOn cmdlet called `New-SqlHADREndpoint` that allows the endpoint to be
created. This requires the port number, owner, encryption algorithm, name, and path. The
path refers to the SQL Server `PSProvider` path of the instance:

```
$port = 5022
$owner = "QUERYWORKS\Administrator"
$endpointName = "AlwaysOnEndpoint"
```

```
$path = "SQLSERVER:\SQL\$($instance)\DEFAULT"

$endpoint = New-SqlHADREndpoint -Port $port `
            -Owner $owner -Encryption Supported `
            -EncryptionAlgorithm Aes `
            -Name $endpointName `
            -Path $path
```

This is equivalent to the following T-SQL code:

```
CREATE ENDPOINT [AlwaysOnEndpoint]
  STATE=STARTED
  AS TCP (LISTENER_PORT = 5022, LISTENER_IP = ALL)
  FOR DATA_MIRRORING
    (
      ROLE = ALL,
      AUTHENTICATION = WINDOWS NEGOTIATE,
      ENCRYPTION = SUPPORTED ALGORITHM AES
    )
```

Once the endpoint has been created, we will start the endpoint:

```
Set-SqlHADREndpoint -InputObject $endpoint -State "Started"
```

In addition to starting the endpoint, we also need to ensure that the account we're using for AlwaysOn has the CONNECT privileges to the endpoint. To do this, we need to get a handle to the endpoint and use an ObjectPermissionSet variable to provide the privileges that we want to assign to that endpoint:

```
#make sure this account is added as principal
#to the SQL Server instance
$endpointAccount = "QUERYWORKS\sqlservice"

#assign the CONNECT permission
$permissionSet = New-Object
Microsoft.SqlServer.Management.Smo.ObjectPermissionSet(
[Microsoft.SqlServer.Management.Smo.ObjectPermission]::Connect)

$endpoint.Grant($permissionSet,$endpointAccount)
```

This is equivalent to the following T-SQL command:

```
GRANT CONNECT
ON ENDPOINT::AlwaysOnEndpoint
TO [QUERYWORKS\sqlservice]
```

## There's more...

Additional information on how to create a database mirroring endpoint can be found at `https://msdn.microsoft.com/en-us/library/ms190456.aspx`.

## See also

▶ The *Granting the CONNECT permission to the HADR endpoint* recipe.

# Granting the CONNECT permission to the HADR endpoint

In this recipe, we will grant the CONNECT permission to an existing SQL Server principle.

## Getting ready

Identify the SQL Server principle that you will use for AlwaysOn that will need the CONNECT permission.

## How to do it...

Perform the following steps to grant the CONNECT permission to an endpoint:

1. Open **PowerShell ISE** as an administrator.

2. Add the following script and run it:

```
Import-Module SQLPS -DisableNameChecking

$instanceName = "SQL01"
$endpointName = "AlwaysOnEndpoint"
$endpointAccount = "QUERYWORKS\sqlservice"

$server = New-Object Microsoft.SqlServer.Management.Smo.Server
$instanceName
$endpoint = $server.Endpoints[$endpointName]

#identify the Connect permission object
$permissionSet = New-Object Microsoft.SqlServer.Management.Smo.
ObjectPermissionSet(
[Microsoft.SqlServer.Management.Smo.ObjectPermission]::Connect)

#grant permission
$endpoint.Grant($permissionSet,$endpointAccount)
```

## How it works...

To assign permissions to an endpoint using PowerShell, a handle to the server instance needs to be created:

```
$server = New-Object Microsoft.SqlServer.Management.Smo.Server
$instanceName
```

Once the server object has been created, we can connect directly to the endpoint by referencing the endpoint's name:

```
$endpoint = $server.Endpoints[$endpointName]
```

Once this is done, an `ObjectPermissionSet` object can be created. This accepts a series of permissions. In our example, we are only passing it the `[Microsoft.SqlServer.Management.Smo.ObjectPermission]::Connect` enumeration value:

```
#identify permission
$permissionSet = New-Object
Microsoft.SqlServer.Management.Smo.ObjectPermissionSet(
[Microsoft.SqlServer.Management.Smo.ObjectPermission]::Connect)
```

Additional permissions can be easily seen in PowerShell ISE, thanks to the **Intellisense** feature introduced in PowerShell V3:

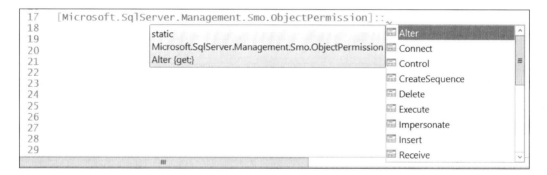

The last step is to invoke the `Grant()` method from the endpoint object to persist the new permission set:

```
#grant permission
$endpoint.Grant($permissionSet,$endpointAccount)
```

This is equivalent to the following T-SQL command:

```
GRANT CONNECT
ON ENDPOINT::AlwaysOnEndpoint
TO [QUERYWORKS\sqlservice]
```

## There's more...

Read the *Set Up Login Accounts for Database Mirroring or AlwaysOn Availability Groups (SQL Server)* article to understand the permissions required for AlwaysOn at `https://msdn.microsoft.com/en-ca/library/ms366346.aspx`.

## See also

▶ The *Creating and enabling the HADR endpoint* recipe.

# Creating an AlwaysOn Availability Group

In this recipe, we will create an Availability Group in the primary instance.

## Getting ready

It is worth having a refresher on some of the AlwaysOn terminology:

▶ A **primary** is the active instance and is the source of all the updates. This was referred to as the principal in database mirroring.

▶ A **secondary** is the instance that receives all the updates from the primary. In database mirroring, this was referred to as the mirror and was unreadable because it was left in the restoring state. In AlwaysOn, there can be up to four secondary replicas with different synchronization modes. Secondary replicas can also be readable.

▶ An **Availability Group** defines the unit of a failover. This includes defining the group of user databases called **availability databases**, which will failover together. According to MSDN, *an availability group supports a set of primary databases and one to eight sets of corresponding secondary databases*. An availability group also identifies the specific SQL Server instance.

▶ An **availability replica** maintains a local copy of each database in the availability group. There are two types of availability replicas: primary and secondary. There can only be one primary replica that will host the user databases that are readable and writeable. There can be up to four secondary replicas.

▶ The **availability mode** identifies whether the replicas will use synchronous or asynchronous commit mode. In **synchronous commit mode**, the primary replica will wait for an acknowledgement from the secondary replica that the transaction has been written to the log. This prevents data loss; however, this may result in blocking because the primary replica will not process transactions until the acknowledgement is received or the timeout period is reached. In **asynchronous commit mode**, the primary replica does not wait for any confirmation from the secondary replica. This may, however, result in data loss.

▸ The **failover mode** identifies how the secondary replica can take over the primary replica's role if the primary replica fails. During a failover, a role reversal will take place. If the availability mode is in synchronous-commit mode, a failover can be automatic or manual. If the mode is in asynchronous-commit mode, only a manual failover is available.

For this recipe, make sure that you have access to the environment that will host AlwaysOn. In the following recipe, the following nodes are ready to be utilized for AlwaysOn:

▸ SQL01 as a primary replica

▸ SQL02 as a secondary replica

▸ SQL03 as a secondary replica

In addition, you should also back up the database in the primary instance that you want to use as part of the availability group. Choose an existing database from the first node and add $db to the name of that database. You can store the instance name of the primary node in another variable called $primary.

You can use the following script to back up your database:

```
Import-Module SQLPS -DisableNameChecking

$backupDirectory = "\\SQL01\Backups"

$fullBackup = Join-Path $backupDirectory "$db.bak"
$txnBackup = Join-Path $backupDirectory "$db.trn"

#create a full backup
Backup-SqlDatabase $db $fullBackup `
-ServerInstance $primary -BackupAction Database

#create a transaction log backup
Backup-SqlDatabase $db $txnBackup `
-ServerInstance $primary -BackupAction Log
```

## How to do it...

Perform the following steps to create the AlwaysOn Availability Group as well as the primary and secondary replicas:

1. Open **PowerShell ISE** as an administrator.

2. Add the following script and run it:

```
Import-Module SQLPS -DisableNameChecking
```

```
$AGName = "SQLAG"
$db = "QueryWorksDB"

#create primary replica
$primaryReplica = New-SqlAvailabilityReplica `
-Name "SQL01" `
-EndpointUrl "TCP://SQL01:5022" `
-AsTemplate -FailoverMode Automatic `
-AvailabilityMode SynchronousCommit `
-Version 12

#create first secondary replica
$secondaryReplica1 = New-SqlAvailabilityReplica `
-Name "SQL02" `
-EndpointUrl "TCP://SQL02:5022" `
-AsTemplate -FailoverMode Automatic `
-AvailabilityMode SynchronousCommit `
-Version 12

#create second secondary replica
$secondaryReplica2 = New-SqlAvailabilityReplica `
-Name "SQL03" `
-EndpointUrl "TCP://SQL03:5022" `
-AsTemplate -FailoverMode Manual `
-AvailabilityMode AsynchronousCommit `
-Version 12

#PSProvider path of primary instance
$primaryPath = "SQLSERVER:\SQL\SQL01\DEFAULT"

#create availability group in primary instance
New-SqlAvailabilityGroup `
-Path $primaryPath -Name $AGName `
-AvailabilityReplica ($primaryReplica, $secondaryReplica1,
$secondaryReplica2) `
-Database $db
```

3. Once the query is executed, you can check **SQL Server Management Studio**. Go to the **AlwaysOn High Availability** node and you will see the **SQLAG** Availability Group. Under it, you will find the replicas:

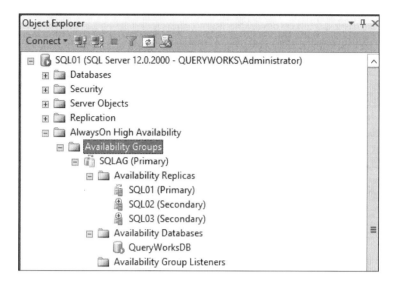

## How it works...

In this recipe, we accomplished a few tasks. First, we created our primary replica. To create a replica using PowerShell, we can use the New-SqlAvailabilityReplica cmdlet:

```
#create primary replica
$primaryReplica = New-SqlAvailabilityReplica `
-Name "SQL01" `
-EndpointUrl "TCP://SQL01:5022" `
-AsTemplate -FailoverMode Automatic `
-AvailabilityMode SynchronousCommit `
-Version 12
```

The New-SqlAvailabilityReplica cmdlet accepts the replica name, endpoint URL, failover mode, availability mode, and version as parameters. The available FailoverMode values are: Automatic, Manual, and Unknown. The AvailabilityMode values are: AsynchronousCommit, SynchronousCommit, and Unknown. The -AsTemplate parameter creates the definition of the replica in memory, which is needed to create the Availability Group.

Additional parameters available with New-SqlAvailabilityReplica include the following:

- ▸ SessionTimeout
- ▸ ConnectionModeInPrimaryRole
- ▸ ConnectionModeInSecondaryRole
- ▸ BackupPriority
- ▸ ReadOnlyRoutingList
- ▸ ReadOnlyRoutingConnectionUrl

The syntax for creating the secondary replicas is similar to the syntax for creating the primary replicas, with changes to the endpoint URL and the failover and availability modes:

```
$secondaryReplica1 = New-SqlAvailabilityReplica `
-Name "SQL02" `
-EndpointUrl "TCP://SQL02:5022" `
-AsTemplate -FailoverMode Automatic `
-AvailabilityMode SynchronousCommit `
-Version 12

#create second secondary replica
$secondaryReplica2 = New-SqlAvailabilityReplica `
-Name "SQL03" `
-EndpointUrl "TCP://SQL03:5022" `
-AsTemplate -FailoverMode Manual `
-AvailabilityMode AsynchronousCommit `
-Version 12
```

Once the replicas are set up, the availability group can be created using the `New-SqlAvailabilityGroup` cmdlet. This cmdlet accepts the SQL Server `PSProvider` path of the primary instance, the availability group name, the list of secondary replicas, and the availability database:

```
#PSProvider path of primary instance
$primaryPath = "SQLSERVER:\SQL\SQL01\DEFAULT"

#create availability group in primary instance
New-SqlAvailabilityGroup `
-Path $primaryPath -Name $AGName `
-AvailabilityReplica ($primaryReplica, $secondaryReplica1,
$secondaryReplica2) `
-Database $db
```

The equivalent T-SQL statement for creating the Availability Group is as follows:

```
CREATE AVAILABILITY GROUP [SQLAG]
FOR DATABASE [QueryWorksDB]
REPLICA ON

N'SQL01' WITH
(ENDPOINT_URL = N'TCP://SQL01:5022',
FAILOVER_MODE = AUTOMATIC,
AVAILABILITY_MODE = SYNCHRONOUS_COMMIT),

N'SQL02' WITH
(ENDPOINT_URL = N'TCP://SQL02:5022',
```

```
FAILOVER_MODE = AUTOMATIC,
AVAILABILITY_MODE = SYNCHRONOUS_COMMIT),

N'SQL03' WITH
(ENDPOINT_URL = N'TCP://SQL03:5022',
FAILOVER_MODE = MANUAL,
AVAILABILITY_MODE = ASYNCHRONOUS_COMMIT);
GO
```

If some of the replica settings need to be changed later on, you can use the `Set-SqlAvailabilityReplica` cmdlet to make the changes to existing replicas.

## There's more...

There is an MSDN page dedicated to creating Availability Groups in PowerShell, which can be found at `https://msdn.microsoft.com/en-us/library/gg492181.aspx`.

# Joining the secondary replicas to Availability Group

In this recipe, we will join the secondary replicas to an existing Availability Group.

## Getting ready

Before we proceed with this recipe, the availability group needs to be created. Let's take a look at the *Creating an AlwaysOn Availability Group* recipe.

As documented on MSDN, the prerequisites to join the secondary replicas are as follows:

- The primary replica should be online
- The join command to join the secondary replicas to the availability group needs to take place at the secondary server instance that hosts the secondary replicas
- The secondary instance must be able to connect to the database mirroring endpoint of the primary instance

Since we need to execute the command on the secondary instances, we can use PowerShell remoting to send the command to the remote hosts. Ensure that `PSRemoting` is turned on in every node. If `PSRemoting` is disabled, log in to each of the nodes, launch PowerShell or PowerShell ISE as an administrator, and enable remoting using the following script:

```
Enable-PSRemoting -Force
```

## How to do it...

The following steps walk you through how to join the secondary replicas to the availability group:

1. Open **PowerShell ISE** as an administrator.

2. Add the following script and run it:

```
#secondary nodes list
$secondaryList ="SQL02,SQL03".Split(",")

$cred = Get-Credential

#execute command for each node
foreach ($secondary in $secondaryList)
{
    Invoke-Command -ComputerName $secondary -Credential $cred
-ScriptBlock {
        Import-Module SQLPS -DisableNameChecking
        $instance = $env:COMPUTERNAME
        $path = "SQLSERVER:\SQL\$($instance)\DEFAULT"
        $AGName = "SQLAG"

        #join current node to availability group
        Join-SqlAvailabilityGroup `
        -Path $path `
        -Name $AGName
    }
}
```

3. Once the script has been executed, you can check whether the secondary replicas, SQL02 and SQL03, are now online and part of the SQLAG Availability Group from **SQL Server Management Studio**:

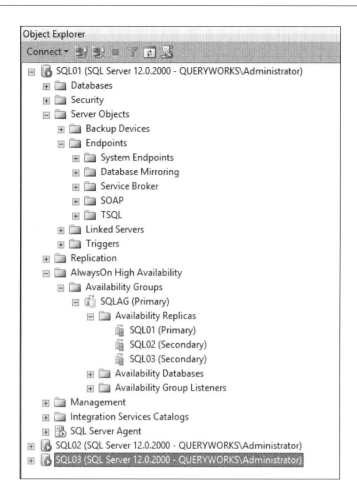

## How it works...

After a secondary replica is added to an AlwaysOn Availability Group, it must be joined to the Availability Group. To do this, we can use the `Join-SqlAvailabilityGroup` cmdlet, which accepts the SQL Server `PSProvider` path and the Availability Group name:

```
$instance = $env:COMPUTERNAME
$path = "SQLSERVER:\SQL\$($instance)\DEFAULT"
$AGName = "SQLAG"

#join current node to availability group
Join-SqlAvailabilityGroup `
-Path $path `
-Name $AGName -Verbose
```

Since there are no parameters that target the node to execute this on, this command needs to be executed on the secondary instance. You can do this by either logging in to the secondary instance and running the preceding code there or using PowerShell remoting to essentially accomplish the same task.

After the secondary replicas are joined to the availability group, the database should be restored to each secondary instance. You can use the following script to restore the database from backup files created before the availability group was created:

```
Import-Module SQLPS -DisableNameChecking

#list of secondary replicas
$secondaryList = @("SQL02", "SQL03")
$cred = Get-Credential

#execute code to each instance
foreach ($secondary in $secondaryList)
{
    Invoke-Command -ComputerName $secondary
-Credential $cred -ScriptBlock {
        Import-Module SQLPS -DisableNameChecking

        $instance = $env:COMPUTERNAME
        Write-Host "Processing $instance"
        $db = "QueryWorksDB"
        $backupDirectory = "\\SQL01\Backups"

        #compose full file path
        $fullBackup = Join-Path $backupDirectory "$db.bak"
        $txnBackup = Join-Path $backupDirectory "$db.trn"

        #restore full backup
        Restore-SqlDatabase -Database $db `
        -BackupFile $fullBackup `
        -ServerInstance $instance `
        -RestoreAction Database -NoRecovery

        #restore transaction log backup
        Restore-SqlDatabase -Database $db `
        -BackupFile $txnBackup `
        -ServerInstance $instance `
        -RestoreAction Log `
        -NoRecovery
    }
}
```

**There's more...**

Read the *Join a secondary replica to an Availability Group (SQL Server)* article to learn more about the prerequisites and syntax to perform the join from MSDN at `https://msdn.microsoft.com/en-us/library/ff878473.aspx`.

**See also**

▸   The *Creating an AlwaysOn Availability Group* recipe.

# Adding an availability database to an Availability Group

In this recipe, we will add an availability database to an Availability Group.

**Getting ready**

Before we proceed with this recipe, ensure that you have already created the availability group in the primary instance.

The prerequisites for adding an availability database, as documented on MSDN, are as follows:

▸   You must be connected to the server instance that hosts the primary replica

▸   The database must reside on the server instance that hosts the primary replica and comply with the prerequisites and restrictions for availability databases

**How to do it...**

Perform the following steps to add an availability database to an existing availability group:

1.  Open **PowerShell ISE** as an administrator.

2.  Add the following script and run it:

```
Import-Module SQLPS -DisableNameChecking

$AGName = "SQLAG"
$dbName = "QueryWorksDB"
$secondaryList = @("SQL02", "SQL03")
$cred = Get-Credential
```

```
foreach ($secondary in $secondaryList)
{

    $server = New-Object Microsoft.SqlServer.Management.Smo.Server
$secondary

    #get handle to availability group
    $ag = $server.AvailabilityGroups[$AGName]

    #add database
    Add-SqlAvailabilityDatabase -InputObject $ag `
    -Database $dbName

}
```

3.  When the script finishes the execution, you can check **SQL Server Management Studio** and see the availability database in the **AlwaysOn High Availability** node:

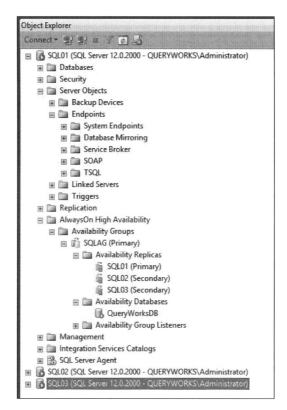

## How it works...

The availability database needs to be added to each secondary instance. To do this, we created a list of the secondary instances:

```
$secondaryList = @("SQL02", "SQL03")
```

Instead of listing the secondary instances like this, we can also save them in a file and use the `Get-Content` cmdlet to read them to the array.

Once the array has been populated with the list, we need to loop through each instance. For each instance, we create an SMO Server object:

```
$server = New-Object Microsoft.SqlServer.Management.Smo.Server
$secondary
```

From the server object, we can access the availability group based on the availability group name:

```
#get handle to availability group
$ag = $server.AvailabilityGroups[$AGName]
```

To add the availability database, we can use the `Add-SqlAvailabilityDatabase` cmdlet and pass the Availability Group object and the database name:

```
#add database
Add-SqlAvailabilityDatabase -InputObject $ag `
-Database $dbName
```

## There's more...

▶ Learn more about adding databases by reading the *Add a database to an Availability Group (SQL Server)* article found at `https://msdn.microsoft.com/en-us/library/hh213078.aspx`

▶ For details about adding secondary databases to an availability group, check out the *Join a secondary database to an Availability Group (SQL Server)* article at `https://msdn.microsoft.com/en-us/library/ff878535.aspx`

# Creating an Availability Group listener

In this recipe, we will create an Availability Group listener for an Availability Group.

## Getting ready

We will use the following information for this recipe. You will need to change these values based on your environment configuration:

| Configuration | Value |
|---|---|
| **Availability Group (AG) Name** | SQLAGListener |
| **Primary Replica Instance** | SQL01 |
| **AG Listener Name** | SQLAGListener |
| **AG Listener IP Address** | 192.168.1.200 |
| **AG Listener Subnet Mask** | 255.255.255.0 |
| **AG Listener Port Number** | 1433 |

## How to do it...

Perform the following steps to create and configure an Availability Group listener:

1. Open **PowerShell ISE** as an administrator.

2. Add the following script and run it:

```
Import-Module SQLPS -DisableNameChecking

$AGName = "SQLAG"
$AGListenerName = "SQLAGListener"
$AGListenerPort = 1433
$AGListenerIPAddress = "192.168.1.200"
$AGListenerSubnetMask = "255.255.255.0"
$primary = "SQL01"

#server object
$server = New-Object Microsoft.SqlServer.Management.Smo.Server $primary
```

```
#availability group object
$AG = $server.AvailabilityGroups[$AGName]

#for our recipe, if listener already exists,
#remove it first
if ($AG.AvailabilityGroupListeners[$AGListenerName] -ne
$null)
{
   $AG.AvailabilityGroupListeners[$AGListenerName].Drop()

}

$AGListener = New-Object
Microsoft.SqlServer.Management.Smo.
AvailabilityGroupListener -ArgumentList $AG,
$AGListenerName

$AGListenerIP = New-Object
Microsoft.SqlServer.Management.Smo.
AvailabilityGroupListenerIPAddress
-ArgumentList $AGListener
$AGListener.PortNumber = $AGListenerPort
$AGListenerIP.IsDHCP = $false
$AGListenerIP.IPAddress = $AGListenerIPAddress
$AGListenerIP.SubnetMask = $AGListenerSubnetMask

#add the listener IP
$AGListener.AvailabilityGroupListenerIPAddresses.
Add($AGListenerIP)

#create listener
$AGListener.Create()
```

3. When the script finishes the execution, you will see the Availability Group listener named **SQLAG** listed in SQL Server Management Studio:

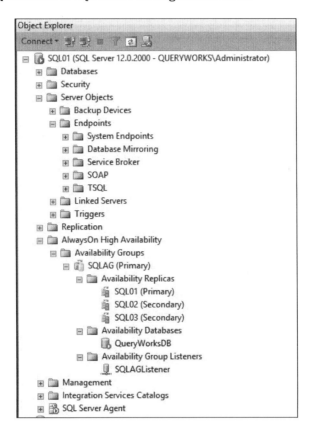

## How it works...

An Availability Group listener is a virtual server name that listens to incoming connections and directs the communication to a readable replica, whether it's the primary or secondary.

The first part of the script is to create variables for all the values that are needed to create the listener:

```
$AGName = "SQLAG"
$AGListenerName = "SQLAGListener"
$AGListenerPort = 1433
$AGListenerIPAddress = "192.168.1.200"
$AGListenerSubnetMask = "255.255.255.0"
$primary = "SQL01"
```

In this example, we are keeping the port number 1433, which is the default SQL Server port number. This simplifies the connection because only the listener name will need to be specified in the application. If you choose to use a nonstandard port, the listener name and port number should be supplied in the following format:

```
<listener name>,<port number>
```

There needs to be an availability group object, and we can access this from the SMO Server object:

```
#server object
$server = New-Object Microsoft.SqlServer.Management.Smo.Server
$primary

#availability group object
$AG = $server.AvailabilityGroups[$AGName]
```

In this recipe, we are utilizing the SMO `AvailabilityGroupListener` class to create the Availability Group listener object:

```
$AGListener = New-Object
Microsoft.SqlServer.Management.Smo.AvailabilityGroupListener
-ArgumentList $AG, $AGListenerName
```

An IP address object also needs to be created using the `AvailabilityGroupListenerIPAddress` class. Using this class, we can also port number, IP address, and subnet mask. We can also specify whether the IP address is **Dynamic Host Configuration Protocol** (**DHCP**) or not, which technically allows dynamic IP addresses; in which case, you will not need to assign a specific IP address:

```
$AGListenerIP = New-Object Microsoft.SqlServer.Management.Smo.
AvailabilityGroupListenerIPAddress -ArgumentList $AGListener
$AGListener.PortNumber = $AGListenerPort
$AGListenerIP.IsDHCP = $false
$AGListenerIP.IPAddress = $AGListenerIPAddress
$AGListenerIP.SubnetMask = $AGListenerSubnetMask
```

This IP address object needs to be added to the AG listener object using the `Add()` method of the `AvailabilityGroupListenerIPAddresses` member:

```
#add the listener IP
$AGListener.AvailabilityGroupListenerIPAddresses.Add
($AGListenerIP)
```

The last action is to invoke the `Create()` method to create the listener:

```
#create listener
$AGListener.Create()
```

The equivalent T-SQL statement to create the listener is as follows:

```
ALTER AVAILABILITY GROUP [SQLAG]
ADD LISTENER N'SQLAGListener'
(
   WITH IP
   ((N'192.168.1.200', N'255.255.255.0')
)
, PORT=1433);
```

Once the listener has been configured, you will be able to connect to the listener from SQL Server Management Studio:

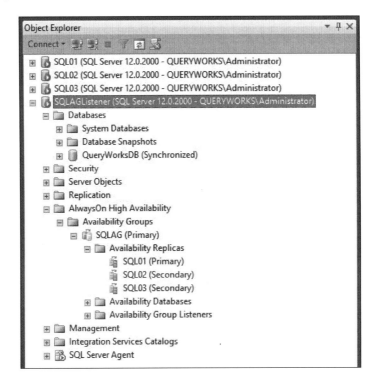

## There's more...

Read more about Availability Group listeners from *Availability Group Listeners, Client Connectivity, and Application Failover (SQL Server)* at `https://msdn.microsoft.com/en-us/library/hh213417.aspx`.

# Testing the Availability Group failover

In this recipe, we will failover our availability group to our secondary replica.

## Getting ready

To follow this recipe, your AlwaysOn availability group should already be set up and the primary/secondary replicas should be functional. If it's not yet set up, you can use the previous recipes in this chapter to set up your AlwaysOn availability group.

In this recipe, we will failover from the primary replica (SQL01) to our secondary replica (SQL02). Before doing this, let's visually check whether the availability group looks like SQL02. Open SQL Server Management Studio and go to the **AlwaysOn High Availability** node. Here is what SQL02 looks like:

Notice that beside the SQLAG availability group name is the indicator **(Secondary)**. This should change to **Primary** after we failover.

## How to do it...

The following steps show you how to failover an Availability Group:

1. Log in to the secondary replica that you want to failover to. In this recipe, it's SQL02.

2. Open **PowerShell ISE** as an administrator.

3. Add the following script and run it:

```
Import-Module SQLPS -DisableNameChecking
$AGName = "SQLAG"
$instanceName = "SQL02"

$path = "SQLServer:\SQL\$($instanceName)\DEFAULT\
AvailabilityGroups\$($AGName)"

#failover
Switch-SqlAvailabilityGroup -Path $path
```

4. Once the script has been executed, check the status of your AlwaysOn availability group in SQL02. You will notice that the indicator beside the SQLAG availability group name will now say **(Primary)**:

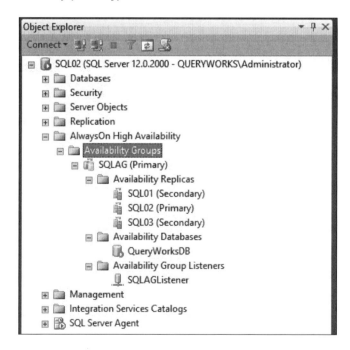

You can also connect to the AG listener to view the AlwaysOn dashboard, as the dashboard in the first node may not be functional right after the failover.

## How it works...

Microsoft provides a cmdlet that allows you to failover an availability group. The `Switch-SqlAvailabilityGroup` cmdlet starts the failover process in the secondary replica you're currently logged on to. We can pass the SQL Server `PSProvider` path to the availability group to this cmdlet:

```
#all in one line
$path = "SQLServer:\SQL\$($instanceName)\DEFAULT\
AvailabilityGroups\$($AGName)"

#failover
Switch-SqlAvailabilityGroup -Path $path
```

A few other parameters that can be used are `AllowDataLoss` and `Force`. The `AllowDataLoss` parameter indicates a force failover, but you will be prompted to confirm that this is the action you want to undertake. The `Force` parameter suppresses the confirmation.

The equivalent T-SQL command to failover is as follows:

```
ALTER AVAILABILITY GROUP [SQLAG] FAILOVER
```

## There's more...

There are a number of resources that will help you learn more about planned and manual failovers with AlwaysOn:

▶ Microsoft documents how to perform planned failovers, including limitations, restrictions, and permissions required before the task can be performed at `https://msdn.microsoft.com/en-us/library/hh231018.aspx`

▶ There is also documentation on how to perform forced manual failovers, including recommendations and tasks to be done after the failover happens, which can be found at `https://msdn.microsoft.com/en-us/library/ff877957.aspx`

# Monitoring the health of an Availability Group

In this recipe, we will see a few snippets that will help us monitor the health of an AlwaysOn Availability Group.

## Getting ready

To follow this recipe, your AlwaysOn availability group should already be set up and the primary/secondary replicas should be functional. If not, you can use the previous recipes in this chapter to set up your AlwaysOn Availability Group.

In PowerShell, there are three cmdlets that we will use to test AlwaysOn health. To use these cmdlets, you need the following permissions:

▶ CONNECT

▶ VIEW SERVER STATE

▶ VIEW ANY DEFINITION

## How to do it...

We will see how to monitor an Availability Group's health using PowerShell by following these steps:

1. Open **PowerShell ISE** as an administrator.

2. Add the following script and run it:

```
Import-Module SQLPS -DisableNameChecking

$instanceName = "SQL01"
$AGName = "SQLAG"

#SMO server object
$server = New-Object
Microsoft.SqlServer.Management.Smo.Server   $instanceName

#test availability group health
$AGPath =
"SQLSERVER:\SQL\$($instanceName)\DEFAULT\AvailabilityGroups
\$($AGName)"
Test-SqlAvailabilityGroup -Path $AGPath

#check all AG properties using SMO
$server.AvailabilityGroups[$AGName] |
Select-Object *

#test availability replica health
$AGReplicaPath =
"SQLSERVER:\SQL\$($instanceName)\DEFAULT\
AvailabilityGroups\$($AGName)\AvailabilityReplicas\$($instanceNa
me)"
```

```
Test-SqlAvailabilityReplica -Path $AGReplicaPath

#check availability replica properties using SMO
$server.AvailabilityGroups[$AGName].AvailabilityReplicas |
Select-Object *

#test availability database replica state health
$AGReplicaStatePath =
"SQLSERVER:\SQL\$($instanceName)\DEFAULT\
AvailabilityGroups\$($AGName)\DatabaseReplicaStates"

Get-ChildItem $AGReplicaStatePath |
Test-SqlDatabaseReplicaState

#check database replica state properties using SMO
$server.AvailabilityGroups[$AGName].DatabaseReplicaStates |
Select-Object *
```

Once this script has been executed, you will see a series of results that provide insight into your AlwaysOn Availability Group's health. The results are discussed in more depth in the *How it works...* section.

## How it works...

Before we dive deep into the script, it's worth mentioning that there is an AlwaysOn dashboard that you can launch from SQL Server Management Studio. When you right-click on the **AlwaysOn High Availability** node, select **Show Dashboard**:

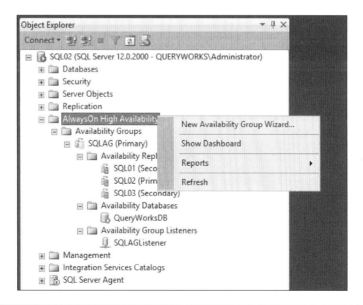

This will reveal a **SQL Server Reporting Services** (**SSRS**) report that provides an overview of the health of the Availability Group and its components:

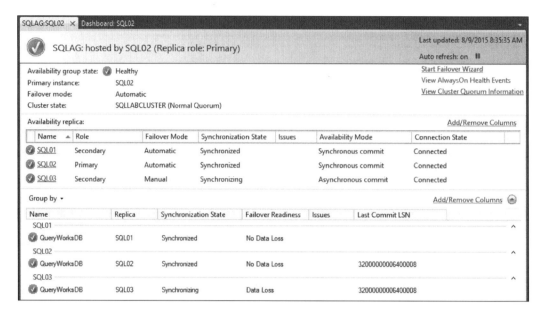

You can get the information this dashboard displays using a PowerShell script. The script in this recipe is a collection of snippets that can be used to monitor AlwaysOn. Let's take a look at them in more detail.

SQL Server provides a few cmdlets that will help you check the operational health of availability groups, replicas, and replica states. PowerShell's Intellisense will pick these up once you start typing `Test-Sql`:

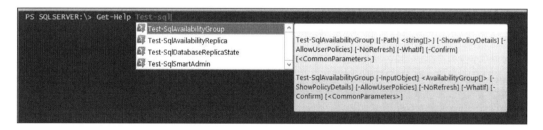

The `Test-SqlAvailabilityGroup`, `Test-SqlAvailabilityReplica`, and `Test-SqlDatabaseReplicaState` cmdlets will test the *health* by executing defined policies against the appropriate AlwaysOn object. The three possible outcomes are: `Healthy`, `Warning`, and `Error`.

To use the cmdlets, either the SQL Server `PSProvider` path can be provided or the appropriate object can be piped to it. We will see both of these variations when we use these cmdlets.

Here is what you can expect when you run the `Test-SqlAvailabilityGroup` cmdlet:

```
PS SQLSERVER:\> Test-SqlAvailabilityGroup -Path $AGPath

HealthState              Name
-----------              ----
Healthy                  SQLAG
```

This cmdlet simply returns whether the availability group is "healthy" or not, based on the results of the policies that were run. This cmdlet also has some additional parameters, including `ShowPolicyDetails`, which will show you the result of each policy evaluation and `AllowUserPolicies`, which runs user policies created under the AlwaysOn policy categories.

If you want to get more information, you can use SMO and create a handle to the Availability Group, pipe the object to the `Select-Object` cmdlet, and pull all available fields:

```
#check all AG properties using SMO
$server.AvailabilityGroups[$AGName] |
Select-Object *
```

The result of the preceding snippet will look like this:

```
Parent                      : [SQL01]
AutomatedBackupPreference   : Secondary
FailureConditionLevel       : OnCriticalServerErrors
HealthCheckTimeout          : 30000
ID                          : 65537
LocalReplicaRole            : Primary
PrimaryReplicaServerName    : SQL01
UniqueId                    : 4053832c-64ab-4ad5-96e1-3e2b6a7f4389
AvailabilityReplicas        : {SQL01, SQL02, SQL03}
AvailabilityDatabases       : {QueryWorksDB}
DatabaseReplicaStates       : {SQLAG, SQLAG, SQLAG}
AvailabilityGroupListeners  : {SQLAGListener}
Name                        : SQLAG
```

Note that from here, we can get additional information, such as `LocalReplicaRole`, `PrimaryReplicaServerName`, `AvailabilityReplicas`, `AvailabilityDatabases` `DatabaseReplicaStates`, and `AvailabilityGroupListeners`.

The second `Test-SqlAvailabilityReplica` cmdlet tests all the replicas. We need to pass the SQL Server `PSProvider` path to the Availability Group replica:

```
#test availability replica health
$AGReplicaPath =
"SQLSERVER:\SQL\$($instanceName)\DEFAULT\
AvailabilityGroups\$($AGName)\AvailabilityReplicas\$($instanceName)"
Test-SqlAvailabilityReplica -Path $AGReplicaPath
```

The result looks like the following screenshot:

If you want more information, you can use SMO to create an object that references the availability replica. You can then display all its properties:

```
#check availability replica properties using SMO
$server.AvailabilityGroups[$AGName].AvailabilityReplicas |
Select-Object *
```

Part of the information this returns for each replica includes `Name`, `Parent` (which is the availability group it belongs to), `AvailabilityMode`, `BackupPriority`, `EndpointURL`, `FailoverMode`, `Role`, and `SessionTimeout`. The following is a partial screenshot of the result:

```
Parent                          : [SQLAG]
AvailabilityMode                : SynchronousCommit
BackupPriority                  : 50
ConnectionModeInPrimaryRole     : AllowAllConnections
ConnectionModeInSecondaryRole   : AllowNoConnections
ConnectionState                 : Connected
CreateDate                      : 8/3/2015 11:32:36 PM
DateLastModified                : 8/3/2015 11:32:36 PM
EndpointUrl                     : TCP://SQL01:5022
FailoverMode                    : Automatic
JoinState                       : JoinedStandaloneInstance
LastConnectErrorDescription     :
LastConnectErrorNumber          : -1
LastConnectErrorTimestamp       : 1/1/1900 12:00:00 AM
MemberState                     : Online
OperationalState                : Online
Owner                           : QUERYWORKS\Administrator
QuorumVoteCount                 : 1
ReadonlyRoutingConnectionUrl    :
Role                            : Primary
RollupRecoveryState             : Online
RollupSynchronizationState      : Synchronized
SessionTimeout                  : 10
UniqueId                        : 3477fd9e-9b6c-4f25-b96c-860ffa3d1afe
ReadonlyRoutingList             : {}
Name                            : SQL01
```

The third `Test-SqlDatabaseReplicaState` cmdlet tests the availability database health of all the replicas. In this example, we use `Get-ChildItem` to get to the `DatabaseReplicaStates` path and then pipe this object to the `Test-SqlDatabaseReplicateState` cmdlet:

```
#test availability database replica state health
$AGReplicaStatePath =
"SQLSERVER:\SQL\$($instanceName)\DEFAULT\AvailabilityGroups\
$($AGName)\DatabaseReplicaStates"

Get-ChildItem $AGReplicaStatePath |
Test-SqlDatabaseReplicaState
```

This cmdlet returns a set of information for each database replica. A sample partial result looks like the following screenshot:

| HealthState | AvailabilityGroup | AvailabilityReplica | Name |
| --- | --- | --- | --- |
| Healthy | SQLAG | SQL01 | QueryWorksDB |
| Healthy | SQLAG | SQL02 | QueryWorksDB |
| Healthy | SQLAG | SQL03 | QueryWorksDB |

If you want to get more information, you can create an SMO object of the `DatabaseReplicaStates` property of the availability group:

```
#check database replica state properties using SMO
$server.AvailabilityGroups[$AGName].DatabaseReplicaStates |
Select-Object *
```

A sample partial result is as follows:

```
Parent                            : [SQLAG]
AvailabilityDateabaseId           : 6cf05ca7-45ad-49f2-af4d-02a34d898cdc
AvailabilityGroupId               : 4053832c-64ab-4ad5-96e1-3e2b6a7f4389
AvailabilityGroupName             : SQLAG
AvailabilityReplicaId             : 3477fd9e-9b6c-4f25-b96c-860ffa3d1afe
DatabaseId                        : 5
EndOfLogLSN                       : 32000000011200001
EstimatedDataLoss                 : 0
EstimatedRecoveryTime             : -1
FileStreamSendRate                : -1
IsFailoverReady                   : True
IsJoined                          : True
IsLocal                           : True
IsSuspended                       : False
LastCommitLSN                     : 31000000042400001
LastCommitTime                    : 8/3/2015 9:55:13 PM
LastHardenedLSN                   : 32000000012000001
LastHardenedTime                  : 1/1/1900 12:00:00 AM
LastReceivedLSN                   : 0
LastReceivedTime                  : 1/1/1900 12:00:00 AM
LastRedoneLSN                     : 0
LastRedoneTime                    : 1/1/1900 12:00:00 AM
LastSentLSN                       : 0
LastSentTime                      : 1/1/1900 12:00:00 AM
LogSendQueueSize                  : -1
LogSendRate                       : -1
RecoveryLSN                       : 4294967295429496729500001
RedoQueueSize                     : -1
RedoRate                          : -1
ReplicaAvailabilityMode           : SynchronousCommit
ReplicaRole                       : Primary
SuspendReason                     : NotApplicable
SynchronizationPerformance        : -1
SynchronizationState              : Synchronized
TruncationLSN                     : 32000000006400001
AvailabilityReplicaServerName     : SQL01
AvailabilityDatabaseName          : QueryWorksDB
```

Note that this provides a lot of detailed information to the **Logical Sequence Number** (**LSN**) details, including `LastCommitLSN`, `LastHardenedLSN`, `LastReceivedLSN`, `LastRedoneLSN`, and `LastSentLSN`.

Overall, these snippets provide a way to peek into your AlwaysOn Availability Group's health. This is just the start. You can pull in additional information and properties that will more accurately provide metrics on your AlwaysOn configuration using additional SQL Server objects and tools.

## There's more...

*   The *Use AlwaysOn policies to view the health of an Availability Group (SQL Server)* article will be helpful in understanding how to monitor AlwaysOn health, which can be found at `https://msdn.microsoft.com/en-CA/library/hh510210.aspx`
*   The official SQL Server AlwaysOn team blog features a two-part series that explains the AlwaysOn health model. The URLs for the articles are as follows:
    *   `http://bit.ly/alwaysonhealth-p1`
    *   `http://bit.ly/alwaysonhealth-p2`

# 9
# SQL Server Development

In this chapter, we will cover the following topics:

- ▶ Importing data from a text file
- ▶ Exporting records to a text file
- ▶ Adding files to FileTable
- ▶ Inserting XML into SQL Server
- ▶ Extracting XML from SQL Server
- ▶ Creating an RSS feed from the SQL Server content
- ▶ Applying XSL to an RSS feed
- ▶ Creating a JSON file from SQL Server
- ▶ Storing binary data into SQL Server
- ▶ Extracting binary data from SQL Server
- ▶ Creating a new assembly
- ▶ Listing user-defined assemblies
- ▶ Extracting user-defined assemblies

## Introduction

SQL Server has seen immense enhancements and support to different components that were traditionally not supported natively in databases, such as XML and **Common Language Runtime** (**CLR**) assemblies. This chapter explores how you can use PowerShell to simplify and automate some of the tasks you need to do with these items.

To do the exercises in this chapter, perform the following steps:

1.  Create a sample database named `SampleDB` and use it for the tasks in this chapter:

    ```
    CREATE DATABASE SampleDB
    ```

2.  Download the files for this chapter from the Packt website and save them to your local drive. You will find the following folders in your downloaded package:

    - ❑   Text files
    - ❑   BLOB files
    - ❑   CLR files
    - ❑   XML files

# Importing data from a text file

In this recipe, we will import some pipe-delimited files into an existing table in our SQL Server instance.

## Getting ready

In this recipe, we will create an empty table called `SampleText` in your database instance:

```
CREATE TABLE [dbo].[SampleText]
(
   [CustomerID] [varchar](20) NOT NULL PRIMARY KEY,
   [LastName] [varchar](50) NOT NULL,
   [FirstName] [varchar](50) NOT NULL,
   [Phone] [char](20) NOT NULL,
   [AddressLine] [varchar](50) NULL,
   [City] [varchar](20) NULL,
   [State] [char](5) NULL,
   [Country] [varchar](10) NOT NULL
)
```

We will import records in the file called `Customers.txt` into the `SampleText` table. The text file is a pipe-delimited text file that contains values for all the columns in the `SampleText` table:

```
1   172-32-1176|White|Johnson|408 496-7223|10932 Bigge Rd.|Menlo Park|CA|USA
2   213-46-8915|Green|Marjorie|415 986-7020|309 63rd St. #411|Oakland|CA|USA
3   238-95-7766|Carson|Cheryl|415 548-7723|589 Darwin Ln.|Berkeley|CA|USA
4   267-41-2394|O'Leary|Michael|408 286-2428|22 Cleveland Av. #14|San Jose|CA|USA
5   274-80-9391|Straight|Dean|415 834-2919|5420 College Av.|Oakland|CA|USA
6   341-22-1782|Smith|Meander|913 843-0462|10 Mississippi Dr.|Lawrence|KS|USA
7   409-56-7008|Bennet|Abraham|415 658-9932|6223 Bateman St.|Berkeley|CA|USA
8   427-17-2319|Dull|Ann|415 836-7128|3410 Blonde St.|Palo Alto|CA|USA
9   472-27-2349|Gringlesby|Burt|707 938-6445|PO Box 792|Covelo|CA|USA
10  486-29-1786|Locksley|Charlene|415 585-4620|18 Broadway Av.|San Francisco|CA|USA
11  527-72-3246|Greene|Morningstar|615 297-2723|22 Graybar House Rd.|Nashville|TN|USA
12  648-92-1872|Blotchet-Halls|Reginald|503 745-6402|55 Hillsdale Bl.|Corvallis|OR|USA
13  672-71-3249|Yokomoto|Akiko|415 935-4228|3 Silver Ct.|Walnut Creek|CA|USA
14  712-45-1867|del Castillo|Innes|615 996-8275|2286 Cram Pl. #86|Ann Arbor|MI|USA
15  722-51-5454|DeFrance|Michel|219 547-9982|3 Balding Pl.|Gary|IN|USA
16  724-08-9931|Stringer|Dirk|415 843-2991|5420 Telegraph Av.|Oakland|CA|USA
17  724-80-9391|MacFeather|Stearns|415 354-7128|44 Upland Hts.|Oakland|CA|USA
18  756-30-7391|Karsen|Livia|415 534-9219|5720 McAuley St.|Oakland|CA|USA
19  807-91-6654|Panteley|Sylvia|301 946-8853|1956 Arlington Pl.|Rockville|MD|USA
20  846-92-7186|Hunter|Sheryl|415 836-7128|3410 Blonde St.|Palo Alto|CA|USA
21  893-72-1158|McBadden|Heather|707 448-4982|301 Putnam|Vacaville|CA|USA
22  899-46-2035|Ringer|Anne|801 826-0752|67 Seventh Av.|Salt Lake City|UT|USA
23  998-72-3567|Ringer|Albert|801 826-0752|67 Seventh Av.|Salt Lake City|UT|USA
```

## How to do it...

The following steps will import a text file into a SQL Server table:

1. Open **PowerShell ISE** as an administrator.

2. Import the SQLPS module as follows:

   ```
   #import SQL Server module
   Import-Module SQLPS -DisableNameChecking
   ```

3. Add the following script and run it:

   ```
   $VerbosePreference = "Continue"

   #change this to the path where you have Customers.txt
   $file = "C:\DATA\Customers.txt"
   $fieldDelimiter = "|"
   $rowDelimiter = "\n"
   $instanceName = "localhost"
   $databaseName = "SampleDB"

   #compose the bcp command
   $bcpcmd = "bcp SampleText in `"$file`" -S $instanceName -d
   $databaseName -T -t `"$fieldDelimiter`" -r `"
   $rowDelimiter`" -c "
   ```

```
#execute the bcp command
Invoke-Expression -Command $bcpcmd

$VerbosePreference = "SilentlyContinue"
```

Once the script finishes the execution, the `SampleText` table will get populated with the records in the file. There should be 23 new records.

## How it works...

There are a few ways to import "clean" text files into SQL Server tables. By *clean*, we mean text files that do not require additional cleaning or transformation. Here are some of the ways to do it:

- The bcp utility
- The `BULK INSERT` T-SQL command
- The Import/Export Wizard from SSMS
- **SQL Server Integration Services** (**SSIS**)
- The .NET `SqlBulkCopy` class

In this recipe, we used the bcp utility, which is a lightweight utility for importing and exporting files. The bcp utility is installed when you install the SQL Server tools. We will use this utility in other recipes in the chapter.

Since we are using an executable utility, we need to first compose the command that we need to execute. The command is as follows:

```
$bcpcmd = "bcp SampleText in `"$file`" -S $instanceName -d
$databaseName -T -t `"$fieldDelimiter`" -r `"$rowDelimiter`" -c "
```

This is the `bcp` command that you will typically run in Command Prompt or a batch file. This will produce a command similar to the following command after the replacement of the variable:

```
bcp SampleText in C:\DATA\Customers.txt" -S localhost -d SampleDB
-T -t "|" -r "\n" -c.
```

This line indicates that we want to import a file called `Customers.txt` into the `SampleText` table in the `SampleDB` database which is in the local SQL Server instance. The field delimiter is a pipe | and row delimiter is a newline \n.

Once the command is composed, we can pass the variable that has the command to the `Invoke-Expression` cmdlet:

```
#execute the bcp command
Invoke-Expression -Command $bcpcmd
```

## There's more...

If you do a fair bit of import and export in SQL Server, it is worthwhile to understand the options available with `bcp`:

▶ Learn more about the bcp utility and all the available switches and parameters from the MSDN page at `https://msdn.microsoft.com/en-ca/library/ms162802.aspx`.

▶ Here is another good article on the *Data Loading Performance Guide* at `https://technet.microsoft.com/en-us/library/dd425070(SQL.100).aspx`.

# Exporting records to a text file

In this recipe, we will export records to a pipe-delimited text file in a SQL Server table.

## Getting ready

For this recipe, choose a table with records that you want to export to a text file.

## How to do it...

The following steps will import a text file into a SQL Server table:

1. Open **PowerShell ISE** as an administrator.

2. Import the SQLPS module as follows:

```
#import SQL Server module
Import-Module SQLPS -DisableNameChecking
```

3. Add the following script and run it:

```
$instanceName = "localhost"
$databaseName = "SampleDB"
$filename = "C:\DATA\Customers.txt"
$delimiter = "|"

Invoke-SqlCmd -Query "SELECT * FROM SampleText"
-ServerInstance $instanceName -Database $databaseName |
Export-Csv -Delimiter $delimiter -NoType $fileName
```

Once the script finishes the execution, check the text file that was created.

## How it works...

As with the import recipe, there are a few ways to export records to text files. Here are some of the ways to do this:

- ▶ The bcp utility
- ▶ The Import/Export Wizard from SSMS
- ▶ SQL Server Integration Services

In this recipe, however, we are taking advantage of the `Invoke-SqlCmd` and `Export-Csv` cmdlets.

First, we run a `SELECT` query on the SQL Server instance via `Invoke-SqlCmd`:

```
Invoke-SqlCmd -Query "SELECT * FROM SampleText" -ServerInstance
$instanceName -Database $databaseName |
Export-Csv -Delimiter $delimiter -NoType $fileName
```

However, instead of displaying the results, we pass the results to the `Export-Csv` PowerShell cmdlet that allows us to specify a few options, including the delimiter:

```
Invoke-SqlCmd -Query "SELECT * FROM SampleText" -ServerInstance
$instanceName -Database $databaseName |
Export-Csv -Delimiter $delimiter -NoType $fileName
```

If you are exporting to the Unicode format, you can simply add the `-Encoding` option:

```
Export-Csv -Delimiter $delimiter -NoType $fileName
-Encoding Unicode
```

Note that this uses a fairly simplistic export. If you need to have more flexibility, you can explore bcp with format files, which is demonstrated in other recipes in this chapter.

## There's more...

Learn more about the bcp utility and all the available switches and parameters from the MSDN page at `https://msdn.microsoft.com/en-ca/library/ms162802.aspx`.

# Adding files to a FileTable

In this recipe, we will programmatically add files to a FileTable.

## Getting ready

Before you proceed with this recipe, you need to have a FileTable in your database. If you do not have one yet, you can follow the *Adding a FileTable* recipe in *Chapter 6, Advanced Administration,* to set one up. Alternatively, you can run the prep file *BO4525 - Ch09 - 03 - Adding Files to FileTable Prep.ps1* from the code bundle.

## How to do it...

Let's take a look at the steps required to add multiple files to our FileTable using PowerShell and SMO:

1. Open **PowerShell ISE** as an administrator.

2. Import the SQLPS module as follows:

```
#import SQL Server module
Import-Module SQLPS -DisableNameChecking
```

3. Add the following script and run it:

```
$instanceName = "localhost"
$databaseName = "FilestreamDB"
$tableName = "MyFiles"

$server = New-Object -TypeName
Microsoft.SqlServer.Management.Smo.Server -ArgumentList
$instanceName
$db = $server.Databases[$databaseName]
$table = $db.Tables[$tableName]

#what is the filetable directory?
$ftdir = "\\" + $server.Name +
         "\"  + $server.FilestreamShareName +
         "\"  + $db.FilestreamDirectoryName +
         "\"  + $table.FileTableDirectoryName

#create a new PSDrive
New-PSDrive -Name target -PSProvider FileSystem -Root
$ftdir | Out-Null

$sourceFolder = "C:\DATA"
```

```
Get-ChildItem -Path $sourceFolder |
Where-Object PSIsContainer -EQ $false |
ForEach-Object {
   $file = $_
   Copy-Item -Path $file.FullName -Destination target:
}


#remove PSDrive when done
Remove-PSDrive target
```

## How it works...

When you want to add files to a FileTable manually, you can simply choose the **Explore FileTable Directory** from SQL Server Management Studio. This opens a network directory where you can drag and drop files. Any files that you add will produce a record in the FileTable with the corresponding metadata.

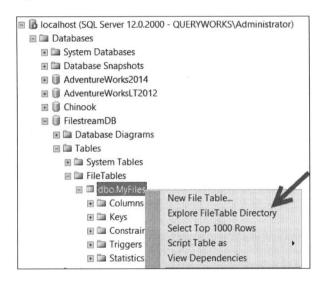

Copying files to local folders using PowerShell is also straightforward:

```
Copy-Item c:\MyFolder c:\MyOtherFolder -Recurse
```

Copying files from the filesystem to SQL Server FileTable requires a little bit more setup.

First, we need to compose the **Uniform Naming Convention** (**UNC**) path to the FileTable in our database. This is how we can do it in PowerShell after we've set up the SMO variables to our server, database, and table:

```
$ftdir = "\\" + $server.Name +
         "\"  + $server.FilestreamShareName +
         "\"  + $db.FilestreamDirectoryName +
         "\"  + $table.FileTableDirectoryName
```

The path will look like the following command:

```
\\Rogue\mssqlserver\FileTable\MyFiles
```

You may be tempted to now use the `Copy-Item` cmdlet to copy your files to this shared directory as follows:

```
$sourceFolder = "C:\DATA"
Get-ChildItem -Path $sourceFolder |
Where-Object PSIsContainer -EQ $false |
ForEach-Object {
   $file = $_
   Copy-Item -Path $file.FullName -Destination $ftdir
}
```

Unfortunately, this will give the following error:

**Error: Copy-Item : Source and destination path did not resolve to the same provider.**

What we need to do is to create a new `PSDrive` and use this as the destination for our `Copy-Item` cmdlet:

```
#create a new PSDrive
New-PSDrive -Name target -PSProvider FileSystem -Root $ftdir |
Out-Null
```

Once we have the new drive, we can now copy all the files to the FileTable using the new PSDrive name:

```
$sourceFolder = "C:\Files"

Get-ChildItem -Path $sourceFolder |
Where-Object PSIsContainer -EQ $false |
ForEach-Object {
   $file = $_
   Copy-Item -Path $file.FullName -Destination target:
}
```

When done, and if you are not going to use `PSDrive` anymore, you can remove it:

```
Remove-PSDrive target
```

## There's more...

Learn more about how to work with directories and paths in FileTables at `https://msdn.microsoft.com/en-us/library/gg492087.aspx`.

## See also

▶ The *Setting up a FileStream filegroup* recipe in *Chapter 6, Advanced Administration*.

▶ The *Adding a FileTable* recipe from *Chapter 6, Advanced Administration*.

# Inserting XML into SQL Server

In this recipe, we will insert the content of some XML files into a SQL Server table that has XML columns.

## Getting ready

We will create a sample table that we can use for this recipe. Run the following script in SQL Server Management Studio to create a table named `SampleXML` that has an XML field:

```
USE SampleDB
GO
IF OBJECT_ID('SampleXML') IS NOT NULL
    DROP TABLE SampleXML
GO

CREATE TABLE SampleXML
(
    ID INT IDENTITY(1, 1) NOT NULL PRIMARY KEY,
    FileName VARCHAR(200) ,
    InsertedDate DATETIME DEFAULT GETDATE() ,
    InsertedBy VARCHAR(100) DEFAULT SUSER_SNAME() ,
    XMLStuff XML ,
    FileExtension VARCHAR(50)
)
```

Create a directory called `C:\DATA\` if it does not exist and copy the sample XML files that come with the book scripts. Alternatively, you can use your own directory and XML files.

## How to do it...

These are the steps required to insert the contents of XML files into SQL Server:

1. Open **PowerShell ISE** as an administrator.

2. Import the SQLPS module as follows:

```
#import SQL Server module
Import-Module SQLPS -DisableNameChecking
```

3. Add the following script and run it:

```
$VerbosePreference = "Continue"

#define variables for directory, instance, database
$xmlDirectory = "C:\DATA\"
$instanceName = "localhost"
$databaseName = "SampleDB"

#get all XML files from your XML directory
Get-ChildItem $xmlDirectory -Filter "*.xml" |
ForEach-Object {

    $xmlFile = $_

    #display XML file currently being imported
    Write-Verbose "Importing  $($xmlFile.FullName) ..."

    #escape single quotes
    #because we are passing the
    #XML content to a T-SQL statement
    [string]$xml =
(Get-Content $xmlFile.FullName) -replace "'", "''"

$query = @"
INSERT INTO SampleXML
(FileName,XMLStuff,FileExtension)
VALUES('$($_.Name)','$xml','.xml')
"@

    Invoke-Sqlcmd -ServerInstance $instanceName
-Database $databaseName -Query $query

}

$VerbosePreference = "SilentlyContinue"
```

When you are done, open SQL Server Management Studio and query the SampleXML table. You will find the XML files inserted into the table:

```
  1  /****** Script for SelectTopNRows command from SSMS   ******/
  2  ⊟SELECT TOP 1000 [ID]
  3        ,[FileName]
  4        ,[InsertedDate]
  5        ,[InsertedBy]
  6        ,[XMLStuff]
  7        ,[FileExtension]
  8    FROM [SampleDB].[dbo].[SampleXML]
```

| | ID | FileName | InsertedDate | InsertedBy | XMLStuff | FileExtensi... |
|---|---|---|---|---|---|---|
| 1 | 1 | books.xml | 2015-05-10 19:02:58.823 | QUERYWORKS\Administrator | `<catalog><book id="bk101"><author>Gambardella, M...` | xml |
| 2 | 2 | sqlmusings_rss.xml | 2015-05-10 19:02:58.857 | QUERYWORKS\Administrator | `<rss xmlns:content="http://purl.org/rss/1.0/modules/co...` | xml |

## How it works...

Inserting the contents of an XML file into a SQL Server XML column can be easily done with a combination of T-SQL and PowerShell.

PowerShell can perform file-related functions, while T-SQL can do the INSERT statements more effectively.

The first step in this recipe is to loop through a set of XML files:

```
Get-ChildItem $xmlDirectory -Filter "*.xml"
```

We then pipe this to a Foreach-Object cmdlet that enables each file to be inserted into the table. In the Foreach-Object cmdlet, we display which file we are importing first:

```
#display XML file currently being imported
Write-Verbose "Importing  $($xmlFile.FullName) ..."
```

We then extract the content of each XML file. As we will pass the content as text back to the server, we need to make sure that we escape all single quotes. Otherwise, the string that we want to insert will be erroneously terminated:

```
[string]$xml = (Get-Content $xmlFile.FullName) -replace "'", "''"
```

Once the XML content is saved in a variable, we can compose an INSERT statement to insert that into our table that has the XML column. Note that our INSERT statement is using a here-string variable:

```
$query = @"
INSERT INTO SampleXML
```

```
(FileName,XMLStuff,FileExtension)
VALUES('$($_.Name)','$xml','.xml')
"@
```

 Remember that a `here-string` variable allows you to easily create variables containing multi-line text. The text needs to start with `@"`, and end with `"@` in a line by itself. There should be no characters before the ending `"@`.

To perform the insert, we can use the `Invoke-SqlCmd` cmdlet and pass our `INSERT` query:

```
Invoke-Sqlcmd -ServerInstance $instanceName -Database
$databaseName -Query $query
```

## There's more...

Learn more about SQL Server XML support from MSDN at `http://msdn.microsoft.com/en-us/library/ms187339.aspx`.

Learn more about variable expansion in strings and here-strings from the Windows PowerShell blog at `http://blogs.msdn.com/b/powershell/archive/2006/07/15/variable-expansion-in-strings-and-herestrings.aspx`.

## See also

▸ The *Extracting XML from SQL Server* recipe of *Chapter 9, SQL Server Development*

# Extracting XML from SQL Server

In this recipe, we will extract the XML content from SQL Server and save each record in individual files in the filesystem.

## Getting ready

For this recipe, we will use the table that we created in the previous recipe, *Inserting XML into SQL Server*, to extract files. Feel free to use your own tables that have XML columns; just ensure that you change the table name in the script.

## How to do it...

These are the steps required to extract XML from SQL Server:

1. Open **PowerShell ISE** as an administrator.

2. Import the SQLPS module as follows:

```
#import SQL Server module
Import-Module SQLPS -DisableNameChecking
```

3. Add the following script and run it:

```
$VerbosePreference = "Continue"
$instanceName = "localhost"
$databaseName = "SampleDB"
$sourceFolder = "C:\ XML Files\"
$destinationFolder = "C:\XML Files\"

#we will save all retrieved files in a new folder
$newFolder = "XML $(Get-Date -format 'yyyy-MMM-dd-hhmmtt')"
$newfolder = Join-Path -Path "$($destinationFolder)" -ChildPath
$newFolder

#if the path exists, will error silently and continue
New-Item -ItemType directory -Path $newFolder -ErrorAction
SilentlyContinue

#query to get XML content from database
$query = @"
SELECT FileName, XMLStuff
FROM SampleXML
WHERE XMLStuff IS NOT NULL
"@

Invoke-Sqlcmd -ServerInstance $instanceName -Database
$databaseName -Query $query -MaxCharLength 99999999 |
ForEach-Object {
    $record = $_
   Write-Verbose "Retrieving $($record.FileName) ..."
   [xml]$xml = $record.XmlStuff
   $xml.Save((Join-Path -Path $newfolder -ChildPath
"$($record.FileName)"))
}
```

```
#open folder with the files
explorer $newFolder

$VerbosePreference = "SilentlyContinue"
```

4. When you are done, go to your folder and you will see something similar to the following screenshot:

## How it works...

SQL Server has a great support for querying and manipulating XML stored in SQL Server tables, but needs external support if these files need to be extracted and saved in the filesystem. PowerShell can definitely help in this area.

We first create a new timestamped folder where we can store our retrieved XML files. This will help us keep track of the files that were downloaded at any specific time. We use the `New-Item` cmdlet to create this new folder. If the folder already exists, no error will be displayed since we specified the `-ErrorAction SilentlyContinue` parameter:

```
#we will save all retrieved files in a new folder
$newFolder = "XML $(Get-Date -format 'yyyy-MMM-dd-hhmmtt')"
$newfolder = Join-Path -Path "$($destinationFolder)"
-ChildPath $newFolder

#if the path exists, will error silently and continue
New-Item -ItemType directory -Path $newFolder -ErrorAction
SilentlyContinue
```

We then construct our T-SQL statement to retrieve the XML data from our table:

```
$query = @"
SELECT FileName, XMLStuff
FROM SampleXML
WHERE XMLStuff IS NOT NULL
"@
```

We can pass this to the `Invoke-Sqlcmd` cmdlet to retrieve all our XML records. We also have to specify a big number for the `MaxCharLength` variable, which defines the maximum number of characters returned for columns, because the content of the XML files that we want to retrieve will be big. By default, the `MaxCharLength` value is `4000`:

```
Invoke-Sqlcmd -ServerInstance $instanceName -Database
$databaseName -Query $query -MaxCharLength 99999999 |
ForEach-Object {
    $record = $_
  Write-Verbose "Retrieving $($record.FileName) ..."
  [xml]$xml = $record.XmlStuff
  $xml.Save((Join-Path -Path $newfolder -ChildPath
"$($record.FileName)"))
}
```

For each record returned in our query result, we save the content in a strongly typed XML variable by putting `[xml]` right beside our `$xml` variable:

```
Invoke-Sqlcmd -ServerInstance $instanceName -Database
$databaseName -Query $query -MaxCharLength 99999999 |
ForEach-Object {
    $record = $_
  Write-Verbose "Retrieving $($record.FileName) ..."
  [xml]$xml = $record.XmlStuff
  $xml.Save((Join-Path -Path $newfolder -ChildPath
"$($record.FileName)"))
}
```

The XML variable, because it is an XML object, will inherit a `Save` method that allows you to save the content in the filesystem:

```
Invoke-Sqlcmd -ServerInstance $instanceName -Database $databaseName
-Query $query -MaxCharLength 99999999 |
ForEach-Object {
    $record = $_
  Write-Verbose "Retrieving $($record.FileName) ..."
  [xml]$xml = $record.XmlStuff
  $xml.Save((Join-Path -Path $newfolder -ChildPath
"$($record.FileName)"))
}
```

## See also

▶  The *Inserting XML into SQL Server* recipe.

# Creating an RSS feed from SQL Server content

In this recipe, we will create an RSS feed from SQL Server content.

## Getting ready

For this recipe, we will use a simple query to populate our RSS feed. We will list our database list from `sys.databases` and use it as fictional content for our RSS file.

## How to do it...

These are the steps required to create an RSS feed using T-SQL and PowerShell:

1. Open **PowerShell ISE** as an administrator.

2. Import the SQLPS module as follows:
```
#import SQL Server module
Import-Module SQLPS -DisableNameChecking
```

3. Add the following script and run it:
```
$instanceName = "localhost"
$databaseName = "SampleDB"
$timestamp = Get-Date -format "yyyy-MMM-dd-hhmmtt"
$rssFileName = "C:\XML Files\rss_$timestamp.xml"

#values to be used for RSS
$rssTitle = "QueryWorks Latest News"
$rssLink = "http://www.queryworks.ca/rss.xml"
$rssDescription = "What's new in the world of QueryWorks"

#use r as date formatter to get
#date in RFC1123Pattern
$rssDate = (Get-Date -Format r)
$rssManagingEditor = "info@queryworks.ca"
$rssGenerator = "SQL Server 2014 XML and PowerShell"
$rssDocs = "http://www.queryworks.ca/rss.xml"

$query = @"
DECLARE @rssbody XML
SET @rssbody = ( SELECT
                name AS 'title' ,
```

```
                         collation_name AS 'description' ,
                         'false' AS 'guid/@isPermaLink' ,
                         'http://www.queryworks.ca/?p=' +
                   CAST(database_id AS VARCHAR(5)) AS 'guid'
                       FROM
                   sys.databases
                       FOR XML PATH('item') , TYPE)
       SELECT @rssbody
       "@


       $rssFromSQL = Invoke-Sqlcmd -ServerInstance $instanceName
       -Database $databaseName -Query $query


       #extract the RSS from the SQL Server result
       [string] $rssBody = $rssFromSQL.Column1.ToString()


       #create the final RSS
       $rsstext = @"
       <?xml version="1.0" encoding="UTF-8" ?>
       <rss version="2.0" xmlns:atom="http://www.w3.org/2005/Atom">
       <channel>
         <title><![CDATA[$rssTitle]]></title>
           <atom:link href="http://www.queryworks.ca/rss.xml"
       rel="self" type="application/rss+xml" />
           <link>$rssLink</link>
           <description><![CDATA[$rssDescription]]></description>
           <pubDate>$rssDate</pubDate>
           <lastBuildDate>$rssDate</lastBuildDate>
           <managingEditor>$rssManagingEditor</managingEditor>
           <generator>$rssGenerator</generator>
           <docs>$rssDocs</docs>
           $rssBody
       </channel>
       </rss>
       "@
       [xml] $rss = $rsstext
       $rss.Save($rssFileName)
```

4. When the script has finished executing, open the RSS file. The content of the file should look similar to this:

```
  rss_2015-May-10-0723PM.xml
1    <?xml version="1.0" encoding="UTF-8"?>
2    <rss version="2.0" xmlns:atom="http://www.w3.org/2005/Atom">
3      <channel>
4        <title><![CDATA[QueryWorks Latest News]]></title>
5        <atom:link href="http://www.queryworks.ca/rss.xml" rel="self" type="application/rss+xml" />
6        <link>http://www.queryworks.ca/rss.xml</link>
7        <description><![CDATA[What's new in the world of QueryWorks]]></description>
8        <pubDate>Sun, 10 May 2015 19:23:07 GMT</pubDate>
9        <lastBuildDate>Sun, 10 May 2015 19:23:07 GMT</lastBuildDate>
10       <managingEditor>info@queryworks.ca</managingEditor>
11       <generator>SQL Server 2014 XML and PowerShell</generator>
12       <docs>http://www.queryworks.ca/rss.xml</docs>
13       <item>
14         <title>master</title>
15         <description>SQL_Latin1_General_CP1_CI_AS</description>
16         <guid isPermaLink="false">http://www.queryworks.ca/?p=1</guid>
17       </item>
18       <item>
19         <title>tempdb</title>
20         <description>SQL_Latin1_General_CP1_CI_AS</description>
21         <guid isPermaLink="false">http://www.queryworks.ca/?p=2</guid>
22       </item>
23       <item>
24         <title>model</title>
25         <description>SQL_Latin1_General_CP1_CI_AS</description>
26         <guid isPermaLink="false">http://www.queryworks.ca/?p=3</guid>
27       </item>
28       <item>
29         <title>msdb</title>
30         <description>SQL_Latin1_General_CP1_CI_AS</description>
31         <guid isPermaLink="false">http://www.queryworks.ca/?p=4</guid>
32       </item>
```

To validate, w3.org has an RSS feed validator at `http://validator.w3.org/feed/?`. Use the **Validate by Direct Input** tab and copy the contents of the file to the text area. Click on the **Validate** button. If it is validated, you will see a message similar to this:

Congratulations!

VALID RSS✔ This is a valid RSS feed.

## How it works...

SQL Server has embraced support for XML since Version 2005. While creating the content for RSS feeds is doable using T-SQL in SQL Server, there are still some challenges with composing the RSS file. For example, the RSS file should have the following header:

```
<?xml version="1.0" encoding="UTF-8" ?>
```

Although adding this line at the beginning of the content is doable in SQL Server, it is not very straightforward. It will take few CAST to get your RSS feed content properly formatted. When you are done with the formatting, you will still need to use another means or tool to save this in an XML file.

Combining T-SQL with PowerShell allows you to accomplish creating the RSS feed file with ease.

The first thing we do is define a timestamped filename:

```
$timestamp = Get-Date -format "yyyy-MMM-dd-hhmmtt"
$rssFileName = "C:\DATA\rss_$timestamp.xml"
```

We then have to define the parameters we want to use to populate our RSS header. These include the `title`, `link`, `description`, `date`, `managingEditor`, `generator`, and `docs` variables. We will insert these variables later in the actual RSS feed string:

```
#values to be used for RSS
$rssTitle = "QueryWorks Latest News"
$rssLink = "http://www.queryworks.ca/rss.xml"
$rssDescription = "What's new in the world of QueryWorks"

#use r as date formatter to get
#date in RFC1123Pattern
$rssDate = (Get-Date -Format r)
$rssManagingEditor = "info@queryworks.ca"
$rssGenerator = "SQL Server 2014 XML and PowerShell"
$rssDocs = "http://www.queryworks.ca/rss.xml"
```

To retrieve data from our SQL Server table, we define a here-string query. Note that in order to get the content in the XML format, we use FOR XML PATH with our query:

```
$query = @"
DECLARE @rssbody XML
SET @rssbody = ( SELECT
                    name AS 'title' ,
                    collation_name AS 'description' ,
                    'false' AS 'guid/@isPermaLink' ,
                    'http://www.queryworks.ca/?p=' +
               CAST(database_id AS VARCHAR(5)) AS 'guid'
                   FROM
               sys.databases
                   FOR XML PATH('item') , TYPE)
SELECT @rssbody
"@
```

This query will give you a result similar to this:

```
<item>
  <title>master</title>
  <description>SQL_Latin1_General_CP1_CI_AS</description>
  <guid isPermaLink="false">http://www.queryworks.ca/?p=1</guid>
</item>
<item>
  <title>tempdb</title>
  <description>SQL_Latin1_General_CP1_CI_AS</description>
  <guid isPermaLink="false">http://www.queryworks.ca/?p=2</guid>
</item>
```

When we execute the query, we can use the `Invoke-Sqlcmd` cmdlet and capture the result using another PowerShell variable:

```
$rssFromSQL = Invoke-Sqlcmd -ServerInstance $instanceName
-Database $databaseName -Query $query
```

Remember that our result from our `Invoke-Sqlcmd` cmdlet is still a table, so we need to extract just the XML content from the result. We do this by extracting what's been returned in `Column1` (that is, the first column of the result) and saving this as a string:

```
#extract the RSS from the SQL Server result
[string] $rssBody = $rssFromSQL.Column1.ToString()
```

Once we have all the information, we can formulate the RSS file. Note that we are using `here-string` as the main template, and each tag is populated by the values that we set for our RSS-related variables. These are the variables (shown in bold) embedded in `here-string`:

```
#create the final RSS
$rsstext = @"
<?xml version="1.0" encoding="UTF-8" ?>
<rss version="2.0" xmlns:atom="http://www.w3.org/2005/Atom">
<channel>
  <title><![CDATA[$rssTitle]]></title>
    <atom:link href="http://www.queryworks.ca/rss.xml" rel="self"
type="application/rss+xml" />
    <link>$rssLink</link>
    <description><![CDATA[$rssDescription]]></description>
    <pubDate>$rssDate</pubDate>
    <lastBuildDate>$rssDate</lastBuildDate>
    <managingEditor>$rssManagingEditor</managingEditor>
    <generator>$rssGenerator</generator>
    <docs>$rssDocs</docs>
    $rssBody
```

```
</channel>
</rss>
"@
```

To validate and create the file, we need to create a strongly typed XML variable. We are trying to accomplish multiple goals this way. This can check for well-formed XML. If the XML is not well formed, we will get an error when we try to assign our content to the XML variable:

```
#this can validate the RSS file
[xml] $rss = $rsstext
```

The XML object also comes with a `Save` method that allows us to save the content to a file on a disk:

```
$rss.Save($rssFileName)
```

## There's more...

**Really Simple Syndication** (**RSS**) allows items such as blog entries and news items to be syndicated or published automatically and consumed by RSS readers from different devices. An RSS feed is nothing more than a specific-formatted XML file that contains specific information such as author, title, description, and so on.

- ► Learn more about RSS feeds and their variations at `http://cyber.law.harvard.edu/rss/rss.html` and `http://www.rss-specifications.com/rss-specifications.htm`.

- ► On the SQL Server side, to learn more about creating XML documents from your records, check out the FOR XML clause at `http://msdn.microsoft.com/en-us/library/ms190922.aspx`.

## See also

- ► The *Applying XSL to an RSS feed* recipe.

# Applying XSL to an RSS feed

In this recipe, we will create a styled HTML file based on an existing RSS feed and XSL (stylesheet).

## Getting ready

The files needed for this recipe are included in the downloadable book scripts from the Packt website. Once you've downloaded the files, copy the `XML Files\RSS` folder to your local `C:\` directory. This folder will have two files: one sample RSS feed (`sample_rss.xml`) and one XSL file (`rss_style.xsl`).

## How to do it...

These are the steps required for styling an RSS feed:

1. Open **PowerShell ISE** as an administrator.

2. Add the following script and run it:

```
#replace these with the paths of the files in your system
Set-Alias ie "$env:programfiles\Internet"

#remove $rss variable if it already exists
if ($rss)
{
    Remove-Variable -Name "rss"
}

#replace these with the paths of the files in your system
$xsl = "C:\DATA\RSS\rss_style.xsl"
$rss = "C:\DATA\RSS\sample_rss.xml"
$styled_rss = "C:\DATA\RSS\sample_result.html"

$xslt = New-Object System.Xml.Xsl.XslCompiledTransform
$xslt.Load($xsl)
$xslt.Transform($rss, $styled_rss)

#load the resulting styled html
#in Internet Explorer
Set-Alias ie "$env:programfiles\Internet
Explorer\iexplore.exe"

ie $styled_rss
```

3. When done, an Internet Explorer browser will open and show a page similar to this:

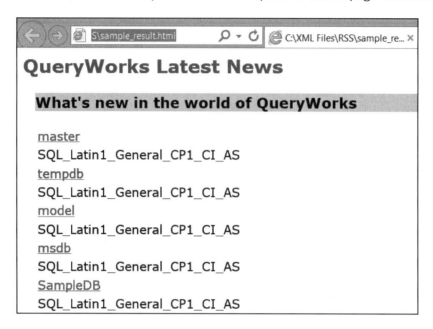

## How it works...

**Extensible Stylesheet Language** (**XSL**) is a stylesheet, which is similar to its "cousin" CSS that defines how an XML document can be styled and potentially transformed.

Although this recipe may not be directly related to SQL Server, knowing how to apply this may benefit the SQL Server professional.

To style our RSS feed, we will first create some variables that contain our .xsl and .xml files (or the RSS feed file). For our recipe, we will style the RSS to produce an HTML file, so we will create a variable to reference this new file as well:

```
$xsl = "C:\DATA\RSS\rss_style.xsl"
$rss = "C:\DATA\RSS\sample_rss.xml"
$styled_rss = "C:\DATA\RSS\sample_result.html"
```

The content of our XSL file looks like this:

```
rss_style.xsl
 2  <xsl:stylesheet version="1.0" xmlns:xsl="http://www.w3.org/1999/XSL/Transform">
 3  <xsl:template match="/rss">
 4  <html>
 5  <head>
 6      <style type="text/css">
 7      body {
 8          font-family: Verdana,"sans-serif";
 9      }
10      h2 a, h2 a:link
11      {
12          text-decoration:none;
13          color: #990000;
14      }
15      .channeldescrip
16      {
17          background-color: #FFCC66;
18      }
19      </style>
20  </head>
21  <body>
22      <div id="rssheader">
23          <h2>
24          <xsl:element name="a">
25              <xsl:attribute name="href">
26                  <xsl:value-of select="channel/link" />
27              </xsl:attribute>
28              <xsl:value-of select="channel/title" />
29          </xsl:element>
30          </h2>
31      </div>
32      <div class="rsscontents" style="border-width:0; background-color:#FFF; margin:1em">
33          <div class="channeldescrip">
34          <h3>
35              <xsl:value-of select="channel/description" />
36          </h3>
37          </div>
```

It is important to show you a sample section of the XSL to help visually map where the RSS items are incorporated.

The styling of the XML with XSL is done using the `XslCompiledTransform` .NET class:

```
$xslt = New-Object System.Xml.Xsl.XslCompiledTransform
```

To transform our RSS feed, which is a simple XML file, into a styled HTML file, the XSL (stylesheet) needs to be loaded using the `Load` method of the `XslCompiledTransform` variable:

```
$xslt.Load($xsl)
```

The actual transformation and styling happens when the `Transform` method of the `XslCompiledTransform` object is invoked and passed to the XML content and a handle (or variable) to the resulting HTML file:

```
$xslt.Transform($rss, $styled_rss)
```

The last piece of code we added is just to display the resulting HTML file in Internet Explorer. We create an alias for Internet Explorer using the `Set-Alias` cmdlet, and use it to open our resulting HTML file:

```
#load the resulting styled html
#in Internet Explorer
Set-Alias ie "$env:programfiles\Internet Explorer\iexplore.exe"
ie $styled_rss
```

## There's more...

▶ To learn more about XSL, visit the w3.org official XSL documentation at `http://www.w3.org/Style/XSL/WhatIsXSL.html`.

▶ In addition, check out the MSDN documentation on the `XslCompiledTransform` .NET class at `http://msdn.microsoft.com/en-us/library/system.xml.xsl.xslcompiledtransform.aspx`.

## See also

▶ The *Creating an RSS feed from SQL Server content* recipe.

# Creating a JSON file from SQL Server

In this recipe, we will create a JSON file from records that we retrieve from SQL Server.

## Getting ready

For this recipe, choose a table with records that you want to export to a JSON file.

## How to do it...

The following steps walk you through how to create a JSON file from SQL Server records using PowerShell:

1. Open **PowerShell ISE** as an administrator.

2. Import the `SQLPS` module as follows:

```
#import SQL Server module
Import-Module SQLPS -DisableNameChecking
```

3. Add the following script and run it:

```
$VerbosePreference = "Continue"

$instanceName = "localhost"
$databaseName = "SampleDB"
$fileName = "C:\DATA\Customers.json"

Invoke-SqlCmd -Query "SELECT * FROM SampleText"
-ServerInstance $instanceName -Database $databaseName |
ConvertTo-Json -Depth 1   |
Out-File -FilePath $fileName

$VerbosePreference = "SilentlyContinue"
```

4. When you are done, check the file created. The JSON file will look like this:

```
[
    {
        "RowError":  "",
        "RowState":  1,
        "Table":  "",
        "ItemArray":  "172-32-1176 White Johnson 408 496-7223        10932 Bigge Rd. Menlo Park CA    USA",
        "HasErrors":  false,
        "CustomerID":  "172-32-1176",
        "LastName":  "White",
        "FirstName":  "Johnson",
        "Phone":  "408 496-7223        ",
        "AddressLine":  "10932 Bigge Rd.",
        "City":  "Menlo Park",
        "State":  "CA   ",
        "Country":  "USA"
    },
    {
        "RowError":  "",
        "RowState":  1,
        "Table":  "",
        "ItemArray":  "213-46-8915 Green Marjorie 415 986-7020        309 63rd St. #411 Oakland CA    USA",
        "HasErrors":  false,
        "CustomerID":  "213-46-8915",
        "LastName":  "Green",
        "FirstName":  "Marjorie",
        "Phone":  "415 986-7020        ",
        "AddressLine":  "309 63rd St. #411",
        "City":  "Oakland",
        "State":  "CA   ",
        "Country":  "USA"
    },
```

## How it works...

**JavaScript Object Notation** (**JSON**) files are used for data interchange, the same way XML files are used for data interchange. JSON is lightweight and is becoming a popular format, especially for web applications.

PowerShell has a cmdlet called the `ConvertTo-Json` cmdlet, which was introduced in PowerShell V3. One way to easily create a JSON file from records in SQL Server is to use `Invoke-SqlCmd` to retrieve the records:

```
Invoke-SqlCmd -Query "SELECT * FROM SampleText" -ServerInstance
$instanceName -Database $databaseName |
ConvertTo-Json -Depth 1   |
Out-File -FilePath $fileName
```

The result of the `Invoke-SqlCmd` cmdlet can be piped to the `ConvertTo-Json` cmdlet:

```
Invoke-SqlCmd -Query "SELECT * FROM SampleText" -ServerInstance
$instanceName -Database $databaseName |
ConvertTo-Json -Depth 1   |
Out-File -FilePath $fileName
```

Lastly, the result of the `ConvertTo-Json` cmdlet can be piped to the `Out-File` cmdlet, which produces the actual `.json` file:

```
Invoke-SqlCmd -Query "SELECT * FROM SampleText" -ServerInstance
$instanceName -Database $databaseName |
ConvertTo-Json -Depth 1   |
Out-File -FilePath $fileName
```

## There's more...

Learn more about the `ConvertTo-Json` cmdlet from the MSDN page at `https://technet.microsoft.com/en-us/library/hh849922.aspx`.

# Storing binary data in SQL Server

In this recipe, we will store some binary data, including some images, a PDF, and a Word document, in SQL Server.

## Getting ready

Let's create a sample table that we can use for this recipe. Run the following script in SQL Server Management Studio to create a table called `SampleBLOB` that has a BLOB, or `VARBINARY(MAX)`, field:

```
USE SampleDB
GO
IF OBJECT_ID('SampleBLOB') IS NOT NULL
    DROP TABLE SampleBLOB
GO

CREATE TABLE SampleBLOB
(
    ID INT IDENTITY(1, 1) NOT NULL PRIMARY KEY,
    FileName VARCHAR(200) ,
    InsertedDate DATETIME DEFAULT GETDATE() ,
    InsertedBy VARCHAR(100) DEFAULT SUSER_SNAME() ,
    BLOBStuff VARBINARY(MAX) ,
    FileExtension VARCHAR(50)
)
```

Create a directory called `C:\DATA\` if it doesn't already exist and copy the sample BLOB files that come with the book scripts, or use your own directory and BLOB files.

## How to do it...

These are the steps required to save binary data in SQL Server:

1. Open **PowerShell ISE** as an administrator.

2. Import the SQLPS module as follows:
   ```
   #import SQL Server module
   Import-Module SQLPS -DisableNameChecking
   ```

3. Add the following script and run it:
   ```
   $VerbosePreference = "Continue"
   $instanceName = "localhost"
   $databaseName = "SampleDB"
   $folderName = "C:\DATA\"
   ```

```
#get all files
Get-ChildItem $folderName |
Where-Object PSIsContainer -eq $false |
ForEach-Object {
    $blobFile = $_
    $fileExtension = $blobFile.Extension
    #learn more about Write-Verbose from Appendix A and
    #https://technet.microsoft.com/en-us/library/hh849951.aspx
    Write-Verbose "Importing file $($blobFile.FullName)..."

$query = @"
INSERT INTO SampleBLOB
(FileName, FileExtension, BLOBStuff)
SELECT '$blobFile','$fileExtension',*
FROM OPENROWSET(BULK N'$folderName$blobFile', SINGLE_BLOB)
as tmpImage
"@

Invoke-Sqlcmd -ServerInstance $instanceName -Database
$databaseName -Query $query

#wait for query to finish
Start-Sleep -Seconds 2

}
$VerbosePreference = "SilentlyContinue"
```

4. After the script has run, open SQL Server Management Studio and query the
   `SampleBLOB` table. You will find the BLOB files inserted into the table:

## How it works...

Inserting the contents of a binary file into a SQL Server table can be made easier with the combination of T-SQL and PowerShell.

In this recipe, we have a few files: a PDF, Word document, and few images that we want to store in SQL Server.

To start, we first need to define from which folder we are importing and to which instance and database we are importing:

```
$instanceName = "localhost"
$databaseName = "SampleDB"
$folderName = "C:\DATA\"
```

We then pipe a series of cmdlets to accomplish our task. First, we use the Get-ChildItem cmdlet to get all our files. In our recipe, we import all the files in C:\BLOB\ Files:

```
#get all files
Get-ChildItem $folderName |
Where-Object PSIsContainer -eq $false  |
```

We exclude folders by specifying Where-Object PSIsContainer -eq $false. Of course, you have an option of filtering by file extensions if you want. You can just add the -Include parameter to Get-ChildItem and specify which extensions you want to import, as follows:

```
Get-ChildItem -Path "C:\DATA\*.*" -Include *.jpg,*.png
```

The Foreach-Object cmdlet then takes each file we retrieve and composes a T-SQL statement that inserts the file into our SampleBLOB table. We use OPENROWSET to import the contents of the binary file as SINGLE_BLOB:

```
    $blobFile = $_
    $fileExtension = $blobFile.Extension
    Write-Verbose "Importing file $($blobFile.FullName)..."

$query = @"
INSERT INTO SampleBLOB
(FileName, FileExtension, BLOBStuff)
SELECT '$blobFile','$fileExtension', *
FROM OPENROWSET(BULK N'$folderName$blobFile', SINGLE_BLOB)
as tmpImage
"@
```

This T-SQL statement is then passed to the `Invoke-Sqlcmd` cmdlet, which executes the statement on our instance. We also sleep for two seconds to give the command some time to complete:

```
Invoke-Sqlcmd -ServerInstance $instanceName -Database
$databaseName -Query $query
Start-Sleep -Seconds 2
```

## There's more...

Read more about the OPENROWSET method at `http://msdn.microsoft.com/en-us/library/ms190312.aspx`.

## See also

▸  The *Extracting binary data from SQL Server* recipe.

# Extracting binary data from SQL Server

In this recipe, we will extract the binary content from SQL Server and save it back to individual files in the filesystem.

## Getting ready

For this recipe, we will use the table that we created in the previous recipe, *Storing binary data in SQL Server*, to extract files. Feel free to use your own tables that have the VARBINARY(MAX) columns; just ensure that you change the table name in the script.

In addition to our SampleBLOB table, we will create an empty table with a single VARBINARY(MAX) table. We will use this to facilitate the creation of a format file we need to export binary data out of SQL Server using bcp:

```
USE SampleDB
GO
IF OBJECT_ID('EmptyBLOB') IS NOT NULL
    DROP TABLE EmptyBLOB
GO
CREATE TABLE EmptyBLOB
(
    BLOBStuff VARBINARY(MAX)
)
```

## How to do it...

These are the steps required to extract binary data from SQL Server:

1. Open **PowerShell ISE** as an administrator.

2. Import the `SQLPS` module as follows:

```
#import SQL Server module
Import-Module SQLPS -DisableNameChecking
```

3. First, we will create a `bcp` format file. Add the following script and run it:

```
$instanceName = "localhost"
$databaseName = "SampleDB"

$timestamp = Get-Date -format "yyyy-MMM-dd-hhmmtt"
$emptyBLOB = "SampleDB.dbo.EmptyBLOB"
$formatFileName = "C:\DATA\blob$($timestamp).fmt"
$fmtcmd = "bcp `"$emptyBLOB`" format nul -T -N  -f `"
$formatFilename`" -S $instanceName"

#create the format file
Invoke-Expression -Command $fmtcmd

#now there is a problem, by default the format file
#will use 8 as prefix length for varbinary
#we need this to be zero, so we will replace
(Get-Content $formatFileName) |
ForEach-Object {
    $_ -replace "8", "0"
} |
Set-Content $formatFileName
```

4. After our format file is created, we will export our BLOB content from SQL Server to files in our filesystem. Run the following script:

```
$folderName = "C:\DATA\"
$newFolderName = "Retrieved BLOB $timestamp"

$newFolder = Join-Path -Path "$($folderName)" -ChildPath
$newFolderName

#if folder does not exist, create
if(!(Test-Path -Path $newFolder))
{
```

```
        New-Item -ItemType directory -Path $newFolder
    }

    $query = @"
SELECT ID, FileName
FROM SampleBLOB
"@

    Invoke-Sqlcmd -ServerInstance $instanceName -Database
    $databaseName -Query $query |
    ForEach-Object {
        $item = $_
        Write-Verbose "Retrieving $($item.FileName) ..."

        $newFileName = Join-Path $newFolder $item.FileName

    #query
    $blobQuery = @"
SELECT BLOBStuff
FROM SampleBLOB
WHERE ID = $($item.ID)
"@

    #bcp command
    $cmd = "bcp `"$blobQuery`" queryout `"$newFileName`" -S
    $instanceName -T -d $databaseName -f `"$formatFileName`""

    Invoke-Expression $cmd

    }

    #show retrieved files
    explorer $newFolder
    $VerbosePreference = "SilentlyContinue"
```

5.  When you are done, you will see the files in the folder that the script created:

| Name | Date modified | Type | Size |
|------|---------------|------|------|
| This PC ▸ Local Disk (C:) ▸ BLOB Files ▸ Retrieved BLOB 2015-May-10-0840PM | | | |
| Hello SQLSaturday 114.docx | 5/10/2015 8:40 PM | Office Open XML ... | 292 KB |
| speakerevals.jpg | 5/10/2015 8:40 PM | JPEG image | 73 KB |
| sqlsat108.png | 5/10/2015 8:40 PM | PNG image | 92 KB |
| SSRS CheatSheet.pdf | 5/10/2015 8:40 PM | PDF File | 45 KB |

# How it works...

To retrieve a BLOB, or binary large object, from SQL Server and save it back to the filesystem, we utilize a combination of T-SQL and PowerShell cmdlets.

The most important part of retrieving binary data and saving it back to a file format is preserving the raw format and encoding. We export our data using bcp with a format file. To help us create this format file, we created a simple table in our prep section that has a single `VARBINARY(MAX)` column.

To create the format file, we first use the dynamically built `bcp` command that will create the format file:

```
$fmtcmd = "bcp `"$emptyBLOB`" format nul -T -N  -f `"
$formatfilename`" -S $instanceName"
```

A fully composed command will look similar to the following command:

```
bcp "SampleDB.dbo.EmptyBLOB" format nul -T -N  -f "C:\BLOB
Files\blob2015-May-10-0840PM.fmt" -S localhost
```

The options we specified in our `bcp` are (based on books online) mentioned in the following table:

| Option | Description |
| --- | --- |
| format nul –f | This specifies the non-XML format file |
| -T | This indicates a trusted connection |
| -N | This specifies to perform bcp using native data types for noncharacter data and Unicode character data |

To create the file, we can use the `Invoke-Expression` command to execute the `bcp` command against the server:

```
Invoke-Expression -Command $fmtcmd
```

The format file will look like this:

```
1  12.0
2  1
3  1        SQLBINARY        0     0     ""   1     BLOBStuff         ""
4
```

Unfortunately, the `bcp` command that creates the format file automatically assigned a prefix length of eight (8)for our `SQLBINARY` data. This will create problems for our binary file because it adds additional characters to our file, which can "corrupt" the file. We want to replace this prefix length with zero (0), and we do it using the following code:

```
(Get-Content $formatFileName) |
ForEach-Object {
    $_ -replace "8", "0"
} |
Set-Content $formatFileName
```

Once our format file is ready, we create our timestamped folder:

```
$newFolderName = "Retrieved BLOB $timestamp"

$newFolder = Join-Path -Path "$($folderName)" -ChildPath
$newfoldername

#if folder already exists, will error silently and continue
New-Item -ItemType directory -Path $newfolder -ErrorAction
SilentlyContinue
```

We then get all the records from our `SampleBLOB` table. We will first only get the `ID` and `FileName` variables:

```
$query = @"
SELECT ID, FileName
FROM SampleBLOB
"@

Invoke-Sqlcmd -ServerInstance $instanceName -Database
$databaseName -Query $query |
```

For each record we retrieve that contains the `ID` and `FileName` variables, we query SQL Server again, but this time for the binary content. We use this query in another `bcp` command we are constructing. This `bcp` command uses the format file that we created in the previous section. We pass this `bcp` command again to the `Invoke-Expression` cmdlet to create the binary file in the filesystem:

```
ForEach-Object {
    $item = $_
    Write-Verbose "Retrieving $($item.FileName) ..."
    $newFileName = Join-Path $newFolder $item.FileName

$blobQuery = @"
SELECT BLOBStuff
FROM SampleBLOB
```

```
WHERE ID = $($item.ID)
"@

#bcp command
$cmd = "bcp `"$blobQuery`" queryout `"$newFileName`" -S
$instanceName -T -d $databaseName -f `"$formatFileName`""

Invoke-Expression $cmd


}
```

## There's more...

Read more about bcp at http://msdn.microsoft.com/en-us/library/ms162802. aspx.

## See also

▸ The *Storing binary data in SQL Server* recipe.

# Creating a new assembly

In this recipe, we will create a new user-defined assembly.

## Getting ready

Create a folder named C:\CLR Files and copy the QueryWorksCLR.dll file that comes with the book's sample files to this folder.

We will load this to the SampleDB database. Feel free to use a database accessible to you; just ensure that you replace the database name in the script.

## How to do it...

These are the steps required to create a new assembly in SQL Server:

1.  Open **PowerShell ISE** as an administrator.
2.  Import the SQLPS module as follows:

    ```
    #import SQL Server module
    Import-Module SQLPS -DisableNameChecking
    ```

3.  Add the following script and run it:

```
$instanceName = "localhost"
$databaseName = "SampleDB"
$assemblyName = "QueryWorksCLR"
$assemblyFile = "C:\CLR Files\QueryWorksCLR.dll"

#this is for SAFE assemblies only
$query = @"
CREATE ASSEMBLY $assemblyName
FROM '$assemblyFile'
WITH PERMISSION_SET = SAFE
"@

Invoke-Sqlcmd -ServerInstance $instanceName -Database
$databaseName -Query $query
```

When you are done, open **SQL Server Management Studio**. Go to the database and navigate to **Programmability | Assemblies**. Check whether the assembly has been created or not, as shown in the following screenshot:

## How it works...

Starting with Version 2005, SQL Server has supported integration with the **Common Language Runtime** (**CLR**). This means that you can create .NET code in your language of preference, compile it into **Dynamic Linked Library** (**DLL**) files, and create these as SQL Server database objects called assemblies.

Creating an assembly in SQL Server can be straightforward. In this recipe, we looked at the simplest case, where we create an assembly with the SAFE access.

To create the assembly, we need to specify where the DLL is located and pass it to a CREATE ASSEMBLY T-SQL statement:

```
$assemblyFile = "C:\CLR Files\QueryWorksCLR.dll"

#this is for SAFE assemblies only
$query = @"
CREATE ASSEMBLY $assemblyName
FROM '$assemblyFile'
WITH PERMISSION_SET = SAFE
"@
```

Once the parameters are defined, we simply use the Invoke-Sqlcmd cmdlet to create the assembly:

```
Invoke-Sqlcmd -ServerInstance $instanceName -Database
$databaseName -Query $query
```

> Note that in SQL Server, an assembly can be successfully created and database objects can be created from it (for example, SQLCLR functions and stored procedures), but these will not be usable until SQLCLR integration has been enabled in your instance. This can be done using the T-SQL system stored procedure, sp_configure, or using PowerShell.

To enable SQLCLR using T-SQL, we can use the following command:

```
EXEC sp_configure 'show advanced options', 1
GO
RECONFIGURE
GO
EXEC sp_configure 'clr enabled', 1
GO
RECONFIGURE
GO
```

To do the same thing using PowerShell, we can use the following snippet after we create the $server SMO object:

```
$server.Configuration.IsSqlClrEnabled.ConfigValue = 1
$server.Alter()
```

## There's more...

CLRs can be very powerful components in a SQL Server environment, so we need to control what is allowed and not allowed. A lot of this can be controlled through **Code Access Security** (**CAS**). There are three security levels, and simply put, these are the differences between them:

| Permission setting | Description |
|---|---|
| SAFE | ▸ This is restricted to internal computation and local SQL Server access |
| | ▸ This cannot access external resources, such as files, folders, and so on |
| EXTERNAL_ACCESS | ▸ This allows external access to files, registry, networks, and so on |
| | ▸ By default, this executes as the SQL Server service account |
| UNSAFE | ▸ This is the least restrictive |
| | ▸ This can potentially do anything CLRs can do |

We have only covered how to deploy the SAFE assemblies. EXTERNAL_ACCESS and UNSAFE can be a bit more complicated and will require creating certificates, logins, and symmetric/asymmetric keys.

> Check out the section on creating EXTERNAL_ACCESS and UNSAFE assemblies from the MSDN article *CLR Integration Code Access Security* at http://msdn.microsoft.com/en-us/library/ms345101.aspx.
>
> Note that this article strongly encourages *not* to set the TRUSTWORTHY property of your database to ON.

## See also

▸ The *Listing user-defined assemblies* recipe.

▸ The *Extracting user-defined assemblies* recipe.

# Listing user-defined assemblies

In this recipe, we will list the user-defined assemblies in a SQL Server database.

## Getting ready

We can use the `SampleDB` database that we used in the previous recipe, or you can substitute this with any database that is accessible to you that has some user-defined assemblies.

## How to do it...

These are the steps required to list user-defined assemblies:

1.  Open **PowerShell ISE** as an administrator.

2.  Import the `SQLPS` module as follows:

    ```
    #import SQL Server module
    Import-Module SQLPS -DisableNameChecking
    ```

3.  Add the following script and run it:

    ```
    $instanceName = "localhost"

    $server = New-Object -TypeName
    Microsoft.SqlServer.Management.Smo.Server -ArgumentList
    $instanceName

    $databaseName = "SampleDB"
    $database = $server.Databases[$databaseName]

    #list assemblies except system assemblies
    $database.Assemblies |
    Where-Object IsSystemObject -eq $false
    ```

## How it works...

Listing user-defined assemblies is a straightforward task.

After importing the `SQLPS` module, we create a server handle and database handle:

```
$instanceName = "localhost"

$server = New-Object -TypeName
Microsoft.SqlServer.Management.Smo.Server -ArgumentList
$instanceName

$databaseName = "SampleDB"
$database = $server.Databases[$databaseName]
```

An assembly is a database-level object, which means that we can access assemblies through our database variable. We also want to filter out any system assemblies:

```
$database.Assemblies |
Where-Object IsSystemObject -eq $false
```

## There's more...

Learn more about SQLCLR assemblies from MSDN at `http://msdn.microsoft.com/en-us/library/ms254498.aspx`.

## See also

> ▸ The *Extracting user-defined assemblies* recipe.

# Extracting user-defined assemblies

In this recipe, we will extract user-defined assemblies and resave these back to the filesystem as DLLs.

## Getting ready

We can use the `SampleDB` database that we used in the previous recipe, or you can substitute this with any database that is accessible to you that has some user-defined assemblies.

## How to do it...

These are the steps required to extract user-defined assemblies:

1. Open **PowerShell ISE** as an administrator.

2. Import the SQLPS module as follows:

```
#import SQL Server module
Import-Module SQLPS -DisableNameChecking
```

3. First, we will create a bcp format file. Add the following script and run it:

```
$VerbosePreference = "Continue"
$instanceName = "localhost"

$timestamp = Get-Date -format "yyyy-MMM-dd-hhmmtt"
$emptyBLOB = "SampleDB.dbo.EmptyBLOB"

$formatFileName = "C:\CLR Files\clr$($timestamp).fmt"

$fmtcmd = "bcp `"$emptyBLOB`" format nul -T -N  -f `"
$formatfilename`" -S $instanceName"

#create the format file
Invoke-Expression -Command  $fmtcmd

#now there is a problem, by default the format file
#will use 8 as prefix length for varbinary
#we need this to be zero, so we will replace
(Get-Content $formatFileName) |
ForEach-Object {
    $_ -replace "8", "0"
} |
Set-Content $formatFileName
```

4. Add the following script and run it:

```
$databaseName = "SampleDB"
$folderName = "C:\CLR Files\"
$newFolderName = "Retrieved CLR $timestamp"

$newFolder = Join-Path -Path "$($folderName)" -ChildPath
$newFolderName

#if the path exists, will error silently and continue
New-Item -ItemType directory -Path $newfolder -ErrorAction
SilentlyContinue

#get all user defined assemblies
$query = @"
SELECT
```

```
            af.file_id AS ID,
            a.name + '.dll' AS FileName
    FROM
            sys.assembly_files af
            INNER JOIN sys.assemblies a
            ON af.assembly_id = a.assembly_id
    WHERE
            a.is_user_defined  = 1
    "@

    Invoke-Sqlcmd -ServerInstance $instanceName -Database
    $databaseName -Query $query |
    ForEach-Object {
        $item = $_
        Write-Verbose "Retrieving $($item.FileName) ..."

        $newFileName = Join-Path $newFolder $item.FileName

    $blobQuery = @"
    SELECT
            af.content
    FROM
            sys.assembly_files af
    WHERE
            af.file_id = $($item.ID)
    "@

    #bcp command
    $cmd = "bcp `"$blobQuery`" queryout `"$newFileName`" -S
    $instanceName -T -d $databaseName -f `"$formatFileName`""

    Invoke-Expression $cmd

    }

    #display files
    explorer $newFolder
    $VerbosePreference = "SilentlyContinue"
```

5. Once done, you can check out the file you generated. Your extracted file(s) will look similar to this:

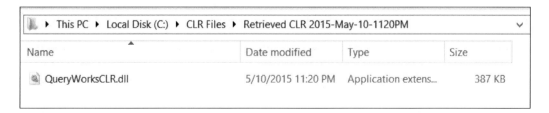

This PC ▸ Local Disk (C:) ▸ CLR Files ▸ Retrieved CLR 2015-May-10-1120PM

| Name | Date modified | Type | Size |
|---|---|---|---|
| QueryWorksCLR.dll | 5/10/2015 11:20 PM | Application extens... | 387 KB |

## How it works...

When we deploy SQLCLR assemblies, the definition of each assembly is saved in the target database. There may be times when you want to extract these back to their DLL binary forms. Retrieving and saving the DLL back into the filesystem is similar to retrieving and saving BLOB data back into the filesystem.

The first thing we do is to create a format file.

> Refer to the *Extracting binary data from SQL Server* recipe for details on creating the format file for BLOB retrieval.

Once we have the format file, we create a timestamped folder where we will store our retrieved DLLs. This will help us keep track of what we extracted and when:

```
$folderName = "C:\CLR Files\"
$newFolderName = "Retrieved CLR $timestamp"

$newFolder = Join-Path -Path "$($folderName)" -ChildPath
$newFolderName

#if the path exists, will error silently and continue
New-Item -ItemType directory -Path $newfolder -ErrorAction
SilentlyContinue
```

We construct a T-SQL statement to retrieve all user-defined assemblies in our target database. We can get the definition of the assemblies from `sys.assembly_files`. To get only user-defined assemblies, we must filter `sys.assembly` for `is_user_defined  = 1`. If we do not filter, we may potentially get other files that were deployed with this assembly, such as debug files, especially when the assembly is deployed from SQL Server data tools. Alternatively, if you want to export only a selection, you can include a filter in your `SELECT` statement:

```
#get all user defined assemblies
$query = @"
SELECT
        af.file_id AS ID,
        a.name + '.dll' AS FileName
FROM
        sys.assembly_files af
        INNER JOIN sys.assemblies a
        ON af.assembly_id = a.assembly_id
WHERE
        a.is_user_defined  = 1
"@
```

We then pass this T-SQL statement to the `Invoke-Sqlcmd` cmdlet:

```
Invoke-Sqlcmd -ServerInstance $instanceName -Database
$databaseName -Query $query |
```

For each record returned to us, we then compose another query that will retrieve the binary contents of the current DLL from `sys.assembly_files` by passing its `file_id`, and save this back to the filesystem using bcp and the format file that we created at the beginning of the recipe:

```
ForEach-Object {
    $item = $_
    Write-Verbose "Retrieving $($item.FileName) ..."

    $newFileName = Join-Path $newFolder $item.FileName
$blobQuery = @"
SELECT
        af.content
FROM
        sys.assembly_files af
WHERE
        af.file_id = $($item.ID)
"@

#bcp command
$cmd = "bcp `"$blobQuery`" queryout `"$newFileName`" -S
$instanceName -T -d $databaseName -f `"$formatFileName`""

Invoke-Expression $cmd
}
```

To ensure that we have maintained the integrity of the DLL file, we can use a decompiler to peek into what is in the DLL file. There are a few free ones, such as JetBrains dotPeek or Telerik JustDecompiler. If all is well, you will be able to see all the classes and the definition of the methods when you open this file in the decompiler. Otherwise, the decompiler will not be able to load this file.

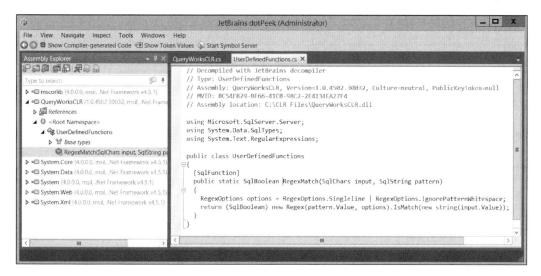

## See also

▶ The *Listing user-defined assemblies* recipe.

▶ The *Creating a new assembly* recipe.

# 10
# Business Intelligence

In this chapter, we will cover the following topics:

- Listing items in your SSRS Report Server
- Listing SSRS report properties
- Using `ReportViewer` to view your SSRS report
- Downloading an SSRS report in Excel and as a PDF
- Creating an SSRS folder
- Creating an SSRS data source
- Changing an SSRS report's data source reference
- Uploading an SSRS report to Report Manager
- Downloading all SSRS report RDL files
- Adding a user with a role to an SSRS report
- Creating folders in an SSIS package store and MSDB
- Deploying an SSIS package to a package store
- Executing an SSIS package stored in a filesystem or a package store
- Downloading an SSIS package to a file
- Creating an SSISDB catalog
- Creating an SSISDB folder
- Deploying an ISPAC file to SSISDB
- Executing an SSIS package stored in SSISDB

- ▶ Listing SSAS cmdlets
- ▶ Listing SSAS instance properties
- ▶ Backing up an SSAS database
- ▶ Restoring an SSAS database
- ▶ Processing an SSAS cube

# Introduction

Over the years and various versions, SQL Server has increased its **Business Intelligence (BI)** support and capabilities. Its BI stack—reporting services, integration services, and analysis services have become strong players in today's BI market.

PowerShell offers capabilities to automate and manage any BI-related tasks from rendering **SQL Server Reporting Services (SSRS)** reports, to deploying the new **SQL Server Integration Services (SSIS)** 2012 ISPAC files, to backing up and restoring **SQL Server Analysis Services (SSAS)** cubes.

# Listing items in your SSRS Report Server

In this recipe, we will list items in an SSRS Report Server that is configured in native mode.

## Getting ready

Identify your SSRS 2014 Report Server URL. We will need to reference the `ReportService2010` web service, and you can reference it using:

```
<ReportServer URL>/ReportService2010.asmx
```

For this recipe, we will use the default Windows credential to authenticate to the server.

## How to do it...

Let's explore the code required to list items in your SSRS Report Server that is configured in native mode:

1. Open **PowerShell ISE** as an administrator.
2. Add the following script and run it:

```
$reportServerUri =
"http://localhost/ReportServer/ReportService2010.asmx"
```

```
$proxy = New-WebServiceProxy -Uri $reportServerUri
-UseDefaultCredential

#list all children
$proxy.ListChildren("/", $true) |
Select-Object Name, TypeName, Path, CreationDate |
Format-Table -AutoSize

#if you want to list only reports
$proxy.ListChildren("/", $true) |
Where-Object TypeName -eq "Report" |
Select-Object Name, TypeName, Path, CreationDate |
Format-Table -AutoSize
```

Here is a sample result:

```
Name              TypeName    Path                                       CreationDate
----              --------    ----                                       ------------
Customer Reports  Folder      /Customer Reports                          5/31/2015 9:21:59 PM
Customer List     Report      /Customer Reports/Customer List            5/31/2015 9:22:00 PM
Customer Sales    Report      /Customer Reports/Customer Sales           5/31/2015 9:24:56 PM
Data Sources      Folder      /Data Sources                              5/31/2015 9:21:59 PM
AdventureWorks2014 DataSource /Data Sources/AdventureWorks2014           5/31/2015 9:21:59 PM
```

## How it works...

The SSRS `ReportService2010` web service provides an API that allows objects in the Report Server to be managed programmatically, whether the Report Server is configured for native mode or SharePoint integrated mode.

This recipe assumes a SQL Server Reporting Services native mode install, although listing reports in SSRS SharePoint integrated mode should employ a similar approach.

 Learn more about the differences between SSRS native mode versus SharePoint integrated mode from the deployment guide document at `https://technet.microsoft.com/en-us/library/bb326345.aspx`.

The first step is to get a handle to create a web service proxy. A web service proxy in PowerShell allows you to manage the web service as you would for any other PowerShell object. To create a new web service proxy, you need to use the `New-WebServiceProxy` cmdlet and pass to it the web service URL as follows:

```
$reportServerUri  =
"http://localhost/ReportServer/ReportService2010.asmx"
$proxy = New-WebServiceProxy -Uri $reportServerUri
-UseDefaultCredential
```

To display all the items in the Report Server, we just need to call the `ListChildren` method of the `ReportingService2010` web proxy object. This will list all items it can find in the path that we specified; in this case, the root `"/"`:

```
#list all children
$proxy.ListChildren("/", $true) |
Select-Object Name, TypeName, Path, CreationDate |
Format-Table -AutoSize
```

If you want to list just the reports, we can pipe the results of the `ListChildren` method and filter for `TypeName = "Report"`. Note that in the old version of the web service, the `ReportService2005` property was called `Type` instead of `TypeName`:

```
#if you want to list only reports
$proxy.ListChildren("/", $true) |
Where-Object TypeName -eq "Report" |
Select-Object Name, TypeName, Path, CreationDate |
Format-Table -AutoSize
```

## There's more...

Learn more about the SSRS Report Server web service endpoints from MSDN at `http://msdn.microsoft.com/en-us/library/ms155398.aspx`.

In addition, the following articles will be helpful when you are working with SSRS programmatically using PowerShell:

- ▶ Check out the MSDN articles for *New-WebServiceProxy* at `http://msdn.microsoft.com/en-us/library/dd315258.aspx`.
- ▶ Check out the MSDN articles for *Report Server Namespace Management Methods* at `http://msdn.microsoft.com/en-us/library/ms152872`.

## See also

- ▶ The *Listing SSRS report properties* recipe.

# Listing SSRS report properties

In this recipe, we will list a single SSRS report's properties.

## Getting ready

To follow this recipe, first identify your SSRS 2012 Report Server URL. We will need to reference the `ReportService2010` web service, and you can reference it using

```
<ReportServer URL>/ReportService2010.asmx
```

You also need to specify your Report Manager URI in the `$reportServerUri` variable.

Lastly, pick a report deployed in your SSRS 2012 Report Manager. Note the path to the report item, and replace the `$reportPath` variable with your own path.

## How to do it...

Here are the steps required to list SSRS report properties:

1. Open **PowerShell ISE** as an administrator.

2. Add the following script and run it:

```
$reportServerUri   =
"http://localhost/ReportServer/ReportService2010.asmx"
$proxy = New-WebServiceProxy -Uri $reportServerUri
-UseDefaultCredential

$reportPath = "/Customer Reports/Customer List"

#list this report's properties
$proxy.ListChildren("/", $true) |
Where-Object Path -eq $reportPath
```

A sample result is as follows:

```
ID                         : 7078384d-066f-40f4-ae58-f23b2c06f2a6
Name                       : Customer List
Path                       : /Customer Reports/Customer List
VirtualPath                :
TypeName                   : Report
Size                       : 11320
SizeSpecified              : True
Description                :
Hidden                     : False
HiddenSpecified            : False
CreationDate               : 5/31/2015 9:22:00 PM
CreationDateSpecified      : True
ModifiedDate               : 5/31/2015 9:24:56 PM
ModifiedDateSpecified      : True
CreatedBy                  : QUERYWORKS\Administrator
ModifiedBy                 : QUERYWORKS\Administrator
ItemMetadata               : {}
```

## How it works...

To get SSRS 2014 report properties, we must first get a web service proxy:

```
$reportServerUri   =
http://localhost/ReportServer/ReportService2010.asmx
$proxy = New-WebServiceProxy -Uri $reportServerUri
-UseDefaultCredential
```

We must also identify which report we want to display properties for:

```
$reportPath = "/Customer Reports/Customer List"
```

Once we get a proxy and we know which report we are querying, we need to get the catalog items that are related to this Report Server instance. We do this using the `ListChildren` method of the proxy object and by specifying a path to traverse starting from the root `"/"` path recursively. We specify a recursive lookup by passing the `Boolean` value `$true` as a second parameter to `ListChildren`:

```
$proxy.ListChildren("/", $true) |
Where-Object Path -eq $reportPath
```

To narrow down the displayed properties to just our report's, we can pipe the result of the `ListChildren` method to the `Where-Object` cmdlet and filter only by reports that match `$reportPath`:

```
$proxy.ListChildren("/", $true) |
Where-Object Path -eq $reportPath
```

Note that a report in the `ReportServer2010` web service is a `CatalogItem` class, not a `Report` class, which was available in previous SSRS versions. If you pipe the preceding code to the `Get-Member` cmdlet, you will see the `TypeName` at the beginning of the displayed results:

```
TypeName:
Microsoft.PowerShell.Commands.NewWebserviceProxy.
AutogeneratedTypes.WebServiceProxy1tServer_Report
Service2010_asmx.CatalogItem
```

## There's more...

To learn more about the `CatalogItem` class, check out http://msdn.microsoft.com/en-us/library/reportservice2010.catalogitem

## See also

▶ The *Listing items in your SSRS Report Server* recipe.

# Using ReportViewer to view your SSRS report

This recipe shows how to display a report using the `ReportViewer` redistributable.

## Getting ready

In previous versions of SSRS, the `ReportViewer` redistributable was a separate download and this needed to be installed on your machine prior to following this recipe. As of SSRS 2014, the ReportViewer 2014 runtime is part of the **SQL Server Data Tools** (**SSDT-BI**) installation. At the time of writing, SSDT-BI for SQL Server 2014 and Visual Studio 2013 can be found at `https://msdn.microsoft.com/en-us/library/mt204009.aspx`.

You will also need to identify your SSRS 2014 Report Server URL. We will need to reference the `ReportService2010` web service, and you can reference it using:

```
<ReportServer URL>/ReportService2010.asmx
```

Lastly, pick a report you want to display using the `ReportViewer` object. Identify the full path, and replace the value of the `$reportViewer.ServerReport.ReportPath` variable in the script.

## How to do it...

This list shows how we can display a report using the `ReportViewer` object:

1. Open **PowerShell ISE** as an administrator.

2. Load the assembly for `ReportViewer` as follows:

```
#load the ReportViewer WinForms assembly
Add-Type -AssemblyName "Microsoft.ReportViewer.WinForms,
Version=12.0.0.0, Culture=neutral,
PublicKeyToken=89845dcd8080cc91"

#load the Windows.Forms assembly
Add-Type -AssemblyName "System.Windows.Forms"
```

Add the following script and run it:

```
$reportViewer = New-Object
Microsoft.Reporting.WinForms.ReportViewer
$reportViewer.ProcessingMode = "Remote"
$reportViewer.ServerReport.ReportServerUrl =
"http://localhost/ReportServer"
$reportViewer.ServerReport.ReportPath =
"/Customer Reports/Customer List"

#adjust report size
$reportViewer.Height = 600
$reportViewer.Width = 800
$reportViewer.RefreshReport()

#create a windows new form
$form = New-Object Windows.Forms.Form

#we're going to make the just slightly bigger
#than the ReportViewer
$form.Height = 610
$form.Width= 810

#form is not resizable
$form.FormBorderStyle = "FixedSingle"

#do not allow user to maximize
$form.MaximizeBox = $false

$form.Controls.Add($reportViewer)

#show the report in the form
$reportViewer.Show()

#show the form
$form.ShowDialog()
```

3. After you run the script, here is a sample result. Notice how the top bar is similar to the top bar in your Report Manager:

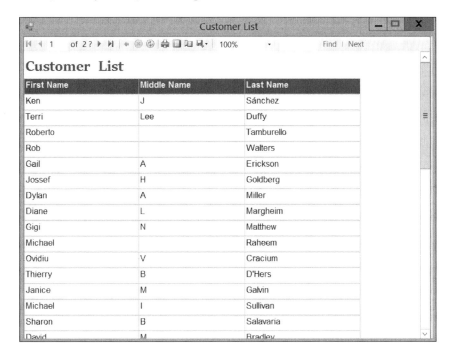

## How it works...

The `ReportViewer` object is a control that allows you to embed and display an SSRS report into a web or Windows form, and supplies the user with a familiar interface they might be accustomed to seeing when using the Report Manager. This control always connects back to the Report Server when processing and rendering the report.

The `ReportViewer` object is a redistributable package that does not come with Reporting Services installations; you will need to download and install this separately. Refer to the *Getting ready* section.

In this recipe, we are displaying a specific report in a Windows form.

To start, we have to load the assemblies related to `ReportViewer` and Windows forms:

```
#load the ReportViewer WinForms assembly
Add-Type -AssemblyName "Microsoft.ReportViewer.WinForms,
Version=12.0.0.0, Culture=neutral,
PublicKeyToken=89845dcd8080cc91"

#load the Windows.Forms assembly
Add-Type -AssemblyName "System.Windows.Forms"
```

We need to load the strong name of the `ReportViewer.WinForms` assembly using the `Add-Type` cmdlet, that is, to load it with the assembly name, version, culture, and public key token information. To determine the strong name, you can open `C:\Windows\assembly` and check the properties of the `Microsoft.ReportViewer.WinForms` assembly. Note that you may get multiple versions of the assembly if you have different versions of the `ReportViewer` redistributable installed on your system. In the following screenshot, you can see that there are two `WinForms` assembly:

Once the assembly is loaded, we then have to create a `ReportViewer` object:

```
$reportViewer = New-Object
Microsoft.Reporting.WinForms.ReportViewer
```

We also need to set some properties that specify where and how the report is going to be fetched:

```
$reportViewer.ProcessingMode = "Remote"
$reportViewer.ServerReport.ReportServerUrl =
"http://localhost/ReportServer"
$reportViewer.ServerReport.ReportPath =
"/Customer Reports/Customer List"
```

The `ProcessingMode` property can either be `Local` or `Remote`. The `ReportServerUrl` and `ReportPath` properties are properties of the `ServerReport` object, and these should point to your report server and the full path to your report. Should you need to specify the credentials to connect to the Report Manager, you will need to set the `ReportCredentials` property as follows:

```
$reportViewer.ServerReport.ReportServerCredentials.
NetworkCredentials= New-Object
System.Net.NetworkCredential("username", "password")
```

We then also specify the `ReportViewer` dimensions:

```
$reportViewer.Height = 600
$reportViewer.Width = 800
$reportViewer.RefreshReport()
```

For this recipe, we embedded the `ReportViewer` object in a Windows form, and lastly, showed it as a dialog form. Since we have preset the size of the report to 800 X 600, we are going to disable the maximize button and the *resizability* of the window to prevent users from resizing the form and seeing only empty spaces when the form is resized:

```
#create a windows new form
$form = New-Object Windows.Forms.Form

#we're going to make the just slightly bigger
#than the ReportViewer
$form.Height = 610
$form.Width= 810

#form is not resizable
$form.FormBorderStyle = "FixedSingle"

#do not allow user to maximize
$form.MaximizeBox = $false

$form.Controls.Add($reportViewer)

#show the report in the form
$reportViewer.Show()

#show the form
$form.ShowDialog()
```

## There's more...

▶ To learn more about the *ReportViewer Class*, visit `http://msdn.microsoft.com/en-us/library/microsoft.reporting.winforms.reportviewer.aspx`.

▶ Refer to the *ReportViewer Properties* at `http://msdn.microsoft.com/en-us/library/microsoft.reporting.webforms.reportviewer_properties`.

▶ To learn more about *ReportViewer Web Server and Windows Forms Controls*, check out `http://msdn.microsoft.com/en-us/library/ms251771.aspx`.

## See also

▶ The *Downloading an SSRS report in Excel and as a PDF* recipe.

# Downloading an SSRS report in Excel and as a PDF

This recipe shows you how to download an SSRS report in Excel and PDF format.

## Getting ready

In previous versions of SSRS, the `ReportViewer` redistributable was a separate download and this needed to be installed on your machine prior to following this recipe. As of SSRS 2014, the Report Viewer 2014 runtime is part of the SSDT-BI installation. At the time of writing, SSDT-BI for SQL Server 2014 and Visual Studio 2013 can be found at `https://msdn.microsoft.com/en-us/library/mt204009.aspx`.

After installing the `ReportViewer` control, select a report that you wish to download as an Excel or PDF version.

This recipe demonstrates how to download a report published to a local Report Server and export it to Excel and as a PDF. The report is in the `/Customer Reports/Customer List` path. Alternatively, choose a report you wish to download and replace the `$reportViewer.ServerReport.ReportPath` variable with the report path in your environment.

## How to do it...

Let's explore the code required to view your report in Excel and as a PDF:

1. Open **PowerShell ISE** as an administrator.

2. Load the `ReportViewer` assembly:

```
Add-Type -AssemblyName "Microsoft.ReportViewer.WinForms,
Version=12.0.0.0, Culture=neutral,
PublicKeyToken=89845dcd8080cc91"
```

3. Add the following script to create and open the Excel file:

```
$reportViewer = New-Object Microsoft.Reporting.WinForms.
ReportViewer

$reportViewer.ProcessingMode = "Remote"

$reportViewer.ServerReport.ReportServerUrl = "http://localhost/
ReportServer"

$reportViewer.ServerReport.ReportPath = "/Customer Reports/
Customer List"

#required variables for rendering
$mimeType = $null
$encoding = $null
$extension = $null
$streamids = $null
$warnings = $null

#export to Excel
$excelFile = "C:\Temp\Customer List.xls"
$bytes = $reportViewer.ServerReport.Render("Excel", $null,
                 [ref] $mimeType,
                 [ref] $encoding,
            [ref] $extension,
            [ref] $streamids,
            [ref] $warnings)
$fileStream = New-Object System.IO.FileStream($excelFile, [System.
IO.FileMode]::OpenOrCreate)
$fileStream.Write($bytes, 0, $bytes.Length)
$fileStream.Close()

#open the generated excel document
$excel = New-Object -comObject Excel.Application
$excel.visible = $true
$excel.Workbooks.Open($excelFile) | Out-Null
```

4.  Add the following script to create and open the PDF file:

```
#export to PDF
$pdfFile = "C:\Temp\Customer List.pdf"
$bytes = $reportViewer.ServerReport.Render("PDF", $null,
                    [ref] $mimeType,
                    [ref] $encoding,
              [ref] $extension,
              [ref] $streamids,
              [ref] $warnings)


$fileStream = New-Object System.IO.FileStream($pdfFile,
[System.IO.FileMode]::OpenOrCreate)
$fileStream.Write($bytes, 0, $bytes.Length)
$fileStream.Close()

#open the PDF file using the default PDF application
[System.Diagnostics.Process]::Start($pdfFile)
```

## How it works...

For this recipe, we need to load the `ReportViewer` assembly, which will render the SSRS report from the Report Manager into different formats:

```
Add-Type -AssemblyName "Microsoft.ReportViewer.WinForms,
Version=12.0.0.0, Culture=neutral,
PublicKeyToken=89845dcd8080cc91"
```

We also need to set the properties of the report:

```
$reportViewer = New-Object
Microsoft.Reporting.WinForms.ReportViewer

$reportViewer.ProcessingMode   = "Remote"

$reportViewer.ServerReport.ReportServerUrl =
"http://localhost/ReportServer"

$reportViewer.ServerReport.ReportPath =
"/Customers/Customer Contact Numbers"
```

There are also a few variables that we need to declare to render our report. We need to declare these because they need to be passed by reference to the `Render` method of `ReportViewer`:

```
#required variables for rendering
$mimeType = $null
```

```
$encoding = $null
$extension = $null
$streamids = $null
$warnings = $null
```

We need to render the report first as an Excel file. The `ReportViewer` handle has a `Render` method that allows the report to be rendered in different formats, including Excel, PDF, and image. To render a report to Excel, we must invoke the `ServerReport.Render` method. The first parameter that we pass is for the format and it should be `"Excel"`. We will also pass five output parameters for MIME type, encoding, extension, stream IDs, and warnings, respectively. We need to assign the result of this method's invocation to a byte variable:

```
#export to Excel
$excelFile = "C:\Temp\Customer List.xls"
$bytes = $reportViewer.ServerReport.Render("Excel", $null,
                [ref] $mimeType,
                [ref] $encoding,
         [ref] $extension,
         [ref] $streamids,
         [ref] $warnings)
```

To create an Excel file based on what was rendered, we should use a `System.IO.FileStream` object:

```
$fileStream = New-Object System.IO.FileStream($excelFile,
[System.IO.FileMode]::OpenOrCreate)
$fileStream.Write($bytes, 0, $bytes.Length)
$fileStream.Close()
```

When done, we create an `Excel.Application` COM object. We pass the filename, and open the workbook using the Excel object's `Workbooks.Open` method:

```
#let's open up our excel document
$excel = New-Object -comObject Excel.Application
$excel.visible = $true
$excel.Workbooks.Open($excelFile) | Out-Null
```

To render the report in PDF format, the same `ServerReport.Render` method can be invoked, but this time, we pass `"PDF"` instead of `"Excel"` as the first parameter:

```
$pdfFile = "C:\Temp\Customer List.pdf"
$bytes = $reportViewer.ServerReport.Render("PDF", $null,
                   [ref] $mimeType,
                   [ref] $encoding,
            [ref] $extension,
            [ref] $streamids,
            [ref] $warnings)
```

Saving the rendered PDF document also requires using the `System.IO.FileStream` object:

```
$fileStream = New-Object System.IO.FileStream($pdfFile,
[System.IO.FileMode]::OpenOrCreate)
$fileStream.Write($bytes, 0, $bytes.Length)
$fileStream.Close()
```

The `[System.Diagnostics.Process]::Start` method is then used to open the PDF using the default application installed to run PDFs:

```
#let's open up our PDF application
[System.Diagnostics.Process]::Start($pdfFile)
```

## There's more...

> ▸ To learn more about *ReportViewer Web Server and Windows Form Controls*, visit `http://msdn.microsoft.com/en-us/library/ms251771.aspx`.

> ▸ To learn more about the *ServerReport.Render Method*, visit `https://msdn.microsoft.com/en-us/library/microsoft.reporting.webforms.serverreport.render.aspx`.

## See also

> ▸ The *Using ReportViewer to view your SSRS report* recipe.

# Creating an SSRS folder

In this recipe, we create a timestamped SSRS folder.

## Getting ready

Identify your SSRS 2014 Report Server URL. We will need to reference the `ReportService2010` web service, and you can reference it using

```
<ReportServer URL>/ReportService2010.asmx
```

## How to do it...

Let's explore the code required to create an SSRS folder programmatically:

1. Open **PowerShell ISE** as an administrator.

2. Add the following script and run it:

```
$reportServerUri  =
"http://localhost/ReportServer/ReportService2010.asmx"
$proxy = New-WebServiceProxy -Uri $reportServerUri
-UseDefaultCredential

#A workaround we have to do to ensure
#we don't get any namespace clashes is to

#capture automatically generated namespace
#this is a workaround to avoid namespace clashes
#resulting in using -Class with New-WebServiceProxy
$type = $Proxy.GetType().Namespace

#formulate data type we need
$datatype = ($type + '.Property')

#display datatype, just for our reference
$datatype

#create new Property
#if we were using -Class SSRS, this would be similar to
#$property = New-Object SSRS.Property
$property = New-Object ($datatype)
$property.Name = "Description"
$property.Value = "Created by PowerShell"
$folderName = "Sales Reports " +
(Get-Date -format "yyyy-MMM-dd-hhmmtt")

#Report SSRS Properties
#http://msdn.microsoft.com/en-us/library/ms152826.aspx
$numProperties = 1
$properties = New-Object ($datatype + '[]')$numProperties
$properties[0] = $property

$proxy.CreateFolder($folderName, "/", $properties)

#display new folder in IE
Set-Alias ie "$env:programfiles\Internet
Explorer\iexplore.exe"
```

```
ie "http://localhost/Reports"

#uncomment below if your browser does not open
#start "http://localhost/Reports"
```

Once done, Internet Explorer will open your SSRS Report Manager. You can verify that the folder has been created, as shown in the following screenshot:

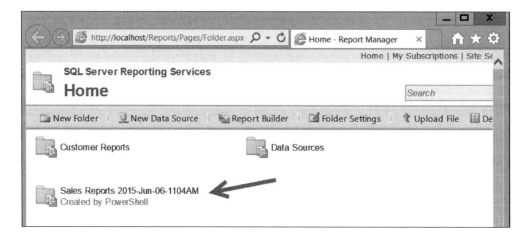

## How it works...

To create a folder, or any item, in your Report Server, we have to first create a handle to the Report Server web service by creating a proxy:

```
$reportServerUri  =
"http://localhost/ReportServer/ReportService2010.asmx"
$proxy = New-WebServiceProxy -Uri $reportServerUri
-UseDefaultCredential
```

Typically, when you check the sample code, you will find that the -Class switch is specified with the New-WebServiceProxy cmdlet, as follows:

```
$proxy = New-WebServiceProxy -Uri $reportServerUri
-UseDefaultCredential -Class SSRS2008
```

We don't use -Class in this recipe because of a couple of issues, which are as follows:

> When run from the PowerShell console, the script runs once and does not run subsequent times in the same session. You will have to close the shell (CLI) to release the previously created proxy object that holds that namespace. As far as the web server proxy is concerned, this namespace has already been created and we will not recreate it again. Remember that what we created is just a proxy. The actual object was allocated not in our session but on the server.

▸ When run from the PowerShell ISE, you will get a different host of issues, including errors that say the namespace cannot be recognized.

Refer to `http://www.sqlmusings.com/2012/02/04/resolving-ssrs-and-powershell-new-webserviceproxy-namespace-issue/` for more details on using the `-Class` switch for the `New-WebServiceProxy` cmdlet.

On the other hand, if we do not use a namespace, a different issue arises. The automatically generated namespace is *unpredictable*. For example, a sample namespace is as follows:

```
PS C:\Users\Administrator> $Proxy.GetType().Namespace
Microsoft.PowerShell.Commands.NewWebserviceProxy.
AutogeneratedTypes.WebServiceProxy1tServer_ReportService2010
_asmx
```

This poses a problem because we need to refer to this namespace when we create any `ReportService2010` object. To work around this issue, we can omit the `-Class` and dynamically capture the namespace, and subsequently use it when creating our SSRS objects.

In the following script, we are creating a `Property` object that we are going to use for our folder:

```
#capture automatically generated namespace
#this is a workaround to avoid namespace clashes
#resulting in using -Class with New-WebServiceProxy
$type = $Proxy.GetType().Namespace

#formulate data type we need
$datatype = ($type + '.Property')

#display datatype, just for our reference
$datatype

#create new Property
#if we were using -Class SSRS, this would be similar to
#$property = New-Object SSRS.Property
$property = New-Object ($datatype)
```

Once we have created the `Property` object, we can assign the values. One property that we can set for a folder is `Description`:

```
$property.Name = "Description"
$property.Value = "Created by PowerShell"
$folderName = "Sales Reports " +
(Get-Date -format "yyyy-MMM-dd-hhmmtt")
```

We then need to add this to a `Property[]` array, which is what the `CreateFolder` method of the proxy accepts. Note that when we create this array, we still need to create this dynamically, which is similar to how we created our `Property` object:

```
#Report SSRS Properties
#http://msdn.microsoft.com/en-us/library/ms152826.aspx
$numProperties = 1
$properties = New-Object ($datatype + '[]')$numProperties
$properties[0] = $property
```

When done, we can create the folder using the `CreateFolder` method that accepts the folder name, parent, and properties array:

```
$proxy.CreateFolder($folderName, "/", $properties)
```

The last step in this recipe is to create an alias for IE and launch our Report Manager to verify that the folder has been created:

```
#display new folder in IE
Set-Alias ie "$env:programfiles\Internet Explorer\iexplore.exe"
ie "http://localhost/Reports"
```

## There's more...

To learn more about the namespace collision issue mentioned in this recipe when dealing with `New-WebServiceProxy`, check out http://www.sqlmusings.com/2012/02/04/resolving-ssrs-and-powershell-new-webserviceproxy-namespace-issue/.

Check out the `ReportService2010.CreateFolder` method at http://msdn.microsoft.com/en-us/library/reportservice2010.reportingservice2010.createfolder.aspx.

## See also

- The *Creating an SSRS folder* recipe.

# Creating an SSRS data source

In this recipe, we will create an SSRS data source.

## Getting ready

In this recipe, we will create a data source called `Sample` that is stored in the `/Data Sources` folder. This data source uses integrated authentication and points to the `AdventureWorks2014` database.

Before we start, we will need to identify the typical information needed for a data source, which is shown in the following table:

| Property | Value |
|---|---|
| Data source name | Sample |
| Data source type | SQL |
| Connection string | Data Source=localhost;Initial Catalog=AdventureWorks2014 |
| Credentials | Integrated |
| Parent (that is, a folder where this data source will be placed; it must already exist) | /Data Sources |

 Note that the /Data Sources folder is the default folder that gets created when you deploy reports to Report Server via SSDT.

These are the same pieces of information that you will find when you go to a data source's properties in your Report Manager:

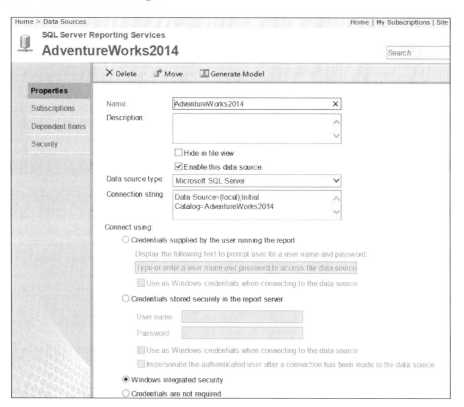

## How to do it...

These are the steps required to create an SSRS data source using PowerShell:

1. Open **PowerShell ISE** as an administrator.

2. Add the following script and run it:

```
$reportServerUri  = "http://localhost/ReportServer/
ReportService2010.asmx"
$proxy = New-WebServiceProxy -Uri $reportServerUri
-UseDefaultCredential
$type = $Proxy.GetType().Namespace

#create a DataSourceDefinition
$dataSourceDefinitionType =
($type + '.DataSourceDefinition')
$dataSourceDefinition =
New-Object($dataSourceDefinitionType)
$dataSourceDefinition.CredentialRetrieval = "Integrated"
$dataSourceDefinition.ConnectString =
"Data Source=localhost;Initial Catalog=AdventureWorks2014"
$dataSourceDefinition.extension = "SQL"
$dataSourceDefinition.enabled = $true
$dataSourceDefinition.Prompt = $null
$dataSourceDefinition.WindowsCredentials = $false

#NOTE this is SSRS native mode
#CreateDataSource method accepts the following parameters:
# 1. datasource name
# 2. parent (data folder) - must already exist
# 3. overwrite
# 4. data source definition
# 5. properties

$dataSource = "Sample"
$parent = "/Data Sources"
$overwrite = $true

$newDataSource =
$proxy.CreateDataSource($dataSource, $parent, $overwrite,$dataSour
ceDefinition, $null)
```

3. When done, open your Report Manager and confirm that the data source has been created:

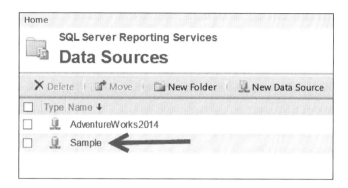

## How it works...

To create a data source programmatically, we first need to get a web service proxy:

```
$reportServerUri  =
"http://localhost/ReportServer/ReportService2010.asmx"
$proxy = New-WebServiceProxy -Uri $reportServerUri
-UseDefaultCredential
```

We then need to capture the automatically generated namespace. We will use this in later steps:

```
$type = $Proxy.GetType().Namespace
```

We then need to create a DataSourceDefinition object. We start with using our automatically generated namespace to help us create a new DataSourceDefinition object:

```
#create a DataSourceDefinition
$dataSourceDefinitionType = ($type + '.DataSourceDefinition')
$dataSourceDefinition = New-Object($dataSourceDefinitionType)
```

 Refer to the *How it works...* section of the *Creating an SSRS folder* recipe for additional details on automatically generated namespace issues.

We then need to specify the properties of `DataSourceDefinition`:

- ▸ `CredentialRetrieval`: This specifies how to retrieve credentials when Report Server needs to connect to the data source. It can be one of the following: `None`, `Prompt`, `Integrated`, or `Store`.

- ▸ `ConnectionString`: This is the connection string to the data source.

- ▸ `Extension`: This is the data source extension and can be either: `SQL`, `OLEDB`, `ODBC`, or a custom extension.

We also set the prompt property to false so that the report does not prompt for credentials when run, and set `WindowsCredentials` to false so that the report does not pass credentials as Windows credentials:

```
$dataSourceDefinition.CredentialRetrieval = "Integrated"
$dataSourceDefinition.ConnectString = "Data Source=localhost;Initial
Catalog=AdventureWorks2014"
$dataSourceDefinition.extension = "SQL"
$dataSourceDefinition.enabled = $true
$dataSourceDefinition.Prompt = $null
$dataSourceDefinition.WindowsCredentials = $false
```

To create a data source in native mode, we need to use the `CreateDataSource` method, which accepts five parameters:

- ▸ Data source name
- ▸ Parent
- ▸ Overwrite
- ▸ Data source definition
- ▸ Properties

The code is as follows:

```
$dataSource = "Sample"
$parent = "/Data Sources"
$overwrite = $true

$newDataSource = $proxy.CreateDataSource($dataSource, $parent,
$overwrite,$dataSourceDefinition, $null)
```

## There's more...

To learn more about the `ReportService.DataSourceDefinition` class, visit `http://msdn.microsoft.com/en-us/library/reportservice2010.datasourcedefinition.aspx`.

## See also

▸ The *Creating an SSRS folder* recipe.

▸ The *Changing an SSRS report's data source reference* recipe.

# Changing an SSRS report's data source reference

In this recipe, we will update an SSRS report's data source.

## Getting ready

In this recipe, we will change the data source of the /Customer Reports/Customer Sales report, which originally uses the data source reference /Data Sources/ AdventureWorks2014 to point to /Data Sources/Sample.

Alternatively, pick an existing report in your environment and the data source you want this report to reference. Note the names and path to these items.

## How to do it...

Let's take a look at the steps to change an SSRS report's data source:

1. Open **PowerShell ISE** as an administrator.

2. Add the following script and run it:

```
$reportServerUri  =
"http://localhost/ReportServer/ReportService2010.asmx"
$proxy = New-WebServiceProxy -Uri $reportServerUri
-UseDefaultCredential

#get autogenerated namespace
$type = $proxy.GetType().Namespace

#specify which report's data source to change
$reportPath = "/Customer Reports/Customer Sales"

#look for the report in the catalog items array
#note we are using PowerShell V3 Where-Object syntax
$report = $proxy.ListChildren("/", $true) |
          Where-Object Path -eq $reportPath

#get current data source name
```

```
#this needs to be the same name in the RDL
$dataSourceName   = $($proxy.GetItemDataSources($report.Path)).Name

#specify new data source reference
$newDataSourcePath  = "/Data Sources/Sample"

#dynamically create data types based on the new
#autogenerated namespace
$dataSourceType = ($type + '.DataSource')
$numItems = 1
$dataSourceArrayType = ($type + '.DataSource[]')
$dataSourceReferenceType = ($type + '.DataSourceReference')

#create a data source array containing
#the new data source path
$dataSourceArray = New-Object
($datasourceArrayType)$numItems
$dataSourceArray[0] = New-Object ($dataSourceType)
$dataSourceArray[0].Name = $dataSourceName
$dataSourceArray[0].Item = New-Object
($dataSourceReferenceType)
$dataSourceArray[0].Item.Reference = $newDataSourcePath

#set the new data source
$proxy.SetItemDataSources($report.Path, $dataSourceArray)
```

You can confirm the changes by opening the Report Manager and opening that report's Data Sources. Ensure that the data source reference now points to the correct path:

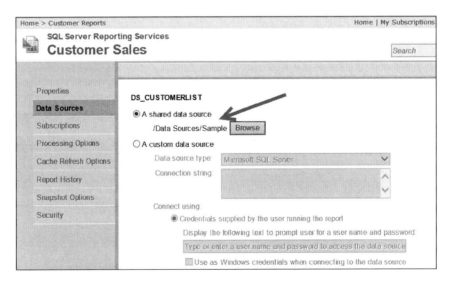

# How it works...

In order to change a report's data source, we must first get a handle to this report.

The first step is to create a web server proxy:

```
$reportServerUri  =
"http://localhost/ReportServer/ReportService2010.asmx"
$proxy = New-WebServiceProxy -Uri $reportServerUri
-UseDefaultCredential
```

In this recipe, we will also create a few `ReportService2010` objects, so we will need to capture the dynamically generated namespace:

```
$type = $proxy.GetType().Namespace
```

 Refer to the *How it works...* section of the *Creating an SSRS folder* recipe for additional details on automatically generated namespace issues.

We then need to get a handle to the report. In order to do this, we need to capture all the Report Server objects and extract the report that matches the path we specified:

```
#look for the report in the catalog items array
#note we are using PowerShell V3 Where-Object syntax
$report = $proxy.ListChildren("/", $true) |
         Where-Object Path -eq $reportPath
```

We also need to capture the report's current data source name using the `GetItemDataSources` method of the proxy object. We need to keep the same name, even if we change the data source path it references.

 Note that paths, report names, data source names, and references are case sensitive.

In the following code, we are capturing the current data source name from the current report's data source:

```
#get current data source name
#this needs to be the same name in the RDL
$dataSourceName  = $($proxy.GetItemDataSources($report.Path)).Name

#specify new data source reference
$newDataSourcePath  = "/Data Sources/Sample"
```

The next step is to create a data source array (`DataSource[]`) object. As we have a dynamically generated namespace, we must first compose the data types dynamically based on the namespace stored in the `$type` variable:

```
#dynamically create data types based on the new
#autogenerated namespace
$dataSourceType = ($type + '.DataSource')
$numItems = 1
$dataSourceArrayType = ($type + '.DataSource[]')
$dataSourceReferenceType = ($type + '.DataSourceReference')
```

To create a data source array, we use the new types:

```
#create a data source array containing
#the new data source path
$dataSourceArray = New-Object ($datasourceArrayType)$numItems
$dataSourceArray[0] = New-Object ($dataSourceType)
$dataSourceArray[0].Name = $dataSourceName
$dataSourceArray[0].Item = New-Object ($dataSourceReferenceType)
$dataSourceArray[0].Item.Reference = $newDataSourcePath
```

We are now ready to call the `SetItemDataSources` method of the proxy object to change our report's data source reference. This method accepts a catalog item name path and data source array:

```
$proxy.SetItemDataSources($report.Path, $dataSourceArray)
```

## There's more...

To learn more about the `SetItemDataSources` method, check out `http://msdn.microsoft.com/en-us/library/reportservice2010.reportingservice2010.setitemdatasources.aspx`.

## See also

- ▶ The *Creating an SSRS folder* recipe.
- ▶ The *Creating an SSRS data source* recipe.

# Uploading an SSRS report to Report Manager

In this recipe, we will upload an SSRS report (`.rdl` file) to the Report Manager.

## Getting ready

You can use the sample RDL file that comes with this cookbook and save it in the `C:\SSRS` folder. The sample RDL file uses the `AdventureWorks2014` sample database. Alternatively, use an RDL file that is readily available to you. Make sure to update the RDL file reference in the script to reflect where your report file is located.

## How to do it...

These are the steps required to upload an RDL file to the Report Manager:

1. Open **PowerShell ISE** as an administrator.

2. Add the following script and run it:

```
$reportServerUri  =
"http://localhost/ReportServer/ReportService2010.asmx"
$proxy = New-WebServiceProxy -Uri $reportServerUri
-UseDefaultCredential
$type = $proxy.GetType().Namespace

#specify where the RDL file is
$rdl = "C:\SSRS\Customer Contact List.rdl"

#extract report name from the RDL file
$reportName =
[System.IO.Path]::GetFileNameWithoutExtension($rdl)

#get contents of the RDL
$byteArray = Get-Content $rdl -Encoding Byte

#The fully qualified URL for the parent folder that will
contain the item.
$parent = "/Customer Reports"
$overwrite = $true
$warnings = $null

#create report
$report = $proxy.CreateCatalogItem("Report", $reportName,
$parent, $overwrite, $byteArray, $null, [ref]$warnings )

#data source name must match what's in the RDL
$dataSourceName = "DS_CUSTOMERLIST"

#data source path should match what's in the report server
```

```
$dataSourcePath = "/Data Sources/AdventureWorks2014"

#when we upload the report, if the
#data source from the source is different
#or has a different path from what's in the
#report manager, the data source will be broken
#and we will need to update

#create our data type references
$dataSourceArrayType = ($type + '.DataSource[]')
$dataSourceType = ($type + '.DataSource')
$dataSourceReferenceType = ($type + '.DataSourceReference')

#create data source array
$numDataSources = 1
$dataSourceArray = New-Object
($dataSourceArrayType)$numDataSources
$dataSourceReference =
New-Object ($dataSourceReferenceType)

#update data source
$dataSourceArray[0] = New-Object ($dataSourceType)
$dataSourceArray[0].Name = $dataSourceName
$dataSourceArray[0].Item =
New-Object ($dataSourceReferenceType)
$dataSourcearray[0].Item.Reference = $dataSourcePath
$proxy.SetItemDataSources($report.Path, $dataSourceArray)
```

## How it works...

First, we create a web service proxy object:

```
$reportServerUri  =
"http://localhost/ReportServer/ReportService2010.asmx"
$proxy = New-WebServiceProxy -Uri $reportServerUri
-UseDefaultCredential
$type = $Proxy.GetType().Namespace
```

We then need to specify the path to the RDL file. In this recipe, we will keep the filename the same as the RDL filename, without the extension:

```
#specify where the RDL file is
$rdl = "C:\SSRS\Customer Contact List.rdl"

#extract report name from the RDL file
$reportName =  [System.IO.Path]::GetFileNameWithoutExtension($rdl)
```

We need to extract the contents of the RDL file to create the report programmatically. To do so, we will use the `Get-Content` cmdlet, but using the `-Encoding` switch will ensure that we preserve the encoding used in the report:

```
#get contents of the RDL
$byteArray = Get-Content $rdl -Encoding Byte
```

To create the report, we need to use the `CreateCatalogItem` method of the proxy object that accepts the catalog item type, report name, parent, overwrite `Boolean` flag, contents of the RDL file, and warnings variable:

```
#The fully qualified URL for the parent folder that will contain
#the item.
$parent = "/Customer Reports"
$overwrite = $true
$warnings = $null

#create report
$report = $proxy.CreateCatalogItem("Report", $reportName, $parent,
$overwrite, $byteArray, $null, [ref]$warnings )
```

The supported `CatalogItem` types in native mode are as follows:

- Report
- DataSet
- Resource
- DataSource
- Model

At this point, the report is already uploaded to the server. However, if the data source path stored in the report is different from where the data source is located in the server, the report will still not be usable.

To change the data source, we must create a `DataSource` array and change only the `DataSourceReference`. We change the report's data source reference using the `SetItemDataSources` method of the proxy object:

```
#data source name must match what's in the RDL
$dataSourceName = "DS_CUSTOMERLIST"

#data source path should match what's in the report server
$dataSourcePath = "/Data Sources/AdventureWorks2014"

#when we upload the report, if the
#data source from the source is different
#or has a different path from what's in the
```

```
#report manager, the data source will be broken
#and we will need to update

#create our data type references
$dataSourceArrayType = ($type + '.DataSource[]')
$dataSourceType = ($type + '.DataSource')
$dataSourceReferenceType = ($type + '.DataSourceReference')

#create data source array
$numDataSources = 1
$dataSourceArray = New-Object ($dataSourceArrayType)$numDataSources
$dataSourceReference = New-Object ($dataSourceReferenceType)

#update data source
$dataSourceArray[0] = New-Object ($dataSourceType)
$dataSourceArray[0].Name = $dataSourceName
$dataSourceArray[0].Item = New-Object ($dataSourceReferenceType)
$dataSourcearray[0].Item.Reference = $dataSourcePath
$proxy.SetItemDataSources($report.Path, $dataSourceArray)
```

 Refer to the *Changing an SSRS report's data source reference* recipe for more details on the steps.

## There's more...

Check out more information on the `CreateCatalogItem` method at `http://msdn.microsoft.com/en-us/library/reportservice2010.reportingservice2010.createcatalogitem.aspx`.

## See also

▸ The *Using ReportViewer to view your SSRS report* recipe.

▸ The *Downloading an SSRS report in Excel and as aPDF* recipe.

# Downloading all SSRS report RDL files

This recipe shows how you can download all RDL files from your Report Server.

## Getting ready

In this recipe, we will download all RDL files from the SSRS Report Server into `C:\SSRS\` in a subfolder structure that mimics the folder structure in the Report Server.

Identify your SSRS 2012 Report Server URL. We need to reference the `ReportService2010` web service, and you can reference it using the following command:

```
<ReportServer URL>/ReportService2010.asmx
```

## How to do it...

Let's explore the code required to download the RDL files from your Report Server:

1. Open **PowerShell ISE** as an administrator.

2. Add the following script and run it:

```
$VerbosePreference = "Continue"
$reportServerUri  = "http://localhost/ReportServer/
ReportService2010.asmx"
$proxy = New-WebServiceProxy -Uri $reportServerUri
-UseDefaultCredential

$destinationFolder = "C:\SSRS\"

#create a new folder where we will save the files
#we'll use a time-stamped folder, format similar
#to 2012-Mar-28-0850PM
$ts = Get-Date -format "yyyy-MMM-dd-hhmmtt"
$folderName = "RDL Files $($ts)"
$fullFolderName = Join-Path -Path "$($destinationFolder)"
-ChildPath $folderName

#If the path exists, will error silently and continue
New-Item -ItemType Directory -Path $fullFolderName -ErrorAction
SilentlyContinue

#get all reports
#second parameter means recursive
#CHANGE ALERT:
#in ReportingService2005 - Type
#in ReportingService2010 - TypeName
$proxy.ListChildren("/", $true) |
Select-Object TypeName, Path, ID, Name |
Where-Object TypeName -eq "Report" |
ForEach-Object {
    $item = $_
    [string]$path = $item.Path
    $pathItems=$path.Split("/")

    #get path name we will mirror structure
    #when we save the file
```

```
        $reportName = $pathitems[$pathItems.Count -1]
        $subfolderName = $path.Trim($reportName)

        $fullSubfolderName = Join-Path -Path "$($fullFolderName)"
-ChildPath $subfolderName

        #If the path exists, will error silently and continue
        New-Item -ItemType directory -Path $fullSubfolderName
-ErrorAction SilentlyContinue

        #CHANGE ALERT:
        #in ReportingService2005 - GetReportDefinition
        #in ReportingService2010 - GetItemDefinition
        #use $Proxy | gm to learn more
        [byte[]] $reportDefinition = $proxy.GetItemDefinition($item.
Path)

        #note here we're forcing the actual definition to be
        #stored as a byte array
        #if you take out the @() from the
        #MemoryStream constructor,
        #you'll get an error
        [System.IO.MemoryStream] $memStream = New-Object System.
IO.MemoryStream(@(,$reportDefinition))

        #save the XML file
        $rdlFile = New-Object System.Xml.XmlDocument
        $rdlFile.Load($memStream) | Out-Null

        $fullReportFileName = "$($fullSubfolderName)$($item.Name).rdl"
        Write-Verbose "Saving $($fullReportFileName)"
        $rdlFile.Save($fullReportFileName)

}

Write-Verbose "Done downloading your RDL files to
$($fullFolderName)"
$VerbosePreference = "SilentlyContinue"
```

## How it works...

This recipe will recreate the entire folder structure of the Report Manager and save the appropriate RDL files in their respective folders.

To do this, we first create a proxy to the `ReportService2010` web service:

```
$reportServerUri  = "http://localhost/ReportServer/ReportService2010.
asmx"
$proxy = New-WebServiceProxy -Uri $reportServerUri
-UseDefaultCredential
```

We also need to specify where we want to store the downloaded RDL files:

```
$destinationFolder = "C:\SSRS\"
```

We also need to create a new `timestamped` folder where we will store the RDL files:

```
$ts = Get-Date -format "yyyy-MMM-dd-hhmmtt"
$folderName = "RDL Files $($ts)"
$fullFolderName = Join-Path -Path "$($destinationFolder)" -ChildPath
$folderName
```

We then get all report items. Note that we have to filter these to return only items with
`TypeName = Report`:

```
$proxy.ListChildren("/", $true) |
Select-Object TypeName, Path, ID, Name |
Where-Object TypeName -eq "Report" |
ForEach-Object {
```

We can pass all the `Report` items to the `Foreach-Object` cmdlet so that we can download
each RDL file from Report Manager. For each report, we need to investigate the path. If the
path contains a series of folders, we need to recreate these folders in our destination folder:

```
    $item = $_
    [string]$path = $item.Path
    $pathItems=$path.Split("/")

    #get path name we will mirror structure
    #when we save the file
    $reportName = $pathitems[$pathItems.Count -1]
    $subfolderName = $path.Trim($reportName)

    $fullSubfolderName = Join-Path -Path "$($fullFolderName)"
-ChildPath $subfolderName

    #If the path exists, will error silently and continue
    New-Item -ItemType directory -Path $fullSubfolderName -ErrorAction
SilentlyContinue
```

Once we have created the folder structure, we can get the report definition using the `GetItemDefinition` method of the proxy object. This needs to be stored in a byte array in order to ensure that we store unaltered, raw bytes of the report:

```
#CHANGE ALERT:
#in ReportingService2005 - GetReportDefinition
#in ReportingService2010 - GetItemDefinition
#use $Proxy | gm to learn more
[byte[]] $reportDefinition = $proxy.GetItemDefinition($item.Path)

#note here we're forcing the actual definition to be
#stored as a byte array
#if you take out the @() from the
#MemoryStream constructor,
#you'll get an error
[System.IO.MemoryStream] $memStream = New-Object System.
IO.MemoryStream(@(,$reportDefinition))
```

We can then store the memory stream in an `XmlDocument` object, which in turn can save the file back in the filesystem, if given a complete file path and name:

```
#save the XML file
$rdlFile = New-Object System.Xml.XmlDocument
$rdlFile.Load($memStream) | Out-Null

$fullReportFileName = "$($fullSubfolderName)$($item.Name).rdl"
Write-Verbose "Saving $($fullReportFileName)"
$rdlFile.Save($fullReportFileName)
```

The script will display all the reports it is downloading and provide a message once all downloads are complete:

```
Mode                LastWriteTime         Length Name
----                -------------         ------ ----
d-----        6/6/2015    2:55 PM                Customer Reports
VERBOSE: Saving C:\SSRS\RDL Files 2015-Jun-06-0255PM\Customer Reports\Customer Contact List.rdl
VERBOSE: Saving C:\SSRS\RDL Files 2015-Jun-06-0255PM\Customer Reports\Customer List.rdl
VERBOSE: Saving C:\SSRS\RDL Files 2015-Jun-06-0255PM\Customer Reports\Customer Sales.rdl
VERBOSE: Done downloading your RDL files to  C:\SSRS\RDL Files 2015-Jun-06-0255PM
```

## There's more...

Check out these MSDN articles:

▶ The `GetItemDefinition` method, which is available at http:// msdn.microsoft.com/en-us/library/reportservice2010. reportingservice2010.getitemdefinition.aspx.

- The `MemoryStream` class, which is available at `http://msdn.microsoft.com/en-us/library/system.io.memorystream.aspx`.

## See also

- The *Using ReportViewer to view your SSRS report* recipe.
- The *Downloading an SSRS report in Excel and as a PDF* recipe.

# Adding a user with a role to SSRS report

In this recipe, we will add a user with a few roles to SSRS.

## Getting ready

In this recipe, we will add `QUERYWORKS\tstark` as a browser and Content Manager to the customer list report.

For your environment, you can identify a user you want to add to an existing report and which roles you want to assign to them.

## How to do it...

Let's explore the code required to add a user with a role to SSRS:

1. Open **PowerShell ISE** as an administrator.
2. Add the following script and run it:

```
$reportServerUri  = "http://localhost/ReportServer/
ReportService2010.asmx"
$proxy = New-WebServiceProxy -Uri $reportServerUri
-UseDefaultCredential
$type = $Proxy.GetType().Namespace

$itemPath = "/Customer Reports/Customer List"

#this will hold all the group/users for a report
$newPolicies = @()
$inherit = $null

#list current report users
$proxy.GetPolicies($itemPath, [ref]$inherit)

#NOTE that when we change policies, it will
```

```
#automatically break inheritance
#ALSO NOTE that when you programmatically mess
#with policies, you will need to "re-add" users that were
#already there, if you want them to keep on having access
#to your reports

#this gets all users who currently have
#access to this report
#need pass $inherit by reference
$proxy.GetPolicies($itemPath, [ref]$inherit) |
ForEach-Object {
    #re-add existing policies
  $newPolicies += $_
}

$policyDataType = ($type + '.Policy')
$newPolicy = New-Object ($policyDataType)

#use a domain account that exists in your system
$newPolicy.GroupUserName = "QUERYWORKS\tstark"

#alternatively you can use:
#$newPolicy.GroupUserName = $env:username

#a policy must have roles
$roleDataType = ($type + '.Role')
$newRole = New-Object ($roleDataType)
$newRole.Name = "Browser"

#add the role to the policy
$newPolicy.roles += $newRole

#a policy must have roles
$roleDataType = ($type + '.Role')
$newRole = New-Object ($roleDataType)
$newRole.Name = "Content Manager"

#add the role to the policy
$newPolicy.roles += $newRole

#check if this user already exists in your policy array
#if user does not exist yet with current role, add policy
if ($($newPolicies |
```

```
        ForEach-Object {$_.GroupUserName}) -notcontains $newPolicy.
GroupUserName)
{
  $newPolicies += $newPolicy
}


#set the policies
$proxy.SetPolicies($itemPath,$newPolicies)


#list new report users
$proxy.GetPolicies($itemPath, [ref]$inherit)
```

When done, check the report that you just added a user to, from Report Manager. Go to its **Properties** and take a look at its security settings. Note that the user has been added, but inheritance is broken, as illustrated by the checkboxes, and the extra menu item called **Revert to Parent Security** has been added.

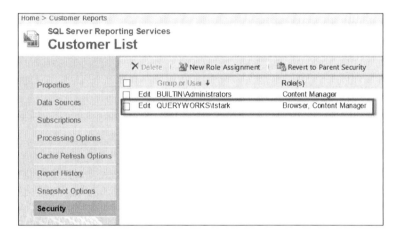

## How it works...

When adding or changing users in an SSRS report programmatically, we will need to get a handle to the whole policy object, add or change the users or roles, and then reapply the policy. Because this is manually changing a single item's security, inheritance is automatically broken for this item.

First, we need to create a proxy and extract the dynamically created namespace:

```
$reportServerUri  = "http://localhost/ReportServer/ReportService2010.
asmx"
$proxy = New-WebServiceProxy -Uri $reportServerUri
-UseDefaultCredential
$type = $proxy.GetType().Namespace
```

[

Refer to the *How it works...* section of the *Creating an SSRS folder* recipe for additional details on automatically generated namespace issues.
]

We also need to specify the path of the report we want to change:

```
$itemPath = "/Customer Reports/Customer List"
```

To change policies, we will need to resave existing policies. We will do this by retrieving the current users and roles using the `GetPolicies` method of the proxy object and saving them to an array. The `$inherit` variable will hold whether that item inherits its security policy from its parent or not:

```
$newPolicies = @()
$inherit = $null

#this gets all users who currently have
#access to this report
#need pass $inherit by reference
$proxy.GetPolicies($itemPath, [ref]$inherit) |
ForEach-Object {
    #re-add existing policies
  $newPolicies += $_
}
```

We then need to specify the account we are adding. This needs to be held in a `ReportingService2010.Policy` object and can either be a user or group name:

```
$policyDataType = ($type + '.Policy')
$newPolicy = New-Object ($policyDataType)
$newPolicy.GroupUserName = "QUERYWORKS\tstark"
```

Next, we add the roles that will be associated with this group or user:

```
#a policy must have roles
$roleDataType = ($type + '.Role')
$newRole = New-Object ($roleDataType)
$newRole.Name = "Browser"

#add the role to the policy
$newPolicy.roles += $newRole

#a policy must have roles
$roleDataType = ($type + '.Role')
$newRole = New-Object ($roleDataType)
```

```
$newRole.Name = "Content Manager"

#add the role to the policy
$newPolicy.roles += $newRole
```

Once the new account and roles are in place, we need to add it to our policy array, which contains all existing policies for the item:

```
#check if this user already exists in your policy array
#if user does not exist yet with current role, add policy
if ($($newPolicies | ForEach-Object {$_.GroupUserName}) -notcontains
$newPolicy.GroupUserName)
{
   $newPolicies += $newPolicy
}
```

When everything is set, we can call the SetPolicies method of the proxy object:

```
#set the policies
$proxy.SetPolicies($itemPath,$newPolicies)
```

## There's more...

Check out these MSDN articles:

▶ The GetPolicies method, which is available at http://msdn.microsoft.com/en-us/library/reportservice2010.reportingservice2010.getpolicies.

▶ The SetPolicies method, which is available at http://msdn.microsoft.com/en-us/library/reportservice2010.reportingservice2010.setpolicies.

▶ The InheritParentSecurity method, which is available at http://msdn.microsoft.com/en-us/library/reportservice2010.reportingservice2010.inheritparentsecurity.

# Creating folders in an SSIS package store and MSDB

In this recipe, we will see how to create a folder in the SSIS instance and package store.

## Getting ready

For this recipe, we will create a timestamped folder prefixed with the word QueryWorks. Feel free to replace it with your folder name by changing the $newFolder variable.

## How to do it...

These are the steps required to create folders in the package store and SSIS instance:

1. Open **PowerShell ISE** as an administrator.

2. Add the ManagedDTS assembly as follows:

```
#add ManagedDTS assembly
Add-Type -AssemblyName "Microsoft.SqlServer.ManagedDTS,
Version=12.0.0.0, Culture=neutral, PublicKeyToken=89845dcd8080
cc91"
```

3. Add the following script and run it:

```
$server = "localhost"

#create new app
$app = New-Object  "Microsoft.SqlServer.Dts.Runtime.Application"
$ts = Get-Date -format "yyyy-MMM-dd-hhmmtt"
$newFolder = "QueryWorks File System $($ts)"

#folder in package store
#will appear under "Stored Packages > File System"
if (!$app.FolderExistsOnDtsServer("\File System\$($newFolder)",
$server))
{
    $app.CreateFolderOnDtsServer("\File System\", $newFolder,
$server)
}

#folder in SSIS instance
#will appear under "Stored Packages > MSDB"
$newFolder = "QueryWorks SSIS $($ts)"
if (!$app.FolderExistsOnSqlServer($newFolder, $server, $null,
$null))
{
    $app.CreateFolderOnSqlServer("\", $newFolder, $server, $null,
$null)
}
```

When the script finishes the execution, connect to the **Integration Services** instance. Expand both the **File System** and **MSDB** nodes and confirm that the folders have been created, as shown in the following screenshot:

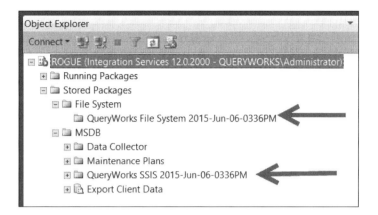

## How it works...

The `Microsoft.SqlServer.ManagedDTS` assembly exposes SSIS 2005 and 2008 objects for programmatic access. Although this can be considered "legacy" SSIS when SQL Server 2012 was introduced, this method is still supported and will still be used by developers.

To create folders in the package store and SSIS instance, we must first load the `ManagedDTS` assembly. We need to do this explicitly because this assembly does not come with the `SQLPS` module:

```
#add ManagedDTS assembly
Add-Type -AssemblyName "Microsoft.SqlServer.ManagedDTS,
Version=12.0.0.0, Culture=neutral, PublicKeyToken=89845dcd8080cc91"
```

We then need to create an application object, which contains the methods to create the folders:

```
$server = "localhost"

#create new app
$app = New-Object ("Microsoft.SqlServer.Dts.Runtime.Application")
```

To create the folder in the SSIS package store, we first check whether the folder is already created. If not, we create the folder using the `CreateFolderOnDtsServer` method of the `DTS Application` object, which accepts the parent path, new folder name, and server name:

```
#folder in package store
#will appear under "Stored Packages > File System"
if (!$app.FolderExistsOnDtsServer("\File System\$($newFolder)",
$server))
{
    $app.CreateFolderOnDtsServer("\File System\", $newFolder, $server)
}
```

Creating the folder in the SSIS instance is very similar to creating folders in the package store. However, the methods to check and create the instance folders accept more parameters. Both the `FolderExistsOnSqlServer` and `CreateFolderOnSqlServer` methods of the DTS application object accept two extra parameters for the username and password used to authenticate to SQL Server:

```
#folder in SSIS instance
#will appear under "Stored Packages > MSDB"
$newFolder = "QueryWorks SSIS $($ts)"
if (!$app.FolderExistsOnSqlServer($newFolder, $server, $null, $null))
{
    $app.CreateFolderOnSqlServer("\", $newFolder, $server, $null,
$null)
}
```

## There's more...

To learn more about the `Application` class, visit `http://msdn.microsoft.com/en-us/library/ms211665`.

## See also

The *Creating an SSISDB folder* recipe.

# Deploying an SSIS package to the package store

In this recipe, we will deploy an SSIS package (`.dtsx`) to the SSIS package store.

## Getting ready

In this recipe, we will use a `Customer Package.dtsx` package saved in `C:\SSIS` and deploy this to our SSIS instance. The package will be saved in the `\File System\QueryWorks` package folder.

To follow this recipe, use a `.dtsx` package that is readily available in your environment and decide where you want it deployed.

## How to do it...

Let's explore the code required to deploy an SSIS `.dtsx` file:

1. Open **PowerShell ISE** as an administrator.

2. Add the `ManagedDTS` assembly as follows:

   ```
   #add ManagedDTS assembly
   Add-Type -AssemblyName "Microsoft.SqlServer.ManagedDTS,
   Version=12.0.0.0, Culture=neutral, PublicKeyToken=89845dcd8080
   cc91"
   ```

3. Add the following script and run it:

   ```
   $server = "localhost"

   #create new app
   $app = New-Object "Microsoft.SqlServer.Dts.Runtime.Application"

   #specify package to be deployed
   $dtsx = "C:\SSIS\Customer Package.dtsx"
   $package = $app.LoadPackage($dtsx, $null)

   #where are we going to deploy?
   $SSISPackageStorePath = "\File System\QueryWorks"
   $destinationName = "$($SSISPackageStorePath)\$($package.Name)"

   #save to the package store
   $app.SaveToDtsServer($package, $events, $destinationName, $server)
   ```

When done, log in to the SSIS instance in Management Studio and confirm that the package has been deployed:

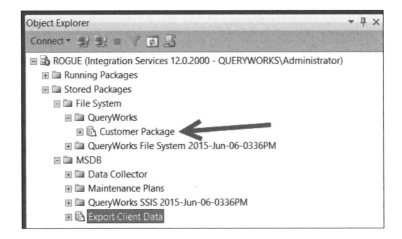

## How it works...

Deploying a .dtsx file to the package store in the filesystem, or the msdb database, is considered a "legacy" way of deploying SSIS packages in SQL Server 2012. This is now referred to as a Package Deployment model.

> Refer to the *Deploying an ISPAC file to SSISDB* recipe for more details on deploying SSIS Projects in SQL Server 2014.

Although this may be considered "legacy" already, this may still be the preferred way to deploy packages in some environments for a while.

To deploy programmatically, we must first create a handle to the ManagedDTS assembly:

```
#add ManagedDTS assembly
Add-Type -AssemblyName "Microsoft.SqlServer.ManagedDTS,
Version=12.0.0.0, Culture=neutral, PublicKeyToken=89845dcd8080cc91"
```

After loading the ManagedDTS object, we need to create an Application object:

```
$server = "localhost"

#create new app
$app = New-Object "Microsoft.SqlServer.Dts.Runtime.Application"
```

We then need to load the SSIS `.dtsx` package into a variable using the `LoadPackage` method of the `DTS Application` object. We will load the package from the `C:\SSIS` folder where we saved the `Customer Package.dtsx`:

```
#deploy a package
$dtsx = "C:\SSIS\Customer Package.dtsx"
$package = $app.LoadPackage($dtsx, $null)
```

We also need to specify where the package is going to be deployed. If the package is to be deployed to the filesystem, we prefix the path with `\File System\`; if to the database, we prefix `\MSDB\`:

```
#where are we going to deploy?
$SSISPackageStorePath = "\File System\QueryWorks"
$destinationName = "$($SSISPackageStorePath)\$($package.Name)"

#save to the package store
$app.SaveToDtsServer($package, $events, $destinationName, $server)
```

If you want to save it in the `MSDB` folder, you will have to use the `SaveToSQLServer` method instead of the `SaveToDtsServer` method.

## There's more...

Check out the `Application.LoadPackage` method documentation from MSDN at `http://msdn.microsoft.com/en-us/library/ms188550.aspx`.

## See also

The *Deploying an ISPAC file to SSISDB* recipe.

# Executing an SSIS package stored in a package store or filesystem

In this recipe, we will execute an SSIS package using PowerShell.

## Getting ready

In this recipe, we will execute the `Customer Package`, which is saved in the package store, and we will also execute the `C:\SSIS\SamplePackage.dtsx` file directly from the filesystem.

Alternatively, you can locate an available SSIS package in your system that you want to execute instead. Identify whether this package is stored in the filesystem or in the SSIS package store.

## How to do it...

Let's explore the code required to execute an SSIS package programmatically using PowerShell:

1. Open **PowerShell ISE** as an administrator.

2. Add the `ManagedDTS` assembly as follows:

```
#add ManagedDTS assembly
Add-Type -AssemblyName "Microsoft.SqlServer.ManagedDTS,
Version=12.0.0.0, Culture=neutral, PublicKeyToken=89845dcd8080
cc91"
```

3. Add the following script and run it:

```
$server = "localhost"

#create new app we'll use for SSIS
$app = New-Object "Microsoft.SqlServer.Dts.Runtime.Application"

#execute package in SSIS Package Store
$packagePath = "\File System\QueryWorks\Customer Package"
$package = $app.LoadFromDtsServer($packagePath, $server,$null)
$package.Execute()

#execute package saved in filesystem
$packagePath = "C:\SSIS\Customer Package.dtsx"
$package = $app.LoadPackage($packagePath, $null)
$package.Execute()
```

## How it works...

In SQL Server 2012, SSIS packages are deployed with their corresponding parameters and environments to the `SSISDB` catalog. SQL Server 2012 and 2014 still support the "legacy" way of storing packages, which is through the filesystem, package store, or MSDB.

The default package store is in `<SQL Server Install Directory>\120\DTS\Packages`.

The first step is to load the `ManagedDTS` assembly and create an `Application` object:

```
#add ManagedDTS assembly
Add-Type -AssemblyName "Microsoft.SqlServer.ManagedDTS,
Version=12.0.0.0, Culture=neutral, PublicKeyToken=89845dcd8080cc91"

#create new app we'll use for SSIS
$app = New-Object "Microsoft.SqlServer.Dts.Runtime.Application"
```

To load a package stored in the package store, we need to use the `LoadFromDtsServer` method of the `DTS Application` object and supply it with three parameters: the path to the package relative to the filesystem, server name, and a third parameter for events, which we will leave as `null`:

```
$packagePath = "\File System\QueryWorks\Customer Package"
$package = $app.LoadFromDtsServer($packagePath, $server,$null)
```

If a package is stored in the filesystem, we have to use the `LoadPackage` method of the `DTS Application` object and pass the path of the package to it:

```
$packagePath = "C:\SSIS\Customer Package.dtsx"
$package = $app.LoadPackage($packagePath, $null)
```

If you still have packages deployed in MSDB, you can also execute these packages using the `LoadFromSqlServer` method of the `DTS Application` object:

```
$packagePath = "\MSDB\SamplePackage"
$package = $app.LoadFromSqlServer($packagePath, $server, $null, $null,
$null)
$package.Execute()
```

## There's more...

Before a package can be executed, it must first be loaded. Check out different methods to load an SSIS package:

- The *LoadFromSqlServer Method* can be found at `http://msdn.microsoft.com/en-us/library/microsoft.sqlserver.dts.runtime.application.loadfromsqlserver.aspx`.

- The *LoadFromDtsServer Method* can be found at `http://msdn.microsoft.com/en-us/library/microsoft.sqlserver.dts.runtime.application.loadfromdtsserver.aspx`.

- The *LoadPackage Method* can be found at `http://msdn.microsoft.com/en-us/library/microsoft.sqlserver.dts.runtime.application.loadpackage.aspx`.

The *Executing an SSIS package stored in SSISDB* recipe.

# Downloading an SSIS package to a file

This recipe will download an SSIS package back to a `.dtsx` file.

## Getting ready

Locate a package stored in the package store that you want to download to the filesystem. Note the path to this package.

## How to do it...

These are the steps required to download an SSIS package:

1. Open **PowerShell ISE** as an administrator.

2. Add the ManagedDTS assembly as follows:

```
#add ManagedDTS assembly
Add-Type -AssemblyName "Microsoft.SqlServer.ManagedDTS,
Version=12.0.0.0, Culture=neutral, PublicKeyToken=89845dcd8080
cc91"
```

3. Add the following script and run it:

```
$server = "localhost"

#create new app
$app = New-Object "Microsoft.SqlServer.Dts.Runtime.Application"

$timestamp = Get-Date -format "yyyy-MMM-dd-hhmmtt"
$destinationFolder = "C:\SSIS\SSIS $($timestamp)"

#If the path exists, will error silently and continue
New-Item -ItemType Directory -Path $destinationFolder -ErrorAction
SilentlyContinue

$packageToDownload = "Customer Package"
$packageParentPath = "\File System\QueryWorks"

#download the specified package
```

```
#here we're dealing with package in
#the SSIS Package store
$app.GetDtsServerPackageInfos($packageParentPath,$server) |
Where-Object Flags -eq "Package" |
ForEach-Object {
    $package = $_
    $packagePath = "$($package.Folder)\$($package.Name)"

    #check if this package does exist in the Package Store
    if($app.ExistsOnDtsServer($packagePath, $server))
    {
        $fileName = Join-Path $destinationFolder "$($package.
Name).dtsx"
        $newPackage = $app.LoadFromDtsServer($packagePath,
$server,$null)
        $app.SaveToXml($fileName, $newPackage, $null)
    }
}
```

## How it works...

The first step is to load the ManagedDTS assembly and create an application object:

```
#add ManagedDTS assembly
Add-Type -AssemblyName "Microsoft.SqlServer.ManagedDTS,
Version=12.0.0.0, Culture=neutral, PublicKeyToken=89845dcd8080cc91"
$server = "KERRIGAN"

#create new app
$app = New-Object "Microsoft.SqlServer.Dts.Runtime.Application"
```

We will also define our variables for the timestamp, destination folder, and the package that we want to download:

```
$timestamp = Get-Date -format "yyyy-MMM-dd-hhmmtt"
$destinationFolder = "C:\SSIS\SSIS $($timestamp)"

#If the path exists, will error silently and continue
New-Item -ItemType Directory -Path $destinationFolder -ErrorAction
SilentlyContinue

$packageToDownload = "Customer Package"
$packageParentPath = "\File System\QueryWorks"
```

We then retrieve all packages using the `GetDtsServerPackageInfos` method of the DTS application object:

```
$app.GetDtsServerPackageInfos($packageParentPath,$server) |
Where-Object Flags -eq "Package" |
ForEach-Object {
```

For each package, we check whether this matches the package we wanted to download. If it does, we can use the `LoadFromDtsServer` method to load the package, and use the `SaveToXml` method to save the package back to the filesystem. Remember that a `.dtsx` file is simply an XML file:

```
ForEach-Object {
    $package = $_
    $packagePath = "$($package.Folder)\$($package.Name)"

    #check if this package does exist in the Package Store
    if($app.ExistsOnDtsServer($packagePath, $server))
    {
        $fileName = Join-Path $destinationFolder "$($package.Name).
dtsx"
        $newPackage = $app.LoadFromDtsServer($packagePath,
$server,$null)
        $app.SaveToXml($fileName, $newPackage, $null)
    }
}
```

Note that the file will be saved in our timestamped folder. You can definitely change this filename to whatever suits your requirements.

## There's more...

Learn more about the following MSDN articles:

- The *Application.SaveToXml Method*, which is available at `http://msdn.microsoft.com/en-us/library/microsoft.sqlserver.dts.runtime.application.savetoxml.aspx`.

- The *LoadFromDtsServer Method*, which is available at `http://msdn.microsoft.com/en-us/library/microsoft.sqlserver.dts.runtime.application.loadfromdtsserver.aspx`.

## See also

The *Deploying an SSIS package to the package store* recipe.

# Creating an SSISDB catalog

In this recipe, we will create an `SSISDB` catalog.

## Getting ready

To create an `SSISDB` catalog, we must first enable `SQLCLR` on the instance. Log in to SQL Server Management Studio, and use the system stored procedure `sp_configure` to enable CLR. Execute the following T-SQL script:

```
sp_configure 'clr enabled', 1
GO
RECONFIGURE
GO
```

## How to do it...

These are the steps required to create `SSISDB` programmatically:

1.  Open **PowerShell ISE** as an administrator.

2.  Import the SQLPS module as follows:

    ```
    Import-Module SQLPS -DisableNameChecking
    ```

3.  Load the `IntegrationServices` assembly as follows:

    ```
    Add-Type -AssemblyName "Microsoft.SqlServer.Management.
    IntegrationServices, Version=12.0.0.0, Culture=neutral, PublicKeyT
    oken=89845dcd8080cc91"
    ```

4.  Add the following script and run it:

    ```
    $instanceName = "localhost"
    $connectionString = "Data Source=$instanceName;Initial
    Catalog=master;Integrated Security=SSPI"

    $conn = New-Object System.Data.SqlClient.SqlConnection
    $connectionString

    $SSISServer = New-Object Microsoft.SqlServer.Management.
    IntegrationServices.IntegrationServices $conn

    if(!$SSISServer.Catalogs["SSISDB"])
    {
    ```

```
#constructor accepts three (3) parameters:
#parent, name, password
$SSISDB = New-Object Microsoft.SqlServer.Management.
IntegrationServices.Catalog ($SSISServer, "SSISDB", "P@ssword")
    $SSISDB.Create()
}
```

## How it works...

SQL Server 2012 introduced the SSIS catalog for Integration Services. The catalog is implemented as a database called SSISDB that stores Integration Services objects (projects, packages, and parameters) and logs when projects are deployed using the new Project Deployment model. This database is accessible from **SQL Server Management Studio (SSMS)** and can be queried like any regular database. The following screenshot shows where SSISDB is in SSMS:

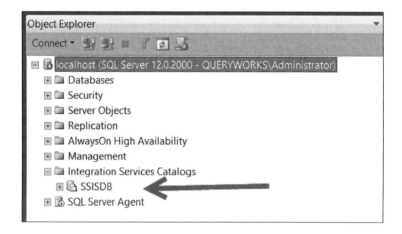

To create SSISDB programmatically, we must first load the IntegrationServices assembly. This assembly exposes the SSIS Catalog Managed Object Model to allow programmatic access to the new SSIS objects:

```
Add-Type -AssemblyName "Microsoft.SqlServer.Management.
IntegrationServices, Version=12.0.0.0, Culture=neutral, PublicKeyToken
=89845dcd8080cc91"
```

To figure out the version and public key token, you can check out `C:\Windows\assembly`, and check the properties of this assembly:

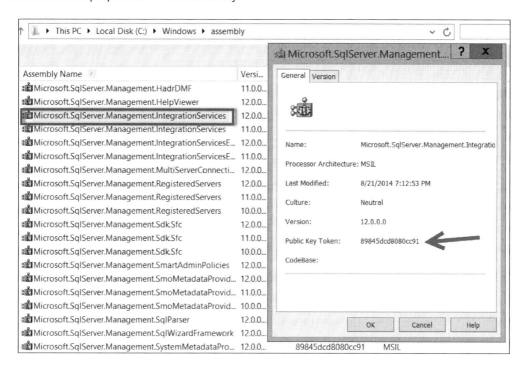

First, we need to create a `SQLConnection` object that we need to pass to the `IntegrationServices` constructor:

```
$instanceName = "localhost"
$connectionString = "Data Source=$instanceName;Initial
Catalog=master;Integrated Security=SSPI;"
$conn = New-Object System.Data.SqlClient.SqlConnection
$connectionString
```

We then need to create an `IntegrationServices` object:

```
$SSISServer = New-Object Microsoft.SqlServer.Management.
IntegrationServices.IntegrationServices $conn
```

To create an `SSISDB` catalog, we create a new `Catalog` object, which accepts three parameters: the `IntegrationServices` server object, name of the catalog (`SSISDB`), and a password:

```
if(!$SSISServer.Catalogs["SSISDB"])
{
    #constructor accepts three (3) parameters:
    #parent, name, password
    $SSISDB = New-Object Microsoft.SqlServer.Management.
IntegrationServices.Catalog ($SSISServer, "SSISDB", "P@ssword")
    $SSISDB.Create()
}
```

## There's more...

▶ Check out additional information about SQL Server 2012 SSIS at `http://msdn.microsoft.com/en-us/library/gg471508.aspx`.

▶ To learn more about the SSISDB catalog from MSDN, visit `http://msdn.microsoft.com/en-us/library/hh479588.aspx`.

▶ Refer to the properties and methods for the new `IntegrationServices` assembly at `http://msdn.microsoft.com/en-us/library/microsoft.sqlserver.management.integrationservices(v=sql.110).aspx`.

## See also

The *Deploying an ISPAC file to SSISDB* recipe.

# Creating an SSISDB folder

In this recipe, we will create a folder in the SSISDB catalog.

## Getting ready

In this recipe, we assume that the SSISDB catalog has been created. We will create a folder called `QueryWorks` inside the `SSISDB` catalog.

## How to do it...

These are the steps required to create a folder in SSISDB:

1. Open **PowerShell ISE** as an administrator.

2. Import the SQLPS module as follows:

```
#import SQL Server module
Import-Module SQLPS -DisableNameChecking
```

3. Load the `IntegrationServices` assembly as follows:

```
Add-Type -AssemblyName "Microsoft.SqlServer.Management.
IntegrationServices, Version=12.0.0.0, Culture=neutral, PublicKeyT
oken=89845dcd8080cc91"
```

4. Add the following script and run it:

```
$instanceName = "localhost"
$connectionString = "Data Source=$instanceName;Initial
Catalog=master;Integrated Security=SSPI"
$conn = New-Object System.Data.SqlClient.SqlConnection
$connectionString
$SSISServer = New-Object Microsoft.SqlServer.Management.
IntegrationServices.IntegrationServices $conn
$SSISDB = $SSISServer.Catalogs["SSISDB"]

#create QueryWorks catalog folder here
$folderName = "QueryWorks"
$folderDescription = "New SSISDB folder"
$SSISDBFolder = New-Object Microsoft.SqlServer.Management.
IntegrationServices.CatalogFolder ($SSISDB, $folderName,
$folderDescription)
$SSISDBFolder.Create()
```

When done, log in to Management Studio and connect to your database engine. Expand **Integration Services Catalog**, and check whether the folder has been created under the **SSISDB** node:

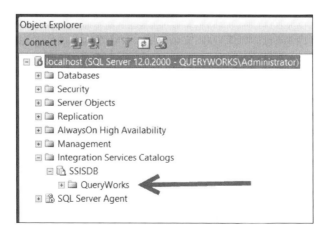

## How it works...

A folder in an `SSISDB` catalog can hold multiple projects and environments.

To create a folder inside `SSISDB`, also called a catalog folder, we must first get a handle to `SSISDB`. The core code required to do this is as follows:

```
$SSISServer = New-Object Microsoft.SqlServer.Management.
IntegrationServices.IntegrationServices $conn
$SSISDB = $SSISServer.Catalogs["SSISDB"]
```

Once we have the `SSISDB` handle, creating the folder is straightforward. It requires creating a new `CatalogFolder` object. The constructor takes the `SSISDB` object, name of the catalog folder, and description:

```
#create QueryWorks catalog folder here
$folderName = "QueryWorks"
$folderDescription = "New SSISDB folder"
$SSISDBFolder = New-Object Microsoft.SqlServer.Management.
IntegrationServices.CatalogFolder ($SSISDB, $folderName,
$folderDescription)
```

The `Create()` method will persist the catalog folder in `SSISDB`:

```
$SSISDBFolder.Create()
```

## There's more...

Check out the properties and methods supported by the `CatalogFolder` class at `http://msdn.microsoft.com/en-us/library/microsoft.sqlserver.management.integrationservices.catalogfolder.aspx`.

## See also

▶ The *Creating an SSISDB catalog* recipe.

▶ The *Deploying an ISPAC file to SSISDB* recipe.

# Deploying an ISPAC file to SSISDB

You will see how to deploy an ISPAC file to SSISDB.

## Getting ready

In this recipe, we will deploy a deployment `Customer Package Project.ispac` package file. Alternatively, pick an available ISPAC file in your environment that you want to use. In this recipe, change the `$ispacFilePath` variable's value to reflect your file.

## How to do it...

Let's explore the code required to deploy an ISPAC file:

1. Open **PowerShell ISE** as an administrator.

2. Import the SQLPS module as follows:

   ```
   #import SQL Server module
   Import-Module SQLPS -DisableNameChecking
   ```

3. Load the `IntegrationServices` assembly as follows:

   ```
   Add-Type -AssemblyName "Microsoft.SqlServer.Management.
   IntegrationServices, Version=12.0.0.0, Culture=neutral, PublicKeyT
   oken=89845dcd8080cc91"
   ```

4. Add the following script and run it:

   ```
   $instanceName = "localhost"
   $connectionString = "Data Source=$instanceName;Initial
   Catalog=master;Integrated Security=SSPI"
   $conn = New-Object System.Data.SqlClient.SqlConnection
   $connectionString
   $SSISServer = New-Object Microsoft.SqlServer.Management.
   IntegrationServices.IntegrationServices $conn
   $SSISDB = $SSISServer.Catalogs["SSISDB"]

   $SSISDBFolderName = "QueryWorks"
   $SSISDBFolder = $SSISDB.Folders[$SSISDBFolderName]

   $ispacFilePath = "C:\SSIS\Customer Package Project.ispac"
   [byte[]] $ispac = [System.IO.File]::ReadAllBytes($ispacFilePath)

   $SSISDBFolder.DeployProject("Customer Package Project", $ispac)
   ```

When done, log in to Management Studio and expand **Integration Services Catalogs**. Under **SSISDB**, open the **QueryWorks** folder, and confirm that the **Customer Package Project** has been deployed, as shown in the following screenshot:

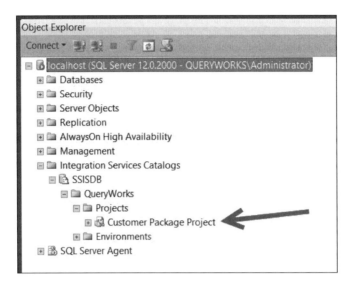

## How it works...

SQL Server 2012 supports two deployment models: the Package Deployment model and Project Deployment model. The Package Deployment model is the older, "legacy" way of deploying, where packages are deployed as standalone entities. The newer Project Deployment model is the default mode supported when you create a new SSIS project in **SQL Server Data Tools** (**SSDT**), previously known as **Business Intelligence Development Studio** (**BIDS**).

In the Package Deployment model, everything that is needed to deploy a project is packaged into a single file with an `.ispac` extension. This file is created when you deploy the SSIS 2012 project. Although it appears to be a single file, you will discover that this is a series of files that have been compressed. Simply change the `.ispac` extension to `.zip` and extract the file. You will see something similar to the files shown in the following screenshot:

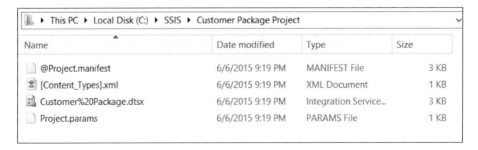

A package manifest has been created when the SSIS was built in SSDT, in addition to the package files and parameter file.

To deploy the `.ispac` file programmatically using PowerShell and the new SSIS object model, we first need to load the `IntegrationServices` assembly and create a handle to the `IntegrationServices` object:

```
Add-Type -AssemblyName "Microsoft.SqlServer.Management.
IntegrationServices, Version=12.0.0.0, Culture=neutral, PublicKeyToken
=89845dcd8080cc91"

$instanceName = "localhost"
$connectionString = "Data Source=$instanceName;Initial
Catalog=master;Integrated Security=SSPI"
$conn = New-Object System.Data.SqlClient.SqlConnection
$connectionString
$SSISServer = New-Object Microsoft.SqlServer.Management.
IntegrationServices.IntegrationServices $conn
```

The next step is to get a handle to the folder where the ISPAC file will be deployed. This means that we need to get a handle to each object in the hierarchy that leads to the folder, that is, create a handle to `SSISDB` and then to the folder:

```
$SSISDB = $SSISServer.Catalogs["SSISDB"]

$SSISDBFolderName = "QueryWorks"
$SSISDBFolder = $SSISDB.Folders[$SSISDBFolderName]
```

Once we have a handle to the folder, we need to read the byte content of the ISPAC file, and use the `DeployProject` method of the `SSISDB` folder object available with the catalog folder object:

```
$ispacFilePath = "C:\SSIS\Customer Package Project.ispac"
[byte[]] $ispac = [System.IO.File]::ReadAllBytes($ispacFilePath)
$SSISDBFolder.DeployProject("Customer Package Project", $ispac)
```

## There's more...

▸ To learn more about the specification, check out *[MS-ISPAC]: Integration Services Project Deployment File Format* structure specification, visit `http://msdn.microsoft.com/en-us/library/ff952821`.

▸ Refer to the properties and methods for the new `IntegrationServices` assembly at `http://msdn.microsoft.com/en-us/library/microsoft.sqlserver.management.integrationservices.aspx`.

## See also

▸ The *Creating an SSISDB catalog* recipe.

▸ The *Creating an SSISDB folder* recipe.

# Executing an SSIS package stored in SSISDB

In this recipe, we execute a package stored in SSISDB.

## Getting ready

In this recipe, we execute the package that comes with the customer package project that was deployed in the *Deploying an ISPAC file to SSISDB* recipe. Alternatively, replace the variables for folder, project, and package names.

## How to do it...

Let's explore the code required to execute a package in SSISDB:

1. Open **PowerShell ISE** as an administrator.

2. Import the SQLPS module as follows:

```
#import SQL Server module
Import-Module SQLPS -DisableNameChecking
```

3. Load the `IntegrationServices` assembly as follows:

```
Add-Type -AssemblyName "Microsoft.SqlServer.Management.
IntegrationServices, Version=12.0.0.0, Culture=neutral, PublicKeyT
oken=89845dcd8080cc91"
```

4. Add the following script and run it:

```
$instanceName = "localhost"
$connectionString = "Data Source=$instanceName;Initial
Catalog=master;Integrated Security=SSPI;"
$conn = New-Object System.Data.SqlClient.SqlConnection $constr
$SSISServer = New-Object Microsoft.SqlServer.Management.
IntegrationServices.IntegrationServices $conn
$SSISDB = $SSISServer.Catalogs["SSISDB"]

$SSISDBFolderName = "QueryWorks"
$SSISDBFolder = $SSISDB.Folders[$SSISDBFolderName]
```

```
$projectName= "Customer Package Project"
$packageName= "Customer Package.dtsx"
$SSISDBFolder.Projects[$projectName].Packages[$packageName].
Execute($false, $null)
```

Once the script finishes the execution, it will return the process ID of the execution.

1. Confirm this process ID against the execution of the report.

2. Connect to Management Studio and go to **Integration Services Catalog**. Right-click on the package that you executed using the script and go to **Reports | Standard Reports | All Executions**.

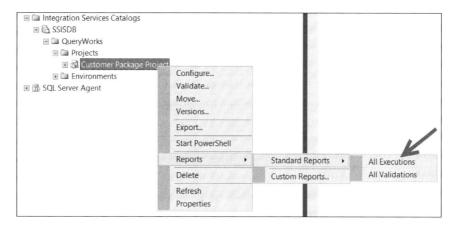

3. You will see the **All Executions** report rendered. Confirm that the ID returned by the script is in the report. You can also check the execution start time (not shown in the following screenshot, but it is in the third, rightmost column of the report).

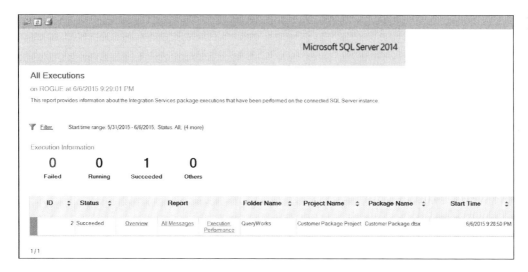

## How it works...

To execute a package stored in the `SSISDB` catalog, we need to first get a handle to the package. To get a handle to the package, we must first get to the `SSISDB` catalog:

```
$connectionString = "Data Source=$instanceName;Initial
Catalog=master;Integrated Security=SSPI;"
$conn = New-Object System.Data.SqlClient.SqlConnection $constr
$SSISServer = New-Object Microsoft.SqlServer.Management.
IntegrationServices.IntegrationServices $conn
$SSISDB = $SSISServer.Catalogs["SSISDB"]
```

We also need to have access to the folder where the package is saved:

```
$SSISDBFolderName = "QueryWorks"
$SSISDBFolder = $SSISDB.Folders[$SSISDBFolderName]
```

To execute, we must trace where the package is and invoke the `Execute` method of the `Package` object. The method accepts two parameters: a `Boolean` value for `use32RuntimeOn64` and an `EnvironmentReference`:

```
$projectName= "Customer Package Project"
$packageName= "Customer Package.dtsx"
$SSISDBFolder.Projects[$projectName].Packages[$packageName].
Execute($false, $null)
```

This method returns the process ID of the execution.

## There's more...

Check out the MSDN articles related to `PackageInfo` at `http://msdn.microsoft.com/en-us/library/microsoft.sqlserver.management.integrationservices.packageinfo.aspx`.

## See also

The *Executing an SSIS package stored in a package store or filesystem* recipe.

# Listing SSAS cmdlets

This recipe lists the available SSAS cmdlets in SQL Server 2014.

## How to do it...

Let's explore the code required to list the SSAS cmdlets:

1. Open **PowerShell ISE** as an administrator.

2. Add the following script and run it:

```
Get-Command -Module SQLASCmdlets
```

   This will give a result similar to this:

```
CommandType     Name                            Version   Source
-----------     ----                            -------   ------
Cmdlet          Add-RoleMember                  1.0       SQLASCmdlets
Cmdlet          Backup-ASDatabase               1.0       SQLASCmdlets
Cmdlet          Invoke-ASCmd                    1.0       SQLASCmdlets
Cmdlet          Invoke-ProcessCube              1.0       SQLASCmdlets
Cmdlet          Invoke-ProcessDimension         1.0       SQLASCmdlets
Cmdlet          Invoke-ProcessPartition         1.0       SQLASCmdlets
Cmdlet          Merge-Partition                 1.0       SQLASCmdlets
Cmdlet          New-RestoreFolder               1.0       SQLASCmdlets
Cmdlet          New-RestoreLocation             1.0       SQLASCmdlets
Cmdlet          Remove-RoleMember               1.0       SQLASCmdlets
Cmdlet          Restore-ASDatabase              1.0       SQLASCmdlets
```

## How it works...

A handful of SSAS cmdlets were introduced in SQL Server 2012 and carried over to SQL Server 2014. You can import the SQLASCMDLETS module to start using the new cmdlets.

To list the new AS cmdlets, simply use Get-Command:

**Get-Command -Module SQLASCmdlets**

You will notice that some of the common SSAS tasks have been wrapped in cmdlets, such as Backup-ASDatabase, Restore-ASDatabase, Invoke-ASCmd, Invoke-ProcessCube, and so on.

## There's more...

Check out these MSDN articles:

▶ *Analysis Services PowerShell*, which is available at http://msdn.microsoft.com/en-us/library/hh213141.aspx.

▶ *Analysis Services PowerShell Reference*, which is available at http://msdn.microsoft.com/en-us/library/hh758425.aspx.

## See also

The *Listing SSAS instance properties* recipe.

# Listing SSAS instance properties

We will list SSAS instance properties in this recipe.

## How to do it...

Let's explore the code required to list SSAS instance properties:

1. Open **PowerShell ISE** as an administrator.

2. Import the `SQLASCmdlets` module as follows:

   ```
   Import-Module SQLASCmdlets -DisableNameChecking
   ```

3. Add the following script and run it:

   ```
   #Connect to your Analysis Services server
   $SSASServer = New-Object Microsoft.AnalysisServices.Server

   $instanceName = "localhost"
   $SSASServer.connect($instanceName)

   #get all properties
   $SSASServer |
   Select-Object *
   ```

   You will see a result similar to this:

   ```
   ConnectionString          : localhost
   ConnectionInfo            : Microsoft.AnalysisServices.ConnectionInfo
   SessionID                 : 778FE4F2-49B7-4E7D-ABE1-D329A4F94B9A
   CaptureXml                : False
   CaptureLog                : {}
   Connected                 : True
   SessionTrace              : Microsoft.AnalysisServices.SessionTrace
   Version                   : 12.0.2000.8
   Edition                   : Developer64
   EditionID                 : 2176971986
   ProductLevel              : RTM
   Databases                 : {}
   Assemblies                : {System, EXCELXLINTERNAL, VBAMDXINTERNAL, VBAMDX...}
   Traces                    : {FlightRecorder}
   Roles                     : {Administrators}
   ServerProperties          : {DataDir, TempDir, LogDir, BackupDir...}
   ProductName               : Microsoft SQL Server Analysis Services
   ServerMode                : Multidimensional
   DefaultCompatibilityLevel : 1100
   ServerLocation            : OnPremise
   IsLoaded                  : True
   CreatedTimestamp          : 6/4/2015 9:52:35 AM
   LastSchemaUpdate          : 6/4/2015 9:52:35 AM
   Description               :
   Annotations               : {}
   ID                        : ROGUE
   Name                      : ROGUE
   ```

## How it works...

To get SSAS instance properties, we first need to load the `SQLASCmdlets` module:

```
Import-Module SQLASCmdlets -DisableNameChecking
```

We then need to create an `Analysis Server` object and connect to our instance:

```
#Connect to your Analysis Services server
$SSASServer = New-Object Microsoft.AnalysisServices.Server

$instanceName = "localhost"
$SSASServer.connect($instanceName)
```

Once we get a handle to our SSAS instance, we can display its properties:

```
#get all properties
$SSASServer |
Select-Object *
```

Note that in SQL Server 2012, there are two flavors of Analysis Services: multidimensional and tabular. You can identify this by checking the `ServerMode` properties.

## There's more...

Check out these MSDN articles related to the SQL Server Analysis Services class at `http://msdn.microsoft.com/en-us/library/microsoft.analysisservices.server.aspx`.

## See also

The *Listing SSAS cmdlets* recipe.

# Backing up an SSAS database

In this recipe, we will create an SSAS database backup.

## Getting ready

Choose an SSAS database you want to back up, and replace the `-Name` parameter in the recipe. Ensure that you are running PowerShell with administrator privileges to the SSAS instance.

## How to do it...

These are the steps required to create an SSAS database backup:

1.  Open **PowerShell ISE** as an administrator.

2.  Import the `SQLASCmdlets` module as follows:

    ```
    #import SQLASCmdlets module
    Import-Module SQLASCmdlets -DisableNameChecking
    ```

3.  Add the following script and run it:

    ```
    $instanceName = "localhost"
    $backupfile = "C:\Temp\AWDW.abf"
    Backup-ASDatabase -BackupFile $backupfile -Name "AWDW" -Server
    $instanceName -AllowOverwrite -ApplyCompression
    ```

## How it works...

The `Backup-ASDatabase` cmdlet allows multidimensional or tabular SSAS databases to be backed up to a file. In this recipe, we chose to do a compressed backup for the AWDW SSAS database to an Analysis Services Backup file (`.abf`):

```
$instanceName = "localhost"
$backupfile = "C:\Temp\AWDW.abf"
Backup-ASDatabase -BackupFile $backupfile -Name "AWDW" -Server
$instanceName -AllowOverwrite -ApplyCompression
```

Other switches that can be set using the `Backup-ASDatabase` cmdlet are as follows:

*   ▶ `-BackupRemotePartitions <SwitchParameter>`
*   ▶ `-FilePassword <SecureString>`
*   ▶ `-Locations <Microsoft.AnalysisServices.BackupLocation[]>`
*   ▶ `-Server <string>`
*   ▶ `-Credential <PSCredential>`

## There's more...

To learn more about the `Backup-ASDatabase` cmdlet, visit `http://msdn.microsoft.com/en-us/library/hh479574.aspx`.

## See also

The *Restoring an SSAS database* recipe.

# Restoring an SSAS database

You will see how to restore an SSAS database in this recipe.

## Getting ready

Locate your SSAS backup file, and replace the backup file parameter with the location of your file.

## How to do it...

Let's explore the code required to restore an SSAS database:

1. Open **PowerShell ISE** as an administrator.

2. Import the SQLASCmdlets module as follows:

   ```
   #import SQLASCmdlets module
   Import-Module SQLASCmdlets -DisableNameChecking
   ```

3. Add the following script and run it:

   ```
   $instanceName = "localhost"
   $backupfile = "C:\Temp\AWDW.abf"
   Restore-ASDatabase -RestoreFile $backupfile -Server $instanceName
   -Name "AWDW" -AllowOverwrite
   ```

## How it works...

The Restore-ASDatabase allows multidimensional or tabular SSAS databases to be restored when provided with a backup file:

```
$instanceName = "localhost"
$backupfile = "C:\Temp\AWDW.abf"
Restore-ASDatabase -RestoreFile $backupfile -Server $instanceName
-Name "AWDW" -AllowOverwrite
```

## There's more...

To learn more about the Restore-ASDatabase cmdlet, visit http://msdn.microsoft.com/en-us/library/hh510169.aspx.

## See also

The *Backing up an SSAS database* recipe.

# Processing an SSAS cube

In this recipe, we will process an SSAS cube.

## Getting ready

Choose a cube that is readily available in your SSAS instance.

## How to do it...

Let's explore the code required to process an SSAS cube:

1. Open **PowerShell ISE** as an administrator.

2. Import the SQLASCmdlets module as follows:

   ```
   #import SQLASCmdlets module
   Import-Module SQLASCmdlets -DisableNameChecking
   ```

3. Add the following script and run it:

   ```
   $instanceName = "localhost"
   Invoke-ProcessCube -Name "AW" -Server $instanceName
   -Database "AWDW" -ProcessType ([Microsoft.AnalysisServices.
   ProcessType]::ProcessFull)
   ```

To check whether the cube has been processed, perform the following steps:

1. Go to **Management Studio** and connect to **SQL Server Analysis Services**.
   Right-click on the cube you just processed and go to **Properties**:

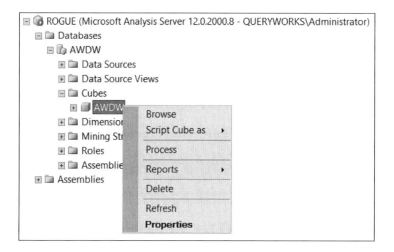

2. In the **General** section, check the **Last Processed** value. It should be updated to when the script finished executing, as shown in the following screenshot:

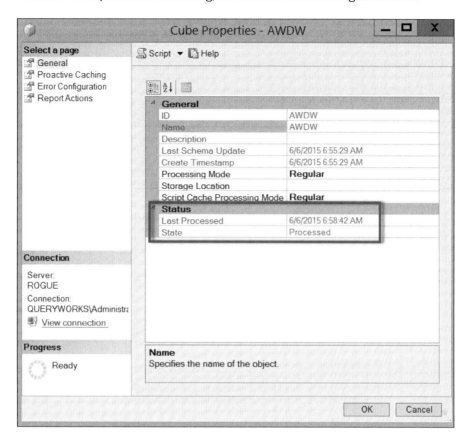

## How it works...

Processing, or reprocessing, a cube is a common task that needs to be done in an SSAS environment on a regular basis. Processing a cube ensures that your cube has the latest data that has been loaded to the source data warehouse, and ensures any changes to the cube's structure are in place.

The `Invoke-Process` cmdlet simplifies this process if you are doing this task using PowerShell:

```
Invoke-ProcessCube -Name "AWDW" -Database "AWDW" -ProcessType
([Microsoft.AnalysisServices.ProcessType]::ProcessFull)
```

All that we need to specify is the cube name and SSAS database where this cube belongs. Processing cubes requires administrative privileges on the SSAS instance.

There are different processing types that can be specified with the `-ProcessType` switch, including `ProcessFull`, `ProcessAdd`, and `ProcessUpdate`.

## There's more...

▸ Check out the MSDN articles related to the `Invoke-ProcessCube` cmdlet at `http://msdn.microsoft.com/en-us/library/hh510171.aspx`.

▸ To learn more about the different processing options and settings for Analysis Services, check out `http://msdn.microsoft.com/en-us/library/ms174774.aspx`.

## See also

▸ The *Backing up an SSAS database* recipe.

▸ The *Restoring an SSAS database* recipe.

# 11
# Helpful PowerShell Snippets

In this chapter, we will cover the following topics:

- ▶ Documenting the PowerShell script for Get-Help
- ▶ Getting history
- ▶ Getting a timestamp
- ▶ Getting more error messages
- ▶ Listing processes
- ▶ Getting aliases
- ▶ Exporting to CSV and XML
- ▶ Using Invoke-Expression
- ▶ Testing regular expressions
- ▶ Managing folders
- ▶ Manipulating files
- ▶ Compressing files
- ▶ Searching for files
- ▶ Reading an event log
- ▶ Sending an e-mail
- ▶ Embedding C# Code

- ▸ Creating an HTML report
- ▸ Parsing XML
- ▸ Extracting data from a web service
- ▸ Using PowerShell remoting

# Introduction

In this chapter, we tackle a variety of recipes that are not SQL Server-specific; but you may find them useful as you use PowerShell with SQL Server. Often, you will need to compress (or zip) files, create timestamped files, analyze event logs for recent system errors, export a list of processes to CSV or XML, or even access web services. Here, you will find code snippets that you can use in existing or new scripts, or whenever you need them.

# Documenting PowerShell script for Get-Help

In this recipe, we will take a look at how to use header comments in your script. Formatting the header comments in a specific way will enable them to be utilized by the `Get-Help` cmdlet.

## How to do it...

In this recipe, we will explore the comment-based help:

1. Open **PowerShell ISE** as an administrator.
2. Add the following script:

```
<#
.SYNOPSIS
    Creates a full database backup
.DESCRIPTION
    Creates a full database backup using specified instance name
and database name
    This will place the backup file to the default backup directory
of the instance
.PARAMETER instanceName
    instance where database to be backed up resides
.PARAMETER databaseName
    database to be backed up
.EXAMPLE
```

```
    PS C:\PowerShell> .\Backup-Database.ps1 -instanceName
"QUERYWORKS\SQL01" -databaseName "pubs"
.EXAMPLE
    PS C:\PowerShell> .\Backup-Database.ps1 -instance "QUERYWORKS\
SQL01" -database "pubs"
.NOTES

    To get help:
    Get-Help .\Backup-Database.ps1

#>

param
(
    [Parameter(Position=0)]
    [alias("instance")]
    [string]$instanceName,
    [Parameter(Position=1)]
    [alias("database")]
    [string]$databaseName
)
function main
{
    #this is just a stub file
}

#clear the screen
cls

#get general help
Get-Help "C:\PowerShell\Backup-Database.ps1"

#get examples
Get-Help "C:\PowerShell\Backup-Database.ps1" -Examples
```

3.  Save the script as `C:\PowerShell\Backup-Database.ps1`.

4.  Execute the script from the PowerShell ISE without any parameters.

 Check *Appendix A, PowerShell Primer,* for more information on how to execute scripts from the PowerShell console.

Here is a sample result:

```
PS C:\Windows\system32> Get-Help "C:\PowerShell\Backup-Database.ps1"

NAME
    C:\PowerShell\Backup-Database.ps1

SYNOPSIS
    Creates a full database backup

SYNTAX
    C:\PowerShell\Backup-Database.ps1 [[-instanceName] <String>] [[-databaseName] <String>] [<CommonParameters>]

DESCRIPTION
    Creates a full database backup using specified instance name and database name
    This will place the backup file to the default backup directory of the instance

RELATED LINKS

REMARKS
    To see the examples, type: "get-help C:\PowerShell\Backup-Database.ps1 -examples".
    For more information, type: "get-help C:\PowerShell\Backup-Database.ps1 -detailed".
    For technical information, type: "get-help C:\PowerShell\Backup-Database.ps1 -full".
```

## How it works...

Introduced in PowerShell V2, the **comment-based help** enables you to provide additional information of a script or cmdlet by creating comment blocks that follow a specified format. This help content can be viewed when you use the `Get-Help` cmdlet.

For this to work, the comment block must be the first section in a script or the first lines in a function. Once it has been composed, the script or the function name can be passed as a parameter to `Get-Help`.

Some of the common keywords and sections of the comment-based help are as follows:

```
<#
.SYNOPSIS
    summary
.DESCRIPTION
    Description
.PARAMETER parameter1Name
    Parameter description
.PARAMETER parameter1Name
    Parameter description
.EXAMPLE
    Usage example; Appears when you use -examples
.EXAMPLE
    Usage example; Appears when you use -examples
.NOTES
    Additional notes; Appears when you use -full
#>
```

Additional sections that can be used, as documented in MSDN, are as follows:

▸ `.INPUTS`: Microsoft .NET Framework types of objects that can be piped to the function or script

▸ `.OUTPUTS`: Microsoft .NET Framework types of objects that the cmdlet returns

▸ `.LINK`: Related topic

▸ `.ROLE`: User role for the help topic

## There's more...

▸ Learn more about the comment-based help from the MSDN page at `https://technet.microsoft.com/en-us/library/hh847834.aspx`.

▸ Refer to Microsoft guidelines on how to write cmdlet help at `https://msdn.microsoft.com/en-us/library/aa965353(VS.85).aspx`.

▸ Although a little bit outdated, Don Jones' article on how to write the help documentation, *WTFM: Writing the Fabulous Manual,* is still relevant and informative, which is available at `https://technet.microsoft.com/en-us/magazine/ff458353.aspx`.

# Getting history

You can recall the commands you typed in the PowerShell console using the `Get-History` cmdlet.

## How to do it...

This is how to redisplay the console history:

1. Open **PowerShell ISE** as an administrator.
2. Run the following command:

```
Get-History
```

## How it works...

By default, PowerShell will keep 64 previous commands in the buffer and allow you to recall these commands when you run `Get-History`. The `Get-History` command will display the last 32 commands, but you can also specify how many lines you want to display by specifying the `-Count` parameter:

```
#get last 10
Get-History -Count 10
```

If you want to reexecute any of the commands that you see in your history, you can use the `Invoke-History` cmdlet and provide it with the history ID. For example, if you want to re-execute ID 7, you can use the following command:

```
Invoke-History -ID 7
```

# Getting a timestamp

In this recipe, we simply get the system's current timestamp.

## How to do it...

This is how we will get the timestamp:

1.  Open **PowerShell ISE** as an administrator.
2.  Add the following script and run it:

    ```
    $timestamp = Get-Date -Format "yyyy-MMM-dd-hhmmtt"

    #display timestamp
    $timestamp
    ```

Here is a sample result:

```
2015-May-23-1152AM
```

## How it works...

Often, we find ourselves needing the timestamp to append to different files we create or modify. To get the timestamp in PowerShell, we simply have to use the `Get-Date` cmdlet, which gives the following default format:

```
Saturday, May 23, 2015 11:51:31 AM
```

To change the format, we can use the `-Format` switch, which accepts a format string. In this recipe, we used the `yyyy-MMM-dd-hhmmtt` format.

There are a number of standard format strings that return preformatted datetimes, or you can also compose your own format string. The common format strings, as documented in MSDN, are as follows:

| Format pattern | Description |
| --- | --- |
| tt | AM/PM designator |
| ss | Seconds with leading zero |
| mm | Minutes with leading zero |
| dd | Day of month with leading zero |
| dddd | Full name of the day of the week |
| hh | 12-hour clock with leading zero |
| HH | 24-hour clock with leading zero |
| dd | Day of month with leading zero |
| dddd | Full name of the day of the week |
| MM | Numeric month with leading zero |
| MMM | Abbreviated month name |
| MMMM | Full month name |
| yy | Two-digit year |
| yyyy | Four-digit year |

## There's more...

The following links are helpful to understand how to use and format dates in PowerShell:

- The *DateTimeFormatInfo Class* at `http://msdn.microsoft.com/en-us/library/system.globalization.datetimeformatinfo.aspx`.

- *Standard Date and Time Format Strings* at `http://msdn.microsoft.com/en-us/library/az4se3k1.aspx`.

- The *Windows PowerShell Tip of the Week—Formatting Dates and Times* at `http://technet.microsoft.com/en-us/library/ee692801.aspx`.

- MSDN *Get-Date* at `http://technet.microsoft.com/en-us/library/hh849887`.

# Getting more error messages

In this recipe, we will learn how to display additional error messages.

## How to do it...

Let's take a look at how to display additional error messages:

1. Open **PowerShell ISE** as an administrator.

2. Add the following script and run it:

```
Clear-Host
$error[0] | Format-List -Force
```

## How it works...

PowerShell supports some variables called automatic variables that store the state information or environment information, such as arguments, events, user directories, profile information, or error codes. The $error is an automatic array variable that holds all the error objects that are encountered in your PowerShell session. To display the last error message, you can use the following code:

```
$error[0] |
Format-List -Force
```

This method is particularly useful when you are working with SQL Server and you encounter an exception. When you run this command, you get the full stack trace; therefore, you get a more complete picture of exactly what went wrong. For example, when you run your script, it just reports that there is an exception in a certain line. When you use $error, you might find out that the constraint you are trying to create already exists in the table.

To check the number of errors contained in your variable, you can use the following code:

```
$error.Count
```

The $error works like a circular buffer. By default, the $error stores the last 256 errors in your session. If you want to increase the number of error objects the array can store, you can set the $MaximumErrorCount variable to a new value:

```
$MaximumErrorCount = 300
```

If you want to clear all the errors, you can use the clear method:

```
$error.Clear()
```

To get more information about variables that are set in your session, you can use the following command:

```
Get-Variable |
Select-Object Name, Value, Options |
Format-Table -AutoSize
```

A partial list of special variables is presented in the following table:

| Special Variable | Description |
| --- | --- |
| $_ | Current pipeline object |
| $args | Arguments passed to a function |
| $error | Stores the last error |
| $home | User's home directory |
| $host | Host information |
| $match | Regex matches |
| $PSHome | Install directory of PowerShell |
| $pid | **Process ID** (**PID**) of PowerShell process |
| $pwd | Present working directory |
| $true | Boolean true |
| $false | Boolean false |
| $null | Null value |

# Listing processes

In this recipe, we will list processes in the system.

## How to do it...

Let's list processes using PowerShell:

1. Open **PowerShell ISE** as an administrator.

2. Add the following script and run it to list processes on the screen:

```
#list all processes to screen
Get-Process

#list 10 most recently started processes
Get-Process |
Sort-Object -Property StartTime -Descending |
Select-Object Name, StartTime, Path, Responding -First 10
```

3. Add the following script and run it to list and save the processes to a text file:

```
#save processes to a text file
$txtFile = "C:\Temp\processes.txt"

Get-Process |
Out-File -FilePath $txtFile -Force

#display text file in notepad
notepad $txtFile
```

4. Add the following script and run it to save the processes to a CSV file:

```
#save processes to a csv file
$csvFile = "C:\Temp\processes.csv"

Get-Process |
Export-Csv -Path $csvFile -Force -NoTypeInformation

#display first five lines in file
Get-Content $csvFile -totalCount 5
```

5. Add the following script and run it to save the processes to XML:

```
$xmlFile = "C:\Temp\processes.xml"

#get top 5 CPU-heavy processes that start with S
Get-Process |
Where-Object ProcessName -like "S*" |
Sort-Object -Property CPU -Descending |
Select-Object Name, CPU -First 5 |
Export-Clixml -path $xmlFile -Force

#display in Internet Explorer
Set-Alias ie "$env:programfiles\Internet Explorer\iexplore.exe"

ie $xmlFile
```

## How it works...

In this recipe, we have used the `Get-Process` cmdlet to display processes in the system. We explored a few variations in this recipe.

The first example lists all processes:

```
Get-Process |
```

The second example is slightly different. We pipe the results of `Get-Process` and get only the 10 most recently started processes. We achieve this by sorting the `StartTime` in descending order and selecting only the top 10:

```
Sort-Object -Property StartTime -Descending |
Select-Object Name, StartTime, Path, Responding -First 10
```

Note that this will throw some errors because there are system processes that are not accessible to nonelevated users.
Following is an example access error:

```
Sort-Object : Exception getting "StartTime": "Access is denied"
At line:6 char:1
+ Sort-Object -Property StartTime -Descending |
+ ~~~~~~~~~~~~~~~~~~~~~~~~~~~~~~~~~~~~~~~~~~~~~~
    + CategoryInfo          : InvalidResult: (System.Diagnostics.Process (Idle):PSObject) [Sort-Object]
ception
    + FullyQualifiedErrorId : ExpressionEvaluation,Microsoft.PowerShell.Commands.SortObjectCommand
```

Refer to the article for more information on this security issue at `http://blogs.technet.com/b/heyscriptingguy/archive/2010/08/07/weekend-scripter-boot-tracing-with-windows-powershell.aspx`.

The results of `Get-Process` can be piped to other cmdlets and exported to different file formats, such as a text file, CSV file, or XML.

To pipe results to a text file, we can use the `Out-File` cmdlet:

```
$txtFile = "C:\Temp\processes.txt"

Get-Process |
Out-File -FilePath $txtFile -Force

#display text file in notepad
notepad $txtFile
```

To create a CSV file, we can use the `Export-Csv` cmdlet. In this sample, we also read back the first five lines of the CSV file that we just created:

```
$csvFile = "C:\Temp\processes.csv"

Get-Process |
Export-Csv -Path $csvFile -Force -NoTypeInformation

#display first five lines in file
Get-Content $csvFile -totalCount 5
```

If you require an XML format, you can achieve this using the `Export-Clixml` cmdlet. In this recipe, we also filter for only processes that start with `S`, and we only get the top five CPU-heavy processes:

```
$xmlFile = "C:\Temp\processes.xml"

#get top 5 CPU-heavy processes that start with S
Get-Process |
Where-Object ProcessName -like "S*" |
Sort-Object -Property CPU -Descending |
Select-Object Name, CPU -First 5 |
Export-Clixml -path $xmlFile -Force

#display in Internet Explorer
Set-Alias ie "$env:programfiles\Internet Explorer\iexplore.exe"

ie $xmlFile
```

The last two lines simply create an alias for Internet Explorer, and then display the XML file.

## There's more...

▸ To learn more about *Using the Get-Process Cmdlet*, check out `http://msdn.microsoft.com/en-us/library/ee176855.aspx`.

▸ Refer to MSDN *Get-Process*, which is available at `http://msdn.microsoft.com/en-us/library/hh849832`.

## See also

The *Exporting to CSV and XML* recipe.

# Getting aliases

In this recipe, we take a look at aliases in PowerShell.

## How to do it...

Let's check out aliases in PowerShell:

1. Open **PowerShell ISE** as an administrator.

2. Add the following script and run it:

```
#list all aliases
Get-Alias

#get members of Get-Alias
Get-Alias |
Get-Member

#list cmdlet that is aliased as dir
$alias:dir

#list cmdlet that is aliased as ls
$alias:ls

#get all aliases of Get-ChildItem
Get-Alias -Definition "Get-ChildItem"
```

## How it works...

An alias in PowerShell is a different name that you can use for a cmdlet. Some cmdlets already come with a handful of aliases, but you can create your own aliases for cmdlets as well.

The Get-Alias returns all PowerShell aliases. PowerShell's building blocks are cmdlets that are named using the <Verb-Noun> convention. For example, to list contents of a directory, we use Get-ChildItem. There are, however, better-known ways to get this information such as dir if running the Windows Command Prompt and ls if running in a Nix environment. Aliases allow most well-known commands to run from within PowerShell. To list all aliases, use the following code:

```
#list all aliases
Get-Alias
```

To get the members of Get-Alias, we can pipe the result of Get-Alias to Get-Member:

```
Get-Alias |
Get-Member
```

If there is a well-known command, such as dir or ls that is supported in PowerShell, and if you are curious to know which cmdlet it refers to, you can use the following command:

```
#list cmdlet that is aliased as dir
$alias:dir

#list cmdlet that is aliased as ls
$alias:ls
```

On the other hand, if you want to know all aliases for a cmdlet, you can use the following command:

```
Get-Alias -Definition "Get-ChildItem"
```

PowerShell also allows you to create your own alias. For example, if you want to use the `gci2` alias instead of `Get-ChildItem`, you can use the `Set-Alias` cmdlet to do so:

```
Set-Alias gci2 Get-ChildItem
```

To confirm, you can either use `Get-Alias` to see all the aliases that are now available in your system, or you can specify the alias you just created:

```
Get-Alias gci2
```

## There's more...

To learn more about the `Get-Alias` cmdlet, visit `http://msdn.microsoft.com/en-us/library/hh849948`.

# Exporting to CSV and XML

In this recipe, we pipe the results of the `Get-Process` cmdlet to a CSV and XML file.

## How to do it...

These are the steps required to export to CSV and XML:

1. Open **PowerShell ISE** as an administrator.

2. Add the following script and run it:

```
$csvFile = "C:\Temp\sample.csv"
Get-Process |
Export-Csv -path $csvFile -Force -NoTypeInformation

#display text file in notepad
notepad $csvFile


$xmlFile = "C:\Temp\process.xml"
Get-Process |
Export-Clixml -path $xmlFile  -Force

#display text file in notepad
notepad $xmlFile
```

## How it works...

PowerShell provides a few cmdlets that support exporting data to files of different formats. The `Export-Csv` cmdlet saves information to a comma-separated value file, and the `Export-Clixml` cmdlet exports the piped data to XML:

```
$csvFile = "C:\Temp\sample.csv"
Get-Process |
Export-Csv -path $csvFile -Force -NoTypeInformation

#display text file in notepad
notepad $csvFile



$xmlFile = "C:\Temp\process.xml"
Get-Process |
Export-Clixml -path $xmlFile  -Force

#display file in notepad
notepad $xmlFile
```

The `Export-Csv` cmdlet converts each object passed to it from the pipeline into a row in the resulting CSV file. Although the default delimiter is a comma, this can be changed to other characters using the `-Delimiter` switch. You can also start appending data using the `-Append` switch, which was added in PowerShell V3.

The `Export-Clixml` cmdlet converts data passed to it into XML and saves it to a file. The resulting XML is similar to what the `ConvertTo-Xml` cmdlet would return.

## There's more...

The following links are helpful in learning more about `Export-Csv` and `Export-Clixml`:

▸ Refer to MSDN *Export-Csv*, which is available at `http://msdn.microsoft.com/en-us/library/hh849932`.

▸ Refer to MSDN *Export-Clixml*, which is available at `http://msdn.microsoft.com/en-us/library/hh849916`.

# Using Invoke-Expression

In this recipe, we will use the `Invoke-Expression` cmdlet to compress some files using a free compression utility.

## Getting ready

For this recipe, we will use the 7-Zip application to compress some files. Download 7-Zip from `http://www.7-zip.org/`.

## How to do it...

Let's check out the `Invoke-Expression` cmdlet:

1.  Open **PowerShell ISE** as an administrator.
2.  Add the following script and run it:

```
$VerbosePreference = "Continue"

$program = "`"C:\Program Files\7-Zip\7z.exe`""

#arguments
$7zargs = " a -tzip "
$zipFile = " `"C:\Temp\new archive.zip`" "
$directoryToZip = " `"C:\Temp\old`" "

#compose the command
$cmd = "& $program $7zargs $zipFile $directoryToZip "

#display final command
Write-Verbose $cmd

#execute the command
Invoke-Expression $cmd

$VerbosePreference = "SilentlyContinue"
```

## How it works...

The `Invoke-Expression` cmdlet allows PowerShell expressions to run from PowerShell. These expressions can consist of other PowerShell statements and functions, or they can contain executables and arguments.

In this recipe, we are composing the command to run `7z.exe` and passing a folder name to it, which needs to be compressed into a ZIP file.

The challenge faced most often with using `Invoke-Expression` is to make sure that the full path of the program, or the full arguments, are all properly escaped. In our recipe, we individually compose the strings for the executable and arguments. All the strings are escaped with a back tick:

```
$program = "`"C:\Program Files\7-Zip\7z.exe`""

#arguments
$7zargs = " a -tzip "
$zipFile = " `"C:\Temp\new archive.zip`" "
$directoryToZip = " `"C:\Temp\old`" "

#compose the command
$cmd = "& $program $7zargs $zipFile $directoryToZip "

#display final command
Write-Verbose $cmd
```

When we display the command, we will see that the double quotes are preserved:

```
VERBOSE: & "C:\Program Files\7-Zip\7z.exe" a -tzip  "C:\Temp\new archive.zip"  "C:\Temp\old"
```

The preceding ampersand is considered a call operator, and this whole expression is meant to run `7z.exe` and compress the `C:\Temp\old` folder into a file called `new archive.zip`.

Finally, running the expression requires using the `Invoke-Expression` cmdlet and passing the string command argument:

**`Invoke-Expression $cmd`**

## There's more...

Learn more about the `Invoke-Expression` cmdlet from the MSDN page at `http://msdn.microsoft.com/en-us/library/hh849893`.

# Testing regular expressions

In this recipe, we are going to explore some ways to use and test regular expressions.

## How to do it...

Let's check out regular expressions in PowerShell:

1. Open **PowerShell ISE** as an administrator.
2. Add the following script and run it:

```
$VerbosePreference = "Continue"

#check if valid email address
$str = "info@sqlbelle.com"
$pattern = "^[A-Z0-9._%+-]+@[A-Z0-9.-]+\.(?:[A-Z]{2}|com|org|net|g
ov|ca|mil|biz|info|mobi|name|aero|jobs|museum)$"

if ($str -match $pattern)
{
    Write-Verbose "Valid Email Address"
}
else
{
  Write-Verbose "Invalid Email Address"
}

#another way to test
[Regex]::Match($str, $pattern)

#can also use regex in switch
$str = "V1A 2V1"
$str = "90250"

switch -regex ($str)
{
    "(^\d{5}$)|(^\d{5}-\d{4}$)"
    {
        Write-Verbose "Valid US Postal Code"
    }
    "[A-Za-z]\d[A-Za-z]\s*\d[A-Za-z]\d"
    {
```

```
            Write-Verbose "Valid Canadian Postal Code"
        }
        default
        {
            Write-Verbose "Don't Know"
        }
    }


    #use regex and extract matches
    #to create named groups - use format ?<groupname>
    $str = "Her number is (604)100-1004. Sometimes she can be reached
    at (604)100-1005."

    $pattern = @"
    (?<phone>\(\d{3}\)\d{3}-\d{4})
    "@

    $m = [regex]::Matches($str, $pattern)

    #list individual phones
    $m |
    Foreach-Object {
        Write-Verbose "$($_.Groups["phone"].Value)"
    }

    $VerbosePreference = "SilentlyContinue"
```

## How it works...

A regular expression is a string pattern—for example, a pattern for a valid ZIP code or an e-mail address that can be used to compare strings.

We have looked at a few ways to use and test regular expressions in this recipe.

Here are some of the common patterns:

| Pattern | Description |
|---------|-------------|
| \ | Escape character |
| ^ | Beginning of line |
| $ | End of line |
| * | Matches zero or many times |
| ? | Matches zero or one time |
| + | Matches one or more times |

| Pattern | Description |
|---|---|
| . | Matches a single character except newline |
| pattern1\|pattern2 | Matches either of the patterns |
| pattern{m} | Matches a pattern exactly m times |
| pattern{m,n} | Matches minimum m to a maximum n times |
| pattern{m, } | Matches minimum m times |
| [abcd] | Matches any character in a set |
| [a-d] | Matches any character in a range |
| [^abcd] | Matches characters NOT in a set |
| \n | Newline |
| \r | Carriage return |
| \b | Word boundary |
| \B | Non-word boundary |
| \d | Digits: 0-9 |
| \D | Non-digit |
| \w | Word character; equivalent to [A-Za-z0-9_] |
| \W | Non-word character |
| \s | Space character |
| \S | Non whitespace character |

PowerShell has the `-match` and `-replace` operators that allow strings to be matched or replaced against a pattern. PowerShell also supports the static methods of the `Regex` class, such as `[regex]::Match` and `[regex]::Matches`.

In the first example, we will check for a valid e-mail address and we will use the `-match` operator:

```
#check if valid email address
$str = info@sqlbelle.com

$pattern = "^[A-Z0-9._%+-]+@[A-Z0-9.-]+\.(?:[A-Z]{2}|com|org|net|gov|c
a|mil|biz|info|mobi|name|aero|jobs|museum)$"

if ($str -match $pattern)
{
   Write-Verbose "Valid Email Address"
}
else
{
  Write-Verbose "Invalid Email Address"
}
```

Regular expressions can also be used in a `switch` statement. In our example, we will check whether our string is either a valid US or Canadian postal code:

```
#can also use regex in switch
$str = "V1A 2V1"

switch -regex ($str)
{
    "(^\d{5}$)|(^\d{5}-\d{4}$)"
    {
        Write-Verbose "Valid US Postal Code"
    }
    "[A-Za-z]\d[A-Za-z]\s*\d[A-Za-z]\d"
    {
        Write-Verbose "Valid Canadian Postal Code"
    }
    default
    {
        Write-Verbose "Don't Know"
    }
}
```

If there is a possibility of multiple matches, we can use the `[regex]::Matches` operator, and pipe the result to a `Foreach-Object` cmdlet to display the group matches:

```
#use regex and extract matches
#to create named groups - use format ?<groupname>
$str = "Her number is (604)100-1004. Sometimes she can be reached at
(604)100-1005."

$pattern = @"
(?<phone>\(\d{3}\)\d{3}-\d{4})
"@

$m = [regex]::Matches($str, $pattern)

#list individual phones
$m |
Foreach-Object {
    Write-Verbose "$($_.Groups["phone"].Value)"
}
```

The pattern we are using is a named group that is specified by the `(?<phone>)` label. Anything that is matched by the pattern in the parenthesis can later be referred to by the `phone` label.

## There's more...

The following links are useful in learning more about regular expressions in general and in the context of PowerShell:

- ▸ For more information on *Regex Methods*, visit `http://msdn.microsoft.com/en-us/library/axa83z9t`.

- ▸ Refer to *Regular Expression Language—Quick Reference*, which is available at `http://msdn.microsoft.com/en-us/library/az24scfc.aspx`.

- ▸ Refer to the PowerShell admin regex article, which is available at `http://www.powershelladmin.com/wiki/Powershell_regular_expressions`.

# Managing folders

In this recipe, we will explore different cmdlets that support folder management.

## How to do it...

Let's take a look at different cmdlets that can be used for folders:

1. Open **PowerShell ISE** as an administrator.

2. Add the following script and run it:

```
#list folders ordered by name descending
$path = "C:\Temp"

#get directories only
Get-Childitem $path |
Where-Object PSIsContainer

#create folder
$newFolder = "C:\Temp\NewFolder"
New-Item -Path $newFolder -ItemType Directory -Force

#check if folder exists
Test-Path $newFolder

#copy folder
$anotherFolder = "C:\Temp\NewFolder2"
Copy-Item $newFolder $anotherFolder -Force
```

```
#move folder
Move-Item $anotherFolder $newFolder

#delete folder
Remove-Item $newFolder -Force -Recurse
```

## How it works...

Here are some cmdlets that support folder manipulation:

| Cmdlet | Description |
|---|---|
| Get-ChildItem | This lists all directories in a path:<br><br>`#get directories only`<br>`Get-Childitem $path \| Where PSIsContainer` |
| Test-Path | This checks whether a folder exists:<br><br>`Test-Path $newFolder` |
| New-Item | This creates a new folder:<br><br>`PS> NewItem -Path $newFolder -ItemType Directory -Force` |
| Copy-Item | This copies a folder:<br><br>`Copy-Item $newFolder $anotherFolder -Force` |
| Move-Item | This moves a folder to a different location:<br><br>`Move-Item $anotherFolder $newFolder` |
| Remove-Item | This deletes a folder and all its contents:<br><br>`Remove-Item $newFolder -Force -Recurse` |

## There's more...

Refer to the following links to understand how to work with files and folders via scripting languages:

▶ *Files and Folders, Part 1* (TechNet, by the Microsoft Scripting Guys) at http://technet.microsoft.com/en-us/library/ee176983.

▶ *Files and Folders, Part 2* (TechNet, by the Microsoft Scripting Guys) at http://technet.microsoft.com/en-us/library/ee176985.

▶ *Files and Folders, Part 3* (TechNet, by the Microsoft Scripting Guys) at http://technet.microsoft.com/en-us/library/ee176988.

## See also

The *Manipulating files* recipe.

# Manipulating files

In this recipe, we will take a look at different cmdlets that help you manipulate files.

## How to do it...

Let's explore different ways to manage files:

1. Open **PowerShell ISE** as an administrator.
2. Add the following script and run it:

```
#create file
$timestamp = Get-Date -format "yyyy-MMM-dd-hhmmtt"
$path = "C:\Temp\"
$fileName = "$timestamp.txt"
$fullPath = Join-Path $path $fileName

New-Item -Path $path -Name $fileName -ItemType "File"

#check if file exists
Test-Path $fullPath

#copy file
$path = "C:\Temp\"
$newFileName = $timestamp + "_2.txt"
$fullPath2 = Join-Path $path $newFileName

Copy-Item $fullPath $fullPath2

#move file
$newFolder = "C:\Data"
Move-Item $fullPath2 $newFolder

#append to file
Add-Content $fullPath "Additional Item"

#show contents of file
notepad $fullPath
```

```
#merge file contents
$newContent = Get-Content "C:\Temp\processes.txt"
Add-Content $fullPath $newContent
#show contents of file
notepad $fullPath

#delete file
Remove-Item $fullPath
```

## How it works...

Here are some of the cmdlets that support file manipulation:

| Cmdlet | Description |
|---|---|
| Test-Path | This checks whether a file exists:<br><br>`Test-Path $fullpath` |
| Join-Path | This combines a path and child path:<br><br>`Join-Path $path $fileName` |
| New-Item | This creates a new file:<br><br>`New-Item -Path $path -Name $fileName -ItemType "File"` |
| Get-Content | This retrieves the content of a file:<br><br>`Get-Content "C:\Temp\processes.txt"` |
| Add-Content | This appends the content to a file:<br><br>`Add-Content $fullPath $newContent` |
| Copy-Item | This copies a file:<br><br>`Copy-Item $fullPath $fullPath2` |
| Move-Item | This moves a file to a different location:<br><br>`Move-Item $fullPath2 $newFolder` |
| Remove-Item | This deletes a file:<br><br>`Remove-Item $fullPath` |

## There's more...

Refer to the following links to understand how to work with files and folders via scripting languages:

- ▸ *Files and Folders, Part 1* (TechNet, by the Microsoft Scripting Guys):
- ▸ `http://technet.microsoft.com/en-us/library/ee176983.`
- ▸ *Files and Folders, Part 2* (TechNet, by the Microsoft Scripting Guys):
- ▸ `http://technet.microsoft.com/en-us/library/ee176985.`
- ▸ *Files and Folders, Part 3* (TechNet, by the Microsoft Scripting Guys):
- ▸ `http://technet.microsoft.com/en-us/library/ee176988.`

## See also

The *Managing folders* recipe.

# Compressing files

In this recipe, we will use the `Compress-Archive` cmdlet to compress or ZIP some files.

## How to do it...

The following steps walk you through compressing files using PowerShell:

1. Open **PowerShell ISE** as an administrator.
2. Add the following script and run it:

```
#replace the variable values with your
#folder and destination file values

#search for file with specific extension
$folderToCompress = "C:\Temp\MyFiles"
$destinationFile = $folderToCompress + ".zip"

Compress-Archive -Path $folderToCompressfolderToCompress -
DestinationPath $destinationFile –CompressionLevel Fastest -Update
```

## How it works...

PowerShell V5 introduces a new cmdlet that compresses files. `Compress-Archive` is an elegant way to archive or ZIP files. It accepts a folder or list of files to be zipped and the destination file. If you want to specify multiple files, you need to list them separated by a comma:

```
Compress-Archive -LiteralPath C:\Data\Resume.docx, C:\MyFiles\
CoverLetter.pdf –CompressionLevel Optimal -DestinationPath C:\Data\
MyApplication.Zip
```

You can also specify the compression level to be `Fastest`, `Optimal`, or `NoCompression`.

If you need to unzip or expand the files, you can use the complementing `Expand-Archive` cmdlet, which is also introduced in PowerShell V5.

# Searching for files

In this recipe, we will search for files based on filenames, attributes, and content.

## How to do it...

Let's explore different ways to use `Get-ChildItem` to search for files:

1. Open **PowerShell ISE** as an administrator.

2. Add the following script and run it:

```
#search for file with specific extension
$path = "C:\Temp"
Get-ChildItem -Path $path -Include *.sql -Recurse

#search for file based on date creation
#use LastWriteTime for date modification
[datetime]$startDate =  "2015-05-01"
[datetime]$endDate =  "2015-05-24"

#note date is at 12 midnight
#sample date Sunday, May 24, 2015 12:00:00 AM

#search for the file
Get-ChildItem -Path $path -Recurse |
Where-Object CreationTime -ge $startDate |
Where-Object CreationTime -le $endDate |
Sort-Object -Property LastWriteTime
```

```
#list files greater than 10MB
Get-ChildItem $path -Recurse |
Where-Object Length -ge 10Mb |
Select-Object Name,
@{Name="MB";Expression={"{0:N2}" -f ($_.Length/1MB)}} |
Sort-Object -Property Length -Descending |
Format-Table –AutoSize

#search for content of file
#search TXT, CSV and SQL files that contain
#the word "QueryWorks"
$pattern = "QueryWorks"
Get-ChildItem -Path $path -Include *.txt, *.csv, *.sql -Recurse |
Select-String -Pattern $pattern
```

## How it works...

The Get-ChildItem cmdlet displays contents of a given path:

**Get-ChildItem**

You can also use the gci, ls, or dir aliases instead of Get-ChildItem when typing this command.

We can pipe the results of Get-ChildItem to a Where-Object cmdlet to filter the results. For example, if we want to look for only .sql files, we will use the following command:

```
#search for file with specific extension
$path = "C:\Temp"
Get-ChildItem -Path $path -Include *.sql -Recurse
```

To get files created within a date range, we pipe the results, and in the Where-Object cmdlet, we filter based on the CreationTime property. Note that dates are automatically assigned a timestamp of midnight, and the following example actually gets all files created between May 1 and May 24:

```
#search for file based on date creation
#use LastWriteTime for date modification
[datetime]$startDate =  "2015-05-01"
[datetime]$endDate =  "2015-05-24"

#note date is at 12 midnight
#sample date Sunday, May 24, 2015 12:00:00 AM
```

```
Get-ChildItem -Path $path -Recurse |
Where-Object CreationTime -ge $startDate |
Where-Object CreationTime -le $endDate |
Sort-Object -Property LastWriteTime
```

To filter files based on file size, we can filter the files using the Length property. Note that PowerShell supports the KB (kilobyte), MB (megabyte), GB (gigabyte), TB (terabyte), and PB (petabyte) constants:

```
#list files greater than 10MB
Get-ChildItem $path -Recurse |
Where-Object Length -ge 10Mb |
Select Name,
@{Name="MB";Expression={"{0:N2}" -f ($_.Length/1MB)}} |
Sort-Object -Property Length -Descending |
Format-Table –AutoSize
```

The last example showcases the use of the –Include switch with the Get-ChildItem cmdlet, which allows the cmdlet to selectively include only specific files based on the pattern that was passed. This example also highlights how we can search not only filenames and paths, but the actual contents of the file using the Select-String cmdlet. The Select-String cmdlet can only search for text files; however, it cannot search for other proprietary formats such as .doc, .docx, and .pdf:

```
#search for content of file
#search TXT, CSV and SQL files that contain
#the word "QueryWorks"
$pattern = "QueryWorks"
Get-ChildItem -Path $path -Include *.txt, *.csv, *.sql -Recurse |
Select-String -Pattern $pattern
```

## There's more...

To learn more about *Get-ChildItem*, visit http://msdn.microsoft.com/en-us/library/hh849800.

## See also

The *Getting aliases* recipe.

# Reading an event log

In this recipe, we will read the event log.

## How to do it...

Let's take a look at how we can read the Windows event log from PowerShell:

1. Open **PowerShell ISE** as an administrator.
2. Add the following script and run it:

```
Get-EventLog -LogName Application -Newest 20 -EntryType Error
```

## How it works...

Reading the event log is straightforward in PowerShell. We can do this using the `Get-EventLog` cmdlet. This cmdlet accepts a few switches that includes `LogName` and `EntryType`:

```
Get-EventLog -LogName Application -Newest 20 -EntryType Error
```

Some of the possible `LogName` values are follows:

▸ Application
▸ HardwareEvents
▸ Internet Explorer
▸ Security
▸ System
▸ Windows PowerShell

You can alternatively pass the name of a custom log that is available in your system to it.

The `EntryType` can be of the following types:

▸ Error
▸ FailureAudit
▸ Information
▸ SuccessAudit
▸ Warning

In this recipe, we also use the `-Newest` switch to filter only for the newest 20 error events.

An alternative way of using `Get-EventLog` is `Get-WinEvent`. Many administrators prefer this method, including our technical reviewer, Chrissy LeMaire, because it is more robust and faster. To use `Get-WinEvent` in order to get the five most recent entries in your `Application` log, you can use this command:

```
Get-WinEvent -LogName "Application" -MaxEvents 5 |
Sort-Object -Property TimeCreated -Descending
```

## There's more...

To learn more about the *Get-EventLog* cmdlet, visit `http://msdn.microsoft.com/en-us/library/hh849834`.

To learn more about *Get-WinEvent*, visit `https://technet.microsoft.com/en-us/library/hh849682.aspx`.

# Sending an e-mail

In this recipe, we send an e-mail with an attachment.

## Getting ready

Before proceeding, identify the following in your environment:

- An SMTP server
- A recipient's e-mail address
- A sender's e-mail address
- An attachment

## How to do it...

These are the steps required to send an e-mail:

1. Open **PowerShell ISE** as an administrator.
2. Add the following script and run it:

```
$file = "C:\Temp\processes.csv"
$timestamp = Get-Date -format "yyyy-MMM-dd-hhmmtt"

#note we are using backticks to put each parameter
#in its own line to make code more readable
```

```
Send-MailMessage `
-SmtpServer "queryworks.local" `
-To "administrator@queryworks.local" `
-From "powershell@sqlbelle.local" `
-Subject "Process Email - $file - $timestamp" `
-Body "Here ya go" `
-Attachments $file
```

## How it works...

One way to send an e-mail using PowerShell is using the `Send-MailMessage` cmdlet. Some of the switches it accepts are as follows:

- ► `-SmtpServer`
- ► `-To`
- ► `-Cc`
- ► `-Bcc`
- ► `-Credential`
- ► `-From`
- ► `-Subject`
- ► `-Body`
- ► `-Attachments`
- ► `-UseSsl`

## There's more...

To learn more about the `Send-MailMessage` cmdlet, visit `http://msdn.microsoft.com/en-us/library/hh849925.aspx`.

# Embedding C# code

In this recipe, we will embed and execute C# code in our PowerShell script.

## How to do it...

Let's explore how to embed C# code in PowerShell:

1. Open **PowerShell ISE** as an administrator.

2. Add the following script and run it:

```
#define code
#note this can also come from a file

$code = @"
using System;
public class HelloWorld
{
    public static string SayHello(string name)
    {
        return (String.Format("Hello there {0}", name));
    }
    public string GetLuckyNumber(string name)
    {
        Random random = new Random();
        int randomNumber = random.Next(0, 100);
        string message = String.Format("{0}, your lucky" +
                        " number for today is {1}",
                        name, randomNumber);
        return message;
    }
}
"@

#add this code to current session
Add-Type -TypeDefinition $code

#call static method
[HelloWorld]::SayHello("belle")

#create instance
$instance = New-Object HelloWorld

#call instance method
$instance.GetLuckyNumber("belle")
```

## How it works...

We can use C# code from within PowerShell. This will require constructing a class in a `here-string` and adding this class as a type to the session using the `Add-Type` cmdlet. The `Add-Type` cmdlet allows the construction of the class in the session, or to all sessions, if created within the PowerShell profile. This method of embedding C# code has been supported since PowerShell V2.

In the recipe, we use a very simple class defined in a `here-string`:

```
$code = @"
using System;
public class HelloWorld
{
    public static string SayHello(string name)
    {
        return (String.Format("Hello there {0}", name));
    }
    public string GetLuckyNumber(string name)
    {
        Random random = new Random();
        int randomNumber = random.Next(0, 100);
        string message = String.Format("{0}, your lucky" +
                        " number for today is {1}",
                        name, randomNumber);
        return message;
    }
}
"@
```

This code does not have to be built and hardcoded within the script. It can be read from another file using the `Get-Content` cmdlet and stored in the `$code` variable.

To put this class in effect in the current session, we use the `Add-Type` cmdlet:

```
#add this code to current session
Add-Type -TypeDefinition $code
```

Note that this class has both a static and nonstatic method. To call the static method, we must use the class name:

```
#call static method
[HelloWorld]::SayHello("belle")
```

To call the nonstatic method, we must first instantiate an object and then call the method using the object:

```
#call instance method
$instance.GetLuckyNumber("belle")
```

## There's more...

Refer to MSDN *Add-Type*, which is available at `http://msdn.microsoft.com/en-us/library/hh849914`.

# Creating an HTML report

In this recipe, we will create an HTML report based on the system's services.

## How to do it...

These are the steps required to create an HTML report using PowerShell:

1. Open **PowerShell ISE** as an administrator.

2. Add the following script and run it:

```
#simple CSS Style
$style = @"
<style type='text/css'>
  td {border:1px solid gray;}
  .stopped{background-color: #E01B1B;}
</style>
"@


#let's get content from Get-Service
#and output this to a styled HTML
Get-Service |
ConvertTo-Html -Property Name, Status -Head $style |
Foreach-Object {
    #if service is running, use green background
    if ($_ -like "*<td>Stopped</td>*")
    {
      $_ -replace "<tr>", "<tr class='stopped'>"
    }
    else
    {
      #display normally
      $_
    }
  } |
Out-File "C:\Temp\sample.html" -force

#open the page in Internet Explorer
Set-Alias ie "$env:programfiles\Internet Explorer\iexplore.exe"
ie "C:\Temp\sample.html"
```

The following screenshot shows a sample result:

## How it works...

In this recipe, we piped the result of the Get-Service cmdlet, which returns all services, into the ConvertTo-HTML cmdlet. The ConvertTo-HTML cmdlet formats the results as HTML. This cmdlet also allows you to configure what goes into an HTML <head> tag. This is where you can typically add your CSS styles and JavaScript.

Once the file has been created, we set an alias to Internet Explorer and just display the resulting HTML file in the browser.

## There's more...

To learn more about the *ConvertTo-HTML* cmdlet, visit http://msdn.microsoft.com/en-us/library/hh849944.

# Parsing XML

In this recipe, we will parse sample XML using PowerShell.

## Getting ready

In this recipe, we will use Vancouver's 2012 daily weather data, which can be downloaded from `http://www.climate.weatheroffice.gc.ca/climateData/dailydata_e.html?Prov=BC&StationID=889&Year=2012&Month=4&Day=30&timeframe=2.`

## How to do it...

Let's take a look at how we can parse XML files:

1. Open **PowerShell ISE** as an administrator.

2. Add the following script and run it:

```
$vancouverXML = "C:\XML Files\eng-daily-01012012-12312012.xml"

$uri = "http://climate.weather.gc.ca/climateData/bulkdata_e.html?f
ormat=xml&stationID=889&Year=2012&Month=4&Day=1&timeframe=2&submit
=Download+Data"

#download Vancouver weather into XML file
Invoke-WebRequest -Uri $uri -OutFile $vancouverXML

[xml] $xml = Get-Content $vancouverXML

#get number of entries
$xml.climatedata.stationdata.Count

#store max temps in array
$maxtemp = $xml.climatedata.stationdata |
Foreach-Object
{
    [int]$_.maxtemp."#text"
}

#list all daily max temperatures
$maxtemp |
Sort-Object -Descending

#get max temperature recorded in 2012
$maxtemp |
Sort-Object -Descending |
Select-Object -First 1
```

## How it works...

Using `Invoke-WebRequest`, we can download the data we want to work with, to an XML file that is saved locally on our system:

```
$vancouverXML = "C:\XML Files\eng-daily-01012012-12312012.xml"

$uri = "http://climate.weather.gc.ca/climateData/bulkdata_e.html?format=xml&stationID=889&Year=2012&Month=4&Day=1&timeframe=2&submit=Download+Data"

#download Vancouver weather into XML file
Invoke-WebRequest -Uri $uri -OutFile $vancouverXML
```

One of the key things to do when working with XML data is to make sure the data is stored as an XML object. In our recipe, we get the contents of the file using `Get-Content`, and store it in the strongly typed `$xml` variable. We know that it is strongly typed because we have placed the `[xml]` data type at the time of declaring a variable :

```
$vancouverXML = "C:\XML Files\eng-daily-01012012-12312012.xml"
[xml] $xml = Get-Content $vancouverXML
```

The following screenshot is an example of how the file is formatted:

```
<?xml version="1.0" encoding="UTF-8"?>
- <climatedata
xsd:schemaLocation="http://www.climate.weatheroffice.gc.ca/climateData/bulkxml/bulkschema.xsd"
xmlns:xsd="http://www.w3.org/TR/xmlschema-1/">
    <lang>ENG</lang>
  - <stationinformation>
        <name>VANCOUVER INT'L A</name>
        <province>BRITISH COLUMBIA</province>
        <latitude>49.20</latitude>
        <longitude>-123.18</longitude>
        <elevation>4.30</elevation>
        <climate_identifier>1108447</climate_identifier>
        <wmo_identifier/>
        <tc_identifier>YVR</tc_identifier>
    </stationinformation>
  + <legend>
  - <stationdata year="2012" month="1" day="1">
        <maxtemp units="°C" description="Maximum Temperature">6.4</maxtemp>
        <mintemp units="°C" description="Minimum Temperature">1.3</mintemp>
        <meantemp units="°C" description="Mean Temperature">3.9</meantemp>
        <heatdegdays units="°C" description="Heating Degree Days">14.1</heatdegdays>
        <cooldegdays units="°C" description="Cooling Degree Days">0.0</cooldegdays>
        <totalrain units="mm" description="Total Rain">0.2</totalrain>
        <totalsnow units="cm" description="Total Snow">0.0</totalsnow>
        <totalprecipitation units="mm" description="Total Precipitation">0.2</totalprecipitation>
        <snowonground units="cm" description="Snow on Ground">0</snowonground>
        <dirofmaxgust units="10s Deg" description="Direction of Maximum Gust"/>
        <speedofmaxgust units="km/h" description="Speed of Maximum Gust"><31</speedofmaxgust>
    </stationdata>
```

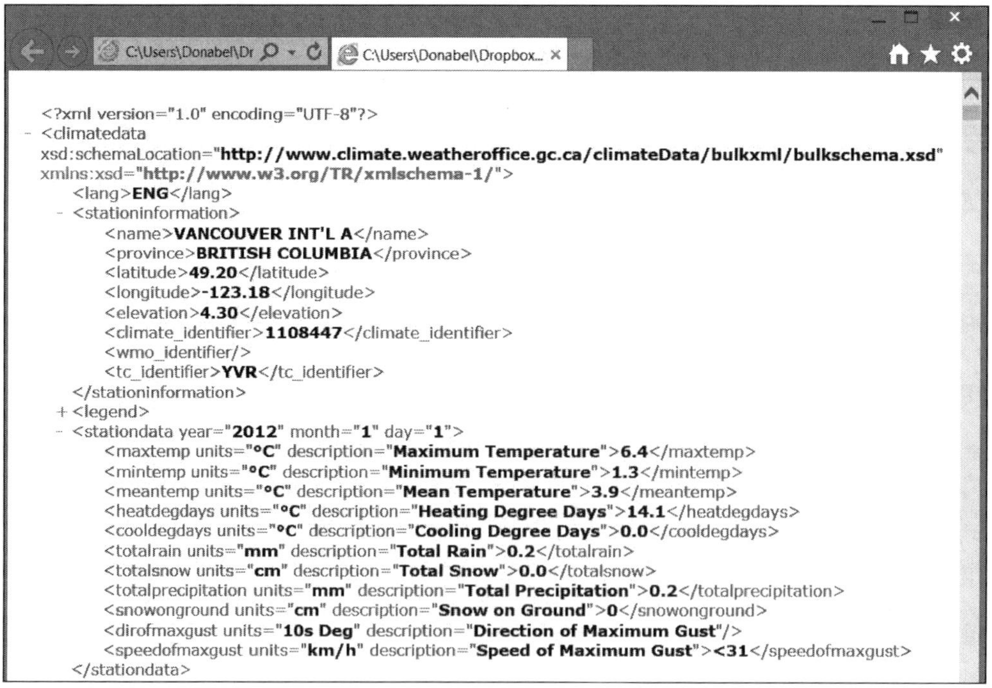

To know how many records are in the file, we can traverse the `stationdata` nodes and count the records:

```
#get number of entries
$xml.climatedata.stationdata.Count
```

To manipulate the `maxtemp` data, we can loop through all the nodes and extract the values to an array:

```
#store max temps in array
$maxtemp = $xml.climatedata.stationdata |
Foreach-Object
{
    [int]$_.maxtemp."#text"
}
```

In an array, we can further manipulate it. For example, we can now easily sort as needed, or get the overall maximum value if required:

```
#list all daily max temperatures
$maxtemp |
Sort-Object -Descending

#get max temperature recorded in 2012
$maxtemp |
Sort-Object -Descending |
Select-Object -First 1
```

# Extracting data from a web service

In this recipe, we will extract data from a free, public web service.

## How to do it...

Let's explore how to access and retrieve data from a web service:

1. Open **PowerShell ISE** as an administrator.

2. Add the following script and run it:

```
#delayed stock quote URI
$stockUri = "http://ws.cdyne.com/delayedstockquote/
delayedstockquote.asmx"
```

```
$stockproxy = New-WebServiceProxy -Uri $stockUri
-UseDefaultCredential

#get quote
$stockresult = $stockProxy.GetQuote("MSFT","")

#display results
$stockresult.StockSymbol
$stockresult.DayHigh
$stockresult.DayLow
$stockresult.LastTradeDateTime
```

## How it works...

To work with a web service, we first need to create a proxy object that will allow us to access the methods available in a web service. We can achieve this using the `New-WebProxy` cmdlet, which accepts the web service URI:

```
$stockUri = "http://ws.cdyne.com/delayedstockquote/delayedstockquote.asmx"
```

This URI points to a free web service that provides delayed stock quote values. If we go to this URI from the browser, this is what we are going to see:

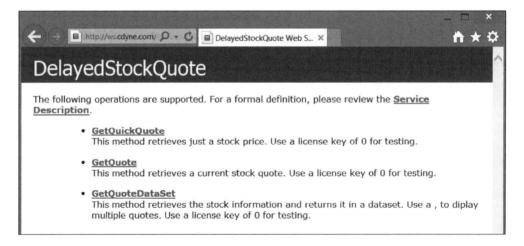

We can see that this web service has a method called `GetQuote`, which retrieves the current stock quote. This accepts a stock symbol and license key. In our script, we call this method using our proxy object:

```
#get quote
$stockresult = $stockProxy.GetQuote("MSFT","")
```

If we were to plug these values into the browser, this is a sample result that we might get:

To display these in our script, we simply need to know how to traverse the nodes, from the root to the values we want to display. In our case, we want to display to `StockSymbol`, `DayHigh`, `DayLow`, and `LastTradeDateTime`:

```
#display results
$stockresult.StockSymbol
$stockresult.DayHigh
$stockresult.DayLow
$stockresult.LastTradeDateTime
```

## There's more...

To learn more about the `New-WebServiceProxy` cmdlet, visit `http://msdn.microsoft.com/en-us/library/hh849841`.

If you encounter errors on namespaces, you may need to dynamically generate them in your PowerShell script instead of relying on the default namespace. Here is an article on how to resolve dynamic namespaces in SSRS at `http://sqlbelle.com/2012/02/04/resolving-ssrs-and-powershell-new-webserviceproxy-namespace-issue/`.

Patrik Lindström also addressed a similar issue on how to resolve namespaces in Stack Overflow at `http://stackoverflow.com/questions/12516512/in-powershell-to-consume-a-soap-complextype-to-keep-a-soap-service-hot/12528404#12528404`.

# Using PowerShell remoting

In this recipe, we will use PowerShell remoting to execute commands on a remote machine.

## Getting ready

To work with remoting in PowerShell, we first need to identify which remote machine we want to use. In this recipe, we will assume that there are two machines in the same domain that we can use.

Log in to the machine you want to use for remoting. We will refer to this as `<Remote Machine Name>`. PowerShell remoting needs to be enabled on this machine.

 Check out the system and permission requirements for running PowerShell remoting from MSDN *about_Remote_Requirements* (`http://msdn.microsoft.com/en-us/library/hh847859.aspx`).

To turn on remoting, open the PowerShell console in `<Remote Machine Name>` using elevated privileges. Right-click on the PowerShell console and go to **Run as Administrator**. Execute the following command:

```
PS> Enable-PSRemoting
```

You will be prompted to confirm the changes a couple of times. Answer `A` (or `Yes to All`) to these questions.

The remote computer `<Remote Machine Name>` also needs to be added as a trusted host. Open a PowerShell console as an administrator from the local machine and run the following command:

```
Set-Item wsman:localhost\client\trustedhosts -value <Remote Machine Name>
```

## How to do it...

Let's explore how to access and retrieve data from a web service:

1. Open a PowerShell console as an administrator from the local machine. Right-click on the PowerShell console icon and select **Run as administrator**.

2. Let's first execute a remote command:

```
Invoke-Command -ComputerName <Remote Machine Name> -Credential
"QUERYWORKS\Administrator" -ScriptBlock {
   Get-Wmiobject win32_computersystem
}
```

3. Next, let's start an interactive remoting session to the remote machine name. We will provide our credentials to the machine by specifying the `-Credential` parameter:

```
Enter-PSSession -ComputerName <Remote Machine Name> -Credential
"QUERYWORKS\Administrator"
```

Note that as soon as we are authenticated, the prompt changes to indicate that we are now in the remote machine.

4. Let's execute a simple command in our remoting session. Execute the following command:

```
Get-Wmiobject win32_computersystem
```

You will see the results of Get-WmiObject, but note that the prompt still displays the remote machine name.

5. Exit out of the session by typing exit.

## How it works...

PowerShell remoting allows you to connect and execute PowerShell commands on remote machines. PowerShell remoting uses **Web Services for Management** (**WSMan**) to communicate with a remote machine, and **Windows Remote Management** (**WinRM**) service on the remote machine to listen for incoming WSMan requests.

There are different ways to execute remote commands. We can use the `Invoke-Command` cmdlet to establish a remote connection, execute our command(s) and get our results, and disconnect. The command(s) we want to execute can either be placed in the `-ScriptBlock` parameter or in a file specified with the `-FilePath` parameter. In our recipe, we used `-ScriptBlock`:

```
Invoke-Command -ComputerName <Remote Machine Name> -Credential
"QUERYWORKS\Administrator" -Authentication Negotiate -ScriptBlock {
   Get-Wmiobject win32_computersystem
}
```

We have also chosen to provide our credentials to `<Remote Machine Name>` by specifying the `-Credential` parameter. You can choose to prompt for both username and password using the `Get-Credential` cmdlet, and passing this to the `Invoke-Command`:

```
$credential = Get-Credential
```

Another way to execute a remote command is by establishing an interactive session in a remote machine. We do this using the `Enter-PSSession` cmdlet:

```
Enter-PSSession -ComputerName <Remote Machine Name> -Credential
"QUERYWORKS\Administrator" -Authentication Negotiate
```

Once the remoting interactive session is started, you will notice that the PowerShell prompt changes to show the remote computer's name. We can then start executing commands in this session.

What we've shown in this recipe is just a very brief example of how you can use PowerShell remoting. To learn more about PowerShell remoting, including system and permission requirements, how to set up HTTPS, and so on, make sure that you check the recommended additional resources in the *There's more...* section.

## There's more...

The following links will help you understand and work with PowerShell remoting:

- ▶ MSDN remoting requirements are available at `http://msdn.microsoft.com/en-us/library/hh847859.aspx`.

- ▶ *Layman's Guide to PowerShell 2.0 Remoting* by Ravikanth Chaganti `http://www.ravichaganti.com/blog/?p=1305`.

- ▶ *An Introduction to PowerShell Remoting* (5-part series):
    - ❏ `http://blogs.technet.com/b/heyscriptingguy/archive/2012/07/23/an-introduction-to-powershell-remoting-part-one.aspx`
    - ❏ `http://blogs.technet.com/b/heyscriptingguy/archive/2012/07/24/an-introduction-to-powershell-remoting-part-two-configuring-powershell-remoting.aspx`
    - ❏ `http://blogs.technet.com/b/heyscriptingguy/archive/2012/07/25/an-introduction-to-powershell-remoting-part-three-interactive-and-fan-out-remoting.aspx`

- ❏ http://blogs.technet.com/b/heyscriptingguy/
  archive/2012/07/26/an-introduction-to-powershell-
  remoting-part-four-sessions-and-implicit-remoting.aspx

- ❏ http://blogs.technet.com/b/heyscriptingguy/
  archive/2012/07/27/an-introduction-to-powershell-
  remoting-part-five-constrained-powershell-endpoints.aspx

▸ *Secrets of PowerShell Remoting* at https://www.penflip.com/
  powershellorg/secrets-of-powershell-remoting.

# PowerShell Primer

In this appendix, we will cover the following topics:

- Understanding the need for PowerShell
- Setting up the environment
- Running PowerShell scripts
- Learning PowerShell basics
- Understanding a scripting syntax
- Converting scripts into functions
- Listing notable PowerShell features
- Learning more about PowerShell

## Introduction

This appendix is a very short primer to get you up and running with PowerShell. We cover the basics of the language and syntax; however, we will not go into in-depth details and variations.

## Understanding the need for PowerShell

PowerShell is both a scripting environment and scripting language meant to support administrators and developers alike in automating and integrating processes and environments.

You may already be familiar with other tools or languages that will help you accomplish your task, and you may be asking why you should even bother learning PowerShell. It is important to note that PowerShell is just another tool, but it can be a very powerful one if used in the appropriate situations.

There are different reasons for using PowerShell, which are as follows:

- **Running a script is faster than clicking on an application's user interface**: If we minimize clicks, or eliminate them in some cases, the task can potentially be done much faster. Think about compressing, copying, archiving, and renaming multiple files. If we had to rely on the UI, this task may take much longer. However, if we can bake the logic into a script that performs all the steps, we can run this script when we need to do the same task. We would be faster and more efficient in accomplishing this task.

- **Learning and mastering one language instead of five or ten**: Instead of using a duct-taped mishmash of scripting languages (batch file for some items, VBScript, Perl, and COM), we can now use one single language to handle most tasks. PowerShell is supported by different Microsoft applications through libraries of cmdlets that come with applications, such as Microsoft Exchange, SharePoint, and SQL Server. This makes integration and automation among these products easier and more seamless.

- **Leveraging the .NET library**: The .NET library provides a rich collection of classes that pretty much covers most programmatic items you can think of such as forms, database connectivity, networking, and so on.

- **Taking advantage of the fact that PowerShell is already built into and supported in different applications**: More and more Microsoft products are being shipped with a growing number of PowerShell cmdlets because PowerShell scripting is part of Microsoft's **Common Engineering Criteria** program (`https://technet.microsoft.com/en-us/library/ff460855.aspx`). Windows Server, Exchange, Active Directory, SharePoint, and SQL Server, to name a few, all have some PowerShell support.

# Setting up the environment

Before we can start talking about PowerShell, we first need to make sure you have access to an environment that has PowerShell.

PowerShell V5 comes natively with these operating systems: Windows 8 and Windows Server 2012. You can also install PowerShell V5 on Windows 7, Windows Server 2008, and Windows Server 2008 R2 by installing the Windows Management Framework 5.0, which contains PowerShell V5.

# Running PowerShell scripts

It is now time to run your script. In the following sections, we will see how you can run your PowerShell scripts through the command shell or the **Integrated Scripting Environment** (**ISE**).

## Through shell or through the ISE

You can run ad hoc commands using the shell or the **Integrated Scripting Environment** (**ISE**).

Depending on your operating system, you may have a different navigation path to open the PowerShell console. An easy way is to use Windows **Search** to look for **Windows PowerShell**. Often, when managing your servers or performing administrative tasks, you will need to run PowerShell as an administrator. To do this, right-click on PowerShell and select **Run as administrator**.

Once the console is ready, you can type your commands and press *Enter* to see the results. For example, to display 10 running processes, you can use the `Get-Process` cmdlet, as shown in the following screenshot:

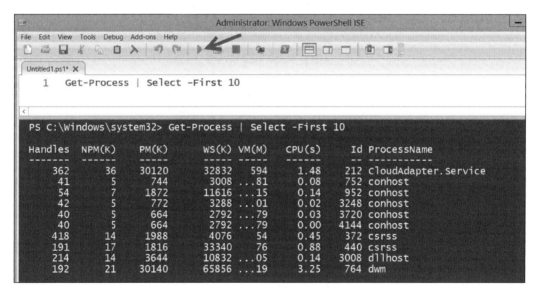

You can also use the ISE to perform this task. Search for the PowerShell ISE and launch it as an administrator. The ISE comes with a script editor, where you can type your command and press the run button (the green arrow icon).

Typically, you can save your commands in a script file with the `.ps1` extension, and run them from the shell in any of a few different ways:

1.  From the PowerShell console, run the following command:

    ```
    PS C:\PowerShell> .\My Script.ps1"
    ```

2.  From the PowerShell console, using the (`&`) call operator:

    ```
    PS C:\ >&"C:\PowerShell\My Script.ps1"
    ```

3.  From the PowerShell console, using dot sourcing. Dot sourcing simply means that you prepend a dot and space to your invocation. You can invoke your script using dot sourcing to persist variables and functions in your session:

    ```
    PS C:\PowerShell > . ".\My Script.ps1"
    PS C:\> . "C:\PowerShell\My Script.ps1"
    ```

4.  From Command Prompt, run the following command:

    ```
    C:\ >powershell.exe -ExecutionPolicyRemoteSigned -File
    "C:\PowerShell\My Script.ps1"
    ```

> Learn more about advantages and disadvantages of dot sourcing from the article by Ed Wilson, also known as the Microsoft Scripting Guy, in his article *Hey, Scripting Guy! Why Would I Even Want to Use Functions in My Windows PowerShell Scripts?* at `http://blogs.technet.com/b/heyscriptingguy/archive/2009/12/23/hey-scripting-guy-december-23-2009.aspx`.

# The execution policy

PowerShell scripts are not authorized to *just run*. We learned in IT that *trusting* scripts and authorizing them to launch and run automatically can create havoc in systems, particularly because of the prevalence of malicious scripts and code. Remember the infamous *I Love You* virus (`https://en.wikipedia.org/wiki/ILOVEYOU`). It took off because, at that time, it was so easy to launch a script just by double-clicking on the `.vbs` file.

To avoid problems such as these, PowerShell scripts by default are blocked from running. This means that you cannot just accidentally double-click on a PowerShell script and execute it.

The rules that determine which PowerShell scripts can run are contained in the execution policy. This will need to be set ahead of time. The different settings are explained in the following table:

| | |
|---|---|
| `Restricted` | This is the default execution policy. PowerShell will not run any scripts. |
| `AllSigned` | PowerShell will run only signed scripts. |
| `RemoteSigned` | PowerShell will run signed scripts or locally created scripts. |
| `Unrestricted` | PowerShell will run any scripts, signed or not. |
| `Bypass` | PowerShell will not block any scripts and will prevent any prompts or warnings. |
| `Undefined` | PowerShell will remove the set execution policy in the current user scope. |

To determine what your current setting is, you can use the `Get-ExecutionPolicy` cmdlet:

```
PS C:\>Get-ExecutionPolicy
```

If you try to run a script without setting the proper execution policy, you may get an error, which is similar to the following:

**File C:\Sample Script.ps1 cannot be loaded because the execution of scripts is disabled on this system. For more information, see about_execution_policies.**

To change the execution policy, use `Set-ExecutionPolicy` as follows:

```
PS C:\>Set-ExecutionPolicyRemoteSigned
```

Typically, if you need to run a script that does a lot of administrative tasks, you will run the script as an administrator.

To learn more about execution policies, run the following script:

```
helpabout_execution_policies
```

For more information on how to sign your script, use the following command:

```
helpabout_signing
```

# Learning PowerShell basics

Let's explore some PowerShell basic concepts.

# Cmdlets

**Cmdlets**, pronounced as **"commandlets"**, are the foundation of PowerShell. Cmdlets are *small commands* or specialized commands. The naming convention for cmdlets follows the verb-noun format, such as `Get-Command` or `Invoke-Expression`. PowerShell V3 boasts a lot of new cmdlets, including cmdlets to manipulate JSON (`ConvertFrom-Json` and `ConvertTo-Json`), web services (`Invoke-RestMethod` and `Invoke-WebRequest`), and background jobs (`Register-JobEvent`, `Resume-Job`, and `Suspend-Job`). In addition to built-in cmdlets, there are also downloadable community PowerShell extensions such as SQLPSX, which can be downloaded from `http://sqlpsx.codeplex.com/`.

Many cmdlets accept parameters. Parameters can either be specified by a name or position. Let's take a look at a specific example. The syntax for the `Get-ChildItem` cmdlet is as follows:

```
Get-ChildItem [[-Path] <string[]>] [[-Filter] <string>]
[-Include <string[]>] [-Exclude <string[]>]
[-Recurse] [-Force] [-Name]
[-UseTransaction] [<CommonParameters>]
```

The `Get-ChildItem` cmdlet gets all the *children* in a specified path. For example, to get all files with a `.txt` extension in the `C:\Temp` folder, we can use `Get-ChildItem` with the –`Path` and –`Filter` parameters:

```
Get-ChildItem-Path"C:\Temp"-Filter"*.csv"
```

We can alternatively omit the parameter names by passing the parameter values by position. When passing parameters by position, the order in which the values are passed matters. They need to be in the same order in which the parameters are defined in the `Get-ChildItem` cmdlet:

```
Get-ChildItem"C:\Temp""*.csv"
```

To learn the order in which parameters are expected to come, you can use the `Get-Help` cmdlet:

```
Get-Help Get-ChildItem
```

# Learning PowerShell

The best way to learn PowerShell is to explore the cmdlets and try them out as you learn them. The best way to learn is to explore. Young Jedi, you need to get acquainted with these three cmdlets: `Get-Command`, `Get-Help`, and `Get-Member`.

## Get-Command

There are a lot of cmdlets and this list is just going to get bigger. It will be hard to remember all the cmdlets except for the handful that you use day in and day out. To help you look for cmdlets, besides using the search engine, you can use the `Get-Command` cmdlet.

To list all cmdlets, run this command:

```
Get-Command
```

To list cmdlets with names that match some string patterns, you can use the `-Name` parameter and the asterisk (*) wildcard:

```
Get-Command-Name"*Event*"
```

To get cmdlets from a specific module, run the following command:

```
Get-Command-ModuleSQLASCMDLETS
```

## Get-Help

Now that you've found the command you're looking for, how do you use it? The best way to get help is to use `Get-Help` (no pun intended). The `Get-Help` cmdlet provides the syntax of a cmdlet, examples, and some additional notes or links wherever available:

```
Get-Help Backup-SqlDatabase
Get-Help Backup-SqlDatabase-Examples
Get-Help Backup-SqlDatabase-Detailed
Get-Help Backup-SqlDatabase-Full
```

The different parameters: `Examples`, `Detailed`, `Full`, and `Online` will determine the amount of information that will be displayed. The `Online` parameter opens up the online help in a browser.

You may get prompted to download the updated help. You can download it when you are prompted, or you can preempt this by downloading the help files before you use `Get-Help` using the `Update-Help` cmdlet.

You can find the syntax for `Get-Help` at `https://technet.microsoft.com/en-us/library/hh849720.aspx`.

Only certain topics are supported using the `-Online` switch. This is a known issue. You can find more information on the Microsoft Connect item at `https://connect.microsoft.com/PowerShell/feedback/details/781697/get-help-online-doesnt-work-for-some-topics`.

## Get-Member

To really understand a command or object and explore what's available, you can use the `Get-Member` cmdlet. This will list all the properties and methods of an object, or anything incoming from the pipeline:

```
$dt= (Get-Date)
$dt| Get-Member
```

## Starter notes

We're almost ready to start learning the syntax. However, here are a few last notes, some things to keep in mind about PowerShell as you learn it. Keep a mental note of these items, and you're ready to go full-steam ahead.

### PowerShell is object-oriented and works with .NET

PowerShell works with objects and can take advantage of the objects' methods and properties. PowerShell can also leverage the ever-growing .NET framework library. It can import any of the .NET classes, and reuse any of the already available classes.

You can find out the base class of an object using the `GetType` method, which comes with all objects:

```
$dt= Get-Date
$dt.GetType() #DateTime is the base type
```

To investigate an object, you can always use the `Get-Member` cmdlet:

```
$dt| Get-Member
```

To leverage the .NET libraries, you can import them in your script. A sample import of the .NET libraries is as follows:

```
#load the Windows.Forms assembly
Add-Type -AssemblyName"System.Windows.Forms"
```

There will be cases when you may have multiple versions of the same assembly name. In these cases, you will need to specify the strong name of the assembly with the `Add-Type` cmdlet. This means that you will need to supply the `AssemblyName`, `Version`, `Culture`, and `PublicKeyToken` parameters:

```
#load the ReportViewerWinForms assembly
Add-Type -AssemblyName"Microsoft.ReportViewer.WinForms,
Version=12.0.0.0, Culture=neutral,
PublicKeyToken=89845dcd8080cc91"
```

To determine the strong name, you can open `C:\Windows\assembly` and navigate to the assembly you want to load. You can either check the displayed properties or right-click on the particular assembly and select **Properties**.

| Assembly Name | Version | Cu... | Public Key Token | Proce... |
|---|---|---|---|---|
| Microsoft.ReportViewer.ProcessingO... | 12.0.0.0 | | 89845dcd8080cc91 | MSIL |
| Microsoft.ReportViewer.ProcessingO... | 10.0.0.0 | | b03f5f7f11d50a3a | MSIL |
| Microsoft.ReportViewer.WebDesign | 12.0.0.0 | | 89845dcd8080cc91 | MSIL |
| Microsoft.ReportViewer.WebForms | 12.0.0.0 | | 89845dcd8080cc91 | MSIL |
| Microsoft.ReportViewer.WebForms | 10.0.0.0 | | b03f5f7f11d50a3a | MSIL |
| Microsoft.ReportViewer.WinForms | 12.0.0.0 | | 89845dcd8080cc91 | MSIL |
| Microsoft.ReportViewer.WinForms | 10.0.0.0 | | b03f5f7f11d50a3a | MSIL |
| Microsoft.ServiceHosting.Tools.Deve... | 1.0.0.0 | | 31bf3856ad364e35 | MSIL |

## Cmdlets may have aliases or you can create one

We may already know some scripting or programming languages and may already have preferences on how we do things. For example, when listing directories from Command Prompt, we may be on autopilot when we type `dir`. In PowerShell, listing directories can be accomplished by the `Get-ChildItem` cmdlet. Don't worry, you can still use `dir` if you prefer. If there is another name you want to use instead of `Get-ChildItem`, you can create your own alias.

To find out aliases of a cmdlet, you can use `Get-Alias`. For example, to get the aliases of `Get-ChildItem`, you can execute the following command:

```
Get-Alias-Definition"Get-ChildItem"
```

To create your own alias, you can use `New-Alias`:

```
New-Alias"list" Get-ChildItem
```

Here are some of the common aliases already built-in in PowerShell:

| Cmdlet | Alias |
|---|---|
| Foreach-Object | %, Foreach |
| Where-Object | ?, Where |
| Sort-Object | Sort |
| Compare-Object | compare, diff |

| Cmdlet | Alias |
|---|---|
| Write-Output | echo, write |
| Get-Help | help, man |
| Get-Content | cat, gc, type |
| Get-ChildItem | dir, gci, ls |
| Copy-Item | copy, cp, cpi |
| Move-Item | mi, move, mv |
| Remove-Item | del, erase, rd, ri, rm, rmdir |
| Get-Process | gps, ps |
| Stop-Process | kill, spps |
| Get-Location | gl, pwd |
| Set-Location | cd, chdir, sl |
| Clear-Host | clear, cls |
| Get-History | h, ghy, history |

## You can chain commands

You can take the result from one command and use it as an input to another command. The operator to chain commands is a vertical bar ( | ) called a pipe. This feature to chain commands makes PowerShell really powerful. This can also make your statements more concise.

If you are familiar with the Unix/Linux environment, pipes are must-haves and are incredibly valuable tools.

Let's take a look at an example. Let's export the newest log entries (only time and source fields) to a text file in the JSON format:

1. We need to get the newest log entries:

   ```
   Get-EventLog -LogNameApplication -Newest 10
   ```

2. We need only the time and source fields. Based on what we get from the previous step, we need to execute the following command:

   ```
   Select Time, Source
   ```

3. We need to convert to JSON. Using the previous step's results as input, we need to execute this command:

   ```
   ConvertTo-Json
   ```

4. We need to save it to a file. We now want to take what we have in step 3 and put it into a file:

   ```
   Out-File-FilePath"C:\Temp\json.txt"-Force
   ```

5. The complete command will be as follows:

```
Get-EventLog -LogNameApplication -Newest 10|
Select-ObjectTime,Source|
ConvertTo-Json|
Out-File -FilePath"C:\Temp\json.txt" -Force
```

This is just a simple example of how you can chain commands, but this should give you an idea of how it can be done.

## Filter left, format right

When you chain commands, especially when your last actions are for formatting the result, you want to do this as efficiently as possible. Otherwise, you may use a lot of resources to format data and end up only needing to display a few. It is best to first trim your data, before you pass them down the pipeline for formatting.

## Package and reuse

Functions and modules allow you to package up the logic you built in your scripts and put it in reusable structures. A function can be simply described as a "*callable*" code block. A module allows you to put together a library of variables and functions that can be loaded into any session and allows you to use these variables and functions.

Your goal should be to package up most of what you've already built in scripts, put it into functions, and later compile them into a module. As a best practice, you should make a habit of making your functions return objects so that they can be combined with other scripts and behave like regular cmdlets.

 Converting your scripts into functions is tackled at a later section in this appendix.

## Common cmdlets

Typically, cmdlets are categorized into their main purpose or functionality based on the verb used in their name. Here is a partial list of cmdlets to explore. Note that many cmdlet names are self-documenting:

| Utility | ▸ ConvertFrom-Csv |
| --- | --- |
| | ▸ ConvertFrom-Json |
| | ▸ ConvertTo-Csv |
| | ▸ ConvertTo-Html |
| | ▸ ConvertTo-Json |
| | ▸ ConvertTo-Xml |
| | ▸ Export-Clixml |
| | ▸ Export-Csv |
| | ▸ Format-List |
| | ▸ Format-Table |
| | ▸ Get-Alias |
| | ▸ Get-Date |
| | ▸ Get-Member |
| | ▸ Import-Clixml |
| | ▸ Import-Csv |
| | ▸ Read-Host |
| Management | ▸ Get-ChildItem |
| | ▸ Get-Content |
| | ▸ Get-EventLog |
| | ▸ Get-HotFix |
| | ▸ Get-Process |
| | ▸ Get-Service |
| | ▸ Get-WmiObject |
| | ▸ New-WebServiceProxy |
| | ▸ Start-Process |
| | ▸ Start-Service |
| Security | ▸ ConvertFrom-SecureString |
| | ▸ ConvertTo-SecureString |
| | ▸ Get-Credential |
| | ▸ Get-ExecutionPolicy |
| | ▸ Set-ExecutionPolicy |

# Scripting syntax

We will now dive into the specifics of the PowerShell syntax.

## Statement terminators

A semicolon is typically a mandatory statement terminator in many programming and scripting languages. PowerShell considers both a **newline** and **semicolon** as statement terminators, although using the newline is more common. The caveat for using the newline is that the previous line must be a complete statement before it gets executed.

## Escape and line continuation

The **backtick** (`` ` ``) is a peculiar character in PowerShell, and it has a double meaning. You can typically find this character on your keyboard above the left *Tab* key, and it is on the same key as the tilde ~ symbol.

The backtick is the escape character in PowerShell. Some of the common characters that need to be escaped are as follows:

| Escaped character | Description |
|---|---|
| `` `n `` | Newline |
| `` `r `` | Carriage return |
| `` `' `` | Single quote |
| `` `" `` | Double quote |
| `` `0 `` | Null |

PowerShell also uses the backtick (`` ` ``) as a line continuation character.

A technical reviewer, Chrissy LeMaire, points out an interesting fact about the backtick. It is used as a line continuation character because it actually escapes the newline. Interesting tidbit!

You may find yourself writing a long chain of commands and may want to put different parts of the command into different lines to make the code more readable. If you do so, you need to make sure to put a backtick at the end of each line you are continuing; otherwise, PowerShell treats the newline as a statement terminator. You also need to make sure that there are not any extra spaces after the backtick:

```
Invoke-Sqlcmd `
-Query $query `
-ServerInstance $instanceName `
-Database $dbName
```

## Variables

Variables are placeholders for values. Variables in PowerShell start with a dollar ($) sign:

```
$a=10
```

By default, variables are loosely and dynamically typed, which means that the variable assumes the data type based on the value of the content:

```
$a=10
$a.GetType()    #Int32

$a="Hello"
$a.GetType()    #String

$a=Get-Date
$a.GetType()    #DateTime
```

Note how the data type changes based on the value we assign to the variable. You can, however, create strongly typed variables:

```
[int]$a=10
$a.GetType()    #Int32
```

When we have a strongly typed variable, we can no longer just haphazardly assign it any value. If we do, we will get an error:

```
$a="Hello"

<# Error
Cannot convert value "Hello" to type "System.Int32". Error: "Input
string was not in a correct format."
At line:3char:1
+ $a = "Hello"
+ ~~~~~~~~~~~~
```

```
    + CategoryInfo          : MetadataError: (:) [],
ArgumentTransformationMetadataException
    + FullyQualifiedErrorId : RuntimeException
#>
```

We have also mentioned in the previous section that PowerShell is object oriented. Variables in PowerShell are automatically created as objects. Depending on the data type, variables are packaged with their own attributes and methods. To explore what properties and methods are available with a data type, use the Get-Member cmdlet:

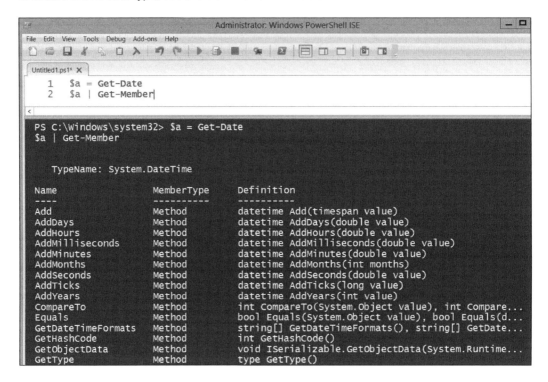

## Here-string

There may be times when you need to create a string variable that will contain multiple lines of code. You should create these as here-string.

A here-string data type is a string that often contains large blocks of text. It starts with @" and must end with a line that contains only "@ . For here-string terminating characters, make sure this is placed in its own line and there are no other characters and no spaces before or after it:

```
$query=@"
INSERT INTO SampleXML
```

```
(FileName,XMLStuff,FileExtension)
VALUES('$xmlfile','$xml','$fileextension')
"@
```

## String interpolation

When working with strings, you need to remember that using a double quote evaluates enclosed variables, that is, variables are replaced with their values. For example, run the following code snippet:

```
$today= Get-Date
Write-Host "Today is $today"

#result
#Today is 07/04/2015 19:48:24
```

This behavior may sometimes cause issues especially if you need to use multiple variables in continuation; as in the following case, where we want to combine $name, underscore (_), $ts, and .txt to create a timestamped filename:

```
$name = "belle"
$ts = Get-Date -Format yyyy-MMM-dd
$filename = ""$name_$ts.txt""


$filename = "$($name)_$($ts).txt"
Write-Host $filename
```

This will give an incorrect result because it will look for $name_ and $ts, but since it cannot find $name_, the final filename that we get is 2015-Jul-04.txt and not belle_2015-Jul-04.txt.

To resolve this issue, we can use any of the following to ensure proper interpolation:

```
$filename = "$($name)_$($ts).txt"
Write-Host $filename

$filename = "${name}_${ts}.txt"
Write-Host $filename

$filename = "{0}_{1}.txt" -f $name, $ts
Write-Host $filename
```

A single quote, on the other hand, preserves the actual variable name and does not interpolate the value:

```
$today= Get-Date
Write-Host 'Today is $today'

#result
#Today is $today
```

You can also store actual commands in a string. However, this is treated as a string unless you prepend it with an ampersand (`&`), which is PowerShell's invoke or call operator:

```
$cmd="Get-Process"

$cmd#just displays Get-Process, treated as string
&$cmd#actually executes Get-Process
```

## Operators

The operators used in PowerShell may not be readily familiar to you even if you have already done some programming before. This is because the operators in PowerShell do not use the common operator symbols.

| PowerShell | Traditional | Meaning |
|---|---|---|
| `-eq` | `==` | Equal to |
| `-ne` | `<> or !=` | Not equal to |
| `-match`<br>`-notmatch` | | Match using regex; searches anywhere in a string |
| `-contains`<br>`-notcontains` | | Check whether the match exists in the collection or array. |
| `-like`<br>`-notlike` | | Wildcard match<br>asterisk (*) for zero or more characters<br>question mark (?) for any single character |
| `-clike`<br>`-cnotlike` | | Case-sensitive wildcard match |
| `-not` | `!` | Negation |
| `-lt` | `<` | Less than |
| `-le` | `<=` | Less than or equal to |
| `-gt` | `>` | Greater than |
| `-ge` | `>=` | Greater than or equal to |

| PowerShell | Traditional | Meaning |
|---|---|---|
| -and | && | Logical and |
| -or | \|\| | Logical or |
| -bor | \| | Bitwise or |
| -band | & | Bitwise and |
| -xor | ^ | Exclusive or |

Note that many operators perform case-insensitive string comparisons by default. If you want to do case-sensitive matching, prepend with c. For example, -ceq, -clike, and -cnotlike.

## Displaying messages

Often, we will need to display or log messages as our scripts execute. PowerShell provides a few cmdlets to help us accomplish this:

```
Get-Command -Name "*Write*" -CommandTypeCmdlet
```

This will give a list of our Write-related cmdlets:

| Cmdlet | Description |
|---|---|
| Write-Debug | This displays a debug message on the console. It is typically used with $DebugPreference = "Continue". |
| Write-Error | This displays a nonterminating error message on the console. |
| Write-EventLog | This writes a message to the Windows event log. |
| Write-Host | This displays a string message on the host. |
| Write-Output | This writes an object to the pipeline. |
| Write-Progress | This displays a progress bar. |
| Write-Verbose | This displays a verbose message on the console. It is typically used with $VerbosePreference = "Continue". |
| Write-Warning | This displays a warning message on the console. |

Although some of these cmdlets seem similar, there are some fundamental differences. For example, Write-Host and Write-Output seem to display the same messages on the screen. The Write-Host cmdlet, however, simply displays a string, but Write-Output writes objects that have properties that can be queried and can eventually be used in the pipeline.

We use `Write-Verbose` a fair bit in the recipes in this book. `Write-Verbose` does not automatically display messages on the host. It relies on the `$VerbosePreference` setting. By default, `$VerbosePreference` is set to `SilentlyContinue`, but it can also be set to `Continue`, which allows us to display messages used with `Write-Verbose` on the screen:

```
$VerbosePreference = ""Continue""
$folderName = ""C:\BLOB Files\""

#using PowerShell V2 style Where-Object syntax
Get-ChildItem $folderName |
Where-Object {$_.PSIsContainer -eq $false}   |
ForEach-Object {
   $blobFile = $_
   Write-Verbose ""Importing file $($blobFile.FullName)...""

}
$VerbosePreference = "SilentlyContinue"
```

This is an elegant way of turning all messages on or off, without needing to change the script.

## Comments

Comments are important in any programming or scripting language. Comments are often used to document logic and sometimes a chain of changes to the script.

Single-line comments start with a hash sign (#):

```
#this is a single line comment
```

Block comments start with <# and end with #>:

```
<#
this is a block comment
#>
```

PowerShell also supports what's called **Comment-Based Help**. This feature allows you to put a special comment block at the start of your script, or in the beginning of your function, that allows the script or function to be looked up using `Get-Help`. A sample of this type of comment block is as follows:

```
<#
.SYNOPSIS
   Creates a full database backup
.DESCRIPTION
   Creates a full database backup using specified instance name
and database name
```

```
    This will place the backup file to the default backup directory
of the instance
.PARAMETER instanceName
    instance where database to be backed up resides
.PARAMETER databaseName
    database to be backed up
.EXAMPLE
    PS C:\PowerShell> .\Backup-Database.ps1 -instanceName
"QUERYWORKS\SQL01" -databaseName"pubs"
.EXAMPLE
    PS C:\PowerShell> .\Backup-Database.ps1 -instance
"QUERYWORKS\SQL01" -database "pubs"
.NOTES

    To get help:
    Get-Help .\Backup-Database.ps1
.LINK
    http://msdn.microsoft.com/en-us/library/hh245198.aspx
#>
```

To look up the help, you can simply type a `Get-Help` cmdlet followed by the script filename or function name:

```
PS>Get-Help .\Backup-Database.ps1
```

## Special variables

PowerShell also has some special variables. These special variables do not need to be created ahead of time; they are already available. Some of the special variables are as follows:

| Special variable | Description |
| --- | --- |
| $_ | Current pipeline object |
| $args | Arguments passed to a function |
| $error | An array that stores all errors |
| $home | User's home directory |
| $host | Host information |
| $match | Regex matches |
| $profile | Path to a profile, if available |
| $PSHome | Install a directory of PowerShell |
| $PSISE | PowerShell Scripting Environment object |
| $pid | Process ID (PID) of a PowerShell process |

| Special variable | Description |
|---|---|
| `$pwd` | Present Working Directory |
| `$true` | Boolean true |
| `$false` | Boolean false |
| `$null` | Null value |

## Special characters

A few more special characters worth noting down are explained in the following table, which you may find in many scripts you work with:

| Character | Name | Description |
|---|---|---|
| \| | Pipe | Command chaining; the output from one command to input to another |
| ` | Backtick | An escape or continuation character |
| @ | At sign | An array |
| # | Hash sign | A comment |
| [] | Square brackets | For indexes and strongly typed variables |
| () | Parentheses | For array members; for calling functions |
| & | Ampersand | A call operator |
| * | Start or asterisk | A wildcard character |
| % | Percent | An alias for `Foreach-Object` |
| ? | Question mark | An alias for `Where-Object` |
| + | Plus | Addition; a string concatenation operator |

## Conditions

PowerShell supports conditional statements using `if-else` or `switch` statements. These two constructs allow you to check for a condition, and consequently execute different blocks of code if the condition is met or not. Note that PowerShell treats null/empty as false.

Let's take a look at an example of an `if-else` block:

```
$answer=Read-Host"Which course are you taking?"

if ($answer-eq"COMP 4677")
{
Write-Host"That's SQL Server Administration"
```

```
}
elseif ($answer-eq"COMP 4678")
{
Write-Host"That's SQL Server Development"
}
else
{
Write-Host"That's another course"
}
```

 Note that the `elseif` and `else` blocks are optional. They don't need to be defined if you do not have a separate code to execute if the condition is not met.

An equivalent `switch` block can be written for the preceding code:

```
$answer=Read-Host"Which course are you taking?"

switch ($answer)
{
"COMP 4677"
    {
Write-Host"That's SQL Server Administration"
    }
"COMP 4678"
    {
Write-Host"That's SQL Server Development"
    }
default
    {
Write-Host"That's another course"
    }
}
```

Note that these two constructs can be functionally equivalent for simple comparisons. The choice to use one over the other hinges on preference and readability. If there are many choices, the switch can definitely make the code more readable.

## Regular expressions

Regular expressions, more commonly referred to as regex, specify a string pattern to match. Regex can be extremely powerful and is often used when dealing with massive amounts of text. The area of bioinformatics, for example, tends to rely heavily on regular expressions for gene pattern matching.

Regex can also be quite confusing especially for beginners. It has its own set of patterns and wildcards, and it is up to you to put these together to ensure that you are matching what you need to be matched.

 Refer to the *Testing regular expressions* recipe in *Chapter 11, Helpful PowerShell Snippets*.

## Arrays

Arrays are collections of items. Often, we find ourselves in situations where we need to store a group of items, either for further processing or for exporting:

```
#ways to create an array
$myArray= @() #empty
$myArray=1,2,3,4,5
$myArray= @(1,2,3,4,5)
#array of processes consuming >30% CPU
$myArray= (Get-Process|Where-Object  CPU -gt30 )
```

Arrays can either be a fixed size or not. Fixed-size arrays are instantiated with a fixed number of items. Some of the typical methods such as Add or Remove cannot be used with fixed-size arrays:

```
$myArray= @()
$myArray+= 1,2,3,4,5
$myArray+=6,7,8
$myArray.Add(9) #error because array is fixed size
```

Removing an item from a fixed array is a little bit tricky. Although arrays have the Remove and RemoveAt methods to remove entries based on a value and index, respectively, we cannot use these with fixed-size arrays. To remove an item from a fixed-size array, we will need to reassign the new set of values to the array variable:

```
#remove 6
$myArray=$myArray-ne6

#remove 7
$myArray=$myArray-ne7
```

To create a dynamic-sized array, you will need to declare the array as an array list and add items using the `Add` method. This also supports removing items from the list using the `Remove` method:

```
$myArray=New-ObjectSystem.Collections.ArrayList
$myArray.Add(1)
$myArray.Add(2)
$myArray.Add(3)
$myArray.Remove(2)
```

We can use indexes to retrieve information from the array:

```
#retrieve first item
$myArray[0]

#retrieve first 3 items
$myArray[0..2]
```

We can also retrieve information based on some comparison or condition:

```
#retrieving anything > 3
$myArray-gt3
```

## Hash tables

A hash table is also a collection. This is different from an array, however, because hashes are collections of key-value pairs. Hashes are also called associative arrays or hash tables:

```
#simple hash
$simplehash= @{
"BCIT"="BC Institute of Technology"
"CST"="Computer Systems Technology"
"CIT"="Computer Information Technology"
}
$simplehash.Count

#hash containing process IDs and names
$hash= @{}

Get-Process|
Foreach-Object {
    $hash.Add($_.Id,$_.Name)
}

$hash.GetType()
```

To access items in a hash, we can refer to the hash table variable and retrieve information based on the stored key:

```
$simplehash["BCIT"]
$simplehash.BCIT
```

# Loops

A loop allows you to repeatedly execute block(s) of code based on some condition. There are different types of loop support in PowerShell. For all intents and purposes, you may use all of these types, but it's always useful to be aware of what's available and doable.

This is a `while` loop, where the condition is tested at the beginning of the block:

```
$i=1
while($i-le5)
{
#code block
$i
$i++
}
```

There is also support for the `do while` loop, where the condition is tested at the bottom of the block:

```
$i=1
do
{
#code block
$i
$i++
} while($i-le5)
```

The `for` loop allows you to loop a specified number of times, based on a counter that you create in the `for` header:

```
for($i=1; $i-le5; $i++)
{
$i
}
```

There is yet another type of loop, a `foreach` loop. This loop is a little bit different because it works with arrays or collections. It allows a block of code to be executed for each item in a collection:

```
$backupcmds=Get-Command -Name "*Backup*" -CommandTypeCmdlet
foreach($backupcmdin$backupcmds)
{
$backupcmd|Get-Member
}
```

If you're a developer, this code might look very familiar to you. In PowerShell, however, you can use pipelining to make your code more concise:

```
Get-Command -Name "*Backup*" -CommandTypeCmdlet|
Foreach-Object
{
    #recall that $_ is the current pipeline object
$_|Get-Member
}
```

Use the `foreach` loop operator when the collection of objects is small enough so that it can be loaded into memory. For example, an array of 20 string values.

Use the `ForEach-Object` cmdlet when you want to pass only one object at a time through the pipeline, minimizing the memory usage. For example, a directory containing 10,000 files.

## Error handling

When developing functions or scripts, it is important to think beyond just the functionality you are trying to achieve. You also want to handle exceptions, or errors, when they happen. We all want our scripts to gracefully exit if something goes wrong, rather than displaying some rather intimidating or cryptic error messages.

Developers in the house will be familiar with the concept of `try/catch/finally`. This is a construct that allows us to put the code we want to run in one block (`try`), exception handling code in another (`catch`), and any must-execute housekeeping blocks in a final block (`finally`):

```
$dividend =20
$divisor =0

try
{
    $result = $dividend/$divisor
}
```

```
catch
{
Write-Host ("======"*20)
Write-Host"Exception $error[0]"
Write-Host ("======"*20)


}
finally
{
Write-Host"Housekeeping block"
Write-Host"Must execute by hook or by crook"
}
```

# Converting scripts into functions

A function is a reusable, callable code block(s). A function can accept parameters and can produce different results.

A typical anatomy of a PowerShell function looks like this:

```
function Do-Something
{
<#
        comment based help
    #>
param
    (
#parameters
    )
#blocks of code
}
```

To illustrate, let's create a very simple function that takes a report server URL and lists all items in that report server.

When naming functions, it is recommended that you adhere to the verb-noun convention. The verb also needs to be approved; otherwise, you may get a warning similar to when you import the SQLPS module:

**WARNING**: The names of some imported commands from the 'sqlps' module include unapproved verbs that might make them less discoverable. To find the commands with unapproved verbs, run the Import-Module command again with the verbose parameter. For a list of approved verbs, type Get-Verb.

This function will take in a parameter for the report server URL and another switch called $ReportsOnly, which can toggle displaying between all items or only report items:

```
function Get-SSRSItems
{
<#
        comment based help
    #>
param
    (
        [Parameter(Position=0,Mandatory=$true)]
        [alias("reportServer")]
        [string]$ReportServerUri,
        [switch]$ReportsOnly
    )

    Write-Verbose "Processing $($ReportServerUri) ..."
    $proxy = New-WebServiceProxy -Uri $ReportServerUri
-UseDefaultCredential
    if ($ReportsOnly)
    {
        $proxy.ListChildren("/", $true) |
        Where-Object TypeName -eq"Report"
    }
    else
    {
        $proxy.ListChildren("/", $true)
    }
}
```

To call this function, we can pass in the value for –ReportServerUri and also set the –ReportsOnly switch:

```
$server = "http://server1/ReportServer/ReportService2010.asmx"

Get-SSRSItems -ReportsOnly -ReportServerUri $server |
Select-Object Path, TypeName |
Format-Table -AutoSize
```

To allow your function to behave more like a cmdlet and work with the pipeline, we will need to add the [CmdletBinding()] attribute. We can also change the parameters to enable values to come from the pipeline using ValueFromPipeline=$true. Inside the function definition, we will need to add three blocks:

▶ BEGIN: Preprocessing; anything in this block will be executed once when the function is called

▶ PROCESS: Actual processing that is done for each item that is passed in the pipeline

▶ END: Post-processing; this block will be executed once before the function terminates executing

We will also need to specify in the parameter block that we want to accept input from the pipeline.

A revised function is as follows:

```
function Get-SSRSItems
{
<#
    comment based help
  #>
  [CmdletBinding()]
param
   (
     [Parameter(Position=0,Mandatory=$true,
ValueFromPipeline=$true,
ValueFromPipelineByPropertyName=$true)]
     [alias("reportServer")]
     [string]$ReportServerUri,
     [switch]$ReportsOnly
   )
  BEGIN
  {
  }
  PROCESS
  {
     Write-Verbose "Processing $($ReportServerUri) ..."
     $proxy = New-WebServiceProxy `
             -Uri $ReportServerUri -UseDefaultCredential
     if ($ReportsOnly)
     {
       $proxy.ListChildren("/", $true) |
       Where-Object TypeName -eq"Report"
     }
     else
     {
       $proxy.ListChildren("/", $true)
     }
  }
```

```
    END
    {
        Write-Verbose "Finished processing"
    }
}
```

To invoke, we can pipe an array of servers to the `Get-SSRSItems` function, and this automatically maps the servers to our `-ReportServerUri` parameter as we specified `ValueFromPipeline=$true`. Note that `Get-SSRSItems` will get invoked for each value in our array:

```
$servers = @("http://server1/ReportServer/ReportService2010.asmx",
"http://server2/ReportServer/ReportService2010.asmx")

$servers |
Get-SSRSItems -Verbose -ReportsOnly |
Select-Object Path, TypeName |
Format-Table -AutoSize
```

# Listing notable PowerShell features

Before you dive deeper into PowerShell, it's worth noting down the features that have been added to PowerShell over the last few versions. They are as follows:

**Improvements to the Integrated Scripting Environment** (**ISE**): Many of the improvements such as Intellisense, autocomplete (tab completion), command window, and live syntax checking were introduced in PowerShell V3. Although subtle, the ISE has kept on improving through the versions.

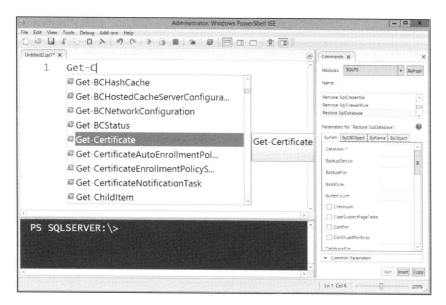

**OneGet**: PowerShell's `OneGet` has been added in PowerShell V5 to ease the process of finding, listing, managing, and installing packages from web-based repositories and installing them. If you have worked with *nix machines and environments before, this new feature is similar to `apt-get` or **Red Hat Package Manager(RPM)**.

> In Windows 10, this module has been renamed as PackageManagement. To learn more about this module, visit `http://blogs.technet.com/b/packagemanagement/archive/2015/04/29/introducing-packagemanagement-in-windows-10.aspx`.

To use `OneGet`, simply import the module:

```
Import-Module -Name OneGet
```

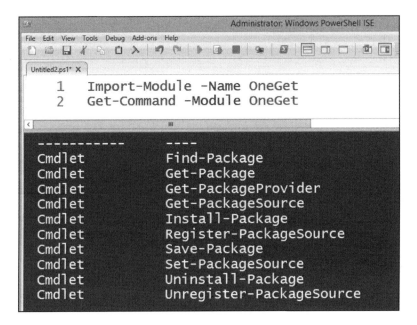

The `OneGet` feature by default, works with the default provider, PowerShellGallery.

> To learn more about the PowerShellGallery, visit `https://www.powershellgallery.com/pages/GettingStarted`.

It can also work with the Chocolatey repository (`https://chocolatey.org/`), a community-driven machine package manager. The PowerShell team does mention that support for additional repositories are in their roadmap.

To search for packages that can be installed using `OneGet`, you can run the following command:

```
Find-Package -Source Chocolatey
```

To install a package, `MagicDisc`, you can use the following command:

```
Find-Package -Name MagicDisc | Install-Package
```

PowerShell will also keep you updated on the progress of the installation in a command-line fashion:

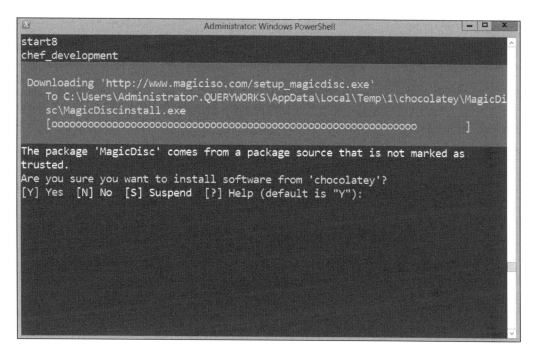

To check how many packages are available to be installed via `OneGet`, you can use the following command:

```
@(Find-Package).Count
```

At the time of writing this appendix, there are 2,649 packages available.

With this great power (`OneGet`), comes great responsibility. Make sure that you understand what this feature does for you, what the security risks are, and evaluate packages before you download and install them.

BoeProx, PowerShell MVP, has a blog post that discusses `OneGet` in more detail. You can refer to `http://learn-powershell.net/2014/04/03/checking-out-oneget-in-powershell-v5/`.

**PowerShellGet**: The `PowerShellGet` package is very similar to `OneGet`. The `PowerShellGet` package is a wrapper around `OneGet` and provides more PowerShell-specific package management. At the time of writing this book, you can search for modules using `Find-Module` of the `PowerShellGet` package and look for the **Desired State Configuration(DSC)** sources using `Find-DscResource` of the `PowerShellGet` package.

**PowerShell Classes**: While PowerShell has always been object-based, there has been no true support for creating true classes, until now. Starting V5, PowerShell supports the creation of user-defined classes using constructs that you would use in an object-oriented programming language. Here is a very simple example that creates a class with one property and one method:

```
class CustomClass
{
    [Int] $NumProcessors

CustomClass([Int]$p_NumProcessors)
    {
        $this.NumProcessors = $p_NumProcessors
    }

    #method
    [void] SetNumProcessors([Int] $p_NewNum)
    {
        $this.NumProcessors = $p_NewNum
    }
}

$myClass = [CustomClass]::new(4)

#display
$myClass

#change
$myClass.SetNumProcessors(8)
```

**PowerShell debugging**: PowerShell V5 comes with a number of improvements that will help you with debugging:

▸ You can now break into the debugger from either the console (*Ctrl + B*) or from the ISE (*Ctrl + B*)

▸ You can do remote debugging from the ISE

▸ You can debug runspaces using runspace-specific cmdlets:

❑ `Get-Runspace`

❑ `Debug-Runspace`

❑ `Enable-RunspaceDebug`

❑ `Disable-RunspaceDebug`

❑ `Get-RunspaceDebug`

**Network Switch cmdlets**: PowerShell V5 introduces a number of cmdlets that allow you to configure, manage, and support Windows Server 2012 R2 logo-certified network switches. Here is a partial list of Network Switch-related cmdlets in PowerShell V5:

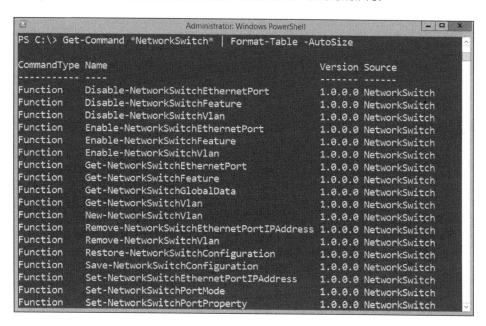

**Transcription and logging**: The `Start-Transcript` and `Stop-Transcript` cmdlets help you record and capture all the commands that you issue in a PowerShell session. These are supported in the console but not in the ISE. In PowerShell V5, these two cmdlets work within the ISE as well.

**Archive cmdlets**: There is no need for you to go out and look for another tool to help you zip and unzip your files and folders. PowerShell V5 comes with two cmdlets that will help you do this from PowerShell: `Compress-Archive` and `Expand-Archive`. Here is a simple example of how you can compress files from a folder:

```
#code all in one line
Compress-Archive -Path C:\MyFiles\* -DestinationPath
C:\Temp\MyFiles.zip
```

**Desired State Configuration**: An introduction of **Desired State Configuration** (**DSC**) was one of the highlights of PowerShell V4. DSC is defined in MSDN (`https://msdn.microsoft.com/en-ca/library/dn249912.aspx`) as "*a new management platform in Windows PowerShell that enables deploying and managing configuration data for software services and managing the environment in which these services run.*" DSC has extended PowerShell to allow you to declaratively specify your *"desired configurations"*. To get a list of functions and cmdlets related to DSC, you can use the following command:

```
Get-Command –Module PSDesiredStateConfiguration
```

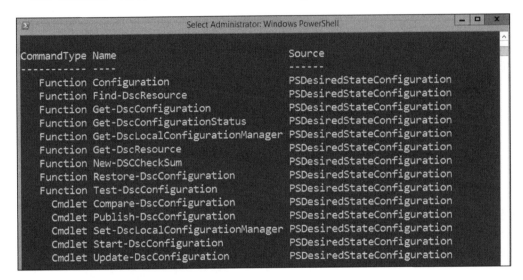

```
                                Select Administrator: Windows PowerShell

CommandType  Name                                    Source
-----------  ----                                    ------
   Function  Configuration                           PSDesiredStateConfiguration
   Function  Find-DscResource                        PSDesiredStateConfiguration
   Function  Get-DscConfiguration                    PSDesiredStateConfiguration
   Function  Get-DscConfigurationStatus              PSDesiredStateConfiguration
   Function  Get-DscLocalConfigurationManager        PSDesiredStateConfiguration
   Function  Get-DscResource                         PSDesiredStateConfiguration
   Function  New-DSCCheckSum                         PSDesiredStateConfiguration
   Function  Restore-DscConfiguration                PSDesiredStateConfiguration
   Function  Test-DscConfiguration                   PSDesiredStateConfiguration
     Cmdlet  Compare-DscConfiguration                PSDesiredStateConfiguration
     Cmdlet  Publish-DscConfiguration                PSDesiredStateConfiguration
     Cmdlet  Set-DscLocalConfigurationManager        PSDesiredStateConfiguration
     Cmdlet  Start-DscConfiguration                  PSDesiredStateConfiguration
     Cmdlet  Update-DscConfiguration                 PSDesiredStateConfiguration
```

The current list is as follows:

**Updateable help**: Instead of bundling the help files with the PowerShell installation, which often remains static and easily becomes outdated, PowerShell help files can be downloaded and updated on demand in PowerShell V3. Using the `Update-Help` cmdlet, the most up-to-date help files will be installed on your system.

**Workflows**: Introduced in PowerShell V3, **PowerShell Workflows** (**PSWF**), as stated in MSDN (`http://msdn.microsoft.com/en-us/library/jj134242.aspx`), *"help automate the distribution, orchestration, and completion of multi-computer tasks, freeing users and administrators to focus on higher-level tasks"*. PSWF leverages Windows Workflow Foundation 4.0 for the declarative framework but using familiar PowerShell syntax and constructs. Check out the MSDN article on how to get started with Windows PowerShell Workflow.

**Robust sessions**: In PowerShell V3, sessions can be retained amidst network interruptions. These sessions will remain open until they time out.

**Module auto loading**: In PowerShell V3, modules can be autoloaded, that is, they don't have to be explicitly loaded. If you use a cmdlet that belongs to a module that hasn't been loaded yet, this will trigger PowerShell to search `PSModulePath` and load the first module that contains this cmdlet. This is something we can easily test:

```
#=====================================
#TEST 1
#=====================================
#check current modules in session
Get-Module

#use cmdlet from CimCmdlets module, which
#is not loaded yet
Get-CimInstancewin32_bios

#note new module loaded CimCmdlets
Get-Module


#=====================================
#TEST 2
#=====================================
#use cmdlet from SQLPS module, which
#is not loaded yet
Invoke-Sqlcmd -Query "SELECT GETDATE()" -ServerInstance"localhost"

#note new modules loaded SQLPS and SQLASCmdlets
Get-Module
```

**PSCustomObject**: In PowerShell V3, you can create custom objects more cleanly using `PSCustomObject`. Creating custom objects are quite useful especially when you need to bring together properties from different objects or components. Here is a simple example:

```
[PSCustomObject] @{
    Database = $db.Name
FileGroup = $fg.Name
FileName = $file.FileName
}
```

**Web service support**: PowerShell V3 introduced the `Invoke-WebRequest` cmdlet that sends HTTP or HTTPS requests to a web service and returns the object-based content that can be easily manipulated in PowerShell. You can download websites using PowerShell (check out Lee Holmes' article on this at `http://www.leeholmes.com/blog/2012/03/31/how-to-download-an-entire-wordpress-blog/`).

**Simplified language syntax**: In PowerShell V3, some syntax has been simplified.

What you used to write in V1 and V2 with curly braces and $_ like this:

```
Get-Service | Where-Object { $_.Status -eq'Running' }
```

This can now be rewritten in V3 onward as follows:

```
Get-Service | Where-Object Status -eq'Running'
```

 Read more about the Windows Management Framework V5.0 announcement at `http://blogs.technet.com/b/ windowsserver/archive/2014/04/03/windows- management-framework-v5-preview.aspx`.

# Exploring more PowerShell

We have barely touched PowerShell basics, but this appendix should give you an idea how to use PowerShell. To learn more about PowerShell, pick up a book or two that dives deep into the PowerShell syntax and its intricacies. There are also a number of sites and blogs that have collections of articles on PowerShell. The following are a few resources you might find useful with your PowerShell adventure:

- PowerShell team:Windows PowerShell Blog: `http://blogs.msdn.com/ powershell/`
- PowerShell.com: `http://www.powershell.com`
- PowerShell Magazine: `http://www.powershellmagazine.com/`
- MSDN Channel 9 PowerShell Webcasts: `http://channel9.msdn.com/tags/ PowerShell/`
- PowerScripting Podcasts: `http://powerscripting.wordpress.com/`

# B

# Creating a SQL Server VM

In this appendix, we will cover the following topics:

- ▶ Terminologies
- ▶ Downloading software
- ▶ VM details and accounts
- ▶ Creating an empty virtual machine
- ▶ Installing Windows Server 2012 R2 as a guest OS
- ▶ Installing VMWare tools
- ▶ Configuring a domain controller (optional)
- ▶ Creating domain accounts
- ▶ Installing SQL Server 2014 on a VM
- ▶ Configuring Reporting Services in native mode
- ▶ Installing sample databases
- ▶ Installing PowerShell V5

# Introduction

One of the best ways to learn and understand SQL Server and the components that interact with it is by creating a virtual machine that has the version of SQL Server you want to use. I typically use SQL Server virtual machines for my development and administration classes. I want the students to have full autonomy over the machines they are using so that they can try different features and configurations without worrying about affecting the host machines too much. If anything goes awry, they can simply remove the offending VM and recreate it.

This appendix is a simple guide to help you create virtual machines to work with SQL Server and PowerShell. This can be considered a starting point for more complex virtual machine configurations you may want to explore.

If you want to be up and running faster, you can also consider some predefined template environments; you can check out companies such as CloudShare that enables you to build production-like environments in a short time for a fee. Check out their template library at `http://www.cloudshare.com/cloudshare-template-library`.

# Terminologies

Let's start off with some terminologies:

| Terminology | Description |
|---|---|
| Virtual machine, or VM | This is essentially a standalone computer installed within another platform/OS. |
| | A virtual machine is also sometimes called a **guest machine**. This typically provides a complete system platform with its own set of operating system, hardware configurations, and installed software packages, but it still runs on top of a "host" machine that has the main OS (operating system) and the physical hardware. |
| | There are different applications that can create and run virtual machines. A partial list includes the following: |
| | ▸ *VMware Workstation Player* (free) which is available at `http://www.vmware.com/products/player/`. |
| | ▸ *VMware Workstation Pro* or other VMWare products which is available at `http://www.vmware.com/products/workstation/overview.html`. |
| | ▸ Windows Server Hyper-V Server 2012 R2 which is available at `https://www.microsoft.com/en-us/evalcenter/evaluate-hyper-v-server-2012-r2`. |
| | ▸ VirtualBox which is available at `https://www.virtualbox.org/wiki/Downloads`. |
| | ▸ Microsoft Azure Virtual Machines which is available at `http://azure.microsoft.com/en-us/services/virtual-machines/` |

| Terminology | Description |
|---|---|
| ISO file | This is a disk image; an archive file of an optical disc in a format defined by the **International Organization for Standardization** (**ISO**). This contains archived CD/DVD content. |
| | In a VM, an ISO file can be treated as a "real" CD/DVD. All you need to do is to point the CD/DVD settings to the ISO file path. |
| | If you need to, you can also burn the ISO file to CD/DVD, or you can create ISO files using any CD/DVD image file processing tool, such as: |
| | ► PowerISO from `http://www.poweriso.com/` link. |
| | ► MagicISO from `http://www.magiciso.com/` link. |
| | ► Free ISO Creator from `http://www.minidvdsoft.com/isocreator/` link. |
| | ► Nero Burning Software from `http://www.nero.com/enu/` link. |
| Service account | This is the account used to run services running on a Windows operating system. To learn more about service accounts, visit `https://msdn.microsoft.com/en-ca/library/windows/desktop/ms686005.aspx`. |

# Downloading software

We will use VMware Player, a free virtual machine application, and the trial versions for Windows Server 2012 R2, SQL Server 2014, Windows Management Framework, and optionally Visual Studio 2010:

1. Download and install VMware player from `http://www.vmware.com/products/player/`. You can find the VMWare player documentation at `http://www.vmware.com/support/pubs/player_pubs.html`.

2. Download the Windows Server 2012 R2 trial version ISO file (or if you have a licensed copy, use that) from `https://www.microsoft.com/en-us/evalcenter/evaluate-windows-server-2012-r2`.

3. Download the SQL Server 2014 trial version ISO file (or if you have a licensed copy, use that) from `https://www.microsoft.com/en-us/evalcenter/evaluate-sql-server-2014`.

4. Download the Windows Management Framework 5. At the time of writing this book, Windows Management Framework 5 Preview April 2015 is available at `https://www.microsoft.com/en-us/download/details.aspx?id=46889`.

5. Download SQL Server Data Tools and SQL Server Data Tools Business Intelligence (optional) from `https://msdn.microsoft.com/en-us/library/mt204009.aspx`.

6. If you are planning to create some SQLCLR assemblies, you will need Visual Studio Professional (optional). SQL Server Data Tools (SSDT) is not sufficient for creating the assemblies. You can download Visual Studio from `https://www.visualstudio.com/en-us/products/vs-2015-product-editions.aspx`.

# VM details and accounts

You will need to identify your virtual machine details, such as a virtual machine name, instance name, and service account. The following table is a sample form that you can use as a reference:

| Item | Description |
|---|---|
| Virtual machine name | `SQL2014VM` |
| Virtual machine computer name | `PHOENIX` |
| Domain | `QUERYWORKS` |
| Virtual machine computer administrator account | **UserName:** `Administrator`<br>**Password:** `P@ssword` |
| SQL Server instances | **Default:** `PHOENIX` (localhost can also be used)<br>**Named:** `PHOENIX\SQL01` |
| SQL Server service account | **UserName:** `QUERYWORKS\sqlservice`<br>**Password:** `P@ssword` |
| SQL Server agent account | **UserName:** `QUERYWORKS\sqlagent`<br>**Password:** `P@ssword` |
| Additional domain accounts | `QUERYWORKS\tstark`<br>`QUERYWORKS\srogers`<br>`QUERYWORKS\todinson` |

You need to log in to the VM when it's ready:

For logging in to the VM navigate to **Player | Send Ctrl + Alt + Del**.

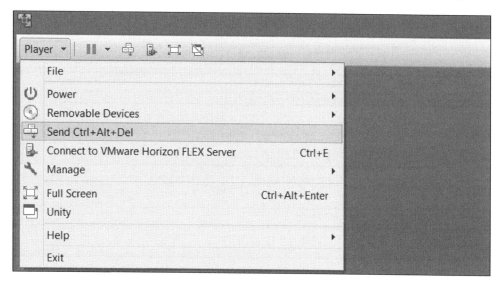

Additional VMWare shortcuts can be found at `http://www.vmware.com/support/ws55/doc/ws_learning_keyboard_shortcuts.html`.

# Creating an empty virtual machine

Once you have downloaded the software packages, you need to configure your virtual machine. Once ready, we will create our empty virtual machine. We will call our virtual machine `SQL2014VM`:

1. Launch VMware Player.

2. On the initial screen, click on the **Create New Virtual Machine** button.

3. You can also do this by navigating to **File** | **Create New Virtual Machine**.

4. On the **New Virtual Machine Wizard** screen, select **I will install operating system later**. This option will allow you to have more flexibility to configure the operating system later.

5. On the **Select a Guest Operating System** screen, select **Microsoft Windows** for the guest operating system, and select **Windows Server 2012** from the **Version** drop-down menu.

6. Choose a name for your virtual machine. We will name our virtual machine
   `SQL2014VM`. If you prefer, you can also change the location of your VM:

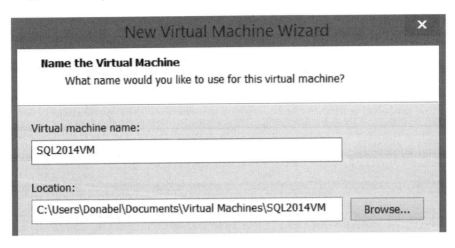

7. We will allocate hard drive space for our virtual machine. In this tutorial, we will
   allocate 40 GB disk space and choose to split the virtual disk into 2 GB files. Feel free
   to adjust it as you see fit for your own use. You can allocate a bigger disk space if you
   want to use this VM for some data warehouses and cubes:

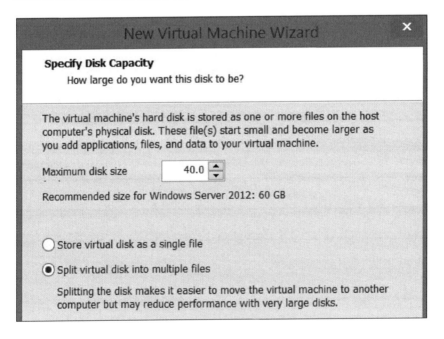

8. On the **Ready to Create Virtual Machine** screen, click on **Finish**.

# Installing Windows Server 2012 R2 as guest OS

To install the operating system, we first need to mount the Windows Server ISO and play the virtual machine. After this, we can follow the installation wizard:

1. Launch VMware Player.

2. Select **SQL2014VM** and then select **Edit virtual machine settings**.

3. Let's increase the memory settings—adjust this based on your available hardware configurations. For our purposes, we will increase the memory to 4 GB (or 4096 MB), but you can definitely set this higher if you wish. Just make sure you have enough memory still left for your host OS and other VMs that you may be running simultaneously:

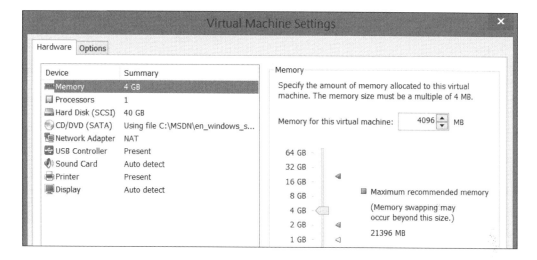

4. Select **CD/DVD** and choose the **Use ISO image file** button. Navigate to **Windows Server 2012 R2 ISO** and click on **OK**.

5. Go back to the main VMWare Player screen, and while **SQL2012VM** is selected, click on **Play Virtual Machine**.

6. Since we've mounted the ISO, the Windows Server installation screen will be displayed when the VM starts. Now, we'll need to follow the installation for Windows Server 2012 R2.

7. For the installation language, we will select **English** and keyboard will be **US**.

8. When prompted to install, select **Install Now**.

9. When asked about the operating system to install, we will choose **Windows Server 2012 R2 Standard (Server with a GUI)**, but feel free to choose a different edition that you want to explore.

> The Server Core edition is bare-bones version of Windows Server, which many administrators prefer, because of the lower overhead and removal of unnecessary services for certain server roles. This may become the recommended edition for production systems in future. To learn more about Server Core, visit `https://msdn.microsoft.com/en-us/library/dd184075.aspx`.

10. Accept the license terms and click on **Next**.

11. When prompted for the type of installation, select **Custom: Install Windows only (advanced)**. This installs a new copy of Windows on your blank virtual machine.

12. In the **Install Windows** dialog box, select **Disk 0 Unallocated space**.

13. Let the installation complete. Note that the VM will be restarted a few times by the installation process.

14. In one of the restarts, you will be prompted to change the password. Type in the administrator password. When done, click on the arrow. You will now be able to log in to your new VM.

15. By default, the **Server Manager** dashboard screen will be displayed when you first log in. On this screen, you can manage the server, add roles and features, and configure:

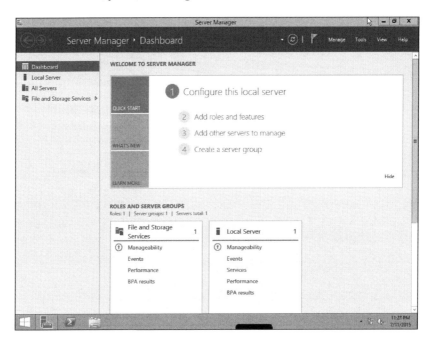

16. Click on **Local Server**, which is in the left-hand pane. Click on **Computer Name** to change the computer name and computer description and set the following options:

    1. In the **Computer description** textbox, type SQL2014 VM.

    2. Click on the **Change** button.

    3. In the **Computer name** textbox, type your computer name. For this tutorial, we will use PHOENIX.

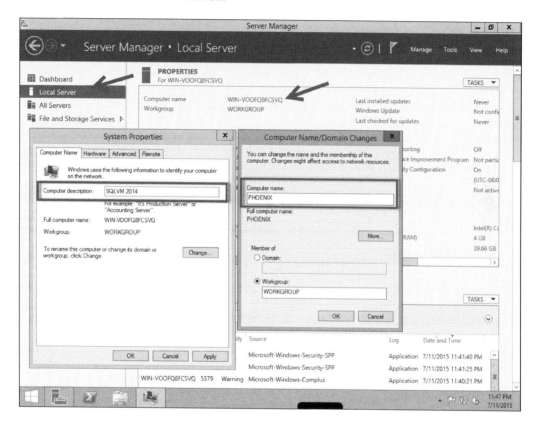

17. Click on **Ok** and then **Apply**. You will be prompted to restart the VM; select **Restart Later**.

18. For our purposes, disable the firewall. In the **Customize Settings** dialog box, choose to turn off Windows firewall for both private and public networks. This is definitely not recommended on production systems, but for our exercises, this will be sufficient.

19. Activate windows. Leave the **Serial Number** textbox blank and click on **Activate**. Once the activation has been successful, and if you've used the trial version of the operating system, you will see a window indicating that your license is valid for 180 days.

20. Restart the VM.

21. We are almost ready. In the **Server Manager** window, click on **Local Server**, which is in the left-hand pane, and then click on **Windows Update** from the **Properties** screen. Currently, it should say **Not configured**.

22. Click on **Let me choose my settings**, which is the link below **Turn on automatic updates**. By doing this, we will disable automatic, ongoing updates for this VM.

23. Under **Important Updates**, choose **Never check for updates** and click on **OK**.

24. In the **Properties** window, click on **Last installed updates**. It should currently say **Never**. Click on **check updates**. If there are any important updates, we need to install them. Otherwise, you will see the message **Your pc is up to date. No updates are available**.

25. When prompted to restart, click on **OK**. Once the VM has restarted, log in to the VM.

26. Now, let's disable **IE Enhanced Security Configuration**. In **Server Manager**, click on **Local Server**, which is in the left-hand pane, and then click on the option beside **IE Enhanced Security Configuration**. This is by default set to **On**.

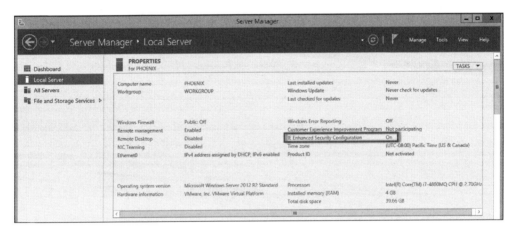

27. Choose **Off** for both **Administrators** and **Users**. Click on **OK**.

28. Restart your VM.

# Installing VMware tools

For an enhanced VM experience, we need to install VMware tools:

1. Launch VMWare Player.
2. Play **SQL2014VM**.
3. In the **Player** menu, select **Install VMWare Tools**.
4. When the **AutoPlay** dialog comes up, click on **Run setup.exe**.
5. Select the **Typical** setup type and click on **Next**. Follow the wizard to completion.
6. Once the installation is done, you will be prompted to restart. Click on **Yes**.

# Making a snapshot as a baseline

Once you have your base virtual machine set up, it is a good idea to take a snapshot if your VM application allows it. You may want to create a snapshot to preserve the current state of your snapshot and to enable you to go back to this state later on.

VMware workstation allows you to take snapshots. The option is accessible from the menu item:

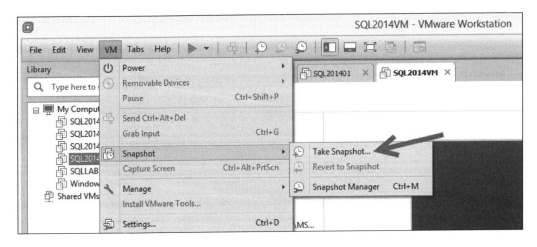

When you take a snapshot, all you need to provide is the name and optionally a description:

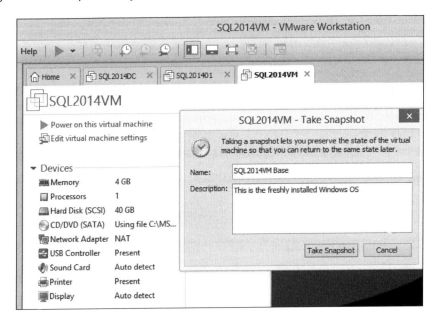

You can check the following YouTube video for VMware Snapshot Best Practices at `https://www.youtube.com/watch?v=A8KOh4CzmQc`.

VMware also has an article on *Understanding virtual machine snapshots in VMware ESXi and ESX*, which is available at `http://kb.vmware.com/selfservice/microsites/search.do?language=en_US&cmd=displayKC&externalId=1015180`.

# Configuring a domain controller (optional)

In a production environment, it is not recommended that you install the domain controller with any of your other server software. Doing so will have a negative impact on your SQL Server installation, as outlined in `https://msdn.microsoft.com/en-us/library/ms143506.aspx#DC_support`.

It is still helpful to have access to a domain controller to get a feel of how a "production environment" works, or understand how to create and manage domain accounts, among other tasks. If you have a spare VM (or if you can create another one), it would be best to install your domain controller on a different VM. However, if you are working with only a single VM, we can install this role on the same machine. Make sure you note down the limitations as specified in `https://msdn.microsoft.com/en-us/library/ms143506.aspx#DC_support`.

If you want to mimic a production setup, you can create another Windows Server 2012 R2 VM with a different computer name, and perform the following steps:

1. Launch VMWare Player.
2. Play **SQL2014VM**.
3. Log in to the VM.

4. In **Server Manager**, click on the **Manage** menu item and select **Add Roles and Features** from the drop-down menu. This will launch the **Add Roles and Features Wizard**.

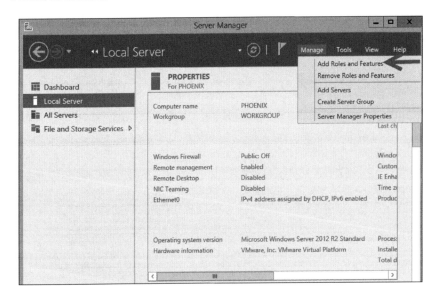

5. On the **Select installation type** screen, choose **Role-based or feature-based installation**, which will configure a single server by adding roles and role services and features:

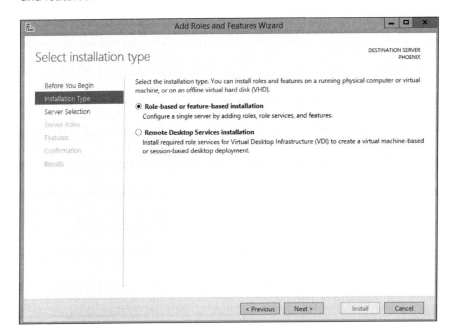

6.  On the **Select destination server** screen, select the current server:

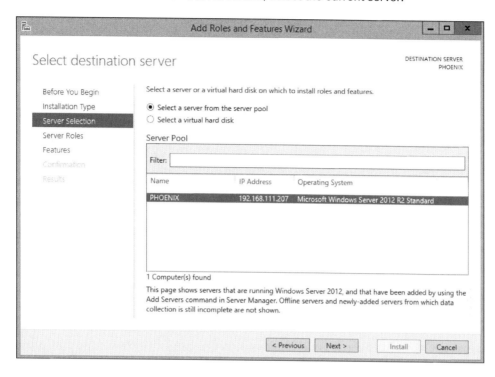

7.  On the **Select server roles** screen, choose **Active Directory Domain Services**.

8.  This action will trigger the display of another window, prompting **Add features that are required for Active Directory Domain Services**. Click on **Add Features**.

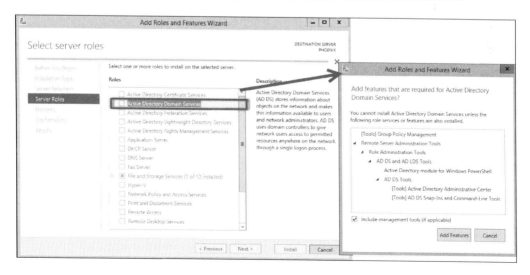

9. Click on **Next** until you get to the **Confirm installation selections** screen. Check **Restart the destination server automatically if required** and click on **Install**.

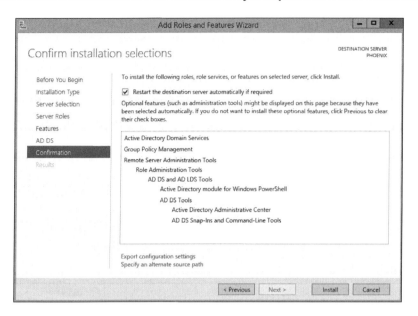

10. Once the **Active Directory Domain Services** feature has been installed, a link will appear on the result screen.

11. Click on **Promote this server to a domain controller** link on the result screen.

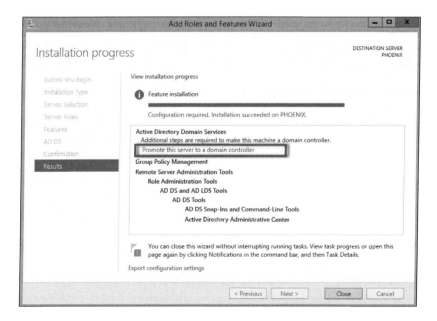

12. Select **create a new forest**. Type `queryworks.local` in the **Root domain name** textbox and click on **Next**.

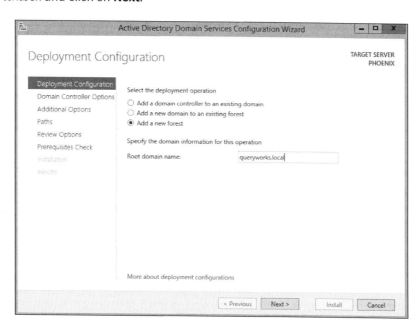

13. In **Forest functional level**, select **Windows Server 2012 R2**. In **Type the Directory Services Restore Mode (DSRM) password** textbox, type a password and click on **Next**.

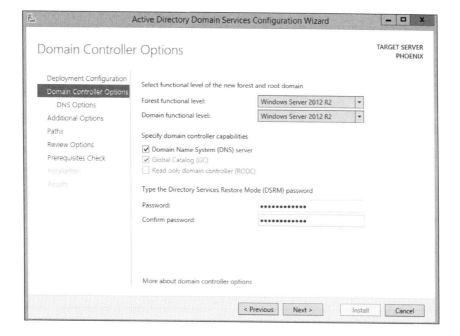

14. Under **DNS Options**, you will receive a warning about a DNS delegation that cannot be created because of a missing authoritative parent zone. For purposes of our exercise, you can ignore this warning since we will not be integrating this server to an existing DNS infrastructure.

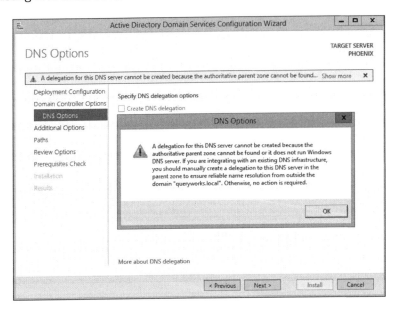

15. On the **Additional Options** screen, confirm the **NETBIOS domain name**. In our case, it should be QUERYWORKS.

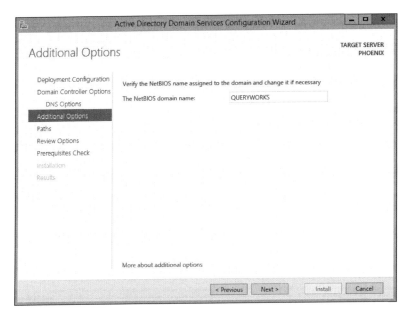

16. Review and confirm the paths for the AD DS database and SYSVOL.

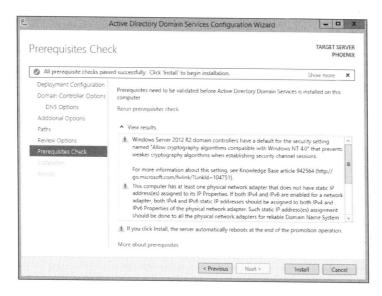

17. On the **Review Options** screen, review to ensure that all the options are correct and click on **Next**.

18. On the **Prerequisites Check** screen, you may receive some warnings. One warning is about the server having a dynamically assigned IP address. For our purposes, this is acceptable. Note that if this option is chosen, it is assumed that a DHCP server is already available on the network. Otherwise, the server will use an APIPA scheme, or **Automatic Private IP Addressing** (**APIPA**), which does not work well with domain controllers.

19. Click on **Install** to complete the Active Directory Domain Services configuration. The server will be restarted.

20. Once the virtual machine is back online, you will notice that the login screen now shows the domain information **QUERYWORKS\Administrator**.

# Creating domain accounts

In this section, we will create some domain accounts that we will use for our exercises. We will create the following domain accounts:

 ▶  QUERYWORKS\sqlservice

 ▶  QUERYWORKS\sqlagent

 ▶  QUERYWORKS\tstark

 ▶  QUERYWORKS\srogers

 ▶  QUERYWORKS\todinson

To add these accounts, perform the following steps:

1. Launch SQL2014VM and log in.

2. In **Server Manager**, click on the **Tools** menu item and select **Active Directory Users and Computers**.

3. In the **Active Directory Users and Computers** window, expand **queryworks.local**. Right-click on **Users** and navigate to **New | User**.

4. In **Full Name** and **User logon name**, type sqlservice and click on **Next**, as shown in the following screenshot:

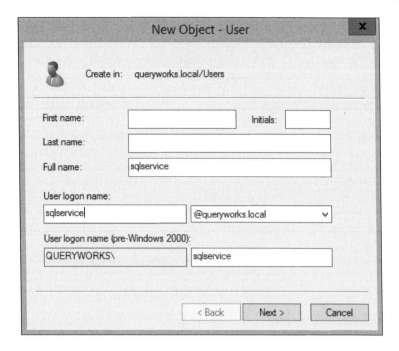

5.  Type the password and then check **User cannot change password** and **password never expires**, as shown in the following screenshot:

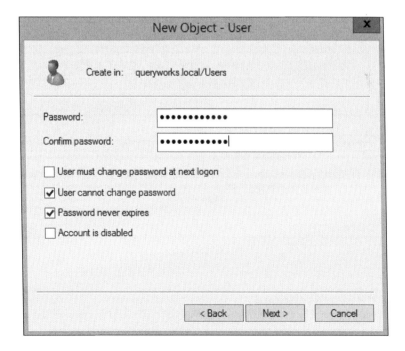

6. Click on **Next** and then on **Finish**.

7. Repeat steps 3-6 for creating the rest of the users and any additional ones you identify:

```
sqlagent

tstark

srogers

todinson
```

# Installing SQL Server 2014 on a VM

Before we install SQL Server 2014, we need to ensure that .NET 3.5 and .NET 3.5 Service Pack 1 are installed on your VM.

.NET 3.5 is a feature you can install from Server Manager.

.NET 3.5 Service Pack 1 can be downloaded from `https://www.microsoft.com/en-ca/download/details.aspx?id=22`.

Once these are installed, the following steps will walk you through installing SQL Server 2014 on your virtual machine:

1. Launch VMWare Player.

2. Play `SQL2014VM` and log in using the administrator domain account.

3. Go to **Player | Removable Devices | CD/DVD | Settings**.

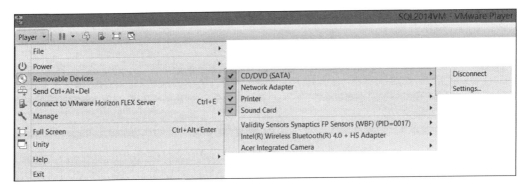

4. Change the ISO image file path to the SQL Server 2012 ISO file and click on **OK**.

5. Once you click on **OK**, the **Autoplay** window will appear. Click on **Run SETUP.EXE**. If **Autoplay** does not appear, open Windows Explorer and navigate to the DVD drive to run `setup.exe`. This will open the **SQL Server Installation Center** window.

6. Select **Installation** from the left-hand pane and choose **New SQL Server stand-alone installation or add features to an existing installation**.

7. In the **Product Key** window, accept the default values and click on **Next**.

8. In the **License Terms** window, select **I accept the license terms** and click on **Next**.

9. In the **Microsoft Update** window, select **User Microsoft Update to check for updates (recommended)**.

10. In the **Install Rules** window, possible issues may be flagged. For our purposes, we expect to see a warning because of the domain controller and the firewall, as shown in the following screenshot:

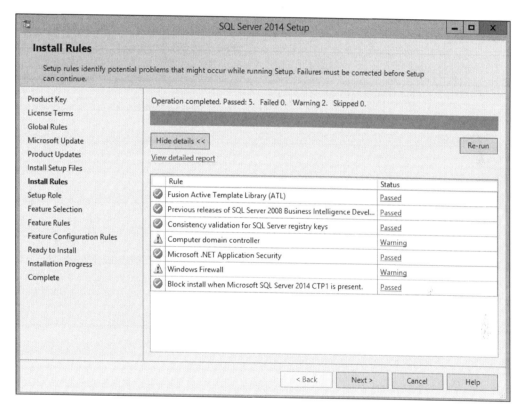

For security reasons, it is recommended that you do not install SQL Server on top of the domain controller, as discussed in the article at `http://msdn.microsoft.com/en-us/library/ms143506.aspx`. For our purposes, however, it is acceptable.

11. On the **Setup Role** screen, select **SQL Server Feature Installation**, as shown in the following screenshot:

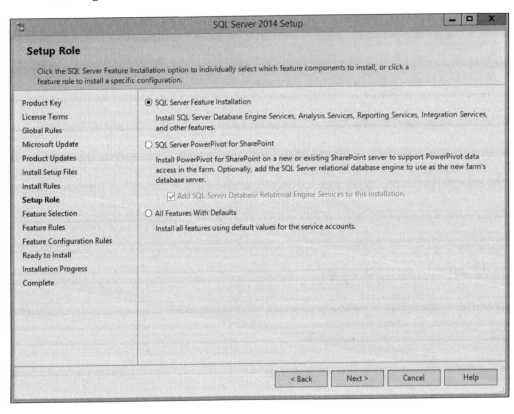

12. In the **Feature Selection** window, make sure that you choose the following options:

- **Database Engine Services** (all components)
- **Analysis Services**
- **Reporting Services - Native**
- **Client Tools Connectivity**
- **SQL Server Data Tools**
- **Integration Services**
- **Documentation Components**
- **Management Tools - Basic**
- **Management Tools - Complete**

Feel free to choose additional features you want to try. In addition, adjust the directories if you want to store the SQL Server files somewhere other than the default directories. When done making adjustments, click on **Next**.

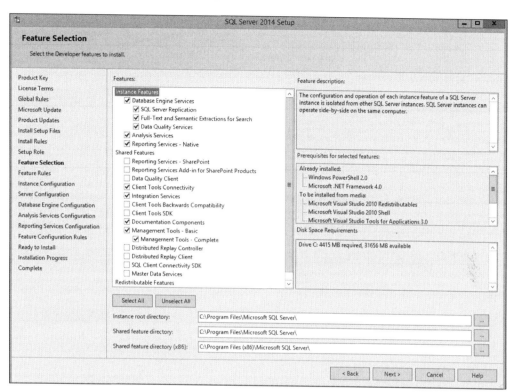

13. The installation wizard will now check **Feature Rules**. If there are any errors reported, make sure that you resolve them before continuing with the installation. Click on **Next**.

14. In the **Instance Configuration** window, select **Default instance**.

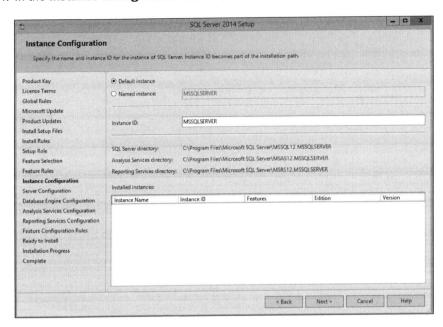

15. In the **Server Configuration** window, in the **Service Accounts** tab, set up the service accounts.

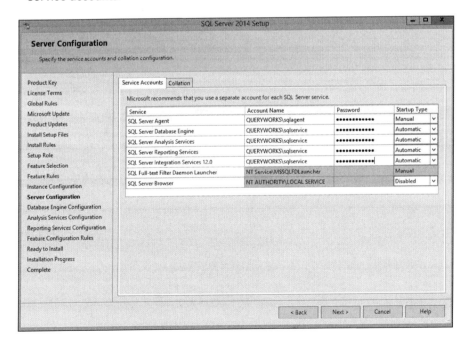

16. In the **Server Configuration** window, under the **Collation** tab, keep the default settings as is: **SQL_Latin1_General_CP1_CI_AS** for **Database Engine** and **Latin1_General_CI_AS** for **Analysis Services**.

17. In the **Database Engine Configuration** window, under the **Server Configuration** tab, keep the default settings for **Windows authentication mode** as is and click on **Add Current User**.

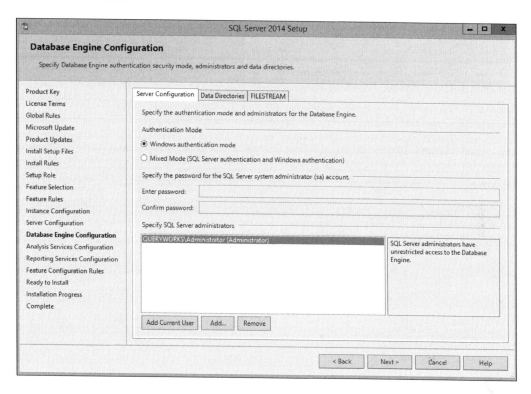

18. In the **Database Engine Configuration** window, under the **Data Directories** tab, keep the default settings.

19. In the **Database Engine Configuration** window, under the **FILESTREAM** tab, check all checkboxes to enable filestream.

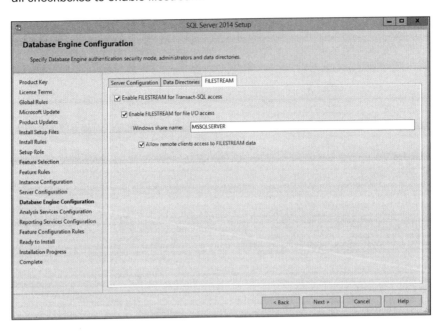

20. In the **Analysis Services Configuration** window, under the **Server Configuration** tab, select **Multidimensional and Data Mining Mode** and click on **Add Current User**.

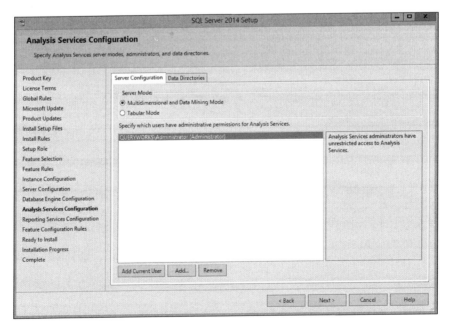

21. In the **Analysis Services Configuration** window, under the **Data Directories** tab, keep the default settings.

22. In the **Reporting Services Configuration** window, under the **Reporting Services Native Mode** section, select **Install only**.

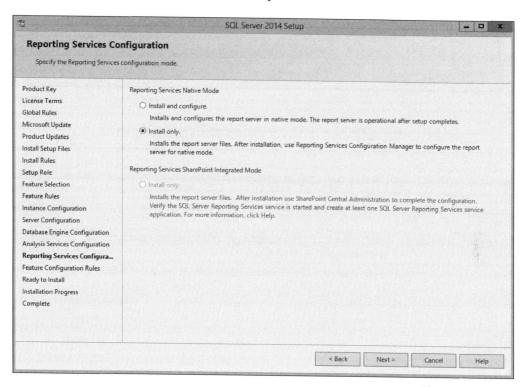

23. Click on **Next** to go to the **Feature Configuration Rules** window. If there are any errors, you need to address them before you proceed.

24. Click on **Next** to go to the **Ready to Install** window. Review all the features, and click on **Install** once all the features have been reviewed and confirmed.

25. Once the installation is complete, close the setup window.

# Configuring Reporting Services in native mode

Once SQL Server 2014 is installed, we can configure Reporting Services in native mode.

 You can learn more about the differences between SSRS native mode and SharePoint integrated mode from the deployment guide document available at `https://technet.microsoft.com/en-us/library/bb326345.aspx`.

1.  Open **SQL Server 2014 Reporting Services Configuration Manager**.

2.  Connect to the default instance:

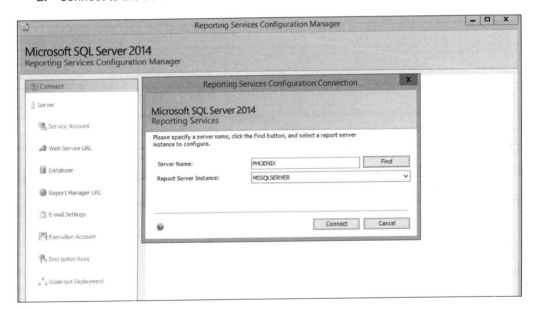

3. Click on **Service Account**. Double-check the service account assigned to run Reporting Services. If it is properly set, we do not need to make any changes in this window.

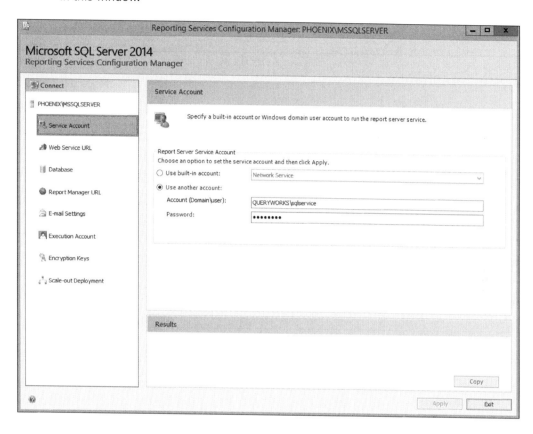

4.  Click on **Web Service URL**. We will accept the default values and then click on **Apply**.

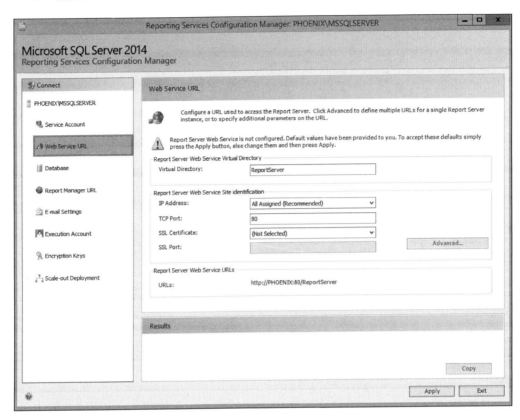

5.  Click on **Database** and then click on the **Change Database** button. This will launch another set of windows.

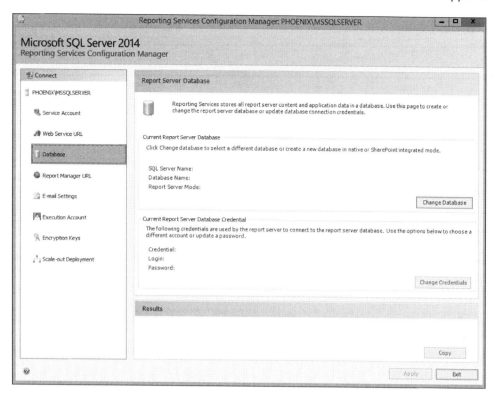

6.  Select **create a new report server database**, as shown in the following screenshot:

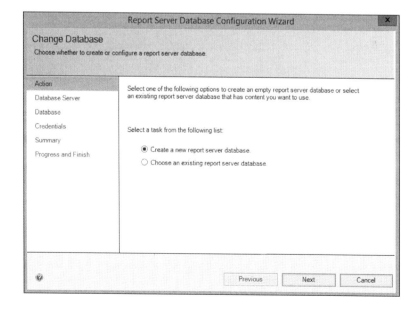

7. Leave the default database name as **Report Server** and click on **Next**.

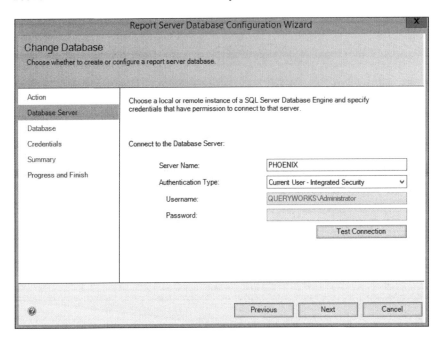

8. For **Authentication Type**, select **Service Credentials** and then click on **Next**.

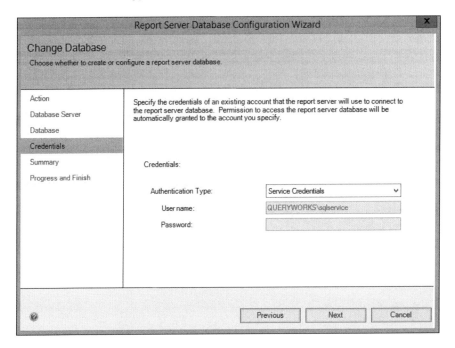

9.  Review your summary and click on **Next**.

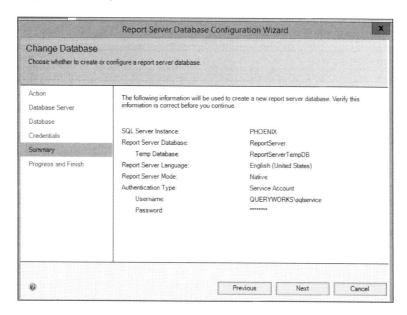

10. When the configurations have been successfully applied, click on **Finish**. Note that the original **Report Server Database** screen will now be populated with the newly configured values.

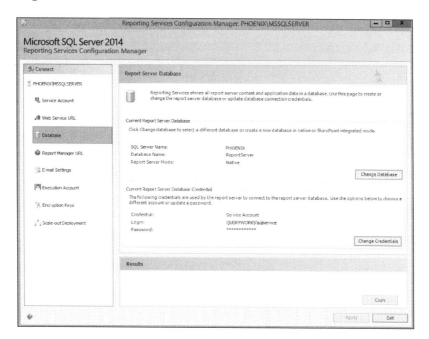

11. Click on **Report Manager URL** and then click on **Apply**.

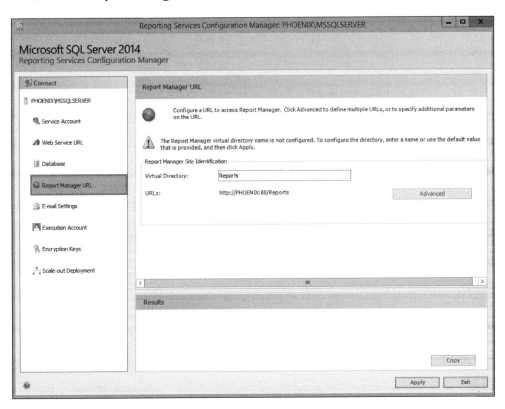

12. Test the URL by launching Internet Explorer. In the browser, type `http://localhost/Reports` (this is the same URL as `http://PHOENIX:80/Reports`):

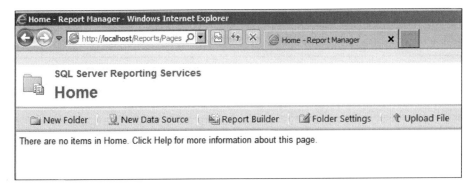

# Installing sample databases

The SQL Server sample databases can be found at `http://msftdbprodsamples.codeplex.com/`.

You can choose to install both SQL Server 2014 OLTP and DW samples. If you are going to try the recipes that involve Analysis Services cubes, then you definitely have to install the DW samples.

Complete instructions on how to install the sample databases can be found at `http://social.technet.microsoft.com/wiki/contents/articles/3735.sql-server-samples-readme-en-us.aspx#Readme_for_Adventure_Works_Sample_Databases`.

# Installing PowerShell V5

As Windows Server 2012 R2 does not natively come with PowerShell V5, at the time of the writing this book, we will need to install it separately.

1.  Launch VMWare Player.

2.  Play **SQL2014VM**, and log in.

3.  Download and install the Windows Management Framework 5. This will install PowerShell V5, including the PowerShell V5 ISE (Integrated Scripting Environment). At the time of writing this book, this framework can be downloaded from `https://www.microsoft.com/en-us/download/details.aspx?id=46889` and the binary is **WindwosBlue-KB3055381-x64.msu**.

4.  After the installation is complete, restart your VM.

5.  Confirm that PowerShell V5 is installed by launching the PowerShell console. Type `$host.version` in the console, and you will see the value **5** for the **Major** build, as shown in the following screenshot:

```
                                                    Administrator: Windows PowerShell
Windows PowerShell
Copyright (C) 2015 Microsoft Corporation. All rights reserved.

PS C:\Users\Administrator> $host.version

Major  Minor  Build  Revision
-----  -----  -----  --------
5      0      10105  0
```

# Using SQL Server on a Windows Azure VM

If you are interested in using SQL Server on a Windows Azure VM, you can check out the Microsoft Virtual Academy video on *SQL Server in Windows Azure Virtual Machines Jump Start*, which can be found at `https://www.microsoftvirtualacademy.com/en-us/training-courses/sql-server-in-windows-azure-virtual-machines-jump-start-8293?l=2OlYzCYy_1004984382`.

# Index

## Thank you for buying
## SQL Server 2014 with PowerShell v5 Cookbook

# About Packt Publishing

Packt, pronounced 'packed', published its first book, *Mastering phpMyAdmin for Effective MySQL Management*, in April 2004, and subsequently continued to specialize in publishing highly focused books on specific technologies and solutions.

Our books and publications share the experiences of your fellow IT professionals in adapting and customizing today's systems, applications, and frameworks. Our solution-based books give you the knowledge and power to customize the software and technologies you're using to get the job done. Packt books are more specific and less general than the IT books you have seen in the past. Our unique business model allows us to bring you more focused information, giving you more of what you need to know, and less of what you don't.

Packt is a modern yet unique publishing company that focuses on producing quality, cutting-edge books for communities of developers, administrators, and newbies alike. For more information, please visit our website at www.PacktPub.com.

# About Packt Enterprise

In 2010, Packt launched two new brands, Packt Enterprise and Packt Open Source, in order to continue its focus on specialization. This book is part of the Packt Enterprise brand, home to books published on enterprise software – software created by major vendors, including (but not limited to) IBM, Microsoft, and Oracle, often for use in other corporations. Its titles will offer information relevant to a range of users of this software, including administrators, developers, architects, and end users.

# Writing for Packt

We welcome all inquiries from people who are interested in authoring. Book proposals should be sent to author@packtpub.com. If your book idea is still at an early stage and you would like to discuss it first before writing a formal book proposal, then please contact us; one of our commissioning editors will get in touch with you.

We're not just looking for published authors; if you have strong technical skills but no writing experience, our experienced editors can help you develop a writing career, or simply get some additional reward for your expertise.

## SQL Server 2012 with PowerShell V3 Cookbook

ISBN: 978-1-84968-646-4          Paperback: 634 pages

Increase your productivity as a DBA, developer, or IT Pro, by using PowerShell with SQL Server to simplify database management and automate repetitive, mundane tasks

### SQL Server 2012 with PowerShell V3 Cookbook

Increase your productivity as a DBA, developer, or IT Pro, by using PowerShell with SQL Server to simplify database management and automate repetitive, mundane tasks

Donabel Santos

1. Provides over a hundred practical recipes that utilize PowerShell to automate, integrate and simplify SQL Server tasks.

2. Offers easy to follow, step-by-step guide to getting the most out of SQL Server and PowerShell.

3. Covers numerous guidelines, tips, and explanations on how and when to use PowerShell cmdlets, WMI, SMO, .NET classes or other components.

## PowerShell for SQL Server Essentials

ISBN: 978-1-78439-149-2          Paperback: 186 pages

Manage and monitor SQL Server administration and application deployment with PowerShell

### PowerShell for SQL Server Essentials

Manage and monitor SQL Server administration and application deployment with PowerShell

Donabel Santos

1. Create scripts using PowerShell to manage and monitor server administration and application deployment.

2. Automate creation of SQL Database objects through PowerShell with the help of SQL Server module (SQLPS) and SQL Server snapins.

3. A fast paced guide, packed with hands-on examples on profiling and configuring SQL Server.

Please check **www.PacktPub.com** for information on our titles

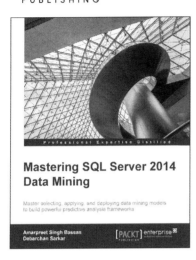

**Mastering SQL Server 2014**

# Mastering SQL Server 2014 Data Mining

ISBN: 978-1-84968-894-9          Paperback: 304 pages

Master selecting, applying, and deploying data mining models to build powerful predictive analysis frameworks

1.  Understand the different phases of data mining, along with the tools used at each stage.

2.  Explore the different data mining algorithms in depth.

3.  Become an expert in optimizing algorithms and situation-based modeling.

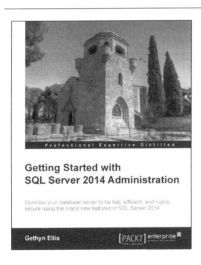

# Getting Started with SQL Server 2014 Administration

ISBN: 978-1-78217-241-3          Paperback: 106 pages

Optimize your database server to be fast, efficient, and highly secure using the brand new features of SQL Server 2014

1.  Design your SQL Server 2014 infrastructure by combining both onpremise and WindowsAzurebased technology.

2.  Implement the new InMemory OLTP database engine feature to enhance the performance of your transaction databases.

3.  This is a handson tutorial that explores the new features of SQL Server 2014 along with giving real world examples.

Please check **www.PacktPub.com** for information on our titles